PUENTES . . . Building Bridges between Courses and Cultures

Puentes: Spanish for Intensive and High-Beginner Courses, **Fifth Edition,** is a proven program that successfully moves your students to the next level of Spanish-language proficiency.

Known for its dynamic power-pacing organization, easily accessible grammar and vocabulary presentations, rich integration of culture, and full array of supplemental resources, *Puentes* provides you with adaptable, flexible teaching options that address the specific needs of your students.

The *Puentes* program—the first of its kind for the course—offers a unique approach that

- bridges the gap between beginning- and intermediate-level courses;
- propels students to the next level of proficiency;
- connects students to the richness of Hispanic cultures.

This time-tested program embraces the National Standards for Foreign Language Learning. Through engaging speaking, listening, reading, and writing activities, *Puentes* enables learners to quickly communicate with confidence in meaningful contexts. Cultural presentations and activities allow students to further connect with the people and cultures of the Spanish-speaking world.

PUENTES

Spanish for Intensive and High-Beginner Courses

Patti J. Marinelli
Lizette Mujica Laughlin

FIFTH EDITION

Your special chapter preview begins now.

Puentes strikes the perfect balance between everyday topics and transactional situations.

The proven *Puentes* program has nine chapters, plus a preliminary *Paso*. Each chapter consists of two or three *Pasos,* each with their core content of vocabulary, functional language, grammar, and activities.
- **Odd-numbered chapters** consist of **three** *Pasos* and focus on everyday topics such as family, university life, and pastimes.
- **Even-numbered chapters** include **two** *Pasos* and explore Spanish in practical situations such as making travel arrangements, eating in a restaurant, and dealing with minor medical problems.

Numerous hints, suggestions, ideas for implementation, and explanations have been added to this **Annotated Instructor's Edition.**

Chapter-opening *Objetivos* outline chapter content and list reading and writing strategies presented in the **Student Activities Manual.** Each chapter emphasizes the cultures of a particular Spanish-speaking country or region.

¡De viaje!

CAPÍTULO

OBJETIVOS

Speaking and Listening
▸ Telling time and giving dates
▸ Making travel and hotel arrangements
▸ Using numbers from hundreds to millions

Culture
▸ Mexico
▸ Popular vacation destinations in Spanish-speaking countries

Grammar
▸ Verb phrases (conjugated verb + infinitive)
▸ Stem-changing verbs in the present tense (e → ie; o → ue; e → i)
▸ Irregular verbs in the present tense

Video
▸ En la Hacienda Vista Alegre: Episodio 2
▸ Imágenes de México

Gramática suplementaria
▸ El futuro

Cuaderno de actividades
Reading
▸ Strategy: Scanning for detail

Writing
▸ Strategy: Keys to composing social correspondence

Playlist
🌐 www.cengage.com/spanish/puentes

*A **primera vista** sections introduce each chapter's topic through the compelling use of art or music.*

A primera vista

Buscándola

Los viajes nos pueden llevar *(can take us)* **a Europa, Asia, África, Oceanía, América del Sur o América del Norte. ¿Cuáles de los continentes has visitado** *(have you visited)* **en tus viajes?**

En la canción "Buscándola", un joven vuela *(flies)* por todo el mundo buscando *(looking for)* a la chica que se le escapó *(the girl that got away)*. Escucha la canción e indica todos los destinos mencionados.

☐ África   ☐ Japón

☐ Cancún   ☐ Katmandú

☐ China   ☐ Los Ángeles

☐ Honolulu   ☐ Nueva York

☐ Italia   ☐ París

Puentes playlist available on iTunes

HABLANDO DE LA MÚSICA

Together with the human voice, musical instruments create the myriad sounds we enjoy as music. The innumerable musical styles of Spain and Hispanic America may be created with familiar instruments such as **la guitarra, el clarinete, la flauta, la trompeta, el piano, el violín, el sintetizador, el teclado** *(keyboard)* or **la batería** *(drums)*. Other musical styles employ unique instruments indigenous to a particular region, such as these:

- **la ocarina:** This simple flute-like instrument made of ceramic or wood dates to ancient Aztec and Mayan times. It may have 4 to 12 finger holes.

- **la marimba:** This sweet-toned percussion instrument is played in parts of Mexico and throughout many cou[...] series of w[...] piano, tha[...]

- **el charango:** This guitar-like instrument with fiv[...] cords evolved in the Andean regions as a small, [...] version of the Spanish guitar. Traditionally, the [...] soundbox was made from the dried shell of an a[...]

This short, thematic introduction to the chapter topic now alternates between two formats. In odd-numbered chapters, the focus on paintings and art has been retained. **New to this edition,** the even-numbered chapters now feature songs in a variety of musical styles, along with key information on musical terminology, musicians, and instruments.

MANÁ (GRUPO MUSICAL, 1987–)

Nacionalidad: mexicano

Obras y premios: Su primer gran éxito *(first big hit)* fue "Rayando el sol". En 2008, hacen una gira mundial *(world tour)* y sacan un DVD grabado en vivo *(recorded live)*. Sus premios incluyen cuatro Grammys, cinco Latin Grammys y varios Premios MTV Latinoamérica.

De interés: Varios músicos *(musicians)* han formado este conjunto *(musical group)* en las tres décadas de su existencia. Se considera un conjunto de pop/rock pero a veces sus melodías tienen elementos de reggae o calipso.

BUSCÁNDOLA
canción de Maná

Conecto un avión para buscarte
pues te me escapaste.

Europa, Asia y el Oriente, ¿dónde?
En eso un secuestro al avión ¡ah!

qué loca situación, nos dirigimos
hacia Cuba al reventón.

Students can purchase songs by artists featured in the text via an **iTunes®** playlist, accessible at the text's **Premium Website** and **iLrn™: Heinle Learning Center.**

iTunes is a trademark of Apple, Inc., registered in the U.S. and other countries.

From *Vocabulario temático* to *Gramática,* each chapter of *Puentes* is designed to help students progress quickly as they build upon their knowledge base.

Vocabulario temático

Las fechas *(Expressing days and dates)*

—¿Cuándo salimos para *Mérida?*

—Salimos el *lunes, 28 de junio.*

—¿Cuándo regresamos?

—Regresamos el *viernes, 2 de julio.*

—¿Cuándo está abierto *el museo?*

—Está abierto *todos los días, de lunes a sábado.*

—¿Cuándo está cerrado?

—Está cerrado *los domingos.*

Los días de la semana *(Days of the week)*

—¿Qué día es hoy?

—Hoy es *lunes.*

| lunes | martes | miércoles | jueves | viernes | sábado | domingo |

Los meses del año *(Months of the year)*

—¿Cuál es la fecha de hoy?

—Es el *25 (veinticinco) de noviembre.*

enero	julio
febrero	agosto
marzo	septiembre
abril	octubre
mayo	noviembre
junio	diciembre

| L | M | M | J | V | S | D | | L | M | M | J | V | S | D |
| 1 | 2 | 3 | 4 | 5 | 6 | | | 1 | 2 | 3 | 4 | 5 | 6 |

Use the cardinal numbers for most dates: **el cinco (5) de octubre, el veinte (20) de diciembre.** But say **primero** for the first day of the month: **el primero de febrero.** Give years as any other large number, NOT in groups of two: **1935 = mil novecientos treinta**

The *Vocabulario temático* presents thematically related vocabulary in authentic contexts. Sentence templates in this section include ready-to-use phrases as well as models of upcoming grammatical structures.

The clear, new layout of this section helps focus learners' attention on key "chunks" of information and facilitates classroom presentation of the material. Models have also been slightly shortened to allow for more rapid coverage.

Ponerlo a prueba

CD1
Track 12

2-5 El conserje. Tres turistas tienen reservaciones para el Hotel Sevilla Palace en el Distrito Federal de México. Escucha y escribe en español toda la información.

Nombre	Número de personas	Habitación sencilla (*single*) o doble (*double*)	Día y fecha de llegada	Hora de llegada
1.				
2.				
3.				

2-6 Los exploradores. El Club de Viajes ofrece varias excursiones este año. ¿Cuándo son? Lee la información y completa las oraciones de una manera lógica. Escribe los números en palabras.

> MODELO   El tour a Panamá sale <u>el seis de septiembre</u> y regresa <u>el veinticuatro de septiembre.</u>

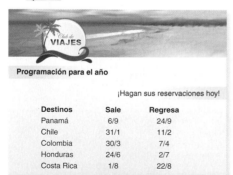

Programación para el año

¡Hagan sus reservaciones hoy!

Destinos	Sale	Regresa
Panamá	6/9	24/9
Chile	31/1	11/2
Colombia	30/3	7/4
Honduras	24/6	2/7
Costa Rica	1/8	22/8

1. El tour a Chile sale _____ y regresa _____.
2. Salimos para Colombia _____ y regresamos _____.
3. La excursión a Honduras sale _____ y regresa _____.
4. Salimos para Costa Rica _____ y regresamos _____.

 2-7 Nuestras preferencias. Conversa con un(a) compañero(a) de clase sobre sus días y meses favoritos.

1. ¿Qué día de la semana prefieres? ¿Por qué te gusta? ¿Qué día te gusta menos?

2-8 Una atracción popular. Estás en México, D.F., y quieres visitar unas atracciones populares de la capital. Lee este anuncio para el Museo Nacional de Antropología. Con tu compañero(a), contesta las preguntas.

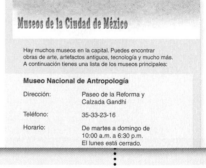

Museos de la Ciudad de México

Hay muchos museos en la capital. Puedes encontrar obras de arte, artefactos antiguos, tecnología y mucho más. A continuación tienes una lista de los museos principales:

Museo Nacional de Antropología

Dirección:	Paseo de la Reforma y Calzada Gandhi
Teléfono:	35-33-23-16
Horario:	De martes a domingo de 10:00 a.m. a 6:30 p.m. El lunes está cerrado.

Carefully sequenced *Ponerlo a prueba* practice activities follow each vocabulary and grammar presentation.

In this edition, particular emphasis is given to providing more opportunities for self-expression and open-ended response in both paired and small-group contexts. Short new readings in every chapter provide informative and entertaining content while serving as a springboard for conversation.

Gramática sections provide concise explanations of the major grammatical structures students need to advance to the intermediate level of proficiency.

Each grammar explanation is preceded by a model conversational exchange (also recorded), which directs students' attention to the grammar point of study and provides an opportunity for inductive learning.

Grammar Tutorial notations prompt students to access a virtual instructor who explains structures whenever they need additional support. **Video grammar tutorials** are available at the **Premium Website** and in **iLrn™: Heinle Learning Center.**

🌐 **Heinle Grammar Tutorial:** The present indicative tense

🌐 **Heinle Grammar Tutorial:** The present indicative tense

Here the **e** in the stem changes to **ie**.

Here the **e** in the stem stays the same.

Gramática

Los verbos con cambio en la raíz en el tiempo presente

Listen and read along as Marcos and Laura discuss their plans for the upcoming break. Find examples in the present tense of the following verbs: **empezar, pensar, poder, preferir, querer, volver.** What looks different about the way these verbs are conjugated?

MARCOS: Oye, Laura. Las vacaciones empiezan muy pronto. ¿Qué piensas hacer?

LAURA: Voy a la playa Progreso. Salgo el próximo domingo y vuelvo el sábado.

MARCOS: Todos dicen que es un pueblo muy tranquilo.

LAURA: Sí, es cierto. Puedo dormir y descansar *(rest)* toda la semana ¿Y tú, Marcos? ¿Qué vas a hacer?

MARCOS: Bueno, yo prefiero las vacaciones más activas. Quiero ir a Tulum y explorar las ruinas mayas.

A. Verbos con cambios en la raíz. In Spanish, all infinitives are composed of two parts: a stem (or root) and an ending.

Infinitive	Stem	+	Ending
pensar	pens-		ar
volver	volv-		er
preferir	prefer-		ir

When certain verbs are conjugated in the present tense, the stressed vowel in the stem undergoes a change. For example, the **e** in **pensar** changes to **ie**:

Infinitive	Stem	Stem change	Example of conjugated form
pensar	pens-	piens-	¿Qué pie**n**sas hacer?

B. Los tres tipos de verbos. There are three basic patterns of "stem-changing verbs" or *verbos con cambio en la raíz.* They are identified in the glossary and in most dictionaries with cues in parentheses, like this: **pensar (ie); volver (ue); servir (i).** Notice that the stem changes occur when the verb is conjugated in any person except **nosotros** and **vosotros.**

¿Adónde **piensan** ir Uds.?	*Where do you (plural) plan on going?*
Pensamos ir a Tulum.	*We're planning on going to Tulum.*

Stem change e → ie
pensar (ie) *(to think, to plan [to do something])*

yo	**pie**nso	nosotros(as)	pensamos
tú	**pie**nsas	vosotros(as)	pensáis
Ud./él/ella	**pie**nsa	Uds./ellos/ellas	**pie**nsan

Gramática suplementaria

🌐 **Heinle Grammar Tutorial:** The future tense 25

El futuro

The tour guide is explaining to your group what you will be doing on your excursion to Mexico City tomorrow. What are three of the planned activities? Identify three verbs that refer to the future.

Su tour empezará con un corto viaje en autobús. Después, nosotros visitaremos la hermosa catedral. Yo les recomendaré varios restaurantes donde ustedes podrán probar los platos típicos de la región. Por la tarde, iremos al Museo de Antropología.

A. La función del futuro. The future tense (**el futuro**) is used in two ways:

▸ to describe what will happen or what somebody will do in the future.
Notice that the English word *will* is not translated, but expressed through the *verb ending* in Spanish.

Su tour **empezará** con un corto viaje en autobús.	*Your tour **will begin** with a short trip by bus.*
Después, nosotros **visitaremos** la hermosa catedral.	*Afterward, we **will visit** the beautiful cathedral.*

▸ to speculate about what is *probably going on* or what *will probably take place* in the near future.
In English, probability is expressed by using separate words such as *probably* or *must,* while in Spanish the notion of probability is conveyed by the use of the future tense.

—¿Qué hora es, mamá?	*What time is it, Mom?*
—No sé, hija. **Serán** las cinco.	*I don't know, daughter. **It must be** five o'clock.*
—¿Cuándo va a llegar papá?	*When is Dad coming home?*
—No te preocupes. **Llegará** pronto.	*Don't worry. **He will probably arrive** soon.*

B. La formación del futuro. To form the future tense of most verbs, add the appropiate verb endings to the entire infinitive. Notice in the following examples that the same set of endings is used for **-ar, -er,** and **-ir** verbs.

El futuro: verbos regulares

		viajar *(to travel)*	volver *(to return)*	ir *(to go)*
yo	-é	viajaré	volveré	iré
tú	-ás	viajarás	volverás	irás

Gramática suplementaria, formerly found at the end of the **Student Activities Manual,** has been significantly revised and is now conveniently located at the end of the textbook. Instructors may pick and choose from these sections to supplement the grammatical content of the course as they wish.

Cultural information is woven throughout all thematic presentations and accompanying activities. Each chapter emphasizes the culture of a particular Spanish-speaking country.

Puente cultural

¿Adónde van los jóvenes de vacaciones?

Jimena Escamilla

🌐 MÉXICO

En México es muy común visitar las playas, como Acapulco o Veracruz, en la época de verano (*summer*). El invierno (*winter*) ofrece la oportunidad de pasar más tiempo con la familia.

Gabriella Paracat

🌐 ARGENTINA

Bariloche; es una región muy popular en el sur de Argentina, cerca a la cordillera de los Andes. Los jóvenes van allí en el invierno para esquiar. Si es verano, pueden hacer excursiones y practicar el alpinismo (*mountain climbing*).

Mauricio Mbomio

🌐 GUINEA ECUATORIAL

Depende de cada uno. Muchos jóvenes viajan a sus pueblos para visitar a sus abuelos o padres. Otros se quedan en la ciudad estudiando o trabajando.

🌐 Go to the *Puentes* Premium Website to view the **Puente cultural** interviews.

En comparación. Completa la tabla con la información necesaria.

	En México	En Argentina	En Guinea Ecuatorial	En los Estados Unidos

A hallmark of the *Puentes* program, *Puente cultural* highlights the cultural practices and products of the Hispanic world as seen through the eyes of college-aged students native to Spain, Africa, Central and South America, and the Caribbean. Accompanying activities are designed to help students learn about and appreciate facets of day-to-day culture and to compare them with their own customs and habits.

Chapter-ending *Panorama cultural* focuses on a specific Spanish-speaking country and presents rich cultural content on history, geography, customs, and famous personalities. This presentation is accompanied by an all-new travelogue-style video program, *Imágenes de…*.Video segments are available on **DVD** and online at the **Premium Website** and **iLrn™: Heinle Learning Center.**

In addition to these cultural components, brief *Comentario cultural* readings discuss cultural phenomena.

Each chapter ends with *Un paso más,* which features optional sections that will boost your students' speaking and comprehension skills.

Un paso más

¡Vamos a hablar!

Estudiante A

Contexto: Imagine that you (**Estudiante A**) and a friend are traveling together in Mexico. You are now in Puerto Vallarta and want to participate in an eco-tour in the area. Each of you has an advertisement for a different tour. Exchange information about the tours, and then decide together which one the two of you will take.

You will begin by asking: **¿Adónde va el tour de Eco-Discovery?**

Eco-Discovery

▸ Destino: _____

▸ Días disponibles *(available):* _____

▸ Hora de salida: _____

▸ Duración: _____

▸ Precio: _____

▸ Teléfono (para las reservaciones): _____

▸ Aspectos interesantes: _____

Aventuras Tiroleso

Tour de canopy

¡Observe la flora y la fauna de la selva tropical desde una perspectiva única! Con la asistencia de nuestros guías especializados, Ud. puede transportarse de un árbol

Vocabulary: **árbol** *tree;* **poleas** *pulleys.*

Go to the **Un paso más** section in the *Cuaderno de actividades* for reading, writing, and listening activities that correlate with this chapter.

¡*Vamos a hablar!* is an information-gap activity, designed for pairs of students to complete for additional speaking practice.

¡Vamos a ver! | Episodio 2

En la Hacienda Vista Alegre

Anticipación

A. Hablando se entiende la gente. Habla con un(a) compañero(a).

¿Adónde te gusta ir de vacaciones? ¿Qué te gusta hacer durante las vacaciones? ¿Qué lugares prefieres visitar?

B. ¿Cómo se dice... ? Relaciona *(Match)* las oraciones de la primera columna con las expresiones de la segunda columna.

____ 1. ¿Qué hora es?

____ 2. Vamos a otro hotel. Este es muy caro.

____ 3. ¿Ya podemos salir de casa? ¿Necesitan más tiempo?

____ 4. ¿Vienes con nosotros?

____ 5. Este coche es muy caro y no es demasiado bueno.

a. Está bien. **Ya estamos listos.** *We are ready.*

b. **No vale la pena** comprarlo. *It's not worth buying it.*

c. **Son las once en punto.** *It's 11 o'clock (sharp).*

d. Sí, **vamos todos juntos.** *Let's go together.*

e. Sí, es verdad. **Estoy de acuerdo contigo.** *I agree with you.*

Vamos a ver

C. De paseo por la Hacienda Vista Alegre. Mira el Episodio 2 del video y completa las oraciones. ¿Qué van a hacer los amigos en San Juan?

1. Javier va a _____.
2. Alejandra quiere _____.
3. Sofía piensa _____.
4. Valeria va a _____.
5. Antonio va a _____.

D. Después de ver el episodio. Contesta las siguientes preguntas sobre el episodio.

1. ¿Por qué los chicos están enojados con Valeria?

¡*Vamos a ver!* features *En la Hacienda Vista Alegre* video segments with accompanying pre-viewing, viewing, and post-viewing comprehension and speaking activities. This reality-based video follows the lives of five strangers brought together to live and learn in a Spanish-speaking culture. Video segments are available on **DVD,** and online at the **Premium Website** and **iLrn™: Heinle Learning Center.**

Learners continue building their reading and writing skills through the following sections, located in the **Student Activities Manual:**
• ¡*Vamos a leer!* that includes articles from newspapers, magazines, and the Internet
• ¡*Vamos a escribir!* that offers process-approach writing activities

iLrn™: Heinle Learning Center
Printed Access Card ISBN: 978-0-495-90315-4
See the inside front cover and visit iLrn.Heinle.com for more information.

QUIA™ Online Student Activities Manual
Printed Access Card ISBN: 978-0-538-48650-7
QUIA is a complete online **Student Activities Manual** (with audio). Learn more at **books.quia.com.**

Companion Website
www.cengage.com/spanish/puentes
This site features complimentary access to self-correcting grammar and vocabulary quizzes; the **Text Audio Program;** guided Web exploration of chapter topics; and more.

Personal Tutor
Personal Tutor gives your students access to live, one-on-one, online tutoring help from a subject-area expert.

Premium Website
Printed Access Card ISBN: 978-0-495-90603-2
The **Premium Website** makes it easy for you and your students to access all of the resources from the **Companion Website** PLUS premium password-protected content that includes the **SAM** Audio Program, Video Program, links to the playlist in *iTunes* (for songs featured in *A primera vista* sections), **Heinle Grammar Tutorials**, and **Heinle iRadio podcasts.** For instructors, additional password-protected resources, including the SAM Answer Key/Audio Script, are provided.

Video on DVD
ISBN: 978-0-495-90241-6
The video includes two segments for each chapter. *En la Hacienda Vista Alegre* footage follows the lives of five strangers brought together to live and learn in a Spanish-speaking culture and is featured in the *¡Vamos a ver!* section of the textbook. The new geo-cultural video, *Imágenes de...*, presents travelogue-style clips from the Spanish-speaking countries featured in each chapter's *Panorama cultural* section.

Annotated Instructor's Edition (with Audio CDs)
ISBN: 978-0-495-90060-3

Introductory Situation Cards for Oral Evaluation
ISBN: 978-0-03-026769-7
These handy cards provide additional role-playing opportunities and can be used for in-class practice or for oral testing.

PowerLecture™: Instructor's Resource CD-ROM + Testing Audio CD Package
PowerLecture™ ISBN: 978-0-495-90620-9
This essential resource includes helpful teaching tips, explanations on lesson organization, and suggestions for syllabus planning, as well as how to integrate program components. **The Placement Exam,** customizable **Testing Program,** and **Testing Audio CD** are also provided.

Student Activities Manual (SAM)
Cuaderno de actividades
ISBN: 978-0-495-90199-0
Comprehensively revised, this essential manual features easy-to-check activities specifically correlated to the text's vocabulary and grammar sections, as well as activities of more open-ended and personalized design. *Vamos a leer* sections include updated strategies and new readings. *Vamos a escribir* sections feature more step-by-step guidance to improving writing skills and additional real-life writing tasks. Listening practice and additional video activities that complement those in the text are also provided.

SAM Audio Program
ISBN: 978-0-495-90366-6

SAM Answer Key/Audio Script
ISBN: 978-0-495-90200-3
Available for purchase by students at instructor's discretion.

Text Audio Program (Stand-alone Version)
ISBN: 978-0-495-90688-9

Preface

Welcome to the Fifth Edition of *Puentes*

Puentes is a unique Spanish program designed especially for high-beginning college students. From its inception—and as its title implies—it has been created to serve as a bridge for these students in three key ways:

To bridge the gap between beginning- and intermediate-level courses High-beginning students have typically studied Spanish for one to three years in high-school or middle school. They know more than true beginners, but may not be ready to function in an intermediate-level college course. *Puentes* provides instruction and practice specially geared towards these learners, so that they may quickly build upon their knowledge base instead of "starting over" in a beginners' program.

To serve as a bridge to the next level of proficiency High-beginning students are often at the Novice-mid to Novice-high level of proficiency on the ACTFL scale. At this level, learners communicate minimally by responding to questions with words, phrases, and some sentences. The goal of the *Puentes* program is to move these students into the Intermediate-low level of proficiency. At this level, students will be able to participate simply, but consistently and fully, in conversations in the present time frame on everyday, personal topics and to handle themselves in basic travel situations.

To act as a bridge to the richness of Hispanic cultures *Puentes* interweaves culture into every lesson and introduces students to the varied geography, history, music, art, personalities, customs, and literatures of Spanish-speaking lands. High-interest topics stimulate greater student involvement in the course while level-appropriate activities build confidence in these learners.

Philosophy and approach

Puentes reflects the authors' extensive experience in teaching high-beginning students, their work in proficiency-oriented instruction and course design, and their familiarity with coordinating the work of graduate teaching assistants and adjunct faculty.

The authors have developed the eclectic approach of the *Puentes* program to accomplish the following:

▶ move students from receptive to productive use of the language

▶ allow sufficient time and practice for students to master the essential structures needed to function at the intermediate level of proficiency while laying the foundation for more advanced levels

▶ interweave vocabulary, linguistic functions, and grammar into activities that practice language in natural, authentic tasks

▶ focus upon communicative activities while at the same time integrating reading, writing, and culture into a balanced program of study

▶ provide a clearly-designed program that is user-friendly for both new and experienced teachers

▶ present sufficient material to allow for flexibility and choice

What's new to the Fifth Edition of *Puentes*?

This new edition of *Puentes* builds on the strengths of the previous editions while introducing significant innovations that will enhance student learning and simplify teaching.

Vocabulario temático The backbone of this vocabulary presentation consists of model questions and answers on everyday topics. Novice-level learners can easily memorize and adapt these key phrases for immediate communication, even as they internalize the structural patterns presented. In this edition, the clear new layout of this section helps focus learner's attention on key "chunks" of information and facilitates classroom presentation of the material. The models have also been slightly shortened to allow for more rapid coverage.

Gramática Since key grammatical structures are embedded in the *Vocabulario temático* sections, students work with the grammar before practicing it more formally in the *Gramática* sections. In this edition, each grammar explanation is preceded by a model conversational exchange (also available as an audio recording) that directs students' attention to the grammar point of study and provides an opportunity for inductive learning. Explanations have been streamlined, with an emphasis on the most common uses; exceptions and more advanced points are provided in instructor annotations.

Ponerlo a prueba A carefully designed sequence of practice activities follows each vocabulary and grammar presentation. In this edition, particular emphasis is given to providing more opportunities for self-expression and open-ended response in both paired and small-group contexts. Short new readings in every chapter provide informative and entertaining content while serving as a springboard for conversation.

A primera vista This short thematic introduction to the chapter topic now alternates between two formats: In odd-numbered chapters, we have retained the well-received focus on paintings and art. New to this edition, the even-numbered chapters now feature songs in a variety of musical styles, along with key information on musical terminology, musicians and instruments. The popular songs featured in the even-numbered chapters are available for purchase from iTunes™.

Puente cultural A hallmark feature of the *Puentes* program, the *Puente cultural* highlights the cultural practices and products of the Hispanic world as seen through the eyes of college-aged students native to Spain, Africa, Central and South America. In the text, the all-new survey focuses on these students' responses to a more general question, while their answers to a more personal question on the same topic are available as video clips on the *Puentes* Premium Website.

Panorama cultural Each *Panorama cultural* spotlights a particular Spanish-speaking country and presents attention-grabbing photographs along with fascinating facts about history, geography, customs, and famous persons. This presentation is accompanied by an all-new travelogue-style video program.

Annotations Recognizing that many teaching assistants and others new to the profession will be using *Puentes*, we have added numerous hints, suggestions, ideas for implementation and explanation. We hope that novice teachers will profit from these tips, gleaned from more than thirty years of teaching experience at this level. For additional ease of reference, annotations are labeled according to the type of information provided.

Cuaderno de actividades The student activities manual has been comprehensively revised, per your requests, with increased numbers of student practice activities and much greater ease-of-grading. Each *Paso* is now comprised of 5 to 7 activities specifically correlated to the vocabulary and grammar sections, in easy-to-check formats (true-false, multiple-choice, etc.), along with 1 or 2 activities of more open-ended, personalized design. The *Vamos a leer* sections have been extensively rewritten, with updated strategies and numerous new readings. Similarly, the *Vamos a escribir* sections have been completely rewritten and now feature more step-by-step guidance to improving writing skills and more real-life writing tasks.

Gramática suplementaria This section, formerly found at the end of the student activities manual, is now located at the end of the textbook. Instructors may pick and choose from these sections to supplement the grammatical content of the course as they wish. Explanations and practices have been completely revamped to provide a closer tie-in to the main body of each chapter.

Hallmark features of the *Puentes* program

Power pacing The first half of *Puentes,* which contains material more familiar to the high-beginner student, presents the major vocabulary, functions, and grammar in a concentrated and condensed fashion. Activities in the first half focus on getting students to actively use the language that they already recognize. The second half, which presents less familiar material, features smaller chunks of information and more extensive practice activities. Many of these activities lay the foundation for higher levels of proficiency while others continue to work towards the goal of Intermediate-low level proficiency.

Balance of everyday topics and transactional situations Odd-numbered chapters are slightly longer (with three *Pasos*) and focus on everyday topics such as family, university life, and pastimes. Even-numbered chapters are shorter (with two *Pasos*) and focus on using Spanish in practical situations, such as making travel arrangements, eating in a restaurant, dealing with minor medical problems, and shopping for clothing or souvenirs.

Natural language in context In *Puentes*, students can see immediately how the language is used because the vocabulary is organized thematically and presented in sentences that reflect everyday spoken language. The study of grammar is a logical extension of the linguistic structures already modeled in these lexical/functional presentations.

Selective grammar presentations *Puentes* emphasizes the grammatical structures that students need to master in order to reach the intermediate level of proficiency. At the same time, it introduces and practices additional structures that lay the groundwork for achieving higher levels of proficiency. For those who prefer a more in-depth grammatical presentation, the *Gramática suplementaria* section, at the back of the textbook, provides additional instruction and practice.

Extensive listening program Two separate audio programs provide a wealth of listening practice. The Text Audio program contains recordings of all in-text listening activities as well as the conversation models before each grammatical explanation. Annotations provide an instant correlation between listening activities in the text and their corresponding audio tracks on the CDs or on the Premium Website. These listening activities, designed to be assigned for homework, provide comprehensible input of the vocabulary presented in each *Paso*. The Lab Audio program in the *Cuaderno de actividades* provides entertaining radio-style listening practice in addition to pronunciation practice.

Integrated study of culture Cultural information is woven into all thematic presentations and accompanying activities. In the Fifth Edition, each chapter emphasizes the culture of a particular Spanish-speaking country; readings and activities throughout the chapter are centered on this country of focus. The *Panorama cultural* at the end of each chapter continues the cultural presentation through a brief timeline of important historical events that have shaped the country's culture, carefully captioned photos of prominent persons and important places, and a travelogue-style video shot on location.

Another key cultural component, *Puente cultural,* brings culture to life and bridges the gap between students' culture and that of the people they meet in this cultural section. Drawn from authentic interviews with real, college-aged Spanish-speakers, *Puente cultural* highlights cultures and comparisons addressed by ACTFL's National Standards for Foreign Language Learning. Activities are designed to help students learn about and appreciate facets of day-to-day culture and to compare them with their own customs and habits.

The chapter-opening *A primera vista* section features a painting by a Spanish-speaking artist or a song by an Hispanic musician along with biographical information. This edition also presents key artistic and musical terminology and a brief exercise that ties the content of the painting or song with the theme of the chapter.

In addition to all these cultural components, brief *Comentario cultural* boxes discuss cultural phenomena relevant to surrounding activities throughout each chapter.

Learning strategies *Puentes* systematically presents explicit instruction and practice for learning how to read, write, and communicate conversationally in Spanish, as well as tips on how to approach language study and interact with native speakers. These tips appear in *Estrategia* boxes throughout the text. Detailed presentation and practice with reading strategies and process writing are included in the *Un paso más* section of the *Cuaderno de actividades*.

Preface *continued*

National Standards *Puentes* embraces the National Standards for Foreign Language Learning and incorporates appropriate activities and suggestions for implementing the "Five Cs": Communication, Cultures, Comparisons, Connections, and Communities. Communication, as the most prominent of the five standards, is fully addressed through myriad speaking, listening, reading, and writing activities. Cultural products and practices are presented in the context of each chapter, with special attention to comparison of customs in the *Puente cultural* section. The Connections standard is addressed though rich content on art, literature, geography, history, and other fields, as presented through the travelogue-style videos, the *Panorama cultural,* and the *A primera vista* sections. The *Puentes* website allows students to make additional connections by visiting websites of the Spanish-speaking world.

Note to Instructors

Since the number of states that require high school graduates to study a foreign language has increased and many of those graduates are choosing Spanish, a large number of students in our classrooms are high beginners. Because this profile is so challenging and diverse, the authors of *Puentes* hope that you will find the program suitable to meet the needs of your students and give you a wide variety of options to pursue. Please consult the *Instructor's Resource Manual* for specific suggestions on adapting this program to your needs.

Who are high beginners?

The placement of students who have already had some experience, formal or informal, with Spanish has always been a challenge. Some students do well in advanced classes; others, however, need a good review and additional practice in Spanish before continuing their studies at the intermediate level. It is for this latter group of "high beginners" that *Puentes* has been written.

Having taught thousands of high beginners at the University of South Carolina, we recognize that they are a group with varying levels of proficiency in all skills. In general, these learners have some conceptual knowledge of fundamental grammatical points such as verb conjugations in the present tense and noun-adjective agreement. Also, they are usually familiar with core vocabulary, such as colors, days of the week, clothing, and food. Some high beginners are able to function very simply with memorized phrases or expressions or even to reply to basic questions about personal information by recombining memorized information. As a rule, high beginners can recognize quite a bit but cannot produce with accuracy.

Given the current language requirements in the United States, most high beginners come with two years of high school Spanish. Their skill level upon entering our programs varies according to many factors, such as the number of years passed since their language experience, the quality of their language instruction, their unique learning style, and their motivation for learning the language. In general, high beginners are ready for a class with less emphasis on explanations and more emphasis on practicing and using the language in real-life situations.

General organization

The *Puentes* program consists of nine chapters. Each chapter consists of two or three *Pasos*, each with their core content of vocabulary, functional language, grammar and activities. A thematic introduction *(A primera vista)* and extension activities *(Un paso más, Gramática suplementaria)* round out each chapter.

Objetivos The first page of each chapter outlines the chapter objectives and content and lists the reading and writing strategies presented in the student activities manual.

A primera vista The chapter theme is introduced via a work of art (in odd-numbered chapters) or a song (in even-numbered chapters).

Vocabulario temático One of the two major components of each *Paso*, the *Vocabulario temático* presents thematically-related vocabulary in authentic contexts. Odd-numbered chapters emphasize social topics: family, friends, pastimes, academic studies, daily routines, celebrations, and life milestones. Even-numbered chapters focus on common travel situations: making hotel and travel arrangements, ordering meals, shopping, getting directions, handling minor ailments. The unique sentence templates in this section provide students with ready-to-use phrases as well as models of upcoming grammatical structures. A carefully sequenced chain of practice activities follows, with abundant opportunities for self-expression.

Gramática The second major component of each *Paso*, *Gramática* provides concise, level-appropriate explanations of the major grammatical structures that students need to master in order to advance to the Intermediate level on the ACTFL scale of proficiency. Those who wish broader coverage of grammar can pick and choose from the explanations and practices of *Gramática suplementaria*, conveniently located at the back of the textbook and completely coordinated to the chapter themes.

Un paso más The final section of each chapter offers three optional sections. *Vamos a hablar* is an information-gap activity that pairs of students complete for additional speaking practice. *En la Hacienda Vista Alegre* features a reality-T.V. type video with comprehension and speaking activities. Wrapping up this section, *Panorama cultural* focuses on a different Spanish-speaking country in each chapter and presents rich cultural content on history, famous personalities, and customs together with a travelogue-style video of the country.

Additional sections While culture is woven throughout the chapter, additional information is presented in short cultural readings (*Comentario cultural*) and through the results of a survey of customs (*Puente cultural*).

Components of the *Puentes* program

FOR THE STUDENT

Puentes, Fifth Edition, Student Text

Student Activities Manual (SAM)—*Cuaderno de actividades*

SAM Audio Program

Quia eSAM

: Heinle Learning Center

Premium Website www.cengage.com/spanish/puentes The student website offers much opportunity for practice and expansion. The self-correcting quizzes focus on each chapter's grammar and vocabulary *paso*-by-*paso*. A web exploration section allows students to complete guided research of topics that pertain to the chapter of focus, and encourages them to share their results with their instructor or classmates.

Atajo 4.0 CD-ROM Writing Assistant for Spanish

FOR THE INSTRUCTOR

Puentes, Fifth Edition, Annotated Instructor's Edition (AIE), packaged with Text Audio CDs. An instructor's guide at the beginning of the AIE provides the Audio Script for the in-class listening activities.

Instructor's Resource CD-ROM packaged with the Testing Audio CD

New, Expanded Video, available on DVD or on the Premium Website. The video includes two segments for each chapter, *En la Hacienda Vista Alegre* and *Imágenes de...*, a video visit to the country featured in each chapter's Panorama cultural section. Activities to accompany each video segment are found in the Un paso más sections of each chapter in the textbook and the *Cuaderno de actividades*.

Answer Key to the *Cuaderno de actividades* and Lab Audio Script, which can be made available to students.

Chapter Organization

Section	Description	In/Out of Class
Objetivos	Summary of chapter objectives and points of study	Both
A primera vista	Thematic introduction through fine art or music	In
Pasos (odd-numbered chapters have three pasos; even-numbered have two **pasos**). Each **paso** contains three or four presentations of vocabulary and grammar that may be any combination of the following:		
Vocabulario temático	Vocabulary and language functions in context	Both
Gramática	Grammar explanations	Both
Ponerlo a prueba (after each presentation)	Listening, writing, reading, and speaking activities that reinforce and practice the presentation	Both
Puente cultural (at the end of **Paso 1**)	Real-life survey of college-age Spanish speakers from a variety of backgrounds and countries with cross-cultural comparison activities	Both
Interspersed throughout each chapter appear the following sections:		
Estructuras esenciales	Explanations of minor grammar points or previews of more complex structures	Out
Estrategia	Learning and communicative strategies	Either
Comentario cultural	Cultural information	Either
Un paso más appears towards the end of each chapter. It contains:		
¡Vamos a hablar!	Information gap, pair-work speaking activity	In
En la Hacienda Vista Alegre	Reality-TV style video with activities	In
Panorama cultural	Introduction to a different Spanish-speaking country in each chapter	Both
Imágenes de...	Travelogue-style video of the country of focus and comprehension activity	Either
Vocabulario	End-of-chapter vocabulary list	Both

How *Puentes* Works

Component	Description	Usage	Skills: Developed/Practiced	More Information
Student Text	*Preliminary paso* + 9 chapters	Daily, in class and at home	Real-life listening and speaking tasks; integrated culture; selective grammar syllabus	Chapters are divided into manageable study units called *Pasos*; unique alternating chapter structure
Text Audio Program (on CD or Website)	Natural conversations model the vocabulary and linguistic functions; sample dialogues place the grammar in context	Use daily at home; may be used in class at the instructor's discretion	Listening comprehension based on real-life situations: face-to-face conversations, radio advertisements, telephone messages, etc.	Script available to instructors in *Annotated Instructor's Edition*
Student Activities Manual: *Cuaderno de actividades* **(also available online through QUIA™ or iLRN™)**	Features additional practice in all skills; *Imágenes de...* video activities, *¡Vamos a escribir!* process writing activities, *¡Vamos a leer!* applied reading strategies; *Panorama cultural* cultural comparisons activity	Use daily or as needed, depending on number of contact hours	**Reading:** authentic readings from periodical and literary sources; practical strategies; **Writing:** integrative, real-life writing tasks as well as grammar review practices; **Listening:** simulated radio broadcasts and pronunciation	Writing activities correlated with *Atajo 4.0: Writing Assistant for Spanish software* Separate answer key available for purchase and/or packaged with *Cuaderno de actividades*
Lab Audio Program (on CD or Premium Website)	A series of simulated radio broadcasts correlated to the chapter theme; pronunciation practice	Use once per chapter at home; may be used in class at instructor's discretion	Listening comprehension and pronunciation practice	
Website	Self-correcting vocabulary and grammar quizzes; meaningful, task-based web exploration activities	Use once per chapter with *Un paso más*	Real-life tasks; reading comprehension; cultural understanding	Located at: www.cengage.com/spanish/puentes
Premium Website	Multimedia resources and study tools: lab audio program, video program, grammar tutorials, and more	Use daily or as needed	Grammar, vocabulary, culture, and listening	Purchase a passcard for access
iLrn™ Spanish	A powerful and interactive study tool with an audio-enhanced e-book; companion videos, interactive Voice Board, online SAM with audio, interactive enrichment activities, and access to live, online tutoring with a Spanish teaching expert	Use as needed	Reading, writing, listening, grammar and vocabulary	Purchase a passcard for access

Component	Description	Usage	Skills: Developed/Practiced	More Information
Annotated Instructor's Edition	Contains margin notes on implementation of activities, additional practices, answers to activities	Optional usage by instructor	Provides helpful suggestions on how to implement and expand activities throughout text	
Instructor's Resource CD-ROM and Testing Audio CD	Instructor's resource materials, plus a Placement Exam that tests students on listening comprehension, vocabulary recognition, grammar usage, reading comprehension, and writing ability	Before the course begins, in order to evaluate whether or not a student should be placed into a high-beginner course	Listening, reading, writing, vocabulary, grammar	Packaged with Testing Audio CD
Testing Program (on Instructor's Resource CD-ROM)	Two tests per chapter for a total of 20 chapter tests; provides selection of contextualized test items, answer key and listening comprehension scripts; separate oral questions and oral situations for each chapter	Optional, at the end of each chapter	Tests focus on core information; tests assess vocabulary, grammar, reading, writing, culture, and listening comprehension

Oral questions and oral situations included for each chapter. | Answer key provided

Culture questions provided

Gramática suplementaria questions provided |
| **Software: *Atajo 4.0: Writing Assistant for Spanish*** | Word-processing program; bilingual Spanish-English dictionary; reference grammar with 250,000 conjugated verb forms; hard-to-define idiomatic expressions | Use with writing activities in the *Cuaderno de actividades;* optional | Develops writing skills through task-based writing activities | Correlations to appropriate activities provided in the *Cuaderno de actividades* |
| **Text-tied Video Program (on DVD and the Premium Website)** | Nineteen correlated video segments

Two segments per chapter (plus one bonus clip); *En la Hacienda Vista Alegre* focuses on the chapter theme and *Imágenes de...* highlights the country featured in *Panorama cultural* | Students may watch in or out of class; most activities are for in-class practice | All in Spanish; listening comprehension and cultural enrichment | Vocabulary exercises for *Imágenes de...* are in the *Un paso más* section of *Cuaderno de actividades*

Both videos may be viewed with the closed-captioning on or off |

Text Audio Script

Capítulo 1

Paso 1

1-1 Por el campus. [CD1-2]

1. Hola. Soy Luis Delgado. ¿Cómo te llamas?
2. Hola, Tamika. ¿Qué tal?
3. Buenos días, Tamika.
4. ¿Cómo está Ud.?
5. Hablamos más tarde. Hasta luego.
6. ¿Cómo estás, Tamika?

1-7 Dos compañeros. [CD1-3]

FRANCISCO:	Hola, soy Francisco Díaz. ¿Cómo te llamas?
SONIA:	Me llamo Sonia López.
FRANCISCO:	Mucho gusto, Sonia.
SONIA:	Igualmente. Así que... vamos a ser compañeros de clase.
FRANCISCO:	Así parece. A propósito, ¿de dónde eres, Sonia?
SONIA:	Nací en Puerto Rico, pero ahora vivo en Nueva York.
FRANCISCO:	¡Qué casualidad! Yo soy de Puerto Rico también, de Ponce.
SONIA:	Bueno, como somos compañeros en esta clase, déjame apuntar tu nombre en mi agenda. Quizás podemos estudiar juntos.
FRANCISCO:	De acuerdo.
SONIA:	Bien. ¿Cuál es tu nombre completo?
FRANCISCO:	Francisco Díaz Feliciano, pero todos me dicen Paco. ¿Y cuál es tu nombre?
SONIA:	Yo soy Sonia López Cruz. ¿Cuál es tu dirección en el campus?
FRANCISCO:	No vivo en el campus. Mi hermano y yo tenemos una pequeña casa en la calle Rosewood, número treinta y cinco, cincuenta. ¿Y tú? ¿Vives en el campus?
SONIA:	Sí, vivo en la Residencia Barnwell, número dos sesenta.
FRANCISCO:	¿Y tu teléfono?
SONIA:	Mi celular es el seis, noventa y seis, cuarenta y cinco, cincuenta y ocho.
FRANCISCO:	El mío es el seis, setenta y siete, cero, dos, ochenta y seis.
SONIA:	¿Por qué no me das tu dirección de correo-electrónico también?
FRANCISCO:	Muy bien. Es "el jefe nueve seis ocho arroba hotmail punto com."
SONIA:	Y la mía es "sonia veintitrés arroba yahoo punto com".
FRANCISCO:	Bueno, ¿vamos a tomar algo después de clase?
SONIA:	Sí, de acuerdo.

Paso 2

1-15 La foto. [CD1-5]

MODELO (You hear:) Mira, ésta es mi madre, Carmen.
(You write:) a. Carmen, la madre de Mercedes.

Mira esta foto. La sacamos el año pasado cuando fuimos de picnic con mis vecinos.

Mira, ésta es mi madre; Carmen.

Y ésta es mi hermana, Ana, tiene catorce años.

Ésta es Elena, una amiga de mi hermana.

Y éste, pues éste es Paco, mi hermano. Tiene solamente ocho años.

Éste es mi padre, Francisco.

Y ésta es nuestra tía Luisa, la hermana de mi padre.

Éste señor es nuestro vecino, Alberto Guzmán.

Ésta es Teresa, la esposa de Alberto.

Ésta es María, la hija de los vecinos. Es una buena amiga también.

Y ésta, pues, soy yo.

1-19 Una nueva amiga. [CD1-6]

IGNACIO:	Hola, Silvia. ¿Qué tal?
SILVIA:	Hola, Ignacio. ¡Qué gusto verte! Mira, ésta es mi buena amiga Delia. Delia, éste es mi amigo Ignacio.
DELIA:	Mucho gusto, Ignacio.
IGNACIO:	Encantado, Delia.
SILVIA:	Ignacio, Delia es de Puerto Rico.
IGNACIO:	¡No me digas! ¿Estás aquí para visitar a Silvia?

DELIA: Sí, estoy aquí de visita. Tenemos vacaciones en la universidad esta semana.

IGNACIO: ¿A qué universidad asistes?

DELIA: Estoy en mi primer año en la Universidad de Puerto Rico, en Bayamón.

IGNACIO: Y, ¿te gusta?

DELIA: Sí, bastante. Tomo cinco clases este semestre y son muy interesantes.

IGNACIO: ¿Vives en una residencia?

DELIA: No, vivo en casa con mi familia, pero mis amigos y yo pasamos mucho tiempo juntos. Y los fines de semana, trabajo de voluntaria en un hospital.

SILVIA: Oye, ¿vamos a tomar algo en el café? Podemos hablar mejor allí.

IGNACIO: Buena idea. ¡Vamos!

Paso 3

1-26 La clase de inglés. [CD1-8]

1. ¡Hola! Me llamo Marta y soy de Colombia, de Cali. En mis ratos libres me gusta ir al cine y, claro, pasar tiempo con mi novio. También me gusta navegar el Internet y jugar videojuegos.

2. ¡Hola! Soy Cristián y soy de Santiago, Chile. Soy muy deportista. Me gusta mucho practicar el fútbol y otros deportes también... eh, me gusta correr —corro todos los días— y los fines de semana, me gusta ir de fiesta.

3. ¡Hola! Soy Gabriela y soy argentina, de Córdoba. Me gusta mucho leer; me encantan sobre todo las novelas románticas y la poesía. Y también, con frecuencia voy de compras con mis amigas.

4. ¡Hola! Me llamo Antonio. Soy de Guayaquil, Ecuador. En mi tiempo libre, me gusta practicar deportes, —todos— el béisbol, el fútbol, el tenis. También me gusta correr y actualmente me estoy entrenando para un maratón. Tengo muchos amigos en Guayaquil y me gusta pasar tiempo con ellos.

5. ¡Hola! Soy Rosa y vengo de Cuzco, Perú. A mí también me gustan los deportes —me gusta mucho el tenis, más que ningún otro. También me gusta montar a caballo. Y eh (...) me gusta pasar tiempo con amigos e ir a fiestas para bailar.

Capítulo 2

Paso 1

2-1 La estación de autobuses. [CD1-11]

MODELO (You hear) Señores pasajeros, el autobús para Cuernavaca sale a las veintidós horas, de la plataforma número 3.

(You write) 22 (10 P.M.)

1. Señores pasajeros, el autobús para Puebla sale a las 22 horas 45 minutos de la plataforma 5.
2. El autobús para Acapulco sale a las 14 horas 3 minutos, de la plataforma 4.
3. El autobús para Veracruz sale a las 15 horas 36 minutos de la plataforma 1.
4. El autobús para Mérida sale a las 18 horas 15 minutos de la plataforma 8.
5. El autobús para Guadalajara sale a las 19 horas de la plataforma 7.

2-5 El conserje. [CD1-12]

La primera reservación es la de la señora Adela Acosta, para tres personas. Prefiere una habitación doble y llega el viernes, veintiséis de agosto a las cuatro de la tarde. La segunda reservación es la del señor Ramón Cordero, para una persona. Prefiere una habitación sencilla y llega el domingo, treinta y uno de julio a la una y media de la tarde. La tercera reservación es la del señor César Romero, para cuatro personas. Prefiere una habitación doble y llega el jueves, primero de septiembre, a las seis menos cuarto de la tarde.

2-8 El viaje de Daniel. [CD1-13]

G = Sra. Garretón; D = Daniel Vargas, estudiante

G: Agencia Turinam, María Teresa Garretón, a sus órdenes.

D: Sí, señora. Quisiera ir de Guadalajara a Miami.

G: ¿Cuándo desea salir?

D: Prefiero salir el jueves, cinco de agosto.

G: ¿Quiere Ud. un boleto sólo de ida, o de ida y vuelta?

D: Deseo un boleto de ida y vuelta.

G: ¿Cuándo desea regresar?

D: Creo que para el quince de diciembre. Es que... voy a estudiar en los Estados Unidos y el semestre termina en diciembre, pero no estoy seguro.

G: Bueno, no se preocupe. Voy a poner el 15 de diciembre, pero Ud. lo puede cambiar en cualquier momento.

D: Muy bien.

G: ¿Prefiere Ud. viajar de noche o de día?

D: Eh..., me gusta más de día.

G: Bien. Aquí tengo su reservación. Ud. sale el jueves, cinco de agosto, a las diez y cuarto de la mañana en el vuelo número ciento dieciocho de la aerolínea norteamericana Delta. Y su vuelo de regreso el quince de diciembre es a la una menos veinte de la tarde en el vuelo doscientos ochenta. ¿Cómo desea pagar?

D: Voy a pagar con la tarjeta de crédito Visa.

G: Muy bien. Ud. va a recibir los boletos dentro de una semana.

D: Muchas gracias.

G: No hay de qué.

Paso 2

2-15 Una reservación. [CD1-15]

E = empleada; T = turista

E: Hotel Carlton. Buenos días.

T: Buenos días. Quisiera hacer una reservación, por favor.

E: Muy bien, señor. ¿Para cuándo?

T: Bueno, llegamos el próximo jueves; creo que es el día 4 de octubre.

E: Jueves, 4 de octubre. ¿Sabe Ud. más o menos a qué hora va a llegar?

T: Pues sí, creo que vamos a llegar como a las seis de la tarde.

E: A las seis de la tarde. Bueno, y... ¿esta reservación es para Ud. sólo, o sea, para una persona?

T: No, somos dos, mi esposa y yo. Quisiéramos una habitación con cama doble.

E: Muy bien. Una habitación con cama doble.

T: Sí, perfecto... eh, ¿cuánto cuesta, por favor?

E: La tarifa es 158 dólares por día. ¿Piensa pagar con tarjeta de crédito?

T: Sí, con Visa.

E: Muy bien, su nombre y apellidos por favor.

T: Sí... Víctor Fuentes López.

E: Víctor Fuentes López. Muy bien, Sr. Fuentes, entonces confirmamos su reservación para el día 4 de octubre, eh... en una habitación con cama doble.

T: Perfecto. Muchas gracias.

E: A la orden.

2-19 Un viaje a México. [CD1-16]

MODELO (You hear)

SRA. PALA: Quiero hacer una reservación para un hotel en el Distrito Federal. ¿Qué hotel me recomienda?

EL AGENTE: El hotel Presidente Intercontinental. Es un hotel de cuatro estrellas. Un cuarto doble cuesta dos mil doscientos pesos por noche.

(You write) Presidente Intercontinental: 2200 pesos

P = Sra. Pala; A = Agente de viaje

Número 1

P: Me gustaría un hotel más económico.

A: El Hotel Camino Real cuesta sólo 1650 pesos por noche.

Número 2

P: También quiero pasar unos días en Cancún. ¿Son caros los vuelos?

A: Un boleto de ida a Cancún cuesta 2750 pesos.

Número 3

P: ¿Cuánto es el boleto de ida y vuelta a Cancún?

A: Es menos caro. Cuesta 5225 pesos.

Número 4

P: Quiero visitar Acapulco y Taxco. ¿Hay excursiones?

A: Sí, señora. Tenemos viajes que cuestan 8800 pesos.

Número 5

P: También me interesa mucho el ecoturismo. ¿Cuánto cuestan los viajes a la Barranca del Cobre?

A: Una excursión cuesta aproximadamente 10.945 pesos. Este precio incluye el hotel, las comidas, y el viaje a Barranca.

Capítulo 3

Paso 1

3-1 La familia Martínez. [CD1-18]

MODELO (You hear) [A:] Esa señora es muy guapa. ¿Quién es?

[D:] Es nuestra tía Ginette. Es la esposa del hermano de mi padre.

[A:] Ah. ¿Viven tus tíos aquí en Maracaibo?

[D:] Ahora no. Viven en isla Margarita. ¿No ves qué playa más bonita?

(You write: *la tía* in the blank, and select *b. isla Margarita*.)

A – Amiga; D – Dulce

Número 1

A: Entonces... éste es el hermano de tu padre.

D: Sí, ése es nuestro tío Enrique. Se parece mucho a papá, ¿no? Trabaja en un hotel cerca de la playa. Es mi tío favorito, ¿sabes? Siempre tiene tiempo para hablar conmigo, para escuchar mis problemas.

Número 2

A: ¡Qué suerte tienes! Hmm... así que éstos son tus tres primos.

D: Bueno, ya te lo explico. Ésa es mi prima Claudia. Ella está casada y su esposo se llama Alejandro. Ése es el hermano de Claudia, mi primo Felipe. Felipe es estudiante de primer año en la universidad, donde estudia matemáticas.

Número 3

A: Entonces, esta niña, ¿quién es? ¿la hija de Claudia?

D: Sí, es la hija de Claudia y Alejandro; se llama Aurora. Tiene sólo 3 añitos. En esta foto la ves con su gato, Tigre.

A: Es una niña preciosa.

Número 4

A: Bueno: esta última foto parece muy, muy vieja. ¿Quién es este señor tan guapo?

D: Es mi abuelo Francisco, el padre de mi padre. Y esa señora es mi abuela Sofía. Esa niña es Felicia, su hija mayor, en el día de su bautismo.

Número 5

A: Y los otros dos señores, ¿quiénes son?

D: Son los padrinos de Felicia, pero no recuerdo sus nombres. Creo que eran unos buenos amigos de mis abuelos.

A: ¡Qué fotos más interesantes!

3-5 ¿Quién es... ? [CD1-19]

D = Daniela; I = Ignacio

D: Oye, Ignacio, ¿quién es ese chico alto y rubio?

I: ¿El chico que lleva anteojos?

D: Sí, ése es, alto y delgado...

I: Ah, sí, ese chico se llama Antonio. Es estudiante de farmacia en la universidad.

D: Bueno... y ¿quién es esa señora alta?

I: ¿Quién? ¿La chica rubia del pelo largo?

D: No, la señora bien alta y morena, no sé, la que tiene 40 años más o menos.

I: Ésa es Carolina Romero. Es una íntima amiga de mi mamá.

D: ¿Quién es el hombre alto de pelo castaño?

I: ¿Ese hombre guapo que lleva barba?

D: Sí, ése.

I: Ése es mi tío Alejandro. Es de Costa Rica, pero está aquí de vacaciones.

D: ¡Qué lindo! Y ¿quién es esa chica baja, la rubia?

I: ¿La rubia bajita?

D: Sí, es baja y delgada y tiene el pelo corto.

I: Ésa es mi novia, Rosaura. Vamos, te la presento.

Paso 2

3-14 De venta. [CD1-21]

Acabo de encontrar la casa perfecta para Ud. ¡Es fabulosa! Tiene dos pisos con tres dormitorios; uno está en la planta baja y hay dos en el primer piso. Hay dos baños; uno está en la habitación matrimonial y sólo tiene ducha, pero en el otro hay ducha y bañera. La cocina es tan grande que hay espacio para una mesa con sillas, pero, desafortunadamente, no tiene nevera. Sin embargo, hay un garaje enorme... hasta para dos carros. Por suerte, ahora acaban de rebajar el precio de la casa y está casi regalada por $98.000,00 pesos. Debe ir a ver esta casa cuanto antes porque a ese precio se va a vender como pan caliente. ¿Cuándo quiere ir a verla?

3-19 El cuarto de Mayra. [CD1-22]

¡Rodolfo! El apartamento de Mayra es fabuloso; es tan amplio y tan limpio. Es azul como su dormitorio aquí en casa. Lo mejor es que tiene un clóset enorme. También, hay una ventana con una vista muy bonita. Mayra tiene la cama debajo de la ventana. Al lado de la cama, tiene la mesita de noche con su radio y el despertador. A la izquierda de la puerta, Mayra tiene un sillón muy cómodo donde puede estudiar o leer. Delante del sillón, hay una mesita con un televisor. A la derecha de la puerta, hay una cómoda muy pequeña, pero como el clóset es tan grande, no importa. ¡Es fantástico! ¿Cuándo vas a ir conmigo a visitarla?

Paso 3

3-26 Un estudiante de primer año. [CD1-24]

G = Gustavo; M = Madre

M: Hijo, estoy tan contenta de verte. Cuéntame todo. ¿Cómo van tus clases?

G: Pues, todo va bastante bien. Como te puedes imaginar, la vida universitaria es bien diferente de la vida en la escuela secundaria. Pero me gusta muchísimo.

M: ¡Cuánto me alegro! Bueno, cuéntame más. ¿Cómo pasas los días?

G: Primero, me despierto bien temprano, como a las seis y media, y me levanto a las siete menos cuarto.

M: ¡A las seis y media! ¡Qué temprano! Y ¿después qué?

G: Bueno... después de ducharme, voy a la cafetería para el desayuno. Luego tengo tres clases. La primera es a las ocho... Es una clase de filosofía y el profesor es fascinante. Después tengo mis clases de inglés y de sicología.

M: Así que estás muy ocupado por la mañana. ¿Tienes tiempo para almorzar?

G: Sí, por supuesto. Almuerzo con mis amigos a la una, o a la una y media. Después, normalmente voy a la biblioteca para estudiar. Los lunes y miércoles también asisto a un laboratorio de química.

M: ¡Qué día más largo!

G: En realidad, no es tan malo. A veces mis amigos y yo nos divertimos un rato; vamos al gimnasio y jugamos al básquetbol por una hora antes de cenar en la cafetería.

M: Hijo, estás muy ocupado. Pero, recuerda una cosa. Tienes que dormir lo suficiente si quieres sacar buenas notas.

G: Ya lo sé, mamá, no te preocupes. No me acuesto muy tarde, a las once y media, o a veces a la medianoche.

3-34 Los quehaceres. [CD1-26]

M = Mamá; A = Adalberto (husband/dad); S = Samuel (son); P = Pilar (daughter)

M: Hoy es día de limpieza general. Vamos a dividir los quehaceres. Adalberto, mi amor, ¿qué prefieres hacer, limpiar el garaje o ir al supermercado?

A: Bueno, mi amor, es que hay un partido de béisbol entre los Cardenales y los Leones. No puedo limpiar el garaje ahora, pero te prometo que mañana lo limpio.

M: *(Sighs, then turns her attention to her son.)* Bueno, Samuel, los perros tienen hambre. ¿Cuándo piensas darles de comer?

S: Ah... Mami, no tengo tiempo ahora. Tú sabes que todos los sábados yo siempre juego al tenis con Manuel. Pilar puede darles de comer.

P: ¿¡Yo!? ¿Por qué yo? Son tus perros, idiota.

M: Hijos, ¡no peleen! Samuel, antes de salir de esta casa, quiero que les des de comer a los perros.

S: *(dejectedly, but resigned)* Sí, mamá.

M: Y tú, Pilar, ya sabes que tienes que lavar la ropa hoy.

P: Lo sé, mami, pero tengo planes. Voy a salir con mis amigas. Si vuelvo temprano, te prometo que la lavo esta tarde. ¿Está bien?

M: No. No está nada bien. Bueno, como nadie quiere ayudar, yo tampoco voy a trabajar. Entonces en vez de preparar el almuerzo, voy a ir de compras.

Capítulo 4

Paso 1

4-1 En el restaurante La Estancia. [CD1-27]

A = Adriana; H = Hugo; C = Camarero; O = Omar

C: ¿Qué desea, señora?

A: De primer plato, tráigame la sopa de pollo, por favor. Y de segundo, una tortilla. Eh... ¿puede traerme una ensalada verde con la tortilla?

C: Claro que sí. ¿Y para beber?

A: Vamos a ver... para beber quiero agua mineral y... de postre, flan.

C: Muy bien. ¿Y Ud., señor?

O: Por favor, yo quiero biftec... arroz con frijoles y bróculi. De postre, tráigame un helado de fresa, si lo tiene.

C: Sí, señor. ¿Qué desea para beber?

O: Una cerveza nacional, por favor.

C: Muy bien. ¿Y Ud.?

H: Voy a probar el pollo asado, con maíz.

C: Ah, lo siento, señor, no tenemos maíz hoy.

H: Bueno, entonces con papas y una ensalada. Para beber, tráigame una copa de vino. Y de postre... quisiera torta, por favor.

C: Regreso en seguida con las bebidas.

4-6 ¿Qué quieren los clientes? [CD1-28]

C = Camarero(a); M = Cliente (masculino); F = Cliente (femenino)

Conversación 1

F: ¡Camarero!

C: A sus órdenes, señora.

F: Por favor, ¿qué ingredientes tiene la papa a la huancaína?

C: Tiene papas con una salsa de leche y queso. Es un plato delicioso, muy típico de Perú. ¿Quiere probar un poquito?

Conversación 2

M: Camarero, la cuenta, por favor.

C: Aquí la tiene.

M: Señor, ¿está incluida la propina en la cuenta?

C: Sí, aquí se incluye automáticamente.

M: ¿Aceptan Uds. tarjetas de crédito?

C: Sí, señor.

Conversación 3

F: Camarero, por favor.

C: Mande Ud., señora.

F: Mire, la sopa de pollo está fría.

C: Perdone, señora. Le traigo otro plato en seguida.

Conversación 4

C: ¿Qué desean comer?

F: Quiero el biftec a la parrilla con ensalada y pan. Y para beber quisiera una copa de vino tinto.

M: Yo voy a probar el pollo asado con arroz amarillo y platanitos fritos. También quiero una cerveza.

Paso 2

4-14 Servicio a domicilio. [CD1-30]

S = Sra. Santana; R = Roberto

R: Supermercado Sánchez. ¿En qué puedo servirle?

E: Eh, Roberto, ¿eres tú? Soy Amalia Santana.

R: Ah, sí, Sra. Santana. ¿Cómo está Ud. hoy?

S: Muy bien, gracias. ¿Y tú?

R: Yo, muy bien, gracias a Dios. ¿En qué puedo servirle hoy?

S: Necesito algunas cosas y quiero que me las traigan a mi casa.

R: Perfecto, un momento mientras escribo su nombre aquí. Sra. Amalia Santana. Bueno, Ud. vive en la calle Luna, ¿verdad?

S: Sí, calle Luna, número 58.

R: Número 58. Muy bien, y ¿su número de teléfono, por favor?

S: Es el 29-78-03.

E: 29-78-03... Muy bien. ¿Qué desea Ud. hoy?

S: Bueno, primero un pollo, bien grande.

R: Un pollo, que sea grande.

S: Sí, y también, dos kilos de biftec, y lo quiero muy bueno, sin mucha grasa.

R: Claro, dos kilos de biftec.

S: Bueno, vamos a ver... de fruta... necesito un kilo de melocotones.

R: Un kilo de melocotones.

S: Una lechuga, y que sea fresca.

R: Sí, una lechuga... tan fresca como la primavera.

S: Déjame pensar, eh... Necesito un frasco de mayonesa también.

R: Un frasco de mayonesa. ¿Quiere algo más?

S: ¿Tienen pan fresco?

R: Sí, por supuesto.

S: Entonces, una barra de pan. Creo que eso es todo.

R: Muy bien, Sra. Santana. Ahora más tarde le pongo los precios al pedido. ¿Está bien si entregamos todo esto a las once?

S: Sí, a las once está bien. Y muchas gracias, Roberto.

R: A Ud., señora. Hasta pronto.

R: Adiós, Roberto. Hasta pronto.

Capítulo 5

Paso 1

5-1 Las clases de Reinaldo. [CD1-33]

R = Reinaldo; P = Patricia

P: Hola, Reinaldo.

R: Hola, Patricia. ¿Cómo va el semestre?

P: Bastante bien. Tengo un horario muy bueno y me gustan mis profesores.

R: ¿Qué clases estás tomando?

P: Los lunes, miércoles y viernes tengo biología a las nueve. Luego, a las once, tengo física. Los martes y jueves tengo cálculo a las once y un laboratorio de biología a las cuatro.

R: ¡Hombre, sí que tienes un horario muy bueno!

P: ¿Y a ti, cómo te va, Reinaldo? ¿Todavía piensas graduarte este año?

R: Sí, efectivamente, voy a graduarme a finales de noviembre.

P: ¡Qué bien! ¿Y qué tal tu horario este semestre?

R: Me gusta bastante, pero no es tan bueno como el tuyo. Los lunes, miércoles y viernes tengo literatura inglesa a las ocho y literatura norteamericana a las diez. A las doce tengo cinematografía. Los martes y jueves tengo historia del arte a las ocho y antropología a las doce.

P: ¡Pobrecito! Tienes clases todos los días a las ocho.

R: Bueno, en realidad no me importa tanto porque me encantan mis profesores este semestre. A propósito, Patricia, tengo que irme corriendo porque mi clase de antropología empieza en cinco minutos.

P: De acuerdo. ¡Nos vemos pronto!

R: ¡Chao! ¡Hasta pronto!

5-6 ¿Cómo te va? [CD1-34]

E = Elsa; A = Andrés

Número 1

E: Hola, Andrés.

A: Ah, ¡hola, Elsa! ¿Cómo estás?

E: Bien, gracias. ¿Adónde vas con tanta prisa?

A: A la clase de química. Estoy tomando una clase con el profesor Vazques. Es un tipo muy exigente y quisquilloso, ¿sabes? No quiero llegar tarde.

E: Comprendo perfectamente. Tomé una clase con él el semestre pasado y fue pésimo.

Número 2

E: ¿Cómo van tus otras clases?

A: Me encanta mi clase de filosofía. Siempre hablamos de temas muy interesantes en clase.

E: Es mi clase favorita también.

Número 3

E: Oye ¿no estás tomando historia este semestre?

A: Sí, historia medieval. ¡Es fatal! El profesor da unas conferencias muy largas y aburridas. ¿Y tú? ¿Estás tomando historia?

E: No, este semestre no.

Número 4

A: ¿Qué otra clase tienes?

E: Tengo una clase de sociología que me interesa mucho. La profesora no es muy dinámica pero es organizada y muy amable.

A: Mira, Elsa, tengo que irme ahora, pero ¿por qué no nos vemos en el café esta tarde, a eso de las 4:00?

E: ¡De acuerdo! ¡Nos vemos a las 4:00!

A: ¡Hasta entonces!

5-10 Se busca. [CD1-35]

Gracias por su llamada. Las oportunidades de empleo para hoy, el tres de abril, son las siguientes:

Secretaria bilingüe para una compañía multinacional: Se requiere dominio perfecto del español y del inglés y dos años de experiencia.

Director de personal para una tienda de departamentos: Se buscan candidatos con título universitario en negocios y dos años de experiencia.

Consultor técnico: Se requiere un título universitario en informática y tres años de experiencia.

Maestro de primaria: Se prefieren candidatos con especialización en matemáticas y ciencias.

Trabajador social: Se buscan candidatos con experiencia en el área de salud pública.

Para mayor información sobre éstas y otras oportunidades de empleo, llame al 555-8991 de las nueve de la mañana a las cinco de la tarde.

Paso 2

5-15 El primer día de clases de Ernesto. [CD1-36]

M = La madre; E = Ernesto

M: ¡Hola, Ernesto! ¿Cómo te fue todo hoy? ¿Qué tal tus clases?

E: ¿Qué tal, Mamá? ¿Cómo estás?

M: Bueno, ¡cuéntame!

E: Pues, todo bien, Mamá. Esta mañana me levanté a las siete y media de la mañana, me vestí y fui a mi clase de filosofía a las ocho.

M: Y, ¿te gustó?

E: Sí, muchísimo. El profesor es joven y muy dinámico. Además, hay mucha interacción en la clase.

M: ¿A qué otras clases asististe?

E: A las diez y diez asistí a la clase de inglés. Esa clase fue un poco aburrida. Y, hay que leer varias novelas.

M: ¿Qué comiste?

E: Volví a la residencia a eso de la una de la tarde y almorcé en la cafetería. Entonces, estudié un poco antes de ir al laboratorio de química.

M: ¡Hombre! ¡Qué ocupado! Y, ¿cuándo vas a estudiar?

E: Por la noche despues de cenar.

M: Pues, aliméntate bien. Y, hablamos pronto. ¡Cuídate!

E: Sí, Mamá, hasta pronto.

Paso 3

5-25 El viaje al acuario. [CD1-39]

V = Virginia; K = Karina

K: ¡Hola, Virginia! ¿Cómo pasaste el fin de semana?

V: ¿Qué tal, Karina? ¿El fin de semana? Pues, mis amigos y yo condujimos al acuario en Charleston. Nuestro profesor de ciencia marina nos prometió crédito extra. Nos gustó muchísimo. Allí vimos una gran variedad de animales acuáticos. ¡Fue una experiencia fenomenal!

K: ¿Qué hicieron ustedes?

V: El director del acuario nos dio una charla personal. Luego, tuvimos que hacer un resumen de lo que ocurrió porque nuestro profesor dijo que teníamos que entregar un informe escrito para poder recibir el crédito extra.

K: ¡Eso suena maravilloso! ¿Qué animales acuáticos vieron?

V: Quisimos ver los delfines, pero no fue posible. En vez, vimos algunos tiburones. ¡Qué horror! Luego, cuando fuimos a comer pizza antes de regresar a Columbia, yo no tenía hambre.

Capítulo 6

Paso 1

6-1 Una orden por catálogo. [CD2-2]

O = Operadora; C = Cliente

O: Gracias por llamar al servicio de catálogo de JCPenny. ¿En qué puedo servirle?

C: Buenos días, señorita. Me gustaría hacer un pedido.

O: Muy bien. Primero, por favor, ¿cuál es su código de área de teléfono?

C: Es el 216.

O: Dos dieciséis. ¿Y su teléfono?

C: Es el 555-4884.

O: Cinco-cincuenta y cinco-cuarenta y ocho-ochenta y cuatro. Su apellido, por favor.

C: Davis.

O: Y su nombre...

C: Margarita.

O: Su dirección, por favor.

C: Calle Correne, número 1743.

O: En Canton, Ohio, código postal 44718, ¿verdad?

C: Sí, efectivamente.

O: Muy bien, Sra. Davis. El número de su primer artículo.

C: Bien, es... el... R508–1922.

O: Gracias.... una chaqueta. ¿Qué talla quiere?

C: Talla 44.

O: ¿Y el color?

C: Número 35, azul marino.

O: ¿Cuántas quiere?

C: Una.

O: Bien. Para confirmar: una chaqueta, talla 44, en azul marino... por $75.00. Su siguiente selección...

C: Bueno, también quiero pedir una falda... es el número... R484-0641 D.

O: Una falda... ¿en qué talla?

C: En talla 10... y el color número 03, rojo.

O: Talla 10... color 03, rojo, eh... por $58.00. ¿Cuántas quiere?

C: Una.

O: Una... Bien... Su siguiente selección.

C: Bueno, quiero calcetines... R503-0028 C.

O: Calcetines. ¿De qué color?

C: En negro, número 8.

O: Calcetines de hombre, en negro... éstos se venden en paquetes de dos pares y cuestan $15.00 por los dos paquetes. ¿Cuántos quiere?

C: Pues, dos paquetes.

O: Muy bien, dos paquetes por $15.00. Su siguiente selección.

C: Nada más, eso es todo.

O: ¿Mandamos la mercancía a su casa o quiere recogerla en la tienda?

C: Quiero recogerla en la tienda, aquí en Canton.

O: Recoger en Canton, muy bien... ¿Qué tarjeta de crédito quiere usar?

C: Eh... prefiero pagar al contado.

O: Al contado. Muy bien. Este pedido estará en la tienda en Canton el próximo lunes. Gracias por su orden.

C: De nada. Adiós.

6-6 En Madrid Xanadú. [CD2-3]

C = Carla; D = Dependienta (female) 1; D2 = Dependienta (female); N = Narrador

D: Buenos días, señorita. ¿La atienden?

C: Buenos días. Estoy buscando un vestido, uno muy elegante, que sirva para una boda. Es que se casa una de mis amigas...

D: Ah... para una boda... pues tenemos un surtido muy amplio ahora. ¿Qué talla lleva Ud.?

C: Llevo la talla 38.

D: Venga conmigo, señorita, y le enseño los vestidos que tenemos. ¿Buscaba algún color en particular?

C: No, aunque creo que me favorecen más los tonos claros, un azul celeste o un rosado claro, por ejemplo.

D: El azul está muy de moda este año. ¿Qué le parece este modelo en azul celeste? Es de seda.

C: ¡Qué elegante! Esto es exactamente lo que buscaba. Me encanta.

D: ¿Por qué no se lo prueba? El probador está allí, a la izquierda.

N: Unos minutos más tarde...

D: Bueno, ¿cómo le queda?

C: No sé. Creo que me queda grande. ¿Qué le parece a Ud.?

D: Mm... bueno quizás es un poquito... Vamos a consultar con mi colega... Hortensia, por favor, ¿podrías ayudarnos?

D2: Sí, voy... Ah, señorita, ¡pero qué guapa está con ese vestido! ¡El color le queda fenomenal!

D: Sí, pero, ¿qué te parece? ¿No le queda grande?

D2: Bueno... quizás un poquito por aquí, pero nuestra modista puede arreglárselo fácilmente.

C: Bueno... Me encanta de verdad. Entonces, si la modista puede arreglármelo, me lo llevo. ¿Cuánto cuesta?

D: 103 euros.

C: Muy bien. Me lo llevo. Aquí tiene mi tarjeta de crédito.

Paso 2

6-14 Muchos regalos. [CD2-5]

L = Liliana; C = Cristina

L: ¡Hola!

C: ¡Hola, Liliana! Oye, ¡cuántos paquetes tienes!

L: Sí, acabo de volver del mercado. Mira todos los regalos que compré, y todos a muy buen precio.

C: Uy, me gusta ese suéter. ¡Qué bonito!

L: Es para mi hermana; yo sé que le va a encantar. Es de seda y sólo costó 62 euros.

C: ¡Qué bien! Casi te lo regalaron. ¿Qué más compraste?

L: Mira, para mi mamá...

C: Ah ¡qué mantilla bordada más bonita!

L: Imagínate que sólo pagué 120 euros.

C: Es preciosa.

L: Y esta pulsera se la compré a mi abuela por 93 euros.

C: El oro se ve de buena calidad. ¿Y ese cinturón? ¿Para quién es?

L: Es para mi hermano. Es de piel y lo compré por sólo 45 euros.

C: Tú sí que sabes regatear.

L: Luego a mi mejor amiga le compré esta botella de perfume por 57 euros.

C: ¡Increíble! Pero, ¿no te compraste nada para ti?

L: Bueno, no tengo tiempo ahora para contarte todo lo que me compré. Y, no me olvidé de ti. También te traje un pequeño recuerdo de España.

6-18 En el mercado de artesanías. [CD2-6]

C = Cliente   D = Dependiente

Número 1

C: ¿Cuánto cuestan las camisetas?

D: Depende. Hay de varios precios.

C: ¿Cuánto cuesta la blanca que tiene la bandera de España?

D: Ésa cuesta dieciocho euros.

C: Me parece mucho dinero. ¿Me puede hacer un descuento?

D: Sí, se la doy por dieciséis euros.

C: Muy bien. Me la llevo.

Número 2

C: ¿Cuánto valen las castañuelas?

D: Las tengo de diferentes estilos y precios. ¿Cuáles les gustan más?

C: Las que tienen la flor roja.

D: Esas valen doce euros.

C: ¡Qué caras! Le doy ocho.

D: No, ocho euros es muy poco. Diez euros.

C: ¡Muy bien! Diez euros.

Número 3

C: ¿Tiene algún brazalete de plata?

D: Sí, tengo varias pulseras. Aquí están. ¿Cuál prefiere?

C: Me gusta más la que tiene la decoración azul.

D: Ésa cuesta catorce euros.

C: Eso es mucho dinero. ¿Acepta doce?

D: No, doce es muy poco.

C: Entonces, le doy trece euros.

D: Vale.

Capítulo 7

Paso 1

7-1 ¿Quieres ir a... ? [CD2-8]

L = Locutor; P = Patricia; C = Carmen

L: Radio Omega, la mejor emisora de esta región, tiene el placer de anunciar y patrocinar un concierto en el Estadio Ricardo Saprissa el domingo 10 de noviembre, a las ocho de la noche, por el fenomenal Juanes. Compre su boleto por Internet o en la taquilla del Palacio de Bellas Artes. Los boletos cuestan cuarenta mil colones, veintiocho mil colones y dieciséis mil quinientos colones. ¡No se olviden, el 10 de noviembre, Juanes en concierto!

P: Carmen, ¿oíste lo que acaba de anunciar el locutor? Un concierto de Juanes, el guapísimo cantante colombiano.

C: ¡Tranquila, Patricia! Pues, ¿cuándo es?

P: A las ocho de la noche el 10 de noviembre. ¡Vamos, chica!

C: No sé, los boletos están un poco caros. Quiero ahorrar dinero para mis vacaciones.

P: ¡Ay, Carmen! Tienes que ir. Es mi cantante favorito. No vamos a perder esta oportunidad.

C: ¡Paciencia, Patricia! Déjame pensarlo. Quizás mis padres me pueden regalar el boleto para mi cumpleaños.

P. ¡Ojalá! Mira que si no vienes te borro de mi lista...

C: Bueno, Pati ahora tenemos que estudiar para nuestro examen de bioquímica. Hablamos más de esto mañana, ¿de acuerdo?

P: Está bien.

7-6 ¿Qué tal el fin de semana? [CD2-9]

M = Marcos; P = Pilar

P: Hola, Marcos.
M: Hola, Pilar. ¿Qué tal tu fin de semana?
P: Lo pasé muy bien. El sábado Rosa y yo fuimos al lago.
M: ¡Qué suerte! ¿Qué hicieron allí?

P: Los padres de Rosa tienen un barco de vela. Así que paseamos todo el día en el barco, pescamos un poco... En fin, fue un día muy tranquilo pero divertido. ¿Y tú Marcos, qué hiciste?
M: Bueno, en realidad mi fin de semana fue fatal.
P: ¡Ay pobrecito! ¿Qué pasó?
M: El viernes por la noche fui a un festival donde tenían muchas comidas internacionales. Probé un poco de todo y, no sé, alguno de los platos me cayó muy mal. Me enfermé y tuve que quedarme en casa el resto del fin de semana.
P: ¡Qué lástima! ¡Cuánto lo siento!

Paso 2

7-15 El pronóstico para los Estados Unidos. [CD2-11]

El pronóstico para los Estados Unidos hoy, lunes, 25 de noviembre, a las nueve y media de la mañana es el siguiente. Para el Noreste del país, va a hacer sol y frío. Actualmente la temperatura en la Ciudad de Nueva York es de 48 grados. En el Sureste, hay lluvia y viento. En la bella ciudad de Miami la temperatura está a 81 grados. En el norte de la zona central se espera frío con lluvia y nieve. La temperatura hoy en Chicago va a llegar a unos 42 grados. En el sur de la zona central, va a hacer sol y buen tiempo con 74 grados en la ciudad de Houston, Texas. En la costa del Pacífico se espera mucho viento y sol. En la ciudad de Los Ángeles va a hacer viento con 63 grados.

7-19 Días festivos. [CD2-12]

Número 1

MARISA: Me encanta esta época del año, porque me parece que todo el mundo está de buen humor. En mi casa, es motivo para una gran celebración. El día 24, o sea la Nochebuena, nos reunimos en casa de los abuelos y se hace una gran cena; a la medianoche, vamos a la misa de gallo. Luego, al día siguiente, todos vienen a nuestra casa para almorzar y después abrimos nuestros regalos. Lo de los regalos, en realidad, no tiene tanta importancia como antes. Cuando era niña, claro que me gustaba recibir regalos de Papá Noel, pero ahora, para mí, lo esencial es estar entre familia.

Número 2

ROLANDO: Por lo general, es un día normal, como cualquier otro, y no hago nada en especial para celebrarlo, pero el año pasado, mi novia Maritere me hizo una fiesta sorpresa, y para decir la verdad, lo pasé muy bien. Vinieron todos mis amigos, los compañeros de trabajo y bailamos y cantamos toda la noche. Claro, cuando era niño era otra cosa. Siempre había una fiesta para los amiguitos, teníamos una piñata y —lo mejor de todo— yo apagaba las velas del pastel.

Paso 3

7-28 Y luego, ¿qué? [CD2-14]

E = Elisa; M = Mamá (Beatriz)

E: ¡Mamá, mamá!

M: Elisa, ahora voy, no chilles tanto.

E: ¡Mamá, no lo vas a creer! Es horrible... pobre Carlos...

M: Cálmate, Elisa, tranquila. Ahora dime. ¿Qué le pasó a Carlos?

E: Ay, mamá. ¡Carlos se partió una pierna!

M: ¡No me digas! ¿Se partió una pierna? Pero, ¿cómo? ¿Cuándo ocurrió?

E: Hace una hora. Ya sabes que Carlos siempre juega al fútbol los sábados por la mañana. Bueno, esta mañana, mientras jugaba, chocó con un jugador del otro equipo y se rompió la pierna.

M: Ay, no... el pobre. Pero, ¿cómo está? ¿Dónde está ahora?

E: Pues, todavía está en el hospital.

M: ¿En el hospital? ¿En qué hospital? ¿Quién lo llevó allí?

E: Bueno, por suerte, había un médico allí en el campo de fútbol. Era el padre de uno de los otros chicos del equipo. Entonces, ese señor, el médico, examinó a Carlos y dijo que tenía la pierna rota. Luego llegó la ambulancia y lo llevaron a la Clínica de la Merced. Creo que le van a sacar radiografías.

M: Pero, ¿estás segura, hija? ¿Tiene la pierna rota de verdad?

E: Sí, mami. Primero nadie se dio cuenta. Pero cuando Carlos intentó levantarse, el dolor era muy fuerte y se cayó. Es la pierna izquierda.

M: Bueno, Elisa, yo voy al hospital. Tú espera aquí y te llamaré desde el hospital.

E: Ay, mami, por favor, quiero ir contigo. Por favor, déjame ir contigo.

M: Bueno, está bien, puedes venir conmigo. Pero vamos ya.

Capítulo 8

Paso 1

8-1 Unas diligencias. [CD2-17]

Conversación 1

S = Señorita Rosales; R = Recepcionista

S: Quiero mandar estas tarjetas postales a mis amigos. ¿Dónde se puede comprar sellos?

R: El correo está bastante cerca del hotel.

S: ¿Sí? ¿Dónde está, por favor?

R: Está al final de esta calle.

S: Gracias.

Conversación 2

S = Señor Rulfo; R = Recepcionista

R: Buenas tardes, Señor Rulfo. ¿Cómo va su visita de la ciudad?

S: La ciudad es realmente bellísima. Pero, para decirle la verdad, no me encuentro muy bien hoy. ¿Dónde se puede comprar aspirina?

R: Hay una farmacia en la esquina. Pero, si se encuentra mal, le puedo llamar a un médico.

S: No, no. No necesito a un médico. ¿Entonces la farmacia está muy cerca?

R: Sí, está aquí al lado del hotel, en la esquina con la Calle Bolívar. No se puede perder.

S: Muchas gracias.

8-6 ¿Para ir a... ? [CD2-18]

P = Policía; T = Turista

MODELO (You hear:) No está lejos de aquí. Siga por esta calle, la calle Montalvo, por una cuadra. En la primera esquina, en la calle Roca, doble a la derecha. Siga por esa calle por una cuadra, y doble a la izquierda en la próxima esquina. Está a la derecha.

(You write:) *Transportes Otavalo*

Número 1
Siga derecho por la calle Montalvo. En la primera esquina, doble a la izquierda. Camine una cuadra por la calle Roca. Está en la esquina, a la derecha.

Número 2
Siga derecho por la calle Montalvo. Tome la segunda calle a la derecha. Camine dos cuadras y doble a la izquierda en la calle Colón. Vaya una cuadra más y está a la derecha, en la esquina.

Número 3
Siga por esta calle, la calle Montalvo. Camine unas tres cuadras. Está a la derecha, enfrente de la plaza y al lado del Restaurante Copacabana.

Paso 2

8-14 ¿Qué médico me recomienda? [CD2-20]

Número 1
Sí, mi hija de 6 años dice que le duele mucho la garganta. Tiene fiebre y no puede respirar muy bien. También, tiene dolor de cabeza.

Número 2
Mire, tengo 70 años y, generalmente, disfruto de buena salud. Pero, ahora me duele el cuello, el brazo izquierdo y el pecho. Casi no puedo respirar.

Número 3
Sí, por favor, acabo de lastimarme jugando al fútbol. Choqué con un compañero y me lastimé la rodilla y el tobillo. Creo que tengo una fractura.

8-18 ¿Qué le pasa? [CD2-21]

D = Doctora; E = Emilia; M = Miguel; P = Pablo

Conversación 1
E: ¡Ay, doctora! ¡Qué mal me siento!

D: ¿Qué tiene?

E: ¡Es que no puedo comer nada! Estoy aquí de vacaciones. Desde que comí arroz con pollo el primer día, estoy enferma. No tengo fiebre pero me duele el estómago y tengo náuseas.

D: Me parece que tiene una intoxicación. Tome bastantes líquidos durante las próximas 24 horas. Le voy a recetar unas pastillas también. Tome una pastilla cada día y muy pronto se sentirá mejor.

E: ¡Ojalá, doctora!

Conversación 2
M: ¡Doctora, por favor! Hace tres días que estoy enfermo y hoy me siento peor.

D: ¿Qué le pasa?

M: No sé. Tengo una tos muy mala. Creo que tengo un poco de fiebre y me siento mareado.

D: ¿Y qué día se enfermó?

M: El lunes empecé con la tos, el martes con el mareo y hoy que es miércoles con la fiebre.

D: Bueno, tiene la gripe. He tenido muchos pacientes hoy con los mismos síntomas que Ud. Me parece que tiene también una infección en la garganta. Le voy a mandar un antibiótico muy bueno y un jarabe para la tos.

M: Sí, doctora. Muchas gracias.

Conversación 3
P: Hola, doctora.

D: ¿Cómo estás hoy?

P: Bueno, no me siento muy mal, pero estoy un poco preocupado porque pienso ir de vacaciones a la playa este fin de semana y ahora tengo un dolor de cabeza terrible y un poco de dolor de garganta.

D: Bueno, no es nada serio. Toma dos aspirinas con té caliente cada cuatro horas, tres veces al día, y descansa bastante por un par de días para ver si te mejoras. Si no te mejoras o si tienes fiebre, regresa a verme. Si te sientes mejor para el viernes, ve a la playa de vacaciones, pero cuídate.

P: Un millón de gracias, doctora.

Capítulo 9

Paso 1

9-1 ¡Pobre Selena! [CD2-23]

S = Selena; C = Carmen

C: ¿Qué te pasa? Tienes mala cara.

S: Ay, Carmen, estoy agotada. No puedo más.

C: Pero, ¿qué te pasa, mujer? ¿Estás enferma?

S: No, no, no estoy enferma. Es que tengo tanto estrés en mi trabajo ahora.

C: ¿Por qué no te tomas unos días libres? Así puedes descansar.

S: Ay, es imposible. Mi jefe está de vacaciones y por eso tengo que trabajar horas extras. Salgo de casa a las siete de la mañana y vuelvo a las ocho de la noche.

C: Pues, eso sí es mucho trabajo. Deberías tomar más vitaminas. Yo las tomo todos los días y me dan más energía.

S: Bueno, quizás, pero en realidad me alimento muy bien. No creo que me hagan falta más vitaminas.

C: Bueno, en este caso, quizás no. Y, ¿el ejercicio? ¿Haces algún tipo de ejercicio?

S: ¿Ejercicio? No, no tengo tiempo.

C: Mira, yo tengo una clase de ejercicios aeróbicos los sábados por la mañana. ¿Por qué no vas conmigo el próximo sábado?

S: Me parece una idea buenísima. ¿Quieres llamarme el jueves por la noche? Así podemos arreglar dónde encontrarnos.

C: De acuerdo. Te llamo el jueves.

Paso 2

9-14 ¿Qué hay de nuevo? [CD2-26]

A Aurora; G = Gloria

Conversación 1

A: Hola, Gloria. ¿Qué me cuentas?

G: Ay, Aurora, estoy contentísima.

A: ¿Sí? ¿Qué pasa? Cuéntame todo.

G: ¿Te acuerdas de Luis, el estudiante de medicina?

A: Sí, claro. Lo conocí en la fiesta de cumpleaños de Paloma. Es un hombre guapísimo y muy buena persona además.

G: Pues, llevamos casi seis meses saliendo juntos y ¡Luis es el hombre de mis sueños! Creo que vamos a comprometernos pronto.

A: ¡Qué maravilloso! Estoy muy contenta por los dos.

Conversación 2

M = Mariana; R = Rodolfo

R: Oigo.

M: Rodolfo, Mariana aquí. ¿Qué hay de nuevo, cariño?

R: Por aquí no hay mucho que contar. Y a ti, mi amor, ¿cómo te va hoy?

M: Bueno, estoy contentísima. Me acaban de llamar del consultorio del Dr. Ideliso y el análisis es positivo.

R: Mariana, ¡no me digas que vamos a tener un bebé! ¿Cuándo va a nacer? No es una broma, ¿verdad?

M: No, vamos a ser padres en enero. ¿Qué te parece?

R: Es que estoy tan emocionado que no sé qué decir.

Paso 3

9-28 ¿Cómo se siente Raquel? [CD2-29]

R = Raquel; S = Sofía

S: ¿Qué hay de nuevo, Raquel?

R: Oye, Sofía. Yo no sé si puedo aguantar más. Esta vida universitaria es terrible.

S: Uy. ¿Qué ocurrió?

R: Bueno, me pasé la noche entera estudiando para un examen de estadística. Y no sé, creo que salí muy mal.

S: Pero siempre sacas buenas notas en estadística, Raquel. ¿Por qué te sientes tan pesimista esta vez?

R: Es que el examen era muy largo y difícil. No pude terminar la última pregunta.

S: Ay, Raquel, no te preocupes. Yo pienso que todo va a salir bien.

R: No estoy segura; es muy difícil.

PUENTES

Spanish for Intensive and High-Beginner Courses

FIFTH EDITION

Patti J. Marinelli
University of South Carolina

Lizette Mujica Laughlin
University of South Carolina

HEINLE
CENGAGE Learning™

Australia • Brazil • Canada • Japan • Korea • Mexico • Singapore • Spain • United Kingdom • United States

Puentes **Fifth Edition**

Marinelli | Mujica Laughlin

Editor in Chief: PJ Boardman

Publisher: Beth Kramer

Acquisitions Editor: Heather Bradley

Development Editor: Karin Fajardo

Managing Development Editor:
   Harold Swearingen

Senior Content Project Manager: Esther Marshall

Editorial Assistants: David Naden and Sara Dyer

Senior Marketing Manager: Ben Rivera

Marketing Coordinator: Janine Enos

Senior Marketing Communications Manager:
   Stacey Purviance

Media Editor: Morgen Murphy

Senior Print Buyer: Elizabeth Donaghey

Senior Art Director: Linda Jurras

Text Designer: Carol Maglitta/One Visual Mind

Photo Researcher: Jill Engebretson and
   Pre-Press PMG

Permissions Editor: Llanca Letelier

Cover Designer: Hetch Design

Production Service and Compositor:
   Pre-Press PMG

Cover image: Corbis, ©Timothy Winter/Robert
   Harding, World Imagery/Corbis, RM

For product information and technology assistance, contact us at
Cengage Learning Academic Resource Center, 1-800-423-0563

For permission to use material from this text or product,
submit all requests online at **cengage.com/permissions.**
Further permissions questions can be e-mailed to
permissionrequest@cengage.com.

Library of Congress Control Number: 2009934080

Student Edition:

ISBN-13: 978-0-495-80319-5

ISBN-10: 0-495-80319-7

Loose-Leaf Edition:

ISBN-13: 978-0-495-90071-9

ISBN-10: 0-495-90071-0

Heinle Cengage Learning
20 Channel Center Street
Boston, MA 02210
USA

Cengage Learning products are represented in Canada by Nelson Education, Ltd.

For your course and learning solutions, visit
academic.cengage.com.
Purchase any of our products at your local college store or at
our preferred online store **www.ichapters.com.**

Printed in the United States of America
1 2 3 4 5 6 7 13 12 11 10 09

....

To my aunt, Dorothy Marinelli, with love.

P. J. M

....

With sincere gratitude to those students who reversed the teaching process and taught me meaningful life lessons.

L. M. L.

Contents

P · Paso preliminar p. 1

Vocabulario temático	Gramática	Cultura
▸ En la sala de clase	▸ Los sustantivos y los artículos	
▸ El abecedario ▸ Los números de 0 a 39		▸ Los números mayas
▸ Para presentarnos ▸ Las instrucciones del profesor ▸ Cómo hablar con tu profesor(a)		

1 · ¡Así somos! • *Puerto Rico* p. 11

	Vocabulario temático	Gramática	Cultura	Estrategias
A primera vista p. 12			▸ *La calle* de Fernando Botero	
Paso 1 p. 14	▸ Cómo saludar a los compañeros y a los profesores ▸ Información básica ▸ Los números de 40 a 100	▸ Los pronombres personales, el verbo **estar** y los adjetivos ▸ Los verbos **ser, tener, ir**	▸ ¿Cómo demuestran el cariño entre amigos?	
Paso 2 p. 26	▸ La familia y los amigos ▸ Dime más	▸ Cómo indicar la posesión ▸ El tiempo presente de los verbos regulares		▸ Previewing a lesson
Paso 3 p. 36	▸ El tiempo libre	▸ El verbo **gustar** ▸ Las preguntas	▸ Los pasatiempos	
Un paso más p. 47	▸ ¡Vamos a hablar! ▸ ¡Vamos a ver! *En la Hacienda Vista Alegre,* Episodio 1 ▶			
Panorama cultural p. 50			**Imágenes de Puerto Rico** ▶	
Gramática suplementaria p. 333		▸ El presente progresivo		
Cuaderno de actividades				▸ Reading: Deciphering unfamiliar words ▸ Writing: The writing process

Contents *continued*

Contents *continued*

Contents *continued*

8   Somos turistas • *Ecuador*   p. 263

¡Así es la vida! • *Chile* **p. 293**

Contents *continued*

Note to Students

Welcome to *Puentes*

Learning a new language has been called by many "the journey of a lifetime." Along the way, we meet remarkable new people and become acquainted with intriguingly different ways of life. Whether you have studied Spanish for one year or three, **Puentes, Fifth Edition,** will help you cross the bridge into the next level of language proficiency as you continue your journey into the Spanish-speaking world.

Suggestions for Success

Since you have studied Spanish prior to this course, you will discover that you are somewhat familiar with many of the grammatical structures and vocabulary items in this textbook. **Puentes, Fifth Edition,** has been designed to help you move from recognition of the various elements of language to active, practical use of this material.

Learning a language is a lot like learning to drive a car, play a musical instrument, or play a sport. To become successful at any of them, it isn't enough to read a manual about the topic. Ultimately, you have to put in many hours of intense practice to finally learn how to parallel park, play a song on the guitar, or swim across the pool. The same is true for learning to speak, read and write Spanish.

Here are some tips to help you on your way to success:

- Set aside a time each day to study and practice Spanish. It is important to study regularly and not get behind, because much memory work is needed.

- Choose a place that is free of distractions so that you can concentrate.

- During your practice, focus more on **active** tasks: write out sentences, answer questions in the book orally, focus on listening to the audio selections with a purpose in mind.

- Consult regularly the *Vocabulario temático: español e inglés* at the back of your textbook to drill new words and expressions.

- As much as possible, practice speaking Spanish with a classmate in order to improve more quickly and feel more comfortable participating in class.

- Remember that recognizing a point of information does not imply that you have mastered it. You must be able to use the words and grammatical structures to communicate an idea in writing or speech.

- Keep in mind that it is normal to make errors as you learn a new language. Learn to monitor yourself and correct as many errors as you can.

¡Buena suerte! ¡Buen viaje!

P.J.M.

L. M. L.

Acknowledgments

This fifth edition of *Puentes* reflects the dedicated work of the Heinle Cengage Learning team as well as the generous assistance of many colleagues and friends. We are grateful to each of you for your contributions and thank you all for your support.

Our deep appreciation goes to Heather Bradley Cole, Acquisitions Editor, for providing leadership and direction at every step of the revision process. We are especially indebted to Karin Fajardo, developmental editor, whose keen understanding of language, culture, pedagogy, and publishing helped us hone the manuscript into an infinitely stronger work.

The updating of the *Puente cultural* required the generous collaboration of many colleagues. Special thanks go to Clara Mengolini for creating the survey questions and to Cheryl Gil, Carolina Arias and Clara Mengolini for conducting the surveys and filming many of the video segments. A big thank you goes to Bill Fairchild for continually providing his superior technical expertise. We are also grateful to numerous others who made valuable contributions to this feature, including Wendy Schneider, Nina Moreno, Karin Fajardo, Jimena Escamilla, Patricio Daniel Aravena, Romeo Wong Henderson, Mauricio Mbomio, Jahel Pulido, Elvira Zaldivar, Rosalennys Inoa, Lineliz M. Vasallo, Gabriella Paracat, María José Vargas Cevallos, David Valecillos and Federick Rivers.

The cultural content of this edition is much the richer thanks to many colleagues and friends who patiently answered questions, helped us conduct research, and shared their expertise in ways large and small. For their invaluable assistance, we recognize Cheryl Gil, Allison Whitehouse, Carolina Arias, Alejandro Bernal, María Mabrey, Lucile Charlebois, Francisco Sánchez, Paul Malovrh, Nina Moreno, Jorge Camacho, Ana Lorena Cueto, Puri Crowe, Carla Aguado, Lenora Hayes, Cari Kepner, Sheila Benavente, Harriet Nichols, Judy Dent, Leah Miller, Sherry Weeks, Sibela Nye, Stephanie King, Adela Seay, and Andy Corley.

The *Cuaderno de actividades* sports a fresh look in this edition, with numerous new practice activities, strategies and readings—many of which were penned by Karin Fajardo. We are most grateful to Karin for her collaboration in writing this vital component of the program. Special recognition also goes to three colleagues who shared anecdotes and stories for readings in the workbook—Alejandra Madrigal, Gloria Losada, and Clara Mengolini.

The *Puentes* program is greatly enhanced by its top-notch ancillary materials. We extend our sincere thanks and kudos to Katherine Lincoln for writing the eminently practical testing program and to Karen Lopez Alonzo for creating an imaginative and outstanding website. Many thanks also go to Mary McKeon for expertly updating the Instructor's Resource Manual.

The preparation of the manuscript was a formidable job made much easier by the able assistance of Kennedy Watkins and Lucía Vega. Our deep thanks to you for your meticulous work.

From beginning to end, *Puentes* has benefitted from the careful planning and creative solutions of the Heinle team. For their dedication and consummate professionalism we recognize the following team members: Harold Swearingen, Managing Development Editor; Esther Marshall, Senior Content Project Manager; Linda Jurras, Art Director; Ben Rivera, Senior Marketing Manager; John Farrell, Media Producer; Morgen Murphy, Media Editor; and David Naden and Sara Dyer, Editorial Assistants. And, finally, our thanks also go to all the other people involved with the production of this edition and, in particular, Melissa Sacco, Project Manager on behalf of Pre-Press PMG, Lourdes Murray, native reader, Peggy Hines, copyeditor and proofreader.

We would also like to thank our colleagues that provided valuable comments and suggestions throughout the review process.

Eileen Angelini, Canisius College

Barbara Avila-Shah, University at Buffalo: SUNY

Phyllis Bellver, Centre College

Aymara Boggiano, University of Houston

Maria Jose Bordera, Randolph-Macon College

Benita Clarke, University of Kentucky

Barbara Domcekova, Birmingham-Southern College

Maria Dorantes, University of Michigan–Ann Arbor

Jose Fabres, College of Saint Benedict: Saint John's University

David B. Fiero, Western Washington University

Benjamin Fraser, Christopher Newport University

Andrew Gordon, Mesa State College

Margarita Groeger, Massachusetts Institute of Technology

Ann Hilberry, University of Michigan

Ruth Kauffmann, William Jewell College

Sofia Kearns, Furman University

Lina Lee, University of New Hampshire

J. Layne Mayon, USC Union

Jerome Miner, Knox College

Cecilia Montes-Alcalá, Georgia Institute of Technology

Peggy McNeil, Louisiana State University

Edward "Ted" Peebles, University of Richmond

Teresa Perez-Gamboa, University of Georgia

Alicia Ramos, Hunter College, CUNY

Maria Rippon, Furman University

Silvia Rodriguez-Sabater, College of Charleston

Ruth Sanchez-Imizcoz, Sewanee: The University of the South

Timothy Scott, Onondaga Community College

Nancy Smith, Allegheny College

Nohemy Solorzano-Thompson, Whitman College

Jorge Trinchet, Wichita State University

Victoria Uricoechea, Winthrop University

U. Theresa Zmurkewycz, St. Joseph´s University

Finally, for their unwavering support and never-ending supply of love and encouragement, we send our love and thanks to our families.

P. J. M.

L. M. L.

América del Sur

MAR CARIBE

Barranquilla
Cartagena
Maracaibo
Puerto de España
Caracas
TRINIDAD Y TOBAGO

R. Orinoco

Medellín
VENEZUELA
Georgetown
GUYANA
Paramaribo
SURINAM
Cayenne
GUAYANA FRANCESA

OCÉANO ATLÁNTICO

Manizales
Bogotá
Cali
COLOMBIA

Quito
ECUADOR
ECUADOR
Guayaquil
Iquitos
PERÚ
Manaus

R. Amazo
Belem

R. Madeira

Cajamarca

BRASIL

Recife

Machu Picchu
Lima
Ayacucho
Cuzco

Arequipa
L. Titicaca
BOLIVIA
La Paz
Sucre
Arica
Potosí
Iquique

Salvador

Brasilia

Belo Horizonte

OCÉANO PACÍFICO

Antofagasta

PARAGUAY

São Paulo
Río de Janeiro
Santos

Salta
Asunción
CHILE
Tucumán

R. Paraná
R. Uruguay

Porto Alegre

Córdoba
Mendoza
Valparaíso
Santiago
Concepción
ARGENTINA
Rosario
Buenos Aires
La Plata
URUGUAY
Montevideo
Río de la Plata

TRÓPICO DE CAPRICORNIO

Bahía Blanca

Puerto Montt

CORDILLERA DE LOS ANDES

ISLAS MALVINAS

0	200	400	600	800 millas

0	200	400	600	800 kilómetros

Punta Arenas
TIERRA DEL FUEGO
Cabo de Hornos
Estrecho de Magallanes

España

MAR CANTÁBRICO

FRANCIA

Áviles · Gijón
La Coruña · · Santander
PRINCIPADO
DE ASTURIAS · Oviedo
Lugo · **CANTABRIA** · Bilbao · San Sebastián
GALICIA Cordillera Cantábrica **PAÍS**
VASCO Pamplona
· Pontevedra León **COM. FORAL**
DE NAVARRA
· Vigo Palencia · Burgos **LA RIOJA** **ARAGÓN**
Zamora · **CASTILLA Y LEÓN** · Valladolid Sistema Ibérico · Zaragoza
R. Due R. Ebro
· Braga Salamanca
·Oporto Segovia Sierra de Guadarrama
MADRID
PORTUGAL · Avila · Madrid
R. Tajo · Toledo
Coimbra
Cáceres ·
· EXTREMADURA **CASTILLA-LA MANCHA**
Mérida · R. Júcar
· R. Guadiana
Lisboa · Badajoz · Almadén Ciudad Real · Albacete
Setúbal · Sierra Morena
R. Guadalquivir Linares ·
· Córdoba
· Jaén **REGIÓN**
ANDALUCÍA DE MURCIA
· Sevilla · Granada
Huelva · Sierra Nevada
Jerez de la
Frontera · Málaga · Almería
· Cádiz

OCÉANO
ATLÁNTICO
Algeciras ·
Tánger · Ceuta (Esp.)
Melilla (Esp.)

MARRUECOS

ANDORRA

CATALUÑA
Lérida
· Barcelona
Tarragona

MAR
MEDITERRÁNEO

MENORCA

MALLORCA
ISLAS
BALEARES Palma de
Mallorca
EIVISSA (IBIZA)
· Valencia
COMUNIDAD
VALENCIANA FORMENTERA

· Alicante

· Murcia
Cartagena ·

ISLAS CANARIAS LANZAROTE
Arrecife ·
Santa Cruz
de la Palma **FUERTEVENTURA**
LA PALMA · Santa Cruz
TENERIFE · Puerto
del
GOMERA Las Palmas Rosario
GRAN CANARIA

Malabo ★ **CAMERÚN**
GUINEA
ECUATORIAL
ÁFRICA

GABÓN

0   50   100   150 millas
0   50   100   150   250 kilómetros

Estrecho de Gibraltar

PIRINEOS

xvii

México, América Central y el Caribe

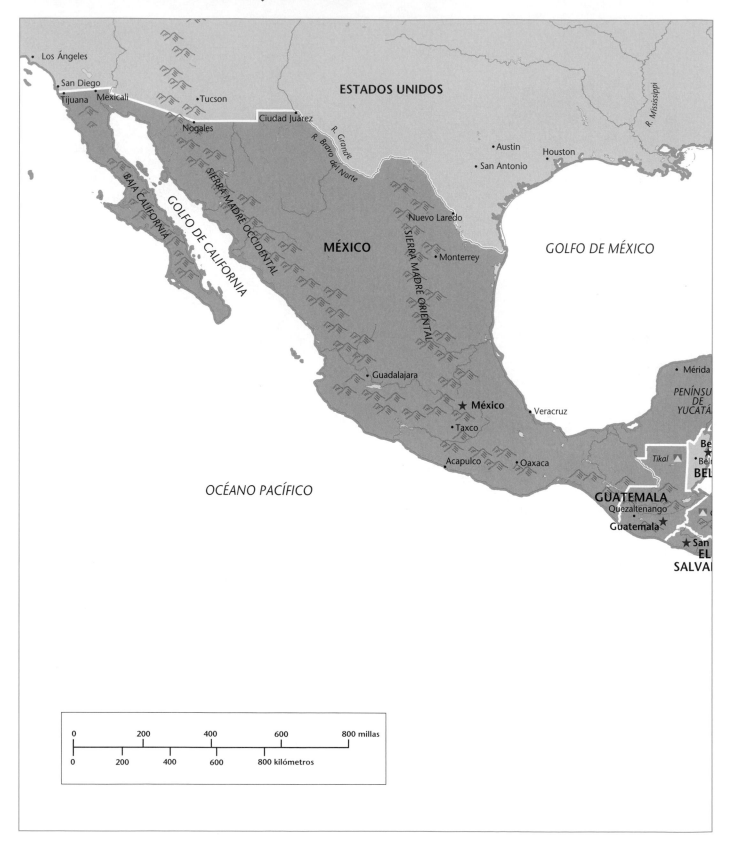

ESTADOS UNIDOS

Los Ángeles

San Diego

Tijuana
Mexicali
•Tucson

Nogales
Ciudad Juárez

R. Grande

R. Bravo del Norte

R. Mississippi

•Austin

Houston

•San Antonio

Nuevo Laredo

MÉXICO

•Monterrey

GOLFO DE MÉXICO

BAJA CALIFORNIA

GOLFO DE CALIFORNIA

SIERRA MADRE OCCIDENTAL

SIERRA MADRE ORIENTAL

•Mérida

PENÍNSULA DE YUCATÁN

•Guadalajara

★ México
•Veracruz

•Taxco

Tikal

Be

Bel

BEL

Acapulco
•Oaxaca

GUATEMALA

Quezaltenango

OCÉANO PACÍFICO

Guatemala

★San

EL
SALVA

0	200	400	600	800 millas

0	200	400	600	800 kilómetros

OCÉANO ATLÁNTICO

Miami

Estrecho de Florida

LAS BAHAMAS

Canal de Yucatán

La Habana
• Matanzas
• Pinar del Río
• Cienfuegos
• Camagüey

CUBA

Santiago de Cuba • Guantánamo

REPÚBLICA
DOMINICANA

HAITÍ

PUERTO RICO

Port-au-Prince
Santo Domingo
San Juan
Mayagüez • Ponce

ISLAS VÍRGENES

INSULA
E
TÁN

Belice
• Belmopán
BELICE

Kingston

JAMAICA

ANTIGUA

GUADALUPE

DOMINICA

MARTINICA

SANTA LUCÍA

SAN VICENTE

HONDURAS

Copán

Tegucigalpa

an Salvador
EL
VADOR

NICARAGUA

MAR DEL CARIBE

BARBADOS

ANTILLAS MENORES

GRANADA

León • Managua

L. de Nicaragua

ARUBA
CURAÇAO
BONAIRE

ISLA DE MARGARITA

TRINIDAD
Y
TOBAGO

COSTA RICA

Canal de Panamá

Puntarenas • San José

Colón

Caracas

Puerto de España

PANAMÁ
• Panamá

R. Magdalena

VENEZUELA

R. Orinoco

GOLFO
DE
PANAMÁ

COLOMBIA

GUYANA

Bogotá

BRASIL

Paso preliminar

Various kinds of instructor's annotations will help guide you through *Puentes.* Those labeled as **More Information** are informational annotations that focus on text features. **Proficiency** explains how activities promote proficiency and what to expect from students. **Teaching Tip** includes suggestions for presentation of new material, implementation of activities, and alternative activities. **Expansion** provides additional practice items and suggested follow-up activities. **Grammar** presents more in-depth grammatical information and tips for those students with a strong background. **Standards** point out how different activities address the National Standards for Foreign Language and Learning. **Vocabulary** and **Regional Vocabulary** provide additional lexical terms and regional variations. **Note** provides information related to art, music, history, customs, usage, and other useful topics.

OBJETIVOS

Speaking and Listening
- Describing a classroom
- Using the alphabet
- Numbers from 0 to 39
- Talking with your professor about class routines

Grammar
- Nouns
- Gender and number of nouns
- Definite and indefinite articles

Culture
- Mayan numbers
- www.cengage.com/spanish/puentes

Go to the *Puentes* website for extra vocabulary practice using the Flashcard program.

The English equivalents of the **Vocabulario temático** sections are found at the back of the book.

More Information: The material in this **Paso** can be easily covered in the first day or two of class, even if some students do not have their books. Your students will be familiar with the vocabulary and grammar, so in-depth explanations are not required.

Vocabulario temático

En la sala de clase *(In the classroom)*

—¿Qué hay en la sala de clase?

—Hay *un reloj, una computadora, una puerta…*

　Tambíen hay *un calendario, un mapa…*

Teaching Tip: Introduce classroom vocabulary with objects found in your room. Your students will know many of the terms, so you may begin by pointing to the items and asking **¿Qué es esto?**. Use the items as a point of departure to practice articles as well as singular and plural nouns.

Note: Both MP3 and MP4 are pronounced as Spanish words: **eme—pe—tres/cuatro.**

Vocabulary: Additional objects found in the classroom: **un sacapuntas** *(a pencil sharpener)*, **una papelera** *(a wastepaper basket)*, **un estante** *(a shelf)*.

Regional Vocabulary: In Spain, the computer is known as **un ordenador**; a cell phone is **un móvil.** In Colombia and Chile, the computer is **un computador** *(masculine)*.

Los sustantivos y los artículos

A. Los sustantivos. The words for people, places, and things—such as **profesor, sala,** and **libro**—are known as nouns. In Spanish, all nouns are classified as masculine or feminine.

- ▶ A noun is masculine if it refers to a male, regardless of its ending: **estudiante, profesor.** For inanimate objects, a noun is generally masculine if it ends in -**o**: **libro, diccionario.**

- ▶ A noun is feminine if it refers to a female, regardless of its ending: **estudiante, profesora.** For inanimate objects, a noun is usually feminine if it ends in -**a**: **mochila, mesa.**

- ▶ Nouns that end in -**e** or a consonant may be masculine or feminine. You must learn the gender of these nouns on a case-by-case basis: **pupitre** (masculine); **reloj** (masculine); **clase** (feminine).

B. Singular y plural. A noun that refers to just one person or thing is **singular;** one that refers to two or more is **plural.**

- ▶ If a noun ends in a vowel, add -**s** to make it plural.
  diccionario + s → diccionario**s**

- ▶ If a noun ends in a consonant, add -**es** to make it plural.
  papel + es → papel**es**

C. Los artículos definidos. The English definite article *the* has four equivalents in Spanish; you must choose the one that matches the noun in gender (masculine or feminine) and in number (singular or plural).

	MASCULINO	FEMENINO
SINGULAR	**el** cuaderno	**la** silla
PLURAL	**los** cuadernos	**las** sillas

D. Los artículos indefinidos. The English indefinite articles *a/an* and their plural *some* also have four equivalents in Spanish; once again, you must choose the indefinite article that matches the noun in gender and number.

	MASCULINO	FEMENINO
SINGULAR	**un** diccionario	**una** mesa
PLURAL	**unos** diccionarios	**unas** mesas

🌐 **Heinle Grammar Tutorial:** Nouns and articles

A few nouns ending in **a** are masculine: **mapa, problema.**

A few nouns ending in -**o** are feminine: **moto, mano** *(hand).*

Ponerlo a prueba

P-1 ¿Qué hay en la sala de clase? Observa el dibujo de la página 2. Para cada oración, selecciona los artículos correctos. Luego di si es cierto o falso *(Then say if it's true or false).*

MODELO	En (el / la) sala de clase hay (un / una) reloj.
	En <u>la</u> sala de clase hay <u>un</u> reloj. Cierto

<u>cierto</u>   1. Hay (un / <u>una</u>) profesora, (el / <u>la</u>) señora Wing.

<u>falso</u>   2. (<u>Los</u> / Las) estudiantes están en (el / <u>la</u>) clase de inglés.

<u>cierto</u>   3. Hay (<u>una</u> / unas) ventana en (el / <u>la</u>) puerta.

<u>falso</u>   4. Hay (<u>un</u> / una) mapa de España en (el / <u>la</u>) sala de clase.

<u>cierto</u>   5. (Un / <u>Una</u>) estudiante usa (<u>el</u> / la) teléfono celular.

<u>falso</u>   6. Hay (<u>unos</u> / unas) borradores en (el / <u>la</u>) silla.

<u>cierto</u>   7. (Un / <u>Una</u>) estudiante escribe mensajes de texto en (<u>el</u> / la) teléfono celular.

<u>cierto</u>   8. Hay (<u>un</u> / una) libro en (el / <u>la</u>) mesa de la profesora.

P-2 ¿Qué hay? Con un(a) compañero(a), mira las fotos y describe qué hay en cada una. Sigue el modelo.

MODELO	En la sala de clase hay un estudiante...
	También hay...
	En el cuarto hay libros,...

Vocabulario temático

El abecedario *(The alphabet)*

—¿Qué es esto?

—Es *un pupitre.*

—¿Cómo se escribe "pupitre"?

—Se escribe *pe-u-pe-i-te-ere-e.*

a	a	Argentina	ñ	eñe	España
b	be	Bolivia	o	o	Omán
	be grande		p	pe	Perú
c	ce	Colombia	q	cu	Quito
ch	che	Chile	r	ere	Rusia
d	de	Dinamarca	s	ese	Suiza
e	e	Ecuador	t	te	Tailandia
f	efe	Francia	u	u	Uruguay
g	ge	Guatemala	v	ve / uve	Venezuela
h	hache	Honduras		ve chica	
i	i	Inglaterra	w	doble ve	Washington
j	jota	Japón		uve doble	
k	ka	Kenia		doble uve	
l	ele	Luxemburgo	x	equis	México
ll	elle	Llano	y	i griega	Yemen
m	eme	Mónaco	z	zeta	Nueva Zelanda
n	ene	Nicaragua			

Teaching Tip: Use this section to practice basic pronunciation as well. Go over the sounds of the vowels and have students work through the pronunciation of the names of the countries and cities.

Note: In 1994, Spanish adopted the universal Latin alphabetical order and consequently, words that begin with **ch** and **ll** are alphabetized under **c** and **l** respectively. Older dictionaries, however, still have separate sections for words that begin with **ch** and **ll**.

Ponerlo a prueba

P-3 El ahorcado (Hangman). Con tu compañero(a), piensa en una palabra conocida e incluye un espacio para cada letra. Luego, escribe la primera letra de la palabra. Entonces, tu compañero(a) debe adivinar (*guess*) el resto de las letras en la palabra. Por cada error que tu compañero(a) comete (*makes*) puedes dibujar una parte de su cuerpo hasta terminar el ahorcado.

MODELO   B_L _ _ RA_ _ *(bolígrafo)*

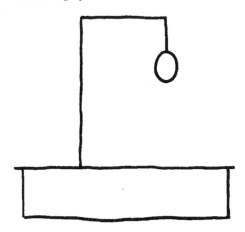

Vocabulario temático

Los números de 0 a 39 *(Numbers from 0 to 39)*

—¿Cuántos pupitres hay en la sala?

—Hay *veinte (20).*

0	cero	14	catorce
1	uno	15	quince
2	dos	16	dieciséis
3	tres	17	diecisiete
4	cuatro	18	dieciocho
5	cinco	19	diecinueve
6	seis	20	veinte
7	siete	21	veintiuno
8	ocho	22	veintidós (veintitrés, veinticuatro…)
9	nueve		
10	diez	30	treinta
11	once	31	treinta y uno (treinta y dos, treinta y tres…)
12	doce		
13	trece	39	treinta y nueve

P-4 El inventario. Con un(a) compañero(a), di *(say)* cuántas de las siguientes cosas/personas hay en tu sala de clase.

> MODELO
>
> ESTUDIANTE A: ¿Cuántas puertas hay?
>
> ESTUDIANTE B: Hay una puerta.

1. cuántas sillas
2. cuántos pupitres
3. cuántas ventanas
4. cuántas computadoras
5. cuántos borradores
6. cuántos estudiantes

COMENTARIO CULTURAL *Los números mayas*

¿Conoces el sistema de números de los mayas? ¿Sabes cómo escribir el número 2 con el sistema de los mayas?

Long before Columbus made his famous first voyage to the New World in 1492, numerous indigenous civilizations were flourishing in the Americas. One of those civilizations is especially well-known for its achievements in mathematics and in the measurement of time.

Muchos años antes de la llegada *(arrival)* de Cristóbal Colón al Nuevo Mundo, existían grandes civilizaciones indígenas en las Américas. Una de las civilizaciones más avanzadas era la de los mayas. Los mayas vivían donde hoy se encuentran México y Centroamérica. Los mayas son famosos por sus cálculos matemáticos; fueron uno de los primeros pueblos *(one of the first peoples)* en usar el concepto del cero. Su sistema de números se basaba en *(was based upon)* el número veinte; se escribía como una serie de puntos y barras. Arriba *(Above)* tienes los números mayas de 0 a 14. ¿Puedes escribir el número 15 según el sistema maya?

Teaching Tip: P-4 is meant for in-class practice.

Teaching Tip P-4: Before moving on to this activity, practice the numbers with simple counting patterns, such as by 2's from 2 to 38 or by 3's backwards from 39. Then, do simple addition and/or subtraction problems with your students. **¿Cuántos son dos y dos? Dos y dos son cuatro. ¿Cuántos son diez menos seis? Son cuatro.**

Grammar: Point out that the interrogative adjective **cuántos** *(how many)* agrees in number and gender with the noun that it modifies. For example, **¿Cuántos libros necesitas este semestre?** and **¿Cuántas sillas hay en tu sala de clase?**

Teaching Tip P-4: If needed, customize the list of items by deleting any items that are not in your room. Mention additional objects in your room for additional practice.

Expansion P-4: In pairs, students interview each other to find out how many of the classroom-related items they have: **¿Cuántos cuadernos tienes? ¿Cuántos bolígrafos tienes? ¿Cuántos libros tienes este semestre?** Introduce the words **tienes** and **tengo** in context; there is no need to conjugate the entire verb at this point.

Note: The first symbol in the drawing "Los números mayas" represents 0.

Vocabulario temático

More Information: Simple introductions are presented here for those who wish to have students introduce themselves the first day of class. Introductions are covered in more detail in the first chapter.

Teaching Tip: Model the introduction. Then have students mingle and meet one another.

Para presentarnos *(Introducing ourselves)*

AMANDA:	Hola. Me llamo *Amanda*.
CHRIS:	Hola, *Amanda*. Soy *Chris*.
AMANDA:	Mucho gusto.
CHRIS:	Igualmente.

Teaching Tip: Introduce this section by saying an expression and then miming the activity. Gesture to students that they should join you in acting out the instructions. If you prefer, introduce these phrases as needed; that is, as you teach the class and have the need to give instructions.

Las instrucciones del profesor *(Classroom instructions)*

Abran los libros.	Cierren los libros.
Repitan.	Escriban el ejercicio.
Contesten en español.	Escuchen.
Lean la información.	Trabajen con un(a) compañero(a).

More Information: Refer to the inside back cover of the textbook for more useful expressions, including phrases that students can use to find and work with partners in pair activities.

Cómo hablar con tu profesor(a) *(Talking with your professor)*

Más despacio, por favor.	Tengo una pregunta.
¿Cómo se dice… ?	¿Qué quiere decir… ?
¿Puede repetir, por favor?	¿En qué página?
Sí. / No.	No sé.
Gracias.	De nada.
Perdón.	Con permiso.

Use **perdón** if you bump into someone or need to interrupt a conversation. Say **Con permiso** when walking or reaching in front of someone.

Ponerlo a prueba

 P-5 ¿Qué se dice? Con un(a) compañero(a), usa una expresión adecuada para reaccionar en cada situación.

Teaching Tip: Activity P-5 may be assigned for homework or completed in class. P-6 is meant for in-class practice.

1. A classmate thanks you for the use of your pen.
   You respond: _____ De nada. _____

2. You want to ask your professor how to say "backpack" in Spanish.
   You ask: _____ ¿Cómo se dice "backpack" en español? _____

3. Your professor wants you to close your book.
   He/She requests: _____ Cierren el libro. _____

4. You need to walk in front of a classmate to get to the blackboard.
   You say: _____ Con permiso. _____

5. You didn't catch the page number.
   You say: _____ ¿En qué página? _____

6. Your partner asks you a question and you don't know the answer.
   You respond: _____ No sé. _____

7. Your professor is speaking very quickly.
   You say: _____ Más despacio, por favor. Or ¿Puede repetir, por favor? _____

8. When moving to sit next to a new partner, you step on someone's foot.
   You say: _____ Perdón. _____

9. You want to ask your professor a question.
   You say: _____ Tengo una pregunta. _____

10. You want to ask your professor the meaning of the word **igualmente.**
    You say: _____ ¿Qué quiere decir igualmente? _____

P-6 En nuestra sala de clase. ¿Qué dicen las personas en esta sala? Escribe pequeños diálogos.

Teaching Tip P-6: Have pairs of students work together on writing short, two-line dialogues and then read them aloud to the class.

Sustantivos

el bolígrafo *ballpoint pen*
el borrador *eraser*
el calendario *calendar*
el cartel *poster*
el (la) compañero(a) *partner*
la computadora *computer*
el cuaderno *notebook*
el diccionario *dictionary*
el (la) estudiante *student*
la hoja de papel *sheet of paper*
la impresora *printer*
el lápiz *pencil*
el libro *book*
el mapa *map*
la mesa *table*
la mochila *backpack*
la pizarra *blackboard*
el profesor / la profesora *professor*
el pupitre *desk*
el reloj *clock*
el reproductor de MP3/MP4 *MP3/MP4 player*
la sala de clase *classroom*
la silla *chair*
el teléfono celular *cell phone*
la tiza *chalk*
la ventana *window*

Expresiones

Abran los libros. *Open the books.*
Cierren los libros. *Close the books.*
¿Cómo se dice...? *How do you say . . . ?*
¿Cómo se escribe...? *How do you write . . . ?*
Con permiso. *Excuse me.*
Contesten. *Answer.*
De nada. *You're welcome.*
Escriban el ejercicio. *Write the exercise.*
Escuchen. *Listen.*
Gracias. *Thank you.*
¿Hay preguntas? *Are there any questions?*
Lean la explicación. *Read the explanation.*
Más despacio, por favor. *More slowly, please.*
Perdón. *Pardon me; Excuse me.*
¿Qué quiere decir...? *What does . . . mean?*
¿Puede repetir, por favor? *Could you repeat that, please?*
Tengo una pregunta. *I have a question.*

Alphabet: p. 5
Numbers 0–39: p. 6

For further review, please turn to **Vocabulario temático: español e inglés** at the back of the book.

Go to the *Puentes* website for extra vocabulary practice using the Flashcard program.

¡Así somos!

Situation Cards: A set of 145 situation cards for oral evaluation or for classroom practice are available through your representative. For classroom use, make photocopies or project the situation to the class. For this chapter, the most appropriate cards are numbers 5, 6, 8, 12, 13, 21.

More Information: Chapters 1, 3, 5, 7, and 9 are slightly longer than Chapters 2, 4, 6, and 8. For fewer contact hours, focus on the three **Pasos** and plan on spending about 4 hours to cover the material. For more contact hours, add **Un paso más** and plan on about 6 class hours.

Gramática suplementaria: This is a complete section, at the end of the textbook, of optional grammar explanations and practices for those who wish a fuller and broader treatment of grammar.

Turn to the *Cuaderno de actividades* for this chapter's reading practice and strategy: Deciphering unfamiliar words.

Turn to the *Cuaderno de actividades* for this chapter's composition practice and writing strategy: The writing process.

OBJETIVOS

Speaking and Listening
▸ Introducing yourself
▸ Greeting others and saying good-bye
▸ Expressing some physical and emotional conditions
▸ Providing basic information about yourself, your family, and friends
▸ Using the numbers from 40 to 100
▸ Talking about some of your daily activities at work, home, and school
▸ Expressing likes and dislikes
▸ Asking questions

Culture
▸ Puerto Rico
▸ Expressions of affection

Grammar
▸ Subject pronouns and adjectives
▸ **Estar, ser, tener,** and **ir** in the present tense
▸ Possessive adjectives
▸ Present tense of regular -**ar**, -**er**, and -**ir** verbs
▸ Basic sentence formation

Video
▸ En la Hacienda Vista Alegre: Episodio 1
▸ Imágenes de Puerto Rico

Gramática suplementaria
▸ El presente progresivo

Cuaderno de actividades
Reading
▸ Strategy: Deciphering unfamiliar words

Writing
▸ Strategy: The writing process

Playlist
🌐 www.cengage.com/spanish/puentes

More Information: The *Cuaderno* contains written activities to reinforce and expand upon the vocabulary and grammar presentations of the text. There are also cultural activities related to the country of focus and the video. In addition, reading and writing strategies are presented and practiced. An additional listening program with radio-style segments and pronunciation practice round out each section.

More Information: Music is incorporated into the lessons for cultural enrichment, and—in some cases—for comprehension. Access the list on iTunes.

A primera vista

La calle *(The Street)*

La interacción es un elemento vital de nuestra existencia. Y, con frecuencia, una nueva relación empieza con un simple saludo *(starts with a simple greeting)*. ¿Cómo saludas tú *(How do you greet)* a una persona que te encuentras en la calle *(run into on the street)*? ¿Cómo se saludan las personas en el cuadro de Botero?

Observa el cuadro *(painting)* y lee *(read)* la información sobre este famoso pintor. Trabaja con un(a) compañero(a) de clase. Completen las oraciones con la información más lógica.

1. Fernando Botero es de (<u>Colombia</u> / Argentina / Venezuela).
2. Botero es pintor y (arquitecto / compositor / <u>escultor</u>).
3. Las figuras de Botero son (<u>voluminosas</u> / realistas / pequeñas).
4. Este cuadro tiene (un / dos / <u>tres</u>) plano(s).
5. En el primer plano, hay (un chico / <u>un chico con su mamá y un señor</u> / muchas casas [*houses*]).

HABLANDO DEL ARTE

Although paintings exist in two dimensions, artists can create the illusion of depth by arranging the elements in different planes: the foreground (**el primer plano**), the middle ground (**el segundo plano**), and the background (**el fondo**).

FERNANDO BOTERO (1932–)

Nacionalidad: colombiano

Otras obras: *La cama, Picadores, El baño, Desayuno en la hierba* (escultura)

Estilo: El estilo de este famoso pintor y escultor contemporáneo es original y creativo. Sus esculturas en bronce son monumentales. Se conoce su obra *(His work is known)* por sus características figuras rotundas, de volumen exagerado. Estas figuras infladas son aparentemente humorísticas, pero algunos piensan *(some think)* que las imágenes de Botero son una sátira política y social.

More Information: In odd-numbered chapters, *A primera vista* features a painting by a Hispanic artist and serves as an introduction to the chapter theme.

Standards Basic art terminology is presented in **Hablando del arte,** which addresses the National Standards in Culture (Products and Perspectives).

Teaching Tip: To implement *A primera vista,* first, draw students' attention to the painting and ask a few basic questions about the artist (name, country, etc.) and the figures in the painting. Next, have students work with a classmate to complete the activity at the top of the page. Point out that they will need to study the painting and read the **Hablando del arte** section to complete this activity. This thematic introduction should take about 5–7 minutes to complete.

Note: Botero struggled for some years before he became a universally acclaimed artist. He made a career choice at an early age and left for Europe, where he studied the masters in Spain and Italy. He also lived in Mexico and the United States. His recent works include controversial pieces depicting the violence in his native Colombia.

La calle (1995) **Fernando Botero**

Paso 1

Vocabulario temático

Las presentaciones familiares *(Introducing yourself to classmates)*

FRANCISCO: Hola. Soy *Francisco Martín.* ¿Cómo te llamas?

ELENA: Me llamo *Elena Suárez Lagos.*

FRANCISCO: Mucho gusto, *Elena.*

ELENA: Mucho gusto, *Francisco.*

Las presentaciones formales *(Introducing yourself to professors)*

RAFAEL: Buenos días. Me llamo *Rafael Díaz.* ¿Cómo se llama usted?

PROFESORA: Soy *Carmen Acosta.*

RAFAEL: Encantado.

PROFESORA: Igualmente.

Los saludos informales *(Greeting classmates and friends)*

MARGARITA: Hola, *Patricia.*

PATRICIA: Hola, *Margarita.*

MARGARITA: ¿Cómo estás?

PATRICIA: *Bien*, gracias. ¿Y tú?

Regular.

Más o menos.

MARGARITA: Muy bien. *Hablamos* más tarde.

PATRICIA: Está bien. *Hasta luego.*

Nos vemos.

Los saludos formales *(Greeting your professors)*

ESTUDIANTE:	Buenas tardes, *profesor(a)*.
PROFESOR(A):	Buenas tardes, *Roberto*.
ESTUDIANTE:	¿Cómo está usted?
PROFESOR(A):	*Estoy bastante bien. ¿Y usted?*
	Ocupado(a), pero bien.
ESTUDIANTE:	*Bien*, gracias. Bueno, nos vemos en clase.
PROFESOR(A):	Adiós. *Hasta mañana.*

Other common titles: **señor** *(Mr.)*, **señora** *(Mrs.)*, **señorita** *(Miss)*, **doctor/doctora** *(Dr.)*.

Más saludos y despedidas *(More ways to greet and say good-bye)*

Buenos días.
(from morning to mid-day)

Buenas tardes.
(from after lunch to dusk)

Buenas noches. *(from dusk on)*

¿Qué tal? *(informal)*

Estoy... estupendo(a)/bastante bien/bien/regular/mal.

Chao. *(informal)*

Hasta pronto.

¡Que pases un buen fin de semana!
(informal)

¡Que pase un buen fin de semana!
(formal)

Vocabulary: High beginner students often have a wide repertoire of greetings. For more advanced groups, offer additional vocabulary choices. For example, for this section on greetings, you might add **¡Que te/le vaya bien!** *(Have a good day!)*; **¿Qué te/le pasa?** *(What's wrong? What's the matter?)*

Teaching Tip: To help your students practice both the informal and formal modes of speech, establish rules for classroom use, such as students using **tú** among themselves, and **usted** with their instructor.

Note: Mention that in many countries (such as Argentina, Uruguay, and Costa Rica) the subject pronoun **vos** and its corresponding verb forms are used instead of **tú** to address friends.

Algunos estados *(Expressing how you feel)*

—¿Cómo estás? (informal)

—Estoy muy *enfermo(a)*. ¿Y tú?

—¿Cómo está Ud.? (formal)

—Estoy un poco *cansado(a)*. ¿Y Ud.?

Use the informal **tú** with friends, family, and peers of your own age group.

Use the formal **Ud.** with professors, bosses, doctors, strangers, and older people.

Otras expresiones *(Related expressions)*

contento/contenta	nervioso/nerviosa
de buen humor	ocupado/ocupada
de mal humor	preocupado/preocupada
enojado/enojada	triste

Teaching Tip: While students may be familiar with the concept of masculine and feminine endings for adjectives, they will not apply them consistently. Use this opportunity to draw attention to the endings for the adjectives. Contrast how two classmates—one male and one female—might respond.

Los pronombres personales, el verbo *estar* y los adjetivos

🌐 **Heinle Grammar Tutorial:** Subject pronouns

A. Los pronombres personales. Subject pronouns identify the person who performs the action or is the topic of a sentence. Notice that there is no Spanish equivalent for the subject pronoun *it*.

yo	*I*	**nosotros(as)**	*we*
tú	*you (informal)*	**vosotros(as)**	*you (plural, informal, used in Spain)*
usted (Ud.)	*you (formal)*	**ustedes (Uds.)**	*you (plural, formal in Spain; both informal and formal in Latin America)*
él	*he*	**ellos**	*they (males, mixed group)*
ella	*she*	**ellas**	*they (females)*

B. Estar *(to be).* To create sentences, you must "conjugate" the verbs. That means you must use the verb form that corresponds to the subject of the sentence. Here is the conjugation of **estar** in the present tense.

estar *(to be)*

yo	**estoy**	nosotros(as)	**estamos**
tú	**estás**	vosotros(as)	**estáis**
usted (Ud.)	**está**	ustedes (Uds.)	**están**
él / ella	**está**	ellos / ellas	**están**

The verb **estar** is used to express how someone feels or where a person or thing is located.

Estoy un poco cansada.	*I'm (feeling) a little tired.*
Mis amigos **están** en casa.	*My friends are at home.*

Subject pronouns are generally not used because the verb ending indicates the subject of the sentence.

¿Cómo **estás?**	*How are you?* (The subject is **tú,** or *you.*)

C. Los adjetivos. Adjectives (**enfermo, cansado, contento,** etc.) have different endings, depending on the word they describe. Use the **-o** ending to refer to a man; the **-a** ending, to a woman. Add an **-s** to either ending to describe two or more people. We refer to this kind of matching as "making adjectives agree in gender and number."

Roberto está enferm**o.**	*Roberto is sick.*
Anita está enferm**a.**	*Anita is sick.*
Roberto y Anita están enferm**os.**	*Roberto and Anita are sick.*

More Information: Estructuras esenciales is placed after **Vocabulario temático** on an as-needed basis. This section helps students review some of the more basic grammar points and the section may be assigned for homework. In a few chapters, this section presents minor points of grammar and may be covered quickly in class. Most students will need continuing practice on these points. For this reason, structures presented in **Estructuras esenciales** and **Vocabulario temático** are practiced together in the **Ponerlo a prueba** section.

Grammar: Provide an example to contrast the use of *it* as a subject in Spanish and English. For example, to say "It's important" in Spanish, you would simply say **Es importante.**

Proficiency: Adjective agreement is covered in greater detail in **Capítulo 3.** By focusing on this point repeatedly and in increments, you will help students assimilate the concept and begin to use agreement with more consistency. This consistent use is needed for students to reach the Intermediate level of proficiency.

Ponerlo a prueba

CD1
Track 2

1-1 Por el campus. Tamika es una estudiante de Arizona. Estudia español en la Universidad de Puerto Rico. Escucha las conversaciones de Tamika. ¿Cómo responde Tamika a las diferentes situaciones?

> **MODELO**
>
> *You hear:* ¡Mucho gusto, Tamika!
>
> *You read and select how Tamika would respond:*

a. Nos vemos en clase.   **b. Me llamo Tamika.**   ©**Mucho gusto.**

1. a. Estoy bien.   ⓑMe llamo Tamika.   c. Mucho gusto.
2. ⓐDe lo mejor. ¿Y tú?   b. Nos vemos en clase.   c. Adiós.
3. a. ¿Cómo estás?   b. Igualmente.   ©Buenos días, profesor.
4. a. Más o menos. ¿Y tú?   b. Encantada.   ©Bien, gracias. ¿Y usted?
5. ⓐEstá bien. Chao.   b. Hola. ¿Cómo te llamas?   c. Estoy enojada.
6. a. Estamos cansados.   ⓑEstoy cansada.   c. Estás cansada.

1-2 En la Universidad de Puerto Rico. Estás en Puerto Rico para estudiar español. ¿Cómo respondes a las situaciones? Escribe tu respuesta.

> **MODELO**
>
> *You read:* Tu profesora de español: Buenos días.
>
> *You write an appropriate response:* Buenos días, profesora.

1. UNA COMPAÑERA DE CLASE: Hola. Me llamo Clarisa Estrada. ¿Cómo te llamas?
2. UN COMPAÑERO DE CLASE: Mucho gusto.
3. TU PROFESOR DE LITERATURA: Nos vemos en clase. Adiós. Hasta pronto.
4. TU AMIGA SILVIA: ¿Cómo estás?
5. TU PROFESORA DE ESPAÑOL: ¡Que pases un buen fin de semana!

1-3 Entre estudiantes. Preséntate *(Introduce yourself)* a tus compañeros de clase. Sigue el modelo.

> **MODELO**
>
> —Hola. Soy Josh Aranson. ¿Cómo te llamas?
>
> —Me llamo Chrissy Hill.
>
> —Mucho gusto, Chrissy.
>
> —Mucho gusto, Josh.

1-4 Mis compañeros de clase. Saluda *(Greet)* a 5–6 compañeros de clase. Sigue el modelo.

> **MODELO**
>
> —Hola, Sam.
>
> —Hola, Megan.
>
> —¿Cómo estás?
>
> —Ocupada, pero bien. ¿Y tú?
>
> —Muy bien, gracias.
>
> —Bueno, hablamos más tarde.
>
> —Hasta luego.
>
> —Chao. Hasta pronto.

To access the audio recordings, visit
www.cengage.com/spanish/puentes

More Information: Students in high-beginner courses can vary widely in their background knowledge and skills. The **Ponerlo a prueba** section provides a variety of practice activities so that you can pick and choose to adapt to the needs of your particular class. In one-semester courses, it is not expected that you would complete all the activities provided.

Standards: Vocabulario temático is followed by a listening input activity, such as Act. 1-1. These activities address the National Standards for Communication (Interpretive). Assign listening activities for homework on a regular basis. Go over the answers quickly in class if you are not using the online component.

More Information: The first and second activities of each **Ponerlo a prueba** section are generally designed for homework. However, if you have more contact hours, you may complete the second activity in class as a quick way to refresh students' memories. The remaining activities in **Ponerlo a prueba** are intended for classroom use. Additional reinforcement practice for homework is available in the *Cuaderno de actividades*.

Sample Answers to 1-2: 1. Me llamo... 2. Mucho gusto / Igualmente. 3. Hasta pronto, profesor. 4. De lo mejor. Bien. Regular, etc. ¿Y tú? 5. Igualmente / Que pase un buen fin de semana.

More Information: Icons identify whether activities are best completed in pairs, in a small group, or as a whole class. Of course you may use your discretion to adapt the practices to the practice mode you prefer.

Standards: Activities such as 1-3 address National Standards – Interpersonal Communication.

Teaching Tip 1-3: Model the activity with a student. Next, have each student introduce himself to someone seated nearby. Then, have all students stand and mingle as they introduce themselves to classmates. After 2–3 minutes, have students be seated. Follow up by finding out how many names they remember as you point and ask: **¿Cómo se llama esta persona?**

Teaching Tip 1-4: Save or reuse this activity for the beginning of the next class period. First, review the names of the students by pointing to individuals and asking the class: **¿Cómo se llama esta persona?.** Then, read the model aloud with a student. Afterwards, have students talk to a classmate seated nearby. Finally, have everyone stand and mingle. If necessary, introduce the phrase: **Perdón, no recuerdo tu nombre.**

1-5 ¿Cómo estás? ¿Cómo te sientes *(do you feel)* en estas situaciones? Responde en oraciones completas con el verbo **estar** y un adjetivo apropiado. Compara tus respuestas con las de un(a) compañero(a) de clase.

nervioso(a)	de buen humor	de mal humor	triste
contento(a)	ocupado(a)	preocupado(a)	
cansado(a)	enojado(a)	enfermo(a)	

MODELO

You read: Tienes un examen importante mañana.

You say how you might feel: Estoy nervioso(a). ¿Y tú?

Your classmate says how he/she might feel: Estoy preocupado(a).

1. Tu compañero(a) de cuarto *(roommate)* usa tu computadora y la daña *(breaks it)*.
2. Necesitas leer tres novelas y escribir tres composiciones para la clase de inglés.
3. ¡Tu profesor(a) de español cancela la clase!
4. Tu perro *(dog)* está muy enfermo.
5. Participas en un maratón.

1-6 En nuestro campus. Trabaja con uno(a) o dos compañeros de clase. Preparen breves diálogos para los dibujos. Después *(Afterwards)*, presenten uno de los diálogos a la clase.

1.   2.   3.

Vocabulario temático

Información básica *(Exchanging basic information with classmates)*

ROBERTO:	**¿Cuál es tu nombre completo?**
VICTORIA:	**Me llamo *Victoria Lourdes Rosati Álvarez*.**

ROBERTO:	**¿Cuál es tu primer nombre?**
VICTORIA:	**Me llamo *Victoria Lourdes*, pero me dicen *Viki*.**

| ROBERTO: | ¿Cuál es tu apellido? |
| VICTORIA: | Mi apellido paterno *es Rosati*, y el materno *es Álvarez*. |

ROBERTO:	¿De dónde eres?
VICTORIA:	Soy de *Nueva York*.
	Nací en *San Juan, Puerto Rico*.

Hispanics use two surnames, or **apellidos.** Lists are alphabetized by the paternal surname.

ROBERTO:	¿Cuál es tu dirección local?
VICTORIA:	Vivo en *la calle Azalea, número 358*.
	los apartamentos Greenbriar, número 6-B
	la residencia Capstone, número 162

Use **tu** to express "your" with friends and family; use **su** with strangers, older persons, and as a sign of respect.

ROBERTO:	¿En qué año de estudios estás?
VICTORIA:	Estoy en *primer* año.
	segundo
	tercer
	cuarto

Regional Vocabulary: In some countries, such as Cuba, it is common to add the article: **Estoy en el primer año.**

| ROBERTO: | ¿Cuántas clases tienes este semestre? |
| VICTORIA: | Tengo *cuatro clases y un laboratorio*. |

Vocabulary: Nicknames are known as **apodos.** For students using a post office box, provide the term **apartado postal.** The symbol @ may be called **signo de arroba** or **arroba.**

Regional Vocabulary: In Spain, a cell phone is called **un móvil.**

ROBERTO:	¿Cuál es tu número de teléfono?
VICTORIA:	En casa, es *el 7-54-26-08 (siete, cincuenta y cuatro, veintiséis, cero, ocho)*.
	Mi celular es el *7-98-46-16 (siete, noventa y ocho, cuarenta y seis, dieciséis)*.

Victoria Lourdes Rosati Álvarez

Calle Azalea, # 358   Tel: 754-2608
Nueva York   Cel: 798-4616
                       Email: Viki278@yahoo.com

| ROBERTO: | ¿Cuál es tu dirección de correo electrónico? |
| VICTORIA: | Es Viki278@yahoo.com *(Viki, dos, siete, ocho, arroba yahoo punto com)*. |

Note: Phone numbers are often given in groups of two, but area codes are often given as single digits.

ROBERTO:	*¿Vamos a un café* más tarde?
	Tomamos algo
	Estudiamos juntos
VICTORIA:	Sí, de acuerdo.

Transparency Bank L-1

Teaching Tip: The numbers from 0 to 39 were presented in the **Paso preliminar.** Review them along with these new numbers. For example, practice counting by twos, by fives, by tens, backwards from 100 using only odd numbers, etc.

Teaching Tip: To practice numbers from 40 to 100, do simple math problems: **Treinta más treinta son... ; Cien menos veinte son... ;** etc. Or, play the game of **Caracoles.** Sitting in groups of 4 or 5, the students must count from 1 to 100, with each student saying in turn the next consecutive number. However, for any number that ends in 7 or is a multiple of 7, the student must say **caracoles** instead of that number (1, 2, 3, 4, 5, 6, caracoles, 8, 9 . . .). Any student who misses three times drops out of the game.

Teaching Tip: Assign 1-7 and 1-8 for homework. Go over the answers quickly in class if you are not using the online component. Choose from the remaining activities for in-class use.

CD1
Track 3

Los números de 40 a 100

40	**cuarenta** (cuarenta y uno, cuarenta y dos...)
50	**cincuenta** (cincuenta y uno, cincuenta y dos...)
60	**sesenta** (sesenta y uno...)
70	**setenta** (setenta y uno...)
80	**ochenta** (ochenta y uno...)
90	**noventa** (noventa y uno...)
100	**cien** (ciento uno, ciento dos, ciento tres...)

Ponerlo a prueba

1-7 Dos compañeros. Es el primer día de clase. Sonia y Francisco son compañeros en la clase de historia. Escucha su conversación. Completa la tabla con la información apropiada.

¿Cuál es su nombre completo?	Sonia López Cruz	Francisco Díaz Feliciano (Paco)
¿De dónde es?	Nueva York	Ponce, Puerto Rico
¿Cuál es su dirección local?	Residencia Barnwell, 260	Calle Rosewood, 3550
¿Cuál es su número de teléfono?	Celular: 696-4558	Celular: 677-0286
¿Cuál es su dirección de correo electrónico?	Sonia23@yahoo.com	Eljefe968@hotmail.com

1-8 El primer día de clase. Vivian y Débora hablan antes de *(before)* clase. ¿Cómo responde Débora a las preguntas de Vivian?

Las preguntas de Vivian	**Las respuestas de Débora**
_b_ 1. ¿Cuál es tu nombre?	a. Mi celular es el 254-6776.
_g_ 2. ¿En qué año estás?	b. Me llamo Débora, pero todos me dicen Debi.
_h_ 3. ¿Cuántas clases tienes este semestre?	c. Nací en Río Grande, pero ahora mi familia vive en San Juan.
_c_ 4. ¿De dónde eres?	d. Sí, de acuerdo. ¿Vamos a Starbucks?
_f_ 5. ¿Cuál es tu dirección local?	e. Es coqui123@yahoo.com
_a_ 6. ¿Cuál es tu número de teléfono?	f. Vivo en la Residencia Maxcy, 45.
_e_ 7. ¿Cuál es tu dirección de correo electrónico?	g. Estoy en mi segundo año.
_d_ 8. ¿Vamos a un café más tarde?	h. Tengo tres clases y dos laboratorios.

1-9 La tarjeta. Recibes esta tarjeta *(business card)* en una recepción. Lee la información y contesta las preguntas.

Viajes Marlo
Calle Colón, 25
San Juan, PR 00919

Tel. (787) 722-8400
Fax (787) 722-8490
Marilú García Romero   Celular (787) 845-6754
Agente   MarilúGR@wepa.com

1. ¿Cuál es el nombre completo de la agente de viajes *(travel agent)*? ¿Cuál es su apellido paterno? ¿Cuál es su apellido materno?

2. ¿Cuál es el nombre y la dirección de la agencia de viajes?

3. ¿Cuál es el número de teléfono de la agencia? ¿Cuál es el número personal de la agente?

4. ¿Cuál es la dirección de correo electrónico de la agente?

 1-10 Un directorio. Habla con varios compañeros de clase y prepara un pequeño directorio con sus datos. Incluye el nombre completo, la dirección, el teléfono y la dirección de correo electrónico.

> **MODELO**   —¿Cuál es tu nombre completo?   —Me llamo Mark Lucas Graciano.
> —¿Cómo se escribe "Graciano"?   —Se escribe ge-ere-a-ce-i-a-ene-o.
> —¿Cuál es tu dirección local?   —Vivo en la residencia…

Nombre completo	Dirección local	Teléfono	Dirección de correo electrónico
1.			
2.			
3.			
4.			

 1-11 Mis compañeros. Habla con tres o cuatro compañeros de clase. Entrevístense con las preguntas y toma apuntes *(take notes)*. ¿Con quién tienes más en común *(more in common)*?

1. ¿Cómo te llamas?

2. ¿De dónde eres?

3. ¿En qué año de estudios estás?

4. ¿Cuántas clases tienes este semestre?

5. (Una pregunta original)

Teaching Tip 1-9: For more advanced classes, you can move directly to this activity to refresh student's memory of the **Vocabulario temático**. Direct the class's attention to the card. Pose each question and call on individuals to respond or seek volunteers.

Teaching Tip 1-10: Before assigning students to small groups for 1-10, tell students your own full name, e-mail, etc. and have them write the information on paper or in your syllabus. Then direct them to do the same with classmates, one at a time.

Teaching Tip 1-11: Have students work in pairs and change pairs every 2 minutes so that they talk with many people. For example, have the class form two circles, one inside the other. Students speak for 2 minutes with a partner; then, the outside circle rotates one position to the right and everyone interviews a new partner. Alternatively, form groups of 3–4 and have students trade information.

Gramática

Los verbos *ser, tener, ir*

Read and listen to the conversation between Marcos and his friend Tomás. Find examples of the following verbs and circle them: **ser, tener, ir.**

—¿De dónde eres, Marcos?

—Soy de Vieques, pero estudio en la Universidad de Puerto Rico aquí en Arecibo.

—Yo también. ¿Tienes muchas clases este semestre?

—Sí, tengo cinco. La clase de física es muy difícil *(difficult)*.

—Yo tengo física también. Mira, voy a clase ahora *(now)*, pero ¿estudiamos juntos más tarde?

—Sí, de acuerdo.

A. Tres verbos importantes. As you have seen in the **Vocabulario temático** section and in the dialogue above, the verbs **ser, tener,** and **ir** are among the most commonly used in Spanish. Here are the conjugations in the present tense.

	tener *(to have)*	**ser** *(to be)*	**ir** *(to go)*
yo	tengo	soy	voy
tú	tienes	eres	vas
usted	tiene	es	va
él/ella	tiene	es	va
nosotros(as)	tenemos	somos	vamos
vosotros(as)	tenéis	sois	vais
ustedes	tienen	son	van
ellos/ellas	tienen	son	van

B. Los usos de *tener, ser, ir*. Here are the main uses of these three verbs.

Tener *(to have)*

▸ ownership

Tengo una computadora.   *I have a computer.*

▸ with **que** + infinitive, for obligation (what you "have to" do)

Tenemos que trabajar ahora.   *We have to work now.*

▸ age

Tengo veinte años.   *I'm twenty (years old).*

▸ special phrases

Tengo (mucho) frío / calor.   *I'm (very) cold/hot.*

Tenemos (mucha) hambre / sed.   *We're (very) hungry/thirsty.*

Tenemos (mucha) prisa.   *We're in a (big) hurry.*

María tiene (mucho) cuidado.   *María is (very) careful.*

¿Tienes (mucho) sueño?   *Are you (very) sleepy?*

¿Tienes (mucho) miedo?   *Are you (very much) afraid?*

(No) Tienen razón.   *They are (not) right.*

(No) Tienen ganas de estudiar.   *They (don't) feel like studying.*

Ser (to be)

▸ before nouns, to identify a person or thing or state someone's nationality, political party, religion, etc.

Marcos y yo somos estudiantes.	*Marcos and I are students.*
Somos puertorriqueños.	*We are Puerto Rican.*

▸ to provide information such as telephone numbers and addresses

¿Cuál es tu teléfono?	*What is your phone number?*
Es el 254-2760.	*It's 254-2760.*

▸ with the preposition **de,** to say where someone or something is from

¿De dónde eres?	*Where are you from?*
Soy de los Estados Unidos.	*I'm from the United States.*

Ir (to go)

▸ with the preposition **a** *(to),* to tell where someone is going

¿Adónde van Uds.?	*Where are you (all) going?*
Vamos a la cafetería.	*We're going to the cafeteria.*

▸ with the preposition **a** + infinitive, to say what somebody is going to do

Vamos a tomar algo.	*We're going to have something to drink.*
Vamos a estudiar juntos.	*We're going to study together.*

Teaching Tip: Some students find it helpful to consider the verb **ser** as an equal sign. For example, **Mi teléfono = 254-6618.**

More Information: Ser and **estar** are contrasted in **Capítulo 3.** We recommend emphasizing forms over uses in this chapter. For a quick rule of thumb, have students remember the rhyme: "How you feel and where you are, always use the verb **estar.**"

More Information: Ir + a + infinitive is practiced more extensively in **Capítulo 2.** In this chapter, emphasize the use of **ir** with destinations.

Ponerlo a prueba

1-12 Una entrevista. Tienes que entrevistar a Miguel y a Felipe, dos estudiantes nuevos *(new)* en tu universidad. Lee la conversación y escoge *(choose)* el verbo más lógico. Escribe el verbo en el tiempo presente.

Teaching Tip: Assign the first activity for homework; choose from the remaining activities for class work.

Tú: Hola, Miguel. Hola, Felipe. Tengo unas preguntas para Uds. Primero, ¿de dónde (ser / ir) 1. __son__ Uds.?

Miguel: Felipe y yo (ser / ir) 2. __somos__ de Bayamón, Puerto Rico.

Tú: No conozco *(I'm not familiar with)* Bayamón. ¿En qué parte de Puerto Rico (estar / ir) 3. __está__ ? ¿(Ser / Tener) 4. __Tiene__ muchas atracciones turísticas?

Miguel: Bueno, Bayamón (estar / ir) 5. __está__ más o menos en la región central de Puerto Rico. Y sí, hay muchas atracciones. Por ejemplo, el parque de ciencias Luis A. Ferré (ser / tener) 6. __es__ muy popular.

Tú: ¡Qué interesante! Bueno, tengo una pregunta más. ¿Qué (ser / ir) 7. __van__ Uds. a estudiar aquí en la universidad?

Miguel: Yo (ser / ir) 8. __voy__ a estudiar farmacia y Felipe (ser / ir) 9. __va__ a estudiar biología.

Tú: Gracias por contestar mis preguntas. ¿(Tener / Ir) 10. __Vamos__ (nosotros) a un café ahora?

Miguel: Sí, de acuerdo.

1-13 En Puerto Rico. Estás en Puerto Rico con tu familia para las vacaciones. Responde a las situaciones con oraciones completas.

> **MODELO**   As you go through the security checkpoint, the guard asks your full name and age.
>
>   *You reply:* Me llamo John Edward Kent. Tengo veinte años.

1. At immigration, the agent asks your profession and country of origin. You reply: _____.

2. The porter helping with the luggage inquires as to what cities you and your family are going to visit (**visitar**) during your stay in Puerto Rico. You reply: _____.

3. At the hotel, the desk clerk asks for your home address and phone number. You reply: _____.

4. During a family excursion later that day, you must tell the taxi driver that you and your family are going to **La Fortaleza** so you say: _____. Then, to add that you are in a hurry, you say: _____.

5. As the taxi cab goes flying through the streets, you decide to show off your Spanish and ask your little brother in Spanish if he is afraid. You ask: _____.

1-14 Una presentación. Preséntate a tus compañeros de clase. Incluye la siguiente información y sigue el modelo:

- Tu nombre completo
- Tu edad *(age)*
- El año de estudios en la universidad
- Tu ciudad *(city)* de origen
- Información interesante sobre *(about)* tu ciudad

> **MODELO**   Me llamo Rita Luisa Quevedo. Tengo diecinueve años y soy estudiante de la Pontificia Universidad Católica de Puerto Rico. Estoy en mi primer año de estudios. Soy de Isla Verde, Puerto Rico. Isla Verde está cerca *(close)* de la capital y es muy popular con los turistas. Tiene playas *(beaches)* bonitas y muchos restaurantes. Con frecuencia, mis amigos y yo vamos a los clubs en el centro de la ciudad.

La Fortaleza, residencia del gobernador de Puerto Rico, es la mansión ejecutiva más antigua de las Américas.

Puente cultural

¿Cómo demuestran el cariño *(How do you show affection)* entre amigos?

Lineliz Marie Vassallo

🌐 **PUERTO RICO**

Los amigos demuestran su cariño con darse un beso en el cachete *(kiss on the cheek)* al saludar y también al despedirse. Como forma de respeto a gente mayor *(older people)*, se dice mucho "Bendición" *(Blessing)* al encontrarse. En Puerto Rico expresamos la amistad más a menudo *(more often)* y tal vez más sentimentalmente que es normal en Estados Unidos.

Jahel Pulido

🌐 **COLOMBIA**

Las mujeres se saludan *(greet one another)* de beso en la mejilla *(a kiss on the cheek)*. Entre hombres se dan la mano *(shake hands)*. Entre hombres y mujeres se dan un beso en la mejilla.

Romeo Wong

🌐 **PERÚ**

Pasar momentos juntos, invitarlos a comer o a tomar algo. En situaciones especiales con algún regalo *(a gift)*. También con palabras amigables *(friendly)*: chochera, compadre, causa. Y con gestos *(gestures)*: abrazos, chocada de manos o puños *(fist bumps)*.

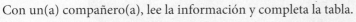 Con un(a) compañero(a), lee la información y completa la tabla.

	En Puerto Rico	En Colombia	En Perú	En los Estados Unidos
¿Cómo demuestran el cariño entre amigos?				

More Information: Each participant in the **Puente cultural** responded to two sets of questions. The written responses to a global, cultural question are included here. The video response to a related, personal question may be found on the *Puentes* Premium Website.

Standards: The **Puente cultural** is offered once each chapter and addresses the National Standards– Culture and Comparisons. The questions focus on the products, practices (or customs), and perspectives (values, beliefs) of the varied Spanish-speaking cultures. College-aged students from three different countries present their views each time to provide for cross-cultural comparisons.

Teaching Tip: Divide the class into groups of 3. Have one person in each group summarize the information for one of the 3 countries. Then have everyone collaborate to describe the customs in the United States. At this early stage you will need to assist students with vocabulary. Allow phrases and words, but work towards complete sentences.

Note: As an example, Lineliz remarked that messages in birthday cards and letters are more sentimental and affectionate in Puerto Rico than in the mainland of the U.S.

Regional Vocabulary: Chochera, causa, compadre are slang words for **amigo, socio, camarada.**

🌐 Go to the *Puentes* Premium Website to view the **Puente cultural** interviews.

► Sharing information about your immediate family, friends, and classmates

► Using some important verbs in conversation and writing

Grammar:

► Possessive adjectives

► Regular -**ar**, -**er**, and -**ir** verbs in the present tense

► Creating basic sentences

Teaching Tip: For classroom practice and quizzes, focus on the objectives listed here. The 3 or 4 points of study within each **Paso** work together to make a "performance unit" that allows students to accomplish the tasks set out in the objectives.

More Information: Estrategia provides students with useful tips on how to become more efficient learners and better speakers of Spanish. Suggestions are provided in every chapter on how to facilitate memorization, approach listening tasks, manage conversations, interact with native speakers, and so on. Assign these sections to be read for homework.

Transparency Bank E-1, E-2, E-3

Use **Este es...** *(This is . . .)* to refer to a male. For more than one person, say **Estos son...**.

Other words for marital status: **estar casado(a)** *to be married;* **estar divorciado(a)** *to be divorced;* **ser viudo(a)** *to be a widow (widower).*

Use **Esta es...** *(This is . . .)* to refer to a female. For more than one, say **Estas son...**.

Grammar: Students often inquire why **ser** is used for certain words of marital status and **estar** for others. This usage, in fact, varies from country to country. A grammatical explanation that works with the usages specified: **casado** and **divorciado** are past participles used as adjectives, and use **estar**; while **soltero** and **viudo** are nouns, and are used with **ser.**

Paso 2

Estrategia *Previewing a lesson*

Previewing the day's lesson before you begin your assignment will help you focus your energies and make the most of your study time. Ask yourself these questions as you start to study and then plan accordingly.

► How many topics are included in the lesson?

► Which topics am I already familiar with?

► Which themes and structures seem to be the most important?

► On which of the sections will I need to spend the most time?

Vocabulario temático

La familia y los amigos *(Family and friends)*

—¿Cómo es tu familia, *Dulce*?

—Aquí tengo una foto. Mira.

Esta es mi tía *Felicia*. Es *soltera* y vive *con nosotros*.

Este es mi hermano mayor, *Carlos*. Tiene *veinte* años.

Este es mi papá. Se llama *Arturo*.

Esta soy yo. Tengo *diecisiete* años.

Esta es mi mamá. Se llama *Beatriz*.

Estos son mis buenos amigos, *Marcos* y *Sara*.

Esta es mi hermana menor, *Elisa*. Tiene *diez* años.

El cumpleaños de Dulce

Otros familiares (Other family members)

los abuelos	los padres	los esposos	los hijos	los tíos
el abuelo	el padre	el esposo	el hijo	el tío
la abuela	la madre	la esposa	la hija	la tía
			los gemelos	

Otros amigos (Other friends and acquaintances)

los novios	unos (buenos) amigos	los vecinos	mis compañeros de clase
el novio	un (buen) amigo	el vecino	mi compañero de clase
la novia	una (buena) amiga	la vecina	mi compañera de clase

ESTRUCTURAS ESENCIALES

Cómo indicar la posesión

A. Los adjetivos posesivos. Possessive adjectives indicate who owns what or show relationships between people or things.

mi(s)	*my*	**nuestro(s) / nuestra(s)**	*our*
tu(s)	*your (informal)*	**vuestro(s) / vuestra(s)**	*your (informal)*
su(s)	*your (formal)*	**su(s)**	*your (informal/formal)*
su(s)	*his/her/its*	**su(s)**	*their*

B. La concordancia. Like all adjectives, possessive adjectives agree in both gender (masculine or feminine) and number (singular or plural) with the noun they describe.

(singular noun: **casa**)	su casa	*their house*
(plural noun: **casas**)	sus casas	*their houses*
(singular, feminine noun: **familia**)	nuestra familia	*our family*

C. "Your." The possessive adjective *your* can be expressed in different ways. When speaking to a friend or family member, use **tu;** with a superior or a stranger, use **su.**

Familiar:	**Tu** hermana es muy simpática, José.
	Your sister is very nice, José.
Formal:	**Su** hermana es muy simpática, Sr. Gómez.
	Your sister is very nice, Mr. Gómez.

More Information: Students will already be familiar with words for common family relationships. Use this opportunity to use the familiar words in sentences and also to focus on the less familiar terms: **mayor/menor, soltero/casado, gemelos, vecinos, novios**.

Teaching Tip: Bring in photos of your family and use sentences similar to those in the lesson to identify who the people are. Have your students do likewise. Persons who don't have photos of their family can bring in photos of celebrities (from the internet) and create fanciful new families.

Note: The Real Academia Española now establishes that demonstrative pronouns (**este, ese, aquel,** etc.) should follow general accent rules, and therefore, not carry written accent marks. Point out to students that in older publications, they will see **éste, ésta, éstos...** with accent marks that were used to distinguish demonstrative pronouns from demonstrative adjectives.

Heinle Grammar Tutorial: Possessive adjectives and pronouns

More Information: Additional family vocabulary is presented in **Capítulo 3** so that students can expand upon this basic and important topic. This is an important topic for students at the Intermediate level of proficiency. However, use sensitivity in class, as some students prefer not to discuss their own families.

D. Su(s). The Spanish word **su** and its plural **sus** can mean *your, his, her, its,* and *their.* When the context is not clear, it is common to replace **su** with a special phrase: **de** + *corresponding subject pronoun* (**él, ella, ellos, ellas, Ud.,** or **Uds.**).

Enrique y Alicia viven en Georgia.	*Enrique and Alicia live in Georgia.*
La casa **de él** está en Atlanta.	***His** house is in Atlanta.*
La casa **de ella** está en Augusta.	***Her** house is in Augusta.*

E. Un caso especial. Spanish never uses 's to indicate relationships and possession. This idea is expressed with the phrase **de** + *person's name.*

la hija **de María**	*María's daughter*
los hermanos **de mi padre**	*my dad's brothers*

Ponerlo a prueba

Teaching Tip: Assign the first two activities for homework.

Answers 1-15: 1. Ana es la hermana de Mercedes. 2. Elena es la amiga de Ana. 3. Paco es el hermano de Mercedes. 4. Francisco es el padre de Mercedes. 5. Luisa es su tía; es la hermana de su padre. 6. Alberto es el vecino. 7. Teresa es la vecina; es la esposa de Alberto. 8. María es la hija de los vecinos. 9. Esta es Mercedes.

CD1
Track 5

1-15 La foto. Mercedes describe una foto a su amiga. Escucha la descripción. Identifica a todas las personas en la "foto". Escribe una oración completa con el parentesco *(relationship)* de cada persona.

MODELO   ***You hear:*** Mira, esta es mi madre, Carmen.
You write a sentence stating the relationship to Mercedes:
Carmen es la madre de Mercedes.

1. Ana	4. Francisco	7. Teresa
2. Elena	5. Luisa	8. María
3. Paco	6. Alberto	9. ¿ ?

1-16 La familia de Gregorio. Gregorio, un estudiante estadounidense, va a estudiar a Venezuela. En una carta a su familia venezolana, Gregorio escribe una descripción de su familia norteamericana. Completa la carta con los adjetivos posesivos más lógicos: **mi(s), tu(s), su(s), nuestro(s), nuestra(s).**

> **(1)**_____ familia no es muy grande. Somos solamente cinco y vivimos en Arlington, Virginia. **(2)**_____ padre se llama Gregorio, como yo. **(3)**_____ mamá se llama Gloria. Ella nació en Cuba pero inmigró a los Estados Unidos con **(4)**_____ padres en 1962. **(5)**_____ hermanos se llaman Ana y Marcos. Como *(Since)* mamá es cubana, Ana, Marcos y yo siempre hablamos español con ella y con **(6)**_____ abuelos maternos.
>
> No estoy casado pero sí tengo una novia, Ángeles. Ella nació en Puerto Rico y ahora vive con **(7)**_____ familia en Arlington. **(8)**_____ apartamento no está muy lejos *(far)* de **(9)**_____ casa y nos vemos *(we see each other)* casi todos los días.

Expansion 1-16: After checking answers, have students create a family tree for Gregorio. Or, ask follow-up questions: **¿Es grande o pequeña la familia de Gregorio? ¿Cómo se llama el padre de Gregorio? ¿Cómo se llama su mamá?, ¿sus hermanos? ¿Con quiénes habla español Gregorio? ¿Cómo se llama la novia de Gregorio? ¿Dónde está el apartamento de ella?**

Answers 1-16: 1. Mi/Nuestra 2. Mi / Nuestro 3. Mi/Nuestra 4. sus 5. Mis 6. nuestros 7. su 8. Su 9. nuestra / mi

1-17 Mi mejor amigo. ¿Quiénes son tus mejores *(best)* amigos? Trabaja con un(a) compañero(a) de clase y entrevístense *(interview each other)* con las preguntas. (Nota: *If you have a photo of your best friend, show it to your classmate as you talk.*)

1. ¿Cómo se llama tu mejor amigo o amiga?
2. ¿De dónde es él / ella?
3. ¿Tiene hermanos o hermanas?
4. ¿Es soltero(a)? ¿Tiene novio(a)?
5. ¿Con quién vive?
6. ¿Cuántos años tiene él / ella?
7. ¿Dónde estudia él / ella?
8. (Haz una pregunta original / *Ask another question.*)

Teaching Tip 1-17: Bring in a photo of a good friend and describe him/her to your students as a model for this activity. Then have students work in pairs to describe their best friends.

1-18 Mi familia. Describe a tu familia a un(a) compañero(a) de clase. ¿Cuál de Uds. tiene la familia más grande?

> **MODELO**
>
> Mi padre se llama Christopher y mi madre se llama Rachel. Están divorciados. Tengo dos hermanos. Mi hermano mayor se llama Eric y tiene 22 años. Mi hermana menor se llama Alyssa y tiene 15 años. Mis abuelos paternos viven en Florida, pero mis abuelos maternos murieron hace unos años *(died a few years ago)*. También tengo cuatro tíos, cinco tías y nueve primos *(cousins)*.

Teaching Tip 1-18: To refresh students' memories on family terms, have them complete orally definitions that you start: **El padre de mi padre es mi... abuelo. La hermana de mi padre es mi... tía,** etc. Then, explain that they will be comparing families with a classmate. Read the model aloud. Then, describe your own family in a similar way. Finally, have students work with their partners. Follow up by comparing family size. Have students bring a family portrait to practice the expressions **"Este es... "** and **"Estos son... ".**

Vocabulario temático

Dime más sobre tu familia *(Tell me more about your family)*

—¿Dónde vive tu familia?
—Mi familia vive en *Dorado, Puerto Rico.*
              un pueblo cerca de San Juan

—¿Dónde trabajan *tus padres?*
—Mi *padre* trabaja *en su propio negocio.*
     madre   *para la compañía Bacardi*

—¿Pasas mucho tiempo con *tus hermanos?*
                      tu familia

—No, porque *viven lejos.*
   Sí, pasamos mucho tiempo juntos.

Dime más sobre la vida estudiantil *(Tell me more about student life)*

—¿A qué universidad asistes?
—Asisto a *la Universidad de Puerto Rico.*

—Vives en una residencia, *¿verdad?*
                      ¿no?

—Sí, vivo en una residencia *con mi buena amiga, Carola.*
   No, vivo *con mi familia.*
            en un apartamento

—¿Cuántas clases tomas este semestre?
—Tomo *cinco* clases *(y un laboratorio).*

—¿Tienes que *leer* mucho para tus clases?
             estudiar

—*Sí,* normalmente tengo que *leer* mucho.
   No, no tengo que *leer* mucho por lo general.

—¿Cuándo trabajas?
—No trabajo.
   Trabajo *por la mañana / por la tarde / por la noche / los fines de semana.*

—Después de *tus clases,* ¿regresas a *la residencia?*
             tu trabajo   *casa*

—*Sí,* regreso *a la residencia* para *descansar.*
   No, voy *a la biblioteca* para *estudiar.*
            al gimnasio   *hacer ejercicio*

—¿Dónde comen tú y tus amigos?
—Por lo general, comemos *en la cafetería.*
                      en restaurantes de comida rápida

Ponerlo a prueba

CD1
Track 6

1-19 Una nueva amiga. Escucha la conversación entre Silvia, Delia e Ignacio. Después, completa las oraciones con la información correcta.

Teaching Tip: Assign the first two activities for homework.

1. Silvia es de _____.

   a. Puerto Vallarta   b. Puerto Rico   c. Costa Rica

2. Delia está en su _____ año de estudios en la Universidad.

   a. primer   b. segundo   c. tercer

3. Este semestre, Delia toma _____.

   a. cuatro clases   b. cinco clases   c. tres clases y dos laboratorios

4. Delia vive _____.

   a. en una residencia   b. en un apartamento   c. con su familia

5. Delia trabaja de voluntaria _____.

   a. los fines de semana   b. por la tarde   c. todos los días

1-20 Katya. Katya describe su vida en la universidad. Relaciona *(Match)* los elementos de las dos columnas para formar oraciones lógicas.

1. Asisto a __b__ .
2. Vivo en una residencia __f__ .
3. Tomo cuatro clases y __h__ .
4. Tengo que estudiar mucho __d__ .
5. Mis amigos y yo comemos __e__ .
6. Los fines de semana, trabajo __c__ .
7. Mi familia vive __g__ .
8. Durante las vacaciones, regreso a casa __a__ .

a. para visitar a mi familia
b. la Universidad de Miami
c. en una oficina
d. para mi clase de física
e. en los restaurantes de comida rápida
f. con mi buena amiga, Cristina
g. un poco lejos de la universidad
h. dos laboratorios

1-21 El estudiante típico. ¿Cómo es tu vida en la universidad? ¿Cómo es la vida del estudiante típico en tu universidad? Completa las oraciones con información lógica.

1. En nuestra universidad, el estudiante típico vive en (una residencia / una fraternidad o sororidad / un apartamento / con sus padres) Yo vivo…

2. Normalmente, los estudiantes aquí (here) toman (tres / cuatro / cinco / seis) clases por semestre. Por lo general, yo tomo…

3. El estudiante típico (trabaja menos de veinte horas por semana / trabaja más de veinte horas por semana / no trabaja). Yo…

4. El estudiante típico come (en la cafetería / en los restaurantes de comida rápida / con su familia) todos los días. Normalmente, yo como…

5. Por lo general, los estudiantes pasan los fines de semana (con sus familias / con sus amigos / en la biblioteca / en su trabajo). Por lo general, yo paso los fines de semana…

1-22 ¿Y tú? Entrevista a un(a) compañero(a) de clase y toma apuntes (take notes). Después, presenta a tu compañero(a) a la clase.

1. ¿Cuál es tu nombre completo?

2. ¿En qué año de estudios estás?

3. ¿Dónde vive tu familia? ¿Pasas mucho tiempo con tu familia?

4. ¿Vives en una residencia en el campus?

5. ¿Cuántas clases tomas? ¿Tienes que estudiar mucho para tus clases?

6. ¿Trabajas? (¿Sí? ¿Dónde? ¿Cuándo?)

MODELO   Esta es mi compañera, Emma. Emma es de Chatanooga, Tennessee. Está en el segundo año de estudios. Este semestre vive en la residencia Whitmore. Toma cuatro clases y un laboratorio. Trabaja en un restaurante los fines de semana.

Gramática

El tiempo presente de los verbos regulares

Heinle Grammar Tutorial: The present indicative tense

Read and listen to this conversation between Silvia and her father. Beside each verb in boldface, write down whether it is an **-ar**, **-er**, or **-ir** verb.

—Bueno, hija, ¿cómo es un día típico para ti?

—Ay, papá, siempre estoy muy ocupada. Primero, **asisto** a mi clase de inglés. En la clase, **leemos, hablamos** y **escribimos** en inglés.

— ¡Qué bien! Vas a aprender mucho así. ¿Tienes otras clases por la mañana? ¿O **regresas** a la residencia después de tu clase de inglés?

—No, generalmente **estudio** un poco en la biblioteca y después **como** en la cafetería con mi compañera de cuarto. Mis otras clases son por la tarde.

Proficiency: Students must master this structure in order to reach the Intermediate level. For this reason, every chapter in *Puentes* provides opportunities for students to converse in the present time frame.

Teaching Tip: Your students will be familiar with the concept of conjugating verbs. Write on the board in three columns the endings **-ar, -er, -ir.** Read aloud each line of the dialogue and have students tell you the corresponding infinitive. Write each in the appropriate column. Ask students to tell you what other verbs they know for each column. Then return to the dialogue and have students give you the subject for each conjugated verb.

A. El tiempo presente. The present tense, or **el presente del indicativo,** is used to express these ideas:

▸ an action that occurs regularly or routinely

> **Estudio en la biblioteca todos los días.**   *I study at the library every day.*

▸ an ongoing action or condition

> **Nuestro amigo vive en una residencia este semestre.**   *Our friend is living in a dorm this semester.*

▸ an action that will take place in the near future

> **Mis compañeros y yo vamos a una fiesta mañana.**   *My classmates and I are going to a party tomorrow.*

B. Los infinitivos. Spanish verbs are classified into three basic groups based upon their infinitive endings (**-ar, -er, -ir**). Each group uses a different set of endings when the verb is conjugated. To use these verbs in a sentence, first you remove the **-ar, -er,** or **-ir,** then you add the ending that matches the subject of the sentence.

	-ar verbs **tomar** *(to take, drink)*	**-er** verbs **comer** *(to eat)*	**-ir** verbs **asistir** *(to attend)*
yo	tom**o**	com**o**	asist**o**
tú	tom**as**	com**es**	asist**es**
usted/él/ella	tom**a**	com**e**	asist**e**
nosotros(as)	tom**amos**	com**emos**	asist**imos**
vosotros(as)	tom**áis**	com**éis**	asist**ís**
ustedes/ellos/ellas	tom**an**	com**en**	asist**en**

Some common regular verbs:

-ar verbs:

escuchar *(to listen to)*	**estudiar** *(to study)*
hablar *(to speak, talk)*	**limpiar** *(to clean)*
mirar *(to watch, look at)*	**necesitar** *(to need)*
pasar *(to spend [time])*	**practicar** *(to play/ practice [sports])*
regresar *(to return, go back)*	**tomar** *(to take, drink)*
trabajar *(to work)*	**visitar** *(to visit)*

-er verbs:

aprender *(to learn)*   correr *(to run)*
comprender *(to understand)*   leer *(to read)*
comer *(to eat)*

-ir verbs:

asistir *(to attend)*   escribir *(to write)*
vivir *(to live)*

C. Cómo formar oraciones. To form a complete sentence (**una oración**), follow these guidelines.

▶ To create a sentence, include a subject, a conjugated verb, and words to complete the thought.

SUBJECT + VERB + THE REST OF THE IDEAS

Juan tiene tres clases este semestre.
Juan has three classes this semester.

▶ To make a sentence negative, add the word **no** before the conjugated verb. English includes the words *do* and *does* in negative sentences, but Spanish does not.

Carla <u>no</u> tiene laboratorios este semestre.
Carla does not (doesn't) have any labs this semester.

▶ If the subject is a pronoun (**yo, tú, él, nosotros,** etc.), you can omit it. The subject is understood from the verb ending.

¿Vives en Ponce?
Do you live in Ponce? (The understood subject is **tú.**)
No, vivimos en Mayagüez.
No, we live in Mayagüez. (The understood subject is **nosotros.**)

▶ Include subject pronouns when you want to **emphasize** or **clarify** the subject. This is commonly done when you give contrasting information for two different subjects.

<u>Él</u> toma cuatro clases, pero <u>ella</u> toma cinco.
*He takes **four** classes but **she** takes **five**.*

D. El presente progresivo. You may be familiar with another present tense in Spanish called the "present progressive." You can recognize it because the conjugated form of **estar** is used together with another verb that ends in **-ando** or **-iendo**. For more information on this tense, see the **Gramática suplementaria** section at the end of your textbook.

¿Qué **estás haciendo,** Pepe?   Nada en particular. **Estoy mirando** la tele.
*What **are you doing,** Pepe?*   *Nothing special. **I'm watching** T.V.*

More Information: Some of your students will have studied this tense previously. It is presented here for recognition, as it is not a key structure for Intermediate level proficiency. If you wish to practice this point, turn to the **Gramática suplementaria** section at the end of the textbook.

Grammar: Point out that, unlike English, Spanish refers to the future with the present tense, not the **presente progresivo: Mañana salgo para España.** Tomorrow I'm leaving for Spain.

Ponerlo a prueba

1-23 Las actividades de mi familia. Iván y su familia pasan mucho tiempo juntos. Completa la descripción de sus actividades. Escoge (*Choose*) el verbo más lógico y escríbelo en el tiempo presente.

Mi familia y yo **(1)** (pasar / regresar) _____ mucho tiempo juntos (*together*). Durante el día, papá y mamá **(2)** (necesitar / trabajar) _____ en el sector turístico. Mis hermanos y yo **(3)** (leer / asistir) _____ a clases. Pero por la noche **(4)** (nosotros: comer / visitar) _____ en casa, **(5)** (conversar / aprender) _____ y **(6)** (mirar / escuchar) _____ televisión. A veces (*Sometimes*) **(7)** (nosotros: regresar / ir) _____ al cine.

Los fines de semana **(8)** (nosotros: ir / ser) _____ más activos. Normalmente yo **(9)** (correr / comprender) _____ los sábados por la mañana. Mis hermanos y papá **(10)** (practicar / tomar) _____ el tenis y mi mamá **(11)** (escribir / limpiar) _____ la casa. Por la tarde, todos nosotros **(12)** (visitar / vivir) _____ a nuestros abuelos.

1-24 Un fin de semana típico. Todos los fines de semana, Fernanda invita a toda la familia a su casa. ¿Qué hacen (*What do they do*) en una fiesta típica? Escribe un mínimo de seis oraciones completas.

MODELO   Por lo general, Fernanda y Mirta preparan la comida para los invitados.

 1-25 Las actividades de mi familia ¿Qué hacen tú y tu familia (o tú y tus amigos) los fines de semana (*on weekends*)? Habla con dos o tres compañeros de clase y descríbanse (*describe to each other*) cinco de sus actividades. ¿Quiénes pasan mucho tiempo juntos? ¿Quiénes son muy activos? ¿Quiénes son menos (*less*) activos?

MODELO   Por lo general, mi familia y yo _____.
También, normalmente _____ y _____.
A veces (*Sometimes*), _____.

In this *Paso* you will practice:

▶ Talking about free-time activities
▶ Expressing likes and dislikes
▶ Asking and answering different types of questions

Grammar:

▶ The verb **gustar**
▶ Question formation

More Information: For classroom practice and quizzes, focus on the objectives listed here. The 3 or 4 points of study within each **Paso** work together to make a "performance unit" that allows students to accomplish the tasks set out in the objectives.

More Information: When presenting this section, focus on new vocabulary and the expression **me gusta.** Other variations with **gustar** are explained in **Gramática.** It is not necessary to go into detail at this point.

To say what you like to do, use **me gusta + infinitive.**

Practicar and **jugar** mean *to play a sport.* **Tocar** means *to play an instrument.*

Transparency Bank G-5, G-6, G-7

Teaching Tip: Direct attention to the second drawing. State whether or not you enjoy the activity pictured: **Me gusta practicar el fútbol. No me gusta practicar el tenis.** Ask 2–3 students **¿Qué deporte te gusta practicar?** Continue in the same way for each drawing.

Vocabulary: Introduce **baloncesto** as an alternative to **básquetbol.** The internet is often referred to by its name in English and always capitalized; depending on the country, to surf the internet may be either expressed as **navegar por Internet** or **navegar en Internet.** Introduce **MP3 (eme pe tres)** as an alternative to ipod.

To say what you AND your friends like to do, use **nos gusta + infinitive.**

Paso 3

Vocabulario temático

El tiempo libre *(Free-time activities)*

¿Qué te gusta hacer en tu tiempo libre?

Me gusta mirar *la televisión (vídeos / películas / partidos de fútbol).*

Me gusta practicar *deportes (el fútbol americano / el básquetbol / el tenis).*

Me gusta escuchar *la radio (la música clásica / la música rock / el jazz / mi ipod).*

Me gusta navegar *por Internet y* **leer** *revistas (poesía / novelas / periódicos).*

Otros pasatiempos *(Other pastimes)*

—¿Qué les gusta hacer en su tiempo libre a ti y a tus amigos?

—Nos gusta *correr en el parque (por el campus).*
         ir al cine (a fiestas / de compras)
         pasar tiempo con los amigos (con los novios[as])
         bailar en clubs
         montar en bicicleta (a caballo)
         jugar videojuegos

Ponerlo a prueba

CD1
Track 8

1-26 La clase de inglés. Los estudiantes en la clase de inglés están presentándose *(are introducing themselves).* Escucha las presentaciones y completa la tabla.

Nombre	Origen	Pasatiempos
1. Marta		
2.	Chile	
3.		leer novelas románticas y poesía, ir de compras
4. Antonio		
5.	Perú	

Teaching Tip: Assign the first two activities for homework. You may wish to occasionally use one of the listening activities as a quiz, to impress upon your students the need to complete them as homework.

Answers 1-26: 1. Colombia, ir al cine, pasar tiempo con su novio, navegar por Internet y jugar videojuegos 2. Cristián, practicar fútbol, correr, ir a fiestas 3. Gabriela, Argentina 4. Ecuador, practicar deportes, correr, pasar tiempo con amigos 5. Rosa, practicar el tenis, montar a caballo, pasar tiempo con amigos, ir a fiestas

1-27 Asociaciones. ¿Qué actividad asocias con estos grupos de palabras? Consulta el **Vocabulario temático** y sigue el modelo.

> **MODELO**   *You see:* "Law & Order," "Sixty Minutes," "Lost"
>
>   *You write:* mirar la televisión

1. *Don Quijote, The Grapes of Wrath, Harry Potter and the Sorcerer's Stone*
2. *Los diarios de motocicleta, Dark Knight, E.T., Casablanca*
3. Tiger Woods, Serena Williams, LeBron James
4. *Newsweek, Sports Illustrated, Glamour, PC World*
5. Sears, Best Buy, Walmart, Barnes & Noble
6. *The New York Times, The Wall Street Journal, The Miami Herald*

Answers 1-27: 1. leer novelas 2. mirar películas / vídeos 3. mirar / practicar deportes 4. leer revistas 5. ir de compras 6. leer periódicos

Expansion 1-27: For follow-up, have students write an original list of items and read them aloud to the class to guess the association.

1-28 Charadas. ¿Eres actor / actriz? Dramatiza una de las actividades a continuación. Tu compañero(a) tiene que adivinar *(guess)* cuál es. Tomen turnos. ¡No se permite hablar!

montar en bicicleta
practicar el tenis
bailar en una fiesta
correr por el campus
practicar el básquetbol
jugar videojuegos
mirar una película de horror
navegar por Internet
leer el periódico
ir de compras

Teaching Tip: Activity 1-28 may be used in lieu of a formal presentation of the **Vocabulario temático.** Begin by pantomiming one activity on the list. After the class guesses the expression, state whether or not you like it: **Me gusta leer el periódico.** Call on volunteers to do the same with other expressions. Continue with expressions not on the list for a greater challenge.

1-29 Nuestras preferencias. ¿Qué les gusta hacer en su tiempo libre a ti y a tu compañero(a) de clase? Habla con un(a) compañero(a) sobre sus preferencias. Sigan el modelo.

MODELO

You ask the question:

¿Qué tipo de música te gusta escuchar? ¿El jazz, la música reggae, la música clásica, el rock, el rap?

Your partner answers and makes a recommendation:

Me gusta escuchar la música reggae. Te recomiendo la música de Bob Marley.

You agree and add another recommendation:

A mí me gusta también. *(Me too.)* Te recomiendo Toot Hibbert.

Or, you disagree and offer an alternative:

No me gusta escuchar la música reggae. Prefiero *(I prefer)* el jazz. Te recomiendo la música de Miles Davis.

1. ¿Qué tipo de música te gusta escuchar? ¿La música clásica, la música reggae, el rock, el jazz, la música alternativa, el hip-hop?

2. ¿Qué tipo de película te gusta mirar? ¿Las películas cómicas, las románticas, las de ciencia-ficción, las de acción, las de terror, las de suspenso?

3. ¿Qué deportes te gusta mirar en la tele? ¿El fútbol americano, el básquetbol, el béisbol, el tenis, el boxeo, el fútbol, el golf?

4. ¿Qué te gusta leer? ¿Las novelas, las biografías, la poesía, la ciencia ficción, las novelas de misterio, las revistas, los blogs sobre la política?

Gimnasio Arias

¡Más de 15 años contigo!

Somos tu gimnasio del barrio y ofrecemos todas las alternativas para mantenerte en forma:

▸ Artes marciales (Karate, Taekwondo)
▸ Pilates y yoga
▸ Aeróbics (con alto y bajo impacto)
▸ Entrenamiento con pesas
▸ Natación
▸ Masajes y sauna
▸ Clases colectivas de baile
▸ Sala cardiovascular
▸ ¡Visita nuestro café dietético!

Dirección: Ave. Ponce de León 1539
San Juan, PR 00925
Teléfono: (787) 274-7642
Email: gimansioarias@gmail.com

1-30 El Gimnasio Arias. Aquí tienes el anuncio *(ad)* para un gimnasio en Puerto Rico. Lee la información y contesta las preguntas. Si quieres, trabaja con un(a) compañero(a) de clase.

1. ¿Cuál es la dirección del Gimnasio Arias?, ¿el número de teléfono?, ¿la dirección de correo electrónico?

2. En tu opinión, ¿tienen una selección variada de actividades y servicios?

3. ¿Cuáles de las actividades te gustan más?

4. ¿Cuáles de estas actividades ofrece el gimnasio de tu universidad?

5. ¿Te gusta más el Gimnasio Arias o el gimnasio de tu universidad? Explica.

Gramática

El verbo *gustar*

CD1
Track 9

Read and listen to the conversation between Marcos and his new roommate Pablo. Find examples of the verb **gustar** and circle them. How many different verb forms do you see?

—Pablo, ¿qué te gusta hacer en tu tiempo libre?

—Me gusta leer. Me gustan mucho las novelas de misterio y las de ciencia ficción. ¿Y a ti te gusta leer?

—No, me gusta más jugar deportes, sobre todo el fútbol. Mis amigos y yo vamos mucho al cine también. Nos gustan las películas de terror.

🌐 **Heinle Grammar Tutorial: Gustar** and similar verbs

Proficiency: The use of **gustar** is a key point for Intermediate level proficiency. Students often struggle with this verb because of its structural pattern. Provide a short explanation before or during the practice activities to clear up questions.

Teaching Tip: Have two students read the dialogue aloud. For each sentence, have students point out the verb form and write on the board the two basic forms: **gusta** and **gustan.** Guide them to explain when each is used by referring to the phrase after each verb. Then, ask them how the **person** who likes something is expressed in Spanish. Point out the examples in the dialogue: **me, te, nos.** Then write sentences about the dialogue and point out the additional indirect object pronouns: **A Pablo le gusta leer. A Marcos le gustan los deportes. A Marcos y a sus amigos les gustan las películas de terror.**

A. Gustar. Unlike other verbs in Spanish, **gustar** *(to like)* commonly uses only two main forms: **gusta** and **gustan.** Another difference: The subject is often placed after the verb.

INDIRECT OBJECT PRONOUN	+	GUSTA/ GUSTAN	+	SUBJECT

Me	gusta	leer.	*I like to read. (Reading is pleasing to me.)*
Me	gusta	el golf.	*I like golf. (Golf is pleasing to me.)*
Me	gustan	los deportes.	*I like sports. (Sports are pleasing to me.)*

▸ Use **gusta** in front of one or more infinitives.

Me gusta ir a fiestas y bailar salsa.
I like to go to parties and to dance salsa. (Literally: Going to parties and dancing salsa are pleasing to me.)

▸ Use **gusta** before **el/la** + singular noun.

Me gusta la música jazz.
I like jazz music. (Literally: Jazz is pleasing to me.)

▸ Use **gustan** before **los/las** + plural noun, or before a series of singular nouns.

Me gustan los deportes.
I like sports. (Literally: Sports are pleasing to me.)

Me gustan el béisbol y el hockey.
I like baseball and hockey. (Literally: Baseball and hockey are pleasing to me.)

B. Otras personas. To express **who** likes a particular activity, you must use **gusta** and **gustan** with a special kind of pronoun called *indirect object pronoun.*

Nos gusta jugar deportes.	*We like to play sports.*
A los niños **les** gusta jugar deportes.	*Children like to play sports.*

I like	**me** gusta (gustan)	*we like*	**nos** gusta (gustan)
you (fam.) like	**te** gusta (gustan)	*you (pl., Spain) like*	**os** gusta (gustan)
you (formal) like	**le** gusta (gustan)	*you (plural) like*	**les** gusta (gustan)
he /she likes	**le** gusta (gustan)	*they like*	**les** gusta (gustan)
(name) likes	**a María le** gusta (gustan)	*(names) like*	**a mis amigos les** gusta (gustan)

More Information: The use of prepositional pronouns is presented for recognition only. We suggest that you focus on the essentials in sections A and B for classroom practice.

C. Aclaración y énfasis. You have seen that with most verbs, we use subject pronouns to clarify or emphasize *who* is doing what.

> **Yo** leo novelas, pero **ella** lee poesía.   *I read novels but **she** reads poetry.*

With the verb **gustar,** however, a special phrasing is used. Prepositional pronouns are used together with the indirect object pronoun.

> **A mí** me gustan las novelas, pero **a ella** le gusta la poesía.
> *I like novels but **she** likes poetry.*

The prepositional phrases used in this way with **gustar** are: **a mí, a nosotros, a ti, a Ud., a Uds., a él, a ella, a ellos, a ellas.**

Vocabulary: Point out that in many countries using **gustar** with a person's name as the subject implies that one is strongly attracted to that person: **Me gusta Julia** = *I am attracted to Julia.* A deep, true, romantic love can also be expressed with **amar: Amo a Julia.**

D. Expresiones afines. While it is correct to use **gustar** to indicate that you like the professional work of musicians, artists, actors, etc., you should choose from the following to say that you like someone *personally.*

> Julia **me cae bien.**   *I like Julia. (Julia strikes me as a nice person.)*
> **Aprecio** a Julia.   *I like Julia. (I hold Julia in esteem and appreciate her.)*

Ponerlo a prueba

1-31 ¿Son compatibles? Óscar y Félix son nuevos compañeros de cuarto. En tu opinión, ¿son compatibles?

Primera parte: Completa las conversaciones con: **me, te, gusta** y **gustan.**

> MODELO   ÓSCAR: ¿Te gustan los deportes?
> FÉLIX: Sí, ¡___me gustan___ mucho!

1. ÓSCAR: ¿Te gustan los deportes?

    FÉLIX: ¡Sí! ___Me gusta___ mucho mirar el boxeo. También ___me gustan___ el fútbol americano y el rugby.

2.   FÉLIX: ¿ _____Te gusta_____ mirar deportes en la televisión?

   ÓSCAR: Bueno, _____me gustan_____ los partidos de fútbol americano, pero no me gusta nada *(not at all)* el boxeo. Prefiero practicar los deportes y no mirarlos *(not watch them)*.

3.   ÓSCAR: ¿ _____Te gusta_____ leer? Yo leo mucha ciencia ficción.

   FÉLIX: Sí, _____me gustan_____ las novelas de Agatha Christie. Y también leo la poesía de Pablo Neruda, pero no _____me gusta_____ la ciencia ficción.

SEGUNDA PARTE: Escribe un resumen *(summary)* de las preferencias de Óscar y Félix. Incluye un mínimo de **cuatro** oraciones completas.

> **MODELO**
>
> A Óscar y a Félix les gusta leer. A Óscar le gusta mucho la ciencia ficción. A Félix le gusta más la poesía...

1-32 Un día en el parque. ¿Qué les gusta hacer a estas personas en el parque? Inventa una oración sobre el dibujo *(the drawing)*. Tu compañero(a) tiene que decidir si tu oración es cierta *(true)* o falsa. Tomen turnos.

> **MODELO**
>
> *You say:* A Augusto le gusta patinar en línea *(roller-blade)*.
>
> *Your partner says:* Falso. A Augusto le gusta practicar el tenis.

1-33 Nuestras actividades favoritas. ¿Qué les gusta hacer a ti y a tus amigos en el tiempo libre? Conversa con dos o tres compañeros de clase y comparen sus actividades favoritas.

> **MODELO**
>
> Mis amigos y yo tenemos mucho en común *(in common)*. Nos gustan mucho las películas románticas. Vamos al cine todas las semanas *(every week)*. También nos gusta bailar en fiestas. A veces bailamos salsa. ¿Qué les gusta hacer a ti y a tus amigos?

Answers 1-31 Segunda parte: Sample responses – A Félix y a Óscar les gustan los deportes. A Félix le gustan el boxeo, el fútbol americano y el rugby. A Óscar no le gusta el boxeo.

Teaching Tip 1-32: Model several sentences before having students work in pairs or small groups. Demonstrate how to turn a false statement into a true one.

Expansion 1-32: For follow up, have students imagine they are studying abroad. Their host family wants to know how Americans spend their leisure time. Working with a partner, they come up with a 1-minute response to the question: **¿Cómo pasan el tiempo libre los norteamericanos, por lo general?**

Gramática

Las preguntas

 Heinle Grammar Tutorial:
Interrogative words

CD1
Track 10

Proficiency: Asking questions is a fundamental skill for Intermediate level proficiency. Your students may already use some memorized or stock questions, such as **¿Cómo estás?** and **¿Cómo te llamas?** This chapter gives considerable emphasis to expanding that repertoire and begins here to encourage students to create original questions.

Teaching Tip: Have two students read the dialogue aloud or play the recording. Have the class identify the two main kinds of questions and note the way each is answered. Write on the board: **Sí/no** and **Información.** Have students tell you other questions they have been using for each category. Ask students to tell you other question words and make a list (**¿Qué? ¿Cuándo?** etc.).

Read and listen to the conversation between Carolina and María, a new acquaintance. Underline all the questions. Which questions could be answered with a "yes" or "no"? Which call for responses with specific information?

CAROLINA:	¿Estudias ciencias marinas aquí?
MARÍA:	Sí, el programa es fabuloso. ¿Y tú? ¿Qué estudias?
CAROLINA:	Biología. Por cierto *(By the way)*, eres puertorriqueña ¿verdad?
MARÍA:	No, mi familia es de Cuba.
CAROLINA:	¿De veras? *(Really?)* Tengo varios amigos cubanos en Miami. ¿Dónde viven Uds.?
MARÍA:	Bueno, mis abuelos viven en Miami pero mis padres y yo vivimos en Carolina del Norte.

A. Las preguntas de *sí* o *no*. A "yes/no question," as its name implies, can be answered by saying **sí** or **no.**

▶ To form a yes/no question, place the subject right after the verb. Notice that English *do* and *does* are not translated in questions. "Upside-down question marks" are placed before the question.

VERBO	+	SUJETO	+	OTROS ELEMENTOS

¿Vive + Martín + en Vieques?
Does Martín live in Vieques?

¿Vives en San Juan?
*Do you live in San Juan? (The subject **tú** is understood.)*

▶ "Tag" questions are another kind of yes/no question, formed by adding a short phrase *(Isn't it?* or *Don't you?)* at the end of a statement. In Spanish, add **¿no?** to the end of an affirmative statement, and **¿verdad?** to the end of a negative or affirmative statement.

María estudia en la universidad, **¿no?**	*María studies at the university, doesn't she?* (Affirmative statement)
No te gustan los deportes, **¿verdad?**	*You don't like sports, do you?* (Negative statement)

▶ To answer yes/no questions in the affirmative, first say **sí.** Then add a related comment to keep the conversation going.

¿Te gustan los deportes? **Sí,** me gustan mucho, especialmente el tenis.	*Do you like sports? Yes, I like them a lot, especially tennis.*

▶ To answer yes/no questions in the negative, first say **no.** To continue, add a negative statement. Or, elaborate by providing the correct information. In the reply below, the first **no** answers the question, while the second **no** is the equivalent of "doesn't" or "isn't."

¿Es María estudiante?	*Is María a student?*
No, María **no** es estudiante.	***No,** María **isn't** a student.*
Trabaja en un banco.	*She works in a bank.*

B. Las preguntas de información. Information questions require a response with specific facts, rather than a simple *yes* or *no*.

| **¿De dónde eres?** | *Where are you from?* |
| **¿Cómo te llamas?** | *What's your name?* |

Teaching Tip: Point out the intonation patterns and have the class repeat the model sentences after you. Yes/no questions in Spanish end in a rising pitch, while information questions end with a falling pitch.

▶ Information questions start with special question words. Each one has an accent mark and uses upside-down question marks at the beginning of the question.

¿Quién? ¿Quiénes? *Who?*	**¿Con qué frecuencia?** *How often?*
¿Qué? *What?*	**¿Cómo?** *How?*
¿Dónde? *Where?*	**¿Cuánto / Cuánta?** *How much?*
¿Adónde? *To where?*	**¿Cuántos / Cuántas?** *How many?*
¿De dónde? *From where?*	**¿Cuál / Cuáles?** *Which one/s?*
¿Cuándo? *When?*	**¿A qué hora?** *At what time?*
¿Por qué? *Why? How come?*	**¿Para qué?** *What for?*

▶ To form an information question, use this word order:

| EXPRESIÓN INTERROGATIVA | + | VERBO | + | SUJETO |
| **¿Dónde** | + | **estudian** | + | **Marcela y Miguel?** |

Where do Marcela and Miguel study?

▶ Place prepositions (**a, de, con,** etc.) **before** the question words.

| **¿De** dónde eres? | *Where are you **from?*** |
| **¿Con** quién hablas? | *Who are you talking **with?*** |

▶ Choose the proper ending for gender and/or number for **cuánto(a), cuántos(as), quién(es),** and **cuál(es).**

| **¿Cuántas** hermanas tienes? | *How many sisters do you have?* |
| **¿Cuáles** son tus hermanos? | *Which ones are your brothers and sisters?* |

> ▶ The expression **¿Cuál es?** is used much more in Spanish than in English, especially to ask for specific information such as names, phone numbers, addresses, favorite books, etc. Notice the English translation "What is . . . ?"
>
> | | |
> |---|---|
> | **¿Cuál es** tu número de teléfono? | *What is your phone number?* |
> | **¿Cuál es** tu película favorita? | *What's your favorite movie?* |
>
> ▶ The expression **¿Qué es... ?** is used to ask for definitions and explanations.
>
> | | |
> |---|---|
> | **¿Qué es** un "coquí"? | ***What is** a "coquí"?* |
> | Es una rana pequeña y un símbolo de Puerto Rico. | *It's a little frog and a symbol of Puerto Rico.* |

Ponerlo a prueba

1-34 ¿Cuál es la pregunta? Esther está en Puerto Rico para estudiar español. Acaba de conocer *(She has just met)* a su familia puertorriqueña. ¿Cuáles son las preguntas de Esther? Escribe las preguntas. (**¡Ojo!** Should Esther use **tú** or **Ud.** with Mr. Maza?)

> **MODELO**
> *You read the reply:* SR. MAZA: Siempre comemos **en casa.**
> *You write the probable question:* ESTHER: ¿<u>Dónde</u> comen Uds.?

1. ESTHER: ¿_____?
   SR. MAZA: Tenemos **tres** hijos. Son Alberto, Cecilia y Martita.

2. ESTHER: ¿_____?
   SR. MAZA: Alberto y Cecilia viven **cerca de aquí** *(here)* pero Martita está en **Río Piedras.**

3. ESTHER: ¿_____?
   SR. MAZA: Vive en Río Piedras **porque es estudiante en la UPR.**

4. ESTHER: ¿_____?
   SR. MAZA: La UPR es **la Universidad de Puerto Rico.**

5. ESTHER: ¿_____?
   SR. MAZA: Trabajo **en el Banco Central** en el departamento de divisas *(foreign currency).*

6. ESTHER: Es un trabajo interesante, ¿_____?
   SR. MAZA: **Sí**, me gusta mucho.

Teaching Tip: Assign the first activity for homework.

Answers 1-34: 1. ¿Cuántos hijos tienen Uds.? 2. ¿Dónde viven? 3. ¿Por qué vive / está Martita en Río Piedras? 4. ¿Qué es la UPR? 5. ¿Dónde trabaja Ud.? 6. ¿verdad? / ¿no?

1-35 Lotería biográfica. Tú y tus compañeros van a jugar a la lotería. El objetivo es encontrar a personas que hagan estas actividades (*find people who engage in these activities*).

MODELO   ***You ask a yes/no question based on the chart:***
Beth, ¿corres todos los días?
Your classmate may not engage in that activity and replies:
No, no corro.
You ask another classmate the same question:
Brian, ¿corres todos los días?
Your classmate may engage in that activity and replies:
Sí, corro todos los días.
You write that person's name in the chart. (*Ask* ¿Cómo te llamas? *if you don't recall his/her name*).

Lotería biográfica	
practicar muchos deportes	mirar películas de acción
leer un periódico con frecuencia	ir de compras con frecuencia
asistir a clases todos los días	pasar mucho tiempo en el gimnasio
comer en restaurantes vegetarianos a veces	correr todos los días
escribir poesía	vivir en un apartamento

 1-36 Situaciones. Estás en Puerto Rico para estudiar español. ¿Qué preguntas (*What do you ask*) en las siguientes situaciones? Dramatiza las situaciones (en la página 46) con un(a) compañero(a) de clase.

MODELO   *You are studying Spanish at a language institute in San Juan and have just been introduced to your teacher. Ask three questions to keep the conversation going. Your classmate will play the role of your professor and answer the questions.*

Tú:	¿De dónde es Ud.?
Tu compañero(a):	Soy de Arecibo.
Tú:	¿Dónde está Arecibo?
Tu compañero(a):	Está en el norte de la isla.
Tú:	¿Qué le gusta hacer en Arecibo?
Tu compañero(a):	Me gusta ir a la playa (*beach*).

Teaching Tip 1-36: Explain briefly the context and read the model with the class. Point out that the students must ask appropriate questions and answer them to create a conversation. Complete the first item as a class. Then have pairs complete items 2 and 3.

Teaching Tip 1-36: Alternate implementation – Divide students into groups of 4. Two must dramatize the situation, while the other two serve as "prompters" and give tips, corrections, words, etc. if the conversation falters. Model this pattern with several students before having students do this on their own.

1. You have just arrived at the home of your host family in Puerto Rico. Sra./Sr. Fuentes has shown you your room, and you would now like to strike up a conversation with him/her. Ask at least three friendly questions. Your classmate will play the role of Sra./Sr. Fuentes.

2. The Fuentes children—Mayra, 17 years old; and Pablo, 16—have just arrived home from school. You'd like to find out more about the life of teenagers in Puerto Rico. What do you ask them? Your classmate will play the role of Mayra or Pablo.

3. It's your first day on campus and you see a friendly face in the cafeteria. He/She seems to be about your age and you'd like to talk a while. After you introduce yourself, what do you ask? Your classmate will play the role of the new student.

COMENTARIO CULTURAL *Los pasatiempos*

¿Cómo pasas tu tiempo libre? ¿Cuáles son algunos de tus intereses?

La semana laboral *(work week)* es un poco más larga en España y en Latinoamérica que en los EE.UU. Sin embargo *(Nevertheless)*, los españoles y los latinoamericanos siempre buscan la manera de integrar algunas diversiones en su rutina. Los intereses de los hispanos son tan diversos como sus culturas. La pasión por el fútbol es casi universal, aunque el

béisbol también es muy popular, especialmente en el Caribe. En el sur de Chile y Argentina hay importantes centros para esquiar en la nieve *(snow)*, mientras que *(while)* en las costas de México hay oportunidades para practicar muchos deportes acuáticos. Otros pasatiempos comunes incluyen ir al cine, mirar la televisión, salir con los amigos o con la familia y bailar.

Un paso más

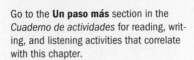

¡Vamos a hablar!

Estudiante A

Contexto: In this activity, you (**Estudiante A**) and your partner will become better acquainted with two celebrities from Puerto Rico. Each one of you has a chart with partial information. By taking turns asking and answering questions, the two of you will share the information needed to complete the chart.

You will begin by asking your partner a question about Daddy Yankee.

MODELO	ESTUDIANTE A:	¿Cuál es el nombre completo de "Daddy Yankee"?
	ESTUDIANTE B:	Se llama…

Daddy Yankee

Nombre completo: _____

Edad *(Age):* _____

Ciudad de origen: _____

Familia: Nombre de su esposa _____

   Número de hijos _____

Profesión: _____

Información de interés: _____

La India

Nombre completo: Linda Viera Caballero

Fecha de nacimiento: 9 de marzo de 1969

Lugar de nacimiento: Río Piedras, Puerto Rico

Familia: Casada con Louis Vega (1989) y divorciada en 1996.

Profesión: Cantante de música salsa y otros géneros. Tiene un estilo emocional y original.

De interés: Empezó *(She began)* su carrera en la ciudad de Nueva York. Ha colaborado con muchos célebres artistas, tales como Tito Puente, Celia Cruz, Gloria Estefan y Marc Anthony.

Go to the **Un paso más** section in the *Cuaderno de actividades* for reading, writing, and listening activities that correlate with this chapter.

More Information: Un paso más provides enrichment opportunities for speaking and cultural study, as well as two video programs: **En la Hacienda Vista Alegre** and **Imágenes de…** Additional enrichment activities in reading, writing, culture, listening are in the *Cuaderno de actividades*. Use these materials as time allows and your course objective dictates. For classes that have fewer contact hours, try alternating reading and writing activities by chapter.

More Information: ¡Vamos a hablar! is an information-gap activity that requires pairs of students to share information to complete the task. Additional activities of this type are in the *Instructor's Resource Manual*.

Teaching Tip: Assign students seated in the left half of the class to be **Estudiante A,** and those seated in the right half to be **Estudiante B.** Show each half of the class which page to use. Review the model, then have each student find a partner from the other half of the class. By asking and answering questions, the pairs complete the profiles on the two celebrities. You may also want to preview with your class the questions they will need to ask: **¿Cuántos años tiene? ¿De dónde es? ¿Cuál es su profesión? ¿Cómo es su familia? ¿Cuál es un aspecto interesante de su carrera?** Point out that partners may need to ask for the spelling of some names: **¿Cómo se escribe…?**

Note: Songs by both musicians are available through iTunes.

Un paso más

¡Vamos a hablar!

Estudiante B

Contexto: In this activity, you (**Estudiante B**) and your partner will become better acquainted with two celebrities from Puerto Rico. Each one of you has a chart with partial information. By taking turns asking and answering questions, the two of you will share the information needed to complete the chart.

Your partner will begin by asking you a question about Daddy Yankee. Look at your chart and provide the answer.

> **MODELO**
> ESTUDIANTE A: ¿Cuál es el nombre completo de "Daddy Yankee"?
> ESTUDIANTE B: Se llama…

Daddy Yankee

Nombre: Raymond Luis Ayala Rodríguez

Fecha de nacimiento: 3 de febrero de 1977

Lugar de nacimiento: San Juan, Puerto Rico

Familia: Casado con Mirredys González. Tres hijos—Yamilet, Jeremy y Jesairis

Profesión: Cantante de reggaetón, actor, empresario (*entrepreneur*).

De interés: Es el mayor proponente del reggaetón: una fusión del reggae y rap, con influencias de salsa, bomba y otros ritmos latinos. Ganó un Grammy Latino en el año 2006 (dos mil seis).

La India

Nombre completo: _____

Edad *(Age):* _____

Ciudad de origen: _____

Familia: Nombre de su ex-esposo _____

Número de hijos _____

Profesión: _____

Información de interés: _____

¡Vamos a ver! | *Episodio 1*

En la Hacienda Vista Alegre

Anticipación

A. Hablando se entiende la gente. Habla con tu compañero(a). Describe a tus cantantes, actores o escritores famosos favoritos. Incluye detalles sobre su origen, edad, estado civil, familia y personalidad. ¿Por qué son tus favoritos?

B. ¿Cómo se dice... ? Expresiones útiles. Relaciona *(Match)* las frases de la primera columna con las expresiones de la segunda.

b 1. ¿Qué te parece la casa?   a. Un poquito largo.

a 2. ¿Qué tal el viaje?   b. Es muy bonita.

d 3. ¡Bienvenido/a!   c. Encantado(a) de conocerte.

c 4. Te presento a Julián.   d. Muchas gracias.

More Information: This appealing video program is loosely based on MTV's *Real World*. Individual episodes may be viewed as time permits.

Teaching Tip: Before showing the video, activate student knowledge with activities A and B. To save time, assign B for homework. Make sure students understand they do not need to watch the video to complete Activity B.

▶ Vamos a ver

C. La Hacienda Vista Alegre. Mira el Episodio 1 del vídeo y observa la foto. ¿Cómo se llaman los personajes *(characters)* del episodio? ¿De qué nacionalidad son?

Nombres: Alejandra, Antonio, Javier, Sofía, Valeria

Nacionalidades: argentino, colombiana, española, mexicano, venezolana

Answers C: Antonio / mexicano, Valeria / venezolana, Alejandra / colombiana, Sofía / española, Javier / argentino

D. ¿Cómo son? Después de ver el episodio, escribe dos o tres oraciones sobre cada personaje. Describe sus estados físicos y emocionales, imagina *(imagine)* cuál es su estado civil, edad y ocupación. Con un(a) compañero(a), compara y comenta tus respuestas.

En acción

E. Charlemos. Comenta con tus compañeros(as).

1. ¿Cómo se saludan los personajes *(characters)*? ¿Cuántos besos *(kisses)* se dan para saludarse? ¿Hay alguna diferencia entre *(between)* la forma hispana de saludarse y la de tu país?

2. A primera vista *(At first glance)*, ¿qué personaje te gusta más? ¿Por qué? ¿Qué te interesa saber sobre los personajes de la *Hacienda Vista Alegre?*

F. 3, 2, 1 ¡Acción! Interpreten la siguiente situación en grupos de 3 ó 4 estudiantes.

Ustedes están en la *Hacienda Vista Alegre* y van a conocer a nuevos amigos. Saluden a sus compañeros. Pregunten de dónde son, dónde viven, su edad, etcétera. Conversen con sus compañeros sobre la familia y los pasatiempos.

Teaching Tip: Preview the questions before showing the video. Complete Activity C as a whole class. Have students work in pairs to complete Activity D.

Teaching Tip: Choose from Activities E and F as time permits. These activities are more challenging, as they involve spontaneous conversation and role playing.

Panorama cultural

DATOS ESENCIALES

Nombre oficial: Estado Libre Asociado *(Commonwealth)* de Puerto Rico

Capital: San Juan

Población: 3 995 000 habitantes

Unidad monetaria: dólar de EE.UU.

Economía: turismo, productos farmacéuticos y electrónicos, textiles, agricultura (caña de azúcar, café, piña)

www.cengage.com/spanish/puentes

Standards: Each **Panorama cultural** spotlights a different Spanish-speaking land. It addresses the National Standards for Connections with other disciplines by providing information about geography, political systems, history, and the arts. In addition, it relates to the standards for Culture (Products, Practices, Perspectives) and Comparisons.

Teaching Tip: Assign the readings and have students complete the corresponding activities in the *Cuaderno de actividades* as homework. Follow up in class by showing the video on Puerto Rico and going over the information and the activities.

Transparency Bank A-3, A-10

Note: Its political status as a commonwealth grants Puerto Ricans U.S. citizenship. However they cannot vote in federal elections, do not pay federal income taxes, and have a nonvoting congressional delegate. The country's autonomy is limited only in aspects of national defense, printing of currency, foreign diplomacy, and the administration of postal services and customs.

Note: Puerto Ricans carry proudly the name given by their Taíno Indian ancestors. They often refer to themselves as **borinqueños** or **boricuas.** Their national anthem is called **"La Borinqueña."**

Puerto Rico es una isla pequeña pero tiene muchas especies de anfibios: 16 de ellas coquíes. El coquí vive en árboles *(trees)* y produce el sonido "co-quí, co-quí". Es el símbolo de Puerto Rico.

Un vistazo a la historia

1493 Cristóbal Colón llega a la isla y empieza la época *(era)* de dominación española.

1898 Con el Tratado *(Treaty)* de París, Puerto Rico pasa a ser posesión de los Estados Unidos.

1952 Puerto Rico obtiene el estatus político de Estado Libre Asociado y se aprueba *(is approved)* una nueva constitución.

1993 El español y el inglés son declarados los idiomas oficiales de Puerto Rico.

1998 El tercer plebiscito sobre el estatus de Puerto Rico indica gran división de opinión entre la estadidad *(statehood)* y el estado libre asociado *(commonwealth).*

2003 Después de años de protesta por las prácticas de bombardeo, la Marina de los Estados Unidos sale de la isla de Vieques.

2009 Sonia Sotomayor, hija de padres puertorriqueños, es confirmada como la primera mujer de origen hispano en ser juez en la Corte Suprema de los Estados Unidos.

Puerto Rico

Guaybaná (¿?–1511)

Este valiente hombre fue un cacique *(leader)* de los taínos, los indígenas de Puerto Rico. Convocó a una reunión a los otros caciques de la isla y organizó una rebelión contra los españoles.

Roberto Clemente (1934–1972)

Este gran deportista y humanitario fue *(was)* la primera superestrella latina del béisbol. En la Serie Mundial de 1971, llevó a su equipo —los Piratas de Pittsburgh— a la victoria con un índice de .414 al bate. Murió *(He died)* en un trágico accidente aéreo durante una misión para llevar ayuda *(to take help)* a las víctimas de un terremoto *(earthquake)* en Nicaragua.

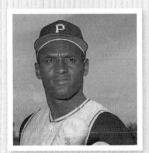

Note: Clemente played for the Pirates from 1955 to 1972 and was the first Latino player inducted into the National Baseball Hall of Fame in 1973.

Note: Puerto Rico officially celebrates religious, Puerto Rican, and U.S. holidays. Among many others are Jan. 6, El Día de los Reyes Magos; Dec. 25, Navidad; Jan. 10, Aniversario de Eugenio María de Hostos; Jul. 18, Aniversario de Muñoz Marín; Feb. 22, Día de Washington; and Julio 4, Día de la Independencia.

Sila María Calderón Serra (1942–)

Sila Calderón ha dedicado su vida al servicio público. Fue la primera mujer *(woman)* en ser gobernadora de Puerto Rico (2001–2005). Antes de ser gobernadora, ocupó varios puestos, entre ellos Alcadesa *(mayor)* de San Juan.

Note: Luis Muñoz Marín was the first governor elected by Puerto Ricans, rather than designated by the U.S. government. He served four terms from 1949 to 1965 and was instrumental in writing the constitution when Puerto Rico became a commonwealth.

Después de mirar el vídeo *Imágenes de Puerto Rico*, contesta estas preguntas con tus compañeros de clase.

1. ¿Cómo es San Juan? *(What is San Juan like?)*

2. Aparte de los indígenas, ¿qué culturas o grupos étnicos han tenido *(have had)* un impacto en Puerto Rico?

3. ¿Cuáles son algunas de las atracciones turísticas de San Juan y Ponce?

Additional activities on Puerto Rico and the **Panorama cultural** may be found in the **Un paso más** section of the *Cuaderno de actividades*.

Suggested Answers: 1. San Juan es una ciudad antigua / vieja. Tiene una muralla vieja y un fuerte español. Las calles son pintorescas. También hay una playa. 2. Los españoles; los africanos. 3. En San Juan: el Fuerte de San Felipe del Morro, las murallas, las artesanías (como las máscaras y las muñecas), la playa de Piñones (con los quioscos de comida). En Ponce: la Catedral de la Guadalupe, el Parque de Bombas, la Guancha.

CAPÍTULO 1

Vocabulario

Sustantivos

la actividad *activity*
el apartamento *apartment*
el apellido *surname, last name*
la biblioteca *library*
la calle *street*
la casa *house*
la comida rápida *fast food*
la compañía *company*
la computadora *computer*
la cosa *thing*
el cuarto *room*
el dato *fact, information*
la dirección *address*
el disco compacto *compact disc*
el ejercicio *exercise*
la familia *family*
la fiesta *party*
el fin de semana *weekend*
el fútbol (europeo) *soccer*
el fútbol americano *football*
el gimnasio *gym*
la gramática *grammar*
el hospital *hospital*
el inglés *English (language)*
la música *music*
el nombre *name*
la novela *novel*
el número *number*
la oficina *office*
el parque *park*
el partido *game*
la película *movie*
el periódico *newspaper*
la poesía *poetry*
la pregunta *question*
el (la) profesor(a) *professor, teacher*
el programa *program, show*
la residencia estudiantil *residence, dormitory*
la respuesta *response, answer*
el restaurante *restaurant*
la revista *magazine*
el semestre *semester*
el supermercado *supermarket*
la televisión *television*

el tenis *tennis*
el tiempo libre *free time*
la tienda *store*
el trabajo *work, job*
la universidad *university*
el (la) vecino(a) *neighbor*
el vídeo *video*

Verbos

aprender *to learn*
asistir *to attend*
bailar *to dance*
comer *to eat*
comprender *to understand*
contestar *to answer*
correr *to run*
escribir *to write*
escuchar *to listen to*
estar *to be*
estudiar *to study*
gustar *to like, to be pleasing*
hablar *to talk, to speak*
hacer ejercicio *to exercise, to do exercise*
ir *to go*
jugar (ue) *to play*
leer *to read*
limpiar *to clean*
mirar *to watch, to look at*
montar en bicicleta (a caballo) *to ride a bike (a horse)*
nacer *to be born*
navegar *to navigate, "surf" (the Internet)*
necesitar *to need*
pasar *to spend (time)*
practicar *to play (a sport), to practice*
regresar *to return, to go back*
ser *to be*
tener *to have*
tener calor / frío *to be hot/cold*
tener cuidado *to be careful*
tener ganas de + infinitive *to feel like (doing something)*
tener hambre/sed *to be hungry/thirsty*
tener miedo *to be afraid*

tener prisa *to be in a hurry*
tener razón *to be right*
tener sueño *to be sleepy*
tomar *to take, to drink*
trabajar *to work*
visitar *to visit*
vivir *to live*

Otras palabras

algo *something, anything*
antes (de) *before*
bien *well, fine*
casado(a) *married*
cerca (de) *close to*
con *with*
después *after*
divorciado(a) *divorced*
juntos(as) *together*
lejos (de) *far (from)*
mal; malo(a) *bad*
mucho(a) *much, a lot*
nuevo(a) *new*
poco(a) *little, not much*
porque *because*
por la mañana *in the morning*
por la noche *in the evening*
por la tarde *in the afternoon*
sí mismo(a) *himself, herself*
soltero(a) *single*
todos los días *every day*
un poco (de)... *a little (of) . . .*
vuestro(a) *your (informal, plural)*
y *and*

Greetings and introductions: pp. 14–15
Titles of address: p. 15
Feelings (Adjectives): p. 15
Numbers: p. 20
Family members and friends: pp. 26–27
Free-time activities: p. 36
Question words: p. 43

For further review, please turn to **Vocabulario temático: español e inglés** at the back of the book.

Go to the *Puentes* website for extra vocabulary practice using the Flashcard program.

¡De viaje!

Situation Cards: 15, 26, 27, 115, 116, 117, 118, 119, 124

More Information: The odd-numbered chapters in *Puentes* focus on developing students' abilities to converse on basic social topics; these chapters have 3 **Pasos**. The even-numbered chapters emphasize preparing students to function in common travel situations; these chapters have 2 **Pasos**.

Proficiency: In order to reach the Intermediate-low level, your students must be able to converse about family, friends, pastimes, and classes; they must also be able to handle basic transactions, such as getting hotel rooms, ordering food in restaurants, or shopping for souvenirs. This chapter focuses on transactions, with the emphasis on making travel arrangements.

Turn to the *Cuaderno de actividades* for this chapter's reading practice and strategy: Scanning for detail.

Turn to the *Cuaderno de actividades* for this chapter's composition practice and writing strategy: Keys to composing social correspondence.

OBJETIVOS

Speaking and Listening
▸ Telling time and giving dates
▸ Making travel and hotel arrangements
▸ Using numbers from hundreds to millions

Culture
▸ Mexico
▸ Popular vacation destinations in Spanish-speaking countries

Grammar
▸ Verb phrases (conjugated verb + infinitive)
▸ Stem-changing verbs in the present tense (e → ie; o → ue; e → i)
▸ Irregular verbs in the present tense

Video
▸ En la Hacienda Vista Alegre: Episodio 2
▸ Imágenes de México

Gramática suplementaria
▸ El futuro

Cuaderno de actividades
Reading
▸ Strategy: Scanning for detail

Writing
▸ Strategy: Keys to composing social correspondence

Playlist
🌐 www.cengage.com/spanish/puentes

A primera vista

Buscándola

Los viajes nos pueden llevar *(can take us)* a Europa, Asia, África, Oceanía, América del Sur o América del Norte. ¿Cuáles de los continentes has visitado *(have you visited)* en tus viajes?

Puentes playlist available on iTunes

More Information: The odd-numbered chapters feature art to introduce the chapter theme, while the even-numbered chapters present the theme through music. These songs are all available on ***Puentes*** iTunes playlist.

Note: How the world is divided into continents is not universally agreed upon. Whereas U.S. geography books generally teach North America and South America as two different continents, most Europeans and Latin Americans regard North and South America as one continent: **América.** Likewise, some people consider Europe and Asia to be one continent: **Eurasia.**

Vocabulary: Although not a common tourist destination, you may wish to introduce the term **Antártida.**

Note: Most destinations in this activity are mentioned in the chorus; Italy is mentioned in one stanza. The first stanza of the song is on the next page.

En la canción "Buscándola", un joven vuela *(flies)* por todo el mundo buscando *(looking for)* a la chica que se le escapó *(the girl that got away)*. Escucha la canción e indica todos los destinos mencionados.

☐ África   ☑ Japón

☑ Cancún   ☑ Katmandú

☐ China   ☐ Los Ángeles

☑ Honolulu   ☑ Nueva York

☑ Italia   ☐ París

HABLANDO DE LA MÚSICA

Together with the human voice, musical instruments create the myriad sounds we enjoy as music. The innumerable musical styles of Spain and Hispanic America may be created with familiar instruments such as **la guitarra, el clarinete, la flauta, la trompeta, el piano, el violín, el sintetizador, el teclado** *(keyboard)* or **la batería** *(drums)*. Other musical styles employ unique instruments indigenous to a particular region, such as these:

- **la ocarina:** This simple flute-like instrument made of ceramic or wood dates to ancient Aztec and Mayan times. It may have 4 to 12 finger holes.

- **la marimba:** This sweet-toned percussion instrument is played in parts of Mexico and throughout many countries of Central America. It is made of a series of wooden bars, arranged like the keys of a piano, that the musician strikes with mallets.

- **el charango:** This guitar-like instrument with five pairs of cords evolved in the Andean regions as a small, portable version of the Spanish guitar. Traditionally, the back of the soundbox was made from the dried shell of an armadillo.

MANÁ (GRUPO MUSICAL, 1987–)

Nacionalidad: mexicano

Obras y premios: Su primer gran éxito (*first big hit*) fue "Rayando el sol". En 2008, hacen una gira mundial (*world tour*) y sacan un DVD grabado en vivo (*recorded live*). Sus premios incluyen cuatro Grammys, cinco Latin Grammys y varios Premios MTV Latinoamérica.

De interés: Varios músicos (*musicians*) han formado este conjunto (*musical group*) en las tres décadas de su existencia. Se considera un conjunto de pop/rock pero a veces sus melodías tienen elementos de reggae o calipso.

Note: In 1995 Maná established Selva Negra, a foundation that works on ecological issues in the Americas.

BUSCÁNDOLA
canción de Maná

Conecto un avión para buscarte pues te me escapaste.

Europa, Asia y el Oriente, ¿dónde?

En eso un secuestro al avión ¡ah!

qué loca situación, nos dirigimos hacia Cuba al reventón.

In this *Paso* you will practice:

► Telling time
► Giving the date
► Making travel arrangements

Grammar:

► Verb phrases
► Stem-changing verbs in the present tense (e → ie; o → ue; e → i)

🌐 Go to the *Puentes* website for extra vocabulary practice using the Flashcard program.

The English equivalents to all **Vocabulario temático** lists are found at the back of the book.

Teaching Tip: The suggested pace for this **Paso** is 1-1/2 class hours.

Teaching Tip: Point out that the preposition **a** must be used in both the question and answer to say **at** what time something takes place.

To tell time up to 30 minutes past the hour, add **y** + *minutes/fraction of the hour:* **la una y cuarto** (1:15); **las dos y veinte** (1:20); **las ocho y media** (8:30). For times greater than 30 minutes, use **menos: las dos menos cuarto** (1:45); **las nueve menos cinco** (8:55).

Teaching Tip: Point out that the phrasing for telling time may vary: **Son las dos y cuarto.** Or, **Son las dos y quince. Son las tres y media.** Or, **Son las tres y treinta. Son las cinco menos cuarto.** Or, with digital time-pieces now being common, **Son las cuatro y cuarenta y cinco** is frequently used.

Use the singular verb form **es** with **una, mediodía,** and **medianoche,** and the plural form **son** with all other hours.

Teaching Tip: Point out that in Spain and Latin America the 24-hour system of telling time is frequently used to give schedules for movies and theater functions as well as arrival and departure times for buses, trains, and planes. For example, if flight #752 arrives at 22:05, it is expected at 10:05 P.M. Practice with several other examples.

Paso 1

Vocabulario temático

Cómo hablar de horarios *(Talking about schedules)*

—¿A qué hora sale *el vuelo 245?*

—Sale a *la una.*

—¿A qué hora llega?

—Llega a *las tres.*

—¿A qué hora abre *el museo?*

—Abre a *las nueve y media.*

—¿A qué hora cierra?

—Cierra a *la una y media.*

Cómo decir la hora *(Telling time)*

—¿Qué hora es?

Perdón, ¿podría decirme la hora?

Es mediodía.   Es la una.   Es la una y media.   Son las dos.

Son las dos   Son las cinco.   Son las ocho   Es medianoche.
y cuarto.   menos veinte.

  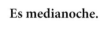

Para expresar "A.M." y "P.M." *(Expressing A.M. and P.M.)*

—¿A qué hora llegamos?
—A las tres de la tarde.

de la mañana *(6 A.M. to noon)*   **de la tarde** *(noon to sundown)*

de la noche *(sundown to midnight)*   **de la madrugada** *(early morning hours)*

Ponerlo a prueba

CD1
Track 11

2-1 La estación de autobuses. En México es muy popular viajar por autobús. Con frecuencia, se usa el sistema de 24 horas para expresar los horarios. Escucha los anuncios en la estación de autobuses. Completa la tabla con las horas adecuadas. Escribe la hora en el sistema de 24 horas y también en el sistema de 12 horas.

MODELO *You hear:* Señores pasajeros, el autobús para Cuernavaca sale de la plataforma número 3 a las veintidós horas.

You write the time two ways: 22 h; 10:00 P.M.

Autobús	Salida (*departure*)	
	Reloj de 24 horas	Reloj de 12 horas
MODELO Cuernavaca	22 h	10:00 P.M.
1. Puebla	22.45 h	10:45 P.M.
2. Acapulco	14.03 h	2:03 P.M.
3. Veracruz	15.36 h	3:36 P.M.
4. Mérida	18.15 h	6:15 P.M.
5. Guadalajara	19 h	7:00 P.M.

2-2 Es cuestión de horas. Completa las conversaciones de una manera lógica. (¡Ojo! *Refer to the times indicated in parentheses and spell out any numbers.*)

1. En el aeropuerto

   TURISTA: Por favor, ¿ _____a_____ qué _____hora_____ sale el vuelo 339 a Cancún?

   AGENTE: Sale a _____las_____ dos y _____media / treinta_____. (2:30)

2. En el hotel

   TURISTA: ¿A qué hora abre el museo?

   EMPLEADO: A _____las nueve_____ (9:00). Y cierra a _____la una_____ (1:00).

3. En la agencia de viajes:

   TURISTA: La excursión a Veracruz sale a las _____once_____, ¿verdad? (11:00)

   AGENTE: Sí, pero es mejor *(it's better)* estar aquí a las _once menos cuarto / quince OR diez y cuarenta y cinco_. (10:45)

4. En el autobús:

   TURISTA: Perdón, ¿ _____a qué_____ hora llegamos?

   CHOFER: Llegamos a Chihuahua _____a_____ las cinco y _____cuarto / quince_____ de la _____tarde_____ (5:15 P.M.).

Teaching Tip: Assign the first two activities for homework; use the remaining two in class.

Regional Vocabulary: In Mexico, **camión** is used for **autobús**.

2-3 Los vuelos. Estás en la capital de México y quieres *(you want)* visitar otras ciudades. Aquí tienes los horarios de varios vuelos en México. Con un(a) compañero(a), inventen diálogos entre tú y un(a) agente de viajes. Sigan el modelo.

MODELO

TÚ: ¿A qué hora sale el vuelo a Guadalajara?

AGENTE: Tenemos dos vuelos a Guadalajara. El primero *(The first one)* sale a las cinco de la tarde y llega a las seis y cuarto. El segundo *(The second one)* sale a las siete y diez de la tarde y llega a las ocho y veinticinco.

TÚ: Gracias.

Aeromexicano

17:00	México DF	10:15	México DF	6:00	México DF
18:15	Guadalajara	11:20	Acapulco	7:30	Monterrey
19:10	México DF	15:15	México DF	11:00	México DF
20:25	Guadalajara	16:20	Acapulco	13:30	Monterrey

2-4 Perdón, ¿podría decirme la hora? Trabajas en el aeropuerto de Miami, Florida, donde varios turistas te preguntan la hora. Con un(a) compañero(a), usa los relojes para contestar sus preguntas.

MODELO

TU COMPAÑERO(A): Perdón, ¿podría decirme la hora?

TÚ: Es la una y veintiocho.

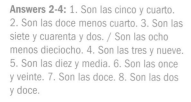

Vocabulario temático

Las fechas *(Expressing days and dates)*

—¿Cuándo salimos para *Mérida?*

—Salimos el *lunes, 28 de junio.*

—¿Cuándo regresamos?

—Regresamos el *viernes, 2 de julio.*

—¿Cuándo está abierto *el museo?*

—Está abierto *todos los días, de lunes a sábado.*

—¿Cuándo está cerrado?

—Está cerrado *los domingos.*

Grammar: Point out how to express *on* with days or dates: The definite article **el** refers to a one-time event; **los,** to an event that occurs regularly on a given day. For example: La fiesta es **el viernes.** *(The party is **(on) Friday.)** Trabajo **los sábados.** *(I work on Saturdays.)*

Los días de la semana *(Days of the week)*

—¿Qué día es hoy?

—Hoy es *lunes.*

lunes	martes	miércoles	jueves	viernes	sábado	domingo

Note: The first day of the week is usually **lunes.**

Los meses del año *(Months of the year)*

—¿Cuál es la fecha de hoy?

—Es el *25 (veinticinco) de noviembre.*

enero
febrero
marzo
abril
mayo
junio

L	M	M	J	V	S	D
	1	2	3	4	5	6
7	8	9	10	11	12	13
14	15	16	17	18	19	20
21	22	23	24	25	26	27
28	29	30				

julio
agosto
septiembre
octubre
noviembre
diciembre

L	M	M	J	V	S	D
	1	2	3	4	5	6
7	8	9	10	11	12	13
14	15	16	17	18	19	20
21	22	23	24	25	26	27
28	29	30	31			

Vocabulary: Other ways of asking the date: **¿En qué fecha estamos? ¿Qué fecha es hoy?**

Teaching Tip: Point out that the day comes before the month in dates. Give examples of how the dates would be written with numerals. For example: **06/09/10 = el seis de septiembre de dos mil diez.**

Use the cardinal numbers for most dates: **el cinco (5) de octubre, el veinte (20) de diciembre.** But say **primero** for the first day of the month: **el primero de febrero.** Give years as any other large number, NOT in groups of two: **1935 = mil novecientos treinta y cinco; 2012 = dos mil doce.**

Ponerlo a prueba

CD1
Track 12

2-5 El conserje. Tres turistas tienen reservaciones para el Hotel Sevilla Palace en el Distrito Federal de México. Escucha y escribe en español toda la información.

Nombre	Número de personas	Habitación sencilla *(single)* o doble *(double)*	Día y fecha de llegada	Hora de llegada
1. Sra. Adela Acosta	3 personas	doble	viernes, 26 de agosto	4 P.M.
2. Sr. Ramón Cordero	1 persona	sencilla	domingo, 31 de julio	1:30 P.M.
3. César Romero	4 personas	doble	jueves, 1 de septiembre	5:45 P.M.

2-6 Los exploradores. El Club de Viajes ofrece varias excursiones este año. ¿Cuándo son? Lee la información y completa las oraciones de una manera lógica. Escribe los números en palabras.

MODELO El tour a Panamá sale <u>el seis de septiembre</u> y regresa <u>el veinticuatro de septiembre.</u>

Programación para el año

¡Hagan sus reservaciones hoy!

Destinos	Sale	Regresa
Panamá	6/9	24/9
Chile	31/1	11/2
Colombia	30/3	7/4
Honduras	24/6	2/7
Costa Rica	1/8	22/8

1. El tour a Chile sale _____ y regresa _____.
2. Salimos para Colombia _____ y regresamos _____.
3. La excursión a Honduras sale _____ y regresa _____.
4. Salimos para Costa Rica _____ y regresamos _____.

2-7 Nuestras preferencias. Conversa con un(a) compañero(a) de clase sobre sus días y meses favoritos.

1. ¿Qué día de la semana prefieres? ¿Por qué te gusta? ¿Qué día te gusta menos? Explica por qué.
2. ¿Qué día de la semana estás superocupado(a) con tus clases y tus actividades? ¿A qué hora sales de casa (o residencia) ese día *(on that day)*? ¿A qué hora regresas?
3. ¿Qué mes prefieres? Explica por qué te gusta.
4. ¿En qué mes te gusta viajar? ¿Adónde te gusta ir?

Teaching Tip: Assign the first two activities for homework. Remind students that they may need to listen to the audio activities several times, particularly when numbers are involved.

Answers 2-6: 1. el treinta y uno de enero, el once de febrero; 2. el treinta de marzo, el siete de abril; 3. el veinticuatro de junio, el dos de julio; 4. el primero de agosto, el veintidós de agosto

Teaching Tip: To practice dates, have pairs of students guess each other's birthday. If the guess is close to the date, the partner says **caliente**; if the guess is not close to the date, the partner says **frío**. This process continues until the correct date is given. Model the activity first by having the entire class guess your birthday.

Teaching Tip: To practice days of the week, ask basic questions about schedules: **¿Qué día de la semana tienes muchas clases? ¿Qué días tienes que trabajar? ¿Qué días sales con tus amigos?**

Vocabulary: Students often want to talk about a "busy day." Point out that **ocupado(a)** is used for people, while **atareado** is used for days or people, and **ajetreado** *(hectic)* is used for days.

To answer question 2, use the irregular verb **salgo: Salgo de casa a las...** *I leave the house at . . .*

2-8 Una atracción popular. Estás en México, D.F., y quieres visitar unas atracciones populares de la capital. Lee este anuncio para el Museo Nacional de Antropología. Con tu compañero(a), contesta las preguntas.

Expansion 2-8: Have students create a brochure advertising their city's most popular attraction.

Note: The **Museo Nacional de Antropología** in Mexico City features pre-Columbian artifacts and is an important center for conferences and courses on these cultures.

Museos de la Ciudad de México

Hay muchos museos en la capital. Puedes encontrar obras de arte, artefactos antiguos, tecnología y mucho más. A continuación tienes una lista de los museos principales:

Museo Nacional de Antropología

Dirección:	Paseo de la Reforma y Calzada Gandhi
Teléfono:	35-33-23-16
Horario:	De martes a domingo de 10:00 a.m. a 6:30 p.m. El lunes está cerrado.
Costo de admisión:	Entrada general $51.00.
Reseña:	Exposiciones sobre la cultura prehispánica y la de los pueblos indígenas actuales, Conferencias y visitas guiadas.

1. ¿Cuándo está abierto el Museo de Antropología? ¿A qué hora abre? ¿A qué hora cierra? ¿Dónde está? ¿Qué número necesitas llamar para más información? ¿Qué exposiciones tienen?
2. ¿Cuál es la atracción más popular de tu ciudad? ¿Qué días está abierto ¿A qué hora abre y cierra? ¿Por qué es tan popular?

COMENTARIO CULTURAL *El calendario maya*

¿Qué culturas indígenas vivían (*lived*) en tu estado antes de la época colonial? ¿Qué sabes sobre su estilo de vida (*way of life*)?

Varias civilizaciones indígenas existían en México y Centroamérica antes de la llegada de los españoles. La civilización de los mayas era una de las más avanzadas. Son famosos por sus investigaciones en el arte, la arquitectura, las matemáticas y la astronomía.

Los mayas tenían varios calendarios. El más importante, el **tzolkin,** tenía 260 días. Otro calendario, el **haab**, tenía 365 días.

Note: The Maya occupied parts of the Yucatan from at least 1600 B.C. The height of their culture, called the Classic Period, occurred from about 250 to 900 A.D. The Mayan writing system is considered the most highly developed and complete of the pre-Columbian civilizations in the Americas. In parts of Guatemala the **tzolkin** calendar continues to be used among descendants of the Maya.

Vocabulario temático

En la agencia de viajes *(Making travel arrangements)*

Quiero is more direct *(I want . . .)*, while **quisiera** *(I'd like)* sounds more polite.

AGENTE:	¿En qué puedo servirle?
TURISTA:	Quisiera *hacer una excursión a Cancún.*
	hacer un viaje a Guadalajara

If you want to rent a car, say: **Quisiera alquilar un carro / un coche.**

AGENTE:	¿Cómo prefiere viajar?
TURISTA:	Me gustaría viajar *por avión.*
	en tren
	en autobús

Both **volver** and **regresar** mean *to return, to come back.*

AGENTE:	¿Qué día piensa salir?
TURISTA:	Pienso salir *el próximo jueves.*
AGENTE:	¿Cuándo quiere volver?
TURISTA:	Quiero volver *el dos de abril.*

Regional Vocabulary: Depending on the country, tickets for transportation may also be called **un billete** or **un pasaje.**

TURISTA:	¿Cuánto es el boleto?
AGENTE:	Un *boleto de ida y vuelta* cuesta *mil pesos.*
	boleto de ida

AGENTE:	¿Necesita un hotel?
TURISTA:	Sí. ¿Qué hotel me recomienda?
AGENTE:	Le recomiendo *el Hotel Miramar.*

Note: Depending on the country, tourists may be able to use a debit card or **tarjeta de débito** and/or withdraw money from an ATM or **cajero automático.**

AGENTE:	¿Cómo quiere pagar?
TURISTA:	Voy a pagar *en efectivo.*
	con tarjeta de crédito
	con cheques de viajero

Planes, preferencias y obligaciones: las frases verbales

A. El futuro. To talk about what you are going to do in the future, use the verb phrase: **ir** + **a** + infinitive.

> **Voy a hacer** una excursión a Taxco en abril.
> *I'm going to take an excursion to Taxco in April.*

B. Los planes. In addition to **ir,** several other verbs can be used to express future plans.

- ▸ **esperar** + infinitive *(to hope to do something)*
  Esperamos visitar el famoso museo en la capital.
  We hope to visit the famous museum in the capital city.

- ▸ **pensar** + infinitive *(to plan on doing something)*
  Pienso salir el viernes y regresar el domingo.
  I plan to leave on Friday and return on Sunday.

C. Las preferencias. Other verb phrases are used to express your wishes or desires. Notice that you must conjugate the first verb, but leave the second one in its infinitive form.

- ▸ **preferir** + infinitive *(to prefer to do something)*
  ¿Prefieren Uds. comer en el hotel o en el restaurante Tío Lucho?
  Do you (pl.) prefer to eat at the hotel or at Tío Lucho's restaurant?

- ▸ **Me gustaría** + infinitive *(I would like to . . .)*
  Me gustaría viajar en primera clase.
  I would like to travel in first class.

- ▸ **querer** + infinitive *(to want to do something)*
  Quiero salir el 8 de junio.
  I want to leave on June 8th.

D. Las obligaciones. Here are three ways to express obligations.

- ▸ **deber** + infinitve *(must/should do something)*
  Debo hacer las reservaciones.
  I should make the reservations.

- ▸ **necesitar** + infinitive *(to need to do something)*
  Necesitamos salir por la mañana.
  We need to leave in the morning.

- ▸ **tener** + **que** + infinitive *(to have to do something)*
  Tengo que hablar con el agente.
  I have to talk with the travel agent.

🌐 **Heinle Grammar Tutorial:** The uses of the infinitive

More Information: This section reviews and expands upon the notion of verb phrases, introduced in the first chapter. Two of the verbs mentioned here—**pensar** and **querer**—are stem-changing; these are explained in more detail later in this **Paso.** For the purposes of this practice, you can postpone practicing full conjugations of these verbs and treat the verb forms as lexical items to be memorized for immediate use.

CD1
Track 13

Ponerlo a prueba

2-9 El viaje de Daniel. Escucha la conversación sobre los planes de Daniel. Completa las oraciones de una manera lógica, según la información.

_b_ 1. En esta conversación, David habla con…

    a. su mamá.   b. una agente de viajes.   c. su mejor amiga.

_b_ 2. Daniel piensa ir a…

    a. los Estados Unidos.   b. México.   c. Canadá.

_a_ 3. Daniel va a viajar…

    a. por avión.   b. en tren.   c. en carro.

_b_ 4. Piensa salir…

    a. el martes, veinticinco de mayo.

    b. el jueves, cinco de agosto.

    c. el viernes, quince de diciembre.

_c_ 5. Daniel va a pagar con…

    a. cheque personal.   b. tarjeta de débito.   c. tarjeta de crédito.

2-10 Un viaje a México. Mariluz habla con un agente para hacer los planes para sus vacaciones. Relaciona las dos columnas de una manera lógica.

AGENTE DE VIAJES	MARILUZ
_b_ 1. ¿En qué puedo servirle?	a. El cuatro de mayo.
_e_ 2. ¿Cómo prefiere viajar?	b. Quisiera hacer un viaje a Acapulco.
_d_ 3. ¿Qué día piensa salir?	c. Para dos personas: mi esposo y yo.
_a_ 4. ¿Cuándo quiere regresar?	d. El veinticinco de abril.
_f_ 5. ¿Necesita un hotel?	e. Por avión. Es más rápido, ¿no?
_g_ 6. ¿Cómo quiere pagar?	f. Sí, uno económico. ¿Cuál me recomienda?
	g. ¿Aceptan Uds. cheques personales?

Teaching Tip 2-11: Model this activity by completing the sentences with your own version of a dream vacation. After students compare ideas, call on several to describe their trips. Be sure to point out that the word for vacation is plural: **vacaciones.**

Expansion: To further practice verb phrases, have students interview each other about their plans for the weekend. Encourage them to provide details for each of these times: **el viernes por la noche, el sábado por la mañana, el sábado por la tarde,** etc. Write these time cues on the board and model the activity by describing your own plans beforehand.

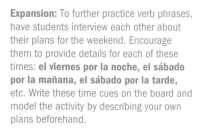

2-11 Unas vacaciones de ensueño (Dream vacation). Participas en un concurso (game show) en la televisión y ganas (you win) $5000 para hacer un viaje fabuloso. Describe tus planes para este viaje. Compara tus planes con los de un(a) compañero(a) de clase.

1. Para mis vacaciones de ensueño, pienso ir a _____. ¿Y tú? ¿Adónde piensas ir?

2. Quiero pasar _____ semanas allí. ¿Y tú? ¿Cuánto tiempo quieres pasar en tu destino?

3. La primera (The first) semana, espero _____ y _____. ¿Y tú? ¿Qué esperas hacer la primera semana de tus vacaciones?

4. El resto del tiempo me gustaría _____ y _____. ¿Y a ti? ¿Qué más (What else) te gustaría hacer?

2-12 ¿Para ir a Morelia, Michoacán? Estás estudiando en México y quieres hacer una excursión a Morelia, en el estado de Michoacán. Completa el diálogo con el agente de viajes.

1. AGENTE: ¿En qué puedo servirle?

   Tú: _____

2. TÚ: ¿ _____?

   AGENTE: El costo del viaje depende del medio de transporte que usted prefiere usar. Por avión, el boleto de ida y vuelta cuesta unos 200 pesos.

3. AGENTE: ¿Cuándo quiere ir?

   Tú: _____

4. TÚ: ¿_____?

   AGENTE: El Hotel Alameda; es muy bueno, pero económico.

5. AGENTE: ¿Cómo quiere pagar?

   Tú: _____

2-13 En la Agencia Venus. La Srta. Salas está hablando con un agente de viajes para hacer los arreglos *(make the arrangements)* para su viaje. Con un(a) compañero(a) de clase, dramatiza la conversación. Tienen que incorporar la información en las imágenes.

Teaching Tip 2-12: To quickly review the typical expressions for making travel arrangements, say a line aloud and ask students to identify who is talking, the tourist or the travel agent.

Teaching Tip: For many students it will be helpful to write out the answers to Activity 2-12 as a way of organizing their thoughts and committing key words to memory. Have pairs collaborate on writing their responses and then reading them aloud. This kind of preparation will make it easier for your students to act out Activtiy 2-13 in a more spontaneous way.

Heinle Grammar Tutorial: The present indicative tense

CD1
Track 14

Gramática

Los verbos con cambio en la raíz en el tiempo presente

Listen and read along as Marcos and Laura discuss their plans for the upcoming break. Find examples in the present tense of the following verbs: **empezar, pensar, poder, preferir, querer, volver.** What looks different about the way these verbs are conjugated?

MARCOS: Oye, Laura. Las vacaciones empiezan muy pronto. ¿Qué piensas hacer?

LAURA: Voy a la playa Progreso. Salgo el próximo domingo y vuelvo el sábado.

MARCOS: Todos dicen que es un pueblo muy tranquilo.

LAURA: Sí, es cierto. Puedo dormir y descansar *(rest)* toda la semana ¿Y tú, Marcos? ¿Qué vas a hacer?

MARCOS: Bueno, yo prefiero las vacaciones más activas. Quiero ir a Tulum y explorar las ruinas mayas.

A. Verbos con cambios en la raíz. In Spanish, all infinitives are composed of two parts: a stem (or root) and an ending.

Infinitive	Stem	+	Ending
pensar	pens-		ar
volver	volv-		er
preferir	prefer-		ir

When certain verbs are conjugated in the present tense, the stressed vowel in the stem undergoes a change. For example, the **e** in **pensar** changes to **ie**:

Infinitive	Stem	Stem change	Example of conjugated form
pensar	pens-	piens-	¿Qué p**ie**nsas hacer?

B. Los tres tipos de verbos. There are three basic patterns of "stem-changing verbs" or **verbos con cambio en la raíz.** They are identified in the glossary and in most dictionaries with cues in parentheses, like this: **pensar (ie); volver (ue); servir (i).** Notice that the stem changes occur when the verb is conjugated in any person except **nosotros** and **vosotros.**

¿Adónde **piensan** ir Uds.?	*Where do you (plural) plan on going?*
Pensamos ir a Tulum.	*We're planning on going to Tulum.*

Stem change e → ie

pensar (ie) *(to think, to plan [to do something])*

yo	p**ie**nso	nosotros(as)	pensamos
tú	p**ie**nsas	vosotros(as)	pensáis
Ud./él/ella	p**ie**nsa	Uds./ellos/ellas	p**ie**nsan

Here the **e** in the stem changes to **ie.**

Here the **e** in the stem stays the same.

Grammar: These verbs are sometimes referred to as "shoe-shaped verbs" because if you draw a line around the verb forms with irregular stems, you end up with a shape that resembles a shoe. Point this out to students as a memory aid.

Stem change o → ue

volver (ue) *(to return, come back)*

yo	v**ue**lvo	nosotros(as)	volvemos
tú	v**ue**lves	vosotros(as)	volvéis
Ud./él/ella	v**ue**lve	Uds./ellos/ellas	v**ue**lven

Stem change e → i

pedir (i) *(to ask for, request)*

yo	p**i**do	nosotros(as)	pedimos
tú	p**i**des	vosotros(as)	pedís
Ud./él/ella	p**i**de	Uds./ellos/ellas	p**i**den

C. Verbos comunes. Here are some common verbs that follow the three stem-changing patterns. All these verbs use the same endings as regular **-ar, -er,** and **-ir** verbs.

Stem change e → ie

empezar (ie) *to begin, to start*	Las vacaciones emp**ie**zan pronto.
pensar (ie) *to plan, to think*	P**ie**nso ir a playa Progreso.
preferir (ie) *to prefer*	Pref**ie**ro las vacaciones activas.
querer (ie) *to want, to love*	Qu**ie**ro ir a las montañas.
recomendar (ie) *to recommend*	Le recom**ie**ndo el Hotel Miramar.

Vocabulary: Querer means *to love* a person; it cannot be combined with infinitives to mean *love to do something*. When used with an infinitive, **querer** means *to want to do something*.

Stem change o → ue

costar (ue) *to cost*	Los boletos c**ue**stan 300 pesos.
dormir (ue) *to sleep*	D**ue**rmo mucho durante las vacaciones.
poder (ue) *to be able, can*	¿P**ue**des salir el jueves?
volver (ue) *to return*	Mis padres v**ue**lven de su viaje mañana.

Stem change e → i

pedir (i) *to ask for, request*	Los turistas p**i**den una recomendación.
seguir (i) *to follow, continue*	Mi amigos s**i**guen el plan del agente.
servir (i) *to serve*	En el tour s**i**rven comida típica.

Grammar: Point out that all the verbs in this category are **-ir** verbs.

The **yo** form of **seguir** also has a spelling change: **sigo.**

D. El verbo jugar. The verb **jugar** is the only verb with a **u →ue** stem change.

jugar (ue) *(to play [a sport or game])*

yo	j**ue**go	nosotros(as)	jugamos
tú	j**ue**gas	vosotros (as)	jugáis
Ud./él/ella	j**ue**ga	Uds./ellos/ellas	j**ue**gan

When using this verb in a sentence, place **a** + definite article before the name of the sport or game.

Juego al vóleibol en la playa.	*I play volleyball on the beach.*

Notice that **a** + **el** forms the contraction **al.**

Ponerlo a prueba

Teaching Tip: Assign the first activity for homework. Complete the other two in class.

2-14 Recuerdos de Guadalajara. Durante un viaje a México, Iván le escribe un mensaje por correo electrónico a su familia. Escribe los verbos entre paréntesis en el tiempo presente.

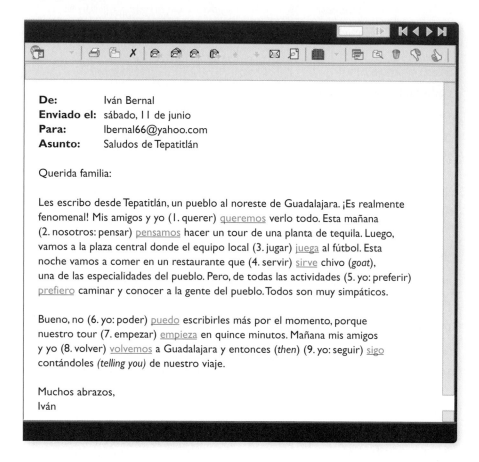

De: Iván Bernal
Enviado el: sábado, 11 de junio
Para: lbernal66@yahoo.com
Asunto: Saludos de Tepatitlán

Querida familia:

Les escribo desde Tepatitlán, un pueblo al noreste de Guadalajara. ¡Es realmente fenomenal! Mis amigos y yo (1. querer) queremos verlo todo. Esta mañana (2. nosotros: pensar) pensamos hacer un tour de una planta de tequila. Luego, vamos a la plaza central donde el equipo local (3. jugar) juega al fútbol. Esta noche vamos a comer en un restaurante que (4. servir) sirve chivo (*goat*), una de las especialidades del pueblo. Pero, de todas las actividades (5. yo: preferir) prefiero caminar y conocer a la gente del pueblo. Todos son muy simpáticos.

Bueno, no (6. yo: poder) puedo escribirles más por el momento, porque nuestro tour (7. empezar) empieza en quince minutos. Mañana mis amigos y yo (8. volver) volvemos a Guadalajara y entonces (*then*) (9. yo: seguir) sigo contándoles (*telling you*) de nuestro viaje.

Muchos abrazos,
Iván

2-15 Las vacaciones. Tú y un(a) compañero(a) de clase van a hablar de las vacaciones. Tomen turnos al hacer y contestar las preguntas.

1. Por lo general, ¿prefieres vacaciones tranquilas o activas? Normalmente, ¿duermes mucho durante las vacaciones? ¿Qué deportes juegas? ¿Qué más (*What else*) te gusta hacer durante las vacaciones?
2. ¿Qué país (*country*) quieres visitar en el futuro? ¿Qué atracciones quieres visitar allí (*there*)? ¿Cuesta mucho hacer un viaje a ese país?
3. Cuando viajas, ¿prefieres ir la playa (*beach*), a las montañas o a las ciudades grandes (*large cities*)? ¿Cuál es tu destino favorito? Por lo general, ¿pides la ayuda (*assistance*) de una agencia de viajes para planear tus viajes?
4. ¿Te gusta viajar por avión? ¿Qué haces durante los vuelos? ¿Duermes? ¿Escuchas música? ¿Qué línea aérea tiene el mejor servicio, en tu opinión? ¿Sirven comida buena?

Expansion: De viaje en México... Set up several ticket windows that display the method of travel (plane, train, bus), the destination, and the schedules, with one student operating each window. The rest of the class plays the roles of travelers buying tickets. While waiting their turn, the travelers should be encouraged to discuss their travel plans with one another.

2-16 Mi próximo viaje. Con dos o tres compañeros(as) de clase, hablen de sus planes para las vacaciones. Incluye muchos detalles:

- adónde vas y con quién(es)
- qué día sales y cuándo vuelves
- qué piensas hacer
- qué necesitas hacer antes de (*before*) salir

Teaching Tip 2-16: Focus the context of this activity on an upcoming break at your institution: **las vacaciones de otoño** (fall break), **las vacaciones de primavera** (spring break), or **las vacaciones en diciembre, marzo,** etc.

Puente cultural

 Go to the *Puentes* Premium Website to view the **Puente cultural** interviews.

¿Adónde van los jóvenes de vacaciones?

Jimena Escamilla

🌐 MÉXICO

En México es muy común visitar las playas, como Acapulco o Veracruz, en la época de verano *(summer)*. El invierno *(winter)* ofrece la oportunidad de pasar más tiempo con la familia.

Gabriella Paracat

🌐 ARGENTINA

Bariloche; es una región muy popular en el sur de Argentina, cerca a la cordillera de los Andes. Los jóvenes van allí en el invierno para esquiar. Si es verano, pueden hacer excursiones y practicar el alpinismo *(mountain climbing)*.

Mauricio Mbomio

🌐 GUINEA ECUATORIAL

Depende de cada uno. Muchos jóvenes viajan a sus pueblos para visitar a sus abuelos o padres. Otros se quedan en la ciudad estudiando o trabajando.

Standards: Although a full discussion in Spanish is not possible at this point, one major purpose of this section is to pique the students' interest on cultural comparisons. Encourage them to think and analyze what they read. Motivate them to find both similiarities and differences across a variety of cultures.

En comparación. Completa la tabla con la información necesaria.

	En México	En Argentina	En Guinea Ecuatorial	En los Estados Unidos
¿Adónde van los jóvenes de vacaciones?				

Paso 2

Proficiency: Getting a hotel room is a key function of the Intermediate-level speaker. Your students need to practice expressing their wishes and asking basic questions in order to deal with this situation.

In many countries, hotels are rated with one to five stars: **un hotel de tres estrellas.**

Vocabulario temático

En el hotel *(Hotel arrangements)*

Para conseguir una habitación *(Getting a room)*

RECEPCIONISTA:	**¿En qué puedo servirle?**
TURISTA:	**Quisiera** *una habitación.*
	hacer una reservación
RECEPCIONISTA:	**¿Para cuántas personas?**
TURISTA:	**Para** *dos.*
RECEPCIONISTA:	**¿Para cuándo?**
TURISTA:	**Para** *el ocho de abril.*
RECEPCIONISTA:	**¿Por cuántas noches?**
TURISTA:	**Por** *tres noches.*
RECEPCIONISTA:	**¿Qué clase de habitación quiere?**
TURISTA:	**Quiero una habitación** *con dos camas.*
	sencilla
	doble
RECEPCIONISTA:	**Su nombre y apellidos, por favor.**
TURISTA:	*Roberto Martín Moreno.*
RECEPCIONISTA:	**Aquí tiene la llave. Su habitación está en el** *tercer* **piso.**
TURISTA:	**Gracias.**

More Information: This section embeds examples of some new irregular verbs which are presented in more detail in **Gramática: saber, conocer, dar, hacer.**

Youth hostels and **pensiones** have more modest amenities. You may want to ask about a private bathroom: **¿Tiene baño privado?**

Preguntas típicas en un hotel *(Common questions in a hotel)*

TURISTA:	**¿Sabe Ud. dónde está** *el banco***?**
RECEPCIONISTA:	**Sí, hay uno** *en la esquina.*
TURISTA:	**¿Conoce Ud. un buen restaurante típico?**
RECEPCIONISTA:	**Sí, hay varios cerca del hotel.** *Casa Lolita* **es uno de los mejores.**
TURISTA:	**¿Dan descuentos para** *estudiantes***?**
RECEPCIONISTA:	*Sí, con la tarjeta de identidad.*
	No, lo siento, no damos descuentos.
TURISTA:	**¿A qué hora** *podemos ocupar* **el cuarto?**
	tenemos que desocupar
RECEPCIONISTA:	**A las** *dos de la tarde.*
TURISTA:	**¿En qué piso está** *la piscina***?**
	el gimnasio
RECEPCIONISTA:	**Está en** *la planta baja.*

Los pisos *(Floors of a building)*

el quinto piso

el cuarto piso

el tercer piso

el segundo piso

el primer piso

la planta baja

The ground floor of a building is often called **la planta baja;** the first floor above ground level is **el primer piso.** To express which floor a room is on, use the verb **estar.**

Estrategia *Memorization tips*

Practice new words with flash cards or lists.
Begin by learning the English equivalents of the Spanish words. Then reverse the procedure and give the Spanish word for the English one. Be sure to practice in both directions and with the words in different orders.

Write sentences with new words from the lesson.
Your memory will be sharper if you include factual information (**Hay tres bolígrafos en mi escritorio**) or invent sentences that are extremely silly (**Los bolígrafos de Bill Gates cuestan $1 000 000**).

Involve several of your physical senses.
As you look at a written word, pronounce it aloud to yourself and create a mental image of the object or action. With verbs (like *repeat* or *write*), pantomime the action as you say the word.

More Information: The **Estrategia** section occurs once per chapter and presents strategies to help students manage their learning and to become more fluent speakers of Spanish. This section should be assigned for homework and then practiced briefly in class whenever possible. With this strategy, you might ask students to generate together a list of techniques they have used for memorizing. For more information on memorization and other kinds of strategies, see Rebecca Oxford's book, *Language Learning Strategies.*

Ponerlo a prueba

CD1
Track 15

2-17 Una reservación. Escucha la conversación entre un turista y el recepcionista del hotel. Completa la información del formulario.

Hotel Carlton

Nombre y apellidos: _____ Víctor Fuentes López _____

Número de personas: _____ 2 _____

Tipo de habitación: ☐ sencilla   ☑ doble   ☐ 2 camas

Fecha / hora de llegada: _____ jueves, 4 de octubre/6:00 P.M. _____

Método de pago: _____ tarjeta de crédito / Visa _____

2-18 El Hotel Miramar. Relaciona *(Match)* las dos columnas de una manera lógica.

RECEPCIONISTA:

_h_ 1. Buenas tardes. ¿En qué puedo servirle?

_a_ 2. ¿Para cuántas personas?

_b_ 3. ¿Por cuántos días?

_g_ 4. ¿Prefiere una habitación con una cama King o con dos camas?

_i_ 5. ¿Está bien una habitación en el quinto piso?

_c_ 6. Su nombre completo, por favor.

_e_ 7. ¿Cómo quiere Ud. pagar?

_d_ 8. Aquí tiene su llave.

TURISTA:

a. Para dos, mi hermano y yo.

b. Solo una noche.

c. Javier Arias Lagos.

d. Gracias. Eh… ¿A qué hora tengo que desocupar el cuarto?

e. Con tarjeta de crédito. ¿Dan descuentos para estudiantes?

f. ¿Hay varios cerca del hotel?

g. Preferimos una habitación con dos camas.

h. Quisiera una habitación.

i. ¿No tiene una en el primer piso?

Teaching Tip 2-19: Adjust role-play instructions to the level of your class. For less proficient classes, have pairs of students write or dramatize two-line dialogues. (For example, the desk clerk asks one question and the tourist responds.) As students gain in confidence and proficiency, request that dialogue exchanges consist of 4 lines. With more proficient groups, have pairs of students use the drawings as a point of departure to create an entire conversation with 6 or more exchanges.

Teaching Tip 2-19: To review the vocabulary related to lodging and getting around the surrounding area, say a line and have the students guess who says it: the tourist or the desk clerk. For example, you say "**¿A qué hora podemos ocupar el cuarto?**" and your students respond "**el turista.**"

Teaching Tip 2-20: Students often find it more difficult to ask than to answer questions. Your students may benefit from writing the answers to 2-20. With more proficient classes, have pairs of students create short dialogues by asking the required question and then inventing the response of the desk clerk.

Expansion: Have students describe their favorite hotel or resort by completing sentences such as the following: **Mi hotel favorito es *el Grove Park Inn. Está en Asheville, Carolina del Norte.* Me gusta porque es *un hotel viejo y elegante.* También tiene *un restaurante fantástico y un campo de golf maravilloso.***

2-19 En la recepción. Varios turistas están en el Hotel Sierra en Cancún. Con un(a) compañero(a) de clase, dramaticen breves conversaciones para cada uno.

1.

2.

3.

2-20 Con el conserje. Después de completar el registro en tu hotel, necesitas hacerle varias preguntas al conserje. ¿Qué preguntas en cada caso?

1. Nosotros acabamos de llegar *(have just arrived)* a México. Estamos cansados y tenemos mucha hambre. ¿ _____?

2. Mis amigos llegan en unos minutos. Ellos son estudiantes y quieren hospedarse *(to stay)* cerca de aquí, pero no tienen mucho dinero. ¿ _____?

3. Necesito cambiar *(exchange)* mis cheques de viajero. ¿ _____?

4. Nuestro vuelo sale el sábado a las seis de la tarde. ¿ _____? ¿Podemos salir un poco más tarde?

5. Mis amigos y yo queremos hacer un poco de ejercicio *(exercise)*. ¿ _____?

Vocabulario temático

Los números de 100 a 10 000 000 *(Numbers from 100 to 10,000,000)*

—¿Cuánto cuesta *una habitación doble?*
        una excursión

—*Mil cien (1100) pesos.*

100	**cien**	900	**novecientos**	
101	**ciento uno**	1000	**mil**	
200	**doscientos**	5000	**cinco mil**	
300	**trescientos**	10 000	**diez mil**	
400	**cuatrocientos**	100 000	**cien mil**	
500	**quinientos**	750 000	**setecientos cincuenta mil**	
600	**seiscientos**	1 000 000	**un millón**	
700	**setecientos**	2 000 000	**dos millones**	
800	**ochocientos**	10 500 000	**diez millones quinientos mil**	

Note: The **Real Academia** recommends that the periods (or commas) separating every three digits of large numbers be replaced by spaces, to conform to international standards. Numbers composed of four digits are written without spaces. The decimal position may be indicated by a comma or a period: **98,6 grados** = 98.6 degrees.

Unlike their English equivalents, Spanish **mil** *(one thousand)* and **cien** *(one hundred)* do not use **un** *(one)* before the number: **mil turistas** = one thousand tourists; **cien pesos** = one hundred pesos.

Teaching Tip: Point out that the words for hundreds have masculine and feminine forms, depending on the noun they modify: **doscientos pesos** vs. **doscientas islas**. Also, after whole millions, the preposition **de** is added: **tres millones de turistas**.

Ponerlo a prueba

CD1
Track 16

2-21 Un viaje a México. La Sra. Pala quiere irse de vacaciones. Ahora está hablando con un agente de viajes. Escucha la conversación. Después escribe el precio *(price)* para los siguientes arreglos *(arrangements)*.

Teaching Tip: Assign the first two activities for homework. Choose from the others to complete in class.

Note: At the time of publication, 1 American dollar was being exchanged for about 15 Mexican pesos.

Note: Copper Canyon **(Barranca del Cobre)**, located in the western Sierra Madre mountain range, is a popular destination for ecotourism enthusiasts. Guided tours often include a scenic rail trip through the canyon and visits with local indigenous peoples. The colonial town of Taxco is known for its charming, winding streets and jewelry stores stocked with unique silver creations. Acapulco is a popular beach resort known as **la Perla del Pacífico**.

> **MODELO** *Escuchas la conversación.*
>
> SRA. PALA: Quiero hacer una reservación para un hotel en el Distrito Federal. ¿Qué hotel me recomienda?
>
> EL AGENTE: El hotel Presidente Intercontinental. Es un hotel de cuatro estrellas. Un cuarto doble cuesta dos mil doscientos pesos por noche.
>
> *Escribes:* Hotel Presidente Intercontinental: 2200 pesos

1. Hotel Camino Real	1650 pesos
2. boleto de ida a Cancún	2750 pesos
3. boleto de ida y vuelta a Cancún	5225 pesos
4. excursión a Acapulco y Taxco	8800 pesos
5. excursión a Barranca del Cobre	10 945 pesos

2-22 Fechas importantes. Aquí tienes algunas fechas (dates) importantes en la historia de México o "Nueva España". Primero, escoge el año apropiado para cada evento. Después, escribe el año en palabras.

MODELO Cristóbal Colón llega al Nuevo Mundo: 1000 / 1492 / 1593
1492 = mil cuatrocientos noventa y dos

1. Los aztecas fundan la ciudad de Tenochtitlan (sitio de la futura capital de México): 1325 / 1667 / 1831
2. Hernán Cortés y los españoles llegan a Centroamérica: 1020 / 1275 / 1519
3. Se consagra la Catedral Metropolitana, la primera catedral de "Nueva España": 1368 / 1667 / 1925
4. La revolución para la independencia empieza: 1492 / 1810 / 1969
5. Hay una guerra (war) con los Estados Unidos: 1600 / 1846 / 1945
6. La revolución social mexicana empieza con una rebelión contra la dictadura de Porfirio Díaz: 1910 / 1975 / 2000

2-23 Una excursión a Ixtapa. Estás en Guadalajara y quieres visitar Ixtapa. Lee el anuncio y contesta las preguntas en la página 75. (¡Ojo! *The prices are given in* **pesos mexicanos.**)

EXCURSIONES A IXTAPA

HOTEL	3 NOCHES	4 NOCHES	7 NOCHES
Posada Real	2740	2950	4320
Radisson	2990	3420	4590
Riviera Beach	3100	3500	4760

Incluye:
- HOSPEDAJE: EN HABITACIÓN DOBLE
- AVIÓN: VIAJE REDONDO DESDE GUADALA JARA
- TRASLADO: DEL AEROPUERTO — HOTEL — AEROPUERTO
- PROPINAS: MALETEROS Y CAMARISTAS
- DESAYUNO: BUFFET

NOTA: EN PLAN TODO INCLUIDO
- DESAYUNOS, COMIDAS Y CENAS TIPO BUFFET
- BEBIDAS NACIONALES SIN LÍMITE

Se aplican cargos por cancelación o cambios de fecha.
Horarios y días de vuelos sujetos a cambio sin previo aviso.
Vigencia: 7 de julio al 10 de agosto.

1. ¿Qué tipo de transporte está incluido en el precio *(price)* de la excursión?

2. ¿Qué comidas *(meals)* están incluidas en el plan "normal"?, ¿en el plan "todo incluido"?

3. ¿En qué meses son aplicables los precios?

4. De todos los hoteles, ¿cuál es es el más económico por tres noches? ¿Cuánto cuesta?

5. ¿Cuánto cuesta la excursión más cara *(expensive)* de todas? ¿Cuántas noches incluye? ¿Cómo se llama el hotel?

6. Si quieres pasar siete noches, ¿cuál de los hoteles prefieres? ¿Por qué? ¿Cuánto cuesta?

2-24 En el Hotel Fiesta Americana. La familia Ortiz piensa alquilar un cuarto en el Hotel Fiesta Americana, en la Ciudad de México. Con un(a) compañero(a), contesta las preguntas a continuación. Luego, dramatiza un diálogo entre el Sr. Ortiz y el recepcionista. (**¡Ojo!** *The prices are given in **pesos mexicanos.***)

PRIMERA PARTE

1. ¿En qué ciudad está la familia Ortiz?

2. ¿Cómo se llama el hotel?

3. ¿Cuánto cuesta una habitación sencilla en este hotel?, ¿una habitación doble?

4. ¿Cuál es el número de la habitación de la familia Ortiz? ¿En qué piso está?

5. ¿Cómo es su cuarto?

6. ¿Cuánto tienen que pagar los Ortiz por noche?

SEGUNDA PARTE

Con tu compañero(a), dramaticen un diálogo entre el Sr. Ortiz y el recepcionista. Incluye los precios *(prices)* en la conversación.

CD1
Track 17

Gramática

Algunos verbos irregulares

Listen and read along as Carolina describes her upcoming trip. Find examples of the following verbs: **conocer, hacer, saber, salir, ver.** What do you notice about the **yo** forms of these verbs?

ADRIANA: ¿Adónde vas de vacaciones, Carolina?

CAROLINA: Voy a Mérida. Conozco a muchas personas allí y siempre hacemos cosas divertidas.

ADRIANA: ¿Qué día sales?

CAROLINA: Salgo el domingo. ¡No veo la hora! *(I can't wait!)* Sé que va a ser un viaje fabuloso.

A. Verbos con la forma irregular *yo*. When some verbs are conjugated in the present tense, the **yo** form is irregular. In many cases the other verb forms are regular; in a few cases there may also be stem changes.

Group 1: *-go* verbs

Only the **yo** form is irregular. The other persons use the same endings as regular verbs.

Infinitive	Yo form	Other forms
hacer *(to do, make)*	**hago**	haces, hace, hacemos, hacéis, hacen
poner *(to put, place)*	**pongo**	pones, pone, ponemos, ponéis, ponen
salir *(to leave, go out)*	**salgo**	sales, sale, salimos, salís, salen
traer *(to bring)*	**traigo**	traes, trae, traemos, traéis, traen

Group 2: *-go* verbs with stem changes

	tener *(to have)*	**venir** *(to come)*	**decir** *(to say, tell)*
yo	**tengo**	**vengo**	**digo**
tú	**tie**nes	**vie**nes	**di**ces
Ud./él/ella	**tie**ne	**vie**ne	**di**ce
nosotros(as)	tenemos	venimos	decimos
vosotros(as)	tenéis	venís	decís
Uds./ellos/ellas	**tie**nen	**vie**nen	**di**cen

Group 3: Other verbs

Infinitive	Yo form	Other forms
conducir *(to drive)*	**conduzco**	conduces, conduce, conducimos, conducís, conducen
conocer *(to know, meet)*	**conozco**	conoces, conoce, conocemos, conocéis, conocen
dar *(to give)*	**doy**	das, da, damos, dais, dan
saber *(to know)*	**sé**	sabes, sabe, sabemos, sabéis, saben
ver *(to see, to watch)*	**veo**	ves, ve, vemos, veis, ven

B. El significado. Several verbs have special or alternate meanings. For example, the verbs **saber** and **conocer** both mean *to know* in Spanish, but they are not interchangeable.

▸ Use **conocer** to indicate that you know or are familiar with people or places. It is also used to express *to meet,* as in to be introduced to someone for the first time.

Mis padres **conocen** a tu agente de viajes.	*My parents **know** your travel agent.*
Yo no **conozco** Nueva York.	*I don't **know** / am not familiar with New York. (I haven't been there.)*

▸ Use **saber** to indicate that you know specific information. Or, use it with an infinitive to express what you know how to do.

Sabemos hacer los arreglos del viaje.	***We know** how to make the travel arrangements.*
No **sé** el número de teléfono del hotel.	***I don't know** the phone number of the hotel.*

Grammar: With the structure **saber + infinitive,** point out that Spanish does not use **como** to say *how* to do something.

▸ Often verbs are combined with other words to create idioms—set expressions that vary from the original meaning of the verb. Here are a few you might use when traveling.

dar *to give*
    dar un paseo   *to take a walk*

hacer *to do, to make*
    hacer la maleta   *to pack the suitcase*
    hacer un viaje   *to take a trip*

poner *to put, to place*
    poner la tele (la radio)   *to turn on the TV/radio*

ver *to see, to watch*
    no ver la hora   *to not be able to wait (for something); to be eager*

More Information: These very few examples are meant as an introduction to the notion of idioms or **modismos.** Others will be introduced as the context demands.

Ponerlo a prueba

Teaching Tip: Assign the first activity for homework. Complete the rest in class.

2-25 Querido diario. Estás en Cancún de vacaciones y decides escribir en tu diario. Completa la información con el presente de los verbos.

Querido diario:

Estoy en Cancún. ¡Eso me parece increíble! Mañana (1. yo: salir) ____salgo____ para Isla Mujeres. Mi amigo Jorge (2. venir) ____viene____ conmigo. Jorge (3. decir) ____dice____ que él (4. conocer) ____conoce____ muy bien la isla. Yo (5. saber) ____sé____ que vamos a divertirnos mucho. ¡No (6. yo: ver) ____veo____ la hora de salir!

Ahora (7. yo: tener) ____tengo____ que hacer todo los arreglos. Primero, (8. yo: hacer) ____hago____ todas las reservaciones por computadora. Después, (9. yo: poner) ____pongo____ pocas cosas necesarias en mi mochila porque siempre (10. yo: traer) ____traigo____ muchos regalos (gifts) de regreso. ¡Qué emocionante!

Answers 2-26: Suggested responses:
1. Hago / No hago; 2. Traigo / No traigo; 3. Pongo / No pongo; 4. Salgo / No salgo; 5. Conduzco / No conduzco

2-26 Mis preferencias. Expresa tus preferencias en los viajes. Describe lo que (what) haces y lo que no haces cuando viajas. Compara tus ideas con las de un(a) compañero(a) de clase.

> **MODELO** hacer las reservaciones con un agente de viajes
> Yo no hago las reservaciones con un agente de viajes.
> Hago mis propias (own) reservaciones. ¿Y tú?

1. hacer las reservaciones por Internet
2. traer dos maletas
3. poner los boletos de avión en una mochila
4. salir para el aeropuerto muy temprano
5. conducir al aeropuerto

2-27 Y, ¿cuándo llegas? Con un(a) compañero(a), comenta lo que hacen ustedes una vez que llegan (once you arrive) al lugar de vacaciones.

1. Para conocer bien el lugar, ¿sales con un guía (tour guide) o prefieres explorar el lugar solo(a) (alone)?
2. En el hotel, ¿le das propinas (tips) generosas al botones (the bellboy)?
3. Generalmente, ¿haces reservación en restaurantes elegantes?
4. Respecto al transporte, ¿conduces un carro, tomas un taxi o caminas?
5. Normalmente, ¿ves los lugares más famosos el primer día del viaje o esperas unos días?
6. Si (If) no conoces el lugar, ¿qué haces?

Un paso más

¡Vamos a hablar!

Estudiante A

Contexto: Imagine that you (**Estudiante A**) and a friend are traveling together in Mexico. You are now in Puerto Vallarta and want to participate in an eco-tour in the area. Each of you has an advertisement for a different tour. Exchange information about the tours, and then decide together which one the two of you will take.

You will begin by asking: **¿Adónde va el tour de Eco-Discovery?**

Eco-Discovery

▶ **Destino:** _____

▶ **Días disponibles** *(available):* ___ _____

▶ **Hora de salida:** _____

▶ **Duración:** _____

▶ **Precio:** _____

▶ **Teléfono (para las reservaciones):** _____

▶ **Aspectos interesantes:** _____

Aventuras Tiroleso

Tour de canopy

¡Observe la flora y la fauna de la selva tropical desde una perspectiva única! Con la asistencia de nuestros guías especializados, Ud. puede transportarse de un árbol a otro empleando poleas sobre cables horizontales.

¡Experimente la emoción hoy!

Tours:	Diario a las 8:30, 10:30 y 1:30.
Duración:	4 ½ horas
Precio:	$89 USD
Incluye:	Transporte, agua embotellada, tour por las copas de los árboles con 14 plataformas.

Nuestra reserva ecológica está a 45 minutos de Puerto Vallarta.

Para hacer reservaciones, llame al: 2-97-53-47.

Go to the **Un paso más** section in the *Cuaderno de actividades* for reading, writing, and listening activities that correlate with this chapter.

Teaching Tip: Divide the class into pairs; direct one person in each pair to be **Estudiante A** and the other **Estudiante B.** Explain that they must share information about the tours without looking at each other's pages. After completing the information, the two should discuss which tour they will take and explain why they have chosen it. Before setting students to work, review with the entire class the questions they might use to obtain information about the tours. **¿Adónde va el tour? ¿Qué días hay tours? ¿A qué hora sale el tour? ¿Cuánto cuesta?** etc.

Vocabulary: **árbol** *tree;* **poleas** *pulleys.*

Un paso más

¡Vamos a hablar!

Estudiante B

Contexto: Imagine that you (**Estudiante B**) and a friend are traveling together in Mexico. You are now in Puerto Vallarta and want to participate in an eco-tour in the area. Each of you has an advertisement for a different tour. Exchange information about the tours, and then decide together which one the two of you will take.

Your classmate will begin by asking: **¿Adónde va el tour de Eco-Discovery?** Look at your ad and provide the answer.

Eco-Discovery

Avistamiento de Ballenas y
Tour de las Islas Marietas

¡La aventura de su vida!

En esta expedición Ud. puede observar la belleza y armonía de estos mamíferos marinos en su hábitat natural. También puede explorar las playas e islas en la Bahía de Banderas.

Tours:	De lunes a sábado; los tours salen a las 9:00 a.m.
Duración:	7 horas
Precio:	$98 USD ($115 con almuerzo)
Incluye:	Transporte, guías y tour
Llame hoy al:	297–7915

Aventuras Tirolesa

▸ **Destino:** _____

▸ **Días disponibles** *(available):* _____

▸ **Hora de salida:** _____

▸ **Duración:** _____

▸ **Precio:** _____

▸ **Teléfono (para las reservaciones):** _____

▸ **Aspectos interesantes:** _____

¡Vamos a ver! | *Episodio 2*

En la Hacienda Vista Alegre

Anticipación

A. Hablando se entiende la gente. Habla con un(a) compañero(a).

¿Adónde te gusta ir de vacaciones? ¿Qué te gusta hacer durante las vacaciones? ¿Qué lugares prefieres visitar?

B. ¿Cómo se dice... ? Relaciona *(Match)* las oraciones de la primera columna con las expresiones de la segunda columna.

Teaching Tip: Preview the video by showing a fragment of the episode without sound and have students use visual clues to anticipate content. Stop and rewind the video until they understand the gist of the episode.

_c_ 1. ¿Qué hora es?

_e_ 2. Vamos a otro hotel. Este es muy caro.

_a_ 3. ¿Ya podemos salir de casa? ¿Necesitan más tiempo?

_d_ 4. ¿Vienes con nosotros?

_b_ 5. Este coche es muy caro y no es demasiado bueno.

a. Está bien. **Ya estamos listos.** *We are ready.*

b. **No vale la pena** comprarlo. *It's not worth buying it.*

c. **Son las once en punto.** *It's 11 o'clock (sharp).*

d. Sí, **vamos todos juntos.** *Let's go together.*

e. Sí, es verdad. **Estoy de acuerdo contigo.** *I agree with you.*

▶ Vamos a ver

C. De paseo por la Hacienda Vista Alegre. Mira el Episodio 2 del vídeo y completa las oraciones. ¿Qué van a hacer los amigos en San Juan?

1. Javier va a ___recorrer el centro de la ciudad___.
2. Alejandra quiere ___tomar muchas fotos___.
3. Sofía piensa ___visitar el mercado___.
4. Valeria va a ___ir de compras___.
5. Antonio va a ___visitar la playa___.

D. Después de ver el episodio. Contesta las siguientes preguntas sobre el episodio.

1. ¿Por qué los chicos están enojados con Valeria?
2. ¿Qué cosas se pueden hacer, ver o visitar en San Juan?
3. Describe cómo es la ciudad de San Juan.

En acción

E. Charlemos. Comenta con tus compañeros(as). ¿Qué es lo que te interesa a ti de San Juan? ¿Qué prefieres ver o hacer en la ciudad? ¿Hay muchas diferencias entre las ciudades de los países hispanohablantes y las ciudades de tu país?

F. 3, 2, 1 ¡Acción! Interpreten la siguiente situación en grupos de 3 ó 4 estudiantes.

Ustedes están en la Hacienda Vista Alegre y quieren pasar cinco días en San Juan (u otra ciudad). ¿Cómo van a viajar? ¿Qué actividades van a hacer durante estos días? ¿Dónde piensan alojarse *(to stay overnight)*?

Sample Answers D: 1. Porque lleva mucho tiempo en el baño y los chicos necesitan entrar. Todos tienen que estar preparados para salir a las 9 en punto. 2. ir de compras, visitar la playa y el mercado, visitar edificios históricos, pasear por sus calles 3. *Answers will vary.*

Practice the vocabulary and grammar you have learned in this chapter (**dar y preguntar la hora y la fecha, planificar viajes, reservar una habitación en un hotel y hacer planes**).

Teaching Tip: Have students practice summarizing, describing characters, sequencing events, making comparisons, and giving detailed narrations and descriptions based on what they see in the video.

Panorama cultural

DATOS ESENCIALES

Nombre oficial: Estados Unidos Mexicanos

Capital: México, D.F. (Distrito Federal)

Población: 107 900 000 habitantes

Unidad monetaria: peso mexicano (Mex $)

Economía: exportación de material para manufacturas, petróleo crudo y productos agrícolas; turismo

 www.cengage.com/spanish/ puentes

Transparency Bank A-7

Note: The official language of Mexico is Spanish; estimates on the number of indigenous languages range from 60 to 350.

More Information: It is not possible to do justice to the rich history and culture of Mexico in this summarized form. The objective of this section is to briefly introduce the country to students while offering a point of departure for further study.

Note: The oil industry is completely state-run and provides about one-third of government revenue. Mexico ranks sixth worldwide in oil sales, most of which go to the United States.

Note: Arqueologists do not know which indigenous people constructed Teotihuacan but trace its origins to about 250 B.C. The city declined rapidly in the 7th or 8th century. It is believed that the Toltecs gave the city its name, which means "City of Gods," long after its decline.

Note: According to Aztec legend, the god Quetzalcóatl had promised to return to his people. Cortés was treated by Moctezuma as the god they had been awaiting. They showered him with gifts and invited him into their rich city. By the time the Aztecs realized their mistake, Moctezuma had been taken prisoner and the fall of the empire was well under way. His nephew Cuauhtémoc took over and fought unsuccessfully. By August 1521, Tenochtitlan had been conquered by the Spaniards.

Teotihuacan

La Pirámide del Sol es parte de la zona arqueológica de Teotihuacan, uno de los lugares más visitados de México. Entre los años 150 y 450 d.C. Teotihuacan era el centro urbano más grande de Mesoamérica, con más de 100 000 habitantes. Otras edificaciones importantes en esta ciudad incluyen la Pirámide de la Luna, el Templo de los Jaguares y el Palacio de Quetzalcóatl.

Un vistazo a la historia

1325	Los aztecas fundan Tenochtitlan, la capital de su imperio, en el valle de México.
1519	Llega el español Hernán Cortés, quien inicia la ruina y destrucción del Imperio Azteca.
1821	México finalmente obtiene su independencia de España.
1846	En la guerra *(war)* con los EE.UU., México pierde *(loses)* los territorios que hoy son Texas, Nuevo México, Arizona, Nevada, Utah y California.

1910	Comienzan los levantamientos *(uprisings)* de la Revolución Mexicana.
1992	Se firma el Tratado de Libre Comercio de América del Norte (NAFTA) entre México, Canadá y EE.UU.
2000	La elección de Vicente Fox Quesada a la presidencia termina la era del control del Partido Revolucionario Institucional (PRI).
2009	Se detectan los primeros casos de la pandemia de gripe H1N1 o "gripe porcina".

Note: Vicente Fox, of the **Partido Acción Nacional (PAN),** was the first opposition candidate to win the presidency. Before this, the PRI had dominated politics for 70 years.

México

Emiliano Zapata (1879–1919)

Zapata es uno de los líderes militares más importantes de la Revolución Mexicana. Con el Plan de Ayala de 1911, proclama su visión: "Reforma, Libertad, Justicia y Ley". Lucha *(He fights)* por la reforma agraria durante unos 10 años. Es asesinado en 1919.

Note: Zapata was born in the southern Mexican state of Morelos, where he saw firsthand the hard life of peasants who worked the land but often did not own it. His influence continues today in the revolutionary movements of southern Mexico.

Frida Kahlo (1907–1954)

Esta importante pintora empieza su carrera artística después de un grave accidente. Durante su convalecencia, pinta su primer autorretrato *(self-portrait)*. Su estilo se caracteriza por colores vibrantes, con influencias indígenas y europeas. En 1929 contrae matrimonio con el famoso muralista, Diego Rivera.

Note: Kahlo suffered much physical pain, due to her accident and a bout of polio. She also suffered psychologically from her miscarriages and marital problems. Many of her 143 works, particularly her 45 self portraits, deal symbolically with this pain.

Teaching Tip: Direct students to see the mural by Rivera on p. 157.

Carlos Slim Helú (1940–)

Hijo de padres libaneses, Slim es la persona más rica de México y una de las más ricas del mundo. Es dueño *(owner)* de varios bancos y empresas en México. También es un importante inversionista *(stockholder)* en compañías extranjeras, como Apple Computer. Su fundación filantrópica Telmex apoya *(supports)* la educación y la salud.

Note: Slim is retired but still plays a large decision-making role in his businesses, which are now directed by his children. The Mexican press often refers to him as **"El rey Midas"** or the Warren Buffet of Latin America.

Additional activities on Mexico and the **Panorama cultural** may be found in the **Un paso más** section of the *Cuaderno de actividades*.

Mira el vídeo sobre la capital de México. Después, contesta las preguntas.

1. ¿Cuáles de estas palabras asocias con la arquitectura del Distrito Federal? Explica por qué.

   tradicional   moderna   colonial   antigua

   interesante   aburrida   colorida   monótona

2. Imagina que vas a pasar cuatro horas en la capital. ¿Cuáles de los sitios del vídeo te gustaría visitar?

Note: The capital city of Mexico, known as **el D.F.** or **Distrito Federal**, was built on the ruins of Tenochtitlan, the Aztec capital constructed in 1325 and destroyed in 1521. It is one of the most important economic hubs of Latin America and its population exceeds 19 million people in the greater metropolitan area. The **Zócalo**, also known as the **Plaza de la Constitución**, is the heart of the city and one of the largest public squares in the world.

Sustantivos

la agencia de viajes *travel agency*
el año *year*
el autobús *bus*
el avión *airplane*
el banco *bank*
el baño *bath(room)*
el boleto *ticket*
la cama *bed*
el carro *car*
el cheque de viajero *traveler's check*
el coche *car*
la cuenta *bill, check*
el descuento *discount*
el día *day*
la ducha *shower*
la excursión *trip, tour*
la fecha *date*
la habitación doble *double room*
la habitación sencilla *single room*
el hotel *hotel*
la llave *key*
la llegada *arrival*
la medianoche *midnight*
el mediodía *noon, midday*
el mes *month*
el museo *museum*
la piscina *swimming pool*
el piso *floor*
la reservación *reservation*
la salida *departure*
la semana *week*
la tarjeta de crédito *credit card*
la tarjeta de identidad *identification card*
el tren *train*
el viaje *trip*
el vuelo *airplane flight*

Verbos

abrir *to open*
alquilar *to rent*
cerrar (ie) *to close*
desocupar *to vacate*
hacer un viaje *to take a trip*
ir *to go*
ocupar *to be in (a room)*
pagar *to pay*
pensar (ie) *to plan, to think*
poder (ue) *to be able to, can*
preferir (ie) *to prefer*
querer (ie) *to want, to love*
regresar *to return, to go back*
salir *to leave, to go out*
viajar *to travel*
volver (ue) *to return, to go back*

Otras palabras y expresiones útiles

abierto *opened*
cerrado *closed*
de ida *one-way*
de ida y vuelta *round-trip*
de la mañana A.M., *6 A.M. to noon*
de la madrugada A.M., *early morning*
de la noche P.M., *sundown to midnight*
de la tarde P.M., *noon to sundown*
en efectivo *cash*
hoy *today*
mañana *tomorrow*
privado(a) *private*

Telling time: p. 56
Days of the week: p. 59
Months of the year: p. 59
Ordinal numbers: p. 71
Cardinal numbers: p. 73

For further review, please turn to **Vocabulario temático: español e inglés** at the back of the book.

Go to the *Puentes* website for extra vocabulary practice using the Flashcard program.

Entre familia

Teaching Tip: Use these situation cards for classroom practice or for short oral evaluations: 9, 10, 11, 13, 14, 16, 17, 18, 19, 20, 21, 33, 34, 35, 36, 37, 38, 39, 41, 65, 71, 72

Proficiency: The topics of this chapter are key ones for the development of Intermediate level proficiency. Since some students prefer not to talk extensively about their families, be prepared to refocus activities onto friends or famous families.

Turn to the *Cuaderno de actividades* for this chapter's reading practice and strategy: Skimming for the main idea.

Turn to the *Cuaderno de actividades* for this chapter's composition practice and writing strategy: Creating paragraphs.

OBJETIVOS

Speaking and Listening
▶ Talking about your family, close friends, and pets
▶ Describing people and homes
▶ Making comparisons
▶ Discussing daily routines and activities at home and on campus

Culture
▶ Venezuela
▶ Family life in Spanish-speaking countries

Grammar
▶ Descriptive adjectives
▶ Comparatives and superlatives
▶ Adverbs of location
▶ Uses of **ser, estar**
▶ Reflexive verbs

Video
▶ En la Hacienda Vista Alegre: Episodio 3
▶ Imágenes de Venezuela

Gramática suplementaria
▶ El participio pasado

Cuaderno de actividades
Reading
▶ Strategy: Skimming for the main idea

Writing
▶ Strategy: Creating paragraphs

Playlist
🌐 www.cengage.com/spanish/puentes

A primera vista

Los Duques de Osuna con sus hijos

Padres, hermanos, abuelos y tíos: todos forman parte de la familia. En la época de la cámara digital, es común tener centenares (hundreds) de fotos de estos seres queridos (loved ones). Piensa en (Think about) una foto reciente de tu familia. ¿Cómo se compara con este cuadro de Goya?

Con un(a) compañero(a), estudia el cuadro de Goya y completa las oraciones de una manera lógica.

1. Las figuras en este cuadro representan a (una familia / unos amigos).
2. Estas personas probablemente son de la clase (alta / media / baja).
3. La ropa (clothing) de las personas es (simple / elegante / informal).
4. Las caras (faces) de las personas se ven (look) (oscuras / brillantes).
5. Este cuadro es (una escena folclórica / un retrato).

HABLANDO DEL ARTE

At the time this painting (**el cuadro**) was produced, it was common to paint portraits—**retratos**—of important people, such as the nobility or political leaders. The powerful status of such people was often indicated visually with fine attire, an ornate setting or a commanding pose. Artists sometimes created bright areas of light to focus the viewer's eyes on the faces of the figures.

FRANCISCO DE GOYA Y LUCIENTES (1746–1828)

Nacionalidad: español

Otras obras: *La maja vestida y la maja desnuda, Los caprichos, El tres de mayo, Saturno devorando a su hijo, El parasol*

Estilo: Versátil y apasionado, con una gran sensibilidad sicológica. Pasó por varias etapas (*stages*): entre ellas, el período de escenas folclóricas de la vida diaria y paisajes españoles, la de los retratos de la familia real y su "etapa negra" de imágenes monstruosamente distorsionadas.

Los Duques de Osuna con sus hijos (1789) **Francisco de Goya y Lucientes**

In this *Paso* you will practice:

▶ Talking about your family, close friends, and pets
▶ Describing people
▶ Making comparisons

Grammar:

▶ Descriptive adjectives
▶ Comparatives and superlatives

Teaching Tip: Plan on spending about 1½ class hours per **Paso** and 1 class hour for **Un paso más.** For fewer contact hours, choose from **Un paso más** as time allows.

Teaching Tip: Students often feel overwhelmed by the amount of memory work involved in learning a language. In this chapter, students must master a large number of words in order to describe persons and homes. Be sure to make your expectations clear to students, and create quizzes and tests that reflect the emphasis that you have placed on the material in class.

🌐 Go to the **Puentes** website for extra vocabulary practice using the Flashcard program.

The English equivalents of the **Vocabulario temático** sections are found at the back of the book.

Transparency Bank E-1, E-2, E-3

More Information: The fictional Martínez family is used in several activities in this chapter. To help remember the family names, note that the first letter of each name corresponds to the first 5 letters of the alphabet: Arturo, Beatriz, Carlos, Dulce, Elisa, Felicia. The family's American guest is Gregorio (Greg).

Teaching Tip: Divide the presentation of this material into two parts: family and pets. For family vocabulary, refer to the Martínez family tree, a transparency, or your own family tree. Refer to the visual aid and give an overview of the family, based on the model sentences in the **Vocabulario.** Then, go on to identify each person: **Este es mi tío. Se llama David. Es el hermano de mi padre. Su esposa se llama Margaret. Tienen dos hijos.** etc.

Expansion: For extra practice, have students create a simple family tree labeled with just one name—their own. Students then exchange papers and describe their families to each other. While listening, each student should label the names of his classmate's family tree. To model this, draw or project your own family tree. Have students fill in the names as you describe your family. If you wish, turn this into a more fanciful task, with students using names of celebrities as their family members, and partners asking questions about the famous relatives.

Paso 1

Estrategia *Managing your learning*

Learning another language requires much memorization and recall. Here are some ways to make these tasks more manageable.

▶ Practice actively. Writing sentences and responding aloud to questions will improve your recall much more than reading or reviewing notes.

▶ Review systematically. Set aside special times to review "old" vocabulary and grammar points.

▶ Practice regularly. Short, regular practices are more effective than a single, long study session.

Vocabulario temático

Mi familia *(Talking about your family)*

—¿Cómo es tu familia, *Carlos*?

—Tengo una familia *de tamaño mediano.*
                  grande
                  pequeña

  Somos *seis: mis padres, mis hermanas, mi tía Felicia y yo.*

—¿Cómo son *tus hermanas*?

—*Elisa,* la menor, es una chica *cariñosa.*

  Dulce, la de en medio, es *extrovertida e inteligente.*

—Háblame más de *tu familia.*

—*Tía Felicia* es la hermana *mayor* de mi padre. Es *soltera* y vive con nosotros.

  Mis abuelos *paternos* viven en *Maracaibo.* Nos reunimos con ellos con frecuencia. Pero mis abuelos *maternos* se murieron hace años.

Vocabulary: Provide these additional terms to your more proficient classes or as requested by learners: **tío(a) abuelo(a)** great uncle/aunt; **bisabuelo(a)** great grandfather/grandmother; **bisnieto(a)** great grandson/granddaughter; **suegro(a)** father-in-law/mother-in-law; **cuñado(a)** brother-in-law/sister-in-law; **yerno** son-in-law; **nuera** daughter-in-law.

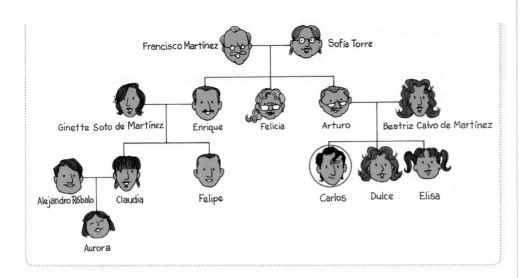

Otros parientes *(Other relatives)*

el abuelo/la abuela	el padrino/la madrina
el nieto/la nieta	el padrastro/la madrastra
el tío/la tía	el medio hermano/la media hermana
el primo/la prima	el hermanastro/la hermanastra
el sobrino/la sobrina	el hijastro/la hijastra

Other terms for step-relationships are common in everyday conversation: **la esposa de mi padre** or **mi madre/ mamá** instead of **madrastra**.

Note: Godparents play an important role in the family life of many Catholic families in Spain and Latin America. The child's mother and godmother are considered to be related as **comadres**; the child's father and godfather, as **compadres**.

Teaching Tip: To present this vocabulary, first tell your class about your own pets. Then, take a poll with a show of hands on who has the different kinds of pets mentioned. Follow up with questions to individual students about their pets: **¿Cómo se llama tu perro? ¿Es grande o pequeño? ¿Vive en casa contigo o fuera en el jardín?**

Vocabulary: Since it is a loan word from English, the **h** in **hámster** is generally pronounced as though it were spelled with the Spanish **jota**. Other common pets: **conejo** (rabbit), **tortuga** (turtle), **serpiente** (snake), **conejillo de Indias/cobayo** (guinea pig). Common names for dogs are **Lobo, Colita, Bobbi, Mancha,** and **Sultán;** for cats, **Tigre, Máximo, Sam, Princesa,** and **Minino.**

Los animales domésticos *(Talking about pets)*

—¿Tienen Uds. animales domésticos?

—No, no tenemos ninguno.

    Sí, tenemos *varios animales domésticos.*

Ponerlo a prueba

3-1 La familia Martínez. Dulce y su mejor amiga miran el álbum de fotos de la familia Martínez. Escucha su conversación. Identifica el parentesco (*relationship/kinship*) de cada persona y contesta las preguntas.

CD1 Track 18

MODELO

Escuchas: LA AMIGA: Esa señora es muy guapa. ¿Quién es?

DULCE: Es nuestra tía Ginette. Es la esposa del hermano de mi padre.

LA AMIGA: Ah. ¿Viven tus tíos aquí en Maracaibo?

DULCE: Ahora, no. Viven en Isla Margarita. ¿No ves qué playa más bonita?

Escribes: Ginette es _la tía_ de Dulce.

Vive en: a. Maracaibo (b.) Isla Margarita c. Maiquetía

1. Enrique es _____ el tío _____ de Dulce.

   Trabaja en: a. un banco b. un hospital (c.) un hotel

2. Claudia y Felipe son _____ los primos _____ de Dulce.

   Felipe es: (a.) estudiante b. profesor c. administrador en una universidad

3. Aurora es _____ la hija _____ de Claudia.

   Aurora tiene: (a.) un gato b. un perro c. un pájaro

4. Francisco es _____ el abuelo _____ de Dulce.

   En la foto, Francisco está con: a. su esposa (b.) su esposa y su hija c. su hija

5. Los otros señores son _____ los padrinos _____ de Felicia.

   Eran (*They were*): (a.) unos amigos b. unos hermanos c. los abuelos maternos

3-2 La familia de Elisa. Elisa está describiendo a su familia para una presentación en su escuela. Completa la descripción con las palabras más lógicas. Consulta el árbol genealógico de la familia Martínez en la página 89.

Yo soy Elisa Martínez Calvo. En mi familia somos seis. Mi **(1)** _____ padre, papá _____ se llama Arturo y mi **(2)** _____ madre, mamá _____ se llama Beatriz. Creo que son los mejores padres del mundo. Tengo dos **(3)** _____ hermanos _____ mayores —Carlos y Dulce— y los quiero mucho (*I love them a lot*). Mi **(4)** _____ tía _____ Felicia es soltera y también vive con nosotros. Aparte de (*Besides*) Felicia, tengo un **(5)** _____ tío _____, Enrique, que vive con su familia en Isla Margarita. Mis dos **(6)** _____ primos _____ se llaman Claudia y Felipe. Mis **(7)** _____ abuelos _____ Francisco y Sofía viven aquí en Maracaibo, cerca de nosotros. Me gusta pasar tiempo con ellos. ¡Claro (*Of course*) que yo soy su **(8)** _____ nieta _____ favorita!

3-3 Mi familia. Trabaja con un(a) compañero(a). Entrevístense con estas preguntas sobre la familia, los amigos y los animales domésticos. (Si prefieres, puedes inventar la información.)

1. ¿Es grande o pequeña tu familia? ¿Cuántos son Uds.? ¿Tienes hermanos mayores o menores? *(Ask your classmate 1–2 additional questions on this topic.)*

2. ¿Viven tus abuelos? ¿Cómo se llaman y dónde viven? ¿Trabajan o están jubilados *(retired)*? ¿Pasas mucho tiempo con tus abuelos? ¿Qué hacen Uds. juntos *(together)*? *(Ask your classmate 1–2 additional questions on this topic.)*

3. ¿Tienes muchos tíos y primos? ¿Tienes más parientes por parte de tu papá o de tu mamá? ¿Con qué frecuencia tienen Uds. reuniones familiares? *(Ask 1–2 additional questions on this topic.)*

4. ¿Qué animales domésticos tienes? ¿Cómo se llaman? ¿Qué animales domésticos te gustan más? Explica por qué son tus favoritos. *(Ask 1–2 additional questions on this topic.)*

5. ¿Tienes un(a) amigo(a) que es como familia *(like family)*? ¿Cómo se llama? ¿Cuántos años tiene? ¿Dónde estudia o trabaja? *(Ask 1–2 additional questions on this topic.)*

3-4 Una familia deportista. Aquí tienes un pequeño artículo sobre una familia extraordinaria. Lee la información y contesta las preguntas con un(a) compañero(a) de clase.

Una familia deportista

Cuatro generaciones de dedicación al wellness, o bienestar total

El año pasado, toda la familia se reunió en la costa para el 90 cumpleaños de Joaquín Ruiz-Giménez. "El abuelo" nadó un kilómetro en el mar para celebrar la ocasión. Y sus 32 nietos siguieron el ejemplo.

Don Joaquín y su esposa Mercedes son los patriarcas de la familia más deportista de España. Él es aficionado al tenis y a la natación; ella—a los 84 años— practica Pilates y monta en bicicleta. Sus 11 hijos, desde pequeños, practican el ciclismo y el submarinismo. Su quinta hija, Guadalupe, es directora de un gimnasio en Marbella.

Parece que el amor al deporte va a pasar a la cuarta generación. Rafa, el bisnieto de Joaquín y Mercedes, ya toma clases en el gimnasio de Guadalupe. Su pregunta más frecuente: "Abuelita, ¿vamos a hacer Pilates?".

1. ¿Cómo es la familia de Joaquín Ruiz: grande, pequeña o de tamaño mediano?

2. ¿Es una familia activa o sedentaria? Explica.

3. ¿Cómo es tu familia, en comparación con los Ruiz? ¿Qué deportes practican los miembros de tu familia?

Vocabulario temático

Las descripciones personales *(Describing people)*

¿Cómo es *Dulce*?

Dulce se parece mucho a su mamá.

No es ni *alta* ni *baja*; es *de estatura mediana.*

Tiene el pelo *castaño* y los ojos *verdes.*

¿Y *Carlos*? ¿Cómo es?

Carlos es bastante *atlético.*

Es menos *trabajador* que *su hermana Dulce.*

Es muy *sociable* y *simpático.*

Beatriz Dulce Arturo Carlos   Felicia Elisa

Rasgos físicos *(Describing physical characteristics)*

Es *alto/bajo.*
   de estatura mediana
   delgado/gordo
   joven/viejo; mayor
   guapo/feo
   calvo

Tiene *barba.*
   bigote
   pecas

Tiene el pelo *negro* y los ojos *azules.*
   rubio   *verdes*
   castaño   *color miel*
   rojo   *castaños*
   canoso

Lleva *gafas/anteojos.*

La personalidad y el carácter *(Describing personality and character traits)*

Es *simpático/antipático.*
   tímido/sociable
   amable/cruel
   educado/maleducado
   cariñoso/frío
   honesto/mentiroso

También, es muy *comprensivo/indiferente.*
   serio/divertido
   bueno/malo
   perezoso/trabajador
   optimista/pesimista
   responsable/irresponsable

Me parezco a... = I look like . . .

To describe persons with an olive skin tone and dark hair, you might say: **Es moreno(a).**

Transparency Bank J-1, J-3, J-4

Teaching Tip: First, read aloud the model sentences and relate them to the drawings. Then, working with the class, form descriptions of the other family members in the drawing. The teacher starts the sentence and the class completes it. For example: (Gesturing) **Arturo es bastante... alto. También es más o menos... delgado. Tiene el pelo... canoso y lleva... anteojos.**

Regional Vocabulary: Common lexical variants include **atractivo(a), bello(a), hermoso(a), bonito(a)** to indicate good looks and **espejuelos** or **lentes** for eyeglasses. In some countries, **Es moreno(a)** refers to persons of black African descent; **color café** may be used instead of **castaño** for hair color.

Vocabulary: For hair, introduce **el pelo rizado/liso** (curly/straight hair) and **el pelo largo/corto** (long/short). Show alternative phrasings: **Tiene el pelo rubio. = Es rubio(a).**

More Information: Adjectives are presented as opposites to assist in memorization. Students will need review of adjective agreement, so provide models: **El gato Garfield es gordo. Jon es delgado. La amiga de Jon es delgada**. With hair color, point out that the color agrees with the word **pelo** and is masculine, even when referring to a woman: **Mi mamá tiene el pelo negro.**

Grammar: Point out that multiple adjectives may be used after the verb. **Es alto y delgado. Tiene el pelo largo y rubio.** Show that **y** changes to **e** before a word beginning with **hi-** or **i-**: **Es guapo e inteligente.**

Teaching Tip: Practice words for physical traits with transparencies, magazine photographs or family snapshots. To introduce personality traits, refer to celebrities from sports, film, television, politics: **El gato Garfield es perezoso; Miss Piggy es extrovertida**; etc.

Los adjetivos

A. La concordancia. Adjectives (like **alto** or **inteligente**) are words that describe, or modify, nouns. In Spanish, adjectives "agree" with the nouns they modify. This means the adjective ending must match the noun in *number* (singular or plural) and *gender* (masculine or feminine).

Heinle Grammar Tutorial: Adjectives

Juan es **alto**; su hermana Rosa es **alta** también.

*Juan is **tall**; his sister Rosa is **tall**, too.*

ADJECTIVE	MASCULINE		FEMININE	
ends in:	*Singular*	*Plural*	*Singular*	*Plural*
-o	alt**o**	alt**os**	alt**a**	alt**as**
-e	amabl**e**	amabl**es**	amabl**e**	amabl**es**
consonant	informa**l**	informa**les**	informa**l**	informa**les**
-dor	trabaja**dor**	trabaja**dores**	trabaja**dora**	trabaja**doras**
-ista	optim**ista**	optim**istas**	optim**ista**	optim**istas**

B. La ubicación. In Spanish, most descriptive adjectives are placed directly after nouns. This is the opposite of what happens in English.

Tiene el <u>pelo</u> **negro** y los <u>ojos</u> **grandes y azules**.

*She has **black** <u>hair</u> and **big, blue** <u>eyes</u>.*

C. Algunos adjetivos especiales. A few descriptive adjectives, such as **bueno** and **malo**, may be placed either before or after a noun. Both of these drop the **-o** ending before a masculine singular noun. The feminine forms and the plural forms of **bueno** and **malo** do not drop any letters.

un **buen** hombre	*a **good** man*
un **mal** ejemplo	*a **bad** example*
unos **buenos** amigos	*some **good** friends*

The adjective **grande** has different meanings depending on its placement. Also, it is shortened to **gran** before a singular noun of either gender.

una **gran** universidad	*a **great** university*
una universidad **grande**	*a **large** university*

Grammar: Point out that **bueno** and **malo** are placed after the noun when accompanied by **muy: Es una persona muy buena.**

CD1
Track 19

3-5 ¿Quién es? Daniela no conoce a muchas personas en la fiesta. Su amigo Ignacio le dice *(tells her)* los nombres de los otros invitados. Escucha su conversación. Identifica a cada persona que describen. Escribe la letra correspondiente al nombre de cada persona.

1. Antonio ___a___   3. Alejandro ___c___

2. Carolina ___d___   4. Rosaura ___f___

a.   b.   c.   d.   e.   f.

3-6 ¿Cómo es la tía Felicia? Mira el dibujo *(drawing)* de la familia Martínez en la página 92. Completa la descripción de Felicia con las palabras más lógicas y apropiadas.

1. Felicia es la hermana de Arturo y se parece (<u>mucho</u> / un poco / poco) a él.

2. Felicia es (alta / de estatura mediana / <u>baja</u>).

3. Según ella *(According to her)*, es un poco (delgada / <u>gorda</u>) y quiere adelgazar *(lose weight)*.

4. Tiene el pelo (<u>largo</u> / corto) y (negro / <u>canoso</u> / rubio).

5. Tiene los ojos (<u>negros</u> / negras) y lleva (<u>anteojos</u> / lentes de contacto).

6. Felicia es bastante (comprensivo / <u>comprensiva</u>) y (generoso / <u>generosa</u>).

7. También es (trabajador / <u>trabajadora</u>) y (cariñoso / <u>cariñosa</u>).

8. Los sobrinos de Felicia la admiran mucho porque es una persona (bueno / <u>buena</u>) y (honesto / <u>honesta</u>).

3-7 Mis ideales. ¿Cómo son las personas ideales? Comparte *(Share)* tus ideas con las de un(a) compañero(a) de clase.

> **MODELO** el profesor ideal
>
> Tú: Para mí *(In my opinion)*, el profesor ideal es organizado, simpático y divertido.
>
> Tu compañero(a): Estoy de acuerdo *(I agree)*. También es inteligente y creativo en clase.

1. el amigo ideal

2. el compañero de cuarto ideal/ la compañera de cuarto ideal

3. los padres ideales

4. el novio ideal/la novia ideal

3-8 Admirable. ¿A cuál de tus parientes admiras mucho? Describe a esta persona con muchos detalles. Explica por qué lo/la admiras. Comparte *(Share)* tus ideas con un(a) compañero(a) de clase. Tu compañero(a) va a hacerte unas preguntas *(ask you some questions)* sobre esta persona, también.

> **MODELO**
>
> Tú: Admiro mucho a mi prima Rachel. Ella es muy inteligente y trabajadora. Estudia medicina y está en el segundo año de su carrera. También, Rachel es muy generosa y cariñosa. Es voluntaria en un hospital para niños.
>
> Tu compañero(a): ¿Cuántos años tiene Rachel? ¿Dónde vive? ¿Visitas a Rachel con frecuencia?

3-9 ¿Quién es? Completa las dos actividades para participar en un juego con tus compañeros.

Primera parte: Escribe una descripción de ti mismo(a). Incluye rasgos físicos y personalidad. No menciones tu nombre.

> **MODELO** *(Susana writes:)*
>
> Soy alta y más o menos *(more or less)* delgada. Tengo el pelo corto y rubio y los ojos verdes. Tengo muchas pecas. Soy extrovertida y un poco perezosa. No soy muy atlética. Me gusta mucho leer e ir a partidos de fútbol americano.

Segunda parte: Tu profesor(a) va a recoger *(collect)* las descripciones y repartírselas *(pass them out)* a diferentes personas. Cada persona tiene que leer la descripción; los compañeros de clase tienen que escuchar e identificar quién es.

Heinle Grammar Tutorial: Comparisons of equality and inequality; Superlatives and irregular comparative and superlative forms

Teaching Tip: Focus especially on making comparisons with adjectives if your time is limited.

CD1
Track 20

Gramática

Los comparativos y los superlativos

Look at the drawings as you listen to and read the descriptions of the three dogs. Identify the expressions that mean *more . . . than, less . . . than,* and *as . . . as.*

Tengo tres perros: Sultán, Preciosa y Lobo. Sultán es el más grande de los tres y es más feroz que Preciosa.

Preciosa es una perra muy tranquila y es menos agresiva que Lobo.

Lobo es el más pequeño de los tres, pero es tan protector como Sultán.

A. Las comparaciones de superioridad e inferioridad. When comparing two people or things, sometimes one has "more" or "less" of a particular quality (or thing) than the other.

▸ To express "more than," use **más + (adjective/adverb/noun) + que.**

adjective (**grande**) Sultán es **más grande que** Preciosa.
  *Sultán is **bigger than** Preciosa.*

adverb (**rápidamente**) Sultán come **más rápidamente que** Preciosa.
  *Sultán eats **more quickly/faster than** Preciosa (does).*

noun (**energía**) Lobo tiene **más energía que** Sultán.
  *Lobo has **more energy than** Sultán does.*

▸ To express "less/fewer than," use **menos + (adjective/adverb/noun) + que.**

adjective (**feroz**) Preciosa es **menos feroz que** Sultán.
  *Preciosa is **not as ferocious as** Sultán.*
    (i.e., "less ferocious")

adverb (**tranquilamente**) Lobo duerme **menos tranquilamente que** Preciosa.
  *Lobo sleeps **less peacefully than** Preciosa.*

noun (**comida**) Preciosa tiene **menos comida que** Sultán.
  *Preciosa has **less food than** Sultan.*

noun (**juguetes**) Lobo tiene **menos juguetes que** Preciosa.
  *Lobo has **fewer toys than** Preciosa does.*

► A few comparative expressions have irregular forms.

younger	**menor**	Elisa es **menor que** Dulce.	*Elisa is **younger than** Dulce.*
older	**mayor**	Carlos es **mayor que** Dulce.	*Carlos is **older than** Dulce.*
better	**mejor**	Gregorio habla inglés **mejor que** Carlos.	*Gregorio speaks English **better than** Carlos does.*
worse	**peor**	Yo canto **peor que** mis hermanos.	*I sing **worse than** my brothers do.*

B. Las comparaciones de igualdad. In another kind of comparison, two people or things have nearly the same amount of a particular quality or thing.

► With an adjective or an adverb: use **tan + (adjective/adverb) + como.**

adjective (**malo**)	Lobo es **tan malo como** Sultán.
	*Lobo is **as bad as** Sultán.*
adverb (**bien**)	Elisa juega al tenis casi **tan bien como** su hermano.
	*Elisa plays tennis almost **as well as** her brother.*

► With a noun: use **tanto/tanta/tantos/tantas + (noun) + como.**

noun: feminine, singular	Lobo tiene **tanta comida como** Preciosa.
	*Lobo has **as much food as** Preciosa.*
noun: masculine, plural	Carlos tiene **tantos hermanos como** Gregorio.
	*Carlos has **as many siblings as** Gregorio.*

► For the idea "as much as" when referring to an action/verb: use **tanto como.**

verb (**come**)	Lobo **come tanto como** Preciosa.
	*Lobo **eats as much as** Preciosa.*

C. Los superlativos. Superlatives refer to the "extremes" within a group: A person or thing may have the "most" of a quality *(the most intelligent student, the smallest, etc.)* or the "least" *(the least difficult professor, the least interesting, etc.).* In these cases, it is necessary to use the definite article (**el, la, los, las**).

► **el/la/los/las (optional noun) + más (adjective) + de (group)**
  Felicia es **la más generosa de** su familia.
  *Felicia is **the most generous one** in the family.*

► **el/la/los/las (optional noun) + menos (adjective) + de (group)**
  Carlos y Elisa son **los menos estudiosos de** la familia.
  *Carlos and Elisa are **the least studious ones** in the family.*

► The irregular forms **mejor, peor, mayor,** and **menor** are also used with definite articles to form the superlative.
  Carlos y Gregorio son **los mejores jugadores de** su equipo.
  *Carlos and Gregorio are **the best players** on their team.*

Ponerlo a prueba

3-10 Dos amigas. Katia y Agnés son amigas en la universidad. Lee las descripciones de las dos jóvenes, y completa las comparaciones con las palabras más lógicas. Sigue el modelo.

> **MODELO**   A Katia le gusta ir a fiestas y salir con muchos amigos. Agnés prefiere las reuniones pequeñas y las actividades solitarias. Katia es _más_ sociable _que_ Agnés.

1. Cuando tiene un examen, normalmente Katia estudia treinta minutos o una hora. Agnés estudia dos o tres horas para un examen típico. Katia es ___menos___ estudiosa ___que___ Agnés.

2. A Katia le gusta ir al gimnasio todos los días. A Agnés no le gustan los deportes y no hace ejercicio. Katia es ___más___ atlética ___que___ Agnés.

3. Las dos chicas necesitan trabajar para pagar los gastos *(expenses)* de la universidad. Katia trabaja veinte horas por semana en un supermercado. Agnés también trabaja veinte horas por semana en un restaurante. Katia es ___tan___ trabajadora ___como___ Agnés.

4. Katia tiene dieciocho años y Agnés tiene diecinueve. Katia es ___menor___ ___que___ Agnés.

5. Katia vive con sus padres y sus tres hermanos. Agnés vive con sus padres, su abuela y sus tres hermanos. Katia tiene ___tantos___ hermanos ___como___ Agnés.

6. Katia tiene un perro, un hámster y un pájaro. Agnés tiene dos gatos. Katia tiene ___más___ animales domésticos ___que___ Agnés.

3-11 Mi amigo(a) y yo. ¿Quién es tu mejor amigo(a)? ¿Son Uds. muy parecidos *(similar)* o muy diferentes? Escribe varias oraciones de comparación entre tú y tu mejor amigo(a). Comparen su aspecto físico y su personalidad.

> **MODELO**   Mi mejor amigo es Allen Martini.
>
> Yo soy más alto(a) que Allen. Los dos *(Both of us)* somos bastante delgados. Allen tiene el pelo negro y yo tengo el pelo rubio.
>
> Los dos somos sociables, pero Allen es un poco más extrovertido que yo. Creo que *(I think that)* yo soy más estudioso(a) que él.

VOCABULARIO ÚTIL: alto(a), delgado(a), atlético(a), responsable, sociable, trabajador(a), optimista, estudioso(a), serio(a)

Teaching Tip: Assign the first two activities for homework. Select from the remaining for in-class practice.

Expansion: For extra practice, have students look at the drawing of the Martinez family on p. 92. As you read aloud the statements, students respond with **cierto** or **falso: 1. Carlos es más calvo que su padre. 2. Beatriz es menos delgada que Dulce. 3. Elisa y Dulce son tan altas como su mamá. 4. Dulce tiene más sed que Carlos. 5. Elisa come tanto como su hermano. 6. La tía Felicia es la mayor de todos. 7. Arturo es el más alto de todos.** Have students continue making true-false statements about this drawing or another that you project.

Expansion 3-11: With more proficient classes, provide a model and have students extend the comparison to activities: **Allen y yo estudiamos mucho pero él estudia menos que yo. Los dos trabajamos, pero Allen trabaja más horas por semana** *(per week)* **que yo.**

3-12 Los animales. ¿Te gustan los animales domésticos? Habla de este tema con un(a) compañero(a) de clase. Usen las preguntas a continuación y crean *(create)* otras preguntas originales también.

1. ¿Tienes un animal doméstico? ¿Cuál? ¿Cómo se llama? ¿Cómo es?

2. ¿Te gustan más los perros o los gatos? ¿Por qué? ¿Qué animales domésticos te gustaría *(would you like)* tener en el futuro?

3. En tu opinión, ¿cuáles son los animales domésticos más inteligentes?, ¿más cariñosos?, ¿menos difíciles de cuidar *(to take care of)*?, ¿mejores para las residencias estudiantiles/los apartamentos?

 3-13 Nuestro campus. Con un(a) compañero(a), comparen sus opiniones sobre los siguientes temas. Completen las frases de una manera lógica. Expliquen sus respuestas.

Teaching Tip 3-13: Complete the model and item 1 with the class; then have partners complete all 3 items. After 2-3 minutes, work with the whole class to compare opinions. Continue orally with items such as: **la residencia más fea y vieja es...; El mejor lugar para aparcar tu coche es...; Los libros menos caros *(expensive)* son...**

> **MODELO**
>
> Tú: La mejor residencia de nuestro campus es *Hampton Hall* porque *es nueva y tiene cuartos grandes y baños privados.*
>
> Tu compañero(a): No estoy de acuerdo. *(I disagree.)* En mi opinión, la mejor residencia de nuestro campus es *Elliott Hall* porque *tiene más actividades sociales para los residentes.*

1. La residencia más divertida de nuestro campus es... porque...
   La más aburrida es... porque...

2. El peor restaurante de nuestro campus es... porque...
   El mejor restaurante es... porque...

3. El mejor lugar *(place)* para estudiar es... porque...
   El peor lugar es... porque...

Puente cultural

¿Qué hacen las familias los fines de semana?

🌐 Go to the **Puentes** Premium Website to view the **Puente cultural** interviews.

🌐 **Standards:** This section addresses the standards for Culture (practices and perspectives) and Comparisons.

David Valecillos

🌐 **VENEZUELA**

Los sábados, los padres se reúnen con amigos para conversar y tomar una bebida. Luego, se van a algún restaurante. Los domingos siempre se va a misa *(mass)* junto con la familia y después todos se reúnen *(get together)* con el resto de los familiares, tíos, primos, etcétera para almorzar. Los almuerzos los domingos casi siempre son en casa de alguno de los familiares.

Jahel Pulido

🌐 **COLOMBIA**

Muchas familias salen a comer, al centro comercial. Van y visitan pueblos cercanos *(nearby)*. Van a la iglesia los domingos y se reúnen con otros familiares.

Mauricio Mbomio

🌐 **GUINEA ECUATORIAL**

Normalmente las familias se reúnen los fines de semana para tratar *(deal with)* asuntos familiares, cenar juntos o simplemente visitar a otras familias que viven en las afueras *(outskirts)* de la ciudad. Los domingos las familias cristianas se reúnen para ir a la iglesia.

Teaching Tip: Form groups of three students, with each person responsible for reading and providing a summary of the information on one country. Then have the group decide what information they would include for the United States.

Comparando a las familias. Con un(a) compañero(a), lee la información y completa la tabla *(complete the chart)*.

	En Venezuela	En Colombia	En Guinea Ecuatorial	En los Estados Unidos
¿Qué hacen las familias los fines de semana?				

Paso 2

Vocabulario temático

In this *Paso* you will practice:

► Talking about houses
► Describing the rooms and furniture of a house
► Reporting the condition of things
► Giving the location of things

Grammar:
► Adverbs of location
► Some uses of **ser** and **estar**

Los cuartos y los muebles *(Describing rooms and furnishings)*

—¿Dónde viven tú y tu familia?
—Acabamos de *comprar* una nueva casa.
    mudarnos a
    alquilar

—¿Cómo es tu (nueva) casa?
—Tiene *dos pisos* y hay *seis cuartos.*
  En la planta baja, hay *una cocina, un comedor* y *una sala.*
  En el primer piso, hay *dos dormitorios grandes* y *un baño.*

Teaching Tip: Spend 1½ to 2 class hours on this **Paso**.

Transparency Bank C-1, C-2, C-4, C-5

Teaching Tip: Introduce the vocabulary by using a transparency or by drawing a sample floor plan of your own house on the board. Name the rooms and what is in each one. **Esta es mi casa. Es de tamaño mediano; no es ni grande ni pequeña. Mi casa tiene siete cuartos. Esta es la cocina. Aquí preparamos la comida. En la cocina hay...**

Grammar: Point out to more proficient groups that the adjective **nueva** is placed before the noun to mean a "different" house, not necessarily a "brand-new" one.

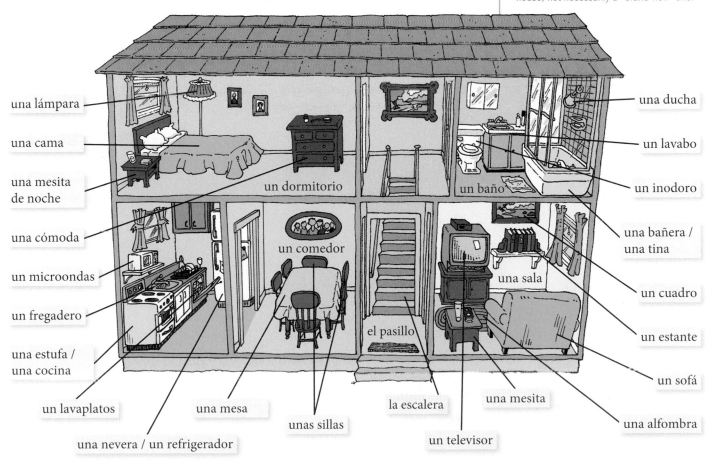

una lámpara
una cama
una mesita de noche
una cómoda
un microondas
un fregadero
una estufa / una cocina
un lavaplatos
una mesa
unas sillas
una nevera / un refrigerador

un dormitorio
un comedor
el pasillo
la escalera
un televisor

una ducha
un lavabo
un inodoro
una bañera / una tina
un cuadro
un estante
un sofá
una alfombra

un baño
una sala
una mesita

CD1
Track 21

Cómo describir algunas características de una casa

Mi casa es *nueva (vieja, de estilo moderno, de estilo tradicional).*

La sala es *grande (de tamaño mediano, pequeña).*

Los muebles son *elegantes (baratos, caros, informales).*

Cómo describir algunas condiciones de una casa

Mi apartamento está *amueblado (en buenas condiciones, en malas condiciones).*

Normalmente, mi dormitorio está *ordenado (desordenado).*

Por lo general, la cocina está *limpia (sucia).*

Por desgracia, el refrigerador está *descompuesto* y la ventana está *rota.*

Ponerlo a prueba

3-14 De venta. Estás hablando con un agente de bienes raíces *(real estate).* Escucha la descripción de la casa y escoge *(choose)* las respuestas correctas.

1. Número de pisos:	1	②	3
2. Número de dormitorios:	2	③	4
3. Número de baños:	1	②	3
4. El baño matrimonial incluye:	(ducha)	bañera	sauna
5. La cocina es:	pequeña	(grande)	de tamaño mediano
6. Otro aspecto positivo es:	(el garaje)	el ático	el patio
7. La casa cuesta _____ pesos.	88 000	(98 000)	198 000

3-15 El nuevo apartamento. Tu amiga Lucía describe un nuevo apartamento.
Relaciona la información de las dos columnas para crear una descripción lógica.

<u>c</u> 1. Acabo de mudarme...

<u>b</u> 2. Me gusta muchísimo porque...

<u>g</u> 3. Tiene tres dormitorios...

<u>d</u> 4. El apartamento está amueblado y...

<u>a</u> 5. En la cocina hay...

<u>e</u> 6. La sala tiene...

<u>h</u> 7. En mi dormitorio hay...

<u>f</u> 8. El baño es un poco pequeño
pero...

a. microondas y lavaplatos.

b. es grande y está cerca del campus.

c. a un nuevo apartamento.

d. los muebles están en buenas condiciones.

e. un sofá, dos sillones y dos mesitas
con lámparas.

f. tiene ducha y bañera.

g. y cada uno tiene su clóset.

h. una cama, una mesita de noche y un
clóset enorme.

3-16 ¿Cómo es esta casa? La familia González acaba de comprar una casa en Miami.
Mira el dibujo y contesta las preguntas con oraciones completas.

1. ¿Cuántos pisos tiene esta casa? ¿Qué hay en cada (each) piso?

2. ¿Qué electrodomésticos (appliances) hay en la cocina? ¿Qué electrodomésticos
necesitan comprar?

3. ¿Cuántos baños hay? ¿Están sucios o limpios? ¿Cuál te gusta más?

4. ¿Cuántos dormitorios hay? ¿Cuál de los dormitorios está desordenado y sucio?
¿Por qué?

5. ¿Cuáles de los muebles están en malas condiciones?

6. ¿Cuál es tu cuarto favorito? Descríbelo.

Teaching Tip 3-16: To prepare students
for this activity have pairs of students quiz
each other on vocabulary. One student says
the word for an appliance or furnishing,
and the other names the room in which it
is commonly found. For example: **mesa:**
Normalmente la mesa está en la cocina
o en el comedor.

3-17 En nuestro campus. ¿Cuál es la mejor residencia en tu campus? ¿Cuáles son los mejores apartamentos para estudiantes cerca del campus? Describe estos lugares (*places*) con detalles y compara tus ideas con las de un(a) compañero(a).

VOCABULARIO ÚTIL:

Para mí...	*In my opinion . . .*
Yo creo que...	*I think that . . .*
(No) Estoy de acuerdo.	*I (dis)agree.*

MODELO

Para mí, los apartamentos de "Millhouse Creek" son los mejores para estudiantes. No están muy cerca de nuestra universidad pero tienen un autobús para llevar a los estudiantes al campus. Todos los apartamentos tienen cocinas grandes y dos baños. Están amueblados con sofás, camas, mesitas, lámparas y más. También hay piscina.

3-18 Una casa para las vacaciones. Tú y tus amigos van a pasar las vacaciones en Isla Margarita, uno de los destinos turísticos más populares de Venezuela. Quieren alquilar una casa por una semana y encuentran (*you find*) este anuncio interesante en Internet. ¿Les gusta la casa? Con un(a) compañero(a) de clase, lean la información sobre la casa y contesten las preguntas.

Prestigiosos townhouses con mucho confort en Playa El Agua

Aquí tiene la perfecta solución tanto para familias como para grupos que viajan juntos. Hermosas casas están a corta distancia de Playa El Agua y a 100 metros de restaurantes, tiendas, bares y mercados. La comunidad cuenta con piscina, áreas sociales y estacionamiento. Todas las casas tienen cocina totalmente equipada, tres habitaciones, dos baños, balcón, terraza y jardín, como también aire acondicionado, TV por cable e Internet gratis via WiFi.

Capacidad para 7 personas máximo.

Precios: desde 490 BsF/día

Pago: 50% al reservar y 50% 15 días antes de llegar.

1. ¿Les gusta la ubicación (*location*) de la casa? Explica.

2. ¿Cuáles de las amenidades (*amenities*) son más atractivas?

3. ¿Es suficientemente grande para Uds.?

4. ¿Es razonable (*reasonable*) el precio?

5. ¿Quieren alquilar la casa? Explica.

Vocabulario temático

Para indicar relaciones espaciales *(Describing where something is located)*

—¿Dónde está el gato?

—Está...

Transparency Bank C-1, C-2, C-4, C-5

Teaching Tip: Introduce spatial relationships by bringing a small stuffed animal (the school mascot is a good choice) and placing it in different locations: on top of your desk, under the desk, beside a student, etc. Use the transparencies for additional practice with essential vocabulary.

Vocabulary: Provide additional words as needed: **en el rincón** *(in the corner)*, **enfrente de** *(opposite, facing, across from)*, **cerca de** *(close to)*.

en las cortinas, **a la izquierda del** estante

en la lámpara, **a la derecha del** estante

encima de la mesita, **detrás del** teléfono

entre los libros

al lado de la computadora

delante del clóset

dentro de la gaveta de la cómoda

sobre la cama

debajo de la cama

en la mochila **en el medio** del cuarto

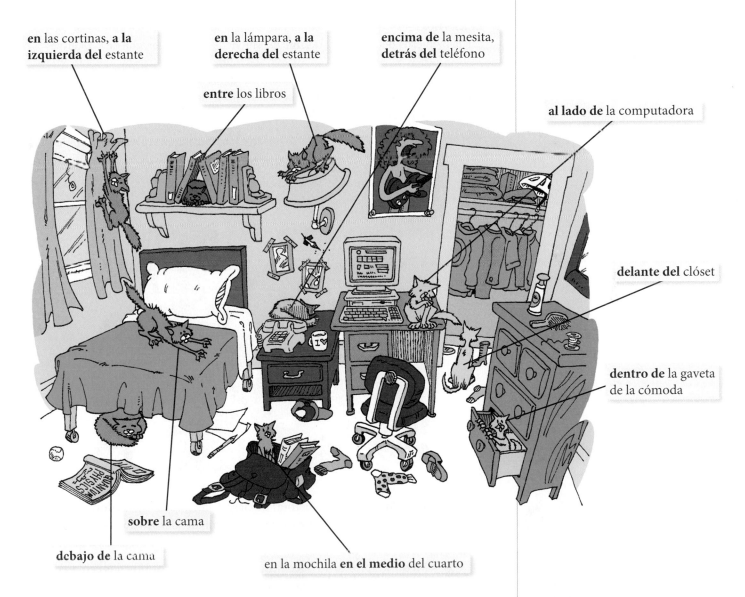

Vocabulary: The preposition **en** may be used to indicate *in* (**El libro está en la caja**), *at* (**Luis está en casa**), and *on* (**La carta está en la mesa**). Other prepositions with multiple meanings include **encima de** *(on top of* or *above)* and **debajo de** *(under* and *below).*

Use **estar** for locations: **El gato *está* dentro de la gaveta de la cómoda.**

Teaching Tip: Assign Activity 3-19 for homework; use the others for in-class work.

CD1
Track 22

Teaching Tip: Have students makes true/false statements about the room on page 105. Use these as models with the entire class before beginning the partner work:

1. La cama está a la izquierda de la ventana.
2. La mesita de noche está entre la cama y el escritorio (*desk*).
3. La computadora está debajo del escritorio.
4. El estante de libros está encima de la cómoda.
5. El teléfono está en la mesita de noche.

3-19 El cuarto de Mayra. Mayra tiene un nuevo apartamento. Su mamá le describe a su esposo el cuarto de Mayra en el nuevo apartamento. Escucha la descripción y contesta las preguntas.

1. La mamá de Mayra piensa que su cuarto es _____.
   (a.) muy grande y bonito   b. pequeño y feo   c. bonito, pero que está sucio

2. A la mamá le gustan mucho _____.
   (a.) el clóset y la ventana   b. la cama y la cómoda   c. el color del cuarto y las plantas

3. La cama está _____.
   a. al lado del clóset   (b.) debajo de la ventana   c. a la izquierda de la puerta

4. El radio y el despertador (*alarm clock*) están _____.
   a. al lado del televisor   b. en el escritorio   (c.) encima de la mesita de noche

5. El televisor está _____.
   a. a la izquierda del clóset   (b.) delante del sillón   c. a la derecha de la puerta

Expansion 3-20: For more practice, "hide" several of your belongings, such as a pen, notebook, textbook, sweater, etc. Have students help you "find" them. **—No sé dónde está mi libro. —Profesor(a), su libro está debajo del escritorio.**

3-20 ¿Dónde está mi... ? Miren el dibujo y dramaticen esta situación en grupos de dos: Tu compañero(a) de cuarto no puede encontrar nada (*can't find anything*). Mira el dibujo y dile (*tell him/her*) dónde están las cosas.

MODELO   Tu compañero(a):   No puedo encontrar mi mochila. ¿Sabes dónde está?

Tú: Sí. Está debajo de la cama.

Tu compañero(a):   No sé dónde está…

Expansion 3-20: Have students describe the location of a piece of furniture in the drawing on p. 101 to their partners. The partner guesses which item is being described. For example: Student A: **Está en la sala, a la derecha del televisor. ¿Qué es?** Student B: **Es el estante de libros.**

Expansion: For extra practice, have each student create an outline of his room, with doors, windows and closets indicated. Then, students swap papers and describe to each other the contents of the room. The partners must draw in the furniture. **Mi cama está al lado del clóset. Hay una mesita de noche a la derecha de mi cama...**

3-21 Mi cuarto. Con un(a) compañero(a) de clase, tomen turnos para describir sus dormitorios. Incluyan 3 ó 4 expresiones, como **encima de, debajo de...,** en la conversación. ¿Qué muebles tienes en tu cuarto? ¿Qué más (*What else*) necesitas o quieres?

MODELO   Mi dormitorio es un poco pequeño pero me gusta. Hay dos camas, dos escritorios, dos cómodas y dos clósets. En un rincón (*In one corner*), tenemos un televisor. Hay un pequeño refrigerador al lado del televisor. Mi computadora está encima de mi escritorio. No tenemos microondas pero queremos comprar uno.

Gramática

Los verbos *ser* y *estar*

CD1
Track 23

Read and listen to Ana's description of her new friend. In each sentence, identify the conjugated forms of **ser** and **estar**. Which of these two verbs is used to describe Berta's personality? Which tells where she is from? Which indicates the location of her room?

Berta es mi nueva amiga en la residencia. Ella es de Arizona, como yo. Berta es muy simpática, responsable y trabajadora. Su cuarto está al lado del mío *(mine)*. Por eso *(So)* estudiamos juntas con frecuencia. Estoy contenta de tenerla como amiga.

A. Los usos del verbo *ser*. Both **ser** and **estar** mean *to be,* but they are used in different ways and may not be interchanged.

Uses of *ser*

▸ With nouns, to identify the subject by relationship, occupation, profession, nationality or other similar categories

Este **es** mi <u>primo</u>.	*This is my cousin.*
Mis padres **son** <u>profesores</u>.	*My parents are professors.*

▸ With adjectives, to describe characteristics and traits of people, places, and things

Elisa y su hermana **son** muy <u>amables</u>.	*Elisa and her sister are very kind.*
Mi casa **es** <u>grande</u> y <u>moderna</u>.	*My house is big and modern.*

▸ With the preposition **de,** to express ownership

La cama **es** <u>de Alicia</u>.	*The bed belongs to Alicia.*

▸ With the preposition **de,** to indicate origin

La lámpara **es** <u>de Italia</u>.	*The lamp is from Italy.*

▸ To tell time and give dates

Es <u>la una de la tarde</u>.	*It's one o'clock in the afternoon.*
Hoy **es** <u>viernes</u>.	*Today is Friday.*

▸ For the location of events (parties, concerts, weddings, classes, etc.)

<u>La fiesta</u> **es** en casa de mi prima.	*The party is at my cousin's house.*

B. Los usos del verbo *estar*. The verb **estar** is used in fewer circumstances.

Uses of *estar*

▸ To indicate the location of persons or things

Gregorio **está** <u>en Venezuela</u>.	*Gregorio is in Venezuela.*
La cama **está** <u>a la derecha del sillón</u>.	*The bed is to the right of the easy chair.*

▸ With adjectives that indicate emotional and physical conditions

Mis padres **están** <u>contentos</u>.	*My parents are happy.*
El refrigerador **está** <u>descompuesto</u>.	*The refrigerator is out of order.*

Heinle Grammar Tutorial: Ser versus **estar**

Answers: es, está, estoy. Personality: ser; where from: ser; location of room: estar.

Teaching Tip: Before discussing the uses of **ser** and **estar**, review their conjugations. Have students attempt to explain why each verb is used in the model sentences before the grammar presentation. Remind them of the "poem": "How you feel and where you are, always use the verb **estar.**"

Teaching Tip: Provide students with an example of how to form a question about possesion: **¿De quién es esta mochila?**

Grammar: When *asking* about how a person feels with regard to a particular topic/event, it is more common to use the verb **sentirse,** although **estar** may be used in the response. **¿Cómo se siente tu papá sobre tu decision? Está muy contento.**

Teaching Tip: Focus on the basic uses in sections A and B. The information in section C is more useful for recognition and understanding of the concept. Few students at this level distinguish the two verbs with accuracy in spontaneous conversation.

Grammar: For more proficient classes, add this explanation: Some adjectives may be used with either **ser** or **estar,** but with different connotations. In these cases, **ser** still describes the essential nature, while **estar** describes a change from the norm. Example: **Juan es muy guapo.** (Everyone considers him handsome. The focus is on a physical trait.) **Juan está muy guapo esta noche.** (John looks especially handsome tonight with his new suit. The focus is on his current condition, rather than on his traits.)

C. Unos contrastes. Although both **ser** and **estar** may be used with descriptive adjectives, the two verbs convey different meanings.

▸ **Ser** is used to describe characteristics, traits, or inherent qualities—the way you normally think of a person or thing. It is generally used with adjectives like **alto, bajo, inteligente, bueno, cómico,** etc.

Nuestra casa **es** grande.   *Our house is big.* (Everyone considers it large because it has twelve rooms.)

▸ **Estar** is used to describe the way a person feels or the current condition of something. **Estar** is generally used with adjectives like **contento, cansado, frustrado, ordenado, roto,** etc.

La sala **está** sucia.   *The living room is dirty.* (We just had a party, so it's a mess.)

▸ **Ser** and **estar** also convey different meanings with the question word **¿cómo?**

ser: ¿Cómo **es** tu mamá?
What is your mother like? (Describe her to me.)

estar: ¿Cómo **está** tu mamá?
How is your mother? (How is she doing? Is she well?)

Ponerlo a prueba

Teaching Tip: Assign Activities 3-22 and 3-23 for homework.

3-22 Análisis. Elisa escribió en su diario sobre *(about)* un evento importante. Lee la descripción en la página 109 y decide por qué es correcto usar **ser** o **estar** para cada frase.

> **MODELO**   *Lees:* Mi prima Inés **es** muy guapa.
>
> *Analizas el uso de **ser** y escribes "c" (expresa una característica).*

Ser

a. delante de un sustantivo *(noun)*: identifica profesiones, nacionalidad, parentesco, etc.
b. la ubicación *(location)* de un evento
c. delante de un adjetivo: expresa una característica
d. delante de la preposición **de**: expresa origen
e. delante de la preposición **de**: expresa posesión
f. la hora, las fechas, las expresiones de tiempo

Estar

g. la ubicación *(location)* de una persona/cosa
h. antes de un adjetivo: expresa una condición/emoción

Querido diario:

La boda (*wedding*) de nuestra prima Inés (1) **es** mañana y todos (2) **estamos** muy contentos. El novio de Inés se llama Jorge y (3) **es** de Perú. Yo creo que (4) **es** muy guapo y simpático. Mamá (5) **está** un poco preocupada porque Jorge (6) **es** representante de ventas (*sales rep*) y tiene que viajar mucho por su trabajo. Pero la nueva casa de los novios (7) **está** muy cerca de nuestra casa, así que (*so*) Inés puede visitarnos con frecuencia.

La ceremonia (8) va a **ser** en la Iglesia de San Pedro. Esta mañana, ayudé (*I helped*) a decorar la iglesia, y ahora todo (9) **está** muy elegante. Creo que le va a gustar a Inés.

3-23 Saludos de Venezuela. María del Carmen está de vacaciones con su esposo, Leonardo. Completa la carta que ella le escribe a su amiga Luisa con la forma correcta del tiempo presente de **ser** y **estar**.

De: María del Carmen Fajardo
Enviado el: martes, 09 de octubre
Para: lvalecillos22@yahoo.com
Asunto: Nuestro viaje

Querida Luisa:

¿Cómo (1) ___estás___ (tú)? Yo (2) ___estoy___ superbién aquí en Los Roques, un paraíso tropical.

Las islas Los Roques (3) ___están___ a 150 kilómetros al norte de Caracas. Hay muy pocos norteamericanos aquí. Casi todos los turistas (4) ___son___ de Venezuela y todos (5) ___son___ muy amables. Nuestra habitación en el hotel no (6) ___es___ muy grande, pero (7) ___es___ bonita y tiene una vista fabulosa de la playa.

Hoy (8) ___es___ domingo, el último día de nuestro tour. La fiesta de despedida (*going-away party*) (9) ___es___ en el gran salón del hotel esta noche. Leonardo y yo (10) ___estamos___ un poco cansados pero también muy contentos después de diez días de viaje.

Bueno, por ahora, ¡saludos desde Los Roques!

Abrazos de María del Carmen

3-24 Las diferencias entre el día y la noche. La Sra. Muñoz tiene dos hijos, Armando y Arturo, quienes son tan diferentes como el día y la noche. Con un(a) compañero(a) de clase, describan diferentes aspectos de los cuartos. Usen los verbos **ser** y **estar** en las descripciones. Tomen turnos.

MODELO

TÚ: El cuarto de Armando **es** grande y las paredes **son** azules.

TU COMPAÑERO(A): También, el cuarto de Armando **está** limpio.

TÚ: Sí, y su mamá **está** contenta porque el cuarto **está** ordenado.

TU COMPAÑERO(A): Armando tiene un televisor en su cuarto. **Está** encima de la cómoda.

A.

B.

3-25 Mi domicilio. Con un(a) compañero(a) de clase, conversa sobre el tema de las casas. Usen estas preguntas y crean *(create)* otras preguntas originales también.

1. ¿Vives en una casa o en un apartamento?

2. ¿Dónde está tu casa/apartamento? ¿Te gusta la ubicación *(location)*? Explica por qué sí o por qué no.

3. ¿Cuántos cuartos hay en tu casa/apartamento? ¿Cuáles son?

4. ¿Cuál es tu cuarto predilecto *(favorite)* en tu casa/apartamento? ¿Cómo es? ¿Por qué te gusta?

5. Haz 2–3 preguntas originales *(Ask 2–3 original questions)* sobre la casa / el apartamento de tu compañero(a).

Paso 3

Vocabulario temático

Mi rutina *(My daily routine)*

Por la mañana

**Normalmente, me despierto
a las ocho *(bastante temprano).***

Me levanto *a las ocho y cuarto.*

Me ducho y me visto *rápidamente*.

Salgo de casa *a las nueve menos cuarto.*

Paso el día *en clase*.

In this *Paso* you will practice:

- ▶ Describing daily routines
- ▶ Describing household chores and other family activities
- ▶ Expressing how often you and your family engage in different activities

Grammar:
- ▶ Reflexive verbs in the present tense

Normalmente is an expression of frequency. You'll learn others later in this chapter.

Transparency Bank L-1

Teaching Tip: Present the new vocabulary one drawing at a time. Adapt the sentence to express your own routine. Then call on several students to restate the same sentence with their own routines. For example: **Normalmente, los lunes me despierto a las seis de la mañana. ¿Y tú, Amanda? ¿A qué hora te despiertas los lunes?** Since student schedules vary by the day, it's best to refer to a specific day of the week.

More Information: This section helps familiarize students with reflexive verbs. Do not give lengthy explanations at this point. Point out that **me** is used with many of the verbs that describe daily routines and that you will discuss them in more detail later.

Por la tarde y por la noche

Para divertirnos, mis amigos y yo vamos con frecuencia *a un café (al centro estudiantil, al gimnasio).*

Por lo general, ceno en casa con mi familia *a las ocho y media.*

Por lo general, necesito estudiar por *dos o tres* horas.

Me acuesto *a la medianoche (a la una, bastante tarde).*

Ponerlo a prueba

Teaching Tip: Assign 3-26 and 3-27 for homework.

CD1
Track 24

3-26 Un estudiante de primer año. Gustavo acaba de pasar *(has just spent)* su primer mes en la universidad. Ahora está en casa visitando a su madre. Escucha su conversación y completa la actividad.

1. ¿A qué hora se despierta Gustavo por la mañana normalmente?
   Gustavo se despierta a las ___seis y media / 6:30___ de la mañana y se levanta a las ___siete menos cuarto / 6:45___.

2. ¿Dónde come el desayuno *(breakfast)*?
   Come el desayuno en ___la cafetería___.

3. ¿Cuántas clases tiene por la mañana?
   Tiene ___tres/3___ clases por la mañana.

4. En un día normal, ¿qué hace Gustavo después de almorzar *(after eating lunch)*?
   Normalmente, va a la ___biblioteca___ para ___estudiar___.

5. ¿Qué hacen Gustavo y sus amigos para divertirse?
   Con frecuencia, van al ___gimnasio___ y juegan al ___básquetbol___.

6. ¿A qué hora se acuesta Gustavo?
   Por lo general, se acuesta a las ___once y media/11:30___ o a la ___medianoche___.

3-27 El día de Marta. ¿Cómo es la rutina de Marta? Relaciona las dos columnas de una manera lógica.

Answers 3-27: 1. d; 2. h; 3. c; 4. a; 5. j; 6. i; 7. e; 8. f; 9. g; 10. b

1. Normalmente me despierto...
2. No me levanto inmediatamente...
3. Luego, me ducho...
4. Me visto...
5. Salgo de casa...
6. Paso todo el día...
7. Por la noche, me gusta...
8. A veces (*Sometimes*) mis amigos y yo...
9. También, necesito...
10. Por lo general, me acuesto...

a. rápidamente y como cereal con leche para el desayuno.
b. a la medianoche o a la una.
c. y me lavo el pelo.
d. bastante temprano, a las siete de la mañana.
e. pasar tiempo con mis amigos.
f. vamos al cine o al gimnasio.
g. estudiar para mis clases por dos o tres horas.
h. porque me gusta escuchar la radio por un rato.
i. en clase o en mi trabajo en el Departamento de Psicología.
j. a las ocho y media de la mañana.

3-28 El día más ajetreado. ¿Cuál es tu día más ajetreado (*hectic*) de la semana? Habla con un(a) compañero(a) y comparen sus rutinas para ese día (*for that day*).

1. Mi día más ajetreado es el _____ (*día de la semana*). ¿Cuál es tu día más ajetreado?
2. Normalmente, me despierto a las _____ (*hora*). ¿A qué hora te despiertas tú?
3. Antes de mis clases, (yo) _____ (*actividades*). ¿Qué haces tú?
4. Salgo de casa/mi residencia a las _____ (*hora*). ¿A qué hora sales tú de tu casa/residencia?
5. Por la mañana tengo _____ (*número*) clases y por la tarde tengo _____ (*número*) clases. ¿Y tú? ¿Cuántas clases tienes por la mañana y por la tarde?
7. Por lo general, regreso a casa/mi residencia a las _____ (*hora*). ¿A qué hora regresas tú?
8. Por la noche, con frecuencia _____ (*actividades*). Después (*Afterwards*) me acuesto a las _____ (*hora*). ¿Y tú? ¿Qué haces por la noche? ¿A qué hora te acuestas?

Teaching Tip 3-28: Prepare for partner work in this way: Complete the first statement with your personal info. Call on one student to respond to the question. Repeat the procedure with items 2 and 3. Then have students complete all items with a partner. After 3–4 minutes, follow up by comparing routines for selected items, such as items 1, 2, and 8.

3-29 Los sábados. ¿Cómo es un sábado típico para ti? Conversa con dos o tres compañeros de clase y comparen sus rutinas. Después (*Afterwards*), contesten estas preguntas sobre la rutina de los sábados:

- ¿Tienen Uds. rutinas muy parecidas (*similar*) o muy diferentes?
- ¿Cuál de Uds. se levanta más temprano?, ¿se acuesta más tarde?
- ¿Cuál de Uds. pasa más tiempo estudiando y trabajando?
- ¿Cuál de Uds. pasa más tiempo con los amigos?

Teaching Tip 3-29: Describe your own Saturday routine as a model. Then have students work in pairs. For follow-up, have pairs respond to the bulleted questions in the activity.

COMENTARIO CULTURAL *Las familias en el mundo hispano*

¿A quiénes consideras parte de tu familia? ¿Dónde viven tus abuelos? ¿Tienes padrinos?

Cuando hablamos de la familia en los Estados Unidos, casi siempre pensamos en la familia nuclear: el padre, la madre y los hijos. En cambio, en el mundo hispano, la palabra familia tiene un significado más amplio; generalmente incluye a abuelos, tíos, primos y otros parientes. Los lazos (*ties*) familiares son muy importantes en el mundo hispano. Los hijos casi siempre viven con sus padres hasta que se casan (*until they get married*). A veces, los abuelos u otros parientes viven en la misma casa también. En muchos países los padrinos (*godparents*) se consideran miembros de la familia. No viven en la misma casa, pero asisten a todas las celebraciones familiares.

Teaching Tip: After students read the Comentario, work with the class to place items in a Venn diagram, to indicate whether the following practices refer mostly to the U.S., to Spanish-speaking countries, or both. **La palabra "familia" incluye a los abuelos y tíos. Los hijos viven con sus padres hasta que se casan. Los abuelos viven con sus hijos. Los padrinos se consideran miembros de la familia.** Add other statements based on your own experiences.

Gramática

Los verbos reflexivos

🌐 **Heinle Grammar Tutorial:**
Reflexive verbs

🔊
CD1
Track 25

Read and listen to Bernardo as he describes his morning routine. Many of the verbs—the ones with **me**—are considered "reflexive." Identify each reflexive verb in the paragraph below.

¿Cómo es mi rutina? Pues *(Well)*, todos los días me despierto a las ocho. Pero no me levanto hasta las ocho y cuarto. Primero me lavo los dientes y me ducho. Luego *(Next)*, me visto. No tengo tiempo para desayunar porque mi primera clase es a las nueve.

A. Los verbos reflexivos. Verbs like **me levanto, me ducho,** and **me despierto** are known as reflexive verbs. In most cases, reflexive verbs indicate that the person who performs the action also receives the benefit or impact of the action. For example, when you take a shower, you wash *yourself.* Many verbs can actually be used reflexively or non-reflexively, depending on the meaning of the sentence.

Reflexive: levantarse   **Me levanto** a las seis y media.
(I get up of my own accord, so I both perform and receive the benefit of the action.)

Non-reflexive: levantar   **Levanto** a mi hijo a las ocho.
(I turn on the light and call out my son's name to get him up.)

B. Los pronombres reflexivos. When a verb is used reflexively, you must use a reflexive pronoun that *matches* the subject of the sentence. The pronoun **me** is used when the subject is **yo,** the pronoun **te** is used when the subject is **tú,** and so on.

yo	me	**Me levanto** a las seis.
tú	te	¿A qué hora **te levantas**?
Ud./él/ella	se	Roberto **se levanta** temprano.
nosotros(as)	nos	**Nos levantamos** tarde los domingos.
vosotros(as)	os	¿**Os levantáis** ahora?
Uds./ellos/ellas	se	Mis padres no **se levantan** muy temprano.

► Reflexive pronouns are always placed before a single conjugated verb.

    Me levanto bastante temprano.   *I get up quite early.*

▶ Reflexive pronouns are usually attached to the end of infinitives.

Prefiero **levantarme** temprano.   *I prefer to get up early.*

▶ With reflexive expressions that refer to parts of the body, Spanish uses definite articles (**el, la, los, las**) instead of possessives (**mi, tu, su,** etc.).

Me lavo **el** pelo todos los días.   *I wash **my** hair every day.*

Grammar: Provide an example with **gustar** and point out that the first **me** is the indirect object while the second **me** is the reflexive pronoun: **Me gusta levantarme a las nueve.**

C. Otros verbos reflexivos. Just like all other verbs, reflexive verbs may be regular, stem-changing, or irregular in the present tense.

Verbos regulares:

afeitarse	*to shave*
arreglarse	*to fix oneself up, to get oneself ready*
bañarse	*to take a bath, to bathe*
ducharse	*to take a shower*
levantarse	*to get up*
lavarse el pelo (las manos, la cara)	*to wash one's hair (hands, face)*
lavarse los dientes	*to brush one's teeth*
maquillarse	*to put on make-up*
peinarse	*to comb one's hair*
quitarse	*to take off (clothing)*

Verbos irregulares:

The verb **ponerse** *(to put on)* is irregular only in the **yo** form of the present tense: **me pongo.**

Verbos con cambios en la raíz:

Like all stem-changing verbs, these reflexive verbs change the vowels in all persons except **nosotros** and **vosotros.**

o → ue

acostarse (me acuesto)	*to go to bed*
dormirse (me duermo)	*to fall asleep*

e → ie

divertirse (me divierto)	*to have a good time*
despertarse (me despierto)	*to wake up*
sentarse (me siento)	*to sit down*
sentirse (me siento)	*to feel*

e → i

vestirse (me visto)	*to get dressed*
despedirse (me despido)	*to say good-bye*

Proficiency: Students need to master the present tense to reach the Intermediate level of proficiency. Practice conjugating a few stem-changing verbs in the present tense to review formation for accuracy; follow up with several open-ended activities in class.

Teaching Tip: Assign 3-30 and 3-31 for homework.

Ponerlo a prueba

3-30 Un día típico. Aquí tienes una descripción de la rutina de Vivian y su hermana Fátima. Escoge el verbo más lógico en cada caso y escríbelo en el presente.

MODELO (Yo) (levantarse / despedirse) _Me levanto_ temprano todos los días.

1. Fátima y yo (despertarse / acostarse [ue]) _nos despertamos_ a las siete y media casi todos los días.

2. Yo (ducharse / vestirse [i]) _me ducho_ por la mañana pero mi hermana (ponerse / bañarse) _se baña_ por la noche.

3. Primero (nosotras) (quitarse / vestirse [i]) _nos vestimos_ y luego (salir / regresar) _salimos_ para ir a la universidad. Pasamos todo el día allí.

4. Los fines de semana, (nosotras) (ir / volver [ue]) _vamos_ a fiestas con nuestros amigos y (divertirse [ie] / afeitarse) _nos divertimos_ mucho.

5. Normalmente, mi hermana (acostarse [ue] / moverse [ue]) _se acuesta_ tarde los viernes y (peinarse / levantarse) _se levanta_ tarde los sábados.

6. Pero yo (tener que / poner) _tengo que_ acostarme temprano los viernes porque los sábados (levantarse / dormirse) _me levanto_ temprano para el trabajo.

Teaching Tip 3-31: For in-class follow-up, have students recast the statements into the **yo** form and tell you which products they prefer to use: **Yo siempre me lavo los dientes con..., etc.** Point out the use of the definite article with **dientes** and **pelo**.

3-31 Los productos de aseo personal. Ramón mira la tele con frecuencia, y muchas veces compra los productos de los anuncios comerciales. Completa las oraciones con los verbos más lógicos de la lista; escribe los verbos en el presente.

afeitarse	ducharse	dormirse
lavarse	ponerse	vestirse

MODELO Ramón _se lava_ los dientes con la pasta dental Colgate, con triple acción.

1. Ramón siempre _se ducha_ con el jabón Fa, con desodorante.

2. Ramón _se lava_ el pelo con el champú Biogénesis, con acondicionador.

3. Ramón _se afeita_ con la crema de afeitar Gilette, con mentol.

4. Cuando sale con su novia, Ramón _se pone_ la colonia Brut.

5. Cuando está nervioso Ramón toma una tisana *(herbal tea)* homeopática y _se duerme_ en seguida *(quickly)*.

3-32 La rutina de Carlos. ¿Qué hace Carlos en un día normal? Mira los dibujos y describe su rutina con oraciones completas.

1.

2.

3.

4.

5.

6.

Expansion 3-32: Make true-false statements about Carlos's routine and have students respond. **Carlos se levanta a las 6:30 de la mañana. Normalmente Carlos come el desayuno en casa. Carlos tiene un laboratorio por la mañana. Por la tarde, Carlos se divierte con sus amigos en el gimnasio. Carlos prefiere bañarse. Carlos estudia un poco y se acuesta a las 11:00.**

Proficiency: Prepare the students for Higher level of proficiencies by encouraging them to create longer sentences, elaborate with details, and use expressions of frequency. Provide models of your expectations so that students can imitate easily. **Normalmente, Carlos se levanta a las... No le gustan las mañanas.** etc.

3-33 ¿Quiénes son más compatibles? Imagínate que vas a alquilar un apartamento cerca de la universidad. Necesitas buscar dos compañeros(as) compatibles.

PRIMERA PARTE: Entrevista a dos o tres compañeros de clase para averiguar *(to find out)* si Uds. son compatibles.

1. ¿A qué hora te levantas por la mañana?

2. ¿A qué hora prefieres acostarte?

3. Por lo general, ¿te duchas por la mañana o por la noche?

5. ¿Escuchas música mientras estudias?

6. ¿Normalmente está ordenado o desordenado tu cuarto?

7. Por lo general, ¿pasas los fines de semana aquí o sales de la ciudad?

8. (una pregunta original)

SEGUNDA PARTE: Explica porque Uds. son o **no** son compatibles.

MODELO   Kathryn y yo no somos compatibles porque…

Vocabulario temático

Los quehaceres domésticos *(Household chores)*

¿Cómo dividen Uds. las responsabilidades para los quehaceres?

Todos los días la empleada *limpia la casa* y *lava la ropa.*

Yo siempre *quito el polvo de los muebles* y *le doy de comer al perro.*

Normalmente mi hermana menor *lava los platos.*

De vez en cuando, mi hermana mayor *limpia el garaje.*

Trabaja en el jardín con frecuencia.

Normalmente, mi padre *cocina el almuerzo o la cena.*

Por lo general, *ayuda con los quehaceres.*

Mi hermanito nunca *pone la mesa.*

Nunca quiere *hacer su cama.*

Grammar: Point out that most expressions of frequency may be placed at the beginning or at the end of a statement: **Todos los días hago la cama. Hago la cama todos los días.** Provide more examples of **no... nunca: No hago la cama nunca.**

Mi hermana pone los platos en el lavaplatos. *My sister loads the dishwasher.*

Regional Vocabulary: Words related to homes and household chores vary from country to country. For example: **lavar los platos/los trastes/la vajilla/la loza; el garaje/la cochera; hacer la cama/tender la cama; quitar el polvo de los muebles/sacudir los muebles.**

Place **nunca** before the verb, or follow this pattern: Mi hermanito **no** pone la mesa **nunca.**

EXPRESIONES DE FRECUENCIA

siempre
todos los días
una vez por semana
con frecuencia
de vez en cuando
nunca

Ponerlo a prueba

CD1
Track 26

3-34 Los quehaceres. Hoy es día de limpieza general *(cleaning day)*. Escucha la conversación entre los miembros de la familia Arroyo y completa la actividad.

1. María Luisa, la mamá de la familia, habla primero *(first)* con _____.
   (a.) su esposo   b. su hijo   c. su hija

2. Adalberto no quiere limpiar el garaje porque piensa _____.
   a. leer el periódico   b. jugar al tenis con un amigo   (c.) mirar la televisión

3. Samuel necesita _____ pero quiere salir con Manuel.
   a. ir al supermercado
   (b.) darles de comer a los perros
   c. poner los platos en el lavaplatos

4. Pilar quiere salir con sus amigas pero _____.
   a. va a darles de comer a los perros primero
   b. decide ir al supermercado con su mamá
   (c.) promete lavar la ropa por la tarde

5. La mamá no va a _____ . Decide ir de compras.
   (a.) cocinar   b. lavar los platos   c. hacer las camas

3-35 Los quehaceres. ¿Con qué cuarto o parte de la casa asocias las siguientes actividades? Indica la respuesta correcta.

MODELO   PLANTAR ROSAS: la sala / el comedor /(el jardín)

1. LAVAR LOS PLATOS: el comedor /(la cocina)/ el baño
2. HACER LA CAMA: el jardín /(el dormitorio)/ la sala
3. COCINAR EL ALMUERZO: el comedor /(la cocina)/ la escalera
4. QUITAR EL POLVO DE LOS MUEBLES: el garaje / el baño /(la sala)
5. PONER LA MESA: el jardín / el ático /(el comedor)

3-36 ¿Limpio o sucio? La vida de los estudiantes es muy ajetreada *(hectic)*. ¿Tienen Uds. tiempo para mantener el cuarto limpio y ordenado? Entrevista a un(a) compañero(a) de clase sobre los quehaceres y comparen sus respuestas. ¿Con qué frecuencia hacen Uds. los quehaceres?

MODELO   hacer la cama

TÚ: ¿Con qué frecuencia haces la cama en tu cuarto?

TU COMPAÑERO(A): Hago mi cama todos los días. ¿Y tú?

TÚ: Hago mi cama solo *(only)* cuando mis padres me visitan.

todos los días	una vez por semana	una vez por mes
de vez en cuando	casi nunca	nunca

1. hacer la cama
2. limpiar el baño
3. quitar el polvo de los muebles

4. lavar la ropa
5. cocinar

More Information: Assign the first two activities for homework.

Teaching Tip: For extra vocabulary practice, have students take turns miming an activity while the class guesses what it is. For example, one student pretends to wash dishes. The class responds: **Lavas los platos (**or, **Estás lavando los platos.)**

Note: According to the Real Academia Española, the accent mark is no longer used on **solo**.

3-37 Las amas de casa y la ayuda. Aquí tienes datos sobre los quehaceres domésticos. En la gráfica, hay información sobre dos aspectos importantes de este tipo de trabajo. Contesta las preguntas y compara tus respuestas con las de un(a) compañero(a) de clase.

VOCABULARIO ÚTIL:
barrer *to sweep*

fregar *to scrub*

hacer la compra *to get groceries*

planchar *to iron*

recoger un cuarto *to pick up a room*

1. Según la gráfica de la izquierda, ¿qué tarea *(chore)* les gusta menos a las amas de casa *(housewives)*? ¿Qué tareas prefieren hacer?

2. Según la gráfica de la derecha, ¿qué tareas hacen las amas de casa normalmente con sus parejas *(with their spouses)*? Por lo general, ¿qué tareas hacen las amas de casa sin *(without)* ayuda?

3. En tu familia, ¿qué tarea es la más popular?, ¿la menos popular? Explica tu respuesta.

4. ¿Qué tarea prefieres compartir *(to share)* con otra persona? ¿Por qué?

5. Respecto a los quehaceres, ¿tienes conflictos a veces con tus hermanos o tu compañero(a) de cuarto? Describe los conflictos.

Answers 3-37: 1. Planchar es la menos popular; prefieren lavar la ropa. 2. Normalmente hacen la compra con sus parejas. Nadie les ayuda a planchar o lavar la ropa. *Answers will vary for items 3, 4, 5.*

Expansion 3-37: Follow up with a class discussion on chores and who tends to do them in the students' respective families.

Un paso más

¡Vamos a hablar!

Estudiante A

Contexto: In this activity, you and your partner will try to find 10 differences between the drawings each of you has—without looking at the other person's picture! To do this, take turns describing in detail the scene on your page. Focus on the aspects listed below. You will begin by saying: **En mi dibujo** *(drawing)*, **Elena es rubia y tiene el pelo largo.**

> ▸ the physical appearance of the two girls
>
> ▸ the room and furniture (including location and condition)
>
> ▸ the activities of each girl

Go to the **Un paso más** section in the *Cuaderno de actividades* for reading, writing, and listening activities that correlate with this chapter.

Answers: 1. Length of Elena's hair; 2. Raquel's freckles; 3. Raquel's eyeglasses; 4. Elena is feeding the cat/making the bed. 5. Raquel is putting on make-up/getting dressed. 6. Computer/books on top of desk; 7. Location of easy chair; 8. Condition of TV set; 9. Rug on floor vs no rug; 10. Neat vs messy closet.

Un paso más

¡Vamos a hablar!

Estudiante B

Contexto: In this activity, you and your partner will try to find 10 differences between the drawings each of you has—without looking at the other person's picture! To do this, take turns describing in detail the scene on your page. Focus on the aspects listed below. Your partner will begin by describing Elena.

> ▸ the physical appearance of the two girls
>
> ▸ the room and furniture (including location and condition)
>
> ▸ the activities of each girl

¡Vamos a ver! | *Episodio 3*

En la Hacienda Vista Alegre

Anticipación

A. Hablando se entiende la gente. Tu compañero(a) y tú van a conocerse (*get to know each other*) un poco mejor. Hablen sobre los siguientes temas: ¿Qué aspectos te gustan más de la vida en familia? ¿Qué aspectos no te gustan? ¿Qué aspectos te gustan más de vivir de forma independiente? ¿Y qué aspectos te gustan menos?

Teaching Tip: Assign A and B for homework. If you play the video in class, complete C and D afterwards. Choose from the more challenging E and F, as time allows, for follow-up practice.

B. ¿Cómo se dice? Completa las siguientes oraciones con estas expresiones.

la carrera	una tradición familiar	te da miedo
Si no le molesta	me parezco	

1. Yo _____me parezco_____ mucho a mi abuelo.

2. ¿No _____te da miedo_____ andar solo por la noche?

3. _____Si no le molesta_____, ¿puedo abrir la ventana?

4. Voy a estudiar _____la carrera_____ de medicina.

5. En España es _____una tradición familiar_____ comer todos juntos los domingos.

▶ Vamos a ver

C. De paseo por la Hacienda Vista Alegre. Lee las preguntas. Luego, mira el Episodio 3 del vídeo y completa las actividades.

1. ¿Con quién comparten (*share*) habitación?
   a. Antonio _Javier_   b. Sofía _Alejandra_   c. Valeria _sola/nadie_

2. Selecciona la respuesta correcta.
   a. Gitano y Lady son los (perros / gatos / pájaros) de Alejandra.
   b. Alejandra se parece más a (su padre / su madre / su hermano).
   c. El hermano de Javier es (mayor / menor) que la hermana.
   d. Los hermanos de Javier estudian (medicina / negocios).
   e. La mamá de Valeria (está trabajando de modelo / está jubilada).

D. ¿Qué más comprendes? Contesta las preguntas. ¿Por qué quiere dormir sola Valeria? ¿Por qué estudian la misma carrera todos los hermanos de Javier? ¿Por qué Antonio quiere conocer a las hermanas de Valeria?

Answers to D: Porque le gusta la privacidad y tiene muchas cosas que guardar; Es una tradición familiar; Porque son modelos y piensa que son muy guapas.

En acción

E. Charlemos. ¿Qué te parece la tradición familiar de Javier? ¿Qué tradiciones familiares hay en tu familia? ¿Con quién quieres compartir habitación? ¿Por qué?

F. 3, 2, 1, ¡Acción! Interpreten la siguiente situación en grupos de 3 ó 4 estudiantes. Ustedes están en el salón de la casa de la Hacienda Vista Alegre. Ustedes están hablando, comparando y preguntándose por sus respectivas familias y por sus casas: **¿Cuántos son en su familia? ¿Cómo son sus padres y hermanos? ¿A quién se parecen ustedes más? ¿Tienen animales domésticos? ¿Cómo se llaman? ¿Qué añoran (*to miss*) más de sus casas?**

Teaching Tip: As an alternate to D, use this activity: **Después de ver el episodio, escribe un pequeño resumen (*summary*) sobre las familias de Antonio, Valeria y Alejandra. ¿Cuántos hermanos tienen? ¿A qué se dedican sus familiares? ¿Cómo son físicamente? ¿Tienen mascotas (*pets*)?**

Panorama cultural

DATOS ESENCIALES

Nombre oficial: República Bolivariana de Venezuela

Capital: Caracas

Población: 26 500 000 habitantes

Unidad monetaria: bolívar

Economía: refinerías de petróleo, metales, manufactura de automóviles, agricultura

🌐 **www.cengage.com/spanish/ puentes**

Standards: This section addresses Connections by including a wide variety of information on history, geography, economics, music, and other disciplines.

Note: The falls are named in honor of American aviator Jimmy Angel, who "discovered" them in 1937. The water falls 937 meters and is part of the Churún River system.

Transparency Bank A-14

El Salto del Ángel, con casi 1000 metros de altura, es la cascada más alta del mundo. Está en el sureste de Venezuela, en el Parque Nacional Canaima. Este parque se caracteriza por los tepuyes —grandes mesetas de paredes verticales— donde se encuentran muchas especies de animales y plantas únicas en el planeta.

Un vistazo a la historia

Note: The history of Venezuela has been marked by many dictatorships, military coups, and political and economic instability. A member of OPEC, Venezuela is dependent on fluctuations of the oil market. It is highly urbanized; agriculture employs less than 10% of the population.

Note: Caracas became the capital because of its strategic position: easy access to fertile lands and ports for the export of agricultural products.

1498 Los españoles llegan y encuentran *(find)* más de veinte diferentes tribus indígenas. Estas tribus se resisten a la colonización.

1567 Finalmente los españoles ganan territorio y fundan la ciudad de Santiago de León de Caracas.

1811 Venezuela declara su independencia el 5 de julio. Siguen *(There follow)* muchos años de conflictos.

Note: The lands currently comprised by Venezuela, Ecuador, and Colombia became independent of Spain in 1821 and formed the country known as **la República de la Gran Colombia.**

1960 Se crea la Organización de Países Exportadores de Petróleo (OPEP).

2008 Bajo la presidencia de Hugo Chávez, Venezuela continúa con la nacionalización de varios bancos e industrias.

Note: When the French Emperor Napoleon Bonaparte invaded Spain in 1808, the Spanish throne was in internal turmoil. The ensuing chaos spurred the Caracas City Council, or **cabildo,** to declare itself an independent republic. Simón Bolívar led the fight for independence during the next ten years, a time characterized by a series of failed republics and civil war. In June 1821 the Constitution for the Republic of Gran Colombia was signed and Bolívar became president. In 1829 General Páez led the separation of Venezuela from the joint republic.

Venezuela

Personajes de ayer y de hoy

Simón Bolívar Palacios (1783-1830)

También llamado El Libertador, luchó por *(fought for)* la independencia de Venezuela, Colombia, Ecuador, Bolivia y Perú. Fue el primer presidente de la República de la Gran Colombia y de la República de Venezuela.

Gustavo Dudamel Ramírez (1981-)

Este joven músico es director de la Orquesta Sinfónica Simón Bolívar. Empezó a estudiar violín a los 10 años. Ha actuado como director invitado de las grandes orquestas de Europa y los Estados Unidos. Es conocido por su presencia dinámica y electrizante.

Milka Duno (1972-)

Milka Duno es la primera latinoamericana considerada "experta" en el circuito profesional de carreras de autos *(auto racing)*. Compite en carreras en los Estados Unidos, Europa y Latinoamérica. También tiene un título universitario en ingeniería naval y cuatro maestrías *(master's degrees)* más.

Imágenes de Venezuela

Después de mirar el vídeo, contesta las preguntas con oraciones completas.

1. Caracas es el centro económico de Venezuela. Según el vídeo, ¿en qué se basa la economía del país?
2. Simón Bolívar es famoso por su papel *(role)* en la liberación de Venezuela. ¿Qué lugares en la capital conmemoran *(commemorate)* a Bolívar?
3. ¿Cuáles son algunos de los aspectos modernos de Caracas? ¿Los aspectos históricos o coloniales?
4. ¿Cuáles son algunos lugares *(places)* interesantes para los turistas? ¿Cuál te gustaría visitar? ¿Por qué?

Sustantivos

el almuerzo *lunch*
el (la) amigo(a) *friend*
el carácter *character, personality*
la casa *house*
la cena *supper, dinner*
el (la) chico(a) *boy, girl*
el (la) cliente(a) *customer, client*
el clóset *closet*
el (la) compañero(a) de cuarto
  roommate
el cuarto *room*
el (la) empleado(a) *employee; maid*
la escalera *stairs/staircase*
el familiar *family member*
el jardín *garden, yard*
la madrina *godmother*
los muebles *furniture*
las noticias *news*
el ojo *eye*
el padrino *godfather*
el (la) pariente(a) *relative*
el pelo *hair*
la personalidad *personality*
el piso *floor*
la planta baja *ground/first floor*
el plato *dish*
los quehaceres *household chores*
el retrato *portrait*
el trabajo *work*

Verbos

acabar de (+ infinitivo) *to have just*
  (done something)
acostarse (ue) *to go to bed*
afeitarse *to shave*
alquilar *to rent*
arreglarse *to fix oneself up, to get ready*
ayudar *to help*
bañarse *to take a bath*
cenar *to eat supper*

cocinar *to cook*
comprar *to buy*
dar de comer *to feed*
despedirse (i) *to say good-bye*
despertarse (ie) *to wake up*
divertirse (ie) *to have a good time*
dormirse (ue) *to fall asleep*
ducharse *to take a shower*
hacer la cama *to make the bed*
lavar *to wash*
lavarse el pelo/las manos/la cara
  to wash one's hair/hands/face
levantarse *to get up*
limpiar *to clean*
maquillarse *to put on make-up*
mudarse *to move (one's residence)*
peinarse *to comb one's hair*
poner *to put; to set (the table); to turn*
  on (TV, radio)
ponerse *to put on*
preparar *to prepare*
quitar el polvo *to dust*
quitarse *to take off (clothing)*
salir *to leave, go out*
sentarse (ie) *to sit down*
sentirse (ie) *to feel*
vestirse (i) *to get dressed*

Otras palabras

a veces *sometimes*
amueblado(a) *furnished*
casado(a) *married*
con frecuencia *frequently, often*
de en medio *middle (child)*
de estilo moderno *modern (in style)*
de estilo tradicional *traditionally*
  styled
de tamaño mediano *medium-sized*
de vez en cuando *now and then, from*
  time to time
descompuesto(a) *out of order*

desordenado(a) *messy*
durante *during*
ese/esa *that*
esos/esas *those*
este/esta *this*
estos/estas *these*
hasta tarde *until late*
limpio(a) *clean*
más... que *more . . . than*
mayor *older, oldest*
mejor *better, best*
menor *younger, youngest*
menos... que *less . . . than*
moderno(a) *modern*
normalmente *normally, usually*
nuevo(a) *new*
nunca *never*
ordenado(a) *neat, tidy*
paterno(a) *paternal*
peor *worse, worst*
roto(a) *broken*
siempre *always*
soltero(a) *single*
sucio(a) *dirty*
tan... como *as . . . as*
tanto(a)(s)... como *as much /*
  many . . . as
tarde *late*
temprano *early*

Family members p. 89
Pets p. 89
Descriptions of people p. 92
Rooms of a house p. 101
Furniture and fixtures p. 101
Locations p. 105

For further review, please turn to **Vocabulario temático: español e inglés** at the back of the book.

Go to the ***Puentes*** website for extra vocabulary practice using the Flashcard program.

¡Buen provecho!

Situation Cards: 18, 19, 20, 41, 44, 45, 46, 48, 49, 50, 51, 52, 53, 54, 55, 56

Teaching Tip: Suggested pace is 3–4 class hours for this chapter.

Proficiency: The topic of foods and the functions of ordering food in restaurants and making food purchases are important, basic content for students at the Intermediate-low level of proficiency. Throughout the chapter, the present tense is further reinforced and practiced, as is the art of asking questions. The new grammar—object pronouns—is important for helping students understand aural and written texts and to lay the foundation for more advanced levels of proficiency.

Turn to the *Cuaderno de actividades* for this chapter's reading practice and strategy: Anticipating content.

Turn to the *Cuaderno de actividades* for this chapter's composition practice and writing strategy: Building longer sentences.

OBJETIVOS

Speaking and Listening
▶ Discussing foods, meals, and diet
▶ Ordering a meal in a restaurant
▶ Shopping for food

Culture
▶ Peru
▶ Eating out and delivery

Grammar
▶ Direct objects and direct object pronouns
▶ Indirect objects and indirect object pronouns
▶ Double object pronouns

Video
▶ En la Hacienda Vista Alegre: Episodio 4
▶ Imágenes de Perú

Gramática suplementaria
▶ El presente perfecto

Cuaderno de actividades
Reading
▶ Strategy: Anticipating content

Writing
▶ Strategy: Building longer sentences

Playlist
🌐 www.cengage.com/spanish/puentes

A primera vista

Ojalá que llueva café

¿Las uvas *(grapes)* de Chile? ¿Las bananas de Honduras? En los Estados Unidos importamos muchos productos agrícolas de los países latinoamericanos. La agricultura es un sector muy importante en la economía de estos países y muchos campesinos viven de la tierra *(live off the land)*. La canción "Ojalá que llueva café" *(If only it would rain coffee)* nos recuerda este hecho *(reminds us of this fact)*. ¿De qué país es tu café favorito?

Escucha la canción y completa la primera estrofa *(stanza)* con las palabras de la lista.

campo *countryside*   **queso** *cheese*
miel *honey*   **té** *tea*

Ojalá que llueva café en el _____ campo _____

Que caiga una aguacero de yuca y _____ té _____.

Del cielo una jarina de _____ queso _____ blanco

Y al sur una montaña

de berro y _____ miel _____.

Oh, oh, oh-oh-oh,

Ojalá que llueva café.

HABLANDO DE LA MÚSICA

The Spanish-speaking world abounds with different musical genres or **géneros,** each of which reflects a unique multicultural heritage.

- The Dominican Republic is the birthplace of the catchy dance rhythm called **el merengue.** The three main instruments played in **merengues** reflect the three major cultural influences in that country: the accordion (European), the **tambora** (African drum), and the **güira** (a percussion instrument native to the Dominican Republic).

- Peru is home to **el huayno,** a unique musical style that dates to pre-Columbian times. The main instruments used in **huaynos** are native to the Andean region and include **la quena** (an Andean flute) and **el charango** (a small guitar-like instrument).

- The urban setting of Buenos Aires, Argentina in the late 1800's gave rise to **el tango,** a sensual dance that springs from a fusion of African, Cuban, gaucho, and European elements. The lyrics of tangos are often in **lunfardo,** a dialect of Spanish with many Italian terms—a reflection of the massive Italian immigration of the last half of the 19th century.

Teaching Tip: Supermarkets are now required to list the country of origin of food stuffs. On their next shopping trip, have your students take note of this for the fruits and vegetables they purchase. Make a list on the board of the products and their countries of origin. Alternatively, have one or two students report on their findings when you reach the end of the chapter.

 Puentes playlist available on iTunes

Note: Important coffee-producing countries include Colombia, Mexico, Peru, Guatemala, Honduras, Ecuador, and Costa Rica, among others. Peru is a world leader in fish-related products. Important crops in the Dominican Republic include sugar cane, coffee, rice, and cacao.

Teaching Tip: You may wish to provide a simple paraphrase in English of the stanza and the chorus on the opposite page.

Teaching Tip: Ask students which of these styles they are familiar with and find out which other popular Latin musical genres they might know, such as **salsa.** By way of comparison, point out some musical styles native to the United States and have students speculate on their origins: country music, jazz, blues, gospel music.

Note: "Ojalá que llueva café" is an example of a merengue song.

Note: The **huayno** lives on today in many forms, including a hybrid known as **rock andino.**

JUAN LUIS GUERRA (1957–)

Nacionalidad: dominicano

Obras y premios: "Ojalá que llueva café" fue el primer éxito *(hit)* multinacional de Juan Luis Guerra y su conjunto 4.40. Ganó un Grammy en 1991 por su álbum *Bachata rosa* y otro en 2007 por *La llave de mi corazón*.

De interés: La música de Juan Luis Guerra representa una fusión de merengue con jazz. También popularizó la bachata dominicana y ha escrito baladas. Aparte de la música, dirige la Fundación Juan Luis Guerra, la cual ayuda a los pobres en República Dominicana.

Note: The **bachata** is a unique Dominican variation of the bolero with African influences. Prior to Juan Luis Guerra's popularization, it was often looked down upon as a dance of the lower classes.

Vocabulary: Ombe is an informal, slang word for **hombre; pa' que** is short for **para que;** and **conuco** is a small farm.

OJALÁ QUE LLUEVA CAFÉ
canción de Juan Luis Guerra

Pa' que en el conuco
no se sufra tanto, ay ombe
ojalá que llueva café en el campo
Pa' que en Villa Vásquez
oigan este canto
ojalá que llueva café en el campo
Ojalá que llueva,
ojalá que llueva, ay ombe
ojalá que llueva café en el campo
Ojalá que llueva café
oh, oh, oh-oh-oh...

▸ Talking about some common foods eaten at different meals

▸ Ordering food at restaurants

Grammar:

▸ Direct objects and direct object pronouns

🌐 Go to the *Puentes* website for extra vocabulary practice using the Flashcard program.

The English equivalents of the **Vocabulario temático** sections are found at the back of the book.

Breakfast often consists of a small meal of bread, sweet rolls, and coffee.

Teaching Tip: Introduce the foods by stating some of your likes and dislikes and have students do the same. Use transparencies, drawings, or photographs to support meaning. This lesson contains more vocabulary items than usual so that everyone can discuss his or her favorite foods. In your testing, provide for such choices, rather than testing every item.

Transparency Bank B-1, B-2, N-3, N-4

Proficiency: The vocabulary and functional language of this chapter are key ones for development of the Intermediate level of proficiency. Students need to be able to discuss their preferences, order meals, and make purchases.

More Information: Additional names of fruits are introduced in **Paso 2.**

The midday meal is usually the largest and may consist of 3 to 4 courses.

Vocabulary: Provide additional terms as requested: **las legumbres** (*vegetables*); **los guisantes/los chícharos/las arvejas** (*peas*); **las habichuelas/las judías verdes** (*green beans*); **los espárragos** (*asparagus*); **la calabaza** (*pumpkin*); **las zanahorias** (*carrots*); **las carnes** (*meats*); **el pavo** (*turkey*); **la ternera** (*veal*); **el perro caliente** (*hot dog*); **la salchicha** (*sausage*); **las costillas de puerco/cerdo** (*ribs*); **la carne picada/molida** (*ground beef*); **las bebidas** (*beverages*); **el agua mineral** (*mineral water*); **la limonada** (*lemonade*); **un batido** (*a milkshake*); **la crema de cacahuetes/maní** (*peanut butter*).

Regional Vocabulary: In Mexico, the word for *cake* is **el pastel**; in Costa Rica, **el queque**; and in Colombia, **el ponqué.**

Paso 1

Vocabulario temático

El desayuno *(Breakfast)*

—¿Qué te gusta desayunar?

—Casi siempre como... y bebo...

la mermelada

un vaso de leche

los huevos (revueltos)

el pan tostado

la mantequilla

el jugo de naranja

el cereal

una taza de café con leche y azúcar

El almuerzo *(Lunch / Midday meal)*

—¿Qué almuerzas?

—Por lo general, como... y bebo...

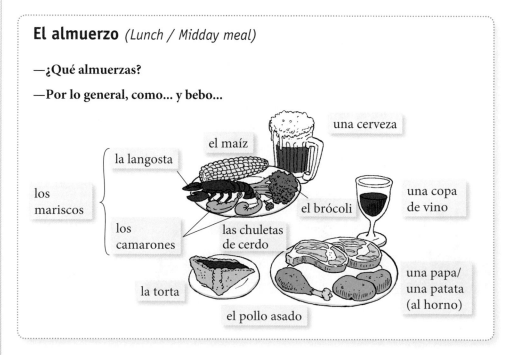

una cerveza

el maíz

la langosta

los mariscos

el brócoli

una copa de vino

los camarones

las chuletas de cerdo

la torta

una papa/ una patata (al horno)

el pollo asado

La merienda (Snack)

—¿Qué meriendas?

—Depende de la hora. Por la mañana, prefiero... Por la tarde, prefiero...

un sándwich de jamón y queso

una taza de té

un helado

un refresco / una gaseosa

una tortilla (de huevos)

unos churros

una hamburguesa

unas galletas

una taza de chocolate

un vaso de té frío

To comment on how delicious the food is, say **¡Qué rico(a)!**

Note: Churros are deep-fried strips of sweet dough sprinkled with sugar. In Spain, **tortillas** are egg omelettes made with potatoes and sometimes onions. In Mexico, an omelette may be called **una tortilla de huevos** since **tortilla** refers to their typical flat, round, bread-like staple.

Teaching Tip: Point out the different verbs for eating: **desayunar, almorzar (ue), merendar (ie), cenar.**

La cena (Supper)

—¿Qué prefieres cenar?

—En los restaurantes pido... En casa como...

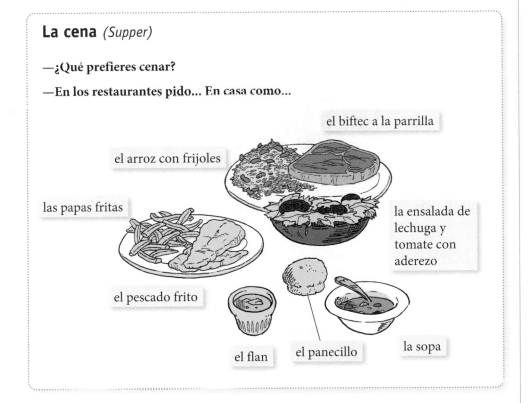

el biftec a la parrilla

el arroz con frijoles

las papas fritas

la ensalada de lechuga y tomate con aderezo

el pescado frito

el flan

el panecillo

la sopa

To wish everyone a good meal, say **¡Buen provecho!** To make a toast with wine or champagne, say **¡Salud!**

Regional Vocabulary: Point out the great variety of foods as well as terms for food. In Peru, the very popular corn-on-the-cob is called **choclo;** soft drinks are called **gaseosas,** and one of the best-known brands is Inca Cola. A common staple, beans, may be called **refritos** in Mexico, **frijoles** in Cuba, or **habichuelas** in Puerto Rico. In Mexico, a **tortilla** is a flat, round corn—or wheat—flour unleavened bread eaten with beans, meat, cheese, and/or vegetables, while in Spain it is an omelette with potatoes and onions. In Spain, fresh fruit juice is called **zumo** and potatoes are called **patatas,** while in many South American countries these would be **jugo** and **papas,** respectively. In some South American countries, **patata** is understood to be a sweet potato.

CD1
Track 27

Estrategia *Reclassifying information*

When you need to memorize a large number of new words, you will recall them more easily if you classify them into meaningful categories. The vocabulary in this section, for example, is organized by meals. You could also classify these words by food types: **carnes** *(meats);* **pescados y mariscos** *(seafood);* **vegetales** or **verduras** *(vegetables)* **y frutas** *(fruits);* **postres** *(desserts);* and **bebidas** *(beverages).*

Try re-categorizing the new vocabulary according to food types. Which system of classification do you find more meaningful? Why? It does not matter which system you use as long as it helps you remember the information.

Ponerlo a prueba

4-1 En el restaurante La Estancia. Tus amigos Omar, Adriana y Hugo están en el restaurante La Estancia. ¿Qué piden *(do they order)?* Escucha su conversación con el camarero y observa bien el dibujo. Escribe las letras que corresponden a la comida.

1. Adriana pide _(sopa-f)_ , _(tortilla-p)_ , _(ensalada-k)_ , _(agua mineral-c)_ y _(flan-t)_ .

2. Omar pide _(biftec-j)_ , _(arroz con frijoles-o)_ , _(brócoli-m)_ , _(helado-r)_ y _(cerveza-a)_ .

3. Hugo pide _(pollo-h)_ , _(papas-n)_ , _(ensalada-k)_ , _(copa de vino-e)_ y _(torta-q)_ .

4-2 Categorías. ¿Qué palabras no corresponden a la categoría indicada? Hay dos en cada ítem.

MODELO   LAS CARNES: la hamburguesa / el jamón /(el pescado)/(la langosta)/ el biftec

1. EL DESAYUNO:(la ensalada con aderezo)/ el cereal con bananas / el jugo de naranja / (las chuletas a la parrilla)/ el pan tostado

2. LOS VEGETALES: el brócoli /(el panecillo)/ el maíz /(los camarones)/ la lechuga

3. LAS BEBIDAS: los refrescos /(las papas)/ la cerveza / el jugo de naranja / (la mantequilla)

4. LOS POSTRES *(DESSERTS):*(el arroz con frijoles)/ el flan / la torta / (los huevos revueltos)/ el helado

4-3 Adivina la comida. Con dos or tres compañeros(as) de clase, tomen turnos para describir y advinar las comidas en los dibujos. Sigan los modelos.

Teaching Tip 4-3: Add a few more examples to model the different ways descriptions may be made; have students guess the answers: **Es algo que comemos el día de nuestro cumpleaños. Es un vegetal blanco que se come al horno o frito. Comemos esta comida en el desayuno, con leche y bananas.**

MODELO

> Tú: Es un plato *(dish)* de huevos y queso.
>
> Compañero(a) 1: Yo sé. Es una tortilla.
>
> Compañero(a) 2: Comemos esta comida por la mañana con mermelada o mantequilla.
>
> Tú: Es el pan tostado.

4-4 ¿Qué comemos? Habla con un(a) compañero(a) de clase sobre sus comidas preferidas. Completa las oraciones y menciona **una variedad** de comidas y bebidas.

Proficiency: Students at this level profit greatly from open-ended activities. Their success depends greatly on the model you provide. By tailoring your language to their level, you set the standard for students to imitate. A good way to do this is to read the model aloud first, then provide your own, additional, personalized model.

MODELO

> Tú: Cuando tengo mucha sed, me gusta beber <u>agua o una bebida energética</u>. ¿Y tú?
>
> Tu compañero(a): Yo prefiero beber <u>refrescos</u>, como la <u>Coca-Cola</u>. A veces bebo <u>agua</u>.

1. Cuando estoy en un restaurante de comida rápida, prefiero comer _____ y beber _____. ¿Y tú?

2. Cuando estoy en un restaurante elegante, por lo general pido _____ . ¿Y tú?

3. Mi desayuno favorito consiste en _____ . ¿Y tú? ¿Qué desayunas?

4. Si tengo hambre entre *(between)* comidas meriendo _____. Y si tengo sed, bebo _____. ¿Y tú? ¿Qué meriendas?

5. Detesto comer _____. ¿Y tú? ¿Qué detestas comer?

4-5 Mis restaurantes favoritos. Habla con dos o tres compañeros(as) sobre sus restaurantes favoritos.

MODELO

> Uno de mis restaurantes favoritos es Grecian Gardens. Tienen ensaladas muy grandes y deliciosas. También me gustan sus pastas italianas. Los platos de pollo con queso parmesán son muy ricos. Una comida típica allí cuesta menos de veinte dólares y el servicio es bastante bueno.
>
> ¿Cuál es uno de tus restaurantes favoritos?

More Information: These restaurant phrases contain examples of direct and indirect object pronouns, which are explained in detail later in this and the next **paso**. For now, let the sentences serve as models of this grammar and postpone explanations. At this level, students will not be able to use object pronouns in spontaneous speech. However, it is important for them to understand their meaning and use so that they can recognize them when listening and reading.

Teaching Tip: To continue to build accuracy in the present tense verbs, point out the stem-changing verbs in the **Vocabulario temático** and refresh students' memories on how to conjugate them: **probar (ue)** (to taste, to try); **recomendar (ie)** (to recommend); **pedir (i)** (to order, ask for).

Teaching Tip: Role-play the lines for the waiter and customer using the menu in Transparency N-1 or with a menu you bring to class.

Meals are eaten in courses: **los entremeses** *(appetizers)*, **el primer plato** *(first course)*, **el segundo plato/ el plato principal** *(main course)*, **el postre** *(dessert)*.

Regional Vocabulary: Depending on the country, a menu may be called **el menú** or **la carta**. In Peru, many restaurants have an economical set menu, similar to a daily special, called **el menú**; one may also order off the regular menu, which is called **la carta**. In Peru, a waiter is called **el mozo**, although that term may be offensive in Colombia and some other countries. Perhaps the "safest" term for waiter is **mesero**.

Vocabulary: Lomo saltado is similar to a stir-fry of beef strips, onion, fried potatoes, and tomatoes served over rice. **Palta rellena** is avocado stuffed with chicken or tuna salad. Highland cuisine often includes potatoes, such as **papa a la huancaína** (boiled potatoes with a milk and cheese sauce), while fish dishes such as **ceviche** (raw fish marinated in lemon juice with seasonings) and **corvina** (sea bass/bream) are popular along the coast. **Sopa a la criolla** contains bits of beef, thin noodles, egg, and vegetables in a spicy broth.

Usually the waiter will not bring out the check until you request it. In some countries, a service charge or tip is included in the bill.

Vocabulario temático

En el restaurante
Antes de pedir *(Before ordering):*

CLIENTE: **¡Camarero! Necesito *un menú*, por favor.**

CAMARERO: **Aquí *lo* tiene.**

CLIENTE: **¿Cuál es el plato del día?**

CAMARERO: **Hoy tenemos *lomo saltado.***

CLIENTE: **¿Qué ingredientes tiene el *lomo saltado*?**

CAMARERO: **Tiene *lomo de res, cebollas, papas, tomates y arroz.***

CLIENTE: **Quiero probar algo típico. ¿Qué me recomienda?**

CAMARERO: **Le recomiendo *el lomo saltado o la palta rellena.***

CLIENTE: **¿Tienen *corvina* hoy?**

CAMARERO: **No, *la* servimos solo los sábados.**

Sí, por supuesto.

Para pedir *(To place an order):*

CAMARERO: **¿Qué desea pedir?**

CLIENTE: **De primer plato, quiero *sopa a la criolla.* De plato principal, deseo *lomo saltado.***

CAMARERO: **¿Y para beber?**

CLIENTE: **Para beber, quisiera *una copa de vino.***

CAMARERO: **¿Quiere algo de postre?**

CLIENTE: **De postre, voy a probar *el flan.***

CAMARERO: **¿Necesita algo más?**

CLIENTE: **¿Me puede traer *unos cubitos de hielo*?**
la sal
la pimienta

Después de comer *(After eating):*

CLIENTE: **La cuenta, por favor.**

CAMARERO: *Se la traigo enseguida.*

CLIENTE: **¿Está incluida la propina en la cuenta?**

CAMARERO: **No, no está incluida.**

Sí, está incluida.

El cubierto *(Place setting)*

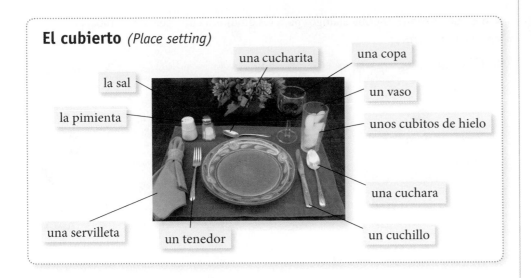

la sal
la pimienta
una cucharita
una copa
un vaso
unos cubitos de hielo
una cuchara
un cuchillo
una servilleta
un tenedor

Ponerlo a prueba

CD1
Track 28

4-6 ¿Qué quieren los clientes? Escucha las cuatro conversaciones. Tienen lugar *(They take place)* en un restaurante. ¿Cuál es la idea principal de cada conversación? Completa las oraciones con la información correcta.

1. En la primera conversación la señora quiere _____.
   a. una recomendación   b. más pan   c. información sobre la comida

2. En la segunda conversación, un señor quiere _____.
   a. pagar *(pay)*   b. una mesa   c. una reservación

3. En la tercera conversación, una señora _____.
   a. pide una sopa típica
   b. tiene un problema con la sopa
   c. necesita una cuchara para la sopa

4. En la cuarta conversación, Ana y Jacinto _____.
   a. desayunan   b. meriendan   c. cenan

4-7 Muchos clientes. Marcos es camarero en el Restaurante San Remo, en Lima, Perú. ¿Cómo les responde él a los clientes? Relaciona las dos columnas de una manera lógica.

Note: **Mazamorra morada** is a typical Peruvian dessert made with purple corn meal and dried fruits. **Papa a la huancaína** consists of boiled potatoes with a milk and cheese sauce.

Teaching Tip: Say a line from the **Vocabulario temático** and have students identify who would say it: **el camarero** or **el cliente**. For example: **¿Qué me recomienda? (el cliente); ¿Están listos para pedir? (el camarero); Tráigame la cuenta. (el cliente);** etc.

Los clientes:

_b_ 1. ¿Cuál es el plato del día?

_e_ 2. Soy vegetariano. ¿Qué me recomienda?

_c_ 3. ¿Me puede traer unos cubitos de hielo para este refresco?

_f_ 4. ¿Qué ingredientes tiene la mazamorra morada?

_a_ 5. El café está frío.

_g_ 6. La cuenta, por favor.

Marcos, el camarero:

a. Lo siento. Enseguida le traigo otro más caliente.

b. Hoy tenemos pollo asado con papas.

c. Se los traigo enseguida.

d. Tenemos jugos, gaseosas, agua mineral, cerveza y vino.

e. La papa a la huancaína tiene leche y queso, pero no tiene carne.

f. Es un postre muy rico de maíz con muchas frutas.

g. Aquí la tiene. La propina ya está incluida.

Expansion 4-8: After students have written their dialogues, select three groups to present their dialogue to the class. The class listens and identifies which of the scenes is being dramatized.

4-8 ¿Qué desean? Escribe diálogos para los dibujos a continuación. Trabaja con un(a) compañero(a).

1.

2.

3.

Teaching Tip 4-9: Before students start work on their role plays, ask questions about the menu: **Si quieres hacer una reservación para comer en el chifa, ¿a qué número debes llamar? ¿Cuántas categorías hay en el menú? ¿Cuáles son? ¿Qué platos conoces? ¿Qué platos no conoces? ¿Puedes adivinar** (guess) **qué son? ¿Cuál es el plato más caro de todos? ¿Cuál es el más barato? ¿Cuándo hay un buffet? ¿A qué hora empieza el buffet? ¿Cuánto cuesta?**

Note: Chaufa is chow-fan, or fried rice; **taufu** is tofu, which is also written **tofu**.

Note: At the time of publication, one Peruvian **nuevo sol** was worth about 32 cents.

4-9 El Restaurante Wa Lok. En Perú, la comida china es muy popular. Aquí tienes el menú de un "chifa"—un restaurante peruano-chino. Con un(a) compañero(a), dramatiza una conversación entre el (la) camarero(a) y el (la) cliente(a).

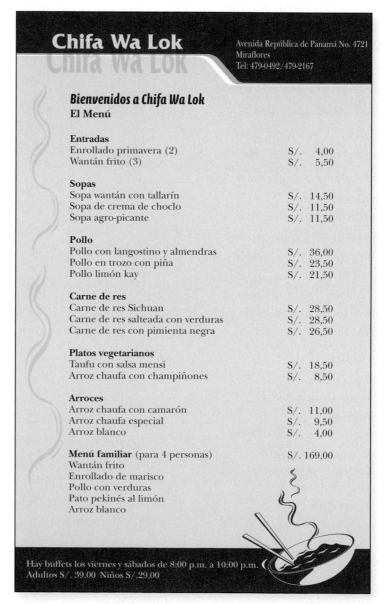

Chifa Wa Lok

Avenida República de Panamá No. 4721
Miraflores
Tel: 479-0492/479-2167

Bienvenidos a Chifa Wa Lok
El Menú

Entradas
Enrollado primavera (2) — S/. 4,00
Wantán frito (3) — S/. 5,50

Sopas
Sopa wantán con tallarín — S/. 14,50
Sopa de crema de choclo — S/. 11,50
Sopa agro-picante — S/. 11,50

Pollo
Pollo con langostino y almendras — S/. 36,00
Pollo en trozo con piña — S/. 23,50
Pollo limón kay — S/. 21,50

Carne de res
Carne de res Sichuan — S/. 28,50
Carne de res salteada con verduras — S/. 28,50
Carne de res con pimienta negra — S/. 26,50

Platos vegetarianos
Taufu con salsa mensi — S/. 18,50
Arroz chaufa con champiñones — S/. 8,50

Arroces
Arroz chaufa con camarón — S/. 11,00
Arroz chaufa especial — S/. 9,50
Arroz blanco — S/. 4,00

Menú familiar (para 4 personas) — S/. 169,00
Wantán frito
Enrollado de marisco
Pollo con verduras
Pato pekinés al limón
Arroz blanco

Hay buffets los viernes y sábados de 8:00 p.m. a 10:00 p.m.
Adultos S/. 39,00 Niños S/. 29,00

Gramática

Los complementos directos

CD1
Track 29

Listen to the conversation between the waitress and the customer while you read the dialogue. The words in boldface type are direct object pronouns. The first one—**los**—refers to **camarones**. What does **La** refer to in this conversation?

CAMARERA: ¿Cómo quiere los camarones: fritos o a la parrilla?

CLIENTE: **Los** quiero fritos, por favor.

CAMARERA: ¿Y la ensalada? ¿**La** quiere con aderezo italiano o francés?

CLIENTE: Bueno... con aderezo francés.

A. Los complementos directos. A complete sentence always has a subject (the person or thing performing the action) and a conjugated verb (the action). It may contain an optional element, such as a *direct object*.

The direct object (**el complemento directo**) receives the action of the verb. It is the word that answers the questions *What?* or *Whom?* and may refer to a thing or a person.

Voy a probar **el flan**.
I'm going to try the flan. (**What** am I going to try? The **flan**: a direct object.)

No veo **a nuestro camarero**.
I don't see our waiter. (**Whom** do I not see? Our **waiter**: a direct object.)

B. Los complementos directos pronominales. To avoid sounding repetitious, we often replace direct object nouns with direct object pronouns (**complementos directos pronominales**).

—¿Cómo quieres **el café**?   *How do you want your coffee?* (What do you want? Coffee/**café**: a direct object noun.)

—**Lo** tomo con azúcar.   *I take it with sugar.* (The direct object pronoun *it/***lo** replaces the direct object noun, coffee.)

In Spanish, direct object pronouns agree in gender (**masculino, femenino**) and number (**singular, plural**) with the nouns they replace.

—¿Haces **las galletas** con frecuencia?   *Do you make cookies very often?*

—Sí, **las** hago todas las semanas.   *Yes, I make them* (feminine, plural) *every week.*

—¿Ves a **nuestra camarera**?   *Do you see our waitress?*

—No, no **la** veo.   *No, I don't see her* (feminine, singular).

Los complementos directos pronominales

me	me	us	nos
you (sing., fam.)	te	you (pl., fam. in Spain)	os
you (sing., formal)	lo, la	you (pl.)	los, las
it	lo, la	them	los, las
him	lo		
her	la		

Heinle Grammar Tutorial: Direct object pronouns

Proficiency: This grammar topic is presented for student understanding and recognition. Spontaneous use of direct object pronouns in speech develops at much higher levels of proficiency. However, working with more structured activities, such as those here, helps students understand sentence structure better and will increase their ability to interpret written texts more accurately.

Answer: ensalada

Grammar: Point out to students that when the direct object is a person, it is preceded by the "personal **a**."

C. La posición en la oración. In English, direct object pronouns are always placed after the verb, but in Spanish the placement depends on the kind of verb used in the sentence.

> ▸ Place a direct object pronoun directly in front of a single, conjugated verb.
>
> —¿Necesitas el menú?   *Do you need the menu?*
> —No, gracias, no **lo** necesito.   *No, thanks, I don't need **it**.*
>
> ▸ With a verb phrase (conjugated verb + infinitive), place the direct object pronoun directly before the conjugated verb or attach it to the end of the infinitive. **Never** place object pronouns between the two verbs.
>
> —¿Vas a servir la torta ahora?   *Are you going to serve the cake now?*
> —No, **la** voy a servir un poco más tarde.
> —No, voy a servir**la** un poco más tarde.   *No, I'm going to serve **it** a little later.*

Ponerlo a prueba

4-10 Un poco de análisis. Lee las conversaciones. En cada conversación, identifica el complemento directo pronominal *(direct object pronoun)* y su antecedente *(the noun it refers to or replaces)*.

> MODELO   SRA. DOMINGO: Necesito un menú, por favor.
>   CAMARERO: Aquí lo tiene.
>   el complemento directo pronominal **lo**; el antecedente **un menú**

1. SR. DOMINGO: La cuenta, por favor.
   CAMARERO: Aquí la tiene.
   el complemento directo pronominal __la__; el antecedente __la cuenta__

2. SR. CARRERAS: ¿Compramos más jugo de naranja?
   SRA. CARRERAS: No, no lo necesitamos.
   el complemento directo pronominal __lo__; el antecedente __el jugo__

3. PACO: ¿Cómo prefieres la pizza? ¿Con salchicha *(sausage)* o con salami?
   SILVIA: ¿Por qué no la pedimos con salchicha?
   el complemento directo pronominal __la__; el antecedente __la pizza__

4. JUANITO: ¡Ay, mamá! ¡Frijoles otra vez!
   MAMÁ: ¿No quieres comerlos? Está bien; puedes comer estas espinacas *(spinach)*.
   el complemento directo pronominal __los__; el antecedente __los frijoles__

5. RITA: Necesito otra servilleta. Hmmm... ¿Dónde está nuestra camarera?
   PENÉLOPE: No sé. No la veo.
   el complemento directo pronominal __la__; el antecedente __nuestra camarera__

4-11 Más complementos directos. Completa las conversaciones con el complemento directo pronominal más lógico: **me, te, nos, lo, la, los** o **las.**

1. CAMARERA: ¿Cómo quiere su hamburguesa?
   PATRICIA: __La__ quiero con lechuga y tomate, por favor.

2. SR. GRISSINI: ¿Dónde está nuestro camarero? No __lo__ veo.
   SRA. GRISSINI: Mira, aquí viene.

3. **PAPÁ:** Hija, ¿no vas a comer los huevos revueltos? Están muy ricos *(delicious)*.
   MARILÚ: No, papá, no voy a comer _los_. Tienen mucha grasa *(fat)*.

4. **JAIME:** ¿Vienes a mi fiesta esta noche *(tonight)*?
   MANOLO: Lo siento, no puedo. Mi novia regresa a su casa esta noche, y necesito llevar_la_ al aeropuerto.

5. **ALICIA:** ¿Me llamas esta noche?
   JORGE: Sí, _te_ llamo a las ocho.

6. **ROSITA:** ¿Quieren tú y Alejandro comer en casa conmigo el domingo?
   CLARA: Lo siento, pero no podemos. Los abuelos siempre _nos_ invitan a comer en su casa los domingos.

4-12 En el restaurante. Mira el dibujo y contesta las preguntas con oraciones completas. Incluye un complemento directo pronominal en las respuestas.

> **MODELO** ¿Quién sirve el café?
> Lo sirve Jaime.

1. ¿Quién paga la cuenta?
2. ¿Quién llama al camarero?
3. ¿Quiénes comen helado?
4. ¿Quién toma leche?
5. ¿Quiénes beben vino?
6. ¿Quién pide pollo?
7. ¿Quién desea camarones?
8. ¿Quién come torta?

 4-13 Las preferencias. Habla con un(a) compañero(a) de tus preferencias culinarias. Contesta las preguntas con oraciones completas. Incluye un complemento directo pronominal.

> **MODELO** —¿Cómo prefieres **las hamburguesas,** con queso o sin *(without)* queso?
> —**Las** prefiero con queso. / **Las** prefiero sin queso. ¿Y tú?

1. ¿Cómo comes **las hamburguesas,** con tomate o sin tomate?
2. ¿Cómo tomas **el té frío,** con azúcar o sin azúcar?
3. ¿Cómo prefieres **las ensaladas,** con aderezo francés o con aderezo italiano?
4. ¿Cómo comes **el cereal,** con bananas o sin bananas?
5. ¿Cómo prefieres **los huevos,** revueltos o fritos?
6. ¿Cómo tomas **el café,** con azúcar, con leche o solo *(black)*?
7. (Haz una pregunta original / *Ask another question.*)

Teaching Tip 4-11: After checking the correct answers, have students contrast and explain the placement of the pronouns in items 3 and 5.

Answers 4-12: 1. El Sr. Gómez la paga./ La paga el Sr. Gómez. 2. Amadeo lo llama./ Lo llama Amadeo. 3. Lourdes y Marina lo comen./Lo comen Lourdes y Marina. 4. Marina la toma./La toma Marina. 5. Ramona y Claudio lo beben./Lo beben Ramona y Claudio. 6. Claudio lo pide./ Lo pide Claudio. 7. Ramona los desea./ Los desea Ramona. 8. Marina la come./La come Marina.

Grammar: When replying to a question with **¿quién?** it is common to place the subject (i.e., the answer to the question) last: **¿Quién bebe leche? La bebe Manolo.**

Teaching Tip: Cut out pictures of foods from magazines or print them from the Internet and distribute them among the class members. Make statements such as: **Necesito el helado. Quiero los sándwiches.** The student with the corresponding pictures hands them to you and says: **Aquí lo (la/ los/las) tiene.**

Teaching Tip 4-13: Present the model to your class, complete the first item with several students, then have pairs complete the remaining items. For follow-up, call on individuals to respond to additional questions such as: **¿Cómo comes las papas al horno *(baked)*, con mantequilla o con margarina? ¿Cómo prefieres el helado, con fruta o sin fruta? ¿Cómo prefieres los camarones, fritos o al vapor *(steamed)*? ¿Cómo tomas los refrescos, con hielo o sin hielo?**

Expansion 4-13: Have students make up similar questions and interview you on your preferences.

Puente cultural

🌐 Go to the **Puentes** Premium Website to view the **Puente cultural** interviews.

¿Qué comen cuando no hay nada en el refrigerador?

Romeo Wong

🌐 **PERÚ**

Voy a un restaurante a comer pollo a la brasa con papas o comida china. Y siempre hay un mercado abierto que tiene frutas y comida fresca. Normalmente me gusta cocinar pollo, arroz, papas, ensaladas.

Rosilennys Mariel Inoa

🌐 **REPÚBLICA DOMINICANA**

Vamos a restaurantes típicos donde podemos encontrar comida dominicana, por ejemplo, tostones, niño envuelto, asopado, sancocho... Un restaurante muy popular es el Pica Pollo.

Note: Sancocho, stew of meat, spices and vegetables, is considered a culinary treat and is often prepared for special occasions. **Niño envuelto** is a rice and meat mixture that is wrapped in a cabbage leaf and cooked in tomato sauce. **Tostones** are fried plantains. **Asopado** (also called **asopao**) is a thick soup of rice and meat or seafood. The popular restaurant chain Pica Pollo specializes in crispy breaded fried chicken.

Clara Mengolini

🌐 **ARGENTINA**

En Argentina pedimos empanadas. Es muy popular el "delivery" de empanadas, que son como "hot pockets" pero el relleno puede ser muy variado: choclo, carne, queso, queso y jamón, queso y cebolla, pollo, etcétera.

Teaching Tip: Form groups of three students, with each person responsible for reading and providing a summary of the information on one country. Then have the group decide what information they would include for the U.S.A.

Comparando las costumbres. Trabaja con un(a) compañero(a). Lee la información y completa la tabla.

	En Perú	En la República Dominicana	En Argentina	En los Estados Unidos
¿Qué comen cuando no hay nada en el refrigerador?				

Paso 2

Vocabulario temático

En el mercado *(In a market)*

VENDEDOR: **¿Qué desea Ud.?**

CLIENTA: **¿Me puede dar *un kilo de manzanas*?**

VENDEDOR: **¿Necesita Ud. algo más?**

CLIENTA: **Sí, quiero *un melón*.**

VENDEDOR: **Se *lo* pongo enseguida. ¿Algo más?**

CLIENTA: **No, gracias. Eso es todo. ¿Cuánto le debo?**

un kilo ~2 lbs.
100 gramos ~4 oz.
un litro ~a quart

Vocabulary: Empacar may also be used in this context, instead of **poner**.

Otras frutas *(Other fruits)*

unas bananas/
unos plátanos

unos melocotones/
unos duraznos

unas peras

unas fresas

una sandía

una piña

Note: The metric equivalencies are meant only for estimates. The more precise measures are 1 liter = 1.05 quarts and 1 kilogram = 2.2 lbs. You may wish to provide Spanish terms for the English system: **galón, cuarto, libra, onza.**

Transparency Bank I-5, I-6, I-7, I-8

Otros comestibles *(Other foods)*

un paquete
de galletas

un litro
de leche

una docena
de huevos

una barra de pan

una bolsa
de arroz

una botella de
agua mineral

un frasco de
mayonesa

Teaching Tip: Introduce the vocabulary with transparencies or with inexpensive toy foods. Provide other terms as desired: **toronja/pomelo** *(grapefruit),* **limón** *(lemon),* **limón verde** *(lime),* **cerezas** *(cherries),* **ciruela** *(plum),* **coliflor** *(cauliflower),* **guisantes** or **arvejas** *(peas),* **judías verdes** or **habichuelas** *(green beans),* **zanahorias** *(carrots),* **pepinos** *(cucumbers).*

Teaching Tip: Assign the first two activities for homework.

CD1
Track 30

Ponerlo a prueba

4-14 Servicio a domicilio. La Sra. Santana habla por teléfono con Roberto, el empleado de un pequeño supermercado. Escucha su conversación. Escribe los datos necesarios para llenar *(to fill out)* el formulario.

Supermercado Sánchez
Entrega a domicilio

Nombre y apellidos : Amalia Santana
Dirección : Calle Luna, 58
Teléfono : 29-78-03

Artículo	Cantidad (Quantity)
pollo	uno
biftec	dos kilos
melocotones	1 kilo
lechuga	una
mayonesa	un frasco
pan	una barra

Note: In both English and Spanish, we speak of a "head," or **cabeza,** of lettuce or cabbage. A "clove of garlic" is **un diente de ajo,** a "tooth of garlic."

4-15 Los ingredientes. ¿Qué ingredientes necesitas para preparar cada plato? Completa los espacios en blanco con las palabras más lógicas de la lista.

MODELO huevos revueltos: una docena de _huevos_, un paquete de _mantequilla_, sal y _pimienta_

Answers 4-15: 1. piña, fresas, bananas; 2. carne picada, queso, salsa picante; 3. pan, jamón, mayonesa; 4. arroz, leche, vainilla

arroz	fresas	mayonesa	queso
bananas	jamón	pan	salsa picante
carne picada	leche	piña	vainilla

1. una macedonia *(salad)* de frutas: una _____, medio kilo de _____, dos o tres _____
2. los tacos: un paquete de tortillas, un kilo de _____, una lechuga, cien gramos de _____, un frasco de _____

Teaching Tip: List the ingredients for a popular dish. Have students guess what you are "cooking." For example: **medio litro de leche, cuatro huevos, un poco de azúcar, vainilla = flan.**

3. unos sándwiches: una barra de _____, un kilo de _____, lechuga, un frasco de _____ o mostaza *(mustard)*
4. el arroz con leche *(rice pudding)*: una bolsa de _____, un litro de _____, unos huevos, una pequeña botella de _____

Expansion 4-16: For additional practice, bring to class plastic fruits and vegetables and play the role of shopkeeper and customer.

4-16 Hacer la compra. Estás en Lima, Perú, donde vives en un apartamento con otros estudiantes. Esta semana te toca *(it's your turn)* comprar los comestibles *(groceries)*. Con un(a) compañero(a), mira los dibujos en la página 143 y prepara diálogos como los del modelo. Nota: En Perú, la moneda es el nuevo sol; hay 100 céntimos en un nuevo sol.

MODELO
—¿Qué desea Ud.?
—Necesito un litro de leche y una bolsa de arroz.
—¿Quiere algo más?
—Sí. ¿Me puede dar un kilo de plátanos?
—Sí, cómo no. ¿Algo más?
—No, gracias, eso es todo. ¿Cuánto le debo?
—Ocho soles con cincuenta céntimos.

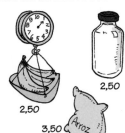

Answers 4-16: Price totals are 1. 43 soles, 50 centavos; 2. 60 soles, 50 centavos.

Note: At the time of publication, the exchange rate was $1.00 = 3,20 nuevos soles.

1.

7,50

4,00

2,00

3,50

Arroz

5,00

21,50

2.

25,00

15,00

8,50

3,50

6,00

2,50

 4-17 En nuestra ciudad. Habla con dos o tres compañeros de clase sobre las tiendas y los supermercados cerca del campus. Comenten estas preguntas.

- ¿Qué supermercado cerca del campus es el más limpio? ¿Cuál tiene los mejores precios (*prices*)?

- ¿Qué alimentos (*foods*) compran los estudiantes con más frecuencia?

- ¿Dónde compras tú los comestibles (*groceries*)? ¿Por qué? ¿Qué frutas compras con más frecuencia?

COMENTARIO CULTURAL *El mercado*

En el momento de comprar comestibles, ¿prefieres ir a un supermercado, al mercado o a una bodega (*small grocery store*)? ¿Por qué?

Uno de los centros comerciales y sociales de cada ciudad es el mercado. Allí se puede comprar de todo: frutas y verduras, carnes y pescados, productos para limpiar la casa y mucho más. Ya que (*Since*) los

hispanos aprecian muchísimo la comida fresca, en algunas familias se va al mercado todos los días. Con el rápido ritmo de la vida actual, muchos prefieren la comodidad (*convenience*) del supermercado.

Aunque los supermercados son muy populares, casi todos los barrios tienen su bodega o pequeña tienda de comestibles. También hay muchas tiendas pequeñas que se especializan en una categoría de comida: por ejemplo, en una carnicería se puede comprar biftec o carne picada (*ground beef*). ¿Qué se puede comprar en una pescadería?, ¿en una panadería?, ¿en una pastelería?

Teaching Tip: After students read the **Comentario cultural,** name various foods and ask in which small store one would purchase them: **una torta (en la pastelería/panadería); unas chuletas de cerdo (en la carnicería),** etc.

Gramática

Los complementos indirectos

Listen to and read the conversation between a customer and a shopkeeper. Then focus on the first sentence and identify the two direct objects. What do you think **me** means in this sentence? In the second line, to whom does **le** refer?

CLIENTE: ¿**Me** puede dar un litro de leche y una barra de pan?

VENDEDOR: ¡Sí, cómo no! ¿**Le** pongo algo más?

CLIENTE: No, gracias. Eso es todo.

A. Los complementos indirectos. While a complete sentence must always have a subject and a verb, it can also contain other elements, such as indirect object pronouns.

> An indirect object (**el complemento indirecto**) tells *to whom* or *for whom* something is done and usually refers to a person. A sentence with an indirect object often has a direct object, too.
>
> **What** do I serve? *Peruvian specialities*   DIRECT OBJECT
>
> Siempre **les** sirvo *especialidades peruanas* a mis invitados.
>
> **To whom** do I serve this food? *To my guests*   INDIRECT OBJECT

B. Los complementos pronominales. Indirect objects may be nouns (for the children, to Sam, for my mother) or pronouns (to me, for us, to her). Here are the indirect object pronouns in Spanish and English.

Los complementos indirectos pronominales			
to/for me	**me**	to/for us	**nos**
to/for you *(sing., fam.)*	**te**	to/for you *(pl., fam. in Spain)*	**os**
to/for you *(sing., formal)*	**le**	to/for you *(pl.)*	**les**
to/for him or her	**le**	to/for them	**les**

C. La posición en la oración. Indirect object pronouns follow the same rules of placement as the direct object pronouns.

> ▸ Place an indirect object pronoun in front of a single, conjugated verb.
>
> ¿Cuánto **le** debo?   *How much do I owe **you**?*
>
> ▸ With a verb phrase consisting of conjugated verb + infinitive, place the pronoun before the conjugated verb or attached to the infinitive.
>
> ¿**Me** puede traer un tenedor? }
> ¿Puede traer**me** un tenedor? }   *Can you bring **me** a fork?*

D. La duplicación. In Spanish, indirect object pronouns and the indirect objects they refer to often appear in the same sentence. When saying a sentence with "to/for person(s)," follow these simple rules.

► Use **le** together with "**a** + singular noun/name."
Siempre **le** sirvo platos vegetarianos **a María.**
*I always serve vegetarian dishes **to María.** / I always serve **María** vegetarian dishes.*

► Use **les** together with "**a** + plural noun/names."
Les voy a servir corvina **a mis invitados.**
*I'm going to serve sea bass **to my guests.** /I'm going to serve **my guests** sea bass.*

Ponerlo a prueba

4-18 Más análisis. Lee las oraciones a continuación. Identifica los complementos directos e indirectos.

Teaching Tip: Assign the first two activities for homework.

> MODELO CLIENTE EN EL RESTAURANTE: ¿Me puede traer una cuchara? Esta está sucia.
>
> Complemento directo: <u>una cuchara</u>   Complemento indirecto: <u>me</u>

1. CLIENTE EN EL RESTAURANTE: Por favor, ¿nos puede traer más pan?

   Complemento directo: _____pan_____   Complemento indirecto: _____nos_____

2. CAMARERO EN EL RESTAURANTE: Les recomiendo a Uds. el arroz con camarones. Está muy rico hoy.

   Complemento directo: __el arroz (con camarones)__   Complemento indirecto: __Les/a Uds.__

3. CLIENTE EN EL MERCADO: ¿Me puede dar dos kilos de naranjas?

   Complemento directo: __dos kilos (de naranjas)__   Complemento indirecto: _____Me_____

4. VENDEDOR EN EL MERCADO: ¿Le pongo unas manzanas también?

   Complemento directo: __unas manzanas__   Complemento indirecto: _____Le_____

5. TU ABUELA, EN CASA: ¿Te sirvo más café?

   Complemento directo: __(más) café__   Complemento indirecto: _____Te_____

4-19 Escenas de la vida. Completa los diálogos con los complementos indirectos pronominales más lógicos: **me, te, le, nos, les.**

1. En la bodega

CLIENTE:	¿ __Me__ puede dar dos litros de jugo de naranja?
EMPLEADO:	¡Claro que sí! ¿Algo más?

2. En el mercado

SRA. GUALTIERI:	Quiero dos kilos de manzanas, por favor.
VENDEDOR:	Muy bien, Sra. Gualtieri. ¿ __Le__ pongo un kilo de uvas también? Tienen buen precio.

3. En el restaurante

JAIME, CON SU NOVIA:	Por favor ¿ __nos/me__ puede traer una botella de vino?
CAMARERO:	Sí, señor. ¿Blanco o tinto?

4. En el restaurante

ALICE, CON SU AMIGA:	Queremos probar un plato típico. ¿Qué nos recomienda?
CAMARERO:	__Les__ recomiendo la corvina *(sea bass)*. Está muy fresca hoy.

5. En la casa de la abuela

JAIME Y JAVIER, LOS NIETOS:	Abuelita, ¿puedes hacer__nos__ una torta?
ABUELITA:	Sí, ¡si se portan bien *(if you behave)*!

4-20 Las costumbres. ¿Qué alimentos *(foods)* asocias con estas situaciones? Compara tus ideas con las de un(a) compañero(a) de clase. Sigan el modelo. (**¡Ojo!** Usa un complemento indirecto pronominal en cada oración.)

MODELO   Cuando estoy enfermo(a) / mi madre *preparar*

TÚ:	Cuando estoy enfermo(a), mi madre **me** prepara sopa de pollo.
TU COMPAÑERO(A):	Cuando estoy enfermo(a), mi madre **me** prepara licuados de fruta *(fruit smoothies)*.

1. Cuando estoy enfermo(a) / con frecuencia mis padres *dar*

2. Cuando mis amigos y yo comemos en la cafetería de la universidad / con frecuencia *(ellos) servir*

3. Cuando invito a mis amigos(as) a comer en mi casa / generalmente *(yo) preparar*

4. Cuando quiero impresionar a mi novio(a) con mis talentos culinarios / *(yo) servir*

5. Cuando mi hermanito(a) no quiere comer los vegetales / *(yo) decir*

4-21 La comida y el cariño. Muchas veces nuestros amigos y nuestros familiares *(family members)* nos compran alimentos especiales, o nos preparan nuestras comidas favoritas, para demostrarnos su cariño *(their affection)*. Con dos o tres compañeros(as), da ejemplos de esta costumbre.

MODELO   Mi abuela siempre **me** prepara galletas con chispas de chocolate *(chocolate chips)*. Yo **le** compro chocolates "Godiva" a mi novia en ocasiones especiales.

Gramática

Dos complementos

🔊
CD1
Track 32

Listen to and read this exchange between a vendor at the market and a customer. Then, decide whether each of the words in boldface type is a direct or an indirect object.

VENDEDORA:	¿Qué desea Ud.?
CLIENTE:	¿**Me** puede dar **dos melones,** por favor?
VENDEDORA:	Enseguida **se los** pongo. ¿Quiere algo más?
CLIENTE:	No, gracias, eso es todo. ¿Cuánto **le** debo?
VENDEDORA:	Quince soles.

A. Dos complementos. Sometimes we use both direct and indirect objects in the same sentence. For example, a child might ask his mother *"When are you going to make me my birthday cake?"*

What will mom make? *The birthday cake* DIRECT OBJECT

Mami, ¿cuándo me vas a hacer la torta de cumpleaños?

For whom will mom make the cake? *For me* INDIRECT OBJECT

It is also possible to have both direct and indirect object *pronouns* in the same sentence. For example, following up to the previous example, the mother might reply: *"I'm going to make it for you this afternoon."*

la = it DIRECT OBJECT PRONOUN, REFERRING TO THE CAKE

Te la voy a hacer esta tarde.

te = for you INDIRECT OBJECT PRONOUN

B. El orden. When both direct and indirect object pronouns are in the same sentence, the indirect object pronoun is placed *in front of* the direct object pronoun. To remember this, think "I.D."

INDIRECT OBJECT PRONOUN   DIRECT OBJECT PRONOUN

¿La pizza? Mamá **nos la** hace todos los sábados.

*Pizza? Mom makes **it for us** every Saturday.*

C. Los complementos *le* y *les*. The indirect object pronouns **le** *(to him/her/you, formal)* and **les** *(to them, to you all)* have a variant: **se.** The variant **se** is used when a direct object pronoun occurs in the same sentence with **le** or **les**.

le	lo				lo
	la				la
+	los	→	se	+	los
les	las				las

—¿Me puede dar una sandía?   *Can you get me a watermelon?*
—Ahora **se la** pongo.   *I'll get **it for you** (formal) right away.*

Ponerlo a prueba

4-22 Escenas diarias. Completa los diálogos con un complemento **indirecto** pronominal (**me, te, nos, se**) o un complemento **directo** pronominal (**lo, la, los, las**).

> **MODELO**
> CLIENTE: ¿Me puede dar una botella de agua mineral?
> VENDEDOR: Sí, señor. Ahora _se_ la pongo.

1. En el mercado   SRA. GONZAGA: ¿Me puede dar una piña?

        VENDEDOR: Ahora __se__ la pongo.

2. En el restaurante   SR. ALBERTI: ¿Me trae otro tenedor, por favor?

        CAMARERO: Sí, señor. Se __lo__ traigo enseguida.

3. En casa   SILVIA: Mamá, ¿cuándo vas a hacerme unas galletas?

        MAMÁ: __Te__ las hago mañana.

4. En casa   CARMEN: Mmm. Me gusta mucho esta torta de chocolate.

        SILVIA: Mamá me __la__ compra todas las semanas porque es mi postre favorito.

4-23 En el mercado. ¿Qué pasa en el mercado hoy? Mira el dibujo y contesta las preguntas. Es necesario usar **dos** complementos pronominales en tus respuestas.

> **MODELO**
> ¿Quién le vende las papas a la Sra. Marini?
> **Se las** vende Edgardo. / Edgardo **se las** vende.

1. ¿Quién le da el dinero a Edgardo? Se lo da la Sra. Marini./ La Sra. Marini se lo da.

2. ¿Quién les vende la piña a Marta y a Rosaura? Se la vende Rafaela. / Rafaela se la vende.

3. ¿Quién le ofrece (*offers*) un helado a Mayra? Se lo ofrece su papá (el Sr. Alberti). / El Sr. Alberti se lo ofrece.

4. ¿Quién le da las galletas a los perros? Se las da Clara./ Clara se las da.

5. ¿Quién le pide los helados a Eduardo? Se los pide la Sra. Cruz. / La Sra. Cruz se los pide.

4-24 Luz, cámara, acción. Mira el dibujo del mercado en la actividad 4-23. Con un(a) compañero(a), dramatiza una de las escenas. (Por ejemplo, una conversación entre Marta y Rafaela.) Tienen que usar dos complementos pronominales en **una** línea del diálogo.

Un paso más

¡Vamos a hablar!

Estudiante A

Contexto: Tú y tu compañero(a) van a completar un crucigrama. Tú tienes las pistas *(the clues)* para las palabras horizontales. Tu compañero(a) las tiene para las palabras verticales. Tomen turnos leyendo las pistas. Tú vas a empezar.

MODELO

> Tú: La pista para el número 1 horizontal es: "Trabaja en un restaurante."
>
> Tu compañero(a): ¿Es "camarero"?
>
> Tú: ¡Sí! ¿Cuál es la pista para el número 1 vertical?

Go to the **Un paso más** section in the *Cuaderno de actividades* for reading, writing, and listening activities that correlate with this chapter.

Teaching Tip: Remind students that they may need to ask **¿Cómo se escribe?** and use the alphabet for this activity.

Teaching Tip: As students work with partners, circulate to make sure they are following the process correctly. Provide sample clues for the last 3 items as needed. For example: 16. Una fruta tropical, muy popular con el cereal o con el helado. 17. El lugar donde venden muchos vegetales y frutas. 18. La necesitas para comer la sopa.

Crucigrama:

1 (horizontal): C A M A R E R O
6 (horizontal): L E C H E
7 (horizontal): L I T R O
8 (horizontal): H E L A D O
9 (horizontal): P R O P I N A
10 (horizontal): M A R I S C O S
11 (horizontal): C U E N T A
14 (horizontal): D E S A Y U N O
16 (horizontal): B A N A N A
17 (horizontal): M E R C A D O
18 (horizontal): C U C H A R A

Horizontal

1. Trabaja en un restaurante.
6. La pones en el cereal.
7. En el sistema métrico, una medida para los líquidos.
8. Un postre frío, de chocolate o fresa.
9. Dinero extra por buen servicio.
10. Esta categoría incluye los camarones y la langosta.
11. La pagas después de comer.
14. La primera comida del día.
16. (Inventa una pista original.)
17. (Inventa una pista original.)
18. (Inventa una pista original.)

Un paso más

¡Vamos a hablar!

Estudiante B

Contexto: Tú y tu compañero(a) van a completar un crucigrama. Tú tienes las pistas *(the clues)* para las palabras verticales. Tu compañero(a) las tiene para las palabras horizontales. Tomen turnos leyendo las pistas. Tu compañero(a) va a empezar.

MODELO	TU COMPAÑERO(A):	La pista para el número 1 horizontal es: "Trabaja en un restaurante."
	TÚ:	¿Es "camarero"?
	TU COMPAÑERO(A):	¡Sí! ¿Cuál es la pista para el número 1 vertical?

Vertical

1. Lo necesitas para comer la carne.
2. Sirves la hamburguesa en esto.
3. Una bebida de frutas.
4. Un producto lácteo, popular en la pizza y en los sándwiches.
5. Un postre típico de leche, huevos y vainilla.
9. Dos condimentos: _____ y sal.
12. (Inventa una pista original.)
13. (Inventa una pista original.)
15. (Inventa una pista original.)

¡Vamos a ver! | *Episodio 4*

En la Hacienda Vista Alegre

Anticipación

 A. Hablando se entiende la gente. Habla con un(a) compañero(a). ¿Te gusta cocinar? ¿Por qué sí o por qué no? ¿Sabes alguna receta de tu familia? ¿Cómo se prepara?

B. Unas palabras clave. Completa las oraciones a continuación con las siguientes expresiones.

la receta	*recipe*	**quemados**	*burnt*
caldo de pollo	*chicken soup*	**¡Buen provecho!**	*Enjoy your meal!*
la lista de la compra	*the shopping list*	**a pesar de**	*despite*

1. No te olvides de coger *(get)* __la lista de la compra__ antes de ir al supermercado.

2. De primer plato, hay __caldo de pollo__ y de segundo, hay pescado frito

3. Ahora mismo les traigo la bebida. ___¡Buen provecho!___

4. Para hacer este pastel de chocolate normalmente sigo ___la receta___ de mi madre.

5. ___A pesar de___ que estoy a dieta, voy a probar este pastel que estás haciendo. Tiene muy buena pinta. *(The cake looks delicious).*

6. Los tomates están un poquito ___quemados___, pero el pollo está muy rico.

▶ Vamos a ver

C. De paseo por la Hacienda Vista Alegre. Lee las preguntas. Luego, mira el Episodio 4 del vídeo y completa las actividades.

1. ¿Qué tipo de comida va a preparar Valeria? ___mexicana/ algo típico mexicano___

2. ¿Qué receta decide preparar? ___Chiles/ chiles___ rellenos al horno.

3. ¿Cuáles de estos ingredientes lleva la receta? Escribe **sí** o **no**.
   a. el arroz blanco ___sí___   c. las cebollitas ___sí___
   b. la mantequilla ___no___   d. los huevos ___no___

4. ¿Qué es el jitomate? __el tomate / Es el nombre que recibe el tomate en el país de Valeria, Venezuela__.

5. La cena fue un desastre porque ___Answers will vary___.

En acción

 D. Charlemos. Comenta con tus compañeros(as).
¿Por qué quiere Valeria preparar esta comida? Describe lo negativo o positivo de la cena. ¿Hay diferencias entre la comida latinoamericana y la comida de tu país? ¿En qué se parecen *(are they similar)* o diferencian?

E. 3, 2, 1 ¡Acción! Interpreten la siguiente situación en grupos de 3 ó 4 estudiantes.
Van a preparar una fiesta sorpresa para uno(a) de sus compañeros(as). Entre todos, decidan qué platos van a preparar y qué ingredientes necesitan. Decidan qué bebidas y accesorios necesitan comprar para la fiesta. Mientras hablan, hagan una lista de la compra *(shopping list)*.

Teaching Tip: Preview the video by showing a fragment of the episode without sound and having students use visual clues to anticipate content. You can stop and rewind the video until they understand the gist of the episode.

Teaching Tip: Have students practice summarizing, describing characters, sequencing events, making comparisons, and giving detailed narrations and descriptions based on what they see in the video.

Panorama cultural

DATOS ESENCIALES

Nombre oficial: República del Perú

Capital: Lima

Población: 28 500 000 habitantes

Unidad monetaria: nuevo sol (S./)

Economía: producción de minerales (cobre, oro, plata, cinc, plomo); petróleo y gas natural; madera *(wood)*; textiles de alpaca; productos pesqueros

🌐 **www.cengage.com/spanish/ puentes**

Transparency Bank A-12

Note: Machu Picchu was named one of the "new" wonders of the world. It is also a UNESCO World Heritage site. There is much discussion over the use of the city, which was "rediscovered" for the outside world by Yale professor Hiram Bingham in 1911.

Note: The capital of the highly developed Inca Empire was Cuzco. Their language was Quechua. Today, both Spanish and Quechua are official languages of Peru.

Note: The Spanish conquistador Francisco Pizarro began exploring the Peruvian coast in 1526. In 1535 he founded the city of Lima. He was killed in 1541.

Note: In 1996 the guerrilla group, Movimiento Revolucionario Túpac Amaru or MRTA, raided a party at the Japanese Ambassador's home in Lima and took 72 hostages for 126 days. Negotiations failed and government troops carefully planned an attack that released the hostages and killed the MRTA leader, among other members of the guerilla group.

Machu Picchu, o "montaña vieja", está en los Andes, en el sur de Perú. Los expertos piensan que esta maravilla de la ingeniería fue un santuario religioso y el palacio de un emperador inca. Hoy es uno de los destinos turísticos más populares del mundo.

Un vistazo a la historia

1100–1500	El avanzado imperio inca se extiende y controla el área andina (Perú y partes de Bolivia, Chile, Ecuador y Argentina).
1533	Pizarro captura y ejecuta al emperador inca Atahualpa.
1824	Perú es liberado por el venezolano Simón Bolívar y el argentino José de San Martín.
1980	Los guerrilleros de Sendero Luminoso y Túpac Amaru empiezan sus ataques; mueren más de 69 000 personas entre 1980 y 2000.
1990	Sube a la presidencia Alberto Fujimori, hijo de inmigrantes japoneses. Dimite *(He resigns)* en 2000 bajo acusaciones de fraude electoral.
2002	Elección de Alejandro Toledo, primer presidente indígena elegido a la presidencia en Perú.
2008	Perú es el primer país andino en firmar un Tratado de Libre Comercio con los Estados Unidos.

Perú

Personajes de ayer y de hoy

Atahualpa (1502–1533)

Fue el último inca (cacique o supremo gobernante) independiente. Gobernó de 1532 a 1533. Fue capturado y ejecutado por Pizarro.

Note: Atahualpa initially shared power with his half brother Huáscar but then used his military power to defeat his brother and take over the empire. The lack of internal unity made it easier for the Inca empire to fall under Spanish rule.

Mario Vargas Llosa (1936–)

Es un conocido novelista, periodista (*journalist*), crítico literario y profesor. Fue candidato a la presidencia de Perú en 1990. Ha ganado múltiples premios literarios como el Ritz Paris Hemingway Award y el Premio Internacional de Literatura Rómulo Gallegos.

Note: Important novels by Vargas Llosa include *La ciudad y los perros*, *La casa verde* and *Conversación en la catedral*. He has taught as a visiting professor in numerous prestigious universities, including Harvard, Princeton and Georgetown.

Sofía Mulánovich Aljovín (1983–)

En 2004, esta joven surfista se convirtió en la primera peruana y sudamericana en ganar un campeonato mundial de surf. Empezó a practicar a los cinco años, en las playas de Punta Hermosa. En 2007 fue admitida al Salón de la Fama del Surf.

Note: Sofía Mulánovich, of Croatian descent, is a national hero in Peru and the subject of a 2004 documentary. The trailer is at www.sofiadoco.com.

Note: The Amazonian **selva** comprises 60% of the territory of Perú, but only 10% of the country's population lives there. More than half of Peru's population is concentrated in cities along the mostly desert-like coast.

Note: Every 4–7 years, the warm equatorial currents move further south than usual. Since this usually happens around Christmas time, this phenomenon is called **El Niño**, for the Christ Child.

Note: Descendants of the Incas comprise 47% of the population and are referred to as **indígenas**. Besides Spanish, commonly spoken languages include quechua and aymara. In the 1850s, many Chinese laborers came to Perú and their descendants are an important cultural influence.

Imágenes de Perú

Después de mirar el vídeo de Perú, contesta las preguntas. Trabaja con un(a) compañero(a).

1. ¿Cuáles son dos datos (*facts*) interesantes sobre la capital de Perú?

2. Describe el distrito de Miraflores. ¿Qué hacen los limeños allí?

3. ¿Qué edificios y plazas nos recuerdan (*remind us*) la historia de Perú?

4. ¿Cuáles de las atracciones turísticas te gustan más?

There are more activities on Peru and the **Panorama cultural** in the **Un paso más** section of the *Cuaderno de actividades*.

Responses may vary; suggested content follows. 1. Es la ciudad más grande de Perú. Fue fundada por los españoles (Francisco Pizarro) en 1535. 2. Es un distrito muy cosmopolita. Hay muchos restaurantes. El Parque Kennedy tiene atracciones como la iglesia Virgen Milagrosa, plazas de juegos infantiles, el Parque del Amor, con una escultura famosa. 3. El Parque de la Muralla tiene una parte de la antigua muralla de Lima. La Catedral y la Iglesia de San Francisco son ejemplos del estilo colonial. La Plaza de San Martín conmemora al héroe de la independencia peruana. 4. Answers may include: el mercado de artesanías, las playas, el barrio chino, las fuentes de agua, etc.

Sustantivos

el almuerzo *lunch*
la barra (de pan) *loaf (of bread)*
la bolsa *bag*
la botella *bottle*
el (la) camarero(a) *waiter/waitress*
la cena *dinner*
la comida *food, meal*
el cubito de hielo *ice cube*
la cuenta *bill*
el desayuno *breakfast*
la docena *dozen*
el frasco *jar*
el kilo *kilo [metric pound]*
el litro *liter*
la mayonesa *mayonnaise*
el menú *menu*
el mercado *market*
la merienda *snack, snacktime*
la palta rellena *avocado stuffed with chicken or tuna salad*
el paquete *package*
la pimienta *black pepper*
el postre *dessert*
el plato principal *main course*
el primer plato *first course*
la propina *tip*
el restaurante *restaurant*
el segundo plato *second course*
la taza *cup (of coffee/tea/hot chocolate)*
la tortilla *omelette; flour tortilla (Mex.)*
el vaso *glass*

Verbos

almorzar (ue) *to eat lunch*
beber *to drink*
cenar *to eat supper*
desayunar *to eat breakfast*
desear *to want, wish for*
merendar (ie) *to snack*
necesitar *to need*
pedir (i) *to ask for; to order*
probar (ue) *to taste; to try*
recomendar (ie) *to recommend*
servir (i) *to serve*
tomar *to take; to drink*

Otras palabras

a la parrilla *grilled*
al horno *baked*
asado(a) *roasted*
frito(a) *fried*
revuelto(a) *scrambled*

Breakfast foods p. 130
Luncheon foods p. 130
Supper/dinner foods p. 131
Snacks p. 131
Place settings p. 135
Other fruits and vegetables p. 141

For further review, please turn to **Vocabulario temático: español e inglés** at the back of the book.

Go to the *Puentes* website for extra vocabulary practice using the Flashcard program.

La vida estudiantil

Situation Cards: 3, 4, 7, 25, 32, 57, 67, 74, 82, 89

More Information: At this point in *Puentes*, your students may find that some of the material is less familiar. For this reason, the information is presented in smaller chunks, thereby allowing for more time on these topics.

Proficiency: In this chapter we continue to develop the students' ability to converse simply in the present time frame but on a new topic—university life. The first **Paso** also focuses on the exchange of simple opinions. At the same time, we begin a new phase of the program, by presenting the basics on how to converse in the past time frame. This lays the foundation for attainment of higher levels of proficiency and helps students understand a greater variety of spoken language and written texts.

Turn to the *Cuaderno de actividades* for this chapter's reading practice and strategy: Understanding a long sentence.

Turn to the *Cuaderno de actividades* for this chapter's composition practice and writing strategy: Developing cohesion.

OBJETIVOS

Speaking and Listening
► Describing everyday routines on campus
► Discussing classes
► Expressing opinions about school life
► Identifying professions and occupations
► Talking about plans for the future
► Narrating actions and events in the past
► Describing a field trip

Culture
► Argentina
► University life in Spanish-speaking countries

Grammar
► Preterite aspect of regular -**ar**, -**er**, and -**ir** verbs
► Spelling-changing verbs in the preterite
► Stem-changing verbs in the preterite
► Preterite of irregular verbs

Video
► En la Hacienda Vista Alegre: Episodio 5
► Imágenes de Argentina

Gramática suplementaria
► El condicional

Cuaderno de actividades
Reading
► Strategy: Understanding a long sentence

Writing
► Strategy: Developing cohesion

Playlist
🌐 www.cengage.com/spanish/puentes

A primera vista

Unidad panamericana

Las artes y las ciencias forman la base de los estudios universitarios. Nos llevan a investigar el mundo, meditar sobre la condición humana y crear nuevas maravillas *(marvels)*. ¿Cuál de las dos áreas prefieres tú estudiar?

En esta obra de Diego Rivera observamos que las dos áreas pueden resultar en grandes logros *(achievements)* para la humanidad. Mira el panel del mural *Unidad panamericana* y completa la actividad con un(a) compañero(a).

1. Según Rivera, el impulso creativo puede resultar en invenciones científicas. ¿Cuáles son dos o tres ejemplos de invenciones prácticas en el mural? el motor, el coche, el barco, el fonógrafo, el telégrafo, la lámpara incandescente
2. Según Rivera, el impulso creativo también resulta en obras *(works)* artísticas. ¿Cuáles son dos o tres ejemplos de obras artísticas en el mural? la escultura, la pintura
3. Los ejemplos en el mural son de los siglos *(centuries)* XIX y XX. ¿Qué ejemplos del siglo XXI pondrías *(would you put)* en un mural? Answers will vary.
4. ¿Qué clase de pintura es *Unidad panamericana*: un mural al fresco o un mosaico? un mural al fresco

HABLANDO DEL ARTE

Before their application to a canvas or other surface, the color pigments of paintings are mixed with water, oil, or synthetic substances. Each of these mixtures produces a different effect in terms of texture and intensity of color. Some of the more common kinds include watercolors (**las acuarelas**) and oil paints (**la pintura al óleo**). Large murals are often created by applying the colors to wet plaster (**la pintura al fresco**). Another technique involves using small pieces of tiles or glass to create mosaics (**los mosaicos**).

DIEGO RIVERA BARRIENTOS (1886–1957)

Nacionalidad: mexicano

Otras obras: *La creación, El reparto de tierras, Hombre en la encrucijada, La historia de la cardiología*

Estilo: Diego Rivera participó en el gran renacimiento *(renaissance)* de la pintura mural. Es muy famoso por sus enormes frescos, sobre la historia y la sociedad mexicana, en edificios públicos. Con frecuencia estos murales reflejan *(reflect)* sus ideas políticas basadas en el comunismo. En sus últimas obras, experimentó con el uso de piedras *(stones)* naturales en la creación de mosaicos.

Detail of "Pan American Unity" Mural © City College of San Francisco
Diego Rivera

In this *Paso* you will practice:

▸ Talking about your schedule, your academic major, and grades
▸ Expressing opinions about different aspects of school life
▸ Identifying professions and occupations
▸ Talking about plans for the future

Grammar:
▸ **Encantar** and **interesar:** Two verbs like **gustar**
▸ Expressing future time: Review of verb phrases

🌐 Go to the *Puentes* website for extra vocabulary practice using the Flashcard program.

The English equivalents of the **Vocabulario temático** sections are found at the back of the book.

Teaching Tip: Begin by practicing names of courses and then complete Activity 5-3. Next, present the basic Q&A by calling on individual students to respond. Follow up with Activities 5-4 and 5-5.

Another way to ask about majors: **¿En qué te especializas?**

Other time expressions: **el próximo año** (next year); **en dos años** (in two years).

Teaching Tip: Many course names are offered here so that students can speak of their own classes. Due to the heavy vocabulary load, consider writing more open-ended test items that allow for a variety of responses.

Teaching Tip: Review the alphabet: Begin spelling a course name letter by letter and have students name the course before you finish spelling it.

Vocabulary: Provide other courses as requested or desired: **enfermería, idiomas, fotografía, geometría, trigonometría, genética, astronomía, geología, criminología, administración de empresas, mercadeo, farmacia, turismo y hotelería, veterinaria.**

Paso 1

Vocabulario temático

Cómo hablar de los horarios y las especializaciones

—¿Qué clases tomas este semestre?

—Este semestre tomo *inglés y literatura.*

—¿Te gusta tu horario?

—Sí, me encanta.

   No, no me gusta porque...

—¿A qué hora empieza tu primera clase?

—Mi primera clase empieza *a las ocho.*

—¿A qué hora termina tu última clase?

—Mi última clase termina *a las dos y media.*

—¿Cuál es tu carrera?

—Todavía no (lo) sé.

   Estudio *economía.*

—¿Cuándo piensas graduarte?

—Pienso graduarme *a finales de mayo.*
                a principios de diciembre

Las asignaturas
Humanidades y bellas artes

arte   literatura
música   teatro

Ciencias sociales

antropología   historia
ciencias políticas   psicología
geografía   sociología

Ciencias naturales

biología   ecología
física   química

Matemáticas

álgebra   cálculo   estadística

Estudios profesionales

negocios   informática
derecho   educación
medicina   periodismo
ingeniería   cinematografía

Note: Point out that in many Spanish-speaking countries, students who want to go on to college must first finish a college-preparatory high school program that gives them a diploma known as **el bachillerato**. An undergraduate university degree is often called **un título universitario** or **una licenciatura**.

Ponerlo a prueba

🔊 **5-1 Las clases de Reinaldo.** Escucha la conversación entre Reinaldo y su amiga Patricia. Completa las actividades.

CD1
Track 33

PRIMERA PARTE: Escoge la mejor respuesta a las preguntas.

_a_ 1. ¿Cómo es el horario de Patricia?
   a. Es bueno. A Patricia le gusta.
   b. Es regular. A Patricia no le gusta mucho.
   c. Es malo. Patricia lo detesta.

_b_ 2. ¿A qué hora empieza la primera clase de Patricia los lunes?
   a. A las ocho.
   b. A las nueve.
   c. A las once.

_c_ 3. La mayoría de las materias de Patricia están relacionadas con...
   a. el periodismo
   b. las humanidades y las bellas artes
   c. las ciencias naturales

_b_ 4. ¿Cuándo piensa graduarse Reinaldo?
   a. El próximo año.
   b. A finales de noviembre.
   c. A principios de junio.

_a_ 5. La mayoría de las materias de Reinaldo están relacionadas con...
   a. las humanidades y las bellas artes
   b. las ciencias sociales
   c. la ingeniería

SEGUNDA PARTE: Vuelve a escuchar *(Listen again)* la conversación e indica las clases de Patricia y Reinaldo.

6. Este semestre, Patricia toma...
   ☑ biología   ☐ geología   ☑ cálculo
   ☑ física   ☐ química   ☐ estadística

7. Este semestre, Reinaldo toma...
   ☑ antropología   ☑ literatura   ☐ teatro
   ☐ sociología   ☑ cinematografía   ☑ historia del arte

Teaching Tip: Assign the first two activities for homework.

Teaching Tip 5-2: Create or have students create additional descriptions for others to guess.

5-2 Las asignaturas. Lee la descripción y escribe el nombre de la asignatura o clase correspondiente.

1. Si quieres programar computadoras, necesitas estudiar ___informática___.

2. Si te gusta leer novelas, cuentos y poemas, debes (*you should*) tomar una clase de ___literatura___.

3. En la clase de ___psicología___ puedes investigar distintas teorías de la personalidad, la conducta de las personas y los procesos mentales.

4. Para aprender más sobre la familia, las clases sociales y las instituciones sociales, puedes tomar una clase de ___sociología___.

5. En ___álgebra___, tienes que formular y resolver series de ecuaciones; es una rama (*branch*) de las matemáticas.

6. Para trabajar en el mundo comercial, es interesante tener una carrera en ___negocios___.

7. Si estudias ___ecología___, vas a aprender mucho sobre el clima, las interacciones de los organismos y los hábitats.

8. La carrera de ___periodismo___ es para los estudiantes que esperan trabajar para un periódico o revista.

Teaching Tip 5-3: This activity recycles superlatives, introduced in Chapter 3. Point out the use of the definite article.

Expansion 5-3: After partners share opinions, engage the class in a simple group discussion. Ask follow-up questions to have students describe in more detail what kinds of activities are common for their favorite and least favorite classes. Note that giving opinions is practiced in more depth in the next **Vocabulario temático**.

5-3 En mi opinión. Completa las frases oralmente para expresar tus opiniones sobre las clases. Compara tus opiniones con las de un(a) compañero(a).

1. En humanidades y bellas artes, la clase más interesante es _____ y la menos interesante es _____. ¿Estás de acuerdo? (*Do you agree?*)

2. En ciencias naturales, la clase más difícil (*difficult*) es _____ y la menos difícil es _____. ¿Qué piensas tú? (*What do you think?*)

3. En ciencias sociales, la clase más aburrida (*boring*) es _____ y la menos aburrida es _____. ¿Estás de acuerdo?

4. De los estudios profesionales, me gusta más _____ y el que menos me gusta es _____. ¿Cuáles son tus preferencias?

5-4 Este semestre. Conversa con un(a) compañero(a) sobre los estudios.

1. ¿Qué clases tomas este semestre? ¿Tienes laboratorios?

2. ¿Te gusta tu horario este semestre? ¿A qué hora empieza tu primera clase? ¿A qué hora termina tu última clase?

3. ¿Cuál es tu carrera? ¿Es una tradición en tu familia seguir (*follow*) esa carrera?

4. ¿Cuándo piensas graduarte? ¿Dónde quieres vivir después de graduarte?

5. Haz una pregunta original. (*Ask an original question on this topic.*)

Standards: Culture, Comparisons
are addressed here. You may wish
to create a Venn diagram with the class to
compare features of American and Hispanic
university systems and experiences.

COMENTARIO CULTURAL · *El sistema educativo*

En el momento de escoger tus clases, ¿tienes mucho control sobre tu horario? En tus clases, ¿hay mucha interacción entre los profesores y los estudiantes? ¿Qué criterio usan tus profesores para determinar la nota final?

Los estudiantes universitarios de España e Hispanoamérica tienen un sistema educativo muy diferente al de los Estados Unidos. En primer lugar, casi siempre tienen que seguir un plan de estudios sin flexibilidad, que no les da oportunidad de tomar muchos cursos electivos. Además, en algunas universidades los profesores no toman asistencia ni tampoco tienen muchas interacciones con los estudiantes en sus clases. Por último, en algunos casos los estudiantes solamente tienen un examen final al concluir el año escolar.

Normalmente las notas en España e Hispanoamérica siguen un sistema numérico del 1 al 10 o con las siguientes descripciones:

sobresaliente *(outstanding)*   bien *(good)*   deficiente *(unsatisfactory)*

notable *(very good)*   aprobado *(passing)*   suspenso *(fail)*

 5-5 Estudiar en Argentina. Este anuncio presenta información sobre un programa de estudios en Argentina. Contesta las preguntas y compara tus preferencias con las de un(a) compañero(a) de clase.

¡Aprende español en Argentina!

Instituto Magnum

Escoge tu destino:
- ❖ Explora el ambiente cosmopolita de Buenos Aires.
- ❖ Disfruta de los deportes en la tranquila ciudad de Mendoza.

Escoge tu curso:
- ❖ Curso intensivo en grupo (20 clases por semana)
- ❖ Clases privadas (10 clases por semana)
- ❖ Curso tango (20 clases de español + 5 clases de tango)

Todos nuestros centros de estudio ofrecen alojamiento en familia o en residencias de estudiantes (habitación doble o individual).

Y para los fines de semana:
- ❖ Visitas a museos y teatros
- ❖ Barbacoas con otros estudiantes
- ❖ Conferencias de literatura, arte y cinematografía
- ❖ Excursiones a Patagonia y el Parque Nacional Nahuel Huapi
- ❖ Actividades de aventura: rafting, trekking, esquí

Precios y más información:
Visítanos en www.escuelamagnum.com
Teléfono (en los Estados Unidos) 1-800-555-8963

Note: Nahuel Huapi is in the lake district of Argentina, in Patagonia. The popular town of Bariloche, within the park, is a tourist base for the area.

1. ¿En qué ciudades ofrecen cursos de español? ¿Cuál prefieres tú? ¿Por qué?
2. ¿Qué curso del Instituto Magnum te gustaría tomar? Explica por qué.
3. ¿Te gustaría más alojamiento *(lodging)* en familia o en residencia de estudiantes?
4. ¿Cuáles de las actividades son más interesantes?

Vocabulario temático

Cómo pedir y dar opiniones sobre las clases

—¿Qué piensas de tus clases este semestre?

—Pienso que mi clase de *microbiología* es *difícil / fácil.*
                                                    interesante / aburrida

Me encanta mi clase de *historia del arte.*

No me gusta nada mi clase de *ciencias marinas.*

Las conferencias de *historia medieval* son *fascinantes / pesadas.*

Me interesa mucho la clase de *genética.* ¿Y tú? ¿Qué piensas?

Opiniones sobre los profesores

—¿Qué tal tus profesores?

—Son *bastante dinámicos(as).*
       muy exigentes
       un poco quisquillosos(as)

Mi profesor de *química* es muy *organizado / desorganizado.*

Las notas *(Grades)*

—¿Cómo te va en *psicología*?

—(No) Me va bien.

Saqué una nota muy buena en *mi presentación.*
                             el último trabajo escrito

(No) Salí muy bien en el examen. Y a ti, ¿cómo te va en tus clases?

ESTRUCTURAS ESENCIALES

Los verbos *encantar* e *interesar*

A. Gustar. As you saw in Chapter 1, the verb **gustar** follows a special sentence pattern:

Indirect object	Verb	Subject
Me	gusta	la clase de inglés.

I like English class. (English class is pleasing to me.)

B. Encantar. The verb **encantar** *(to "love")* follows the same patterns as **gustar**.

me encanta(n)	nos encanta(n)
te encanta(n)	os encanta(n)
le encanta(n)	les encanta(n)

▸ Use **encanta** with infinitives and singular nouns; use **encantan** with plural nouns. Specify *who* loves something with an indirect object pronoun.

   Nos encanta la clase de sociología.   *We **love** sociology class.*

▸ Use **encantar** to talk about things or activities that you enjoy greatly or "love." This verb is *not* used to talk about persons for whom you feel affection.

   A Rita le **encanta** leer.   *Rita **loves** to read.*

   Me **encantan** sus conferencias.   *I **love** her lectures.*

C. Interesar. Use **interesar** to talk about what interests you. This verb follows the same pattern as **gustar** and **encantar**.

me interesa(n)	nos interesa(n)
te interesa(n)	os interesa(n)
le interesa(n)	les interesa(n)

Me interesa mucho la genética.   *I'm very much interested in genetics.*

Ponerlo a prueba

CD1
Track 34

5-6 ¿Cómo te va? Escucha la conversación entre dos estudiantes universitarios, Elsa y Andrés. Escoge las palabras más apropiadas para completar las oraciones, según la información en la conversación.

1. Andrés tiene una impresión (favorable / desfavorable) de su profesor de química porque dice que el profesor es muy (dinámico / exigente).

2. Elsa y Andrés piensan que la clase de filosofía es (fascinante / pesada).

3. A Andrés no le gustan (los exámenes / las conferencias) de la clase de historia.

4. Elsa piensa que su profesora de sociología es (organizada / desorganizada) y (dinámica / un poco aburrida).

5-7 Opiniones contrarias. Gabi y Julia son gemelas pero tienen opiniones contrarias sobre sus clases y sus profesores. Relaciona las dos columnas para ver los contrastes.

A. Gabi

_b_ 1. Me encanta la clase de ciencias marinas.

_a_ 2. El profesor Marini es fascinante.

_c_ 3. Las conferencias son maravillosas; el tiempo pasa volando (*flies by*).

_e_ 4. Los exámenes son un poco difíciles, pero justos (*fair*).

_d_ 5. Tengo muy buenas notas y estoy muy contenta con la clase.

B. Julia

a. Yo creo que es el profesor más aburrido del planeta, además de ser desorganizado.

b. ¡Increíble! Es la clase que menos me gusta.

c. Yo siempre me duermo cuando el profesor empieza a hablar.

d. Saqué una nota muy mala en el último examen. No pienso estudiar ciencias marinas el próximo semestre.

e. ¡Qué dices! Siempre incluyen material insignificante. El profe es demasiado exigente y quisquilloso.

5-8 Opiniones. Conversa con unos(as) compañeros(as) sobre las clases, los profesores y las notas.

1. En tu opinión, ¿son más difíciles las clases de la universidad o las de la escuela secundaria? Explica. ¿Cuál es tu clase más difícil este semestre? Explica por qué es difícil.

2. ¿Quién es tu profesor favorito este semestre? ¿Cuáles son sus características personales y profesionales más admirables? ¿En qué actividades consiste una clase típica de ese profesor? ¿Hay muchas conferencias?

3. Para ti, ¿es importante sacar buenas notas? ¿Para qué clases tienes que estudiar más? ¿En qué clases tienes que hacer muchos trabajos escritos?, ¿hacer muchas presentaciones?

Estrategia *Using simpler language*

Learning another language can be frustrating, especially when you want to communicate sophisticated ideas but find that you don't have all the words you need. At times like that, you may need to simplify your message. To do this, make more general statements and substitute more basic words for picturesque or colloquial speech. Read the example that follows and then complete the chart with your own versions of simplified English and Spanish sentences.

Instead of saying . . .	You might say . . .	And express it in Spanish as . . .
Marie says that her bio-chemistry prof is just awful.	Marie has a very bad chemistry professor.	El profesor de química de Marie es muy malo.
Einstein himself couldn't pass one of my physics professor's tests.		
I haven't declared a major yet, but I'm thinking of going into computers.		

5-9 ¿Qué piensas? Trabaja con un(a) compañero(a). Comparen sus opiniones sobre sus clases y profesores.

MODELO

> TÚ: ¿Qué piensas de tus clases este semestre?
>
> TU COMPAÑERO(A): Me encanta la clase de español porque la profesora Dent es organizada y simpática. Saqué una nota muy buena en el último examen. Me interesa mucho mi clase de...

Vocabulario temático

Las profesiones, los oficios y los planes para el futuro

—¿A qué te quieres dedicar?

—Quiero ser *enfermero(a)*.

—¿A qué se dedican tus padres?

—Mi padre es *dueño de un pequeño negocio*. Mi madre trabaja para *una agencia del estado*.

—¿Qué planes tienes para el futuro?

—No estoy seguro(a) todavía.

Me gustaría *hacer estudios de postgrado.*
            estudiar medicina

Espero trabajar *para el gobierno.*
            con una empresa multinacional

Profesiones y ocupaciones

abogado(a)	dentista	periodista
agente de bienes raíces	director(a) de personal	programador(a)
agricultor(a)	gerente	psicólogo(a)
ama de casa	ingeniero(a)	trabajador(a) social
consejero(a)	maestro(a)	vendedor(a)
consultor(a)	médico(a)	veterinario(a)
contador(a)	obrero(a)	

Teaching Tip: Start by practicing vocabulary for professions: Give definitions or descriptions and have students guess the profession. Also, discuss the professions of prominent Hispanics in your community. Next, introduce the expressions dealing with future plans: Mention a possible course of study (**¿Cuántos de Uds. quieren estudiar derecho?** etc.) and make a tally of how many people are interested in each option.

Use **un(a)** with professions only when an adjective is present. For example: **Es profesor. Es un profesor muy dinámico.**

Vocabulary: Introduce additional professions as needed so that students can describe the work of family members: **arquitecto(a), cocinero(a), corredor(a) de bolsa, psiquiatra, cirujano(a), químico(a), arquitecto(a), mecánico(a), electricista, compositor(a), escultor(a), piloto, secretario(a), fotógrafo(a), músico(a), reportero(a), pastor(a), decorador(a), bailarín (bailarina), astronauta, político(a), banquero(a), biólogo(a).** For complicated professions, encourage students to use simpler phrasing, such as, **Trabaja para...** or **Trabaja con....**

Vocabulary: Provide these expressions as needed: **estar jubilado(a)** *to be retired;* **estar desempleado(a)** *to be unemployed.*

Grammar: Review masculine and feminine forms for various professions. Point out that nouns ending in **-ista** may be masculine or feminine, despite the final **-a.**

CD1
Track 35

ESTRUCTURAS ESENCIALES

Para hablar del futuro: repaso de las expresiones verbales

All of the following expressions may be used to talk about plans for the future. Use the pattern **conjugated verb + infinitive.**

ir a	**Voy a** trabajar en un banco.	*I'm going to work in a bank.*
pensar	**Pienso** hacer estudios de postgrado.	*I plan on doing graduate work.*
querer	**Quiero** estudiar derecho.	*I want to study law.*
esperar	**Espero** trabajar con niños.	*I hope to work with children.*
gustar	**Me gustaría** dedicarme a la investigación.	*I'd like to dedicate myself to research.*

Ponerlo a prueba

5-10 Se busca. La agencia de empleo tiene varias oportunidades. Escúchalas y completa la tabla *(chart)*.

Profesión	Requisitos *(Requirements)*
1. __secretaria bilingüe__	dominio de dos lenguas: ____español____ e ____inglés____; ____2____ años de experiencia
2. __director de personal__	título universitario en ____negocios____; ____2____ años de experiencia
3. __consultor técnico__	título en ____informática____; ____3____ años de experiencia
4. __maestro de primaria__	especialización en ____matemáticas____ y ____ciencias____
5. __trabajador social__	experiencia en ____salud pública____
Para mayor información, llame al teléfono ____555-8991____.	

5-11 Los planes. Karina está hablando con su amigo Mariano sobre sus planes para el futuro. Relaciona las dos columnas de una manera lógica.

Karina:

_b_ 1. ¿En qué te especializas, Mariano?

_d_ 2. ¿Cuándo vas a graduarte?

_a_ 3. ¿Piensas hacer estudios de postgrado?

_c_ 4. ¿A qué te quieres dedicar?

_f_ 5. ¿Dónde esperas trabajar?

_g_ 6. ¿Y si no encuentras ese tipo de empleo?

Mariano:

a. No, quiero buscar empleo después de graduarme.

b. Estudio ciencias naturales, con una especialización en biología.

c. Me gustaría hacer investigación científica.

d. ¡Muy pronto! A finales de este mes.

e. Sí, creo que es muy importante.

f. Espero trabajar en un laboratorio en una universidad.

g. No estoy seguro. Quizás *(Perhaps)* haría trabajo voluntario por unos meses.

5-12 Trabajo voluntario. ¿Te gustaría hacer trabajo voluntario en otro país? Lee el anuncio y contesta las preguntas. Comparte *(Share)* tus ideas con un(a) compañero(a).

Expansion 5-12: Have students investigate possible community service projects in your community. For example, students might read Spanish story books to children at the library, teach simple Spanish words to English-speaking children in kindergarten, complete basic intake information at a free, medical clinic, etc.

Programa de Voluntariado C.E.I. en Córdoba, Argentina

¿Quiere perfeccionar su español? ¿Le interesa ayudar a la gente?
Nuestro programa ofrece la oportunidad de una completa inmersión cultural.

Requisitos para los aspirantes:
Edad mínima: 18 años
Nivel de español: Intermedio o avanzado
Se buscan personas responsables con ganas de aprender
acerca de nuestra cultura.

Duración del programa: Mínimo de 8 semanas y máximo de 6 meses.

Proyectos:
Preservación de reservas naturales
Trabajo con gente sin hogar
Construcción de escuelas
Enseñar inglés o computación a los niños
Leer a los niños en el hospital público
o alimentar a los pacientes

Existen más oportunidades, solamente tiene que hacernos
saber qué le gustaría hacer. Escríbanos al info@cei.com

1. ¿Dónde se ofrece este programa?

2. ¿Qué tipo de persona buscan para participar en este programa?

3. ¿Te gustaría participar en este programa de voluntariado? ¿Tienes los requisitos *(qualifications)*?

4. ¿Cuáles de los proyectos son más interesantes, en tu opinión? ¿Tienes experiencia en hacer trabajo voluntario de ese tipo?

 5-13 Las ocupaciones de mis parientes. Conversa con un(a) compañero(a) sobre las ocupaciones de sus padres, abuelos y hermanos.

Expansion 5-13: Have students discuss people with unusual professions, within their family or in the community.

MODELO

TÚ:	¿A qué se dedican tus padres?
TU COMPAÑERO(A):	Mi padre es ingeniero; trabaja con una compañía en Greenville. Mi madre es maestra; enseña inglés en la Escuela Primaria McCants. ¿Y tus padres? ¿Dónde trabajan?
TÚ:	Mi papá es profesor...

5-14 El futuro. Conversa con un(a) compañero(a) sobre sus planes para el futuro.

1. ¿En qué año vas a graduarte? ¿Piensas hacer estudios de postgrado? ¿Quieres trabajar por unos años antes de continuar tus estudios? *Haz una pregunta original.*

2. ¿A qué te quieres dedicar después de graduarte? Para ti, ¿es más importante ganar *(to earn)* mucho dinero o tener un horario flexible? *Haz una pregunta original.*

3. Después de graduarte, ¿en qué ciudad te gustaría vivir? ¿Esperas vivir cerca de tu familia? *Haz una pregunta original.*

Puente cultural

🌐 Go to the *Puentes* Premium Website to view the **Puente cultural** interviews.

¿Cómo es la vida social en la universidad?

Gabriella Paracat

🌐 **ARGENTINA**

Hay una gran vida social en la universidad. Se trabaja mucho en grupo, haciendo trabajo o dando exposiciones dentro de la universidad. Los estudiantes también se juntan fuera de la universidad. No hay fiestas como en los Estados Unidos pero los estudiantes se reúnen en cafés a charlar.

David Valecillos

🌐 **VENEZUELA**

La vida social en la universidad es muy diferente a la de los Estados Unidos. El campus no está unido. Por ejemplo, si estudias ingeniería, solamente vas a estudiar con estudiantes de tu misma carrera.

María José Vargas Cevallos

🌐 **ECUADOR**

Existe mucha vida social en la universidad en el Ecuador. Por lo general las chicas van muy bien arregladas y se preocupan mucho de su aspecto físico. Lo mismo sucede con los hombres aunque esto se nota menos. Por lo general se forman grandes círculos de amistades (*friendships*) dentro de la universidad a la que se asiste, ya que comúnmente la mayoría de personas que se graduaron de un mismo colegio asisten a una misma universidad.

Comparando países. Lee la información sobre las universidades y completa la tabla. Compara tus respuestas con las de tus compañeros(as) de clase.

	En Argentina	En Venezuela	En Ecuador	En los Estados Unidos
¿Cómo es la vida social en la universidad?				

Vocabulario temático

Cómo hablar del pasado *(Talking about the past)*

¿Qué hiciste ayer?

Primero, me levanté y me vestí.

Después de comer el desayuno, asistí a clases.

Luego, volví a casa y almorcé con mi familia.

Entonces, estudié para mi examen de 3 a 5.

Más tarde salí con mis amigos a un club y nos divertimos muchísimo.

Antes de acostarme, miré la tele por un rato.

Teaching Tip: Introduce the topic by taking a poll of what students did yesterday. Have students respond affirmatively by raising their hands. For example, for a class day you might ask: **¿Cuáles de Uds. fueron a todas sus clases ayer? ¿Cuáles tuvieron que tomar un examen? ¿Cuáles estudiaron más de una hora? ¿Cuáles salieron con sus amigos? ¿Cuáles hicieron ejercicio en el gimnasio?** Then direct attention to the drawings and review what Tomás did yesterday. Have students identify the infinitive that corresponds to each preterite verb form.

The verbs in this section are conjugated in the **preterite,** which is used to refer to past actions, such as what you did yesterday.

Notice that an infintive is used after **después de** and **antes de.**

Proficiency: Narrating past events is a function of Intermediate-high and Advanced-level speakers. Nevertheless, because of the complexity of the task and the large number of irregular preterite verbs, it is important to begin laying the foundation at this point of study. For this reason the proficiency goal is modified to conceptual and partial control; that is, you can expect your students to understand the concept, to learn a number of forms and to apply them in controlled speaking exercises and writing tasks. Do not expect students to speak spontaneously in the past time frame with accuracy.

To specify the order of your activities, use words like **primero** *(first),* **luego** *(next),* **entonces** *(then),* **más tarde** *(later),* **por último** *(last, finally).*

Teaching Tip: This **Paso** introduces students to the past time frame. While most students will be somewhat familiar with the preterite verbs, many will not be able to produce them with much accuracy. For most classes, it is appropriate to allocate the majority of the available practice time to regular verbs along with the most common irregular verbs: **ir/ser, hacer, tener.** Adjust your emphasis according to the incoming level of the students.

More Information: Reflexive verbs were introduced in Chapter 3 and used in the context of daily routine. Here the emphasis is not on past routine, but rather the activities of a particular day, such as **ayer.** Past routines—which require the use of the imperfect—are introduced in Chapter 7.

CD1
Track 36

Teaching Tip: Assign the first two activities for homework.

5-15 El primer día de clases de Ernesto. La madre de Ernesto lo llama por teléfono el primer día de clases. Escucha la conversación y contesta las preguntas.

_b_ 1. ¿A qué hora se levantó Ernesto?

    a. a las siete   b. a las siete y media   c. a las ocho

_c_ 2. ¿Por qué le gustó la clase de filosofía a Ernesto?

    a. El profesor es inteligente.

    b. El profesor es famoso.

    c. El profesor es dinámico.

_b_ 3. ¿Dónde comió Ernesto?

    a. en la residencia   b. en la cafetería   c. en su cuarto

_a_ 4. ¿Qué hizo Ernesto después de comer?

    a. Estudió y fue al laboratorio.

    b. Descansó un poco y fue a la biblioteca para estudiar.

    c. Lavó la ropa y jugó al fútbol.

_b_ 5. ¿Qué clases tuvo Ernesto?

    a. historia, inglés y fisiología

    b. filosofía, inglés y el laboratorio de química

    c. francés, economía y el laboratorio de biología

Teaching Tip: Use Activity 5-16 to build familiarity with the preterite verb forms. After checking answers, have students identify the infinitive that corresponds to each conjugated verb. Next, compare the verb endings for several **-ar** verbs and several **-er/-ir** verbs and have students tell you the appropriate ending for each category.

5-16 El horario de Fátima. Fátima es una profesional muy ocupada. Lee la descripción de sus actividades ayer. Luego, usa los números del 1 al 8 para poner sus actividades en la secuencia correcta.

_3_ a. Antes de llegar a la oficina, desayuné en un café.

_8_ b. Llegué a casa a las seis y media de la tarde.

_7_ c. Antes de irme a casa, fui al gimnasio y corrí por treinta minutos.

_1_ d. Me levanté a las seis de la mañana y me duché.

_6_ e Hablé con varios clientes por la tarde.

_4_ f. Por la mañana, contesté todos mis mensajes electrónicos.

_5_ g. Luego, almorcé con mis colegas.

_2_ h. Después, me vestí y salí para la oficina.

5-17 Ayer. Con un(a) compañero(a), sustituye la información subrayada (*underlined*) en las oraciones para describir tus actividades ayer. (**¡Ojo!** *If there were no classes yesterday, refer to the last day you both had classes.*) ¿Cuál de Uds. tuvo el día más ajetreado *(hectic)*?

1. Ayer me levanté a <u>las siete y media de la mañana</u>. ¿Y tú? ¿A qué hora te levantaste?

2. Salí de mi casa/residencia a las <u>nueve menos cuarto</u>. ¿Y tú? ¿A qué hora saliste?

3. Asistí a <u>dos</u> clases: <u>inglés y biología</u>. ¿Y tú? ¿A cuántas clases asististe?

4. Estudié por <u>tres</u> horas. ¿Y tú? ¿Por cuánto tiempo estudiaste?

5. No volví a casa/la residencia hasta <u>las siete de la noche</u>. ¿Y tú? ¿A qué hora llegaste a casa/la residenica?

Gramática

El pretérito de los verbos regulares y de los verbos con cambios ortográficos

🌐 **Heinle Grammar Tutorial:** The preterite tense

 CD1 Track 37

Read and listen to the conversation between Amanda and Raquel. Identify all the verbs that refer to the past.

AMANDA: ¿Saliste con tus compañeros de clase anoche *(last night)*?

RAQUEL: Sí. Fuimos a un restaurante tailandés para celebrar el fin del curso.

AMANDA: ¡Qué bien! ¿Dónde comieron Uds.? ¿En el Thai Lotus?

RAQUEL: Sí, la comida es superrica allí. Y después de comer, cantamos karaoke. ¿Y tú, Amanda? ¿Qué hiciste?

AMANDA: Pasé la noche en la biblioteca. Tengo un examen esta tarde, ¿sabes?

Teaching Tip: Play the recording or have students read the conversation aloud. Help students use verb forms, expressions of time, and context clues to distinguish past, present, and future time frames.

Answers: Saliste, Fuimos, comieron, cantamos, hiciste, Pasé

A. El pretérito. In Spanish, two kinds of verbs are used to refer to the past—the preterite and the imperfect. In this section you will learn more about one of these: **el pretérito.** The preterite is used to tell what happened or what somebody did with reference to a particular point in time, such as yesterday or last week.

> **Salí** con unos compañeros de clase anoche.
> *I **went out** with some classmates last night.*

B. Verbos regulares. Here are the verb endings for the preterite. Notice that **-er** and **-ir** verbs share the same set of endings.

El pretérito de los verbos regulares

	tomar *(to take)*	**volver** *(to return)*	**salir** *(to leave, go out)*
yo	tom**é**	volv**í**	sal**í**
tú	tom**aste**	volv**iste**	sal**iste**
Ud./él/ella	tom**ó**	volv**ió**	sal**ió**
nosotros(as)	tom**amos**	volv**imos**	sal**imos**
vosotros(a)	tom**asteis**	volv**isteis**	sal**isteis**
Uds./ellos/ellas	tom**aron**	volv**ieron**	sal**ieron**

► Remember that reflexive verbs must be accompanied by a reflexive pronoun.

> **Me desperté** a las siete hoy.   *I **woke up** at seven o'clock today.*

► The verb **gustar** generally uses only two forms in the preterite: **gustó,** with infinitives and singular nouns, and **gustaron,** with plural nouns.

> Me **gustó** mucho el concierto.
> *I **liked** the concert a lot. (The concert **was pleasing** to me.)*

> No me **gustaron** esas dos películas.
> *I **didn't like** those two films. (Those two films **were not pleasing** to me.)*

Teaching Tip: Point out that accent marks are needed over the endings corresponding to **yo** and **Ud./él/ella.** Contrast the difference in pronunciation and meaning in **-ar** verbs between present tense **tomo** and **tomó.** Provide examples to show that context helps us distinguish between present and past time frames with **-ar** and **-ir** verb forms such as **tomamos** or **salimos.**

More Information: Stem-changing **-ir** verbs are introduced later in this chapter. You will probably need to emphasize repeatedly the fact that **o → ue** and **e → ie** stem changes are limited to the present tense, as students tend to overgeneralize and apply this rule to the preterite as well.

Grammar: With more proficient classes, introduce the verb **ver** (to see), which is conjugated as a regular **-er** verb but does not use accent marks: **vi, viste, vio, vimos, visteis, vieron.**

C. Los verbos con cambios ortográficos. There are two main categories of spelling-changing verbs (**verbos con cambios ortográficos**).

1. Infinitives that end in -**car**, -**gar**, or -**zar** change spelling only when the subject is **yo.**

   ► Verbs that end in -**car** (like **tocar, buscar,** and **sacar**) change **c → qu.**

   to**car** *(to play an instrument)*: yo to**qué** (tocaste, tocó, tocamos, tocasteis, tocaron)

   ► Verbs that end in -**gar** (like **llegar, jugar,** and **pagar**) change **g → gu.**

   lle**gar** *(to arrive)*: yo lle**gué** (llegaste, llegó, llegamos, llegasteis, llegaron)

   ► Verbs that end in -**zar** (like **empezar** or **almorzar**) change **z → c.**

   empe**zar** *(to begin)*: yo empe**cé** (empezaste, empezó, empezamos, empezasteis, empezaron)

2. Infinitives that end in "**vowel + -er / -ir**" have spelling changes only when the subject is **Ud./él/ella** or **Uds./ellos/ellas.**

   ► Verbs that end in "vowel + -**er**/-**ir**" (like **leer, creer,** and **caerse**) change **i → y.**

   leer *(to read)*: leí, leíste, leyó, leímos, leísteis, leyeron

Ponerlo a prueba

Teaching Tip: Assign 5–18 and 5–19 for homework to continue providing input on the preterite verb endings.

5-18 El fin de semana pasado. ¿Qué hicieron todos el fin de semana pasado? Escoge el verbo correcto para cada oración.

1. El viernes (yo) fui al cine. (<u>Miré</u> / Miró) una película cómica y después (<u>comí</u> / comió) una pizza.

2. El sábado mis amigos y yo (jugaron / <u>jugamos</u>) al básquetbol por unas horas. Luego, (nosotros) (<u>volvimos</u> / volvieron) a la residencia para estudiar.

3. Mi amiga Katrina (estudiaste / <u>estudió</u>) mucho el domingo para un examen. Después, (corriste / <u>corrió</u>) un poco para despejar la mente *(to clear her head)*.

4. Mis compañeros de cuarto Carlos y Jaime (decidimos / <u>decidieron</u>) salir de la ciudad. (Pasamos / <u>Pasaron</u>) todo el fin de semana en la playa.

5. ¿Y tú? ¿(<u>Trabajaste</u> / Trabajó) mucho este fin de semana? ¿(<u>Saliste</u> / Salió) con amigos?

5-19 El primer día de clases de Gabriel. Usa el pretérito de los verbos para describir el primer día de clases de Gabriel. Escoge el verbo más lógico en cada caso; escríbelo en el pretérito.

> **MODELO**   Este semestre (empezar / sacar) __empezó__ mal para mí.

1. El primer día de clases, el despertador *(alarm clock)* no (sonar / comer) ___sonó___.

2. Por eso *(That's why)* (yo) (levantarse / afeitarse) __me levanté__ muy tarde.

3. Después de vestirme rápidamente, (yo) (jugar / correr) ___corrí___ a mi primera clase.

4. Desafortunadamente, (yo) no (volver / llegar) ___llegué___ a clase a tiempo. ¡No había nadie *(nobody)* en la sala!

5. Más tarde, mis amigos y yo (leer / almorzar) __almorzamos__ en la cafetería.

6. Después de comer, (yo) (empezar / creer) ___empecé___ a sentirme *(to feel)* mal.

7. Entonces, mis amigos y yo (asistir / volver) __volvimos__ a nuestra residencia.

8. Ellos (jugar / mirar) ___jugaron___ videojuegos y (leer / creer) ___leyeron___ sus mensajes electrónicos.

9. Pero yo (leer / acostarse) ___me acosté___ inmediatamente y dormí el resto del día.

5-20 ¿Qué hizo la familia Martínez ayer? Describe las actividades de los miembros de la familia Martínez con oraciones completas. Hay que usar el pretérito y escribir tres o cuatro frases para cada dibujo.

Algunos verbos útiles: asistir, beber, comer, escribir, escuchar, estudiar, explicar, hablar, jugar, mirar, nadar, tomar, trabajar, ver

| MODELO | Ayer don Arturo trabajó en su oficina. Habló con sus clientes por teléfono. También, estudió algunas estadísticas para el banco en su computadora. |

don Arturo

1. 2. 3. 4.

Elisa y Tía Felicia   Beatriz   Dulce y sus compañeros de clase   Carlos y sus amigos

5-21 ¿Qué pasó ayer? Conversa con un(a) compañero(a) sobre sus actividades ayer.

PRIMERA PARTE: Entrevista a un(a) compañero(a) con las siguientes preguntas. Toma apuntes *(Take notes)*. (**¡Ojo!** *If yesterday was not a class day, refer back to the last day you both attended class.*)

1. ¿A cuántas clases asististe ayer?

2. ¿Tomaste un examen o una prueba *(quiz)*? ¿En qué clase?

3. ¿Estudiaste mucho? ¿Para qué clases?

4. ¿Limpiaste tu cuarto? ¿Lavaste la ropa?

5. ¿Saliste con tus amigos? ¿Qué hicieron Uds.?

6. ¿Jugaste algún deporte? ¿Miraste televisión o una película?

7. ¿Pasó algo especial? *(Did anything special happen?)* ¿Algo malo?

8. *Haz una pregunta original.*

SEGUNDA PARTE: Lee los apuntes. ¿Cómo fue el día de tu compañero(a) en comparación con el tuyo? Marca todos los adjetivos aplicables.

☐ ajetreado   ☐ bueno   ☐ rutinario   ☐ triste

☐ aburrido   ☐ divertido   ☐ activo   ☐ difícil

Teaching Tip 5-20: Complete two items together as a class. Begin by creating a short simple sentence on the board or screen; have students focus on the pattern "subject + conjugated verb." Then add details to make the sentences longer. Refocus the students' attention on the time frame—yesterday. Next, have pairs complete the last two items. Encourage friendly competition to see which pair can create the longest sentence or the most information for a drawing.

Vocabulary: Explain that **don** is a title of respect used with the first name, particularly with older persons. The feminine equivalent is **doña.**

Teaching Tip 5-21: Follow up by asking individual students question 7. Elicit details on the special or bad event.

Expansion 5-21: Have students pantomime what they did yesterday, while classmates narrate what they did. For example, one student pantomimes reading a newspaper and the class responds: **Leíste el periódico.**

Expansion: For additional practice, ask students questions about last semester, or last year: **¿Estudiaste en esta universidad el semestre pasado? ¿Qué clases tomaste? ¿Te gustó la clase de ____? ¿Sacaste buenas o malas notas? ¿Viviste en una residencia? ¿Cuál?**

Proficiency: This section continues to lay the groundwork for students' comprehension of the past time frame. Of the two topics presented here, emphasize the uses of the preterite and continue to focus on regular verbs, along with the new stem-changing verbs.

Teaching Tip: Use the party description to introduce the various uses of the preterite. Afterwards, refer to the verbs in boldface print and use them to introduce the topic of stem-changing **-ir** verbs.

Answers: anoche, por horas, cuatro veces.

More Information: Although the imperfect is not introduced until Chapter 7, we mention it here to begin preparing students for its eventual introduction. When speaking in class, feel free to use the imperfect at the appropriate times, as student understanding at this level is based largely on the stem of verbs, rather than the ending.

Gramática

Los usos del pretérito y los verbos con cambios en la raíz

🔊 CD1 Track 38

Listen and read as Isabel describes a party she attended. Identify the following: the word that tells you **when** the party took place; the phrase that expresses **how long** everyone danced; another phrase that tells you **how many times** Paul asked her to dance.

Fui a una fiesta fenomenal anoche. Era una fiesta formal para celebrar el cumpleaños de Sarita y todos **nos vestimos** elegantemente. La fiesta **empezó** a las siete y media. Primero, los padres de Sarita **sirvieron** unos platos deliciosos. Después, la orquesta **empezó** a tocar. ¡Mi amigo Paul me **invitó** a bailar cuatro veces! Todos los invitados **bailaron** por horas y **se divirtieron** muchísimo.

A. Los usos del pretérito. In Spanish, both the preterite and the imperfect are used to talk about the past. You will learn more about the imperfect in Chapter 7. Here are the main uses of the preterite.

▸ To tell what happened or what somebody did on some particular occasion. To specify the occasion or time, add: **ayer, anoche** *(last night),* **la semana pasada** *(last week),* **el año pasado, en 2008.**

  Mis padres me **visitaron la semana pasada.**
  *My parents **visited** me **last week**.*

▸ To say that an action or event occurred several times. To specify the number of times, add: **una vez** *(one time, once),* **dos veces, varias veces** *(several times).*

  Mi mejor amiga me **llamó dos veces** anoche.
  *My best friend **called** me **twice** last night.*

▸ To tell how long an action or event lasted. To specify the amount of time, adapt the phrase "**por** + amount of time": **por veinte minutos, por dos días, por cuatro años.**

  Mi compañero de cuarto y yo **estudiamos por tres horas** anoche.
  *My roommate and I **studied for three hours** last night.*

▸ To sum up an experience, especially at the beginning or end of a story or anecdote.

  Ayer **fue** un día horrible. Primero, me desperté tarde, después...
  *Yesterday **was** a terrible day. First, I got up late; then . . .*

B. Los verbos con cambios en la raíz. Some verbs undergo changes in the stem (the front part of the verb) when they are conjugated in the preterite.

▸ The change takes place only with certain **-ir** verbs.

▸ There are two kinds of stem changes: **e → i** and **o → u.**

▸ The stem change occurs only in the "third person" forms: **Ud./él/ella** and **Uds./ellos/ellas.**

Los verbos con cambios en la raíz en el pretérito

	e → i **divertirse** *(to have fun)*	o → u **dormir** *(to sleep)*
yo	me divertí	dormí
tú	te divertiste	dormiste
Ud./él/ella	se divirtió	durmió
nosotros(as)	nos divertimos	dormimos
vosotros(as)	os divertisteis	dormisteis
Uds./ellos/ellas	se divirtieron	durmieron

Here are some common stem-changing verbs in the preterite along with examples.

e → i

conseguir *(to get, to obtain)*	Paco consiguió boletos para el concierto.
divertirse *(to have fun)*	Todos se divirtieron en la excursión.
pedir *(to ask for, to order)*	Marta pidió camarones en el restaurante.
repetir *(to repeat)*	Los estudiantes repitieron el vocabulario.
servir *(to serve)*	Mi hermana sirvió un postre delicioso anoche.
vestirse *(to get dressed)*	Elena se vistió muy elegantemente para su cita.

o → u

dormir *(to sleep)*	Mi compañero de cuarto durmió todo el día.
morir *(to die)*	Mi perro murió el año pasado.

Ponerlo a prueba

5-22 Una semana desastrosa. Rubén tuvo una semana horrible. Lee las descripciones de qué pasó. Luego, indica por qué se usa el pretérito en cada caso; escribe la letra (a, b, c, d) que corresponde mejor.

a. to express what happened on a particular occasion

b. to say how long an action/event lasted

c. to tell how many times an action took place

d. to sum up the experience

___d___ 1. Esta semana fue *(was)* una de las peores de mi vida.

___a___ 2. El lunes tomé un examen muy difícil en química. Creo que saqué C o D.

___a___ 3. El martes, ¡me robaron *(they stole)* el coche! La policía no tiene pistas *(clues)* y yo no tengo seguro *(insurance)*.

___b/a___ 4. El miércoles esperé a mi novia en la cafetería por dos horas y ella nunca se presentó.

___c/a___ 5. El jueves llamé a mi novia por teléfono cinco veces pero ella no contestó. No sé qué pasa con ella.

___a___ 6. El viernes llegué al trabajo tarde (¡Es difícil llegar a tiempo sin coche!) y el supervisor me despidió *(fired me)*.

Teaching Tip: Students often use "Spanglish" to express the idea "have a good time" with incorrect, invented phrases such as *tener un buen tiempo**. Gently and consistently correct them and encourage the use of *divertirse.*

Teaching Tip: Assign 5-22 for homework to familiarize students with the uses of the preterite and 5-23 to have them practice stem-changing verbs in the preterite.

5-23 El fin de semana de Milagros. Usa la información a continuación para describir las actividades de Milagros y sus amigos. Escoge el verbo más lógico de la lista y escríbelo en el pretérito.

conseguir (i)   **divertirse (i)**   **dormir (u)**

pedir (i)   **servir (i)**   **vestirse (i)**

1. El fin de semana pasado Milagros y sus amigos <u>se divirtieron</u> mucho.

2. El viernes por la noche, fueron a un restaurante con especialidades argentinas. Milagros <u>pidió</u> churrasco *(Argentine barbecued beef)*. ¡Era muy rico!

3. El sábado Ricardo invitó a Milagros a una fiesta. Ella <u>se vistió</u> muy elegantemente para su cita *(date)* porque quería impresionar a Ricardo.

4. Milagros y Ricardo bailaron toda la noche en la fiesta, y ella llegó a casa a las tres de la madrugada. El domingo ella <u>durmió</u> hasta el mediodía.

5. El domingo por la tarde Milagros y sus amigos <u>consiguieron</u> boletos *(tickets)* para un concierto. Después, salieron a comer pizza. ¡Qué fin de semana más divertido!

Teaching Tip 5-24: After giving directions, go over the meaning of the time expressions in **Expresiones útiles** before students work in pairs. Give more examples of how to use **hace + time** to express "ago." Remind the class that the preterite is appropriate here because they are referring to what they did on specific occasions.

Expansion 5-24: If you wish to focus more on this grammatical point, have students write follow-up sentences like this: **Yo saqué una buena nota en historia la semana pasada, y mi compañero Luke sacó una buena nota en inglés hace dos semanas. Yo dormí hasta la una el domingo pasado y mi compañero durmió hasta la una el sábado.**

5-24 ¿Cuándo? Habla con un(a) compañero(a) de clase sobre los temas y comparen respuestas. ¿Cuándo fue la última vez que hicieron estas actividades? *(When was the last time that you did these things?)*

MODELO

Tú: ¿Cuándo tomaste un examen difícil?

Tu compañero(a):   Tomé un examen difícil en historia **la semana pasada**. ¿Y tú?

Tú: Tomé un examen difícil en psicología **hace dos semanas** *(two weeks ago)*.

Expresiones útiles: ayer, la semana pasada, el fin de semana pasado, el mes pasado, el año pasado, hace + *time* ("ago")

1. ¿Cuándo te levantaste tarde para ir a clase?

2. ¿Cuándo sacaste una buena nota en un examen?

3. ¿Cuándo dormiste hasta la una de la tarde?

4. ¿Cuándo te vestiste elegantemente para un evento social?

5. ¿Cuándo pediste un postre exquisito en un restaurante?

6. ¿Cuándo te divertiste mucho con tus hermanos o con tus padres?

Paso 3

Vocabulario temático

In this *Paso* you will practice:

▶ Describing a field trip that you have taken
▶ Talking about actions in the present, past, and future time frames

Grammar:

▶ Preterite of irregular verbs
▶ Summary of past, present, and future time frames

Cómo hablar de las excursiones académicas

¿Hiciste algo interesante la semana pasada?

Sí, el viernes mi clase de *ciencia marina* hizo una excursión *al centro acuático de la universidad.*

Primero, el director del centro dio una presentación sobre *los delfines* y todos tomamos apuntes.

Luego, tuvimos que *recolectar datos* para nuestros proyectos.

Más tarde, fuimos *al observatorio del centro.*

Pudimos observar *varios animales acuáticos.*

Proficiency: In this **Paso** we continue to lay the foundation for more advanced levels of proficiency by continuing to practice expression in the past time frame. Because of the number of irregular verbs, the preterite is a challenging topic; as students begin to memorize these forms, you will find that their proficiency level in the present time frame will suffer temporarily. You may wish to focus on the more common irregular verbs to ease the memory load for your students: **ser/ir, hacer, tener.** Towards the end of the **Paso** we refocus students' attention on the three time frames: past, present, and future.

Teaching Tip: Find out what field trips are commonly taken in your academic institution and use these as a point of departure for this presentation. You might also ask your students about field trips they took in high school.

Vocabulary: Students may enjoy learning the names of some marine animals: **delfín** *(dolphin)*, **tiburón** *(shark)*, **pez** *(fish)*, **pulpo** *(octopus)*, **ballena** *(whale)*, **tortuga marina** *(sea turtle)*.

CD1
Track 39

Ponerlo a prueba

5-25 El viaje al acuario. La clase de ciencia marina hizo una excursión a la costa. Escucha la conversación y completa las oraciones.

_c_ 1. Virginia y sus amigos fueron al acuario porque...
   a. les dieron unos boletos gratis.
   b. tuvieron que hacer unos experimentos.
   c. recibieron un crédito extra.

_a_ 2. En el acuario, el director...
   a. les dio una charla *(talk)* personal a Virginia y a sus amigos.
   b. llevó a Virginia y a sus amigos al observatorio.
   c. ayudó a Virginia y a sus amigos a recolectar datos.

_b_ 3. Virginia y sus amigos tuvieron que...
   a. tomar fotografías de los animales acuáticos.
   b. entregar *(turn in)* un informe escrito.
   c. hacer unos experimentos con los animales acuáticos.

_a_ 4. Durante la visita al acuario, los amigos vieron...
   a. tiburones *(sharks)*.   b. delfines *(dolphins)*.   c. plantas acuáticas.

_b_ 5. Antes de regresar a la universidad, Virginia y sus amigos fueron a...
   a. nadar en el mar.   b. comer en un restaurante.   c. pasear por la playa.

5-26 La excursión al Museo de Arte. Completa la información sobre el viaje al Museo de Arte Moderno de una manera lógica. Relaciona las dos columnas.

_b_ 1. La semana pasada, nuestro profesor nos llevó al Museo de Arte...

_e_ 2. Luego, la directora del museo nos saludó y...

_a_ 3. Más tarde, vimos las exposiciones y...

_c_ 4. Después, tomamos un café y...

_d_ 5. Por último, salimos del museo y...

a. tomamos apuntes sobre las obras.

b. para ver la nueva exposición de Xul Solar.

c. conversamos sobre las obras y los artistas.

d. volvimos a la universidad.

e. nos dio una presentación sobre el artista.

5-27 Una excursión. Piensa en una excursión académica que tomaste en la universidad o en la escuela secundaria. Completa las oraciones con información sobre esa excursión y léeselas *(read them to)* a un(a) compañero(a) de clase. Tu compañero(a) debe hacerte *(ask you)* dos o tres preguntas sobre la excursión.

1. Una vez, hice una excursión académica a _____.
2. Durante la excursión, mis compañeros y yo escuchamos una presentación sobre _____.
3. También, pudimos observar _____.
4. Tuvimos que recolectar datos / tomar apuntes sobre _____.

5-28 Es académico. Conversa con un(a) compañero(a) sobre los temas a continuación.

1. ¿Te gusta hacer excursiones académicas? ¿Cuáles son las excursiones más populares de tu universidad? ¿Vas a hacer alguna excursión académica este semestre? ¿Adónde vas?
2. ¿En qué clases tienes que recolectar datos para experimentos o proyectos? ¿Te gusta hacer este tipo de investigación *(research)*?
3. ¿En qué clases tienes que dar presentaciones? ¿Usas PowerPoint para tus presentaciones o prefieres otra manera de presentar el material? Cuando escuchas presentaciones, ¿tomas muchos apuntes o prefieres concentrarte en el presentador?

Gramática

El pretérito de los verbos irregulares

CD1
Track 40
Read and listen to this description of a class experiment. What infinitive corresponds to each of the verbs in boldface?

Mi clase de sicología **hizo** un experimento interesante. **Tuvimos** que observar a niños interactuando con gatos y perros. El experimento **duró** dos semanas y **fue** muy laborioso. Pero al final, **pudimos** comprobar *(verify)* nuestra tesis. ¡Qué experiencia más fascinante!

A. Los verbos irregulares. The preterite aspect of the past tense has many irregular verbs. To help you memorize them, the verbs are grouped according to patterns they have in common. Note that accent marks are not used with any of the irregular verbs in the preterite.

IR / SER / DAR / VER: **Ser** and **ir** have identical forms, while **dar** and **ver** rhyme.

Irregular Preterite Verbs

	ir *(to go)*	**ser** *(to be)*	**dar** *(to give)*	**ver** *(to see)*
yo	fui	fui	di	vi
tú	fuiste	fuiste	diste	viste
Ud./él/ella	fue	fue	dio	vio
nosotros(as)	fuimos	fuimos	dimos	vimos
vosotros(as)	fuisteis	fuisteis	disteis	visteis
Uds./ellos/ellas	fueron	fueron	dieron	vieron

B. Más verbos irregulares. All the verbs in this section share the same set of endings.

Irregular Preterite Verb Endings: Group 1

yo	-e
tú	-iste
Ud./él/ella	-o
nosotros(as)	-imos
vosotros(as)	-isteis
Uds./ellos/ellas	-ieron

"U-STEM" VERBS: ESTAR / PODER / PONER / SABER / TENER. These verbs all have the letter "u" in the stem (front part) of the verb.

estar *(was / were)*	**poder** *(was/ were able to; managed to)*	**poner** *(put, placed)*	**saber** *(knew, found out)*	**tener** *(had, had to, got)*
estuve	pude	puse	supe	tuve
estuviste	pudiste	pusiste	supiste	tuviste
estuvo	pudo	puso	supo	tuvo
estuvimos	pudimos	pusimos	supimos	tuvimos
estuvisteis	pudisteis	pusisteis	supisteis	tuvisteis
estuvieron	pudieron	pusieron	supieron	tuvieron

More Information: To further emphasize the past time frame, translations for these verbs are given as the most common English equivalent for the preterite. The "meaning changes" are explained in greater detail in section C.

"I-STEM" VERBS: HACER / QUERER / VENIR. These verbs have the vowel "i" in the stem (front part of the verb) and use the same endings as the "u" verbs.

hacer *(made, did)*	querer *(wanted, tried to)*	venir *(came)*
hice	quise	vine
hiciste	quisiste	viniste
hizo	quiso	vino
hicimos	quisimos	vinimos
hicisteis	quisisteis	vinisteis
hicieron	quisieron	vinieron

C. Otros verbos irregulares. The verbs in this second grouping all share the same set of endings. In fact, the endings are nearly the same as those for the first grouping. The only difference is for the subjects **Uds./ellos/ellas.**

Irregular Preterite Verb Endings: Group 2

yo	-e
tú	-iste
Ud./él/ella	-o
nosotros(as)	-imos
vosotros(as)	-isteis
Uds./ellos/ellas	-eron

"J-STEM" VERBS: CONDUCIR / DECIR / TRAER. All these verbs have a "j' in the stem and use the endings above.

conducir *(drove)*	decir *(said, told)*	traer *(brought)*
conduje	dije	traje
condujiste	dijiste	trajiste
condujo	dijo	trajo
condujimos	dijimos	trajimos
condujisteis	dijisteis	trajisteis
condujeron	dijeron	trajeron

Proficiency: These special verbs are provided for recognition in speaking and listening. Most learners become able to use these subtleties at much higher proficiency levels.

Teaching Tip: Remind students that **conocer** means "to know persons," while **saber** means "to know information" or "to know how to do something."

D. Verbos especiales. Some verbs have slightly different translations when they are used in the preterite. Here are some of the common ones. Notice in parentheses the two translations: first, for the present tense; then, for the preterite.

conocer *(to know – "met")*	Anoche **conocí** a mis futuros suegros. *Last night I **met** my future in-laws.*
saber *(to know – "found out")*	**Supe** la mala noticia ayer. *I **found out** the bad news yesterday.*
poder *(to be able – "managed to")*	**Pudimos** recolectar los datos, a pesar de las dificultades. *We **managed to** collect the data, despite the difficulties.*
querer *(to want – "tried")*	Carmen **quiso** ir, pero nevaba demasiado. *Carmen **tried** to go, but it was snowing too hard.*
no querer *(to not want – "refused")*	No **quise** ir a la fiesta. *I **refused** to go to the party.*

Ponerlo a prueba

5-29 En el recinto universitario. Tomás y Lucy están en Buenos Aires para estudiar por un año. Completa su conversación en el pretérito.

TOMÁS: ¿Adónde (1. tú: ir) __fuiste__ el fin de semana pasado? (2. yo: pasar) __Pasé__ por tu casa varias veces pero no estabas.

LUCY: El sábado mis compañeros y yo (3. hacer) __hicimos__ una excursión al barrio *(neighborhood)* de Palermo.

TOMÁS: ¡Qué suerte! ¿Qué (4. ver) __vieron__ Uds. allí?

LUCY: Primero (5. nosotros: visitar) __visitamos__ el Museo de Arte Latinoamericano. La directora (6. dar) __dio__ una conferencia maravillosa sobre la vanguardia artística.

TOMÁS: ¿(7. ir) __Fueron__ Uds. al Planetario Galileo Galilei? Creo que está cerca del museo.

LUCY: Sí, efectivamente. (8. nosotros: poder) __Pudimos__ observar una roca lunar que la misión Apolo XI (9. traer) __trajo__ a la tierra *(earth)* para el planetario.

TOMÁS: Bueno, ¿y el domingo? ¿Qué (10. tú: hacer) __hiciste__?

LUCY: (11. yo: tener) __Tuve__ que recolectar datos para mi clase de genética. (12. yo: estar) __Estuve__ en el laboratorio todo el día. Más tarde (13. nosotros: dar) __dimos__ un paseo *(took a walk)* por los Bosques de Palermo, un parque muy bonito en esa zona.

5-30 La noche del estudiante. ¿Qué hizo Lucy el jueves por la noche? Completa las oraciones con el verbo más lógico de la lista. Escribe los verbos en el pretérito.

divertirse	poder	poner	ser
querer	tener	traer	venir

1. El jueves por la noche (yo) __me divertí__ mucho.
2. Unos amigos __vinieron__ a mi apartamento para una pequeña fiesta.
3. Mis amigos Josué y Rebeca __trajeron__ una pizza.
4. Después de comer, (nosotros) __pusimos__ música para bailar.
5. ¡__Fue__ una noche fabulosa!
6. Por desgracia, mi amigo Tomás no __pudo__ venir porque __tuvo__ que ayudar a su profesor con un experimento.

5-31 Por el campus. Tú y un(a) compañero(a) van a entrevistarse sobre varias de sus actividades. Contesta las preguntas oralmente con oraciones completas.

1. ¿Estuviste muy ocupado(a) ayer con tus actividades? ¿Pudiste hacer todas las cosas en tu agenda ayer? ¿Qué tareas *(tasks)* no hiciste? *Haz una pregunta original.*
2. ¿Quién te dijo una noticia interesante esta semana? ¿Qué te dijo? *Haz una pregunta original.*
3. ¿Diste una presentación en alguna clase recientemente *(recently)*? ¿Sobre qué hablaste? ¿Sacaste una buena nota? *Haz una pregunta original.*
4. ¿Hiciste una excursión en alguna de tus clases el año pasado? ¿Adónde fueron Uds.? ¿Qué vieron Uds. allí? ¿Qué aspecto de la excursión te gustó más? *Haz una pregunta original.*

Teaching Tip: Assign the first two activities for homework.

Note: The **Museo de Arte Latinoamericano de Buenos Aires** focuses especially on twentieth century art and is the only public museum outside of Mexico with an oil painting by Frida Kahlo. The lunar rock in the **Planetario Galileo Galilei** was a gift of former President Nixon. The **Bosques**, officially named **el Parque Tres de Febrero**, is a popular area for walking, cycling and going out in small boats on its three lakes.

Visit the official site of this planetarium at http://www.planetario.gov.ar

Gramática

El presente, el pasado y el futuro: resumen

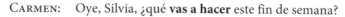

CD1
Track 41

Read and listen to Carmen and Silvia as they talk about classes. Look carefully at each verb or verb phrase in boldface print. Indicate whether the sentence it is in refers to the past (P), the present (PR), or the future (F).

CARMEN: Oye, Silvia, ¿qué **vas a hacer** este fin de semana?

SILVIA: ¡**Voy a estudiar**! La próxima semana **va a ser** muy ajetreada *(hectic)*.

CARMEN: Chica, prácticamente **vives** en la biblioteca.

SILVIA: Sí, **es** cierto. Pero, ¿**sabes**?, **me gusta** estudiar. Mis clases **son** muy interesantes y **me encantan** mis profesores.

CARMEN: ¿Y el Profesor Suárez?

SILVIA: Bueno, él sí **es** quisquilloso. La semana pasada nos **dio** un examen sobre la época medieval y **fue** dificilísimo.

A. Los tres tiempos. In both English and Spanish, everyday conversations generally revolve around three time frames: the past, the present, and the future.

Future:

—¿Qué **vas a hacer** este fin de semana?   *What **are you going to do** this weekend?*

—**Voy a estudiar**.   ***I'm going to study.***

Present:

—Prácticamente **vives** en la biblioteca.   *You practically **live** in the library.*
—Sí... pero **me gustan** mis clases.   *Yes, but I **like** my classes.*

Past:

La semana pasada el profesor nos **dio** un examen difícil.   *Last week the professor **gave** us a difficult test.*

B. El presente. Most conversations about the present time frame refer to our routines or ongoing actions:

▸ Routines or ongoing actions/events → Present tense

   Todos los días **estudio** por dos o tres horas.   *I **study** for 2 or 3 hours every day.*

▸ When speaking about routines, we often use expressions such as **todos los días, generalmente, normalmente**.

C. El futuro. Although Spanish does have a formal future tense, it is common to refer to the future time frame with the verb phrase **ir + a + infinitive**. Notice that the verb **ir** is conjugated in the present tense, but refers to the future.

> ▸ Future actions or plans → **ir + a +** infinitive
> **Voy a estudiar** el próximo fin de semana.   *I'm going to study next weekend.*

> ▸ When speaking about the future time frame, we often use expressions such as **mañana, el próximo martes, la próxima semana, el próximo año.**

> ▸ Other expressions to refer to future plans:
> **esperar** + infinitive *(to hope to . . .)*   **Espero trabajar** en un banco después de graduarme.
>
> **pensar** + infinitive *(to plan to . . .)*   **Pienso vivir** en un apartamento el próximo año.

D. El pasado. Conversations about the past are expressed with a variety of verb tenses. Throughout *Puentes,* you will practice two key ones: the imperfect (in Chapter 7) and the preterite (in this chapter).

> ▸ An action/event that took place on a particular occasion → Preterite
> Ayer **hicimos** una excursión al planetario.   *Yesterday we **took** a field trip to the planetarium.*

> ▸ A series of past actions → Preterite
> Primero, el director **dio** una presentación.   *First, the director **gave** a presentation.*
>
> Luego, **pasamos** al observatorio.   *Next, we **moved into** the observatory.*

> ▸ An action/event that lasted a specified period of time → Preterite
> **Estuvimos** en el planetario por cuatro horas.   *We **were** in the planetarium for 4 hours.*

> ▸ To refer to specific occasions in the past, we often use expressions such as **ayer, la semana pasada, el año pasado, hace cinco años** *(5 years ago).*

> ▸ To specify the order in which actions/events took place, we may say **primero, luego, antes de** +infinitive, **después de**+ infinitive, **más tarde, por último.**

More Information: The future tense is presented in the **Gramática suplementaria** section for Chapter 2 at the end of the textbook.

Teaching Tip: With more proficient groups, mention that the simple present tense can be used to refer to actions in the near future: **Salgo para Córdoba el lunes.** *I'm leaving for Córdoba on Monday.*

More Information: If you have time to go beyond essentials, you may choose to practice the present perfect (Chapter 4) and the past perfect (Chapter 7), which are found in the **Gramática suplementaria** section at the end of the textbook. The core *Puentes* program emphasizes the preterite and imperfect.

5-32 Pasado, presente o futuro.

5-32 Pasado, presente o futuro. Lee el diario de Martika. Escribe los verbos en la forma más adecuada. Conjuga los verbos en el presente o en el pretérito; para expresar acciones en el futuro, usa la expresión **ir + a + infinitivo.**

> Querido diario,
>
> (1. yo: sentirse) _Me siento_ muy frustrada hoy. Ayer (2. yo: estudiar)
> _estudié_ mucho para el examen de fisiología, pero (3. yo: sacar)
> _saqué_ una mala nota. ¡Ahora no (4. yo: saber) _sé_ qué hacer!
> El profesor (5. ser) _es_ muy desorganizado. Me
> (6. gustar) _gusta_ el material, pero (7. ser) _es_ dificilísimo.
> Bueno, (8. yo: hablar) _voy a hablar_ con el profesor la próxima semana
> y pedirle crédito extra.
> Por otro lado (*On the other hand*), mi novio me (9. dar) _dio_ una
> noticia muy buena esta mañana: La multinacional Klas dice que le
> (10. ofrecer) _va a ofrecer/ofreció_ un puesto (*job*) en Buenos Aires. Lo va a
> llamar mañana.

5-33 Mi graduación. Con un(a) compañero(a), conversa sobre la graduación de la escuela secundaria. ¿Tuvieron Uds. experiencias muy parecidas (*similar*)?

1. ¿Cuándo te graduaste de la escuela secundaria?

2. ¿Participaste en una ceremonia formal?

3. ¿Tuviste una fiesta para celebrar? ¿Cuántas personas asistieron?

4. ¿Hiciste un viaje con tus compañeros de clase? ¿Adónde fueron Uds.?

5. ¿Qué regalos recibiste?

6. ¿Cómo pasaste el verano (*summer*) después de tu graduación?

7. *Haz una pregunta original.*

5-34 Una conversación. Con dos o tres compañeros(as), preparen una conversación y preséntenla a la clase.

SITUACIÓN: Tres (o cuatro) estudiantes se encuentran (*run into one another*) por el campus.

- Se saludan (*They greet one other*).

- Hablan un poco sobre sus clases.

- Se preguntan (*They ask one other*) qué hicieron anoche.

- Hablan de sus planes para el próximo fin de semana.

- Se despiden (*They say good-bye*).

Un paso más

¡Vamos a hablar!

Estudiante A

Contexto: Tú (**Estudiante A**) y tu compañero(a) (**Estudiante B**) son investigadores privados. Una novia celosa *(jealous girlfriend)* los contrató *(hired)* para investigar a Felipe Moreno. Tú entrevistaste a Felipe sobre sus actividades del viernes pasado. A continuación hay un resumen *(summary)* de tus apuntes. Tu compañero(a) siguió *(tailed)* a Felipe ese mismo día. Tu tarea es encontrar discrepancias entre lo que Felipe te dijo y lo que tu compañero(a) lo vio hacer. Tomen turnos describiendo las actividades de Felipe y hagan una lista de las actividades que no concuerdan *(don't match)*.

Lunes

1. Por la mañana...

Se levantó temprano; corrió en el parque. Asistió a su

clase de antropología de 8:00 a 9:15.

2. Luego...

Fue a su laboratorio de química. Estuvo allí de

9:30 a 11.30. Después, almorzó en la cafetería

con su amigo Luis.

3. Por la tarde...

Tuvo que estudiar: Fue a la biblioteca y estudió por

varias horas. No habló con nadie en la biblioteca.

Volvió a su cuarto de la residencia y comió un sándwich.

4. Por la noche...

Fue a una discoteca a las 8:30. Habló con sus amigos

Paco y Rosa. Volvió a casa a la 1:00.

Go to the **Un paso más** section in the *Cuaderno de actividades* for reading, writing, and listening activities that correlate with this chapter.

Teaching Tip: Divide the class in half. Explain the instructions for Student A to half the class and the instructions for Student B to the other half. Then have students from the two sides find partners to complete the activity. Focus the groups on the use of the preterite.

Answers: 1. No hay discrepancias. 2. Llegó a clase a las diez, no a las nueve y media. Almorzó con una chica, no con Luis. 3. Habló con otra chica en la biblioteca. Comió en la cafetería con la misma chica. 4. Habló con otra chica en la discoteca. Volvió a casa a las dos, no a la una.

Un paso más

¡Vamos a hablar!

Estudiante B

Contexto: Tú (**Estudiante B**) y tu compañero(a) (**Estudiante A**) son investigadores privados. Una novia celosa *(jealous girlfriend)* los contrató *(hired)* para investigar a Felipe Moreno. Tu compañero(a) entrevistó a Felipe sobre sus actividades del viernes pasado, el mismo *(same)* día que lo seguiste *(tailed him)*. El dibujo representa lo que viste hacer a Felipe. Tu tarea es encontrar discrepancias entre lo que Felipe le dijo a tu compañero(a) y lo que tú viste que hizo. Tomen turnos describiendo las actividades de Felipe y hagan una lista de las actividades que no concuerdan *(don't match)*.

1. Por la mañana...

2. Luego...

3. Por la tarde...

4. Por la noche...

¡Vamos a ver! | *Episodio 5*

En la Hacienda Vista Alegre

Anticipación

A. Hablando se entiende la gente. ¿Qué profesión esperas practicar en el futuro? ¿En el futuro quieres hacer el mismo tipo de trabajo que tienen tus padres? ¿Por qué sí o por qué no? ¿Cómo va a ser tu vida en el futuro?

B. Expresiones. Completa el texto a continuación con las expresiones de la lista.

¡Qué gracioso! *How funny!*

broma *joke*

no estaba para bromas *not in the mood for jokes*

maestría *master's degree*

bromistas *jokers*

Teaching Tip: Preview the video by showing a fragment of the episode without sound and have students use visual clues to anticipate content. Stop and rewind the video until they understand the gist of the episode.

El otro día fui a mi escuela para recoger el diploma de mi (1) __maestría__ .
La secretaria me dijo que no lo encontraba y que lo habían perdido
(had lost). Yo le dije que (2) __no estaba para bromas__ y que necesitaba el
diploma para solicitar *(to apply for)* un trabajo. La secretaria me vio
muy nervioso y me dijo que todo era una (3) __broma__ . "Hoy es el Día
de los Inocentes *(April Fool's Day)*. En esta facultad somos todos muy
(4) __bromistas__ ." Yo le dije sarcásticamente: "(5) __¡Qué gracioso!__ ".

Vamos a ver

C. De paseo por la Hacienda Vista Alegre. Mira el Episodio 5 del vídeo y completa el siguiente cuadro. Escribe la información que escuchas sobre los diferentes temas. **¡Ojo!** No todos los chicos hablan de todos los temas. Pon una X en el cuadro si no dan ninguna información.

Answers to C: Sofía: Filología española; Viajar, leer y escribir; Escribir un libro sobre sus viajes por Latinoamérica. **Javier:** Medicina, Cardiología; La naturaleza, actividades al aire libre, viajar; Abrir una agencia de tours de aventuras naturales. **Alejandra:** Baile, danza y cursos de fotografía; La fotografía, escuchar música y salir con los amigos; X. **Antonio:** Administración de Empresas. Está sacando la maestría.; X; X. **Valeria:** Estudia en la Escuela de Arte y Diseño en Florencia.; X; X.

	SOFÍA	JAVIER	ALEJANDRA	ANTONIO	VALERIA
Estudios:					
Gustos y preferencias:					
Planes:					

En acción

D. Charlemos. Comenta con tus compañeros(as). ¿Con cuál de los chicos y chicas de *La Hacienda* compartes *(do you share)* algún pasatiempo, estudios o planes? ¿Eres una persona bromista? ¿Te gustan las personas bromistas? ¿Por qué sí o por qué no? ¿Sobre qué tema bromea *(jokes)* Sofía con Valeria? ¿Qué broma le gusta Antonio a Valeria? ¿Por qué?

E. 3, 2, 1 ¡Acción! Interpreten la siguiente situación en grupos de 3 ó 4 estudiantes. Ustedes están todos juntos en el salón de la casa la *Hacienda Vista Alegre* y se están conociendo un poco más *(you're getting to know one another better.)* Están hablando sobre sus estudios, gustos, preferencias y planes que tienen para el futuro. Compartan sus ideas y opiniones.

Teaching Tip: Have students practice summarizing, describing characters, sequencing events, making comparisons, and giving detailed narrations and descriptions based on what they see in the video.

Practice the vocabulary and grammar that you learned in **Capítulo 5 (profesiones, asignaturas, hablar del futuro,** etc.).

Panorama cultural

 DATOS ESENCIALES

Nombre oficial: República Argentina

Capital: Buenos Aires

Población: 40 482 000 habitantes

Unidad monetaria: el peso

Economía: producción de ganado *(livestock)* y cereales, maquinaria *(machinery)* y equipo de transporte, petróleo, turismo

 www.cengage.com/spanish/ puentes

Transparency Bank A-8

Note: The area known as Argentina was sparsely settled by a number of indigenous groups, such as the **guaraní**, **quechua**, and **diaguita**. They were all eventually conquered and the land was taken over by Spain.

Note: Argentine society has a European flavor due to the strong influences of immigrants, especially Italians (also French, Swiss, British, Germans, Russians, and Polish). The waves of immigrants continued coming until the middle of the 20th century.

Note: The preparation and serving of mate follows a precise ritual. One person, called the **cebador**, fills the mate vessel and drinks it, to check for the right temperature and quality of the brew. He or she then fills it again and passes it to the next person, who drinks it and then returns the gourd to the server. The server continues to fill the vessel and pass it to the next person in turn.

Note: The Perón era marks a turbulent and fascinating period in Argentine history. A military coup in 1943 made Juan Domingo Perón the nation's new leader. Perón was re-elected in 1951, overthrown in 1955, and returned to power in 1973. His political strength was heightened by the popularity of his second wife, Eva Duarte de Perón. When he died in 1974, his third wife, Isabel (vice president at the time), assumed the presidency; but the military took over in 1976.

Note: Argentina is the second largest country in South America, after Brazil. Important geographical features include the vast, pampas flatlands; Cerro Aconcagua, the highest peak in the western hemisphere; the Cataratas del Iguazú, which are higher than Niagara Falls; and the Perito Moreno glacier.

El mate Beber mate es una actividad social entre amigos, familiares y compañeros de trabajo. El mate es una infusión (similar al té) de agua y las hojas *(leaves)* de la planta yerba mate. Tradicionalmente, se sirve en un recipiente *(container)* especial hecho de una calabaza *(gourd)* y se bebe con una bombilla *(silver straw)*. Todos beben del mismo recipiente y así se forman estrechas *(close)* relaciones personales.

Un vistazo a la historia

1536 Pedro de Mendoza funda Buenos Aires.

1816 Argentina se declara un país independiente.

1850 Principio de la gran inmigración europea, especialmente de España e Italia. El 85% de la población argentina es de origen europeo.

1976 Inicio de la "Guerra Sucia", una época de gran represión. "Desaparecen" unas 30 000 personas entre 1976 y 1983.

Note: The "Dirty War" served to eliminate political opposition and resulted in the death or exile of thousands of trade unionists, students, and other civilians.

1989 Retorno definitivo a la democracia tras *(after)* años de dictaduras militares. Elección del presidente Carlos Saúl Menem.

2007 Elección de Cristina Fernández de Kirschner, primera mujer presidenta de Argentina.

Note: President Cristina Fernandéz de Kirschner is the wife of the previous president, Néstor Kirschner, who oversaw the economic rebound after the economic crisis of 2001. She is the first elected female president; previous female national leaders included President Isabelita Martínez de Perón (1976–1976) and Eva Duarte de Perón.

Argentina

Personajes de ayer y hoy

Jorge Luis Borges (1899–1986)

Brillante autor de poesía, ensayos y cuentos, Borges es uno de los escritores más destacados (*prominent*) del siglo XX. Desde los seis años quería ser escritor y empezó a escribir a los siete años. Entre sus obras más famosas, escritas en español, encontramos *El jardín de los senderos que se bifurcan* y *El Aleph*. Aunque recibió numerosos premios, la Academia Sueca nunca le otorgó el Premio Nobel.

Note: Borges was also an accomplished translator of the works of Oscar Wilde, James Joyce, Walt Whitman, Virginia Woolf, and many others.

Diego Armando Maradona (1960–)

Futbolista extraordinario, Maradona fue elegido el Mejor Jugador del Siglo por la FIFA (Fédération Internationale de Football Association). Entre sus muchos logros (*achievements*), llevó su equipo a la victoria en la Copa Mundial de 1986. En los años 90 tuvo problemas de salud y de adicción a las drogas. En 2008, fue nombrado director técnico (*coach*) de la Selección Argentina de fútbol.

Note: More than a star soccer player, Maradona enjoyed idol status in his home country. He received numerous government commendations and is the subject of many songs. For a short while, after retirement, he hosted a TV show.

Cristina Fernández de Kirschner (1953–)

Esta dinámica abogada y política es la primera mujer en ser elegida presidenta de Argentina. Antes de asumir este cargo en 2007, fue la primera dama (*first lady*) durante la presidencia de su esposo, Néstor Kirschner. Una de las primeras medidas (*measures*) de la nueva Presidenta fue la creación del Ministerio de Ciencia, Tecnología e Innovación Productiva.

Note: Kirschner is a member of the **Partido Justicialista**. She has also served as a legislator and senator.

Note: Singer and actor Carlos Gardel was the foremost proponent of the tango in the first half of the twentieth century.

Note: The Plaza de Mayo was named for the **Revolución de mayo**, when in 1810 the first local government not chosen by the Spanish crown came to power in Buenos Aires. This is considered the start of Argentine independence from colonial rule. In the 1940s it was the site of demonstrations organized by Eva Perón and trade unionists, who demanded the release from prison of Juan Perón. From 1977 to 2006, it was the site of protest of the mothers of the Plaza de Mayo, who demonstrated on behalf of loved ones lost during the Dirty War.

More activities on Argentina and the **Panorama cultural** are found in the **Un paso más** section of the *Cuaderno de actividades*.

Imágenes de Argentina

Mira el vídeo sobre Argentina y contesta las preguntas.

1. ¿Cuáles son algunos aspectos culturales por los cuales (*for which*) es conocida Argentina?

2. ¿Qué es la Plaza de Mayo? ¿Qué importancia tiene en la historia y en el presente?

3. ¿Por qué se le llama a Buenos Aires "el París de Sudamérica"?

Answers for Imágenes de Argentina: 1. El tango, el mate, Gardel, el fútbol; 2. La más conocida de las plazas de Buenos Aires; es un símbolo de los primeros pasos hacia la independencia; es un punto de encuentro y denuncia por los derechos humanos. 3. Porque tiene muchas influencias europeas y es un centro de cultura.

Vocabulario

Sustantivos

los apuntes *notes*
la carrera *major (field of study)*
la compañía multinacional
 multinational company
la conferencia *lecture*
los datos *facts*
la excursión *field trip*
el fin de semana *weekend*
el horario *schedule*
la investigación *research*
la madrugada *dawn, early morning*
la medianoche *midnight*
la nota *grade*
el observatorio *observatory*
el oficio *occupation, trade*
la presentación *presentation*
el proyecto *project*
el rato *while*
la teoría *theory*
la vida marina *marine life*

Verbos

caerse *to fall down*
conseguir (i) *to get, obtain*
creer *to believe, think (opinion)*
dormirse (ue, u) *to fall asleep*
encantar *to love (a thing or an activity)*
graduarse *to graduate*
hacer estudios de postgrado *to go
 to graduate school*
interesar *to be interested in, to interest*
recolectar *to collect*
sacar *to get a grade*
salir (bien/mal) *to do (well/poorly)
 [on a test]*
sentarse (ie) *to sit down*
tocar *to play (a musical instrument);
 to touch*
trabajo escrito *(academic) paper,
 report*

Otras palabras

demasiado(a) *too (much)*
desorganizado(a) *disorganized*
exigente *demanding*
fascinante *fascinating*
mí mismo(a) *myself*
pesado(a) *tedious*
por la mañana *in the morning*
quisquilloso(a) *picky*
regular *average, so-so*
temprano *early*

Expresiones para indicar el tiempo

a finales de *at the end of (a month)*
a principios de *at the beginning of
 (a month)*
antes de *before (doing something)*
ayer *yesterday*
después *afterwards*
después de *after (doing something)*
el año pasado *last year*
el fin de semana pasado *last weekend*
el próximo año *next year*
entonces *then*
hace tres meses *three months ago*
la semana pasada *last week*
luego *then, next*
más tarde *later on*
por fin *finally*
primero *first*

Expresiones útiles

¿A qué te quieres dedicar? *What do
 you want to do for a living?*
¿Cómo te va en...? *How's it going for
 you in . . . ?*
¿Cuál es tu carrera? *What is your
 major?*
Espero trabajar para... *I hope to work
 for . . .*
Me interesa(n)... *I'm interested in . . . /
 . . . interests me.*
(No) estoy seguro(a) todavía. *I'm still
 (not) sure.*
Pienso ser... *I'm thinking about being
 a . . . , I'm planning on being a . . .*
¿Qué piensas de...? *What do you think
 about . . . ?*
¿Qué planes tienes para el futuro?
 What are your plans for the future?
Y tú, ¿qué piensas? *And you, what do
 you think?*

Courses of study pp. 158–159
Professions and occupations p. 165

Go to the **Puentes** website for extra vocabulary
practice using the Flashcard program.

For further review, please turn to **Vocabulario
temático: español e inglés** at the back of the
book.

De compras

More Information: This chapter focuses on two practical functions: shopping for clothing and bargaining for souvenirs and gifts. In addition to the new grammar, the preterite is reinforced in a number of activities so that students will be better prepared for the intensive presentation of past narration and description in Chapter 7.

Situation Cards: 58, 59, 60, 61, 62, 63, 64, 66, 69, 70, 101

Turn to the *Cuaderno de actividades* for this chapter's reading practice and strategy: Consulting a dictionary when reading.

Turn to the *Cuaderno de actividades* for this chapter's composition practice and writing strategy: Consulting a dictionary when writing.

OBJETIVOS

Speaking and Listening
- Naming articles of clothing and colors
- Referring to floors of a building with ordinal numbers
- Handling shopping transactions for clothing, accessories, and souvenirs
- Bargaining for souvenirs

Culture
- Spain
- Fashion in Spanish-speaking countries

Grammar
- More verbs like **gustar: parecer, quedar, importar,** and **faltar**
- Indefinite and negative expressions
- **Por** and **para**

Video
- En la Hacienda Vista Alegre: Episodio 6
- Imágenes de España

Gramática suplementaria
- Las expresiones indefinidas y negativas

Cuaderno de actividades
Reading
- Strategy: Consulting a dictionary when reading

Writing
- Strategy: Consulting a dictionary when writing

Playlist
- 🌐 www.cengage.com/spanish/puentes

A primera vista

El vestido

La ropa, sin duda, tiene fines prácticos: una chaqueta, por ejemplo, nos ofrece protección contra el frío. Pero, con sus múltiples estilos y colores, la ropa también se convierte en una forma de expresión personal. ¿Qué estilo de ropa llevas tú para expresar tu personalidad?

En la canción "El vestido", tanto el vestido como la voz *(voice)* de la cantante son poderosos medios de expresión. Escucha la canción y completa la letra con las palabras de la lista. (**¡Ojo!** Hay dos palabras que se usan dos veces.)

Puentes playlist available on iTunes

nuevo	me pongo	me visto	para	vestido

Solo ___para___ hoy, ___me pongo___ un ___vestido___ ___nuevo___ ;

solo ___para___ hoy, ___me visto___ de ___nuevo___ .

HABLANDO DE LA MÚSICA

The human voice is used in different ways to create music.

- Music that is created primarily with instruments is called **música instrumental**. Music performed primarily by the voice is called **música vocal**.

- In classical music, singing voices are classified according to vocal range, weight, and timbre. Female voices may be **soprano, mezzosoprano, contralto**, while male voices are classified as **tenor, barítono,** and **bajo**.

- In many kinds of music, the quality of the voice is modified in order to express different sentiments. For example, in the flamenco style known as **cante jondo**, the singers modulate their voices to express deep emotion. These singers, known as **cantaores**, may appear overwhelmed by sadness as they sing of death, anguish, and despair.

Teaching Tip: Point out that in this song, Juana Molina uses her voice as an instrument.

Note: Juana Molina accompanies herself with acoustic guitar and keyboard. She is known for looping the sounds in the studio in order to create her unique sound.

JUANA MOLINA (1962–)

Nacionalidad: argentina

Obras y premios: Su segundo álbum, *Segundo,* fue nominado "Best World Music Album 2003" en *Entertainment Weekly. Tres cosas,* su tercer álbum, figura en la lista de "Top Ten Records of 2004" del *New York Times.*

De interés: Empezó su carrera como actriz de televisión en 1988. En 1996 comenzó a componer y cantar sus propias canciones. Su música es difícil de caracterizar; combina ritmos latinoamericanos, electrónicos y orientales. Un aspecto muy notable de su obra: usa su voz *(voice)* como instrumento de percusión.

EL VESTIDO

canción del álbum Un día *de Juana Molina*

Al principio del álbum *Un día*, la cantante explica su estilo: "Un día voy a cantar las canciones sin letra y cada uno podrá imaginar: si hablo de amor, de desilusión, banalidades o sobre Platón".

En tu opinión, ¿qué sentimientos expresa la canción "El vestido"?

Paso 1

Vocabulario temático

De compras en un gran almacén

CLIENTE(A): **Por favor, ¿dónde se encuentran *los zapatos para hombres?***
mujeres
niños(as)
jóvenes

DEPENDIENTE(A): **Están en *la planta baja.***

Los pisos

el sótano

la planta baja

el primer piso (1ᵉʳ)

el segundo piso (2º)

el tercer piso (3ᵉʳ)

el cuarto piso (4º)

el quinto piso (5º)

el sexto piso (6º)

el séptimo piso (7º)

el octavo piso (8º)

el noveno piso (9º)

el décimo piso (10º)

La ropa

un traje   **una camisa**   **unos pantalones**   **una corbata**   **un cinturón**

un vestido   **una falda**   **una blusa**   **unos pantalones cortos**   **una camiseta**

unos vaqueros   **una sudadera**   **unos calcetines**   **un traje de baño**   **unas sandalias**

una chaqueta   **un impermeable**   **un suéter**   **unas botas**   **unos guantes**

Los colores y otros detalles

rojo · rosado · anaranjado · amarillo · verde · azul

azul marino · morado · blanco · negro · gris · marrón

beige · (color) crema · de cuadros · con lunares · de rayas · estampado

LAS TALLAS Y LOS NÚMEROS

CABALLEROS

Zapatos

Estados Unidos	7	8	9	10	11	12	
Europa	39	41	43	44	45	46	

Trajes/Abrigos

Estados Unidos	34	36	38	40	42	44	46	48
Europa	44	46	48	50	52	56	58	60

Camisas

Estados Unidos	14	14½	15	15½	16	16½	17	17½
Europa	36	37	38	39	40	41	42	43

DAMAS

Zapatos

Estados Unidos	4	5	6	7	8	9
Europa	35	36	37	38	39	40

Vestidos/Trajes

Estados Unidos	8	10	12	14	16	18
Europa	36	38	40	42	44	46

More Information: English-speaking students grasp the notion of adjectival agreement easily but have difficulties applying the concept consistently. For this reason adjectives are reviewed here once again. Plan on spending 1–2 minutes to review the concept. Point out the agreement of color words and items of clothing at random intervals throughout the chapter to further heighten student awareness.

Grammar: The word **crema** does not have to agree with the noun because it is derived from a noun, cream. For example, **María llevaba un vestido (color) crema.** Also, agreement is not made when we say **in** what color we would like an item because in this case the color word functions as a noun: **¿Tienen Uds. estos zapatos en negro?**

Teaching Tip: Point out that **ese** (and its variants) refer to a location near the person being spoken to. With more proficient classes, introduce **aquel, aquella, aquellos, aquellas** to refer to locations far from both speakers.

ESTRUCTURAS ESENCIALES

Más sobre los adjetivos

A. Los colores. The words for colors are often used as descriptive adjectives. These words follow the same patterns that you learned in Chapter 3 for words like *alto, bajo, gordo, simpático,* etc.

▸ Place the name of the color **after** the name of the article of clothing.

Quiero una **blusa rosada**.   *I want a **pink blouse**.*

▸ Change the ending of the color word so that it matches the noun in gender and number.

¿Tienen Uds. **vestidos amarillos**?   *Do you have **yellow dresses**?*

B. Los números ordinales. The words for *first, second, third,* etc. are called ordinal numbers.

▸ Place ordinal numbers **before** the noun they modify.

Las blusas están en el **segundo piso**.   *Blouses are on the **second floor**.*

▸ Change the endings of ordinal numbers so that they agree in gender and number with the nouns they are describing.

Me gusta más la **segunda falda**.   *I like the **second skirt** better.*

▸ **Primero** and **tercero** drop the **-o** ending before a masculine singular noun but otherwise follow the rules for agreement of gender and number.

el **tercer** piso   *the **third** floor*

C. Los adjetivos demostrativos. The words *this/these* and *that/those* are called demonstrative adjectives.

▸ Place demonstrative adjectives before the noun in Spanish.

¿Cuánto cuesta **ese vestido**?   *How much does **that dress** cost?*

▸ Choose the form that matches the noun in gender and number.

	this	*these*	*that*	*those*
MASCULINE	este	estos	ese	esos
FEMININE	esta	estas	esa	esas

Estas chaquetas cuestan 80 euros.   ***These jackets** cost 80 euros.*

Ponerlo a prueba

 CD2 Track 2

6-1 Una orden por catálogo. La Sra. Davis quiere pedir algunas cosas del catálogo de JC Penny. Escucha la conversación entre ella y la operadora. Después, completa la información del formulario.

Teaching Tip: Assign the first two activities for homework.

Nombre: ___Margarita___ Apellido: ___Davis___

Dirección: ___Calle Correne, 1743___

Ciudad: ___Canton___ Estado: ___Ohio___ Código postal: ___44718___

Teléfono: ___216-555-4884___

Método de pago: ☐ Cargar a su cuenta # _____ ☑ Al contado

Número de artículo	Artículo	Talla	Color	Cantidad	Precio
R508-1922	chaqueta	44	azul marino	una	$75
R484-0641D	falda	10	rojo	una	$58
R503-0028C	calcetines	grande	negro	dos paquetes	$15

6-2 ¡Cuánta ropa! Basándote en los dibujos, completa las oraciones con los nombres de la ropa y los colores o detalles.

1. Ayer fui de compras a un almacén grande. Compré una ___corbata___ de ___rayas___ para mi papá y un ___suéter___ ___morado___ para mi mamá. También compré una ___camiseta___ con ___lunares___ para mi hermanita.

2. Cuando Carmen fue de compras, perdió una bolsa (*shopping bag*) con todos los artículos que había comprado: una ___falda___ de ___cuadros___, unas ___botas___ ___marrones___ y unos ___pantalones cortos___ ___blancos___.

3. Alberto fue de compras el fin de semana pasado y encontró unas gangas (*bargains*) increíbles: una ___chaqueta___ ___roja___, unos ___guantes___ ___negros___ y un ___traje___ ___gris___.

Teaching Tip 6-3: This activity includes references to the present (items 1-2), future (item 3) and past (item 4), as studied at the end of Chapter 5. Draw attention to these time frames before the students begin their conversation.

6-3 De compras. Con dos o tres compañeros(as) de clase, contesta las preguntas y conversa sobre las compras.

1. ¿Te gusta ir de compras? ¿Vas a los centros comerciales (*shopping malls*) con frecuencia? ¿Qué te gusta comprar por Internet?

2. Por lo general, ¿prefieres comprar la ropa en los grandes almacenes, en las boutiques o en las tiendas de descuentos (*discount stores*)? Explica. ¿Dónde te gusta comprar zapatos y otros accesorios?

3. ¿Qué ropa piensas comprar para la próxima temporada (*next season*)? ¿Qué accesorios vas a comprar? ¿Qué colores o estilos prefieres?

4. ¿Cuándo fue la última vez que fuiste de compras? ¿Qué tiendas visitaste? ¿Qué ropa compraste? ¿Cómo pagaste?

Teaching Tip 6-4: You may also direct students to include physical characteristics of their classmates, in addition to the clothing, to present a fuller description. (Physical characteristics were introduced in Chapter 3.) Alternatively, this activity may be used with more proficient classes in place of a formal presentation of the clothing and color vocabulary.

6-4 Adivina. Con un compañero(a), describe la ropa de las personas en tu clase para que él/ella adivine (*so that he/she can guess*) quién es.

MODELO

Tú: Esta chica lleva pantalones negros, una camiseta blanca y una chaqueta verde. También lleva zapatos marrones con calcetines negros. ¿Quién es?

Tu compañero(a): ¿Es María?

Teaching Tip 6-5: Model additional items in both the singular and the plural before students begin their pair work. **¿Dónde se encuentra el perfume? Está en la planta baja. ¿Dónde se encuentran las camisas para jóvenes? Están en el quinto piso. ¿Dónde se encuentra la agencia de viajes? Está en el primer piso. ¿Dónde se encuentran los cosméticos?** etc. Also, you may need to point out that **B** stands for **planta baja** and **S** for **sótano.**

6-5 En El Corte Inglés. Estás de compras en El Corte Inglés en Madrid, España. Consulta la guía y usa tu imaginación para formar seis pequeños diálogos con un(a) compañero(a). Sigan el modelo.

MODELO

Cliente(a): Por favor, ¿dónde se encuentran las faldas para niñas?

Dependiente(a): Están en el segundo piso.

Cliente(a): Gracias. ¿Y los vaqueros para jóvenes? ¿En qué piso están?

Dependiente(a): Están en el quinto piso.

Note: El Corte Inglés is a major department store with branches in many cities throughout Spain. Their products range from clothing to electronics to housewares. The store directory here features the Madrid location at Calle Preciados, which specializes in fashions. Visit this store's comprehensive online site at www.elcorteingles.es.

Expansion: Have students imagine that you are a student from Spain who is coming to study in your university. Ask individuals what clothing you should bring for different months of the year and different situations: **1. Las clases empiezan en agosto. ¿Qué ropa debo llevar para ir a clase? 2. Me gustaría hacerme socio(a) de una fraternidad. ¿Qué ropa necesito llevar para las fiestas de iniciación? 3. En diciembre quiero visitar** (mention a nearby destination). **¿Qué ropa debo llevar para este viaje? 4. Me dicen que en marzo/abril muchos estudiantes van de vacaciones a** (mention a second location). **¿Qué ropa debo llevar?**

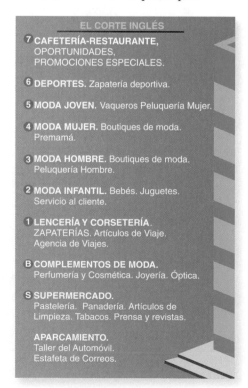

EL CORTE INGLÉS

7 CAFETERÍA-RESTAURANTE, OPORTUNIDADES, PROMOCIONES ESPECIALES.

6 DEPORTES. Zapatería deportiva.

5 MODA JOVEN. Vaqueros Peluquería Mujer.

4 MODA MUJER. Boutiques de moda. Premamá.

3 MODA HOMBRE. Boutiques de moda. Peluquería Hombre.

2 MODA INFANTIL. Bebés. Juguetes. Servicio al cliente.

1 LENCERÍA Y CORSETERÍA. ZAPATERÍAS. Artículos de Viaje. Agencia de Viajes.

B COMPLEMENTOS DE MODA. Perfumería y Cosmética. Joyería. Óptica.

S SUPERMERCADO. Pastelería. Panadería. Artículos de Limpieza. Tabacos. Prensa y revistas.

APARCAMIENTO. Taller del Automóvil. Estafeta de Correos.

Vocabulario temático

Para comprar la ropa

DEPENDIENTE(A): ¿Qué desea?

CLIENTE(A): Estoy buscando un suéter *de lana.*
de algodón
de seda

DEPENDIENTE(A): ¿De qué color?

CLIENTE(A): Quiero un suéter *verde.*

No me importa el color.

DEPENDIENTE(A): ¿Qué talla lleva Ud.?

CLIENTE(A): Llevo la talla *mediana.*
pequeña
(extra) grande

DEPENDIENTE(A): ¿Qué le parece este suéter?

CLIENTE(A): No sé. Me parece *un poco caro.*
demasiado formal

¿Tiene otro *más barato?*
más sencillo

DEPENDIENTE(A): ¿Quiere probarse *este suéter?*

CLIENTE(A): Sí, quiero probárme*lo.* ¿Dónde está el probador?

DEPENDIENTE(A): ¿Cómo le queda *el suéter?*

CLIENTE(A): Me queda *bien/mal.*

¿Tiene una talla más *grande/pequeña?*

CLIENTE(A): ¿Cuánto cuesta?

DEPENDIENTE(A): Está de rebaja. Cuesta *40,00 euros.*

CLIENTE(A): Voy a llevárme*lo.*

DEPENDIENTE(A): Muy bien. ¿Desea algo más?

CLIENTE(A): Eso es todo, gracias.

Transparency Bank I-4, I-10

Teaching Tip: To introduce this vocabulary, bring to class several sweaters and act out the scene with a student, reading the lines in the presentation. Repeat with other items of clothing to demonstrate changes in verb and adjective forms.

Vocabulary: Another way to respond: **Quiero un suéter en verde.**

For shoes, use these expressions: **¿Qué número calza Ud.? Calzo el número 43.**

Teaching Tip: English-speaking students tend to add an incorrect **por** or **para** after **Estoy buscando....** Also, students do not need to know the entire conjugation of the present progressive verb tense in order to use the expression; treat it as a lexical item.

Vocabulary: In some countries **usar** is used with **talla** instead of **llevar.**

Teaching Tip: Point out the reflexive verb **probarse.** Draw attention to the use of the direct object pronoun **lo** to refer to the sweater. Substitute a few other items of clothing and have students tell you which pronouns would be needed. **¿Quiere probarse estos pantalones? Sí, quiero probármelos. ¿Quiere probarse esta chaqueta? Sí, quiero probármela.**

Proficiency: At this level, students find it extremely difficult to manage object pronouns with accuracy in spontaneous speech. They will be able to choose pronouns correctly if you draw attention to them and help them work through word order and agreement.

More Information: The verbs **quedar** and **parecer** are explained later in this **Paso.** With more proficient groups, introduce these additional expressions: **Me queda... apretado** *(tight)* / **ancho** *(wide, big)* / **incómodo** *(uncomfortable).*

Teaching Tip: Review with students methods of payment: **tarjeta de crédito, tarjeta de débito, cheques de viajero, dinero en efectivo.**

Ponerlo a prueba

CD2
Track 3

6-6 En Madrid Xanadú. Carla está de compras en una boutique en Xanadú, un centro comercial en Madrid, España. Escucha la conversación entre ella y una dependienta. Después, contesta las preguntas.

1. ¿Qué tipo de vestido está buscando Carla?
   a. uno para un baile formal
   b. uno para la boda *(wedding)* de una amiga
   c. uno sencillo para el trabajo

2. ¿Qué talla lleva?

   a. 36   b. 48   c. 38

3. ¿De qué color prefiere el vestido?

   a. negro   b. blanco   c. rosado

4. ¿Qué le parece el primer vestido?

   a. Le encanta.   b. Es muy caro.   c. No le gusta.

5. ¿Cómo le queda el vestido que se prueba?

   a. Un poco grande.   b. Perfecto.   c. Un poco pequeño.

6. ¿Cuánto cuesta el vestido que quiere comprar?

   a. 103 euros   b. 113 euros   c. 123 euros

6-7 En una tienda. María Fernanda va de compras. Relaciona las oraciones de las dos columnas de una manera lógica para crear una conversación entre ella y la dependienta.

Dependienta	María Fernanda
b 1. ¿Qué desea?	a. Creo que lleva la talla 38 ó 40.
g 2. ¿Qué le parecen estas blusas?	b. Estoy buscando un regalo para mi madre.
a 3. ¿Qué talla lleva su madre?	c. Con tarjeta de crédito.
f 4. Tenemos esa blusa en verde y amarillo.	d. Quiero probármelo.
e 5. ¿Desea algo más?	e. No, gracias, eso es todo.
c 6. ¿Cómo quiere pagar?	f. Me encanta la verde. ¿Podría envolvérmela?
	g. Son muy elegantes.

6-8 Ropa nueva. Julián quiere comprar ropa nueva para llevar a la universidad. Basándote en el dibujo, completa el siguiente diálogo entre él y el dependiente de la tienda.

DEPENDIENTE: ¿Qué desea, señor?

JULIÁN: (1) _____ .

DEPENDIENTE: ¿Unos pantalones? ¿De qué color?

JULIÁN: (2) _____ .

DEPENDIENTE: ¿Qué talla lleva Ud.?

JULIÁN: (3) _____ .

DEPENDIENTE:	Bueno, aquí tenemos varios modelos en su talla. ¿Qué le parecen estos?
JULIÁN:	(4) _____ . ¿_____?
DEPENDIENTE:	Cuarenta y dos euros. Están de rebaja. ¿Quiere probárselos?
JULIÁN:	(5) _____ . ¿_____?
DEPENDIENTE:	Está allí, en el fondo *(in the back)* a la derecha.
	(Unos momentos después)
DEPENDIENTE:	Bueno… ¿cómo le quedan?
JULIÁN:	(6) _____ . ¿_____?
DEPENDIENTE:	Lo siento, no tenemos ese modelo en una talla más pequeña. Pero vuelva la próxima semana. Tendremos unos modelos nuevos.

6-9 Zara. Lee el artículo sobre esta tienda de España y contesta las preguntas.

Zara: Historia de un éxito comercial

¿Le gusta llevar "lo último" en ropa? ¿Quiere estar de moda sin pagar los precios astronómicos de los grandes diseñadores? Las tiendas Zara le ofrecen la solución. Vende ropa elegante a precios módicos para hombres, mujeres y niños.

Esta cadena española es una de las más populares de España y ha transformado el mundo de la moda. El secreto de su éxito está en su concepto corporativo: Según su página web, Zara "interpreta, adapta las tendencias en tiempo récord y ofrece novedades dos veces por semana". Por eso, los clientes visitan la tienda con frecuencia para comprar sus modelos exclusivos.

La primera tienda Zara abrió sus puertas en La Coruña, al norte de España. Ahora, tiene una presencia en más de 70 países y cuenta con más de 1500 tiendas. Su fundador, el billonario Amancio Ortega Gaona, es uno de los hombres más ricos del planeta, según la revista Forbes.

VOCABULARIO

lo último *the latest*	cadena *chain*	módico *moderate*
de moda *in style*	éxito *success*	novedad *new product*

1. ¿Quiénes son los clientes de las tiendas Zara?
2. ¿Por qué son tan populares estas tiendas?
3. ¿Hay una tienda Zara en tu ciudad o cerca de tu ciudad? ¿Has comprado algo allí?
4. ¿Cuál es tu tienda de ropa favorita? Explica por qué te gusta.

6-10 Un regalo. Dramatiza la situación con un(a) compañero(a) de clase.

Cliente(a): Necesitas comprar un regalo para el cumpleaños de tu tía. No sabes qué comprar y le pides una recomendación al (a la) dependiente(a). Solo puedes gastar *(spend)* $35 y quieres algo bonito y especial. Tú empiezas el diálogo de esta manera: **Necesito comprar un regalo para mi tía. ¿Qué me recomienda?**

Dependiente(a): Hace mucho tiempo *(It's been a long time)* que no vendes nada. Estás preocupado(a) porque trabajas por comisiones. Cuando un(a) cliente(a) te pide una recomendación, intentas venderle muchas cosas.

Teaching Tip 6-9: Although reading activities may be completed individually, students often profit from working with a classmate to interpret and discuss the ideas.

Teaching Tip 6-9: As an alternative activity, have students respond to true/false statements and correct the false ones: **1. En Zara se presentan los modelos de los grandes diseñadores. 2. La ropa en Zara no es muy cara. 3. Zara vende ropa exclusivamente para mujeres y chicas. 4. Los nuevos modelos de ropa salen cuatro veces al año. 5. Zara espera abrir tiendas en otros países en el futuro.**

Note: The reclusive Ortega grew up in a middle-class family and opened his first store in 1976. In 2007, due largely to the success of his stores, he was named by Forbes magazine as the richest man in Spain and the eighth richest in the world. The parent company Inditex now includes other lines of clothing stores as well as home furnishings.

Note: Zara is known for its quick response to customer demand. An idea for a new design may take as little as three weeks to end up in the stores as a finished product. Current styles may be viewed online at www.zara.com.

More Information: Since this verbal structure proves difficult for students to master, it is recycled and expanded upon frequently in *Puentes*. In Chapter 1, **gustar** was introduced; in Chapter 5, **encantar** and **interesar** were presented. Here all these verbs are recycled and four more are introduced.

Answers: te, te, me, me.

Teaching Tip: Use the examples to review the three kinds of subjects and the verb forms that correspond: the singular noun subject with **gusta,** the plural noun subject with **encantan,** the infinitive subject with **interesa**.

Gramática

Otros verbos como *gustar: importar, faltar, quedar* y *parecer*

Read along as you listen to Tania talking with her friend Alejandra as she tries on some clothing in a department store. Find examples of the following verbs: **gustar, encantar, parecer, quedar.** Which pronouns are used with each of these verbs in this conversation?

TANIA:	¿Qué te parecen estos pantalones?
ALEJANDRA:	Pues, creo que te quedan bien.
TANIA:	No sé. Me encanta el estilo, pero no me gusta mucho este color.
ALEJANDRA:	Eso no es problema. Los tienen en otros tonos.

A. Gustar y otros verbos similares. The verb **gustar** *(to like, be pleasing)* follows a special sentence structure. This same pattern is followed by the verbs **encantar** *(to love)* and **interesar** *(to be interested in).*

▸ Only two forms of the verb are commonly used: **gusta** and **gustan.**

▸ An indirect object pronoun (IO) expresses who likes the thing or activity: **me, te, le, nos, os, les.**

IO	VERB	SUBJECT
Nos	gusta	ese vestido.

We like that dress. (That dress is pleasing to us.)

Me	encantan	esos zapatos.

We love those shoes. (Those shoes are "enchanting" to us.)

Le	interesa	diseñar ropa.

He's interested in designing clothing. (Designing clothing interests him.)

B. Otros verbos. The following three verbs follow the same sentence pattern as **gustar, encantar,** and **interesar.**

▸ **importar** *(to care about; to matter)*

A Marisa no **le importa** el precio. *Marisa doesn't care about the price.*

me importa(n)	nos importa(n)
te importa(n)	os importa(n)
le importa(n)	les importa(n)

▸ **faltar** *(to be short, missing, or lacking)*

Les falta un dólar. *They are a dollar short.*

me falta(n)	nos falta(n)
te falta(n)	os falta(n)
le falta(n)	les falta(n)

▸ **quedar** *(to be left; to remain)*

No **nos quedan** más suéteres azules. *We don't have any more blue sweaters left.*

me queda(n)	nos queda(n)
te queda(n)	os queda(n)
le queda(n)	les queda(n)

C. Parecer. Sentences with the verb **parecer** *(to seem, appear)* follow the same pattern but additionally have an adjective. This adjective must "match" the subject of the sentence in gender and number.

IO	VERB	ADJECTIVE	SUBJECT
¿Te	parece	bonita	esa **falda**?

Do you think that skirt is pretty? (Does that skirt seem pretty to you?)

| Nos | parecen | caros | esos **pantalones.** |

Those pants seem expensive to us.

me parece(n) + adjective	**nos parece(n)** + adjective
te parece(n) + adjective	**os parece(n)** + adjective
le parece(n) + adjective	**les parece(n)** + adjective

D. Quedar. The verb **quedar** has a second meaning: *to fit.* When used in this sense, this verb follows a pattern similar to **parecer.**

▶ After the verb **queda(n),** add the adverbs **bien** or **mal** to express that a garment fits well or poorly.

    A Lorenzo le **queda bien** este traje.   *This suit fits Lorenzo well.*

▶ After the verb **queda(n),** add adjectives like **grande, pequeño, estrecho** *(narrow),* **ancho** *(wide),* or **apretado** *(tight)* to describe the fit in more detail. These adjectives must match the subject in gender and number.

(No) IO	VERB	ADVERB/ADJECTIVE	SUBJECT
¿No le	quedan	un poco **apretados**	los zapatos?

Aren't the shoes a little tight on her/him?

▶ With both **parecer** and **quedar,** it is possible to place the subject at the front of a statement instead of at the end.

Este traje le queda bien.	*This suit fits him well.*
Esos zapatos me parecen caros.	*Those shoes seem expensive to me.*

Ponerlo a prueba

6-11 Comentarios. Olivia está de compras con su amiga Cristina. ¿Cómo responde Cristina a los comentarios de Olivia? Relaciona las dos columnas de una manera lógica.

Teaching Tip: Assign the first two activities for homework.

> MODELO
> OLIVIA: Ese vestido es fabuloso.
> CRISTINA: ¡Me encanta! Es realmente bello.

Olivia

_e_ 1. Esos zapatos cuestan $400.

_a_ 2. Necesito la talla mediana.

_f_ 3. ¿Cómo vas a comprar ese traje?

_b_ 4. Chica, no puedes comprar ese vestido de seda para ir al cine.

_d_ 5. ¡Mira! Una camiseta morada con lunares amarillos.

Cristina

a. Sí. La talla grande te queda mal.

b. ¿Por qué no? ¿Te parece demasiado formal?

c. No le interesan. Solo tienes $80.

d. ¡Ay! Me parece muy fea.

e. ¡Uf! Me parecen muy caros.

f. Es verdad. Me faltan $50.

6-12 Más compras. Completa cada oración con el verbo entre paréntesis más lógico y un complemento indirecto apropiado.

> **MODELO** Esa corbata cuesta 40 euros. Quiero comprarla, pero tengo solamente 25 euros.
>
> (faltar / quedar) <u>Me faltan</u> quince euros.

1. Esas botas cuestan 80 euros. Silvia quiere comprarlas, pero tiene solamente 50 euros.

    (interesar / faltar) <u>Le faltan</u> treinta euros.

2. Mis amigas siempre compran los zapatos de Manolo Blahnick.

    Evidentemente no (encantar / importar) <u>les importa</u> el precio.

3. Normalmente Eduardo lleva la talla mediana. Su novia le compró una camiseta en la talla pequeña.

    La camiseta no (gustar / quedar) <u>le queda</u> bien.

4. Mis amigos y yo compramos camisas y pantalones en la tienda Zara.

    (Parecer / Interesar) <u>Nos parecen</u> muy elegantes sus modelos.

5. Quiero comprar este impermeable pero mis tarjetas de crédito están al máximo.

    No (encantar / quedar) <u>me queda</u> dinero.

Note: Manolo Blahnick is a much-acclaimed designer of women's shoes. Born in the Canary Islands, his pricey, high-heeled creations are popular with celebrities around the world.

6-13 Vamos a charlar. Conversa con dos o tres compañeros(as) sobre las compras. Fíjense *(Notice)* en los nuevos verbos: **importar, quedar, parecer.**

1. Cuando compras ropa, ¿**te importa** más el precio, la moda *(fashion)* o la calidad *(quality)*? Explica.

2. ¿Qué estilos y colores están de moda entre tú y tus amigos? ¿Qué **te parecen** los últimos modelos de la temporada *(season)*?

3. ¿Usas la ropa de otras personas a veces, por ejemplo, la ropa de tus hermanos o de tus amigos? ¿Cuáles de sus prendas *(garments)* **te quedan** bien? ¿**Te importa** si tu compañero(a) de cuarto usa tu ropa sin pedirte permiso?

Durante la feria de Sevilla, las chicas llevan vestidos tradicionales, como estos. ¿Qué te parecen?

Puente cultural

¿Qué es vestir elegante en tu país?

Go to the *Puentes* Premium Website to view the **Puente cultural** interviews.

Elvira Zaldívar Santamaría

ESPAÑA

En mi país, los chicos llevan traje y corbata cuando se visten elegantes. Las chicas usan vestidos de tejidos *(fabrics)* más ricos y zapatos de tacón alto *(high heels)*. Normalmente la gente se viste elegante sobre todo para las bodas y los actos religiosos.

Jimena Escamilla

MÉXICO

En México las mujeres se visten con el poder en mente *(power in mind)*, usando en muchas ocasiones trajes y ropa más formal. Aunque muchas veces son incómodos, los tacones *(high heels)* se usan mucho. A los hombres también les gusta lucir *(appear)* poderosos. Ambos *(Both)* sexos siguen la moda de revistas y desfiles *(fashion shows)*.

Clara Mengolini

ARGENTINA

En Argentina se da mucha importancia a la moda europea. Tanto los hombres como las mujeres copian estilos y tendencias que ven en revistas y en desfiles. Las mujeres quieren ser "chic" y modernas, y los hombres también.

 Comparando las costumbres. Trabaja con un(a) compañero(a). Lee la información y completa la tabla.

	En España	En México	En Argentina	En los Estados Unidos
¿Qué es vestir elegante en tu país?				

- Naming souvenirs
- Bargaining in a market

Grammar:

- Indefinite and negative expressions
- **Por** and **para**

Proficiency: This **Paso** practices the function of bargaining for an item in a market place. The grammar points are introduced for conceptual and partial control: Students will be able to use these structures with accuracy in a limited fashion, often only when attention is drawn to them.

Standards: The vocabulary presents an excellent opportunity to introduce native crafts from many countries, thus addressing the National Standards in Culture: Products.

Transparency Bank C-3

Teaching Tip: If possible, introduce these vocabulary items and others of your choosing by bringing in the actual items. Place them all in a bag. Before you pull each one out, describe it simply (shape, color, use, etc.) and have students try to guess what it is.

Regional Vocabulary: A woman's handbag is called **un bolso** or **una cartera,** depending on the country. A bag used to carry groceries or other purchases is **una bolsa** or **una funda.** Names for jewelry also vary widely. Earrings may be called **pendientes** in Spain, **aros** in Argentina and Chile, or **pantallas** in Puerto Rico. A simple ring is **un anillo**, while one with a gemstone setting may be called **una sortija**. In Spain and many Caribbean countries, bracelets are called **pulseras**.

Paso 2

Vocabulario temático

Los recuerdos *(Souvenirs)*

¿Qué se puede comprar en un mercado típico?

un paraguas

una gorra

unas gafas de sol

un bolso de cuero

una guayabera

una billetera

un plato de cerámica

una piñata

un sarape

unas maracas

un sombrero

un collar

unos aretes

un anillo

un brazalete de plata

una cadena de oro

unas castañuelas

un abanico

una boina

la mantilla

Estrategia *Circumlocution*

Circumlocution is the art of talking "around" words that you don't know or don't remember. Here are some ways to circumlocute.

▸ Narrow down the range of items by using a classification:

Es una persona	*It's a person*
una cosa	*a thing*
un lugar	*a place*
un aparato	*a device*

▸ For persons and places, describe an associated activity:

Es una persona que vende ropa en una tienda.
It's a person who sells clothes in a store.

▸ For things, refer to size, shape, color, composition, or use.

Es redondo/de metal/de plástico/de madera.	*It's round/made of metal/ plastic/wooden.*
Se usa para escribir...	*It's used to write . . .*

▸ Explain what it is similar to:

Es parecido a...	*It's similar to . . .*

¿Qué es? Using some of the techniques described above, circumlocute in Spanish some unfamiliar words. Here are a few words to get you started. Your partner should listen and guess which English word corresponds to your Spanish circumlocution.

van	bow tie	consignment shop	DJ
tattoo	cheerleader	mouse (of a computer)	vase
web cam	milkshake	vest	CEO

Ponerlo a prueba

CD2
Track 5

6-14 Muchos regalos. Liliana y su amiga Cristina están de vacaciones en Madrid, España. Un día, Liliana fue al Rastro, un famoso mercado, y compró muchos regalos. Cuando llegó al hotel, le enseñó a Cristina todas sus compras *(purchases)*. Escucha su conversación y completa la tabla.

¿Qué compró?	¿Para quién?	¿Cuánto pagó?
1. suéter de seda	hermana	62 euros
2. mantilla bordada	madre	120 euros
3. pulsera de oro	su abuela	93 euros
4. cinturón de piel	hermano	45 euros
5. botella de perfume	mejor amiga	57 euros

6-15 Muchos recuerdos. ¿Qué palabra **no** corresponde a la categoría?

1. RECUERDOS PARA MUJERES: un brazalete / unos aretes / una guayabera / un abanico

2. RECUERDOS PARA HOMBRES: una boina / una billetera / unas gafas de sol / una mantilla

3. RECUERDOS DE ORO O DE PLATA: un collar / un sarape / un anillo / una cadena

4. RECUERDOS PRÁCTICOS: un bolso / un paraguas / una billetera / unas castañuelas

Teaching Tip: Remind students of other familiar categories: **una clase, una comida, un animal, un pariente, una tienda, un deporte,** etc.

Teaching Tip: Remind students of other descriptive terms they know: **grande, pequeño, rojo, azul, largo, corto, moderno, viejo,** etc.

Expansion: Write a few familiar or new words in Spanish on small pieces of paper. Distribute the words to several students and have them practice circumlocution in Spanish.

Teaching Tip: Assign the first two activities for homework.

6-16 En el mercado de artesanías. Estás de vacaciones en Puerto Rico y visitas el Mercado de Tesoros Puertorriqueños. Usa la información del dibujo para contestar las preguntas.

1. ¿Cómo se llaman los dos puestos *(stalls)* en el Mercado de Tesoros Puertorriqueños?

2. Hoy hace mucho sol y quieres comprar unas gafas de sol. ¿Dónde se venden? ¿Cuánto cuestan? ¿Dónde puedes comprar un paraguas si empieza a llover *(to rain)*?

3. Quieres comprar unas maracas y unas camisetas para tus amigos. ¿Dónde cuestan menos?

4. Tu amiga quiere comprar un bolso de cuero y una billetera también, pero tiene solamente $30.00. ¿Dónde debe comprarlos? Explica.

5. Tienes $30.00 para comprar tres recuerdos: uno para tu padre, uno para tu hermanito(a), uno para tu mejor amigo(a). ¿Qué vas a comprar?

 6-17 En mi comunidad. Con un(a) compañero(a), piensa en un mercado al aire libre *(open-air or flea market)* en tu comunidad y contesta las preguntas.

1. ¿Qué artículos se venden en el mercado de tu comunidad?

2. ¿Cuál es el horario de ese mercado? Por ejemplo, ¿abre todos los días?, ¿los fines de semana?

3. ¿Tienen precios fijos *(set prices)* o es posible regatear *(haggle over prices)*? ¿Te gusta ese sistema? Explica por qué.

4. ¿Qué es lo que más te gusta comprar en ese mercado?

5. Describe la compra *(the purchase)* más memorable que hiciste en ese mercado. ¿Qué compraste? ¿Cuánto pagaste? ¿Tuviste que regatear mucho?

¿Te gusta ir a los mercados al aire libre? Si quieres comprar algo un poco raro, ¿adónde vas?

El Rastro es el mercado al aire libre más antiguo y más grande de España. Su historia se remonta *(dates back to)* a finales del siglo XIX, y hoy en día es tan popular como en el pasado. El Rastro se organiza en el centro histórico de la capital todos los domingos y festivos de nueve a tres.

Miles de madrileños y turistas pasean por las calles y regatean en sus 3500 puestos. En el Rastro se vende un poco de todo: antigüedades, artículos raros, artesanías, libros, mascotas, música y mucho más.

Vocabulario temático

Cómo regatear

CLIENTE(A):   **¿Me puede mostrar *esa camiseta*?**

VENDEDOR(A):   **Aquí *la* tiene.**

CLIENTE(A):   **¿Tiene Ud. *esta camiseta en azul*?**

VENDEDOR(A):   **Lo siento, no nos queda ninguna.**

CLIENTE(A):   **¿Cuánto cuesta *ese anillo*?**

VENDEDOR(A):   ***Cuarenta euros.***

CLIENTE(A):   **¡Uy! ¡Qué caro! ¿Me puede hacer un descuento?**

VENDEDOR(A):   **Bueno… para Ud., se *lo* dejo en *treinta y cinco euros*.**

CLIENTE(A):   **Le doy *treinta euros*.**

VENDEDOR(A):   **No, lo siento. No puedo aceptar menos de *treinta y tres*.**

CLIENTE(A):   **Está bien. Me *lo* llevo.**

Note: The streets that host the **Rastro** are closed to vehicular traffic but packed with people strolling, making purchases, and stopping in the many cafés for food and drink. Tourist information routinely warns that pickpockets also enjoy visiting this popular attraction.

More Information: Bargaining is a practical skill for our students to learn but is also more difficult than making purchases in a store, since it involves negotiating. For this reason it is presented in a simplified version here. Discuss with students the courtesy involved, including that one should begin the bargaining process only when seriously interested in making a purchase.

Choose the direct object pronoun that matches the noun in gender and number: **lo, la, los, las.**

When bargaining, keep counter offers reasonable and be sure not to insult the merchandise.

Teaching Tip: Explain that at this point the merchant may explain why the price cannot go lower: **Este anillo es de plata. Es de muy buena calidad. Está hecho a mano.**

Palabras indefinidas y negativas

A. Las palabras indefinidas y negativas. Words like *something* and *somebody* are known as indefinite words, since they refer to non-specific people or things. Their negative counterparts are words like *nothing* and *nobody*.

INDEFINITE WORDS	NEGATIVE WORDS
algo *something, anything*	**nada** *nothing, not anything*
alguien *somebody, anybody*	**nadie** *nobody, not anybody*
alguno(a, os, as) *some, any*	**ninguno(a, os, as)** *no, none, not any*

B. Usos. Negative and indefinite words are sometimes handled differently in Spanish than in English.

▸ Multiple negative words are frequently used in the same sentence. While this is considered incorrect in English, in Spanish it is the norm.

No conozco a **nadie** aquí.   *I do **not** know **anybody (nobody)** here.*

No nos queda **ninguna.**   *We do **not** have **a single one (none)** left.*

▸ The indefinite word **alguno** must agree in gender and number with the noun it describes or replaces. Before a masculine singular noun, **alguno** becomes **algún.**

¿Hay **algún** mercadillo por aquí?   *Is there **any** open-air market around here?*

Tienen **algunas** camisetas bonitas.   *They have **some** cute T-shirts.*

▸ The negative **ninguno** agrees in gender with the noun it describes or replaces. Before a masculine singular noun, **ninguno** becomes **ningún.** Note that this negative word is not used in the plural in Spanish.

No veo **ningún** anillo de plata.   *I don't see **any** silver rings.*

CLIENTE: ¿Tiene este sombrero en verde?   *Do you have this hat in green?*

VENDEDOR: No me queda **ninguno.**   *I don't have **a single one (any)** left.*

Ponerlo a prueba

CD2
Track 6

6-18 En el mercado de artesanías. En el mercadillo de Toledo, se regatea mucho. Escucha las tres conversaciones entre un cliente y un vendedor. Completa la tabla en la página 211 con:

- el artículo que el cliente quiere comprar
- unos detalles o una descripción del artículo
- el precio original del artículo
- el precio que el cliente paga después de regatear

Artículo	Detalles	Precio original	Precio final
1. camiseta	blanca con bandera	18 euros	16 euros
2. castañuelas	con flor roja	12 euros	10 euros
3. brazalete	de plata con decoración azul	14 euros	13 euros

Teaching Tip: Remind your students that in Spain **pulsera** is the more common term for **brazalete**.

6-19 ¿Qué dices? Estás de compras en el Mercado de Artesanías de Salamanca. Completa las breves conversaciones con las palabras más lógicas.

1.   Tú: ¿Me puede (comprar / <u>mostrar</u> / pagar) esa camiseta?
     Vendedor: Aquí tiene. (<u>Cuesta</u> / Cuestas / Cuestan) quince euros.

2.   Tú: ¿Tiene esta gorra en (<u>negro</u> / negra / negras)?
     Vendedor: Lo siento. No nos queda (ningún / ninguno / <u>ninguna</u>).

3.   Tú: ¿Me puede hacer un (rebaja / <u>descuento</u> / precio)?
     Vendedor: Se lo (hago / digo / <u>dejo</u>) por diez euros.

4.   Tú: ¿Me puede recomendar (<u>algún</u> / alguno / alguna) recuerdo típico?
     Vendedor: (Este / <u>Estos</u> / Estas) platos de cerámica son muy típicos.

5.   Tú: Le (<u>doy</u> / hago / pongo) quince euros.
     Vendedor: No puedo aceptar (más de / <u>menos de</u> / tanto como) dieciocho.

6-20 La cadena de oro. Estás en un mercado y quieres comprar una cadena de oro. Completa la conversación de una manera lógica.

       Tú: (1) _____
   Vendedora: Aquí la tiene.

       Tú: (2) _____
   Vendedora: Cien euros.

       Tú: (3) ¡_____! ¿_____?
   Vendedora: Bueno, se la dejo en noventa y cinco euros.

       Tú: (4) _____.
   Vendedora: Es muy poco, y esta cadena es de oro. No puedo aceptar menos de noventa.

       Tú: (5) _____.

6-21 La venta de garaje. Un sábado por la mañana vas a una gran venta de garaje. ¿Qué quieres comprar? Dramatiza una escena entre tú y el (la) dueño(a) *(owner)*. No se olviden: ¡tienen que regatear!

Teaching Tip 6-20: More proficient classes could dramatize this dialogue spontaneously with a classmate. Less proficient classes may profit more from writing it, individually or with a classmate.

Expansion 6-20: Turn your classroom into a market. Have students "sell" some personal items (book bags, watches, books, sunglasses) to their classmates. Model the activity first with your wristwatch or jewelry. Then have the class mingle to bargain over prices. Afterwards, ask students what they purchased and how much they paid. **¿Qué compraste? ¿Cuánto pagaste?**

Expansion 6-21: Ask students about any yard/garage sales they have held or been to. Discuss what was sold and for how much money. Find out if anyone got any special bargains **(gangas).**

Gramática

Por and *para*

Read along as you listen to the conversation between Iván and Rafael. Which
preposition—**por** or **para**—is used to express the following ideas: *around here, in
order to arrive, along this street, for my best friend?*

> IVÁN: ¿Hay un mercadillo al aire libre por aquí?
>
> RAFAEL: Sí, para llegar al mercadillo, siga derecho por esta calle.
>
> IVÁN: ¿Me puede recomendar algún regalo para mi mejor amigo?
>
> RAFAEL: Sí, tienen camisetas, gorras y *jerseys* de fútbol a buenos precios.

A. Los usos de *por* y *para*. Although the prepositions **por** and **para** are often
translated into English as *for,* they are not interchangeable.

Por:

▸ *for* (an amount of time)

Estuvimos de compras **por** dos horas.	*We were shopping **for** two hours.*

▸ *for, in exchange for*

Compramos esas mantillas **por** 100 euros.	*We bought those mantillas **for** 100 euros.*

▸ *per*

La entrada a la exposición de artesanías cuesta 6 euros **por** persona.	*The admission price to the arts and crafts exhibit is 6 euros **per** person.*

▸ *through, along, beside, by* (places or location)

El domingo di un paseo **por** las Ramblas.	*On Sunday I took a stroll **through** the Ramblas.*

▸ special expressions with **por:**

por ejemplo	*for example*
por eso	*for that reason, therefore*
por fin	*finally, at last*

Para:

▸ *to, in order to* (+ infinitive)

Vamos al mercadillo **para** comprar algunos recuerdos.	*We are going to the market **to** buy some souvenirs.*

▸ *by, for* (a deadline, or certain date)

Necesito comprar el regalo de Susana **para** el viernes.	*I need to buy Susan's gift **by** Friday.*

▸ *for, intended for* (someone)

Estos recuerdos son **para** mi familia.	*These souvenirs are **for** my family.*

▸ *for* (a particular use)

Necesito un botón **para** mi camisa.	*I need a button **for** my shirt.*

Ponerlo a prueba

6-22 Análisis. Lee las oraciones e indica por qué se usa **por** o **para** en cada caso. Escribe la letra de la explicación más apropiada.

Teaching Tip: Assign the first two activities for homework.

POR

a. for (amount of time)

b. for, in exchange for

c. per

d. through, by, along, beside, around (a location)

e. special expressions

PARA

f. to, in order to (do something)

g. by (a deadline, a date)

h. for, intended for (someone)

i. for (a particular use)

1. Ayer fui de compras para (__f__) buscar un regalo para (__h__) mi mamá.

2. Di un paseo por (__d__) el centro comercial por (__a__) cuarenta y cinco minutos.

3. Por (__e__) fin, encontré un bonito cinturón por (__b__) solo quince euros.

4. Me dieron un descuento del 20 por (__c__) ciento

5. Por (__e__) eso, también le compré una cajita *(little box)* para (__i__) poner pendientes.

6-23 El collar de plata. Lee el cuento sobre Andrés y el regalo especial que le compró a su novia. Completa los espacios con **por** o **para**.

Un día, mientras Andrés caminaba (1) ___por___ el mercado de curiosidades, vio un collar de plata muy elegante y pensó: "Ese sería el regalo ideal (2) ___para___ Carmela".

Se acercó al vendedor y le preguntó: —¿Cuánto quiere usted (3) ___por___ ese collar?

El vendedor no dijo nada (4) ___por___ varios largos segundos. Por fin contestó: —Ese collar era de mi esposa que murió hace dos años. Por eso, no se lo vendo a nadie (5) ___por___ todo el dinero del mundo.

Andrés preguntó: —¿Por qué lo tiene aquí si no es (6) ___para___ venderlo?

El vendedor respondió: —Compré ese collar (7) ___para___ mi esposa el día que nos hicimos *(we became)* novios. ¡Imagínese! Nosotros estuvimos casados (8) ___por___ cuarenta años.

Andrés contestó: —Ah, entonces, comprendo... y siguió buscando el regalo perfecto...

6-24 El trabajo. Vas a solicitar empleo en un mercado de artesanías. Debes escribir una carta con tu solicitud de empleo *(job application)*. Completa la carta con **por** o **para**.

> Estimado señor Gómez:
>
> Estoy muy interesado(a) en el empleo que se anuncia en el periódico. Creo que soy el/la candidato(a) ideal (1) __para__ el puesto.
>
> En primer lugar, yo tengo mucha experiencia como vendedor(a). He trabajado en el mismo almacén (2) __por__ cinco años. Normalmente, trabajo veinte horas (3) __por__ semana porque también soy estudiante. Y, no me importa decirle que he trabajado (4) __por__ muy poco dinero. Sin embargo, me gusta mi trabajo porque creo que tengo talento. La semana pasada, (5) __por__ ejemplo, vendí más de mil euros en mercancía.
>
> (6) __Para__ confirmar los datos necesarios también le mando mi currículum vítae con una lista de referencias. Si usted quiere, puedo pasar (7) __por__ su oficina la próxima semana para una entrevista.
>
> Le doy mis gracias (8) __por__ su atención a mi solicitud.
>
> Atentamente,
>
> (firma)

6-25 Charlas. Trabaja con un(a) compañero(a) y contesta las preguntas siguientes. Observa bien los usos de **por** y **para.**

1. LOS REGALOS: ¿Compras muchos regalos? ¿**Para** quiénes los compras con más frecuencia? ¿En qué ocasiones te gusta dar regalos? En tu opinión, ¿es necesario pagar mucho **por** un buen regalo? ¿Qué regalos se pueden comprar **por** poco dinero?

2. LOS ESTUDIOS: ¿**Para** qué clases tuviste que estudiar más este semestre? ¿**Para** qué clase tuviste que escribir muchos trabajos escritos? En general, ¿cuántas horas estudias **por** semana? ¿**Por** cuántas horas estudiaste para tu último examen? ¿Qué se debe hacer **para** tener éxito en los cursos universitarios?

Un paso más

¡Vamos a hablar!

Estudiante A

Contexto: Tú (**Estudiante A**) sabes la ropa que Mario lleva y tienes que descubrir lo que Marta lleva. Tu compañero(a) (**Estudiante B**) sabe la ropa que Marta lleva y tiene que descubrir lo que Mario lleva. Háganse preguntas (*Ask each other questions*) para saber qué ropa llevan Mario y Marta. Tú vas a empezar con la primera pregunta:
¿Lleva Marta un vestido rosado?

Teaching Tip: In this activity pairs of students have to ask each other yes/no questions to discover what clothing the person in the picture is wearing. Student A must find out what Marta is wearing, while Student B must find out what Mario is wearing. Give some examples of appropriate questions: **¿Lleva Mario un traje gris? ¿Lleva unos zapatos de vestir? ¿Lleva Marta un suéter de rayas?**

Go to the **Un paso más** section in the *Cuaderno de actividades* for reading, writing, and listening activities that correlate with this chapter.

Un paso más

¡Vamos a hablar!

Estudiante B

Contexto: Tú (**Estudiante B**) sabes la ropa que Marta lleva y tienes que descubrir lo que Mario lleva. Tu compañero(a) (**Estudiante A**) sabe la ropa que Mario lleva y tiene que descubrir lo que Marta lleva. Háganse preguntas (*Ask each other questions*) para saber qué ropa llevan Mario y Marta. Tu compañero(a) va a empezar con la primera pregunta: **¿Lleva Marta un vestido rosado?**

¡Vamos a ver! | *Episodio 6*

En la Hacienda Vista Alegre

Anticipación

A. Hablando se entiende la gente. ¿Qué piensas del mundo de la moda *(fashion)*? ¿Te gusta vestir a la moda *(to be fashionably dressed)*? ¿Por qué?

B. ¿Cómo se dice… ? Expresiones útiles. Relaciona las siguientes expresiones con la definición adecuada.

Teaching Tip: Preview the video by showing a fragment of the episode without sound and have students use visual clues to anticipate content. Stop and rewind the video until they understand the gist of the episode.

__d__ 1. quedar bien *to fit well*

__c__ 2. estar pasado de moda *to be out of style*

__b__ 3. estar a la moda *to be in fashion*

__a__ 4. disfrazarse de… *to dress up as . . .*

a. Cuando llevas un disfraz *(costume)* de fantasma para una fiesta.

b. Cuando llevas ropa de estilos actuales.

c. Cuando llevas ropa anticuada *(old-fashioned)*.

d. Cuando te pruebas unos pantalones que son exactamente tu talla.

Vamos a ver

C. De paseo por la Hacienda Vista Alegre. Lee las preguntas. Luego, mira el Episodio 6 del vídeo y contesta las preguntas.

1. ¿Qué piensa Alejandra de la ropa de Sofía?

2. Según Alejandra, ¿qué ropa necesita comprar Sofía?

3. ¿Qué estilo te gusta más, el de Alejandra o el de Sofía? ¿Por qué?

Expansion: Tell students to observe what the people are wearing in the video. Afterwards, have them describe the clothing of Sofía, Alejandra, and Javier.

Answers: 1. Piensa que está anticuada, que es demasiado vieja. 2. Una falda y unas sandalias. 3. *Answers will vary.*

Teaching Tip: Have students practice summarizing, describing characters, sequencing events, making comparisons, and giving detailed narrations and descriptions based on what they see in the video.

En acción

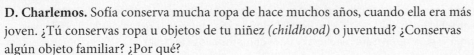

D. Charlemos. Sofía conserva mucha ropa de hace muchos años, cuando ella era más joven. ¿Tú conservas ropa u objetos de tu niñez *(childhood)* o juventud? ¿Conservas algún objeto familiar? ¿Por qué?

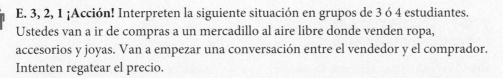

E. 3, 2, 1 ¡Acción! Interpreten la siguiente situación en grupos de 3 ó 4 estudiantes. Ustedes van a ir de compras a un mercadillo al aire libre donde venden ropa, accesorios y joyas. Van a empezar una conversación entre el vendedor y el comprador. Intenten regatear el precio.

Practice the vocabulary and grammar you have learned in this chapter (**ropa, en un gran almacén, en un mercado, cómo regatear**).

CAPÍTULO 6

Panorama cultural

DATOS ESENCIALES

Nombre oficial: Reino de España

Capital: Madrid

Población: 40 500 000 habitantes

Unidad monetaria: el euro

Economía: turismo; exportación de equipos de transporte, productos agrícolas y maquinaria. España es el primer productor mundial de aceite de oliva y uno de los primeros productores de vino.

🌐 **www.cengage.com/spanish/ puentes**

Note: Toledo is especially well known for its colorful ceramics and metalwork, such as swords and knives.

Note: El Greco is the name of the Greek painter, Domenikos Theotokopoulos. Born in 1541, he moved to Spain in 1577 and lived there until his death. One of his most famous works—**El entierro del Conde Orgaz**—is found in the church of Santo Tomé, in Toledo.

Note: After the fall of the Roman Empire in the 5th century, Spain was ruled by the Visigoths, a Germanic tribe, until the invasion of the Moors in 711. The war between the Christians and the Muslims, **La Reconquista**, lasted from 718 to 1492.

Note: The present government is a democratic constitutional monarchy, where the prime minister and heads of the government are elected by popular vote.

Toledo La pequeña cuidad de Toledo es una auténtica joya *(jewel)* de la cultura. Es conocida como "la ciudad de las tres culturas" porque durante la Edad Media *(Middle Ages)* los musulmanes, los judíos y los cristianos convivieron allí. Además, el célebre pintor El Greco vivió allí en el siglo XVI. Hoy en día, muchos turistas visitan Toledo para admirar su arquitectura medieval y para comprar sus artesanías.

Un vistazo a la historia

206 a.C.	La Península Ibérica, originalmente habitada por los íberos, celtas, fenicios, griegos y cartaginenses, pasó a manos de los romanos.
711	Los árabes (moros o musulmanes) del norte de África invadieron la Península Ibérica.
1492	Los reyes católicos, Fernando e Isabel, expulsaron a los árabes. Cristóbal Colón descubrió América en nombre de España.
1936	Estalló la Guerra Civil después de años de dificultades políticas. Con la victoria de los rebeldes franquistas en 1939, Francisco Franco gobernó hasta su muerte en 1975.
1986	España se integró a la Comunidad Europea y a la OTAN.
2004	Un atentado terrorista en los trenes de Madrid resultó en 190 muertos y más de 1400 heridos.
2008	Zapatero anunció su nuevo gabinete, en el que por primera vez hay más mujeres que hombres.

España

Personajes de ayer y de hoy

Miguel de Cervantes y Saavedra (1547-1616)

Fue el autor de la obra maestra de la literatura española, *El ingenioso hidalgo don Quijote de la Mancha*. Nació en 1547. Tuvo una vida llena de vicisitudes: fue herido *(was injured)* en batalla, capturado por piratas, encarcelado *(incarcerated)*. Vivió en la pobreza viajando por el país y conociendo a fondo cada estrato de la sociedad. Su legado *(legacy)* a la literatura mundial fue una joya *(jewel)* llena de realismo, filosofía y extraordinaria calidad artística.

Standards: The *Panorama* may be used as a springboard for further discussion and research in cultural products and practices. Have your students find information and present one-minute talks on figures such as the following: Rafael Nadal, Antonio Banderas, Enrique Iglesias, Paloma Picasso, José Carreras, Néstor Almendros, Pedro Almodóvar. To connect to other disciplines (Connections standard), suggest further research on these Nobel Prize winners: Vicente Aleixandre, Jacinto Benavente, José Echegaray, Juan Ramón Jiménez.

Santiago Ramón y Cajal (1852-1934)

Este célebre médico dedicó su vida a la investigación científica. Desarrolló la revolucionaria "doctrina de la neurona": la teoría de que las neuronas son la estructura básica del sistema nervioso. Ganó el Premio Nobel de Medicina en 1906 por su trabajo en este campo.

Note: Also a skilled artist, Ramón y Cajal produced many illustrations of the nervous system that are still used in textbooks today. He published over one hundred scientific articles and also wrote five science fiction stories.

Penélope Cruz (1974–)

Esta versátil actriz inició su carrera cuando apareció en un vídeo para el conjunto musical Mecano. Es conocida por su trabajo en el cine internacional y ha realizado más de cincuenta películas en varias lenguas. En 2009 se convirtió en la primera actriz española en ganar un Óscar por su trabajo en *Vicky Cristina Barcelona*.

Note: In her youth Cruz trained as a dancer and actor. From a young age her great dream was to work one day with Spanish film director Pedro Almodóvar, a dream she saw fulfilled in 1997 with her role in *Carne trémula*. She won her Oscar for Best Supporting Actress in the Woody Allen film *Vicky Cristina Barcelona*. She has also received several Goyas, the Spanish equivalent of the Oscar.

Imágenes de España

More activities on Spain and the **Panorama cultural** are found in the **Un paso más** section of the *Cuaderno de actividades.*

Mira el vídeo sobre Madrid y contesta las preguntas.

1. ¿Cuáles son dos o tres datos básicos sobre la capital de España?

2. ¿Cuáles son algunos de los atractivos de Madrid?

3. ¿Cuáles son los lugares más interesantes para los turistas? ¿Cuáles te gustaría visitar?

Answers: *Suggested responses:* 1. Está en el centro de la Península Ibérica. Tiene una población de más de tres millones de habitantes. Es un centro financiero y cultural. 2. La Plaza Mayor, los parques y jardines, los museos y restaurantes, la Gran Vía, la Puerta del Sol, los museos del jamón, el Centro de Arte Reina Sofía, el Parque del Retiro. 3. *Answers will vary.*

Vocabulario

Sustantivos

el algodón *cotton*
la artesanía *arts and crafts*
el color *color*
el descuento *discount*
el (gran) almacén *department store*
la lana *wool*
el piso *floor (level)*
la planta baja *ground floor*
la prenda (de vestir) *article of clothing*
el probador *dressing room*
la seda *silk*
el sótano *basement*
la talla *size*
la tienda *store*

Verbos

aceptar *to accept*
buscar *to look for*
calzar *to wear, to take (shoe size)*
encontrar (ue) *to find*
envolver (ue) *to wrap*
faltar *to be short, missing, or lacking*
llevar *to wear (clothing), to take*
mostrar (ue) *to show*
pagar *to pay (for)*
parecer *to seem, to appear*
probarse (ue) *to try on*
quedar *to fit; to remain, to be left*
regatear *to bargain, haggle over a price*

Otras palabras

barato(a) *cheap; inexpensive*
caro(a) *expensive*
esa *that, that one (f.)*
esas *those (f.)*
ese *that, that one (m.)*
esos *those (m.)*
esta *this, this one (f.)*
estas *these (f.)*
este *this, this one (m.)*
estos *these (m.)*
formal *dressy, fancy*
sencillo(a) *simple*

Clothing: p. 194
Ordinal numbers: p. 194
Colors and patterns: p. 195
Jewelry: p. 206
Souvenirs: p. 206

For further review, please turn to **Vocabulario temático: español e inglés** at the back of the book.

Go to the ***Puentes*** website for extra vocabulary practice using the Flashcard program.

¡A divertirnos!

Situation Cards: 22, 23, 24, 28, 29, 30, 67, 73, 74, 75, 76, 77, 79, 80, 81, 83, 84, 85, 86, 87, 90, 91, 92, 93, 97, 98, 99, 102, 103, 104

More Information: This chapter deals with the myriad ways we enjoy ourselves, from sports to holidays. It begins by teaching the simple but practical social skill of issuing oral invitations. Students will continue expanding their ability to ask and answer questions in the present time frame even as they delve further into the more difficult task of describing and narrating in the past time frame.

Proficiency: Although describing and narrating in the past time frame is a characteristic of the Advanced speaker, we must begin now to lay the foundation for that skill. Expect your students to be able to handle more controlled activities in the past, and to respond to your questions in the past when you "intervene;" that is, when you overtly express or direct attention to the past time frame.

Standards: In addition to continuing with the goals for Communication, this chapter addresses numerous Cultural goals in its treatment of holidays and traditional celebrations.

Turn to the *Cuaderno de actividades* for this chapter's reading practice and strategy: Summarizing.

Turn to the *Cuaderno de actividades* for this chapter's composition practice and writing strategy: Writing a personal narrative.

OBJETIVOS

Speaking and Listening
▶ Extending, accepting, and declining invitations
▶ Discussing leisure activities
▶ Talking about the weather and seasons
▶ Describing present and past holidays, celebrations, and memorable experiences
▶ Telling stories about past events
▶ Reacting to stories that others tell

Culture
▶ Costa Rica
▶ Holidays and celebrations

Grammar
▶ Review of the preterite aspect of the past tense
▶ The imperfect aspect of the past tense
▶ Contrast of uses of the preterite and imperfect

Video
▶ En la Hacienda Vista Alegre: Episodio 7
▶ Imágenes de Costa Rica

Gramática suplementaria
▶ El pluscuamperfecto

Cuaderno de actividades
Reading
▶ Strategy: Summarizing

Writing
▶ Strategy: Writing a personal narrative

Playlist
🌐 www.cengage.com/spanish/puentes

A primera vista

Barbacoa para cumpleaños

Las diversiones y las celebraciones nos sacan de la rutina y también nos ofrecen la oportunidad de reforzar los lazos *(reinforce ties)* con la familia, los amigos y la comunidad. ¿Qué celebración familiar te gusta más a ti?

Con un(a) compañero(a), estudien el cuadro de la artista chicana Carmen Lomas Garza y contesten las preguntas.

1. ¿Qué celebran todas estas personas? ¿Quiénes son?

2. ¿Cómo se divierten los niños en esta fiesta? ¿Y los adultos?

3. ¿Cómo son las celebraciones de cumpleaños en tu familia? ¿En qué se parecen a *(How are they similar to)* la del cuadro?

4. Este cuadro se considera un ejemplo del estilo naif porque _____.
   a. tiene un solo plano y predominan los colores brillantes
   b. se parece a *(it looks like)* una fotografía
   c. la artista estudió arte formalmente por muchos años

HABLANDO DEL ARTE

The works of some untrained artists are characterized by bright colors and traditional materials; often the rules of perspective and proportion are not followed. This style, called "naive" or **arte naif,** may also be deliberately used by trained artists, such as Carmen Lomas Garza, as you see in the work on the next page.

CARMEN LOMAS GARZA (1948–)

Nacionalidad: estadounidense (de ascendencia mexicana)

Otras obras: *Cascarones, Camas para sueños, Lotería, En mi familia* (su libro para niños)

Estilo: Rico en colores y detalles, su estilo es de una viveza *(vividness)* refrescante. Las tradiciones familiares cobran vida *(come alive)* en imágenes de la niñez de la autora, pintadas con el orgullo *(pride)* de su herencia chicana. Es un arte lleno de amor y recuerdos íntimos que nos invita a recordar nuestros propios *(own)* momentos especiales en familia.

Teaching Tip: Project other works by the artist and discuss the celebrations and holidays depicted: *Quinceañera, Posadas,* and *Cascarones.*

Note: Carmen Lomas Garza depicts her subject matter with minute detail. Help students focus on each individual, his/her position in the painting, and what he/she is doing. Compare this typical Chicano birthday with a typical birthday in your students' culture(s).

Vocabulary: The paper banners in the background, known as **papel picado,** are a typical Mexican decoration that consists of colorful tissue paper cut into elaborate lace-like designs.

Barbacoa para cumpleaños (1993) **Carmen Lomas Garza**

🌐 Go to the *Puentes* website for extra vocabulary practice using the Flashcard program.

The English equivalents of the **Vocabulario temático** sections are found at the back of the book.

Transparency Bank G-1, G-5

Regional Vocabulary: In some countries, playing cards are called **naipes** or **barajas.** Tickets for social events may be called **boletos** or **entradas.**

Teaching Tip: Remind students of the two words for *play* in Spanish: **tocar** (for instruments) and **jugar** (for sports and games).

Teaching Tip: To introduce this vocabulary, bring a local or Spanish-language newspaper to class and discuss the entertainment possibilities for the coming week. Use the expressions presented here to "invite" several students to a movie or concert as a model for combining the phrases into a complete conversation.

If you want to meet on location, say: **Te espero en *el museo.***

Note: An invitation often implies that the person extending the invitation will pay for all of the expenses related to the activity, particularly when a man invites a woman on a date. However, when groups of friends go out together, usually everyone pays his or her own way; if one person wants to treat the others, he or she will say **"Yo invito."**

Vocabulario temático

El tiempo libre: las invitaciones

Para invitar

¿Quieres ir *al cine* el sábado?
　　　　al teatro
　　　　al museo de arte
　　　　a un concierto

¿Por qué no *vamos de picnic* esta tarde?
　　　　jugamos a las cartas
　　　　damos un paseo
　　　　vamos al partido de fútbol

Para aceptar la invitación

¡Qué buena idea!

¡Cómo no!

¡Me encantaría!

Para declinar la invitación

Lo siento, pero *tengo que estudiar.*

Gracias, pero no puedo. *Estoy cansado(a).*
　　　　Tengo otro compromiso.
　　　　No sé jugar.

Quizás la próxima vez.

Para pedir información y hacer los planes

—¿A qué hora empieza?

—Empieza *a las ocho.*

—¿Dónde nos encontramos?

—Paso por tu casa *a las siete y media.*

—¿Cuánto cuestan los boletos?

— La entrada es gratuita.

Otras preguntas útiles

¿Qué película dan?　　　　¿Quiénes tocan?

¿Qué obra presentan?　　　　¿Quiénes juegan?

Ponerlo a prueba

7-1 ¿Quieres ir a... ? Dos amigas están escuchando la radio y oyen algo interesante. Primero, escucha el anuncio de radio y la reacción de las jóvenes. Luego, completa las oraciones con la información correcta.

c 1. El anuncio es para...
   a. una obra teatral. b. un ballet. c. un concierto.

a 2. El acontecimiento *(event)* va a tener lugar...
   a. el 8 de noviembre. b. el 10 de noviembre. c. el 16 de noviembre.

b 3. El boleto menos caro cuesta…
   a. 8000 colones. b. 16 500 colones. c. 28 000 colones.

c 4. Carmen no está segura si quiere ir porque...
   a. tiene que estudiar para los exámenes.
   b. no le gusta el acontecimiento.
   c. los boletos cuestan mucho dinero.

b 5. Las chicas deciden…
   a. conversar más sobre el evento mañana.
   b. comprar los boletos inmediatamente.
   c. ahorrar *(save)* su dinero para las vacaciones.

7-2 Vamos al teatro. Carolina y Ricardo están haciendo sus planes para el fin de semana. Relaciona las dos columnas de una manera lógica.

Carolina:

c 1. ¿Quieres ir al museo el sábado? Hay una nueva exposición de arte contemporáneo.

g 2. ¡Buena idea! ¿Qué obra presentan?

e 3. ¿Cuánto cuestan los boletos?

f 4. Está bien. ¿A qué hora empieza?

a 5. Bueno. ¿Dónde nos encontramos?

d 6. De acuerdo. Entonces nos vemos el sábado a las 6:45.

Ricardo:

a. Paso por tu casa a las siete menos cuarto.

b. Juegan los equipos de Puntarenas y Liberia.

c. No sé. En realidad, no me interesa mucho. ¿Por qué no vamos al teatro?

d. ¡Hasta pronto!

e. Tres mil colones. Pero hay un descuento para estudiantes.

f. A las ocho.

g. Una tragedia clásica: *Romeo y Julieta.*

7-3 Dos invitaciones. Completa los diálogos de una manera lógica.

1. **Una invitación y una aceptación**

Tu amigo(a): Oye, ¿quieres ir al cine esta noche?

   Tú: ¡_____! ¿_____?

Tu amigo(a): Dan *El Laberinto.*

   Tú: ¿_____?

Tu amigo(a): La primera función *(first showing)* es a las siete y cuarto, y la segunda empieza a las nueve y media.

   Tú: Prefiero _____ porque _____.

Tu amigo(a): De acuerdo. ¿Dónde nos encontramos?

   Tú: _____.

Tu amigo(a): Muy bien. ¡Hasta muy pronto!

Teaching Tip: Assign the first two activities for homework.

Note: The currency of Costa Rica is the **colón,** named after the explorer **Cristóbal Colón.** The rate of exchange at the time of publication was $1 = 570 colones.

2. **Una invitación y una declinación**

TU AMIGO(A): No tengo ganas de ir a clase esta tarde. ¿Por qué no jugamos al tenis?

TÚ: Lo siento, pero _____.

TU AMIGO(A): Ah, pues… ¿quieres ir al partido de básquetbol esta noche?

TÚ: _____.

TU AMIGO(A): Bueno, entonces será la próxima vez.

Teaching Tip 7-4: Have more proficient classes complete this activity orally in pairs. Less proficient groups may profit from writing a dialogue first.

Teaching Tip 7-4: Before pairing students for this practice, ask the class questions about the content of the *agenda cultural:* **¿Qué película dan en el cine Cinépolis? ¿A qué hora empieza? ¿Cuánto es el boleto/la entrada? ¿Qué obra presentan en el Teatro de La Aduana? ¿Qué días la van a presentar? ¿A qué hora empieza? ¿Hay un descuento para estudiantes? ¿Qué van a presentar en el Teatro Nacional? ¿Cuándo? ¿Cuánto cuestan los boletos? ¿Cómo se llama la exposición en la Galería Joaquín García Monge? ¿Qué días está abierta la galería? ¿Es cara esta exposición?**

7-4 ¿Quieres ir? Mira la siguiente agenda cultural de un periódico de San José, Costa Rica. ¿Cuál de los eventos es más interesante? Invita a tu compañero(a) a ese evento.

MODELO

TÚ: ¿Quieres ir a…?

TU COMPAÑERO(A): ¡Buena idea! ¿…?

AGENDA CULTURAL

Cine

El sustituto (drama, mayores de 15 años)
Lugar: Cinépolis VIP
Horario: 3:15, 6:30, 9:45
Entrada: ₡2300 general,
₡1800 estudiantes

Danza

Ballet Nacional de Cuba
Lugar: Teatro Nacional
Horario: viernes y sábado, 8 p.m.
Entrada: ₡4000 a ₡12000

Teatro

Salomé (dirigida por Luis Carlos Vásquez)
Lugar: Teatro de La Aduana
Horario: jueves a sábado, 8 p.m.
Entrada: ₡3000 general, ₡1500 estudiantes

Artes plásticas

OBJETOS DE ARTE, OBJETOS DE LUZ:
Arte lumínico en Costa Rica
Lugar: Galería Joaquín García Monge
Horario: lunes a sábado, de 9 a.m. a 4 p.m.
Entrada: gratuita

7-5 Nuestras preferencias. Conversa con dos o tres compañeros(as) sobre sus actividades favoritas durante el tiempo libre. Contesta las preguntas a continuación y haz *(ask)* otras preguntas originales.

1. **Los deportes:** ¿Cuáles son tus deportes favoritos? ¿Cuáles prefieres jugar y cuáles prefieres mirar? ¿Cuáles son tus equipos *(teams)* preferidos? (Haz una pregunta original.)

2. **El cine y el teatro:** ¿Te gusta más el cine o el teatro? ¿Quiénes son tus actores y actrices favoritos? ¿Qué películas u obras viste recientemente? (Haz una pregunta original.)

3. **Otros pasatiempos:** Después de estudiar mucho, ¿qué haces para relajarte *(to relax)*? ¿Qué prefieres hacer los viernes y los sábados por la noche? (Haz una pregunta original.)

Vocabulario temático

El fin de semana

Un fin de semana divertido

ESTEBAN: ¿Qué tal tu fin de semana?

DIEGO: Me divertí muchísimo.

ESTEBAN: ¿Adónde fuiste?

DIEGO: Fui *a las montañas.*
al lago
a la playa

ESTEBAN: ¿Qué hiciste?

DIEGO: Mi amigo(a) y yo *acampamos.*
paseamos en barco de vela
tomamos el sol

ESTEBAN: ¡Qué bien!

DIEGO: Sí, lo pasamos muy bien. ¿Y tú qué hiciste?

If you didn't do anything special over the weekend you can say **No hice nada en particular** (*nothing in particular*) or **No hice nada especial** (*nothing special*).

Un fin de semana regular/malo

ANA: ¿Cómo pasaste el fin de semana?

LORENA: Lo pasé *fatal.*
más o menos

ANA: ¿Qué pasó?

LORENA: Me enfermé y tuve que quedarme en casa.

ANA: ¡Qué lástima!

LORENA: Sí, pero hoy me siento mejor. ¿Y tú cómo pasaste el fin de semana?

Actividades populares

En las montañas: **escalar en roca, hacer caminatas, acampar, dormir bajo las estrellas**

En la playa: **bucear, esquiar, nadar, pasear en barco de vela, tomar el sol**

En el campo: **montar a caballo, ir de caza, pescar**

En el gimnasio: **correr, levantar pesas, hacer yoga, hacer ejercicio aeróbico**

En un festival: **escuchar música, ver artesanías, probar la comida, bailar**

En casa: **descansar, mirar televisión, relajarse, leer**

Estrategia *Tips on sustaining a conversation*

To sustain a conversation, you need to be an active participant. Express your interest in the topic by asking follow-up questions and by reacting to the news with appropriate phrases, such as the following:

To react to happy news:		To react to a disappointment:	
¡Fantástico!	*That's fantastic!*	¡Qué lástima!	*That's too bad!*
¡Magnífico!	*That's wonderful!*	¡Qué mala suerte!	*What bad luck!*
¡Qué buena suerte!	*What good luck!*	¡Qué pena!	*That's very sad!*
¡Estupendo!	*That's great!*	¡Qué decepción!	*What a disappointment!*

More Information: More phrases and questions to express interest are presented in **Paso 3.**

Teaching Tip: To practice these expressions, tell students what you did and have them respond with an appropriate phrase. For example, you say: **Esquié en las montañas.** A student may respond: **¡Estupendo!**

CD2
Track 9

Ponerlo a prueba

7-6 ¿Qué tal el fin de semana? Pilar y Marcos están hablando de su fin de semana. ¿Qué hicieron? Escucha su conversación y completa las oraciones.

_b_ 1. El fin de semana pasado Pilar…
    a. no hizo nada en particular.   b. se divirtió mucho.   c. lo pasó muy mal.

_a_ 2. Pilar y Rosa fueron…
    a. al lago.   b. a la playa.   c. al campo.

_a_ 3. Pilar y Rosa…
    a. pasearon en barco de vela.   b. hicieron caminatas.   c. tomaron el sol.

_c_ 4. Marcos tuvo un fin de semana…
    a. divertido.   b. tranquilo.   c. malo.

_b_ 5. El viernes, en el festival, Marcos…
    a. vio muchas artesanías.
    b. probó muchas comidas.
    c. escuchó un conjunto nuevo.

_b_ 6. El sábado y el domingo, Marcos…
    a. tuvo que estudiar.
    b. estuvo enfermo.
    c. trabajó en el restaurante.

7-7 Dónde. ¿Dónde hicieron tú y tus amigos estas actividades? Relaciona la información de las dos columnas. **¡Ojo!** Puede haber más de una respuesta correcta.

_b_ 1. Rita tomó el sol y nadó en el mar.

_e, g_ 2. Hice ejercicio aeróbico y levanté pesas.

_a, c_ 3. Mis amigos y yo nos fuimos de caza y también pescamos.

_a, b, c_ 4. Carlos acampó y durmió bajo las estrellas.

_a, b, d_ 5. Silvia y Elena bucearon y esquiaron todo el día.

_a, c_ 6. Alicia y Javier escalaron en roca e hicieron caminatas.

_g_ 7. Jaime se enfermó y se quedó en cama.

_f_ 8. Vimos unas artesanías y bailamos salsa.

a. En las montañas.
b. En la playa.
c. En el campo.
d. En el lago.
e. En el gimnasio.
f. En un festival.
g. En casa.

7-8 Nuestras preferencias. Conversa con tres compañeros(as) sobre sus actividades favoritas en los distintos lugares. Toma apuntes sobre las actividades favoritas de cada persona.

MODELO

Tú: ¿Qué te gusta hacer en las montañas?

Compañero(a) 1:   Me encanta acampar en las montañas. También me gusta escalar en roca. ¿Y a ti? ¿Qué te gusta hacer?

	Compañero(a) 1	Compañero(a) 2	Compañero(a) 3
En las montañas			
En la playa			
En el gimnasio			
En un festival			
En casa			

7-9 El fin de semana. ¿Adónde fueron estas personas el fin de semana pasado? ¿Qué hicieron allí? Para cada ilustración, escribe un mínimo de tres oraciones en el pretérito.

MODELO Laura y su esposo **fueron** a Nueva York. **Comieron** en un restaurante chino una noche. Otro día **visitaron** un museo de arte. También **vieron** una obra de teatro.

1. Paco y sus amigos…

2. Puri…

3. Leonora y David…

7-10 ¿Qué tal? Conversa con un(a) compañero(a) sobre el fin de semana pasado.

MODELO

Tú:	¿Cómo pasaste el fin de semana?
Tu compañero(a):	Lo pasé muy bien.
Tú:	¿Qué hiciste?…

Expansion 7-10: After the pairs finish talking, have them report their findings. Ask questions like **¿Quién pasó un fin de semana divertido?, ¿aburrido?, ¿desastroso?** etc.

Gramática

Repaso del pretérito

Read along as you listen to Roberto describe how he and his wife spent last Saturday. Identify all the verbs in the preterite.

Heinle Grammar Tutorial:
The preterite tense

CD2
Track 10

Carla y yo <u>nos divertimos</u> mucho el sábado. Primero, <u>fuimos</u> a un parque donde <u>dimos</u> un paseo y <u>jugamos</u> al frisbee. Luego <u>fuimos</u> a un festival en el centro de la ciudad. <u>Probamos</u> muchos platos deliciosos y <u>escuchamos</u> un conjunto nuevo. <u>Bailamos</u> por horas y horas. <u>Volvimos</u> a casa a la medianoche, cansados pero contentos.

A. El pretérito. The preterite (**el pretérito**) is one of two important verb forms used in Spanish to talk about past actions and events. To refresh your memory of the different conjugations, see Appendices A, B, C, and D.

▸ **Regular -ar verbs:** pas**é**, pas**aste**, pas**ó**, pas**amos**, pas**asteis**, pas**aron**

▸ **Regular -er and -ir verbs:** com**í**, com**iste**, com**ió**, com**imos**, com**isteis**, com**ieron**

▸ **Spelling-changing verbs in the *yo* form:** -zar → -cé (almorcé, empecé); -car → -qué (busqué, toqué); -gar → -gué (llegué, jugué)

▸ **Stem-changing -ir verbs (e → i and o → u):** pedir, repetir, vestirse, divertirse, servir, conseguir, dormir, morir

▸ **Irregular verbs:** ser, ir, tener, estar, hacer, dar, poder, poner, venir, querer, hacer, decir, traer, conducir

More Information: To accommodate different learning styles, the uses of the preterite and the imperfect are presented in different ways throughout this chapter. In the first two **Pasos,** the two tenses are explained separately with fairly detailed guidelines for use; in the third **Paso,** the tenses are explained together and in a more global way.

B. Los usos del pretérito. In Spanish, both the preterite and the imperfect are used to talk about the past. The preterite is used in the following ways:

▸ To tell what happened or what somebody did at a particular time.
The sentence often includes time expressions such as these: **ayer** *(yesterday)*, **anteayer** *(the day before yesterday)*, **anoche** *(last night)*, **la semana pasada** *(last week)*, **hace dos semanas** *(two weeks ago)*, **el año pasado** *(last year)*, **en 2005, para mi cumpleaños,** etc.

    Mis padres me visitaron **ayer.**   *My parents visited me **yesterday.***

▸ To state that an action or event occurred several times.
The sentence usually contains an expression using **vez** *(time)*, such as **una vez, dos veces, varias veces,** etc.

    Vi la película *El Laberinto del Fauno* **dos veces.**   *I saw the movie* Pan's Labyrinth ***twice.***

▸ To express that an action or event lasted a specific amount of time.
The sentence will often include the expression **por** + *amount of time,* such as **por unos minutos, por dos horas, por varios días, por veinte años, por siglos** *(centuries),* etc.

    Estudié **por tres horas.**   *I studied **for three hours.***

▸ To sum up an experience.
A summary statement is usually placed at the beginning or end of a story or anecdote.

    Ayer **fue** un día horrible. Primero…   *Yesterday **was** a terrible day. First …*

C. Algunos verbos especiales. The preterite is often used to indicate the beginning or end of an action. To reflect this usage, certain verbs need a special translation in English when they are used in the preterite. Here are a few of the more common ones:

conocer	Anoche **conocí** a mis futuros suegros. *Last night I **met** my future in-laws. (That is, I met them for the first time.)*
saber	**Supe** la mala noticia ayer. *I **found out** the bad news yesterday.*
querer	Carmen **quiso** ir, pero nevaba demasiado. *Carmen **tried** to go, but it was snowing too hard.*
no querer	**No quise** ir a la fiesta. *I **refused** to go to the party.*
poder	**Pude** ir a pesar de la lluvia. *I **managed** to go despite the rain.*
tener	Ayer **tuve** una buena noticia. *Yesterday I **got** some good news.*

Ponerlo a prueba

7-11 Una visita a Costa Rica. ¿Qué hicieron Rosaura y sus amigos durante su visita a Costa Rica? Escoge el verbo más lógico y escríbelo en el pretérito.

1. Mi amiga Yensy y yo (hacer/ir) __hicimos__ una excursión a Sarchí, un pueblo famoso por su artesanía.

   Allí (tener/poder) __pudimos__ ver unas carretas *(ox carts)* hechas a mano y muchos artículos de madera *(wood)*.

2. Hernando y Saúl (acampar/alquilar) __alquilaron__ un carro y (conducir/tomar) __condujeron__ al Parque Nacional Volcán Poás.

   Por desgracia, no (conseguir/seguir) __consiguieron__ ver el cráter, porque estaba muy nublado *(cloudy)*.

3. Glenda (correr/ir) __fue__ a un restaurante típico y (pedir/poner) __pidió__ casado, un plato típico con arroz, frijoles, carne y ensalada.

   Pero no (bucear/querer) __quiso__ probar la sopa de mondongo *(tripe)*.

4. Silvia y Patricio (dar/escalar) __dieron__ un paseo en bote para ver las junglas *(jungles)* de Tortuguero.

   Silvia (ducharse/divertirse) __se divirtió__ mucho mirando los animales pero Patricio (dormirse/despertarse) __se durmió__ y no (ver/comer) __vio__ nada.

5. José, Martita y yo (venir/tener) __tuvimos__ la suerte de ver las cavernas subterráneas en el Parque Nacional de Barra Honda.

   ¡No sé por qué nosotros no (traer/hacer) __trajimos__ nuestra cámara!

Teaching Tip: Assign the first activity for homework. Complete the remaining ones in class.

Answers 7-12. 1. Mayo; 2. Para su cumpleaños; 3. A las nueve, flores y un regalo; 4. Un pastel/una torta; 5. El ponche/las bebidas; 6. Al tenis de mesa/al pin-pon; 7. Escucharon música y hablaron; 8. Bailaron; comieron y hablaron; 9. Miraron la tele; 10. *Answers will vary.*

Teaching Tip 7-12: Direct more proficient classes to complete the sentences orally, perhaps with the help of a partner. Less proficient classes will benefit from writing down the answers.

Expansion: Using the drawings in **Capítulo 3,** have students tell what the people did yesterday, last night, last year, etc.

Expansion 7-13: After students converse, draw the group into a discussion of movies and restaurants. Have students recommend their favorites to the group and explain why these are good choices.

Teaching Tip 7-14: Before having students talk about a special party, provide a model by describing a memorable party that you have attended. Adjust the length and sophistication of the description to the level of the class.

7-12 La fiesta de Paloma. Mira la escena de la fiesta de Paloma y contesta las preguntas con oraciones completas.

1. ¿En qué mes fue la fiesta de Paloma?
2. ¿Por qué dio una fiesta?
3. ¿A qué hora llegó Miguel? ¿Qué le trajo Miguel a Paloma?
4. ¿Qué hizo doña Eugenia para la fiesta?
5. ¿Qué sirvió don Patricio durante la fiesta?
6. ¿A qué jugaron Antonio y Felipe?
7. ¿Qué hicieron Neeka y Kelly durante la fiesta?
8. ¿Cómo se divirtieron Ricardo y Margarita? ¿Celso y Bernadette?
9. ¿Cómo pasaron el tiempo en la fiesta Paco y Juan?
10. En tu opinión, ¿quiénes se divirtieron más en la fiesta? ¿Por qué?

7-13 La última vez. Tú y un(a) compañero(a) van a hablar de la última vez *(the last time)* que hicieron algo. Usen las siguientes expresiones y preguntas para entrevistarse.

| ayer | anteayer | la semana pasada | hace *dos semanas* |
| anoche | el año pasado | el mes pasado | hace *dos años* |

1. ¿Cuándo fue la última vez que fuiste al cine? ¿Qué película viste? ¿Te gustó? ¿Adónde fuiste después de ver la película? (Haz una pregunta original).
2. ¿Cuándo fue la última vez que fuiste con tus amigos a un restaurante mexicano? ¿Qué pidieron Uds. para comer? ¿Fue bueno o malo el servicio allí? ¿Tocaron música de mariachi? (Haz una pregunta original).
3. ¿Cuándo fue la última vez que pasaste todo el día en casa? ¿Estuviste enfermo(a) ese día? ¿Hasta qué hora dormiste? ¿Qué hiciste el resto del día? (Haz una pregunta original).

7-14 La fiesta. Conversa con dos o tres compañeros(as) sobre una fiesta especial o memorable. Incluyan la siguiente información:

- ¿Cuándo fue la fiesta?
- ¿Quién dio la fiesta?
- ¿Qué hicieron todos en la fiesta?
- ¿Por qué fue una fiesta especial o memorable?

Puente cultural

¿Cuál es la fiesta o acontecimiento más divertido de tu país?

🌐 Go to the *Puentes* Premium Website to view the **Puente cultural** interviews.

Federick Rivers

🌐 **COSTA RICA**

En Costa Rica las fiestas más divertidas del año son las de Palmares. Son fiestas que se celebran una vez al año, en enero, en el pueblo de Palmares. Consisten en diferentes actividades como tope (desfile de caballos), carnaval y conciertos, entre otros. Lo que las hace tan buenas es la asistencia que tienen. Casi un millón de personas de todas partes del país van a las fiestas y es un llenazo total *(a huge crowd)*.

Gabriella Paracat

🌐 **ARGENTINA**

El carnaval, sin duda, es la celebración más divertida. Todos se disfrazan de cualquier cosa, como acá durante *Halloween*. En los boliches (clubes) populares hay bailes y conciertos con los cantantes del momento. Hay que pagar para entrar y van principalmente las personas jóvenes, desde los adolescentes hasta los que tienen 30 años. La fiesta tarda una semana. La mayoría de la gente no trabaja durante ese tiempo porque los chicos están de vacaciones.

Mauricio Mbomio

🌐 **GUINEA ECUATORIAL**

Yo diría *(I would say)* que es la Navidad. En mi país, la Navidad es considerada tradicionalmente como la fiesta de los niños porque Jesús Cristo nace, así que todos los menores de edad salen a la calle a cantar y a divertirse. También los niños reciben regalos de sus padres y de otros seres queridos.

Lee la información y completa la tabla.

	En Costa Rica	En Argentina	En Guinea Ecuatorial	En los Estados Unidos
¿Cuál es la fiesta o acontecimiento más divertido de tu país?				

Transparency Bank H-1, H-2, H-3, H-4, H-5

Teaching Tip: Introduce this vocabulary with transparencies, by linking the months to the seasons, by describing the weather conditions in your area for each season, or by relating sports activities to seasons and the weather.

Note: Sometimes the wet season is called **el invierno.**

Está nevando and **está lloviendo** describe *current* weather conditions. To describe climate (or the usual weather pattern), use **nieva** (*it snows*) and **llueve** (*it rains*).

Paso 2

Vocabulario temático

Las estaciones

En las zonas templadas:

el otoño   el invierno   la primavera   el verano

En las zonas tropicales:

 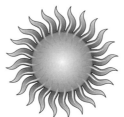

la estación de lluvia   la estación seca

El tiempo

¿Qué tiempo hace hoy?

Hace buen tiempo. Hace sol y mucho calor.

El día está pésimo. Está lloviendo mucho. ¡Detesto la lluvia!

Hace mucho frío. Está nevando. ¡Me gusta la nieve!

Hace fresco hoy. Hace mucho viento. Creo que va a llover.

Otras expresiones de tiempo

Hace *fresco.*
  (mucho) calor
  (mucho) frío
  (mucho) viento
  (muy) buen tiempo
  (muy) mal tiempo

Está *lloviendo.*
  nevando

Está *despejado.*
  nublado

El día está *pésimo.*
  fatal

—¿A cuántos grados estamos?

—Estamos a 20 grados.

—¿Cuál es el pronóstico para mañana?

—Va a *llover.*
  nevar
  haber una tormenta

Vocabulary: **Hay niebla** (*It's foggy*); **Hay granizo** (*It's hailing*).

Note: Point out that in the Caribbean, it is common to have hurricanes **(huracanes)** from June to November. Discuss how climate varies according to altitude, and that the seasons are reversed south of the equator.

Grammar: Briefly review with students the progressive construction. Use **está lloviendo** and **está nevando** as examples. Contrast the meaning of the progressive with the simple present tense of the same verbs: **llueve** and **nieva.**

Vocabulary: There are many ways to give the temperature, including these: **Hace / Está a / Tenemos 20 grados.**

Note: To convert Fahrenheit to Celsius, subtract 32 from the temperature in Fahrenheit (for example: 100 − 32 = 68). Multiply this number by 5 (5 x 68 = 340). Divide by 9 (340 divided by 9 = 37.8). This gives you the equivalent in Celsius. To convert Celsius to Fahrenheit, do the opposite: add 32, multiply by 9 and divide by 5.

Ponerlo a prueba

CD2
Track 11

7-15 El pronóstico para los Estados Unidos. Escucha el pronóstico del tiempo para los Estados Unidos. Para cada zona y ciudad, escribe las letras que corresponden a los símbolos del tiempo. Antes de escuchar el pronóstico, familiarízate bien con los símbolos.

1. Noreste: _a_, _g_. Nueva York: _n_.

2. Sureste: _c_, _f_. Miami: _j_.

3. Zona central norte: _f_, _c_, _e_. Chicago: _k_.

4. Zona central sur: _a_. Houston: _m_.

5. Oeste/Costa del Pacífico: _f_, _a_. Los Ángeles: _f_, _l_.

Teaching Tip: Assign the first two activities for homework.

Expansion: Go on the internet and find weather forecasts for different cities in the United States or for capitals in Central and South America. Hand out copies of the forecast to pairs of students and have each group prepare and present a weather forecast based on the city you have assigned them.

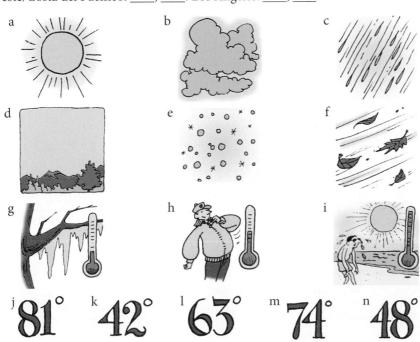

7-16 Mis estaciones favoritas. Relaciona la información de las dos columnas de una manera lógica.

__c__ 1. Me encanta el verano porque…

__a__ 2. Me gusta el invierno porque…

__d__ 3. La primavera es muy agradable *(pleasant)* porque…

__e__ 4. El otoño es mi estación favorita porque…

__b__ 5. En la estación de lluvia…

a. nieva con frecuencia en las montañas y podemos esquiar.

b. llueve por unas horas todos los días.

c. hace sol y calor y siempre vamos a la playa.

d. hace buen tiempo y las plantas florecen *(are in full bloom)*.

e. hace fresco y empieza la temporada de fútbol americano.

7-17 ¿Qué tiempo hace en…? Con un(a) compañero(a), usa la información siguiente para hablar del clima en diferentes lugares.

MODELO

Tú:	¿Qué tiempo hace en primavera en Madrid, España?
Tu compañero(a):	Hace fresco y llueve.
Tú:	¿Cuál es la temperatura media en Madrid en primavera?
Tu compañero(a):	Es de 60 grados (Fahrenheit).

	diciembre enero febrero	marzo abril mayo	junio julio agosto	septiembre octubre noviembre
Madrid, España	45°	60°	85°	60°
Buenos Aires, Argentina	80°	72°	57°	76°
San José, Costa Rica	75°	79°	78°	77°
tu ciudad	?	?	?	?

7-18 Mi estación favorita. Conversa con dos o tres compañeros(as) sobre sus estaciones favoritas. Incluye esta información:

- ¿Cuál es tu estación favorita? ¿Por qué?
- ¿Cómo es el clima en esa estación donde tú vives?
- ¿Cuáles son tus actividades favoritas en esa estación?

Vocabulario temático

Los días festivos y las celebraciones

¿Cómo celebras *el Día de la Independencia?*
el Día de Acción de Gracias
tu cumpleaños

Para celebrar el Día de la Independencia, siempre vamos a ver un desfile en mi pueblo. Cuando era niño(a), me gustaba *ver los fuegos artificiales.*

Para celebrar el Día de Acción de Gracias, normalmente toda la familia se reúne en mi casa. Siempre comemos pavo y pastel de calabaza. Cuando era niño(a), *jugaba al fútbol americano con mis primos.*

Para celebrar mi cumpleaños, con frecuencia salgo a comer con mi familia. Cuando era niño(a), *tenía una fiesta todos los años.*

More Information: This presentation introduces holidays and traditions. Students first practice describing their current customs for celebrating different holidays. Later, they will use the imperfect to describe how they used to celebrate these same holidays when they were younger. The expression **me gustaba** is used here to foreshadow this upcoming practice.

Vocabulary: Other useful terms for Thanksgiving: **salsa de arándanos** *cranberry sauce;* **pavo relleno** *turkey with dressing/ stuffing.*

Regional Vocabulary: In Mexico, turkey is called **guajalote** and sweet potatoes are called **camotes.**

Teaching Tip: To present the new vocabulary, begin with the names of holidays. Ask students what holidays are celebrated in each season. **¿Qué días festivos celebramos en el otoño?** Next, have students provide the corresponding date or month for each holiday. **(El 14 de febrero es... el Día de los Enamorados.)** Then, pick a holiday and, using the present tense, describe 2 or 3 things you do to celebrate. **(Para el Día de Acción de Gracias, toda la familia...)** Call on a student and ask if he/ she celebrates the same way. Finally, using the expression **me gustaba,** mention one thing you used to do as a child to celebrate the same holiday: **Cuando era niño(a), me gustaba...** Call on a student for a similar response.

Las celebraciones y las costumbres

la Navidad	decorar un árbol y cantar villancicos
la Nochebuena	intercambiar regalos
la Janucá	encender las velas del candelabro
la Noche Vieja	brindar con champaña
el Día de Año Nuevo	reunirse con amigos
la Pascua	ir a la iglesia
el Pésaj	ir a la sinagoga
el Día de las Brujas	llevar disfraz y pedir dulces
el Día de los Enamorados	regalar flores o chocolates
el cumpleaños	apagar las velas del pastel de cumpleaños

COMENTARIO CULTURAL *La fiesta de quinceañera*

En tu familia, ¿cómo se marca la transición de niño a adulto? ¿Tienen Uds. una celebración o ceremonia religiosa? ¿Cómo es?

Una de las celebraciones más populares entre las chicas de los países hispanohablantes es la fiesta de los quince años. Este cumpleaños es especial porque marca la transición de niña a mujer. La forma de celebrar varía un poco según el país y los recursos económicos de los padres. En muchos casos, la quinceañera —luciendo un hermoso vestido formal— asiste a una ceremonia religiosa con su familia y sus amigos. Después hay una gran fiesta, donde es tradicional que la chica baile un vals con su padre. Entre las familias más adineradas (*wealthy*), la chica puede escoger entre una fiesta y un viaje. Por ejemplo, algunas chicas hacen un crucero u organizan un viaje a Disneyworld con sus amigos.

Ponerlo a prueba

7-19 Días festivos. Dos latinoamericanos que viven en los Estados Unidos van a describir su día festivo favorito. Escucha las descripciones de sus actividades y completa las actividades.

PRIMERA DESCRIPCIÓN:

1. Marisa describe (<u>la Navidad</u> / el Año Nuevo / la Pascua).

2. Por lo general, Marisa pasa el 24 con (sus tíos / <u>sus abuelos</u> / sus nietos).

3. Cuando Marisa era pequeña, le gustaba (ir a la iglesia / decorar el árbol / <u>recibir regalos de Papá Noel</u>).

SEGUNDA DESCRIPCIÓN:

4. Rolando habla (del Día de las Brujas / <u>de su cumpleaños</u> / del Día de los Enamorados).

5. El año pasado, Rolando (no hizo nada especial / salió a comer / <u>tuvo una fiesta sorpresa</u>).

6. Cuando Rolando era pequeño, le gustaba (comer helado / romper la piñata / <u>apagar las velas del pastel</u>).

7-20 Los días festivos y las tradiciones. ¿Con qué día festivo asocias las siguientes tradiciones? Escoge el día de la lista y escríbelo en el espacio en blanco. También indica cuál de las actividades no corresponde al grupo.

> **MODELO** <u>La Noche Vieja</u>: brindar con champaña / celebrar a la medianoche / <u>pasear en barco de vela</u> / hacer propósitos (*resolutions*)

el cumpleaños   el Día de Acción de Gracias
la Navidad   el Día de los Enamorados
la Noche Vieja   el Día de la Independencia

1. _____la Navidad_____ : cantar villancicos / decorar un árbol / intercambiar regalos / <u>llevar disfraz</u>

2. _el Día de Acción de Gracias_ : comer pavo y jamón / mirar el desfile de Macy's / <u>llover mucho</u> / mirar partidos de fútbol americano

3. _el Día de los Enamorados_ : <u>ir a la sinagoga</u> / regalar una docena de rosas / comer en un restaurante romántico / beber champaña

4. _____el cumpleaños_____ : tener una fiesta / <u>comer un pastel de calabaza</u> / apagar las velas del pastel / reunirse con amigos y con la familia

5. _el Día de la Independencia_ : ver los fuegos artificiales / <u>encender las velas del candelabro</u> / asistir a un concierto de música patriótica / hacer un picnic o una barbacoa

7-21 Juan Santamaría. Lee el artículo sobre este héroe nacional y contesta las preguntas con un(a) compañero(a) de clase.

Juan Santamaría: de tamborilero a héroe nacional

Era joven y muy pobre, pero murió por su país. Con tan solo 16 años y por su valentía, Juan Santamaría se convirtió en el héroe nacional de Costa Rica.

La insólita historia de este soldado empieza en 1855. En ese año, el estadounidense William Walker invadió y tomó control de Nicaragua. Walker quería conquistar varios países centroamericanos y anexarlos a una Confederación Centroamericana. Para avanzar ese objetivo, el día 20 de marzo de 1856 invadió la provincia de Guanacaste, al norte de Costa Rica. Las tropas costarricenses expulsaron a Walker y sus "filibusteros" y los siguieron a la ciudad de Rivas, en el sur de Nicaragua.

El 11 de abril Walker inició otro ataque a Costa Rica. El combate fue feroz, pero los costarricenses no pudieron hacer que Walker abandonara su centro de comando en Rivas, el llamado Mesón de Guerra. Uno de los generales de la Campaña Nacional costarricense decidió prender fuego a este centro de comando. Dos soldados intentaron incendiarlo, pero sin éxito. Entonces fue que el tamborilero Santamaría se ofreció. Con gran valor Santamaría logró quemar el Mesón, y eso llevó a la victoria de los costarricenses.

Hoy en día el 11 de abril es un día festivo nacional, un día para honrar al humilde tamborilero y para recordar la gesta heroica del soldado Juan en contra del filibustero William Walker.

VOCABULARIO ÚTIL:

tamborilero	*drummer (in the army)*
valentía	*courage, bravery*
filibustero	*pirate, plunderer*
prender fuego	*to set fire to*
quemar	*to burn*

1. ¿Cómo se llamaba el tamborilero que llegó a ser un héroe nacional de Costa Rica? ¿Cuándo es el día festivo en su honor?

2. ¿En qué batalla *(battle)* participó? ¿Qué hizo para llevar a las tropas costarricenses a la victoria?

3. ¿Cuándo ocurrió la invasión de William Walker? ¿Por qué quería Walker anexar a Costa Rica?

4. Nombra un héroe nacional de los Estados Unidos. ¿Hay un día festivo en su honor? ¿Qué hizo para convertirse en héroe nacional?

7-22 En Costa Rica. Aquí tienes una lista de los días festivos de Costa Rica. Con un(a) compañero(a), lee la información y contesta las preguntas.

Los días festivos de Costa Rica

1° de enero:	Año Nuevo
19 de marzo:	Día de San José (patrono de la ciudad capital)
marzo/abril:	Semana Santa
11 de abril:	Día de Juan Santamaría (héroe nacional)
1° de mayo:	Día del Trabajo
9 de junio:	Día de San Pedro y San Pablo
25 de julio:	Anexión del Partido de Nicoya
2 de agosto:	Día de la Virgen de los Ángeles (patrona de Costa Rica)
15 de agosto:	Día de la Madre
15 de septiembre:	Día de la Independencia
12 de octubre:	Día de las Culturas
25 de diciembre:	Navidad

Note: In many other countries, October 12 is known as **Día de la Raza;** Costa Rica prefers the more inclusive term, **Día de las Culturas.**

1. ¿Cuáles de los días festivos en Costa Rica son celebraciones religiosas? ¿Cuáles son patrióticos?

2. ¿Cuáles de los días festivos costarricenses celebramos en los Estados Unidos también?

3. ¿Qué días festivos les gustan celebrar a ti y a tu familia? ¿Qué tradiciones tienen Uds. para ese día?

4. ¿Qué días festivos te gustan menos? Explica.

 7-23 Adivina. Juega este juego de adivinanza (*guessing game*) con dos o tres compañeros(as). Primero, uno(a) de Uds. tiene que describir un día festivo sin mencionar el nombre. Después de escuchar, las otras personas tienen que adivinar (*guess*) cuál es. Tomen turnos.

> **MODELO**
>
> Tú: Este día festivo es en el verano. Para celebrarlo, muchas personas van a un lago o a un parque donde comen hamburguesas, perros calientes y sandía. Por la noche, hay muchos fuegos artificiales. Los colores "oficiales" de este día son el rojo, el blanco y el azul. ¿Cuál es este día festivo?
>
> Compañero(a) 2: ¿Es el Día de la Independencia?
>
> Tú: ¡Sí!

Gramática

El imperfecto

Read along as you listen to Robert reminisce about his childhood. Find examples of the following: a family tradition, a description of a person's characteristics, a description of a person's feelings.

Cuando yo era pequeño, siempre pasábamos el Día de la Independencia en la casa de campo de mis abuelos. ¡Cómo nos divertíamos! Nadábamos en el lago, comíamos barbacoa y veíamos fuegos artificiales por la noche. Abuelito era un hombre bonachón (*good-natured*) y todos los nietos lo adorábamos.

Heinle Grammar Tutorial:
The imperfect tense

CD2
Track 13

Teaching Tip: After reviewing the examples of uses of the imperfect, draw students' attention to the verb forms in the model. First, ask if the forms look familiar; next, have them identify the infinitive that corresponds to each verb. Point out that the **-er** and **-ir** verbs have **"ía"** in the endings, while the **-ar** verbs have **"aba."**

Grammar: Point out that the verb **gustar** in the imperfect commonly uses only two forms, just as it does in other verb tenses: **gustaba** and **gustaban.** Also, note that the impersonal form of **haber** is regular: **había** (*there was/were/there used to be*).

A. Una breve introducción. Spanish uses two different verb aspects to narrate and describe past events and actions: the preterite (**el pretérito**) and the imperfect (**el imperfecto**). The two aspects may not be used interchangeably, however. In this section, you will learn how to form and use the imperfect.

B. La formación del imperfecto. To conjugate verbs in the imperfect, drop the infinitive ending and add the following endings to the stem:

El imperfecto de los verbos regulares

	-ar verbs **celebrar**	-er verbs **comer**	-ir verbs **recibir**
yo	celebr**aba**	com**ía**	recib**ía**
tú	celebr**abas**	com**ías**	recib**ías**
Ud./él/ella	celebr**aba**	com**ía**	recib**ía**
nosotros(as)	celebr**ábamos**	com**íamos**	recib**íamos**
vosotros(as)	celebr**abais**	com**íais**	recib**íais**
Uds./ellos/ellas	celebr**aban**	com**ían**	recib**ían**

There are only three irregular verbs in the imperfect.

El imperfecto de los verbos irregulares

	ir *(to go)*	ser *(to be)*	ver *(to see)*
yo	**iba**	**era**	**veía**
tú	**ibas**	**eras**	**veías**
Ud./él/ella	**iba**	**era**	**veía**
nosotros(as)	**íbamos**	**éramos**	**veíamos**
vosotros(as)	**ibais**	**erais**	**veíais**
Uds./ellos/ellas	**iban**	**eran**	**veían**

There are no stem-changing verbs in the imperfect tense.

PRESENTE: Siempre **vuelvo** a casa a las diez.
*I always **return** home at ten.*

IMPERFECTO: Cuando era joven, siempre **volvía** a casa a las ocho.
*When I was young, I **would** always **come** home at eight.*

C. Los usos del imperfecto. Although both the **pretérito** and the **imperfecto** are used to talk about the *past*, each of these refers to different *aspects* of past time. The imperfect is used in the following ways:

▸ To describe customs, habits, and routines in the past: what you used to do or would do. An adverb of frequency often accompanies this use of the imperfect: **generalmente, normalmente, (casi) siempre** *(almost always),* **todos los días, todos los años, con frecuencia, a menudo** *(frequently),* **a veces** *(at times),* **de vez en cuando** *(from time to time).*

> De niño, yo **visitaba** a mis abuelos todos los años.
> *As a child, I **used to visit (would visit)** my grandparents every year.*

▸ To describe people, places, and things in the past: physical appearance (**grande, bonito**, etc.); other qualities (**interesante, difícil**, etc.); mental, physical, and emotional states (**agitado, enfermo, furioso**, etc.); and personal information (name, age, nationality, or religion).

> Mi abuelo **era** alto, inteligente y simpático. **Tenía** setenta años pero **parecía** más joven.
> *My grandfather **was** tall, smart, and nice. He **was** seventy years old but **seemed** younger.*

▸ To provide the background against which other actions take place: the time of day, date, location, or weather.

> **Eran** las once de la noche y **llovía.**　　*It **was** eleven o'clock at night, and it **was raining.***

▸ To express ongoing thought processes, such as *knew, thought,* or *believed.*

> El niño **no creía** en Papá Noel.
> *The boy **didn't believe** in Santa Claus.*

▸ To describe actions that were taking place ("in progress") at some particular point in time in the past. In English, this notion is expressed by the past progressive tense (was/were + -ing form of verb).

> Los niños **miraban** el desfile en la tele.
> *The children **were watching** the parade on TV.*

Teaching Tip: Point out that certain verbs are often used for descriptions of conditions, qualities, and traits, such as **ser, estar, tener.**

Grammar: With more proficient groups, introduce the use of the imperfect to express what somebody reported that he/she was going to do: **Mamá dijo que iba a llamarte.**

Ponerlo a prueba

Teaching Tip: Assign the first activity for homework. Complete the others in class.

7-24 El Día de las Brujas. Completa la historia del Día de las Brujas. Usa el imperfecto de los verbos entre paréntesis.

Cuando yo (1. ser) ____era____ más joven, me (2. encantar) __encantaba__ el Día de las Brujas. Todos los años mi familia y yo (3. invitar) __invitábamos__ a los vecinos a nuestra casa para celebrarlo en grande. Un año, cuando yo (4. tener) ____tenía____ ocho o nueve años, algo muy curioso ocurrió durante la fiesta.

Recuerdo que (5. haber) ____había____ una tormenta esa noche. Mis amigos y yo (6. tener) ____teníamos____ un poco de miedo aunque no (7. querer) ____queríamos____ admitirlo. Nosotros (8. estar) __estábamos__ jugando en mi dormitorio con una tabla de espiritismo *(ouija board)*, cuando de repente oímos un ruido. Miramos hacia el clóset y vimos una luz extraña. (9. Ser) ____Era____ de un color azul brillante y (10. pulsar) ____pulsaba____ débilmente. ¿Habríamos despertado *(Could we have awakened)* algún espíritu?

Nosotros no (11. saber) __sabíamos__ qué hacer. Yo (12. estar) ____estaba____ a punto de llamar a mi mamá cuando la luz desapareció. Aliviados *(Relieved)*, dejamos de jugar con la tabla y fuimos a la sala a reunirnos con los demás.

Expansion 7-25: Engage the class in a discussion of how everyone used to celebrate their birthdays when they were children. **¿Normalmente tenían una fiesta? ¿La fiesta era para la familia y para los amigos? ¿Tenían las fiestas en casa o en otro lugar? ¿Qué hacían en las fiestas? ¿Qué regalos recibían?**

7-25 El cumpleaños de Felicia. Con un(a) compañero(a), mira la ilustración, en la página 245, de una de las fotos más representativas de las fiestas de cumpleaños de Felicia y contesta las preguntas.

1. Cuando Felicia era pequeña, ¿generalmente dónde le hacían su fiesta de cumpleaños?

2. ¿Quiénes asistían normalmente a las fiestas de cumpleaños?

3. ¿Qué servían los padres de Felicia todos los años?

4. Generalmente ¿qué hacían los invitados en la fiesta?

5. ¿Quién encendía siempre las velas de la torta?

6. En la fiesta de cumpleaños de 1955, ¿qué tiempo hacía?

7. ¿Cuántos años tenía Felicia en esta foto? ¿Cómo era ella? ¿Qué ropa llevaba?

8. ¿Qué hacía Felicia en el momento en que se tomó esta foto? ¿Qué hacían los otros niños?

 7-26 Análisis. Con un(a) compañero(a), analiza las preguntas de la Actividad 7-25. Busquen ejemplos *(Find examples)* de los siguientes usos del imperfecto.

1. Usamos el imperfecto para indicar una rutina o una costumbre *(custom)* en las preguntas números <u>1, 2, 3, 4, 5</u>.

2. Usamos el imperfecto para describir a una persona en la pregunta número <u>7</u>.

3. Usamos el imperfecto para describir el tiempo en la pregunta número <u>6</u>.

4. Usamos el imperfecto para indicar una acción "continua" *(in progress)* en la pregunta número <u>8</u>.

7-27 Así era la vida. Conversa con dos o tres compañeros(as) sobre sus actividades cuando eran más jóvenes.

1. **Los días festivos:** Cuando eras niño(a), ¿qué día festivo te gustaba más? ¿Cómo celebraban ese día tú y tu familia normalmente? (Haz una pregunta original).

2. **Las vacaciones:** De niño(a), ¿iban tú y tu familia de vacaciones con frecuencia? ¿Adónde iban por lo general? ¿Te divertías allí? (Haz una pregunta original).

3. **Los veranos:** Cuando eras niño(a), ¿qué te gustaba hacer durante los veranos? ¿Con quiénes jugabas generalmente? ¿Qué hacías cuando llovía? (Haz una pregunta original).

Expansion 7-27: In addition to discussing childhood memories, have students use the questions in Activity 7-27 to discuss their teen years.

Expansion: Have students compare what life was like in high school with what it is like now in college. **En la escuela secundaria estudiaba una o dos horas todos los días. Ahora estudio…**

Paso 3

Teaching Tip: This section demonstrates techniques for telling and reacting to simple personal anecdotes. Introduce the phrases by recounting a personal anecdote. As you tell your story, have a student react with the questions and expressions of **Vocabulario temático.**

Vocabulary: In some countries, the verb **partir** is used instead of **romper** to refer to broken bones: **Gregorio se partió la pierna.** *(Greg broke his leg.)*

More Information: Some of the main uses of the imperfect and preterite are embedded in the stories in this section. The two tenses are contrasted further in the remaining points of the **Paso.**

Vocabulario temático

Cómo contar un cuento

ESTEFANÍA:	¿Qué me cuentas?
EDUARDO:	¿Sabes qué pasó?
ESTEFANÍA:	Dime, dime, ¿qué pasó?
EDUARDO:	*Gregorio se rompió la pierna.*
ESTEFANÍA:	¡No me digas! ¿Cuándo ocurrió?
EDUARDO:	*Anteayer.*
ESTEFANÍA:	¿Dónde estaba?
EDUARDO:	*Estaba en las montañas, de vacaciones.*
ESTEFANÍA:	¿Cómo pasó?
EDUARDO:	*Gregorio hacía una caminata con sus amigos. Como llovía un poco, todo estaba resbaloso. Gregorio se cayó y se rompió la pierna.*
ESTEFANÍA:	Ay, pobrecito.
EDUARDO:	Sí, es una lástima.

Regional Vocabulary: In Costa Rica, phrases to react to a story would include: **¡Qué dicha!** *(Good!),* **¡Qué tirada!** *(Pity!),* **¡Qué torta!** *(What a mess!),* **¡Salado!** *(Tough luck!),* **¿Al chile?** *(Seriously?),* **¡Qué pecado!** *(What a shame!).*

Expresiones de interés

¡No me digas!	*You're kidding!*
¿De veras?	*Really?*
¡Ay, pobrecito!	*Oh, poor thing!*
¡Qué horror!	*How awful!*
¡Qué alivio!	*What a relief!*
Eso es increíble.	*That's incredible.*
¡Menos mal!	*Thank goodness! / That's a relief!*
¡Qué buena (mala) suerte!	*What good (bad) luck!*

Algunas preguntas típicas

¿Dónde estaba?	*Where was he/she?*
¿Cuándo ocurrió?	*When did it happen?*
¿Qué hora era?	*What time was it?*
¿Qué tiempo hacía?	*What was the weather like?*
¿Cómo fue/pasó?	*How did it happen?*
Y luego, ¿qué?	*And then what (happened)?*

Ponerlo a prueba

CD2
Track 14

7-28 Y luego, ¿qué? Escucha la conversación entre Elisa y su mamá. Elisa le está contando lo que le pasó a Carlos. Luego, indica la respuesta correcta para cada una de las preguntas.

Teaching Tip: Assign the first two activities for homework.

1. ¿Cómo estaba Elisa cuando llegó a casa?
   a. contenta   b. triste   c. agitada

2. ¿Cuándo ocurrió el accidente de Carlos?
   a. antes de su partido de fútbol
   b. mientras *(while)* jugaba al fútbol
   c. después de su partido de fútbol

3. ¿Quién examinó a Carlos primero?
   a. el padre de otro jugador
   b. otro jugador del equipo
   c. un auxiliar médico en la ambulancia

4. ¿Adónde llevaron a Carlos?
   a. a casa   b. a un hospital   c. al consultorio médico

5. ¿Qué se rompió Carlos?
   a. la pierna *(leg)* derecha b. la pierna izquierda   c. el pie *(foot)* izquierdo

6. ¿Qué hizo la madre al final de este cuento?
   a. Esperó en casa la llamada del médico.
   b. Llamó a su esposo.
   c. Fue al hospital.

7-29 Entre amigos. Lee las breves conversaciones entre tú y varios amigos. En cada conversación, indica cuál es la reacción más lógica, y después, la pregunta más apropiada.

1. Elsa: ¿Sabes qué pasó? Tuve un accidente de coche.
   Tú: (¡No me digas! / ¡Qué bueno!)
          (¿Cuándo ocurrió? / ¿Y luego qué?)

2. Paco: Saqué una nota muy buena en un examen.
   Tú: (¡Qué horror! / ¿De veras?)
          (¿En qué clase? / ¿Qué tiempo hacía?)

3. José: Quiero contarte algo. Anoche vi un platillo volante *(flying saucer)*.
   Tú: (¡Ay, pobrecito! / ¡Eso es increíble!)
          (¿Se rompió la pierna? / ¿Dónde estabas?)

4. Magda: ¿Sabes qué? Mi novio se rompió el brazo *(arm)*.
   Tú: (¡Qué mala suerte! / ¡Qué alivio!)
          (¿Cómo pasó? / ¿Qué hora era?)

5. Juan: Quiero contarte una noticia. Mi padre se ganó la lotería.
   Tú: (¡Menos mal! / ¡Estupendo!)
          (¿Qué piensa hacer? / ¿Cuándo es?)

7-30 Trágame, tierra. A veces, todos metemos la pata *(put our foot in our mouth)*. En el siguiente artículo, una chica cuenta su historia de "horror". Lee el artículo "Mi 'amigo', el pizzero" y contesta las preguntas.

1. ¿Cuándo ocurrió esta "historia de horror"? Ocurrió/Era un sábado por la noche.

2. ¿Adónde fue la chica? ¿Para qué? Fue al apartamento de Diego para una fiesta.

3. ¿Conocía la chica a las personas en la fiesta? No, había mucha gente que no conocía.

4. ¿Cómo saludó la chica a las personas? Se presentó y les dio un beso.

5. ¿Por qué empezaron todos a reír? La chica le había dado un beso al chico que había llevado la pizza.

Mi "amigo", el pizzero
por Clara Mengolini

Era un sábado por la noche. Mi amiga Soledad me llamó y me dijo que había una fiesta en el apartamento de Diego. Cuando llegué, la puerta del apartamento estaba abierta. Entré y vi mucha gente que yo no conocía. Fui a la cocina para saludar a los que estaban allí, y como es costumbre, me acerqué a cada uno de ellos, me presenté y les di un beso en la mejilla. De pronto, el chico que llevaba camiseta roja y gorra blanca tomó unas monedas y se fue. El resto empezó a reír sin parar: ¡Le había dado (*I had given*) un beso al chico que había llevado la pizza!

VOCABULARIO ÚTIL:	me acerqué	*I went up to / approached*
	un beso	*a kiss*
	la mejilla	*cheek*
	gorra	*cap*
	monedas	*money / coins*
	reír	*to laugh*
	sin parar	*without stopping*

7-31 El robo. Completa la conversación entre Patricia y Gonzalo de una manera lógica. Incluye muchas expresiones de interés y preguntas lógicas.

PATRICIA: Hola, Gonzalo. ¿_____?

GONZALO: ¿Sabes qué pasó?

PATRICIA: _____. ¿_____?

GONZALO: A Rosa le entraron a robar *(rob)* a su casa.

PATRICIA: ¡_____! ¿_____?

GONZALO: La semana pasada, en Nochebuena.

PATRICIA: ¡No! ¡¿_____?! ¿_____?

GONZALO: Bueno, Rosa y su familia habían ido (*had gone*) a misa (*mass*). Cuando volvieron a casa, vieron que la puerta estaba abierta.

PATRICIA: ¡_____! ¿_____?

GONZALO: Llamaron a la policía. Cuando llegaron los agentes, entraron y descubrieron que alguien había robado todos los regalos de Navidad.

PATRICIA: ¡_____!

Gramática

El imperfecto y el pretérito: el primer contraste

🌐 **Heinle Grammar Tutorial:**
The preterite versus the imperfect

Read along as you listen to Alonso describe what happened to him last year during the Fourth of July celebration. Which verbs in the story are in the **imperfecto?** Which are in the **pretérito?**

 CD2 Track 15

Era el cuatro de julio. A las diez de la mañana, el desfile **empezó** puntualmente. **Hacía** un calor insoportable. Después de marchar en el desfile por una hora, yo **me desmayé** (*I fainted*) de tanto calor. Cuando desperté, **vi** a todos mis amigos alrededor de mí. **Estaban** preocupados. "Estoy bien", **dije** con gran esfuerzo.

Answers: Imperfecto: Era, Hacía, Estaban, Pretérito: empezó, me desmayé, vi, dije

A. El imperfecto. The imperfect and the preterite must be carefully woven together to tell a story in the past tense.

We often begin a story by using the **imperfecto** to *set the scene and provide background information* in the following ways:

▸ To establish the time, date, and/or place

Era una noche fría de invierno.
It **was** a cold winter night.

Yo **estaba** en casa, sola y aburrida.
I **was** at home, alone and bored.

Bueno, no **estaba** completamente sola, porque allí a mi lado, **tenía** a mi gato.
Well, I **wasn't** completely alone, because I **had** my cat at my side.

▸ To describe the characters and/or the location

Mi gato **se llamaba** Tigre y **era** un gato de esos egoístas y fríos.
My cat's name **was** Tigre, and he **was** one of those cold, egotistical kinds of cats.

▸ To describe what was customary, habitual, or routine for the characters

Normalmente, Tigre **pasaba** la noche en el dormitorio, donde **dormía** debajo de mi cama.
Tigre **usually spent** the evening in my bedroom, where he **would sleep** under my bed.

▸ To describe what was going on at the particular moment in time

Pero esa noche **parecía** un poco nervioso y **se escondía** detrás de los cojines del sofá.
But that night, he **seemed** a little nervous, and **was hiding** behind the pillows on the sofa.

B. El pretérito. After the scene has been set, the storyteller continues on to the heart of the story. The **pretérito** is used *to move the story line forward* in the following way:

▸ To narrate the main actions or events of the story, to tell what happened

De repente, Tigre **saltó** del sofá y **corrió** a la puerta.
Suddenly, Tigre **leaped** off the sofa and **ran** to the door.

Yo lo **seguí** y **abrí** la puerta con cuidado.
I **followed** him and **opened** the door cautiously.

As you study the explanations, notice that all the examples can be read together as a story.

C. En combinación. As the story continues, both the imperfect and preterite continue to work together until the story comes to a close.

▸ The **imperfecto** is used whenever there is a pause in the action so that further description of the scene or character may be added.

Afuera, **nevaba** un poco.
*Outside, **it was snowing** lightly.*

La luna **brillaba** como el sol, pero no **se veía** a nadie.
*The moon **was shining** like the sun, but you **couldn't see** anyone.*

▸ The **pretérito** is used when the action resumes, and the story line moves forward again.

Cerré la puerta y **volví** a sentarme en el sofá.
*I **closed** the door and **sat down** on the sofa again.*

Ponerlo a prueba

7-32 El Día de los Enamorados. Silvia cuenta lo que pasó el pasado Día de los Enamorados. Lee el cuento; después, cambia los verbos de la columna A al imperfecto y los verbos de la columna B al pretérito.

A: El imperfecto

1. (Ser) __Era__ el 14 de febrero, el Día de los Enamorados, pero yo (estar) __estaba__ en casa, sola y triste.
2. Normalmente mi novio Marcos y yo (salir) __salíamos__ para celebrar ese día, pero como el pobre (estar) __estaba__ enfermo, no (tener) __tenía__ ganas de ir a ninguna parte.

6. Ahora (yo / estar) __estaba__ realmente alarmada. No (saber) __sabía__ qué hacer.

9. Marcos (llevar) __llevaba__ su pijama, pero en los brazos (tener) __tenía__ una docena de rosas.

B: El pretérito

3. (Yo / decidir) __Decidí__ ir a su casa para animarlo *(cheer him up)*.
4. (Yo / vestirse) __Me vestí__ rápidamente y (conducir) __conduje__ a su casa.
5. (Yo / tocar) __Toqué__ el timbre *(doorbell)* tres veces... pero ¡nadie __abrió__ (abrir) la puerta!

7. Por fin, (yo / decidir) __decidí__ volver a mi casa y llamar a los padres de Marcos.
8. Cuando (yo / llegar) __llegué__ a mi casa, (ver) __vi__ a Marcos en el porche.

10. Marcos me (dar) __dio__ las rosas y (pedir) __pidió__ mi mano en matrimonio. Yo (aceptar) __acepté__.
11. Ese Día de los Enamorados (ser) __fue__ el más sorprendente y el mejor de mi vida.

7-33 Análisis. Analiza el uso del imperfecto y el pretérito en el cuento "El Día de los Enamorados" (7-32). Escoge *(Choose)* la explicación más lógica para las frases indicadas.

> **MODELO** **Era** el 14 de febrero...
>
> *c:* Descripción del día, la hora, el tiempo.

1. Normalmente mi novio Marcos y yo **salíamos** para celebrar ese día... a
2. ...pero el pobre **estaba** enfermo... b
3. **Me vestí** rápidamente y conduje... d
4. **Toqué** el timbre tres veces... e
5. Ese Día de los Enamorados **fue** el más sorprendente... f

El imperfecto	El pretérito
a. Las costumbres, tradiciones o rutinas	d. Las acciones que avanzan la trama *(advance the plot)*
b. Identificación y descripción de personas, lugares, cosas, animales	e. Se especifica la duración (**por + período de tiempo**) o el número de repeticiones (**número + veces**)
c. Descripción del día, la hora, el tiempo	f. Para resumir *(sum up)* el cuento

7-34 Las vacaciones de mi niñez. En la siguiente historia, Nuria describe cómo pasaba los veranos cuando era niña. Escribe cada verbo en el tiempo adecuado *(proper verb tense).*

> **MODELO** De niña, yo casi siempre (pasar) <u>pasaba</u> las vacaciones en la playa de Bellavista con mi familia.

1. Bellavista (ser) _____ un lugar muy bonito donde siempre (hacer) _____ sol.
2. Por fortuna *(Luckily,)* mi tío Alfonso (ser) _____ dueño de un pequeño hotel en Bellavista. Su hotel (estar) _____ muy cerca del mar.
3. Todos los días nosotros (salir) _____ en un pequeño barco con papá y (pescar) _____.
4. Pero un año, cuando yo (tener) _____ ocho años, (nosotros: hacer) _____ un viaje a Nueva York.
5. Como *(Since)* nuestro hotel (ser) _____ caro, (nosotros: quedarse) _____ en la ciudad por solo cinco días.
6. Pero (nosotros: poder) _____ hacer *(managed to do)* muchas cosas diferentes.
7. Por ejemplo, un día mis hermanos y yo (ver) _____ un partido de béisbol en el famoso estadio de los Yankees.
8. Otro día, (nosotros: ir) _____ a Broadway para ver una comedia musical.
9. También (nosotros: comer) _____ en muchos restaurantes en el Barrio Chino y el Barrio Italiano.
10. Nuestro viaje a Nueva York (ser) _____ una experiencia inolvidable *(unforgettable)* de mi niñez.

7-35 El mejor viaje de mi vida. Conversa con dos o tres compañeros(as). Hablen sobre el mejor viaje o las mejores vacaciones de su vida. Incluyan la siguiente información:

- Adónde fuiste y con quién(es)
- Cuánto tiempo pasaron allí
- Qué hicieron
- Por qué fueron las mejores vacaciones de tu vida

Expansion 7-34: Have students use the reasons given in the box in 7-33 to analyze the items in 7-34 as well. Answers are provided in the key.

Answers 7-34: 1. era-b; hacía-c; 2. era-b; estaba-b; 3. salíamos a; pescábamos-a; 4. tenía-b; hicimos-d; 5. era-b; nos quedamos-e; 6. pudimos-d; 7. vimos-d; 8. fuimos-d; 9. comimos-d; 10. fue-f

Heinle Grammar Tutorial:
The preterite versus the imperfect

Teaching Tip: Have students continue the story of the princess after working through the contrast of the preterite and imperfect. Encourage them to tell their own version of the princess and the toad.

🔊
CD2
Track 16

Gramática

El imperfecto y el pretérito: el segundo contraste

Read along as you listen to the beginning of a fairy tale. Which three verbs set the scene and provide background information? Which three verbs advance the plot? What was the princess doing when she heard the voice?

Había una vez una princesa muy hermosa. Una tarde de primavera, la princesa **cantaba** y **paseaba** por el parque del palacio cuando de repente **oyó** una voz muy bajita. **Miró** a su alrededor y **vio** a un sapo *(toad)* que le **sonreía** *(was smiling at her)* desde el suelo…

A. Resumen y continuación. The preterite and the imperfect work hand in hand in storytelling. The imperfect answers the question "What was it like?" while the preterite answers the question "What happened?".

Imperfect: What was it like?	Preterite: What happened?
▶ set the scene (day, time, location, weather)	▶ move the story line forward, tell who did what
▶ describe people, places, things, and routines	▶ make a summary statement about the experience
▶ tell what was going on or was in progress	

B. Dos acciones. The actions of a story may be related to one another in three different ways. Each way requires a different combination of tenses.

▶ Use the **imperfecto** to describe two or more simultaneous, ongoing actions. Connect the two actions with **y** *(and)*, **mientras** *(while)*, or **mientras tanto** *(meanwhile)*.

You might visualize these actions with wavy lines, to convey their ongoing aspect.

Ángela **miraba** el desfile en la televisión mientras yo **cocinaba.**

*Angela **was watching** the parade on T.V. while I **was cooking.***

〜〜〜〜〜〜〜〜〜 miraba
〜〜〜〜〜〜〜〜〜 cocinaba } acciones simultáneas

▶ Use the **pretérito** to express a series of completed actions. You can visualize these actions as a series of straight vertical lines.

Después de mirar el desfile, Ángela **llamó** a su amiga y la **invitó** a salir. Primero **fueron** al cine y luego **miraron** los fuegos artificiales en la playa.

*After watching the parade, Angela **called** her friend and **invited** her to go out. First they **went** to the movies and then they **watched** the fireworks display at the beach.*

| | | | |
| llamó | invitó | fueron | miraron } acciones en serie

▸ Sometimes one action interrupts another that was already taking place. Use the **imperfecto** to describe the ongoing action; use the **pretérito** for the action that began, ended, or otherwise interrupted the ongoing one.

Connect the two parts of the sentence with **cuando** (when) or **mientras** (while).

Visualize the ongoing action as a horizontal wavy line and the interruption as a short, straight, vertical line that cuts through the wavy one.

Empezó a llover mientras **hacíamos** nuestro picnic.

*It **began** to rain while we **were having** a picnic.*

~~~~~~~|~~~~~~~~ hacíamos
empezó

Ponerlo a prueba

7-36 La Navidad. En el dibujo *(drawing)* puedes ver a la familia Sosa el día 23 de diciembre del año pasado. Escribe los verbos en el tiempo más apropiado en cada caso.

Teaching Tip: Assign the first two activites for homework.

Acciones simultáneas y "continuas" *(ongoing)*

1. Dorotea (cantar) __cantaba__ villancicos mientras su hermana Juanita (tocar) __tocaba__ el piano.

2. Mientras Dorotea y Juanita (cantar) __cantaban__, Albertico (jugar) __jugaba__ con el perro.

Serie de acciones

3. Papá (envolver, *to wrap*) __envolvió__ los regalos y los (poner) __puso__ bajo el árbol.

4. Abuelito (hacer) __hizo__ unas galletas y se las (servir) __sirvió__ a la familia.

Una acción continua interrrumpida por *(interrupted by)* **otra acción**

5. Mamá (quemarse, *to burn*) __se quemó__ un dedo mientras (encender) __encendía__ la vela.

6. Cuando Albertico (jugar) __jugaba__ con el perro, (romperse) __se rompieron__ sus anteojos.

7-37 La luna de miel (*honeymoon*) de René y Rita. Lee la información que Rita escribió en su diario para describir su luna de miel. Escribe los verbos en el pretérito o en el imperfecto.

DÍA 1

(1. Ser) ___Eran___ *las diez de la noche. Nosotros (2. tener)* ___teníamos___ *hambre. A las diez y media, (3. decidir)* ___decidimos___ *pedir comida del restaurante del hotel. Mientras nosotros (4. esperar)* ___esperábamos___ *la comida, René y yo (5. dormirse)* ___nos dormimos___ *. De repente, alguien (6. tocar)* ___tocó___ *la puerta. René (7. despertarse)* ___se despertó___ *y (8. abrir)* ___abrió___ *la puerta. Allí, (9. haber)* ___había___ *un hombre con una pistola en la mano. El hombre (10. llevar)* ___llevaba___ *un uniforme de prisionero. El hombre (11. entrar)* ___entró___ *en la habitación y (12. repetir)* ___repitió___ *dos veces, "¡Silencio o los mato!". En ese momento, el camarero (13. anunciar)* ___anunció___ *su llegada. Después de un minuto, el prisionero (14. decir)* ___dijo___ *, "¡Váyase! No queremos nada". Poco después, la policía (15. llegar)* ___llegó___ *. En cinco minutos, todo (16. terminar)* ___terminó___ *. Entonces, nosotros (17. saber)* ___supimos___ *(to find out) que el prisionero (18. ser)* ___era___ *un asesino muy conocido.*

DÍA 2

Por la mañana, René y yo (19. despertarse) ___nos despertamos___ *y nos (20. ir)* ___fuimos___ *a casa. ¡Qué luna de miel!*

👥 **7-38 La primera cita (date).** Las escenas de los dibujos representan la primera cita de Ana. Describe cómo fue, contestando las preguntas oralmente con un(a) compañero(a).

1. ¿Qué hacía Ana cuando Ramón la llamó por teléfono? ¿Qué la invitó a hacer? ¿Aceptó ella la invitación?

2. ¿Estaba lista Ana cuando Ramón llegó a su casa? ¿Qué ropa llevaba ella? ¿Qué le trajo Ramón? ¿Qué hacía el papá de Ana mientras los jóvenes hablaban?

3. Cuando Ramón y Ana llegaron a la fiesta, ¿qué hacían sus amigos? ¿Qué clase de música tocaba la orquesta?

4. ¿Qué le pasó a Ramón mientras bailaba con Ana?

5. ¿Adónde tuvo que ir Ramón? ¿Lo acompañó Ana? ¿Le pusieron un yeso *(Did they put a cast on him)*?

6. ¿Adónde fueron Ana y Ramón después de salir del hospital? ¿Qué hicieron? En tu opinión, ¿se divirtieron Ramón y Ana en su primera cita?

Teaching Tip: Have students analyze the use of the preterite and imperfect in items 1, 3, and 5.

Answers 7-38: *Suggested responses:*
1. Se duchaba. La invitó a una fiesta. Ella aceptó la invitación. 2. Sí, estaba lista. Llevaba un bonito vestido rosado. Ramón le trajo flores. El papá los filmaba. 3. Sus amigos bailaban. Tocaban música rock. 4. Se cayó. 5. Tuvo que ir al hospital. Sí, Ana lo acompañó. No, no le pusieron un yeso. 6. Volvieron a la fiesta. Ramón se sentó en una silla. Ana bailó con otros chicos. Sí, se divirtieron. / No, no se divirtieron.

1.

2.

3.

4.

5.

6.

7-39 Cuéntame… Escribe cuentos cortos para cada dibujo. Tienes que usar el imperfecto y el pretérito e incorporar el vocabulario correspondiente: **cuando** *(when)*, **mientras** *(while)*, **de repente** *(suddenly)*.

MODELO

- la hora — Eran las once de la noche.
- la ubicación *(location)* — Miguel estaba en una fiesta.
- qué hacía Miguel — Mientras él bailaba con su amiga Elena,
- qué interrumpió la acción — de repente vio a su ex novia María.
- los sentimientos *(feelings)* — Miguel no quería hablar con María.
- qué pasó — Miguel se escondió *(hid)* detrás de una planta.

Teaching Tip: Complete the first item together as a class. Then have pairs of students use the remaining cues and drawings to write brief stories. Remind students to use connecting words like **cuando, mientras,** and **de repente** to link some sentences together.

1. **El accidente**
   - la estación
   - el tiempo
   - qué hacía José
   - qué interrumpió la acción
   - descripción de la chica
   - qué pasó después

Teaching Tip: If your students need a more structured activity, provide them with the following vocabulary phrases:

1. ser un bonito día de primavera / hacer buen tiempo / José montar en bicicleta en el parque / ver a una chica / la chica ser guapa / correr en el parque / José perder la concentración / chocar contra *(run into)* un árbol
2. ser un día bonito / hacer mucho sol / la familia Cruz decidir ir al campo / hacer un picnic / unos extraterrestres llegar / correr al coche
3. la familia Romero pasear en barco / los niños nadar en el agua / el padre pescar / todo estar tranquilo / un tiburón *(shark)* pasar cerca del barco / la madre gritar *(to shout)*

2. **Un encuentro con extraterrestres**
   - el tiempo
   - la ubicación
   - qué hacía la familia
   - qué interrumpió la acción
   - los sentimientos de las personas
   - qué pasó después

3. **¡Tiburón!** *(Shark!)*
   - el tiempo
   - la ubicación
   - qué hacía la familia ese día
   - qué hacían las distintas personas
   - qué interrumpió esas actividades
   - los sentimientos
   - qué pasó después

Expansion: Bring to class a bag of 5 or 6 unrelated items (for example, a spoon, a ticket, a red sweater, etc.). Show them to the class and have small groups collaborate to create a short story that incorporates all the items.

7-40 Un cuento original. Primero, entrevista a un(a) compañero(a) con las siguientes preguntas. Después, escribe un cuento original que incorpore *(that incorporates)* toda la información de la entrevista.

1. ¿Qué estación del año te gusta más?
2. ¿Quién es tu actor, cantante, artista o escritor favorito?
3. ¿Cuál es tu pasatiempo favorito?
4. ¿Dónde quieres pasar tus próximas vacaciones?
5. ¿A qué animal le tienes miedo?

Un paso más

¡Vamos a hablar!

Estudiante A

Contexto: Tú y tu compañero(a) van a hablar de dos películas. En la primera parte, tú **(Estudiante A)** tienes que leer un resumen *(summary)* de una película a tu compañero(a). Tu compañero(a) **(Estudiante B)** tiene que escuchar y completar las palabras que faltan *(missing words)*. Después, ustedes van a hablar de la película.

En la segunda parte, tu compañero(a) **(Estudiante B)** va a leerte un resumen de otra película, y tú **(Estudiante A)** tienes que escuchar para completar las palabras que faltan.

PRIMERA PARTE

A. El resumen: Era la Nochebuena del año 1946. George Bailey pasaba por una crisis. Su tío Billy había perdido los 8000 dólares que tenía que ingresar en el banco. George y Billy buscaron el dinero por todas partes pero no lo encontraron.

George estaba desesperado y no sabía qué hacer. Decidió dar un paseo por el pueblo para pensar en una posible solución. Por fin llegó al río. Profundamente deprimido *(depressed)*, pensaba suicidarse cuando de repente vio a un anciano caer al agua. George se lanzó al río y salvó al anciano.

Luego, mientras se secaba la ropa mojada *(wet)*, el anciano le dijo a George que era su ángel de la guarda. El ángel le enseñó a George una visión alternativa de cómo Bedford Falls habría sido si George no hubiera nacido *(if he hadn't been born)*.

B. Conversa con tu compañero(a) sobre la película:

- ¿Cómo se llama este drama del distinguido director Frank Capra?
- ¿Has visto esta película?
- ¿Cuál es tu escena favorita?

SEGUNDA PARTE

A. El resumen: Magdalena vivía con su _____ en _____. Ella tenía casi _____ años. Solo pensaba en su fiesta de quinceañera, en el _____ y en la limosina Hummer.

Magdalena tenía un _____ y quedó embarazada *(pregnant)*. Su padre era muy _____ y cuando _____ que su hija estaba embarazada, la echó *(threw her out)* de la _____.

Magdalena se fue a vivir con su _____ _____ Tomás. En la casa de Tomás también _____ su primo Carlos. Los _____ de Carlos no lo _____ porque tenía tendencias _____. Magdalena, Carlos y Tomás _____ a vivir juntos.

B. Conversa con tu compañero(a) sobre la película:

- Esta película se llama *Quinceañera*. ¿A qué se refiere el título?
- ¿Has asistitdo a una fiesta de quince? ¿Cómo fue?
- ¿Te gustaría ver esta película?

Go to the **Un paso más** section in the *Cuaderno de actividades* for reading, writing, and listening activities that correlate with this chapter.

More Information: Additional activities with movies may be found in the Instructor's Resource Manual. These activities feature both a film in Spanish (to broaden students' horizons) and a U.S. classic movie (to enjoy a shared experience).

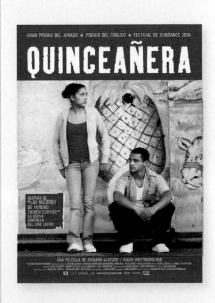

Un paso más

¡Vamos a hablar!

Estudiante B

Contexto: Tú y tu compañero(a) van a hablar de dos películas. En la primera parte, tu compañero(a) **(Estudiante A)** va a leerte un resumen *(summary)* de una película, y tú **(Estudiante B)** tienes que completar las palabras que faltan *(missing words)*. Después ustedes van a hablar de la película.

En la segunda parte, tú **(Estudiante B)** vas a leerle un resumen de otra película a tu compañero(a), y él/ella **(Estudiante A)** tiene que completar las palabras que faltan.

PRIMERA PARTE

A. **El resumen:** Era la _____ del año 1946. George Bailey _____ por una crisis. Su tío Billy había perdido los 8000 dólares que _____ que ingresar en el banco. George y Billy _____ el dinero por todas partes pero no lo _____.

George estaba desesperado y no _____ qué hacer. Decidió dar un _____ por el pueblo para pensar en una posible _____. Por fin _____ al río. Profundamente deprimido *(depressed),* pensaba suicidarse cuando de repente _____ a un anciano caer al agua. George se lanzó al _____ y salvó al anciano.

_____, mientras se secaba la ropa mojada *(wet)*, el anciano le _____ a George que era su _____ de la guarda. El ángel le enseñó a George una _____ alternativa de cómo Bedford Falls habría sido si George no hubiera nacido *(if he hadn't been born)*.

B. Conversa con tu compañero(a) sobre la película.

- ¿Cómo se llama este drama del distinguido director Frank Capra?
- ¿Has visto esta película?
- ¿Cuál es tu escena favorita?

SEGUNDA PARTE

A. **El resumen:** Magdalena vivía con su padre en Los Ángeles. Ella tenía casi quince años. Solo pensaba en su fiesta de quinceañera, en el vestido y en la limosina Hummer.

Magdalena tenía un novio y quedó embarazada *(pregnant)*. Su padre era muy estricto y cuando descubrió que su hija estaba embarazada, la echó *(threw her out)* de la casa.

Magdalena se fue a vivir con su tío abuelo Tomás. En la casa de Tomás también vivía su primo Carlos. Los padres de Carlos no lo querían porque tenía tendencias homosexuales. Magdalena, Carlos y Tomás aprendieron a vivir juntos.

B. Conversa con tu compañero(a) sobre la película:

- Esta película se llama *Quinceañera*. ¿A qué se refiere el título?
- ¿Has asistido a una fiesta de quince? ¿Cómo fue?
- ¿Te gustaría ver esta película?

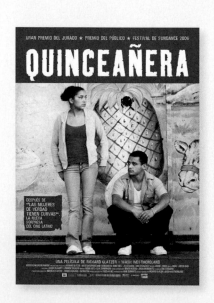

¡Vamos a ver! | *Episodio 7*

En la Hacienda Vista Alegre

Anticipación

 A. Hablando se entiende la gente. Habla con tu compañero(a). Cuando eras pequeño(a), ¿cómo celebrabas tu cumpleaños? ¿Cómo lo celebras ahora? ¿Cuál fue el mejor regalo que recibiste? ¿Por qué lo consideras el mejor?

B. ¿Cómo se dice…? Expresiones útiles. Relaciona las siguientes expresiones con la definición adecuada.

1. tomarse a pecho algo *to take something to heart*
2. tener razón *to be right*
3. estar acostumbrado(a) a comer temprano *be used to (having dinner early)*
4. confites *(sweets)*

a. algo que es verdad
b. se dan en los cumpleaños
c. sentirse criticado *to feel criticized*
d. una acción habitual o rutinaria

Answers-B: 1. c; 2. a; 3. d; 4. b

▶ Vamos a ver

C. De paseo por la Hacienda Vista Alegre. Primero, lee las preguntas. Después, mira el Episodio 7 del vídeo, observa a los personajes y contesta las preguntas.

1. ¿Por qué está triste Valeria?
2. Normalmente, ¿con quiénes celebra Valeria su fiesta de cumpleaños?
3. ¿Cuántos años cumple? *(How old is she going to be?)*
4. ¿Cuántos invitados fueron a su fiesta el año pasado?
5. ¿Qué le regalaba a Valeria su papá?
6. ¿Cómo celebraba Alejandra su cumpleaños cuando era pequeña? ¿Dónde los celebraba? ¿Con quién? ¿Cómo?

Answers-C: 1. Porque es su cumpleaños y nadie la ha felicitado. 2. con muchos primos, amigos, sus padres; 3. 24 años; 4. cien; 5. un ramo de flores; 6. Celebraba el cumpleaños en la escuela con su mamá, sus amigos y su maestra. También con su familia. Su madre le preparaba un bizcocho y llevaba helado y refrescos. También tenía una piñata y repartía bolsitas con confites a sus amigos. Alejandra recibía muchos regalos y esto le gustaba mucho.

En acción

 D. Charlemos. Comenta con tus compañeros(as). ¿Qué le quieres regalar a Valeria el día de su cumpleaños? ¿Y a los otros chicos y chicas de la *Hacienda Vista Alegre*? Explica por qué escogiste *(you chose)* cada regalo.

E. 3, 2, 1 ¡Acción! Interpreten la siguiente situación en grupos de 3 ó 4 estudiantes. Imaginen que están en la *Hacienda Vista Alegre* con sus amigos y se están contando anécdotas de unas vacaciones o de un fin de semana. Deben contar una anécdota *(anecdote)* muy cómica o una situación en la que pasaron mucho miedo *(you were very frightened or scared)*. ¿Qué pasó? ¿Cuándo, dónde, con quién, cómo, por qué pasó? Describan también el lugar, el tiempo *(the weather)* que hacía y las personas que estaban allí.

Practice the vocabulary and grammar that you learned in this chapter (**el tiempo libre, estaciones, el tiempo, narrar un cuento en pasado**).

Panorama cultural

DATOS ESENCIALES

Nombre oficial: República de Costa Rica

Capital: San José

Población: 4 200 500 habitantes

Unidad monetaria: el colón

Economía: exportación de banano, piña, café, flores y energía hidroeléctrica; manufactura de equipo electrónico y médico; turismo, en particular el ecoturismo

🌐 **www.cengage.com/spanish/ puentes**

Transparency Bank A-15

Note: The coffee economy began prospering under government auspices in the early 1800s. In 1843 an English ship stopped at a port in Costa Rica to get some ballast. The excess coffee crop was loaded onto the ship and later sold by the captain, thus beginning coffee trade with Europe. Today there are more than 50,000 coffee plantations in the Central Valley of the country.

Note: Four generations of the Chavarri family have maintained the tradition of constructing and painting ox carts by hand. Today, in addition to the full size ox carts, miniatures are sold as souvenirs. Examples of these **carretas** may be found online at www.sarchicostarica.net.

Note: A variety of indigenous tribes inhabited the area of present-day Costa Rica. Each had their own distinct culture; few had large, organized communities. Today fewer than 1% of the population is of indigenous origin.

Note: In 1824 Costa Rica became a state of the **República Federal de América Central.** After the collapse of the Republic in 1838, Costa Rica became an independent nation.

Note: Costa Rica has reserved 25% of its land for national parks. About 38% of the land of Costa Rica is covered with forest and jungles.

Note: The Constitution of 1949, still in force, also gave women and descendants of Africans the right to vote.

La carreta Estas hermosas carretas (*ox carts*) son un símbolo de tradición e historia en Costa Rica. Se producen en Sarchí, una pequeña ciudad situada al noroeste de la capital. A partir del año 1840 se usaban para transportar el café de las montañas a los puertos en la costa Pacífica. La colorida decoración de las carretas se debe en gran parte a la inspiración de Joaquín Chavarri, quien estableció su fábrica en 1903.

Un vistazo a la historia

1502	Llegó Cristóbal Colón al área, pero como esta no tenía grandes riquezas minerales, la corona española la colonizó lentamente (*slowly*).
1821	Costa Rica se unió a otras naciones centroamericanas y declaró su independencia de España.
1843	Fue uno de los mejores años en la producción de café. Por casualidad (*By chance*) un barco inglés llevó el café costarricense a Europa y la economía del país floreció.
1949	Después de una guerra civil en 1948, la nueva Constitución abolió el ejército, pero se mantuvo una guardia civil.
2000	Por primera vez, el número de turistas a Costa Rica superó un millón.
2009	Entró en vigor el Tratado de Libre Comercio entre Estados Unidos, Centroamérica y República Dominicana (DR-CAFTA, por sus siglas en inglés).

Costa Rica

Óscar Arias Sánchez (1940–)

Este distinguido político ganó las elecciones presidenciales en 1986, una época *(a time)* de grandes conflictos internos en muchos países centroamericanos. Arias promovió la paz, la democracia, la libertad y la protección de los derechos *(rights)* humanos. Preparó en 1987 un plan para la paz, que fue firmado *(signed)* por todos los presidentes centroamericanos. Por estos esfuerzos, ganó el Premio Nobel de la Paz en 1987. En 2006 volvió a ser elegido Presidente del país.

Franklin R. Chang-Díaz (1950–)

Este célebre ingeniero fue el primer astronauta latinoamericano en la NASA. Obtuvo un doctorado en ingeniería nuclear en el Instituto Tecnológico de Massachusetts (MIT) en 1977. Ha dedicado su vida a la investigación de la propulsión basada en plasma. Entre 1986 y 2000 completó siete misiones espaciales. Ha registrado más de 1601 horas en el espacio.

Carmen Lyra (1888-1949)

Carmen Lyra es el pseudónimo de la conocida escritora y educadora María Isabel Carvajal. Los libros de Lyra son considerados como clásicos de la literatura infantil. Entre sus libros más populares está la colección *Cuentos de mi Tía Panchita*. Activista y revolucionaria, Lyra participó en la creación de escuelas y luchó por los derechos de la mujer.

Carmen Lyra
Cuentos de mi Tía Panchita

Imágenes de Costa Rica

¿Qué recuerdas de Costa Rica? Después de mirar el vídeo, contesta las preguntas sobre Costa Rica con un(a) compañero(a) de clase.

1. ¿Qué importancia tiene Costa Rica respecto a la ecología del planeta?

2. Imagina que vas a pasar unos días en San José. ¿Qué lugares interesantes puedes visitar?

3. Describe qué se puede apreciar en dos o tres de los lugares que mencionaste en tu respuesta a la pregunta 2.

Note: The Costa Rican government is characterized by a long-standing tradition of democratic elections. It has the most stable democratic government in Central America, having had only three military coups in 150 years and having enjoyed peace since 1949.

Note: The political turmoil in Central America that President Arias encountered included the fall of the Somoza dictatorship in 1979 and the Sandinista regime in Nicaragua; civil war in Guatemala; internal unrest in El Salvador and Nicaragua; and border tensions among Nicaragua, Honduras, and Costa Rica. His peace plan called for a cease-fire between governments and rebels, amnesty for political prisoners and free, democratic elections.

Note: Chang Díaz was born in San José of a Chinese father and Costa Rican mother. He became a citizen of the United States in 1994. He holds numerous honorary degrees and awards from both the United States and Costa Rica. He is one of the astronauts with the most missions and the most hours in space to date.

Note: In addition to her children's works, Lyra wrote numerous plays, articles, and essays dealing with the economic and societal problems of Costa Rica in the early twentieth century. An active participant in educational reform, she established the first Montessori school in her country. In 1931 she became a founder of the Communist Party and began work in forming unions for women workers and female school teachers. She died in exile in Mexico.

More activities on Costa Rica and the **Panorama cultural** may be found in the **Un paso más** section of the *Cuaderno de actividades*.

Answers: *Suggested responses:* 1. Costa Rica es muy pequeño pero tiene 5% de la biodiversidad del planeta. 2. El Teatro Nacional, el Museo Nacional, el Monumento Nacional, el Parque La Sabana, la Catedral Metropolitana, el Teatro Melico Salazar, el Parque Morazán, el Parque Nacional. 3. El Teatro Nacional es una copia pequeña de la Opera de París. El Museo Nacional tiene arte pre-colombino y de la época colonial. El Monumento Nacional representa la victoria de Costa Rica ante los filibusteros. El Parque La Sabana es un lugar donde se hace deporte o se puede descansar.

Vocabulario

Sustantivos

el árbol *tree*
la artesanía *arts and crafts, handicrafts*
el barco de vela *sailboat*
el campo *country(side)*
el candelabro *Menorah, candelabra*
las cartas *(playing) cards*
la celebración *celebration*
la champaña *champagne*
el cine *cinema, movie theater*
el concierto *concert*
el conjunto *(musical) group*
el cuento *story*
el cumpleaños *birthday*
el desfile *parade*
el día festivo *holiday*
el disfraz *costume*
el equipo *team*
la estación *season (of the year)*
la estrella *star*
la exposición *exhibition*
el festival *festival*
el fin de semana *weekend*
los fuegos artificiales *fireworks*
la función *show*
el gimnasio *gym*
la iglesia *church*
el (la) jugador(a) *player*
el lago *lake*
la lluvia *rain*
la montaña *mountain*
la nieve *snow*
la obra (de teatro) *play, drama*
el pastel de calabaza *pumpkin pie*
el pastel de cumpleaños *birthday cake*
el pavo *turkey*
la película *movie*
la playa *beach*
el pronóstico *forecast*

el regalo *present, gift*
la sinagoga *synagogue*
el teatro *theater*
la temperatura *temperature*
el tiempo *weather*
el tiempo libre *free time*
el trabajo *work, job*
las vacaciones *vacation*
la vela *candle*
el villancico *(Christmas) carol*

Verbos

acampar *to go camping*
acostumbrar a *to be accustomed (to)*
bailar *to dance*
brindar *to make a toast*
bucear *to dive, snorkel*
cantar *to sing*
celebrar *to celebrate*
conocer *to meet, be introduced to*
contar (ue) *to tell (a story)*
dar un paseo *to take a walk*
decorar *to decorate*
disfrutar (de) *to enjoy*
encender (ie) *to light/to turn on*
encontrar (ue) *to meet*
enfermarse *to get sick*
escalar en roca *to climb rocks, to go rock climbing*
esperar *to wait; to hope*
esquiar *to ski*
exhibir *to be on exhibit*
hacer caminatas *to go hiking*
hacer un picnic *to have a picnic*
intercambiar *to exchange*
ir de caza *to go hunting*
ir de picnic *to go on a picnic*
levantar pesas *to lift weights*
llevar *to wear; to carry; to take*

llover (ue) *to rain*
montar a caballo *to go horseback riding*
nadar *to swim*
nevar (ie) *to snow*
ocurrir *to happen, occur*
pasarlo bien *to have a good time*
pescar *to fish*
presentar *to present; to introduce*
probar (ue) *to try (food), to taste*
quedarse *to stay; to remain*
regalar *to give (as a present)*
relajarse *to relax*
recibir *to receive*
romperse *to break*
reunirse *to get together*
salir *to go out (on a social occasion)*
terminar *to finish*
tocar *to play (an instrument); to touch*

Otras palabras

aunque *although*
divertido(a) *funny*
fabuloso(a) *great*
fatal *terrible*
muchísimo(a) *very much*
otro(a) *other; another*
toda *all*

Seasons of the year: p. 234
Weather expressions: pp. 234–235
Holidays and celebrations:
  pp. 237–238
Expressions of interest and empathy:
  p. 246

For further review, please turn to **Vocabulario temático: español e inglés** at the back of the book.

Go the **Puentes** website for extra vocabulary practice using the Flashcard program.

Somos turistas

Situation Cards: 58, 59, 60, 61, 62, 63, 64, 66, 69, 70, 101

More Information: This chapter continues the focus on practical travel situations that was begun in Chapter 2. Here we teach students how to handle two common problems—getting lost and getting sick. The key grammatical topics of the chapter include the formal commands and the present subjunctive with verbs of influence.

Standards: While this chapter focuses on helping students handle small problems and chores related to travel, it also provides a chance to address the Culture and Connections Standards by incorporating information related to the art, architecture, history, climate, and geography of the great cities of the Spanish-speaking world. In addition to showing students photos and videos of cities you have visited, ask your students to prepare brief (1–2 minutes) presentations on capital cities.

Turn to the *Cuaderno de actividades* for this chapter's reading practice and strategy: Recognizing word families.

Turn to the *Cuaderno de actividades* for this chapter's composition practice and writing strategy: Editing and proofreading.

OBJETIVOS

Speaking and Listening
► Locating important tourist destinations
► Asking for and giving directions around a city
► Giving instructions and advice related to travel and health
► Describing symptoms of minor illnesses common to travelers
► Understanding the doctor's orders

Culture
► Ecuador
► Popular tourist and vacation spots

Grammar
► Impersonal and passive **se**
► Formal commands
► Introduction to the present subjunctive

Video
► En la Hacienda Vista Alegre: Episodio 8
► Imágenes de Ecuador

Gramática suplementaria
► Los mandatos familiares

Cuaderno de actividades
Reading
► Strategy: Recognizing word families

Writing
► Strategy: Editing and proofreading

Playlist
🌐 www.cengage.com/spanish/puentes

A primera vista

Ella y él

Cuando viajamos por el mundo, a veces pasa lo inesperado *(the unexpected):* **nos enfermamos, nos perdemos o incluso, nos enamoramos** *(we fall in love).*

 Puentes playlist available on iTunes

En la canción "Ella y él", una chica cubana y un chico estadounidense se conocen y se enamoran mientras están de vacaciones en México. Escucha la canción y completa la tercera estrofa *(third stanza)* con las palabras de la lista.

cristianos	fresas	hamburguesa
cubano	fue	lugar

Él ha comido _____;   ella, un mojito _____.
ella, moros con _____;   Ella se _____ de gira al Yucatán
él, el champagne con sus _____;   y él de vacaciones al mismo _____.

Answers: hamburguesas, cristianos, fresas, cubano, fue, lugar.

Vocabulary: Moros y cristianos is the popular name given to a Cuban dish of black beans and rice. **Mojito** is a fashionable Cuban cocktail made of rum, sugar, lime juice, mint leaves and a splash of soda water.

HABLANDO DE LA MÚSICA

Topical songs are those that comment on social, political, and other current events. This kind of song has been popular around the world, including in Spain and Spanish-speaking America, for centuries.

Note: One of the foremost proponents of the **nueva canción** was Víctor Jara. Jara was kidnapped, tortured, and killed under the Pinochet regime.

Nueva canción: This type of protest song began in Chile in the 1960s and spread rapidly throughout the Andean region. It commonly deals with topics of poverty, democracy, empowerment, and human rights. It is considered the precursor of rock music in Spanish.

Nueva trova: These politically-themed songs incorporate elements of folk music. The government of Fidel Castro used them in the 1960s to help promote the Cuban Revolution. A more contemporary version of the **nueva trova** champions the cause of nationhood for Puerto Rico.

Note: The **narcocorrido** is especially criticized because several drug dealers have commissioned songs exalting their illegal activities as the works of men who are brave and just.

Corrido: These Mexican ballads revolve around love stories, historical events, folk heroes, and natural disasters. The contemporary versions often have a danceable polka rhythm. A recent variation—the **narcocorrido**—has been criticized for glorifying drug dealers.

Note: Arjona's songs are known for their message and social criticism. A highly respected singer and composer, he left the world of music for five years after recording his first song. He spent this time teaching in the countryside and then returned to the world of music. He won two Grammys for his album **Adentro.**

RICARDO ARJONA (1964–)

Nacionalidad: guatemalteco

Obras y premios: Su primer éxito —*Jesús, verbo no sustantivo*— es el álbum más vendido de la historia en varios países de Centroamérica. Sus premios incluyen dos Grammys (2006, 2007), entre muchos otros. Ha vendido más de seis millones de discos.

De interés: Aparte de ser compositor y cantante, Arjona es un gran deportista con una pasión por el baloncesto. Estableció un récord cuando jugó para la Selección Nacional de Guatemala: marcó setenta y ocho puntos en un solo partido.

"ELLA Y ÉL"
canción de Ricardo Arjona

Lo que las ideologías dividen al hombre
el amor con sus hilos los une en su nombre.
Ella mueve su cintura al ritmo de un tan tan
y él se va divorciando del Tío Sam.
Él se refugia en su piel, la quiere para él y
ella se va olvidando de Fidel.
¿Qué sabían Lenin y Lincoln del amor?
¿Qué saben Fidel y Clinton del amor?

- ► Locating important tourist destinations
- ► Asking for and giving directions around a city
- ► Using commands to give instructions and advice related to travel

Grammar:
- ► Impersonal and passive **se**
- ► Formal commands

🌐 Go to the **Puentes** website for extra vocabulary practice using the Flashcard program.

The English equivalents to all **Vocabulario temático** lists are found at the back of the book.

Transparency Bank F-1, F-2, F-3, F-4, F-6

Teaching Tip: Use the transparencies to review old material and to introduce new expressions. Starting with F-1, review the names of public places in a city (**el aeropuerto, la estación de tren, el mercado**, etc.). Use F-3 to practice words of location, including those from **Capítulo 3** (**al lado de, a la izquierda de, a la derecha de, enfrente de, en la esquina**).

Vocabulary: To get the attention of a stranger on the street, say **Disculpe** (Pardon me), **Oiga** (Say there), or **Por favor** (Please). It is also common, but not necessary, to address the stranger with a title such as **señor** or **señora.**

Vocabulary: City blocks are called **cuadras** in much of Spanish-speaking America, and **manzanas** in Spain.

In some larger cities you can travel by subway—**el metro.**

Paso 1

Vocabulario temático

Unas diligencias por la ciudad

TURISTA: Perdone, ¿dónde se puede *comprar sellos?*
cambiar dinero
comprar aspirina
comprar tarjetas postales

RESIDENTE: En *el correo.*
el banco
la farmacia
la papelería

Unos lugares importantes

el aeropuerto	la estación de tren	la parada de autobús
el correo	la comisaría	la papelería
la clínica	la farmacia	la oficina de turismo
la catedral	la iglesia	el parque zoológico

Para indicar la ubicación

TURISTA: Por favor, ¿dónde está el correo?

RESIDENTE: Está *al final de la calle.*
en la esquina
a tres cuadras de aquí

TURISTA: ¿Se puede ir a pie?

RESIDENTE: Sí, está bastante cerca.

No, está lejos de aquí. Es mejor tomar el autobús.

Expresiones de ubicación

detrás de	delante de
a la izquierda de	a la derecha de
al lado de	enfrente de
entre	al otro lado de la calle

ESTRUCTURAS ESENCIALES

El *se* pasivo y el *se* impersonal

A. El *se* pasivo. The subject of a sentence normally expresses *who* performs the action.

> **Rosa** compra sellos en el correo.
> *Rosa buys stamps at the post office.*

Sometimes it is not important to know who performs the action. In this case, English often expresses this idea with the passive voice (is/are + past participle). Spanish uses the construction "**se** + conjugated verb + noun".

> **Se venden** sellos en el correo.
> *Stamps **are sold** at the post office.*

► Use a singular verb when a singular noun follows the verb.

> **Se produce** mucho <u>software</u> en Ecuador.
> *A lot of software **is produced** in Ecuador.*

► Use a plural verb when a plural noun follows the verb.

> También **se cultivan** muchas <u>flores</u>.
> *A lot of flowers **are grown** there also.*

B. El *se* impersonal. A similar "**se** + verb" construction is used in **impersonal** sentences. With impersonal sentences, the person who performs the action is not a specific person, but rather, "people in general." English expresses this idea with the subjects *they, people, you,* and *one.*

> En Ecuador, **se almuerza** a la una.
> *In Ecuador, **people/they eat** lunch at one o'clock.*

> ¿**Se puede** ir a pie?
> *Can **you/one** go on foot?*

With the **se impersonal,** the verb is always used in the singular. It is usually followed by an infinitive or by an adverb.

> ¿Dónde **se puede** comprar aspirina?
> *Where **can one** buy aspirin?*

Ponerlo a prueba

Teaching Tip: Assign the first two activities for homework.

CD2
Track 17

8-1 Unas diligencias. Escucha las conversaciones entre los turistas y el recepcionista del hotel. Completa las oraciones de una manera lógica.

_b_ 1. La señorita Rosales quiere comprar...
    a. tarjetas postales.
    b. unos sellos.
    c. recuerdos para sus amigos.

_a_ 2. Según el recepcionista, la señorita Rosales...
    a. puede ir a pie.
    b. debe tomar un taxi.
    c. necesita ir a la farmacia.

_c_ 3. El señor Rulfo quiere...
    a. ir a la oficina de turismo.
    b. consultar con un médico.
    c. ir a la farmacia.

_c_ 4. Según la recepcionista, ese lugar está...
    a. cerca de la parada de autobuses.
    b. en la esquina.
    c. al lado del hotel.

8-2 En Quito. Imagina que estás de vacaciones en Quito, Ecuador. ¿Cómo responde a tus preguntas el recepcionista del hotel? Relaciona la información de las dos columnas de una manera lógica.

Tú:	El recepcionista del hotel:
_b_ 1. ¿Dónde se puede cambiar dinero?	a. Hay una pequeña tienda aquí en el hotel.
_d_ 2. Mi vuelo sale mañana a las dos de la tarde.	b. El Banco del Pichincha está al final de la calle.
_c_ 3. Quisiera visitar la Catedral Metropolitana. ¿Dónde se encuentra?	c. Está en el centro histórico, en la Plaza de la Independencia. ¡Es magnífica!
_e_ 4. Perdone, ¿hay un parque zoológico en Quito?	d. Bien. Le llamo el taxi a las once y media de la mañana.
_a_ 5. Oiga, ¿dónde se puede comprar tarjetas postales?	e. Está en el Pueblo de Guayllabamba. Es mejor tomar un autobús.

More Information: The present perfect tense is introduced and practiced in the **Gramática suplementaria** section in Chapter 4.

8-3 Las grandes ciudades. Conversa con dos o tres compañeros(as) sobre las vacaciones en las grandes ciudades.

1. ¿Te gusta visitar ciudades grandes cuando vas de vacaciones? ¿Qué ciudades grandes conoces en los Estados Unidos? ¿En otros países? (Haz una pregunta original.)

2. De todas las ciudades grandes que has visitado *(that you have visited)*, ¿cuál prefieres? ¿Qué te gusta hacer cuando estás allí? (Haz una pregunta original.)

3. Cuando estás en una ciudad grande, ¿prefieres tomar el metro, el autobús o un taxi? ¿Por qué? (Haz una pregunta original.)

4. ¿Te has perdido alguna vez *(Have you ever gotten lost)* durante un viaje? ¿Dónde estabas? ¿Cómo resolviste el problema? (Haz una pregunta original.)

5. ¿Qué ciudad grande has visitado *(have you visited)* recientemente? ¿Qué hiciste allí? (Haz una pregunta original.)

8-4 En la ciudad. Con un(a) compañero(a), completa y dramatiza las conversaciones a continuación. Basen sus respuestas en el plano de la ciudad. Sigan el modelo.

MODELO
> TÚ: Por favor, ¿dónde se puede ver una película?
> TU COMPAÑERO(A):   En el cine Colón. Está en la Avenida Patria.

1. Oiga, ¿dónde se puede comprar tarjetas postales?
2. ¿Hay una parada de autobuses cerca de aquí?
3. Perdone, ¿dónde se puede comprar antiácidos?
4. Tengo sed. ¿Hay un café por aquí?
5. Perdone, ¿dónde está el museo de arte?
6. Hace frío hoy. ¿Dónde se venden chaquetas a buen precio?

Expansion: Have your students continue creating dialogues for other locations on the map. Provide additional examples: **Quisiera comprar unas sandalias. ¿Dónde se venden? ¿Hay un hotel económico por aquí?**

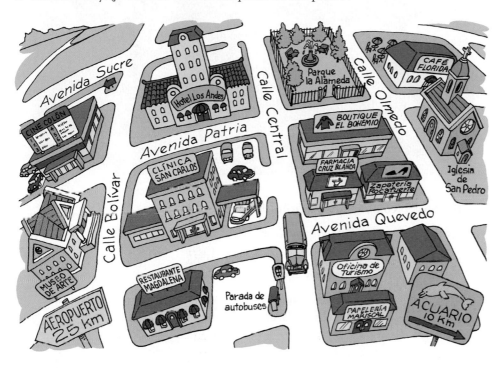

 8-5 Por nuestro campus. Un(a) nuevo(a) estudiante ecuatoriano(a) no conoce bien el campus. Tú tienes que explicarle todo. Dramatiza estas conversaciones con un(a) compañero(a) de clase. Sigan el modelo.

MODELO   nadar y hacer ejercicios
> TU COMPAÑERO(A):   Tengo ganas de hacer un poco de ejercicio. ¿Dónde se puede nadar? ¿Hay un gimnasio o una piscina en el campus?
> TÚ: Sí, hay un nuevo gimnasio muy grande con mucho equipo y una piscina de tamaño olímpico.
> TU COMPAÑERO(A):   ¡Qué bien! ¿Dónde está el gimnasio?
> TÚ: Está en la esquina de la calle Assembly y la calle Blossom. Está enfrente del coliseo.

1. comprar libros de texto
2. consultar a un médico
3. probar comida típica del estado
4. bailar salsa
5. comprar recuerdos con la mascota de la universidad
6. ver películas independientes o internacionales

Vocabulario temático

Para pedir y dar instrucciones

—Por favor, ¿cómo se va a la oficina de turismo?

—Siga todo derecho. Está al final de la calle, a la izquierda.

—Perdone, ¿hay un banco por aquí?

—Sí, el Banco Nacional está bastante cerca. Camine 100 metros por esta calle. Está a la derecha, al lado de la farmacia.

Teaching Tip: Provide students with another way of prefacing their request for directions: **Estoy perdido(a)**.

Look carefully at the last letter of these words: **derecho** means *straight ahead;* **derecha** means *right.*

Otras instrucciones

Vaya a la esquina.

Tome la Avenida de la Independencia.

Tome la segunda calle a la izquierda.

Siga derecho por cuatro cuadras.

Doble a la derecha en la calle República.

Camine cien metros.

Cruce la calle.

Ponerlo a prueba

Teaching Tip: Assign the first two activities for homework.

Note: Otavalo is a small city north of Quito famous for its indigenous market and fine handicrafts.

🔊 CD2 Track 18

8-6 ¿Para ir a...? Aquí tienes el plano *(city map)* de la pequeña ciudad de Otavalo, Ecuador. Un policía y un turista están en el punto indicado con una X en el plano. Escucha las instrucciones del policía. ¿Cuál es el destino del turista en cada caso? (**¡Ojo!** *The directions are given from the perspective of someone looking up Montalvo Street, with his/her back to the train station.*)

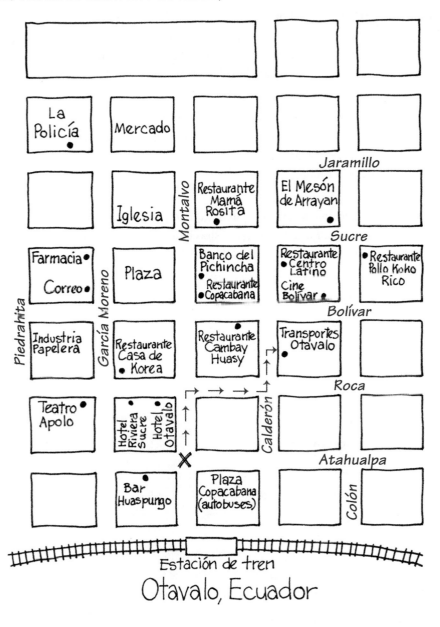

MODELO

ESCUCHAS: No está lejos de aquí. Siga por esta calle, la calle Montalvo, por una cuadra. En la primera esquina, en la calle Roca, doble a la derecha. Siga por esa calle por una cuadra y doble a la izquierda en la próxima esquina. Está a la derecha.

ESCRIBES: Transportes Otavalo

1. ___Restaurante Casa de Korea___   3. ___Banco del Pichincha___

2. ___Restaurante Pollo Koko Rico___

8-7 Por Otavalo. Mira el plano de Otavalo en la página 271 y completa las conversaciones de una manera lógica.

1. TURISTA: Por favor, ¿cómo se (<u>va</u> / van) a la farmacia?

    POLICÍA: (<u>Siga</u> / Doble) derecho por la calle Montalvo. (Camine / <u>Tome</u>) la tercera calle a la izquierda. (<u>Vaya</u> / Cruce) una cuadra más y Ud. verá la farmacia en la (<u>esquina</u> / final).

2. TURISTA: ¿(<u>Hay</u> / Es) un buen restaurante (<u>por</u> / para) aquí?

    POLICÍA: Sí, hay varios. Le (<u>recomiendo</u>/ prefiero) el Mesón de Arrayan. Siga (<u>derecho</u> / a la derecha) por esta calle. En la (segunda / <u>tercera</u>) esquina, doble a la (izquierda / <u>derecha</u>) en la calle Sucre. Camine (<u>dos</u> / tres) cuadras y está a la izquierda.

3. TURISTA: Por favor, ¿(cómo / <u>dónde</u>) está la comisaría?

    POLICÍA: Siga todo (<u>derecho</u> / derecha) por la calle Montalvo. Doble (al / <u>a la</u>) izquierda en la (cuarto / <u>cuarta</u>) esquina. Camine (un /<u>una</u>) cuadra más, y está a la derecha.

Expansion: Play a map game with the students. Start at the X on the map of Otavalo, give directions for a random destination, and ask them where they end up. After several examples, have students continue the activity in pairs.

8-8 Pidiendo instrucciones. Trabaja con un(a) compañero(a) para completar los diálogos a continuación. En cada caso, necesitas contestar la pregunta del turista y también darle instrucciones para llegar al destino indicado. Usen el mapa de Otavalo en la página 271.

1. TURISTA: Por favor, ¿está cerca de aquí el Teatro Apolo?

    POLICÍA: _____.

2. TURISTA: ¿Dónde se puede cambiar dinero?

    POLICÍA: _____.

3. TURISTA: ¿Hay una farmacia por aquí?

    POLICÍA: _____.

4. TURISTA: Quisiera comprar unos recuerdos. ¿Está lejos de aquí el mercado?

    POLICÍA: _____.

5. TURISTA: Por favor, ¿me puede recomendar un hotel?

    POLICÍA: _____.

8-9 Perdón... Unos turistas quieren visitar algunos lugares de tu universidad. Tú te encuentras frente *(in front of)* a la biblioteca de tu universidad. Con un(a) compañero(a), crea *(create)* diálogos con la información que necesitan los turistas.

1. Perdone, ¿dónde está la librería?

2. Por favor, ¿hay un buen restaurante por aquí?

3. Vamos al partido de fútbol americano. ¿Dónde está el estadio?

4. Necesito ir al gimnasio. ¿Cómo se va allá?

5. Mi amigo se encuentra un poco enfermo. ¿Hay una clínica en el campus?

Gramática

Los mandatos formales

Read along as you listen to a frantic tourist seeking advice about his lost passport. Which verbs in this conversation are used to give directions?

SR. ÁLVAREZ:	Se me perdió *(I lost)* el pasaporte. ¿Qué debo hacer?
RECEPCIONISTA:	Tiene que ir al consulado inmediatamente.
SR. ÁLVAREZ:	Por favor, ¿dónde se encuentra?
RECEPCIONISTA:	Doble a la derecha en la esquina. Siga derecho por tres cuadras. Tome la calle Princesa y vaya derecho por dos cuadras. Está allí, a la derecha.

A. Los mandatos formales. Commands are often used to give directions and instructions, as in the following examples:

> **Vaya** a la esquina y **doble** a la derecha.   *Go to the corner and turn right.*
> **Llamen** al consulado inmediatamente.   *Call the consulate immediately.*

Since the understood subject of commands is *you,* Spanish has both familiar (**tú**) and formal (**Ud./Uds.**) commands. In this section you will practice formal commands—those that can be used with persons you normally address as **usted** or **ustedes.**

B. Formación de los mandatos formales. To create formal commands, use this two-step procedure.

Mandatos regulares

	tomar	volver	salir
1. Conjugate the verb in the **yo** form of the present indicative and drop the **-o** ending.	tomø	vuelvø	salgø
2. Add the appropriate ending.			
▸ For the singular **usted** command, add **-e** to **-ar** verbs, and add **-a** to **-er/-ir** verbs.	tom**e**	vuelv**a**	salg**a**
▸ For the plural **ustedes** command, add **-en** to **-ar** verbs and **-an** to **-er/-ir** verbs.	tom**en**	vuelv**an**	salg**an**

▸ To make a command negative, add the word **no** in front of the verb. There is no need to translate the English *don't.*

> **No vuelvan** tarde.   *Don't come back late.*

C. Verbos irregulares y verbos con cambios ortográficos. Certain verbs have irregular command forms that must be individually memorized.

Mandatos irregulares

ir	**Vaya(n)** a la esquina.	*Go to the corner.*
saber	**Sepa(n)** que aquí no se permite fumar.	*Know/Be advised that smoking is prohibited here.*
dar	**Dé (Den)** el pasaporte al recepcionista.	*Give the passport to the desk clerk.*

Heinle Grammar Tutorial: Formal commands

Answers: Tiene que, Doble, Siga, Tome, vaya

More Information: Familiar commands are included in the Gramática suplementaria section.

Proficiency: Expect students to memorize very common commands for everyday use, such as giving directions on the street. Studying commands also facilitates learning the forms of the present subjunctive as well as one of its major uses.

| ser | Sea(n) puntual(es). | *Be punctual.* |
| estar | Por favor, **esté(n)** aquí antes de las seis. | *Please **be** here before six o'clock.* |

Mandatos con cambios ortográficos

	Infinitivo	Mandato formal
Verbs ending in -**gar**, change to -**gue(n)**	lle**gar**	lle**gue(n)**
Verbs ending in -**zar**, change to -**ce(n)**	empe**zar**	empie**ce(n)**
Verbs ending in -**car**, change to -**que(n)**	sa**car**	sa**que(n)**

D. Los mandatos y los complementos. Commands are frequently used with pronouns. Reflexive verbs, such as **acostarse** or **divertirse,** take the pronoun **se.** Most verbs can be used with direct (**me, te, lo, la, nos, os, los, las**) or indirect (**me, te, le, nos, os, les**) object pronouns. Follow these guidelines for pronoun placement with commands.

▸ Attach pronouns to the end of affirmative commands; add an accent mark to the stressed vowel in the third-to-last syllable.

| ¡**Acuéstense** ahora mismo! | *Go to bed right now!* |
| ¿Los cheques? **Cámbielos** en el banco. | *The checks? **Cash them** at the bank.* |

▸ Place pronouns immediately before the verb in negative commands.

| ¡No **se** acuesten en el sofá! | *Don't lie down/go to sleep on the sofa!* |
| ¿Los cheques? No **los** cambie en el hotel. | *The checks? **Don't cash them** at the hotel.* |

Sometimes it is more polite to make requests by using this kind of phrasing:

¿**Podría Ud.** hacerme el favor de llamar antes de venir?
Could you please call before coming over?

¿**Quieres** abrir la ventana?
Will you open the window?

Teaching Tip: Assign the first two activities for homework.

Ponerlo a prueba

8-10 Consejos útiles. Piensas hacer un viaje. ¿Qué consejos *(advice)* te da tu agente de viajes? Escoge el verbo más lógico y escríbelo en la forma de un mandato formal singular (**usted**).

1. (Visitar / Comprar) __Visite__ el parque zoológico.
2. (Comer / Probar) __Coma__ en el restaurante Pito.
3. (Hacer / No salir) __No salga__ a solas *(alone)* por la noche.
4. (Decir / Poner) __Ponga__ el pasaporte en un lugar seguro *(safe)*.
5. (Pagar / Vender) __Pague__ con tarjeta de crédito.
6. (Llevarles / Darles) __Deles__ propina a los camareros.

8-11 El tour de la ciudad. ¿Qué les dice la guía turística *(tour guide)* al grupo de turistas? Escoge el verbo más lógico de la lista y escríbelo en la forma de un mandato formal plural (**ustedes**).

dar   tener   sacar   perder   doblar   volver   observar

1. __Observen__ bien las esculturas en la Galería Nacional.
2. No __saquen__ fotos dentro de la catedral.
3. __Vuelvan__ al hotel antes de las nueve de la noche.
4. No __pierdan__ el pasaporte.
5. __Tengan__ cuidado en el mercado porque hay carteristas *(pickpockets)*.
6. __Den__ un paseo por la Plaza de la Independencia.

8-12 Un viaje a Ecuador. Cuando viajamos, es importante tomar precauciones para tener unas vacaciones saludables *(healthy)*. Primero, lee el artículo para aprender más sobre estas precauciones. Después, crea *(advice)* diálogos con un(a) compañero(a): Tú eres turista y quieres consejos *(consejos)* sobre las vacaciones. Tu compañero(a) es agente de viajes y tiene que darte consejos basados en *(based upon)* la información del artículo. Sigan el modelo. No se olviden de usar mandatos formales.

 MODELO

TÚ: ¿Puedo comer las comidas que se venden por la calle?

TU COMPAÑERO(A):   No, no **coma** las comidas que se venden por la calle. Es mejor comer en restaurantes de aspecto limpio.

1. ¿Puedo tomar agua del grifo *(tap water)*?
2. ¿Y la leche? ¿Puedo beberla?
3. Me encantan el tenis y la natación. ¿Puedo hacer deportes en Quito?
4. ¿Qué más debo hacer para no sufrir los efectos de la altura?
5. Mis amigos dicen que hay muchos mosquitos en la costa. ¿Qué puedo hacer para no enfermarme *(get sick)*?

PARA UN VIAJE SALUDABLE

Consejos esenciales para un viaje a Ecuador

Para disfrutar de sus vacaciones al máximo, le ofrecemos estos consejos para su visita a nuestro país

Sentido común en el momento de comer

Un problema muy común entre los turistas es que la comida o el agua les sienta mal. Es difícil resistir el aroma de la comida preparada por la calle o en los mercados, pero a veces esta comida no ha sido preparada con todas las medidas necesarias de higiene. Es recomendable comer en restaurantes de aspecto limpio, consumir lácteos pasteurizados y tomar agua embotellada.

Evite el mal de altura

Ecuador tiene algunas de las montañas más altas del mundo. Por eso, los turistas tienen que tomar precauciones con los efectos de la altura. Muchos visitantes experimentan dolor de cabeza, insomnio y náusea. Es importante tomar mucha agua y descansar. No es aconsejable correr, hacer deportes o levantar objetos pesados los primeros dos o tres días.

Cuidado con los mosquitos

La Costa y la Amazonia se caracterizan por su clima caliente y húmedo. Por lo tanto, en estas áreas hay mosquitos que transmiten enfermedades. Se recomienda usar repelente contra insectos y llevar ropa adecuada: pantalones largos y camisas de manga larga. En las farmacias del país se venden medicamentos contra la malaria.

 8-13 En mi pueblo. Dos amigos ecuatorianos están de vacaciones en los Estados Unidos y piensan visitarte. ¿Qué consejos y recomendaciones les das? Con un(a) compañero(a), escribe cinco recomendaciones con mandatos formales. Incluyan justificaciones para cada recomendación.

MODELO   **Visiten** la ciudad de Charleston. Es muy hermosa. Tiene casas históricas y restaurantes buenísimos. También, hay muchas tiendas y boutiques en la Calle King...

Teaching Tip 8-12: Before students create their dialogues, go over the main ideas of the article together as a class with these questions: **¿Qué problema se menciona en la primera sección del artículo? ¿Por qué puede ser problemático beber el agua o comer las comidas en la calle? ¿Cómo es el terreno en la parte central de Ecuador? ¿Qué efectos tiene la altura en los turistas? ¿Cuánto tiempo necesitan los turistas para adaptarse a la altura? ¿Cómo es el clima en la costa y en la selva amazónica? ¿Qué enfermedad transmiten los mosquitos?**

Vocabulary: Altitude sickness is known as **soroche.**

Teaching Tip: Provide additional models for your local area; focus on things to do or see on campus, in the city, or in the state. For example: **Vayan** a un partido de fútbol americano. Nuestro equipo está jugando muy bien esta temporada. **Coman** en el restaurante Garibaldi's. Está cerca del campus y es muy elegante. Sirven exquisitos platos franceses e italianos.

Puente cultural

🌐 Go to the *Puentes* Premium Website to view the **Puente cultural** interviews.

Note: Charles Darwin visited the Galapagos Islands in 1835. His observations of several unique species of birds there helped lead to his theory of natural selection.

¿Cuál es el lugar más visitado por turistas en tu país?

María José Vargas Cevallos

🌐 **ECUADOR**

El lugar que más visitan los turistas en el Ecuador son las islas Galápagos. Existen muchas más personas del exterior que conocen las islas Galápagos que ecuatorianos. Les atrae mucho la biodiversidad que existe en cuanto a los animales, la flora y fauna de ese lugar.

Federick Rivers

🌐 **COSTA RICA**

El lugar más visitado es el Parque Nacional Manuel Antonio. Manuel Antonio se encuentra en el Pacífico sur y tiene playa y bosque. Ahí hay una gran cantidad de biodiversidad y por eso atrae a ecoturistas y observadores de aves. Desde que uno llega, puede ver los monos *(monkeys)* en los árboles.

David Valecillos

🌐 **VENEZUELA**

El lugar más visitado es el Parque Nacional Archipiélago Los Roques. Los Roques son unas islas vírgenes al norte del país, como a media hora en avión de Caracas. Es el parque marino más grande de Latinoamérica. Tiene playas de arenas blancas donde se puede practicar muchos deportes acuáticos: windsurf, buceo, pesca deportiva, etcétera.

Lee la información y completa la tabla.

	En Ecuador	En Costa Rica	En Venezuela	En los Estados Unidos
¿Cuál es el lugar más visitado por turistas en tu país?				

Paso 2

Vocabulario temático

In this *Paso* you will practice:

▶ Talking about the human body
▶ Describing symptoms of illnesses common to travelers
▶ Understanding the doctor's orders
▶ Giving advice related to travel and health

Grammar:
▶ Introduction to the present subjunctive

Las partes del cuerpo

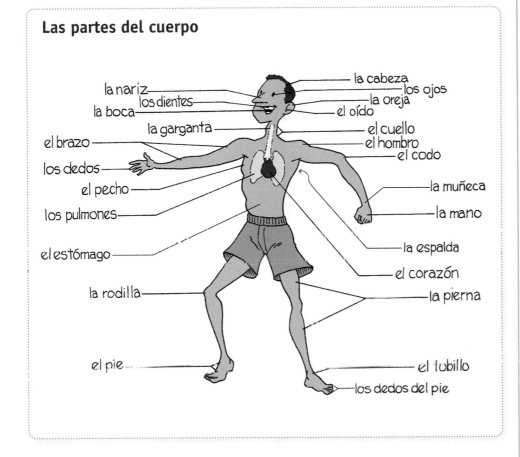

la nariz
los dientes
la boca
la garganta
el brazo
los dedos
el pecho
los pulmones
el estómago
la rodilla
el pie

la cabeza
los ojos
la oreja
el oído
el cuello
el hombro
el codo
la muñeca
la mano
la espalda
el corazón
la pierna
el tobillo
los dedos del pie

Transparency Bank K-1, K-4

Teaching Tip: Introduce parts of the body by pointing and repeating; use the transparencies or yourself as the model. Stop and review the words after every 2 or 3 new items.

Vocabulary: Additional parts of the body: **la cadera** *(hip)*, **los huesos** *(bones)*, **la frente** *(forehead)*, **la cintura** *(waist)*, **la cara** *(face)*. Remind students that the word **oído** is used for inner ear, while **oreja** means ear.

Para indicar lo que te duele

DOCTOR(A):   ¿Qué le duele?

PACIENTE: Me duele el pecho.

Me duelen los oídos.

Tengo dolor de cabeza.

Grammar: Explain to students that the verb **doler** has a structure similar to that of **gustar.**

To say what hurts, use **me duele** + *singular part of the body* or **me duelen** + *plural part of the body.*

Vocabulary: Provide students with these expressions: **Tengo dolor de garganta** *(I have a sore throat)*, **Tengo dolor de estómago** *(I have a stomachache).*

CD2
Track 20

Ponerlo a prueba

8-14 ¿Qué médico me recomienda? Lee los anuncios de algunos médicos en Quito, Ecuador. Luego, escucha los fragmentos de las llamadas telefónicas de varios pacientes. Según los síntomas que describen, ¿qué médico le recomiendas a cada paciente? ¿Por qué? Completa las siguientes frases.

1. A la niña le duele la _____; también tiene dolor de _____. Ella necesita consultar al doctor _____.

2. A la señora le duelen el _____, el _____ izquierdo y el _____. Necesita ver al doctor _____.

3. A este joven le duelen la _____ y el _____. Debe consultar al doctor _____.

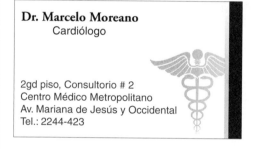

Dr. Alfonso Arcos Barona
Cirujano Dentista

Av. República de El Salvador 525
Edif. Rosanía
2gd piso
Tel.: 4573-268

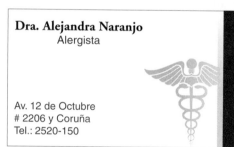

Dr. Alex Sevilla
Neurólogo

Centro Médico Metropolitano
1r piso, Consultorio # 39
Av. Mariana de Jesús y Occidental
Tel.: 2431–524

Dr. Marcelo Moreano
Cardiólogo

2gd piso, Consultorio # 2
Centro Médico Metropolitano
Av. Mariana de Jesús y Occidental
Tel.: 2244-423

Dra. Alejandra Naranjo
Alergista

Av. 12 de Octubre
2206 y Coruña
Tel.: 2520-150

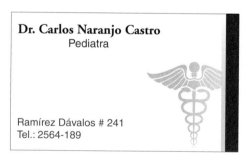

Dr. Carlos Naranjo Castro
Pediatra

Ramírez Dávalos # 241
Tel.: 2564-189

Dr. Stephen Contag
Ortopedista

Edif. Médico Meditrópoli
Consultorio 109
Av. Mariana de Jesús y Occidental
Tel.: 2267-972

8-15 Las partes del cuerpo. Relaciona cada definición con la parte del cuerpo más lógica.

_d_ 1. Conecta el pie con la pierna.

_g_ 2. Son los órganos de la respiración.

_c_ 3. Es la articulación (*joint*) entre la muñeca y el hombro.

_i_ 4. Son los órganos de la vista (*sight*).

_b_ 5. Hay cinco en cada mano.

_a_ 6. Es esencial para la digestión.

_f_ 7. Conecta la cabeza con el tronco.

_h_ 8. Contiene los dientes y la lengua.

a. el estómago

b. los dedos

c. el codo

d. el tobillo

e. el corazón

f. el cuello

g. los pulmones

h. la boca

i. los ojos

Expansion: Give descriptions for different body parts and have students guess which body part it is: **1. Somos necesarios para ver. 2. Sirvo para escribir. 3. Soy necesaria para respirar. 4. Somos necesarios para escuchar música. 5. Necesito Pepto-Bismol® cuando comes mucho. 6. Soy importante para vivir y para amar. 7. No puedes caminar sin nosotros. 8. Me usas para comer y para hablar.**

8-16 Mil excusas. Tus amigos te invitan a participar en muchas actividades pero tú tienes mil excusas. Sigue el modelo y dramatiza las situaciones con un(a) compañero(a). NOTA: Para cada situación, tienes que explicar por qué no puedes aceptar la invitación e incluir la expresión **me duele(n)** y diferentes partes del cuerpo.

MODELO   —¿Quieres salir a bailar con nosotros esta noche?

—Lo siento, no puedo. Me duelen los pies.

1. ¿Quieres ir al karaoke mañana?
2. Vamos a jugar al básquetbol esta tarde. ¿Quieres jugar con nosotros?
3. Pensamos acampar en las montañas este fin de semana. ¿Nos acompañas?
4. Hay una piscina en mi nuevo apartamento. ¿Quieres venir a mi casa para nadar?
5. ¿Por qué no vamos a comer esta noche en el nuevo restaurante mexicano?
6. (Inventen una situación original.)

Expansion: Have students say which parts of the body they associate with the following persons: **un jugador de fútbol, un jugador de básquetbol, una cantante de ópera, un boxeador, un conductor de orquesta, una bailarina de ballet.**

8-17 El viaje inolvidable. Tú y tu familia fueron a Ecuador de vacaciones. ¿Qué síntomas tienen Uds. como consecuencia de sus actividades? Sigue el modelo; usa el verbo **doler** en tu respuesta.

MODELO   *Lees:* Comiste muchos llapingachos (*fried potato-and-cheese patties*) y fritada (*fried pork*).

Respondes: Me duele mucho el estómago.

1. Fuiste a la playa y pasaste todo el día allí. Se te olvidó (*You forgot*) ponerte protector solar.
2. Tus padres subieron (*climbed, went up*) al volcán Pichincha; llevaban (*they were wearing*) sandalias.
3. El vuelo de tu hermana llegó a las tres de la madrugada. La pobre chica no durmió nada.
4. Te lavaste los dientes con el agua del grifo en el hotel.
5. La cama en la habitación de tus padres es muy incómoda. No pudieron pegar ojo (*couldn't sleep a wink*) en toda la noche.
6. Todos Uds. bebieron mucha chicha (*alcoholic fruit drink*).
7. Tu hermano bailó toda la noche en la discoteca.
8. Por su altitud, el aire en Quito tiene poco oxígeno; es problemático porque tu mamá sufre de asma.

Expansion: As a follow-up to Activity 8-17, have students invent three original scenarios and write them on paper. Pairs of students should exchange papers and write down the response of what body part hurts.

Vocabulario temático

Las enfermedades

DOCTOR(A): ¿Qué tiene?

PACIENTE: Me siento mal. Tengo tos y fiebre.

Otros síntomas

Tengo *tos.*
   fiebre
   diarrea
   náuseas
   mareos
   vómitos

Me lastimé *la espalda.*
   el pie

El diagnóstico

PACIENTE: ¿Qué tengo, doctor(a)?

DOCTOR(A): Usted tiene *gripe.*
   un virus
   un resfriado
   una infección
   una intoxicación alimenticia

Los remedios

PACIENTE: ¿Qué debo hacer?

DOCTOR(A): Tome estas pastillas y guarde cama por unos días.

Otros remedios

Le voy a dar unas pastillas para el dolor.

Tome *estos antibióticos dos veces al día.*
   este jarabe para la tos cada cuatro horas

Quiero que Ud. *guarde cama.*
   descanse mucho en casa

Le recomiendo que *tome aspirinas cada cuatro horas.*
   se aplique esta crema tres veces al día

Las farmacias

¿Cómo son las farmacias en tu ciudad? ¿Qué cosas compras allí? En general, ¿vas al médico antes de comprar medicina?

En España y en Latinoamérica, la farmacia o botica es donde puedes comprar medicinas o artículos de uso personal como champú o pasta dentífrica. Generalmente, no hay una gran variedad de artículos como en las farmacias de los Estados Unidos. Sin embargo, si tienes una enfermedad ordinaria y necesitas atención médica, los farmacéuticos te pueden recetar *(prescribe)* medicinas sin necesidad de consultar a un médico. Es aconsejable ir al médico si los síntomas son graves.

Estrategia *Improving your listening*

Listening to recorded materials can be challenging. Here are some tips to help you understand them more easily.

▸ **Listen for the main idea.**

As you listen to a recorded conversation, concentrate on understanding the gist of what is going on. Where is the conversation taking place? Who are the people speaking? What is the main topic?

▸ **Activate background information.**

After you understand the main idea, think about what kinds of information are commonly exchanged in that situation. Try to predict what the speakers might say.

▸ **Listen for key words.**

After you have made a prediction about the content, think about what key words would be used in that sort of conversation. Listen again to the recording in order to confirm or reject your hypothesis.

CD2
Track 21

Ponerlo a prueba

8-18 ¿Qué le pasa? Repasa la estrategia *"Improving your listening"* en la página 281. Después, escucha las conversaciones y completa las actividades.

a.

b.

c.

d.

PRIMERA PARTE: Escucha las tres conversaciones. ¿A qué dibujo le corresponde cada conversación?

CONVERSACIÓN 1: _____d_____

CONVERSACIÓN 2: _____a_____

CONVERSACIÓN 3: _____c_____

SEGUNDA PARTE: Vuelve a escuchar las conversaciones y completa las oraciones.

CONVERSACIÓN 1: La doctora cree que esta paciente tiene _una intoxicación_ . La paciente necesita tomar ___líquidos___ por veinticuatro horas. También debe tomar ___pastillas___ todos los días.

CONVERSACIÓN 2: La doctora piensa que este paciente tiene ___gripe___ y ___una infección___ . Ella le receta dos medicamentos: _un antibiótico_ y _un jarabe para la tos_ .

CONVERSACIÓN 3: Este paciente no tiene nada grave. La doctora le dice que necesita tomar ___té caliente___ y ___aspirinas___ y descansar. Pero, el paciente debe regresar al consultorio médico si tiene ___fiebre___ .

8-19 Historiales. Completa las descripciones de los pacientes con las palabras más lógicas de la lista.

antibióticos	gripe	guardar	infección	pastillas
fractura	jarabe	hacer	intoxicación	resfriado

1. A Sarita le duelen todos los músculos. Tiene fiebre y náuseas. También le duele la cabeza. Sarita tiene ____gripe____. Necesita ____guardar____ cama por unos días.

2. A Enrique le duele un poquito la garganta. Tiene un poco de tos también. Tiene mucha congestión. Probablemente no es nada serio. Él tiene un ____resfriado____. Debe tomar ____jarabe____ para la tos.

3. A Alfonso le duele mucho la garganta. El médico le hizo un análisis y vio que tenía estreptococos. Alfonso tiene una ____infección____. El doctor le va a mandar ____antibióticos____.

4. A Margarita le duele el estómago. Tiene náuseas y diarrea. Anoche comió mariscos en el mercado. Ella tiene una ____intoxicación____ alimenticia. Ella tiene que ir a la farmacia y comprar unas ____pastillas____.

8-20 Remedios. ¿Qué les dice el médico a estos pacientes? Inventa remedios lógicos para cada situación. Usa mandatos formales.

MODELO   ÁNGELES: Me duele mucho la cabeza.

  MÉDICO: Tome dos aspirinas y llámeme en la mañana.

1. Creo que tengo una infección de los oídos.

2. Tengo mucha tos. Me duele el pecho.

3. Creo que estoy resfriado(a).

4. Me lastimé la espalda. No puedo moverme.

5. Fui a la playa y no usé protector solar. Me duelen mucho la espalda y los hombros.

 8-21 ¿Qué te pasó? Tú y tu amiga Julia están en Ecuador de vacaciones. Mientras ustedes estaban escalando en roca, Julia se cayó. Como Julia no habla español, tú tienes que explicarle sus síntomas al médico. Con tu compañero(a), desarrolla una conversación entre tú y el médico.

Gramática

El presente del subjuntivo

Read along as you listen to a caller get recommendations from the doctor on a radio talk show. What expressions does the doctor use to give her advice? One example is provided in boldface type as a model.

RADIO OYENTE: Doctora, pienso hacer un viaje muy pronto a una zona tropical. Dígame, por favor, ¿qué medidas *(measures)* debo tomar para no enfermarme?

DOCTORA (EN LA RADIO): Para no estropear *(to spoil)* sus vacaciones, es importante que Ud. se cuide en todo momento. Por ejemplo, **le recomiendo** que consulte con su propio doctor antes de viajar para averiguar *(find out)* qué vacunas necesita. Para las zonas tropicales, es mejor que tome medicamentos contra la malaria. También es necesario que use repelente contra los mosquitos. Y finalmente, es importante que lleve camisas de manga larga y pantalones largos.

A. Para dar consejos. In both Spanish and English you can give advice and make recommendations in a number of ways.

▸ With a direct, formal command.

 Use esta crema cada seis horas. *Use this cream every six hours.*

▸ With an "embedded" command.

 Es importante que Ud. **use** un bloqueador solar.
 It's important for you to use a sunblock.

B. El subjuntivo. When the formal commands (**Ud.** and **Uds.**) are embedded within a sentence, the verb forms are referred to as the present subjunctive, or **el presente del subjuntivo.**

Mandato	Presente del subjuntivo
Guarde cama.	Es necesario que Ud. **guarde** cama.
Stay in bed.	*It is necessary that you **stay** in bed.*
Beban muchos líquidos.	Es mejor que Uds. **beban** muchos líquidos.
Drink lots of liquids.	*It is better that you **drink** lots of liquids.*

You can also use this new sentence pattern to give advice to persons you address as **tú.** Simply add **-s** to the end of the **Ud.** command form.

 Es necesario que **guardes** cama.
 *It's necessary that **you** (informal) **stay** in bed.*

C. Más sobre el subjuntivo. In order to give advice in this new way, you must create sentences with a special pattern. The present subjunctive is used after the conjunction **que**, in the part of the sentence known as the dependent clause.

			Dependent Clause		
SUBJECT	VERB	*QUE*	NEW SUBJECT	VERB	OTHER ELEMENTS
(Yo)	Quiero	que	(Ud.)	**tome**	estas pastillas.
I	*want*		*you*	***to take***	*these pills.*
	Es importante	que	(tú)	**descanses.**	
It	*is important*	*that*	*you*	***rest.***	

All of the following expressions of advice use this special sentence pattern. Think of these phrases as "triggers" that require the use of the present subjunctive after the **que.**

Le/Te recomiendo que...	*I recommend that you (formal/informal) . . .*
Quiero que...	*I want (you) to . . .*
Es necesario que...	*It is necessary for (you) to . . .*
Es aconsejable que...	*It is advisable that . . .*
Es preferible que...	*It is preferable that . . .*
Es mejor que...	*It is better that . . .*
Es recomendable que...	*It is a good idea for (you) to . . .*
Es importante que...	*It's important that . . .*

Ponerlo a prueba

8-22 En una clínica. Usa las frases adecuadas para completar los diálogos entre los pacientes y los doctores. Escribe los verbos en el presente del subjuntivo (Ud., Uds. o tú).

beber líquidos	guardar cama	comer comida blanda
volver al consultorio	caminar mucho	no salir al sol
tomar Pepto-Bismol®	descansar en casa	aplicarse compresas frías

1. SR. ALONSO: Doctor, no puedo caminar. Me caí y me lastimé el tobillo. Ahora, me duele mucho el pie derecho. ¿Debo regresar a mi país?

   DR. LÓPEZ: ¡Cálmese, Sr. Alonso! Si se lastimó el tobillo, le recomiendo que Ud. _____ por varios días. También es mejor que no _____ por un tiempo.

2. RITA: Dra. Aguilar, me siento mal. Todos en mi familia han tenido gripe. Hace dos días que tengo dolor de cabeza, fiebre y una tos horrible.

   DRA. AGUILAR: Sí, tenemos casi una epidemia de gripe. Te recomiendo que _____. También, quiero que (tú) _____.

3. RAMÓN BLANCO: Doctor, mi esposa y yo somos turistas. Desde que llegamos, hemos tenido problemas estomacales. No podemos comer nada.

   DR. FIGUEROA: Sr. Blanco, su problema es típico de los turistas. Es necesario que ustedes _____. Si no se sienten mejor en dos o tres días, les recomiendo a Uds. que _____.

8-23 ¿Qué me recomienda? Varias personas están enfermas y te piden consejo *(advice)*. ¿Qué remedios caseros *(home remedies)* les recomiendas? Trabaja con un(a) compañero(a); completen los diálogos con sus recomendaciones.

> **MODELO**   SARA: Tengo gripe.
>
>   TÚ: Te recomiendo que <u>comas sopa de pollo</u>.

1. BENJAMÍN: Con frecuencia tengo dolor de cabeza.

    TÚ: Te recomiendo que (tú) _____.

2. ELENA: Sufro de insomnio y no puedo dormir.

    TÚ: Es recomendable que (tú) _____.

3. RAFAEL: Comí mariscos anoche y ahora me duele el estómago.

    TÚ: Es importante que (tú) _____.

4. ROSA: Tengo dolor de garganta.

    TÚ: Es necesario que (tú) _____.

5. CATALINA: Mi padre estaba resfriado y ahora yo estoy resfriada también.

    TÚ: Es mejor que (tú) _____.

8-24 ¿Qué más me recomienda? Imagina que estás trabajando de guía *(tour guide)*. Varios turistas te piden consejos sobre el viaje a las islas Galápagos. ¿Qué les recomiendas? Usa expresiones como **Es importante que...; Es mejor que...; Le recomiendo que...;** etc. **¡Ojo!** Necesitas tratar a los turistas de Ud.

> **MODELO**   —En las islas Galápagos, quiero nadar y tomar el sol.
>
>   —Le recomiendo que use un bloqueador.

1. —¿Qué voy a comer en las islas Galápagos? Soy alérgica a los mariscos.
2. —¿Dónde debo cambiar dinero, aquí o en Ecuador?
3. —Padezco de mareo *(seasickness)*. ¿Qué debo hacer antes de pasear en las lanchas *(boats)*?
4. —Se dice que el clima es muy inestable en esa región.
5. —No sé exactamente cuánto dinero llevar.

Un paso más

¡Vamos a hablar!

Estudiante A

Contexto: Tú (**Estudiante A**) estás de viaje en Ecuador y te enfermas *(get sick)*. Vas a una farmacia y consultas con un(a) farmacéutico(a) (**Estudiante B**) sobre tu problema. Tienes que hacer lo siguiente:

- Basándote en el dibujo, explicar tus síntomas al/a la farmacéutico(a).

- Averiguar *(Find out)* qué tienes.

- Hacer preguntas y pedir consejos.

- Tomar apuntes sobre las respuestas del/de la farmacéutico(a).

Go to the **Un paso más** section in the *Cuaderno de actividades* for reading, writing, and listening activities that correlate with this chapter.

Nota: A temperature of 38 degrees centigrade is equivalent to a fever of just over 100 degrees.

¿Qué tengo?

¿Tengo que guardar cama?

¿Necesito antibióticos?

¿Qué más debo hacer?

¿? ¿? ¿? ¿? ¿? ¿?

Un paso más

¡Vamos a hablar!

Estudiante B

Contexto: Tú (**Estudiante B**) trabajas en una farmacia en Ecuador. Un(a) turista (**Estudiante A**) está enfermo(a) y te pide consejos. Tienes que hacer lo siguiente:

• Saludar al turista.

• Hacerle preguntas sobre sus síntomas.

• Decirle un diagnóstico.

• Darle consejos.

• Apuntar la información.

Síntomas:
☐ Dolor de cabeza
☐ Dolor de garganta
☐ Dolor de estómago
☐ Náuseas
☐ Diarrea
☐ Congestión
☐ Tos
☐ Fiebre

Otros síntomas:

Diagnóstico:

Recomendaciones y medicamentos:

¡Vamos a ver! | *Episodio 8*

En la Hacienda Vista Alegre

Anticipación

A. Hablando se entiende la gente. Habla con un(a) compañero(a). ¿Qué bailes folclóricos hay en tu país? ¿Qué bailes latinos conoces? ¿Qué características tienen estos bailes?

B. ¿Cómo se dice...? Expresiones útiles. Relaciona las siguientes expresiones con la definición adecuada.

Teaching Tip: Preview the video by showing a fragment of the episode without sound and have students use visual clues to anticipate content. Stop and rewind the video until they understand the gist of the episode.

b	1. yeso *(cast)*	a.	Está bien.
c	2. muletas *(crutches)*	b.	Te lo ponen cuando te rompes un hueso.
a	3. De acuerdo. *(All right.)*	c.	Sirven para caminar.

▶ Vamos a ver

C. De paseo por la Hacienda Vista Alegre. Primero, lee las preguntas. Después, mira el Episodio 8 del vídeo, observa a los personajes y completa las actividades.

1. ¿Quién es Víctor? El profesor de baile

2. ¿Qué parte del cuerpo se lastima Alejandra mientras está bailando?
   a. el tobillo
   b. la rodilla
   c. la pierna

3. ¿Qué parte del cuerpo se rompió Alejandra hace un año?
   a. el tobillo
   b. la mano
   c. la pierna

4. ¿Por qué quiere Víctor que Alejandra pare *(stop)* de bailar? Porque le duele el tobillo.

5. ¿Qué condición le pone Alejandra a Víctor? Que ella se va a casa si él la invita a cenar.

En acción

D. Charlemos. Comenta con tus compañeros estos temas. ¿A ti te gusta bailar? ¿Por qué? ¿Qué tipo de música te gusta bailar? ¿Con cuál de los chicos y chicas de la *Hacienda* te gustaría bailar? ¿Por qué? ¿Te rompiste un hueso *(bone)* alguna vez? ¿En qué parte del cuerpo? ¿Cómo fue?

E. 3, 2, 1 ¡Acción! Interpreten la siguiente situación en grupos de 3 ó 4 estudiantes.

Están en Puerto Rico en una clase de baile. ¿Te gusta bailar? ¿Hay alguno de ustedes que conozca *(Are any of you familiar with)* algunos de los siguientes bailes: salsa, tango, vals *(waltz)*, rap, hip-hop? Tomen turnos *(Take turns)* y den indicaciones a sus compañeros(as) para enseñarles a bailar.

Teaching Tip: Have students practice summarizing, describing characters, sequencing events, making comparisons, and giving detailed narrations and descriptions based on what they see in the video.

CAPÍTULO 8

Panorama cultural

DATOS ESENCIALES

Nombre oficial: República de Ecuador

Capital: Quito

Población: 14 573 000 habitantes

Unidad monetaria: dólar estadounidense

Economía: petróleo; exportación de productos químicos, flores y camarones; agricultura (banano, café y cacao); turismo

🌐 **www.cengage.com/spanish/puentes**

Transparency Bank A-12

Note: The traditional currency, **el sucre**, suffered great inflation and instability through the start of the 21st century; in 2000, the American dollar was made the official currency. The use of the dollar is subject to change; consult a local bank or the internet for updated information.

Note: Ecuador has one of the highest percentage of Native Americans in South America. Indigenous groups that still occupy the highlands today are the Quichua, Cañari, Chimborazo, Otavalan, and Saraguro; in other areas are the Auca, Cayapa, Cecoya, Cofan, Colorado, and Shuar. It is said that Quito was the second northern capital of the Incan Empire.

Note: From its beginnings as a republic, Ecuador has had frequent turnover of rulers, and a series of civilian and military governments.

Note: Military encounters have continued sporadically at the Peruvian-Ecuadorean frontier for years. The disputed area in the southern Amazon region is rich in mineral wealth. The border situation is still not resolved.

Note: The word **galápago** means *saddle* and refers to the shape of the tortoise shell. The Galapagos Islands became a base for whalers in the early 1800s. During that time whalers killed and captured thousands of tortoises in order to use their meat on board

Las islas Galápagos Las islas Galápagos son un grupo de islas situadas a unos mil kilómetros de la costa de Ecuador. Es uno de los destinos turísticos más espectaculares del mundo por sus numerosas especies únicas de animales. Su habitante más famoso es la tortuga Galápagos, conocida también como la tortuga gigante. ¡Puede llegar a pesar 700 libras, medir cuatro pies y vivir hasta 150 años!

Un vistazo a la historia

1100– 1500	El avanzado Imperio Inca se extendió y empezó a controlar el área andina: Perú, partes de Bolivia, Chile, Ecuador y Argentina.
1534	Los españoles conquistaron el área y ocuparon Quito. Muchas tribus, como los quechuas, sobrevivieron y hoy ocupan partes de Ecuador.
1822	Los venezolanos Antonio José de Sucre y Simón Bolívar liberaron al Ecuador. Se formó la República de la Gran Colombia, integrada por Venezuela, Ecuador y Colombia.

1830	Ecuador declaró su independencia, pero no había estabilidad política. Gobernaron el país una serie de presidentes, dictadores y juntas militares.
1998	Se firmó un acuerdo que terminó el conflicto fronterizo con el Perú.
2008	Entró en vigor una nueva constitución, la vigésima (*the twentieth*) desde la independencia.

for protein or to extract fat from them. The tortoises are now strictly protected and their numbers have increased as a result of a captive breeding program.

Ecuador

Eugenio Espejo (1747–1795)

Una de las figuras más importantes del Ecuador, este mestizo amerindio se destacó como médico, científico, escritor político-literario, periodista y revolucionario. Espejo luchó por la independencia de Ecuador y fue perseguido *(pursued)* por las autoridades españolas. Hoy en día, Espejo es recordado como "el Duende Sabio" o el "Quijote andino".

Note: Espejo was a noted satirist during Ecuador's colonial period. As a journalist, he criticized the authorities for their corruption, lack of education, and poor handling of the economy. As a scientist and physician, he is noted for his treatise on small pox, one of the most contagious and feared diseases facing Ecuador at the time.

Jefferson Pérez Quezada (1974–)

Considerado el mejor atleta de la historia de Ecuador, Pérez se especializa en la marcha atlética *(race walking)* en la carrera de veinte kilómetros. Ganó la medalla de oro en los Juegos Olímpicos en Atlanta en 1996, la primera y única medalla para un atleta ecuatoriano. Se retiró del atletismo profesional poco después de ganar una medalla de plata en los Juegos Olímpicos de Pekín en el año 2008.

Note: As a child, Pérez helped his mother in the market by selling newspapers. He credits this work with giving him the strength and stamina to excel in his sport. In addition to his Olympic medals, he won three world championships in 2003, 2005, and 2007, all the while battling various ailments, such as a fractured clavicle and herniated disc.

Nina Pacari Vega (1960–)

Esta conocida abogada es una líder del movimiento indígena de Ecuador. La hija mayor de una familia numerosa y humilde, Pacari llegó a ser la primera mujer indígena de Ecuador en graduarse de la universidad en el campo de la jurisprudencia. Se dedica a luchar por los derechos de los indígenas y a resolver los problemas económicos y sociales de su pueblo.

Note: Nina Pacari was born Maria Estela Vega but changed her name to reflect better her indigenous heritage. In Quechua, Nina means *fire* or *light* and Pacari means *dawn*. Pacari is a vocal proponent for land reform, political participation and preservation of cultural identity.

Answers: (Sample responses) 1. Quito está rodeado por volcanes (como Cotopaxi) y la cordillera de los Andes. Tiene un clima primaveral (como la primavera) todo el año. 2. Los incas habitaban el área. Se nota la influencia en el aspecto físico de las personas. También se venden artesanías indígenas en muchos lugares, como el Mercado Mariscal o el parque El Ejido. 3. Hay mucha arquitectura colonial y en el centro histórico se pueden apreciar la Plaza Grande, la Catedral Metropolitana, el Palacio Arzobispal y otros monasterios e iglesias. 4. La parte más moderna está al norte del centro histórico.

More activities on Ecuador and the **Panorama cultural** may be found in the **Un paso más** section of the *Cuaderno de actividades.*

Mira el vídeo sobre Ecuador. Luego, contesta las preguntas.

1. Describe la situación geográfica y el clima de Quito.

2. ¿Qué grupo habitaba el área de Quito hace 1500 años? ¿Qué aspectos de su cultura se notan en el Quito de hoy?

3. ¿Qué aspectos de la época colonial se notan en Quito?

4. ¿Cuáles son algunos contrastes entre el norte de la capital y el centro?

Sustantivos

el aeropuerto *airport*
el antibiótico *antibiotic*
la aspirina *aspirin*
la avenida *avenue*
la calle *street*
la carta *letter*
la clínica *clinic*
la comisaría *police station*
el correo *post office*
la crema *cream*
la cuadra *block (of a street)*
el diagnóstico *diagnosis*
la diarrea *diarrhea*
la esquina *(street) corner*
la estación de tren *train station*
la farmacia *pharmacy*
la fiebre *fever*
la gripe *flu*
la infección *infection*
la intoxicación alimenticia *food poisoning*
el jarabe *(cough) syrup*
el mareo *dizziness, light-headedness, motion/air/sea sickness*
el metro *subway*
la oficina de turismo *tourist information office*
el (la) paciente *patient*
la papelería *stationary store*
la parada de autobús *bus stop*
el parque zoológico *zoo*
la pastilla *pill, tablet*
la receta *prescription*
el resfriado *cold*
el sello *(postage) stamp*
la tarjeta postal *postcard*
la tos *cough*
el vómito *vomiting*

Verbos

aplicarse *to apply, put on oneself*
cambiar *to change; to exchange*
cruzar *to cross*
doblar *to turn*
doler (ue) *to hurt, ache*
guardar cama *to stay in bed*
ir a pie *to go on foot*
lastimarse *to injure oneself, get hurt*
saber *to know (information)*
sentirse (ie; i) *to feel*

Otras palabras

allí mismo *right there*
bastante *quite*
cerca *near(by)*
derecho *straight ahead*
enfrente de *opposite, across from*
grave *severe*
lejos *far*
mejor *better*
peor *worse*

Places or institutions in a city: p. 266
Giving directions: p. 270
Parts of the body: p. 277

For further review, please turn to **Vocabulario temático: español e inglés** at the back of the book.

Go to the **Puentes** website for extra vocabulary practice using the Flashcard program.

¡Así es la vida!

Situation Cards: 31, 32, 44, 72, 92, 100

More Information: In this chapter students learn to express their opinions and concern about common everyday problems as well as to discuss major life events. Special attention is given to managing simple conversations on these topics. The major grammatical focus involves the use of the present subjunctive in noun clauses.

Proficiency: Expressing opinions fully and with support is a Superior-level function. In this chapter we begin to lay the groundwork for this ability by providing students with simpler terms to express their thoughts and opinions about everyday worries and concerns. Keep in mind that your students will be able to use the subjunctive with accuracy only in limited contexts and with your prompting.

Turn to the *Cuaderno de actividades* for this chapter's reading practice and strategy: Distinguishing fact from opinion.

Turn to the *Cuaderno de actividades* for this chapter's composition practice and writing strategy: Creating more complex sentences.

OBJETIVOS

Speaking and Listening
- Discussing everyday problems and concerns
- Giving advice and making suggestions
- Discussing the milestones of life
- Expressing empathy and emotion
- Indicating doubt, denial, uncertainty, and certainty
- Expressing optimism and pessimism

Culture
- Chile
- Daily worries in Spanish-speaking countries

Grammar
- Regular, spelling-changing, stem-changing, and irregular verbs in the present subjunctive
- Uses of the present subjunctive: Noun clauses expressing will and influence; emotion; uncertainty, doubt, and denial
- Using the present indicative to affirm certainty and belief

Video
- En la Hacienda Vista Alegre: Episodio 9
- Imágenes de Chile

Gramática suplementaria
- El subjuntivo en cláusulas adjetivales

Cuaderno de actividades
Reading
- Strategy: Distinguishing fact from opinion

Writing
- Creating more complex sentences

Playlist
- 🌐 www.cengage.com/spanish/puentes

A primera vista

Las tres edades

Los niños sueñan con *(dream of)* **ser adultos, y con frecuencia los ancianos sueñan con ser jóvenes. Por lo visto, cada etapa** *(stage)* **de la vida tiene sus ventajas y desventajas** *(advantages and disadvantages)***. ¿Cuántos años tienes tú? En tu opinión, ¿cuáles son las ventajas y desventajas de tu edad?**

Trabaja con un(a) compañero(a). Estudien el cuadro y lean los datos sobre Salvador Dalí. Después contesten las preguntas.

1. Este cuadro representa las tres edades *(ages)* o fases de la vida. Según el título del cuadro, ¿cuáles son las tres edades? ¿Qué parte del cuadro corresponde a cada una *(each)* de las tres edades?

2. ¿Qué piensas tú? ¿Hay tres edades en la vida? ¿Dividirías *(Would you divide)* la vida de una manera diferente?

3. ¿De cuál de los tres movimientos es representativo este cuadro: del cubismo, del surrealismo o del arte abstracto? Explica.

HABLANDO DEL ARTE

Modern art of the 1900s is comprised of a number of well-known movements.

- Cubism **(el cubismo),** begun by Spanish artist Pablo Picasso in the early part of the twentieth century, features prominent use of geometric forms. The subject is fragmented and depicted from many angles, often simultaneously.

- Surrealism **(el surrealismo),** initiated in France in the 1920s and 1930s, attempts to depict the workings of the subconscious mind. Often weird, dream-like elements are juxtaposed on the canvas.

- Abstract art **(el arte abstracto),** popularized in New York in the 1940s by Jackson Pollock, moves the emphasis from the subject to the act of painting itself—the textures and qualities of paint.

SALVADOR DALÍ (1904–1989)

Nacionalidad: español

Otras obras: *La persistencia de la memoria, El torero alucinogénico, Leda atómica*

Estilo: Dalí es el líder del movimiento surrealista. Pero, ante todo, Dalí fue Dalí: excéntrico y original como pocos. Dalí es un maestro de la técnica y de la perspectiva. En sus cuadros él mezcla la realidad con los sueños *(dreams)*. El mundo que pinta es paradójico, lleno de contradicciones, dobles imágenes y símbolos. Con frecuencia, pinta las imágenes superpuestas *(superimposed)* que ofrecen dos versiones de la misma realidad.

Expansion: Have students identify and describe some of the superimposed or "double" images they see. For example, in the image on the left, the trees on the cliff form part of the head of the old man; his eye, nose, mouth, and chin are all parts of the figure of a woman (in profile). Begin by pointing out several of these correspondences in Spanish: **La cabeza de la mujer es el ojo del hombre. El brazo de la mujer forma la nariz del hombre. La mujer lleva una cesta** *(basket)* **que forma la boca del hombre.** Then have pairs of students collaborate to describe other double images in the remaining figures.

Note: Surrealism originated as a literary movement whose leader was the French poet André Breton. The surrealist style was characterized by the unleashing of the subconscious (following Freud's psychoanalytical method). Its subject matter included the artists' impulses, dreams, and desires. Its objective was to discredit established reality and create a new world, a new human.

Note: Dalí was the most individualistic and prolific of the Surrealists. His dreamlike landscapes and phantasmagoric images are disturbing. His method consisted in merging wakefulness and dreams, of taking the innermost obsessions of his psyche and revealing them on a canvas. He was expelled from the Surrealist group in 1939 over political beliefs. When he created this painting, he had begun to transform his style, leaving the avant-garde and connecting with traditional styles.

Note: The figure of the boy in the sailor suit appears in various of his pictures. He is Dalí himself, as a witness to visions and dreams that date back to childhood.

Las tres edades: la vejez, la adolescencia, la infancia (1940)
Salvador Dalí

In this *Paso* you will practice:

- ▶ Discussing everyday problems and concerns
- ▶ Giving advice and making suggestions

Grammar:

- ▶ Regular, spelling-changing, and irregular verbs in the present subjunctive
- ▶ Using the present subjunctive with expressions of will and influence

Paso 1

🌐 Go to the ***Puentes*** website for extra vocabulary practice using the Flashcard program.

The English equivalents to all **Vocabulario temático** lists are found at the back of the book.

Teaching Tip: To introduce this vocabulary, read aloud each of the common complaints and have students vote on which of these is a problem for them. Tally the results to find out the most common complaint. Then, brainstorm possible solutions or remedies for the complaint. Introduce the phrases for giving advice. Finally, combine all the information into a short conversation.

Vocabulary: Students also find these words useful: **abrumado(a)** *overwhelmed;* **ansioso(a)** *anxious;* **desilusionado(a)** *disappointed;* **enojado(a)** / **enfadado(a)** *angry, mad.*

In everyday spoken language, *procrastinate* is often expressed as **posponer las cosas** *(to put off things)* or **dejar todo para última hora** *(to leave everything until the last minute).* In writing, the more formal **procrastinar** may be used.

Vocabulario temático

Las vicisitudes del estudiante

MANUEL: ¿Qué te pasa?

OCTAVIO: Estoy totalmente estresado por todas mis obligaciones.

MANUEL: Sí, entiendo perfectamente. Debes encontrar la manera de desconectarte un poco.

OCTAVIO: Tienes razón, pero es difícil.

Algunas quejas comunes

Estoy agotado(a) de tanto trabajar.

Necesito volver a ponerme en forma.

Estoy furioso(a) con mi novio(a).

Mi compañero(a) de cuarto y yo no nos llevamos bien.

No tengo dinero para pagar todas mis cuentas.

Tengo que entregar un trabajo escrito mañana y todavía no lo he empezado.

Para dar consejos

Debes...
Tienes que...

dormir ocho horas diarias	buscar una solución
tomarte unos días libres	discutir el problema
comer comidas balanceadas	pedir ayuda
hacer más ejercicio	organizarte mejor
dejar de fumar	dejar de posponer las cosas

Para reaccionar a los consejos

Tienes razón.	Sí, es verdad, pero...
Es buena idea.	Bueno, no sé. No estoy seguro(a).

Ponerlo a prueba

CD2
Track 23

9-1 ¡Pobre Selena! Selena y su amiga Carmen viven en Valparaíso, Chile. Escucha la conversación entre las dos jóvenes y completa las oraciones de una manera lógica.

Teaching Tip: Assign the first two activities for homework.

1. Selena está...
   a. enferma.
   b. furiosa.
   c. estresada.

2. El problema es que...
   a. no le gusta nada su jefe *(boss)*.
   b. trabaja más de doce horas diarias.
   c. todavía no ha empezado su trabajo.

3. Primero, Carmen le recomienda a Selena que...
   a. tome vitaminas.
   b. se tome unas vacaciones.
   c. coma comidas balanceadas.

4. También, le recomienda que...
   a. haga más ejercicio.
   b. discuta el problema con su jefe.
   c. consulte a un especialista.

5. Carmen y Selena deciden reunirse...
   a. esa noche.
   b. el jueves.
   c. el sábado.

9-2 Las quejas y las soluciones. Relaciona las quejas con las recomendaciones más lógicas.

_b_ 1. Necesito volver a ponerme en forma.

_d_ 2. No tengo dinero para pagar todas mis cuentas.

_c_ 3. Tengo que entregar un trabajo escrito y no he empezado.

_a_ 4. Estoy agotado de tanto trabajar.

_e_ 5. Estoy furioso con mi compañero de cuarto.

a. ¿Por qué no te tomas unos días libres?

b. Debes hacer más ejercicio y dejar de fumar.

c. Tienes que dejar de posponer las cosas.

d. Necesitas buscar un trabajo.

e. Debes discutir el problema con él y buscar una solución.

9-3 Las quejas. Conversa con un(a) compañero(a) sobre las quejas típicas de los estudiantes.

Expansion 9-3: After completing the pair work, engage the class in a discussion of the most common sources of stress and the most common problems among roommates. Explore ways in which your students have solved their problems.

1. ¿Estás muy estresado(a)? ¿Cuáles son las fuentes *(sources)* de estrés en tu vida? ¿Qué haces para aliviar el estrés?

2. ¿Te consideras *(Do you consider yourself)* una persona organizada? Cuando tienes que entregar un trabajo escrito, ¿esperas hasta el último momento para empezar? En tu opinión, ¿por qué dejan todo para última hora muchos estudiantes?

3. En general, ¿te llevas bien *(do you get along)* con tu compañero(a) de cuarto? ¿Cuáles son algunas fuentes comunes de fricción o tensión entre compañeros de cuarto? ¿Qué soluciones ves para estos problemas?

Expansion 9-3: For more proficient groups, recycle the imperfect by having your students compare sources of stress in high school versus in college: **Cuando estaba en la escuela secundaria, me preocupaba... Ahora en la universidad, me preocupa más...**

Teaching Tip 9-4: Generate with the class additional questions about health before beginning the survey. Include both good and bad habits, such as: **jugar videojuegos, consumir mucho alcohol, relajarse, practicar yoga,** etc.

Expansion 9-4: After students complete the survey, have them give advice to their classmates on improving their health. Provide models using the expressions **debes** + infinitive and **tienes que** + infinitive: **Marcos, tú comes mucha comida basura. Debes comer más frutas y vegetales.**

9-4 La salud de los estudiantes. ¿Tienen ustedes buena salud? ¿Qué pequeños vicios *(small vices)* y buenos hábitos tienen ustedes? Usa la información a continuación para entrevistar a dos o tres compañeros(as).

MODELO	
Tú:	¿Con qué frecuencia duermes ocho horas diarias?
Tu compañero(a):	Duermo ocho horas diarias de vez en cuando. Normalmente duermo solo 5 ó 6 horas. ¿Y tú?

Expresiones de frecuencia: siempre, todos los días, con mucha frecuencia, de vez en cuando, a veces, casi nunca, nunca

	Compañero(a) 1	Compañero(a) 2	Compañero(a) 3
1. Dormir ocho horas diarias			
2. Comer comida basura *(junk food)*			
3. Fumar			
4. Mirar televisión			
5. Hacer ejercicio aeróbico			
6. Consumir productos con cafeína			

Teaching Tip 9-5: With less proficient groups, have pairs of students write dialogues; choose a few at random to present to the class. With more proficient groups, have pairs of students prepare spontaneous oral dialogues; have several volunteers present to the class after practicing.

9-5 Las quejas de Amanda. Amanda se graduó de la universidad el año pasado. Consiguió un buen empleo en una empresa internacional, pero sus días son muy largos y difíciles. Con un(a) compañero(a), preparen un diálogo entre Amanda y un(a) buen(a) amigo(a). Hay que incluir:

• las quejas de Amanda

• consejos apropiados

• reacciones a los consejos

Gramática

Usos del presente del subjuntivo: cómo influir sobre los demás

CD2
Track 24

Read along as you listen to a patient getting advice from the doctor. What is the patient's problem? Identify three different phrases that the doctor uses to preface her advice to the patient.

—Doctora, sufro de insomnio. Siempre paso toda la noche pensando en mis obligaciones.

—Sí, entiendo. Sé que la vida es muy ajetreada, pero es necesario que usted se desconecte un poco. Es muy importante que se relaje más porque el insomnio crónico puede impactar la salud. Le recomiendo que se tome unos días libres. Luego, quiero que usted lea este folleto *(pamphlet)*. Tiene varias recomendaciones útiles para conciliar el sueño.

⊕ **Heinle Grammar Tutorial:** The present subjunctive

Answers: The patient has insomnia. To preface advice: (accept any three) **es necesario; es muy importante; le recomiendo; quiero.**

A. El presente del subjuntivo. Advice may be phrased in several different ways in Spanish. In **Capítulo 8** you learned two common ways: direct commands and "embedded" commands.

DIRECT COMMAND:

   Tome estas pastillas.   *Take these pills.*

EMBEDDED COMMAND:

   Le recomiendo que **tome** estas pastillas.   *I recommend that you **take** these pills.*

Embedded commands follow a special sentence pattern composed of three parts. The main clause (first part) is connected by the word **que** (second part) to a dependent noun clause (third part). The verb in this third part is conjugated in the present subjunctive (**el presente del subjuntivo**).

1 Main Clause		2	3 Dependent Noun Clause	
Subject	Expression of Advice	*que*	New Subject	Verb in Present Subjunctive
(Yo) *I*	Te aconsejo *advise*	que	(tú) *you*	**dejes** de fumar. *to stop smoking.*
(Yo) *I*	Le recomiendo *recommend*	que *that*	(Ud.) *you*	**lea** este folleto. *read this pamphlet.*

B. Las formas de los verbos. To form the present subjunctive of most verbs, you must follow a two-step process:

▸ Conjugate the verb in the **yo** form of the present tense and drop the **-o** ending.

▸ Add a new ending, according to the chart below.

El presente del subjuntivo	-ar verbs **descansar** (yo descansø)	-er verbs **hacer** (yo hagø)	-ir verbs **salir** (yo salgø)
que yo	descans**e**	hag**a**	salg**a**
que tú	descans**es**	hag**as**	salg**as**
que Ud./él/ella	descans**e**	hag**a**	salg**a**
que nosotros(as)	descans**emos**	hag**amos**	salg**amos**
que vosotros(as)	descans**éis**	hag**áis**	salg**áis**
que Uds./ellos/ellas	descans**en**	hag**an**	salg**an**

Teaching Tip: Introduce the term "present indicative" to refer to the "present tense" so that students can contrast the two moods.

Teaching Tip: Provide examples of these verbs conjugated in different persons: **Mamá nos aconseja que descansemos más. Queremos que duermas ocho horas diarias.**

Grammar: With more proficient groups, introduce the following verbs of influence: **ordenar, rogar (ue), insistir en.**

More Information: This explanation builds upon the introduction given in **Capítulo 8.** Additional uses of the subjunctive in noun clauses are presented throughout this chapter. The use of the subjunctive in adjective clauses is presented and practiced in **Gramática suplementaria.**

Teaching Tip: Assign Activity 9-6 for homework. Activity 9-7 may be assigned for homework or completed in class.

Expansion 9-6: Have students write an original sentence with different advice for each situation.

Answers 9-6: 1. compres; 2. consulte; 3. beba; 4. manejen; 5. hagan.

C. Las expresiones de influencia. When we give advice to others, we are attempting to influence their behavior. We also influence behavior by giving orders, making requests, expressing our preferences, giving permission, or prohibiting someone from doing something.

Here are some common verbs and expressions of influence that trigger the use of the subjunctive in the dependent clause:

aconsejar	Le/Te aconsejo que...	*I advise you to . . .*
recomendar (ie)	Le/Te recomiendo que...	*I recommend that you . . .*
pedir (i)	Le/Te pido que...	*I ask you to . . .*
prohibir	Le/Te prohíbo que...	*I forbid you to . . .*
sugerir (ie)	Le/Te sugiero que...	*I suggest that (you) . . .*
querer (ie)	Quiero que...	*I want (you) to . . .*
preferir (ie)	Prefiero que...	*I prefer that (you) . . .*
	Es preferible que...	*It's preferable that . . .*
	Es mejor que...	*It's better that . . .*
	Es necesario que...	*It's necessary that . . .*
	Es importante que...	*It's important that . . .*

D. Verbos de comunicación. With certain expressions of influence—the verbs of communication—it is common to use an indirect object pronoun in the main clause. This indirect object pronoun refers to the person that you are trying to influence. The most common verbs of communication are **aconsejar, recomendar, pedir, sugerir,** and **prohibir.**

aconsejar	El médico **nos** aconseja que hagamos más ejercicio. *The doctor recommends that **we** do more exercise.*
recomendar	También **le** recomienda a papá que deje de fumar. *He also recommends that **Dad** stop smoking.*

Ponerlo a prueba

9-6 Muchos consejos. El pobre Jaime está muy preocupado por sus problemas y los de sus parientes y amigos. Su amiga Clarisa le da muchos consejos. Relaciona las oraciones de las dos columnas de una manera lógica. Conjuga el verbo entre paréntesis en el presente del subjuntivo.

> MODELO   JAIME: Mi padre trabaja demasiado.
> CLARISA: (c) Es importante que **descanse.**

Los problemas de Jaime:

_b_ 1. Quiero dejar de fumar.

_d_ 2. Mi novia tiene anorexia.

_a_ 3. Mi madre siempre está nerviosa, pero insiste en beber café constantemente.

_f_ 4. Mis amigos beben mucha cerveza.

_e_ 5. Mis compañeros y yo tenemos mucho estrés.

Los consejos de Clarisa:

a. Es mejor que (beber) café descafeinado.

b. Te sugiero que (comprar) los parches *(patches)* de nicotina.

c. Es importante que (descansar).

d. Es necesario que (consultar) a un psicólogo.

e. Les aconsejo que (hacer) más ejercicio.

f. Es importante que no (manejar) si toman bebidas alcohólicas.

9-7 Las compañeras de cuarto. Elena y sus compañeras de cuarto no se llevan muy bien. Según Elena, ¿qué les recomienda su consejera *(advisor)?* Escoge el verbo lógico en cada caso y escríbelo en el presente del subjuntivo.

1. La consejera prefiere que nosotras (discutir / descubrir) <u>discutamos</u> nuestros problemas. Ella no quiere que nosotras (caminar / cambiar) <u>cambiemos</u> de cuarto. Así que *(So)* les voy a dar unas sugerencias.

2. Mari, es necesario que tú (limpiar / ducharse) <u>limpies</u> el baño y que no (poner / procrastinar) <u>pongas</u> tu ropa sucia en el piso.

3. Puri y Tere, es importante que ustedes (hacer / cantar) <u>hagan</u> menos ruido *(noise)* por la noche y que no (invitar / tener) <u>tengan</u> tantas fiestas todos los fines de semana.

4. Yo también acepto responsabilidad por nuestros problemas. Ustedes quieren que yo (lavar / fumar) <u>lave</u> los platos después de comer y que yo no (beber / comer) <u>beba</u> la leche directamente del cartón. Así lo haré *(And that's what I'll do).*

9-8 El diablito. Estás cuidando *(taking care of)* a Ángel, un niño de ocho años que es un poco desobediente. ¿Cómo reaccionas a cada una de las siguientes declaraciones de Ángel? Tienes que incorporar estas expresiones:

Quiero que...	**Te recomiendo que...**	**Te aconsejo que...**
Prefiero que...	**Te pido que...**	**Te prohíbo que...**

MODELO ÁNGEL: Mis amigos no tienen que hacer la cama. Yo tampoco voy a hacerla. Bueno, ¡hasta luego! Voy a salir a jugar.

TÚ: Te prohíbo que salgas a jugar. Quiero que hagas tu cama inmediatamente. Después, puedes salir.

1. ¡Detesto las espinacas! Son tan verdes y tan... tan horribles. No pienso comerlas jamás.

2. ¡Mira! Pepito me dio este vídeo. ¿Quieres mirarlo conmigo? Se llama *Pasión prohibida.*

3. ¿Tarea? ¿Qué tarea? La profesora no nos dio tarea. Además, mañana no tenemos clase.

4. ¿Más leche? Pero si bebí un vaso grande esta mañana en el desayuno. No quiero beber más leche hoy.

5. ¡Hasta luego! Voy a la casa de Pepito. Sus padres le compraron unos fuegos artificiales. ¡Qué suerte! ¡Chao!

6. Quiero navegar por Internet. Mi amigo Marcos me dijo que hay muchas páginas interesantes con rifles y pistolas.

 9-9 Arturo y Elisa. Arturo y su hija Elisa tienen varios malos hábitos de salud. ¿Qué les aconsejas? Con un(a) compañero(a), contesta las preguntas oralmente.

1. ¿Por qué está totalmente estresado Arturo? ¿Qué vicios y malos hábitos tiene? ¿Qué consejos le das para mejorar *(improve)* la salud?

2. ¿Es Elisa una persona activa? ¿Cómo pasa ella su tiempo libre? ¿Qué le gusta merendar? ¿Qué consejos le das para tener una vida más saludable?

Teaching Tip 9-9: With less proficient classes, provide models for advice to Arturo and Elisa: **Es importante que Arturo deje de fumar. Es necesario que Elisa coma comidas balanceadas.**

Gramática

El presente del subjuntivo: verbos con cambios ortográficos y verbos irregulares

 Heinle Grammar Tutorial:
The present subjunctive

CD2
Track 25

Answers: estés (estar); busques (buscar); vayas (ir)

Grammar: Point out to students that **-ar** and **-er** stem-changing verbs do not change their stem in the **nosotros** and **vosotros** forms. Point to **jugar** and **almorzar** here as examples. Stem-changing verbs are explained in detail in **Paso 2.**

More Information: Point out to your students that they learned some of these forms as formal commands in Chapter 8.

Read along as you listen to Rosa give her friend Julia some advice about stress. Identify all the verbs conjugated in the present subjunctive. What infinitive corresponds to each of those conjugated forms?

JULIA: ¡El estrés me está matando! ¿Qué debo hacer?

ROSA: Julia, estoy preocupada por ti. Es importante que estés más calmada. Yo te voy a ayudar. Pero, mira, es necesario que busques una manera de relajarte. No sé, quizás es mejor que vayas al doctor. Si quieres, te acompaño.

A. Los cambios ortográficos. Many verbs use regular endings in the present subjunctive, but undergo spelling changes just before the verb ending. Here are the four major kinds of spelling-changing verbs.

▸ **-car** verbs: c → qu

bus**car** *(to look for):* bus**que**, bus**ques**, bus**que**, bus**que**mos, bus**qué**is, bus**que**n

▸ **-gar** verbs: g → gu

ju**gar** *(to play):* jue**gue**, jue**gue**s, jue**gue**, ju**gue**mos, ju**gué**is, jue**gue**n

▸ **-zar** verbs: z → c

almor**zar** *(to eat lunch):* almuer**c**e, almuer**c**es, almuer**c**e, almor**c**emos, almor**c**éis, almuer**c**en

▸ **-ger** verbs: g → j

esco**ger** *(to choose):* esco**j**a, esco**j**as, esco**j**a, esco**j**amos, esco**j**áis, esco**j**an

B. Los verbos irregulares. The five verbs below have irregular forms in the present subjunctive. Note also that the impersonal form of **haber** in the present subjunctive is **haya** *(there is/are)*.

	ir *(to go)*	ser *(to be)*	estar *(to be)*	saber *(to know)*	dar *(to give)*
que yo	vaya	sea	esté	sepa	dé
que tú	vayas	seas	estés	sepas	des
que Ud./él/ella	vaya	sea	esté	sepa	dé
que nosotros(as)	vayamos	seamos	estemos	sepamos	demos
que vosotros(as)	vayáis	seáis	estéis	sepáis	deis
que Uds./ellos/ellas	vayan	sean	estén	sepan	den

These forms of the present subjunctive are used in the dependent noun clause after expressions of advice and **que.**

Es importante que **haya** más ventilación en este cuarto.
*It's important that **there be** more ventilation in this room.*

Ponerlo a prueba

9-10 Más consejos, por favor. ¿Qué consejos les darías a estas personas? Escoge el verbo más lógico en cada caso y escríbelo en el presente del subjuntivo.

Teaching Tip: Assign the first activity for homework.

1. Luis está un poco gordo y quiere adelgazar *(to lose weight)*. Le recomiendo a Luis que (estar / saber) __esté__ bien informado sobre la nutrición. También, es mejor que él (sacar / saber) __sepa__ cuál es su peso *(weight)* ideal.

2. Eduardo va a graduarse pronto y tiene que buscar empleo. Le sugiero a Eduardo que (empezar / buscar) __empiece__ a solicitar entrevistas. También, es importante que (volver / llegar) __llegue__ a tiempo a las entrevistas.

3. Tonya y Angélica piensan estudiar en el extranjero *(abroad)*. Es necesario que ellas (dar / investigar) __investiguen__ varios programas. También, es mejor que (estar / sacar) __saquen__ pasaporte.

4. Laura y su hermana Francisca sufren de depresión a veces. Es importante que ellas (mirar / buscar) __busquen__ atención médica. También, es preferible que (escoger / eliminar) __escojan__ a un psicólogo con experiencia.

5. Ramón tiene una cita el sábado con una chica que no conoce. Es preferible que él le (pedir / dar) __dé__ flores a la chica. También, es bueno que (ser / saber) __sea__ sincero y cortés *(courteous)*.

COMENTARIO CULTURAL   *El matrimonio*

¿A qué edad normalmente se comprometen las personas en los EE.UU.? Generalmente, ¿cuánto tiempo dura un compromiso en los EE.UU.? ¿Cómo es la ceremonia para celebrar el matrimonio?

En los países hispanohablantes existen algunas prácticas diferentes con respecto al matrimonio. En primer lugar, algunos jóvenes se comprometen más tarde que los jóvenes en los Estados Unidos. A veces el compromiso dura varios años. Los jóvenes se casan después de haberse graduado y de haber ahorrado bastante dinero para montar su propia casa o apartamento. En algunos casos, se casan y viven con sus padres. Muchas veces al casarse, la pareja tiene dos ceremonias: una religiosa y otra civil. En algunos países, la ceremonia religiosa es la tradicional, pero la civil es la legal.

9-11 La procrastinación. Lee este artículo sobre la procrastinación y completa la actividad con un(a) compañero(a).

Tips para
dejar de procrastinar

« Voy a jugar unos videojuegos un rato para relajarme. »
« Tengo que revisar mi correo electrónico primero. »
« Voy a echarme una siesta antes de empezar. »

La procrastinación es algo que afecta a todos hasta cierto punto. Sabemos que deberíamos dar prioridad a ciertas cosas, pero las dejamos para después.

Algunas causas de la procrastinación

¿Por qué procrastinamos? Hay varias razones. Quizás la principal razón es que damos más importancia a los beneficios a corto plazo que a las ventajas a largo plazo. Por ejemplo, realmente no nos gusta hacer investigación y por eso no empezamos ese trabajo escrito que tenemos que entregar en dos semanas. Otra razón es que muchas personas creen que trabajan mejor bajo presión, aunque la realidad es otra: con frecuencia la calidad sufre cuando trabajamos contra reloj. Algunas personas no saben priorizar sus obligaciones y otras se sienten abrumadas por haber procrastinado tanto que no saben por dónde empezar.

Algunos consejos

¿Quiere usted dejar de procrastinar? Aquí tiene unas sugerencias que le pueden ayudar.
• Haga una lista de lo que tiene que hacer y de cuando tiene que finalizarlo.
• Priorice las actividades de la lista: lo esencial va primero.
• Identifique las horas del día cuando usted es más productivo. Intente hacer las actividades más importantes durante ese período de tiempo.
• Divida las tareas grandes en partes más pequeñas y fáciles de terminar.

Con un poco de práctica, Ud. puede dejar de procrastinar y reducir el estrés en su vida.

VOCABULARIO ÚTIL:

echarse una siesta	*to take a nap*
a corto plazo	*in the short term*
a largo plazo	*in the long run*
la calidad	*quality*
abrumadas	*overwhelmed*

1. Según el artículo, ¿qué pequeñas excusas dan muchas personas para procrastinar? ¿Qué excusas usan tú y tus amigos(as) a veces?

2. Según el artículo, ¿por qué procrastinan muchas personas? ¿Qué otras razones (*reasons*) hay, en tu opinión?

3. En el artículo hay cuatro sugerencias para combatir la procrastinación. ¿Cuál es la sugerencia más importante en tu opinión? ¿Qué otras sugerencias tienes tú?

4. Dramatiza esta situación con un(a) compañero(a): Imagina que tienes un(a) amigo(a) que siempre deja todo para última hora. Este(a) amigo(a) te pide consejos porque quiere dejar de posponer las cosas. Basándote en las ideas de este artículo, tú le das consejos para cambiar.

9-12 Querida Ana María. Ana María es una periodista que escribe una columna de consejos sobre los problemas personales. Aquí tienes dos cartas. ¿Cómo las contestarías tú? Escribe tres o cuatro consejos; usa el presente del subjuntivo en tus consejos.

Teaching Tip 9-12: Have students work in pairs to compose their letters. Afterward, have students compare responses in groups of 4–6 and choose the best advice to read to the class.

Querida Ana María:

Soy estudiante de primer año en la universidad. Estoy muy preocupada porque aunque no hago más que estudiar, no saco buenas notas. El estrés en la universidad es increíble. Todas las semanas tenemos exámenes. Además, vivo con mis padres y, por eso, no tengo muchos amigos en la universidad. Espero que tú me puedas ayudar.

María Elena

Estimada Ana María:

Necesito tus consejos. Estoy locamente enamorado de una chica que está en mi clase de cálculo. Desgraciadamente, ella ni se da cuenta de *(has no idea)* que existo. Es que soy un poco tímido y no me atrevo *(I don't dare)* a hablar con ella. ¿Qué debo hacer para conocerla?

José

9-13 Los problemas de mis amigos. Debido a tu reputación como una persona muy sabia *(wise)*, tus amigos siempre consultan contigo cuando quieren resolver sus problemas. Con un(a) compañero(a), analiza cada problema que se presenta en los dibujos, identifica el problema y prepara una solución para cada uno. Para dar consejos, incluye expresiones como: **Es necesario que, Es importante que, Es mejor que, Es preferible que, Le recomiendo que, Le aconsejo que.**

MODELO

Germán tiene muchas obligaciones, pero quiere ir a la fiesta de Mauricio. Es importante que Germán sea responsable y que estudie para sus exámenes. No le recomiendo a Germán que vaya a la fiesta de Mauricio.

1.

2.

Puente cultural

🌐 Go to the *Puentes* Premium Website to view the **Puente cultural** interviews.

¿Qué es lo que más les preocupa a tus compatriotas *(fellow countrymen)*?

Patricio Aravena Carrasco

🌐 **CHILE**

El desempleo *(unemployment)* y la crisis económica son las preocupaciones más importantes que tenemos en Chile. No hay mucha corrupción en nuestro país, pero sí hay algunos casos inquietantes *(disturbing)*.

Rosilennys Mariel Inoa

🌐 **REPÚBLICA DOMINICANA**

Las preocupaciones importantes son la economía y la política. También es motivo de preocupación la inmigración de los haitianos, ya que se teme que estos les quiten *(take away)* los trabajos a los dominicanos.

Jimena Escamilla

🌐 **MÉXICO**

El gobierno mexicano ha tenido varias dificultades en los últimos años debido a *(due to)* enfrentamientos *(confrontations)* con sus ciudadanos. Ha habido varias protestas y demostraciones contra el gobierno. Desafortunadamente, el gobierno mexicano ha sufrido y continúa sufriendo debido a la corrupción.

Lee la información y completa la tabla.

🔵 **Standards:** Cultural comparisons can focus on what people have in common across Spanish-speaking cultures, as well as the similarities with the U.S. culture. You may also want students to explore differences within Spanish-speaking cultures to avoid stereotyping and making the wrong assumption that all Spanish-speaking people live, think, and feel alike.

	En Chile	En la República Dominicana	En México	En los Estados Unidos
¿Qué es lo que más les preocupa a tus compatriotas *(fellow countrymen)*?				

Paso 2

In this *Paso* you will practice:

▸ Talking about the milestones of life

▸ Expressing empathy and emotion

Grammar:

▸ Using the present subjunctive with expressions of emotion

▸ Stem-changing verbs in the present subjunctive

Vocabulario temático

Los grandes momentos de la vida
Buenas noticias

VALERIA: ¿Qué me cuentas?

SEBASTIÁN: Estoy *contentísimo*. ¡Tengo buenas noticias!

VALERIA: ¿Sí? Cuéntame qué pasa.

SEBASTIÁN: *Mi hermana mayor está embarazada y voy a ser tío(a).*

VALERIA: *¡Cuánto me alegro!*

Otros sentimientos

Estoy *orgulloso(a)*.
    emocionado(a)
    enamorado(a)
    muy alegre

Otras noticias buenas

Acabo de conocer al hombre (a la mujer) de mis sueños.

Mi hermana mayor va a graduarse con honores de la universidad.

Mi primo y su novia van a comprometerse.

Mis mejores amigos van a casarse.

Para reaccionar a las buenas noticias

¡Cuánto me alegro!

¡Qué buena noticia!

¡Estupendo!

¡Qué maravilloso!

¡Qué bueno!

Malas noticias

SEBASTIÁN: ¿Todo bien?

VALERIA: En realidad, no. Estoy *muy triste*.

SEBASTIÁN: ¿Sí? ¿Qué te pasa?

VALERIA: Acabo de recibir malas noticias. *Mis padres van a separarse.*

SEBASTIÁN: *¡Cuánto lo siento!*

More Information: The suggested pace for this Paso is 1½ to 2 class hours.

Grammar: Mention to students that **muy** is not used with **contentísimo(a)**.

Teaching Tip: Introduce this vocabulary by putting a time line on the board of some major events in your life. Include events such as graduation from high school or college, engagements and marriages, births, deaths, job changes, etc. Explain in a simple way what happened and how you felt. Then ask for class members to share some good news, such as a new job, an engagement, a birth in the family, etc. Respond with an expression of empathy and an appropriate question to each different event. For bad news, you may refer to the model in the book to avoid discomfort in the classroom. If you prefer not to speak about your personal life, refer to news about celebrities or other well-known families, such as the royal family of Spain or of England.

Teaching Tip: Discuss with students other important milestones in life, both secular and religious, such as baptism, first communion, and confirmation. Mention the importance for many young Hispanic women of the fifteenth birthday, which represents a rite of passage into adulthood.

To congratulate someone, say **¡Felicidades!** or **¡Enhorabuena!**

Otros sentimientos

Estoy *preocupado(a)*.
  deprimido(a)
  desconsolado(a)
  sorprendido(a)

Otras noticias malas

Mi hermano y su novia rompieron su compromiso.

Mis tíos van a divorciarse.

Se murió mi tía abuela.

Para reaccionar a las malas noticias

¡Cuánto lo siento!

¡Qué pena!

¡Lo siento mucho!

¡Ojalá que todo salga bien!

Ponerlo a prueba

CD2
Track 26

9-14 ¿Qué hay de nuevo? Escucha las dos conversaciones sobre las últimas noticias.
Completa las oraciones de una manera lógica.

Conversación 1

1. Gloria está...
 a. preocupada.   (b.) enamorada.   c. desconsolada.

2. Luis es....
 (a.) estudiante de medicina.
 b. el hermano de Paloma.
 c. el director de la compañía.

3. Luis quiere...
 (a.) casarse con Gloria.
 b. consultar a un especialista.
 c. romper su compromiso.

Conversación 2

4. Según el médico, Mariana...
 (a.) está embarazada.
 b. tiene una enfermedad grave.
 c. va a sentirse mejor pronto.

5. Rodolfo es el... de Mariana.
 a. padre   b. hijo   (c.) esposo

6. Cuando oye la noticia, Rodolfo se siente...
 a. muy deprimido.
 (b.) contentísimo.
 c. un poco preocupado.

9-15 Así es la vida. Tus amigos te cuentan muchas noticias. ¿Cómo respondes tú a cada una? Escoge la reacción más apropiada para cada situación.

Las noticias de tus amigos

_e_ 1. Estoy muy orgulloso. Mi hermano mayor va a graduarse con honores de la escuela secundaria.

_a_ 2. Estoy desconsolada. Mi abuelo está muy grave y los médicos piensan que va a morir pronto.

_b_ 3. Estoy emocionada. Pepe pidió mi mano en matrimonio y ¡yo acepté!

_f_ 4. Tengo malas noticias. Por lo visto, mis padres van a separarse.

_c_ 5. ¡Estoy contentísima! Acabo de conocer al hombre de mis sueños.

_d_ 6. Estoy muy preocupado. La compañía de mi padre está pasando por unas dificultades económicas tremendas.

Tus reacciones

a. ¡Lo siento mucho! ¿Puedo acompañarte a visitarlo al hospital?

b. Estoy muy contento(a) por ustedes. ¿Cuándo van a casarse?

c. ¿Sí? ¡Estupendo! ¿Cómo se llama? ¿Cómo se conocieron?

d. Sí, es una situación mala. ¿Piensas que va a perder su empleo?

e. ¡Qué buenas noticias! ¿Cómo van a celebrar su graduación?

f. ¡Qué noticia más triste! ¿Piensas que van a divorciarse?

9-16 Buenas y malas noticias. Aquí tienes varias situaciones, algunas con buenas noticias y otras con malas noticias. Con un(a) compañero(a), lean los diálogos y complétenlos con una expresión apropiada (**¡Qué sorpresa!**) y con una pregunta lógica (**¿Cuándo es la boda?**).

1.   LUPE: ¡Estoy tan emocionada! Tengo una cita para el baile de etiqueta *(formal)* de mi sororidad.

             TÚ: ¡_____! ¿_____?

2.   OCTAVIO: Estoy muy alegre. Mis abuelos van a celebrar su aniversario de boda. Llevan cincuenta años de casados.

             TÚ: ¡_____! ¿_____?

3.   MARIO: ¡Estoy contentísimo! ¿Te acuerdas de *(Do you remember)* la chica que conocí en la fiesta de Enrique el mes pasado? Pues, ¡nos hemos comprometido!

             TÚ: ¡_____! ¿_____?

4.   DALIA: Estoy muy triste. Mi tía se murió anoche.

             TÚ: ¡_____! ¿_____?

5. TU COMPAÑERO(A):   [Inventa una buena noticia.]

             TÚ: ¡_____! ¿_____?

6.   TÚ: [Inventa una mala noticia.]

  TU COMPAÑERO(A):   ¡_____! ¿_____?

Teaching Tip 9-16: Refer to Activity 9-15 for further examples of how one can react to good/bad news and ask follow-up questions.

Expansion 9-16: Have each pair of students select one of the situations and develop it into a full dialogue.

Teaching Tip 9-17: If you need to save time, have students choose between Tema A and Tema B.

9-17 Los grandes momentos de la vida. El matrimonio y el nacimiento de un bebé son acontecimientos muy importantes en la vida. Entrevista a un(a) compañero(a) sobre estos temas.

Tema A: El matrimonio

Piensa en una ceremonia de boda muy memorable.

1. ¿Cuándo fue la boda? ¿Quiénes se casaron?

2. ¿Cómo fue la ceremonia, sencilla *(simple)* o muy elegante? ¿Dónde se celebró?

3. ¿Pasó algo divertido o conmovedor *(moving)* durante la ceremonia o la recepción? Describe lo que ocurrió.

Tema B: El nacimiento de un(a) bebé

Piensa en el nacimiento del (de la) bebé de un familiar o de un(a) amigo(a).

1. ¿Quién tuvo un bebé? ¿Qué nombre le pusieron?

2. ¿Cómo se prepararon los familiares para el nacimiento?

3. ¿Cómo reaccionaste cuando viste al (a la) bebé por primera vez?

Expansion 9-18: Have students think of a special celebration and write an article for it to share with their classmates. Possible topics include: birthdays, anniversaries, engagements, weddings, or significant religious ceremonies.

9-18 Una crónica social. Los anuncios sociales son muy comunes en los periódicos que se publican en los países hispanohablantes. Lee el anuncio a la derecha y contesta las preguntas.

1. ¿Qué ocasión celebra la familia Alonso Fernández?

2. ¿Dónde se celebró el acontecimiento *(event)*?

3. ¿Cuántos padrinos tiene Fernando José? ¿Quiénes son?

4. ¿Cuántos hijos tienen los padres de Fernando José? ¿Quiénes son?

5. ¿Cómo se celebró el evento?

Fernando José y sus orgullos padres, José y Annie Alonso.

Bautizo de Fernando José

El hermoso niño Fernando José Alonso Fernández recibió las sagradas aguas bautismales en ceremonia celebrada en la Iglesia San José de Caguas. Radiantes de felicidad se encontraban sus padres José R. Alonso y la profesora Annie Fernández de Alonso. Fueron padrinos de bautizo la Dra. Irma Santor, Dr. Carlos Fernández, Wanda Fernández y Antonio Delgado. Muy contentas se encontraban las hermanitas de Fernando José, Cristina, Adriana y Viviana. En grande fue festejada la significativa ocasión, con una fiesta en el Colegio de Ingenieros, amenizada por la orquesta de Víctor Roque y la Gran Manzana.

Gramática

Usos del subjuntivo: las emociones

Read along as you listen to the following conversation. How is María feeling? Why? Identify which verbs are in the present subjunctive.

—¿Todo bien, María?

—En realidad, no. Estoy muy preocupada porque mi padre ha perdido su empleo. Tengo miedo de que no encuentre un nuevo trabajo.

—Sí, la crisis económica es muy grave. ¡Espero que todo salga bien!

A. Una breve introducción. There are several ways to express our feelings about important events in our lives. One common way is to say that we feel happy (or concerned, upset, sad, etc.) that something is taking place. To construct a sentence of this type, you must follow the familiar three-part pattern and use the present subjunctive after **que.**

1		2	3	
Main Clause			**Dependent Noun Clause**	
Subject	**Expression of Emotion**	*que*	**New Subject**	**Verb in the Present Subjunctive**
(Yo) *I*	Estoy contentísimo de *am very happy*	que *that*	mi hija *my daughter*	**se case** pronto. *is getting married soon.*
	Es una lástima *It is too bad*	que *that*	su abuela *her grandmother*	**no pueda** ir a la boda. *can't go to the wedding.*

B. Expresiones de emoción. Below are some common expressions of emotion that trigger the use of the present subjunctive in the dependent clause.

- **esperar** *(to hope)*
  Esperamos que tu hermano encuentre empleo pronto.
  We hope that your brother finds work soon.

- **sentir (ie)** *(to regret, to be sorry)*
  Sentimos mucho que Uds. no puedan venir a la boda.
  We're very sorry that you can't come to the wedding.

- **estar** + adjective of emotion + **de**
  Examples: **Estoy orgulloso(a), contento(a), triste, alegre...**
  Ramona **está** muy **orgullosa de** que su hijo se gradúe de la universidad pronto.
  Ramona is very proud that her son is graduating from the university soon.

- **tener miedo de** *(to be afraid of)*
  Tengo miedo de que mi novia quiera romper nuestro compromiso.
  I'm afraid that my fiancée may want to break our engagement.

- **ojalá** *(I hope that/May)*
  Ojalá que sean muy felices.
  *I hope that they are very happy. (**May** they be very happy.)*

🌐 **Heinle Grammar Tutorial:**
The present subjunctive in impersonal expressions

Answers: She is worried, because her father has lost his job and she's afraid he may not find a new one. Verbs in the present subjunctive: **encuentre, salga.**

Grammar: Point out that the present subjunctive can be used only to express events that are taking place now or in the future. Explain that more advanced structures—the past subjunctive or present perfect subjunctive—are needed when we refer to events in that past. For example: **Siento mucho que tu perro haya muerto.** *I'm sorry that your dog died.*

Grammar: Point out that the verb **estar** may be conjugated in any person; for example, **"yo", "mis padres y yo", " Marta"** may all be subjects of the verb.

Grammar: In some regions, it is not necessary to use **que** after **ojalá: Ojalá sean muy felices.**

> ► **es** + adjective or noun of emotion
> Examples: **Es triste, Es bueno, Es ridículo, Es mejor, Es preferible, Es una lástima...**
>
> > **Es ridículo** que Sara no piense asistir a la boda de su hermana.
> > *It's ridiculous that Sara is not planning to attend her sister's wedding.*
>
> *Gustar*-**type verbs:** Sentences with these verbs always include an indirect object pronoun in the first part of the sentence: **me, te, le, nos, os, les.** Use the subjunctive for the verb after **que.**
>
> ► **gustar** *(to like, be pleasing to [someone])*
> > No **nos gusta** que no se casen por la iglesia.
> > *We don't **like** the fact (It displeases us) that they aren't getting married in church.*
>
> ► **alegrar** *(to be glad, make [someone] happy)*
> > A mi padre **le alegra** que yo siga con mis estudios.
> > *My dad **is happy** (It makes my dad happy) that I am continuing with my studies.*
>
> ► **preocupar** *(to worry [someone])*
> > **Me preocupa** que mis padres se separen.
> > *It **worries me** that my parents are separating.*
>
> ► **sorprender** *(to surprise [someone])*
> > ¿**Te sorprende** que se comprometan?
> > *Are you **surprised** (Does it surprise you) that they are getting engaged?*
>
> ► **molestar** *(to bother)*
> > **Les molesta** que no haya una fiesta para celebrar su graduación.
> > *It **bothers them** that there isn't a party to celebrate his/her/their graduation.*
>
> ► **enfadar** *(to anger, to make one mad)*
> > **Me enfada** que no inviten a mi novio a la fiesta.
> > *It **makes me angry** that they're not inviting my boyfriend to the party.*

Ponerlo a prueba

9-19 Las noticias de Juan. ¿Cómo se siente Juan ante los varios acontecimientos de su vida? Lee las oraciones e indica la respuesta más lógica. También escribe el verbo entre paréntesis en el presente del subjuntivo.

1. (Me alegra / <u>Me preocupa</u>) que mi perro (estar) ___esté___ enfermo.
2. (<u>Estoy orgulloso</u> / Estoy triste) de que mi mejor amiga (graduarse) _se gradúe_ con honores de la universidad la próxima semana.
3. (<u>Es una lástima</u> / Es muy bueno) que mis amigos no (poder) _puedan_ encontrar trabajo para el verano.
4. (Estoy contentísimo / <u>Tengo miedo</u>) de que mi novia (querer) _quiera_ romper nuestro compromiso. Todavía estoy enamorado de ella.
5. (Siento mucho / <u>Me gusta</u>) que mis primos favoritos (venir) _vengan_ a visitarme en dos semanas.
6. (<u>Me molesta</u> / Me alegra) que mi compañero de cuarto (leer) ___lea___ mi diario sin pedir permiso.

9-20 Chismes. La Sra. García es la chismosa *(the gossip)* de su barrio en Viña del Mar, Chile. ¿Qué observa y dice ella sobre la vida de los vecinos? Combina las columnas de una manera lógica y escribe seis oraciones con los chismes de la Sra. García. Escribe los verbos entre paréntesis en el presente del subjuntivo.

> **MODELO** Es una lástima que los vecinos de enfrente se divorcien.

A
Me sorprende que
Me molesta que
Es escandaloso que
Me alegra que
Me preocupa que
Estoy contentísima de que
Es una lástima

B
los Ortiz (separarse)
Mimí (llevar) a su novio a su apartamento
el soltero de al lado (casarse) por fin
los Guzmán (celebrar) su aniversario de oro este año
los vecinos de enfrente (divorciarse)
Beto siempre (hacer) tanto ruido *(noise)*
los Garza siempre (decir) que yo soy chismosa

Answers 9-20: *Answers will vary; sample responses follow:* Me sorprende que los Garza siempre digan que yo soy chismosa. Me molesta que Beto siempre haga tanto ruido. Es escandaloso que Mimí lleve a su novio a su apartamento. Me alegra que los Guzmán celebren su aniversario de oro este año. Me preocupa que los Ortiz se separen. Estoy contentísima de que el soltero de al lado se case por fin.

9-21 ¿Qué te parece? ¿Cuáles son tus reacciones a estos acontecimientos (hipotéticos) en tu universidad? Trabaja con dos o tres compañeros(as) y sigan el modelo. **¡Ojo!** Hay que usar el presente del subjuntivo.

> **MODELO** Aumentan la matrícula *(tuition)* el próximo año.
> TÚ: Me enfada que **aumenten** la matrícula otra vez. Es la segunda vez en tres años. ¿Cómo se sienten Uds. con esta situación?

Me alegra que...   **Me preocupa que...**
Estoy contentísimo(a) de que...   **Me enfada que...**
Me gusta que...   **Me molesta que...**
Es ridículo que...   **Es una lástima que...**
Me sorprende que...   **Es increíble que...**

1. Las nuevas residencias son "verdes" y utilizan muchos materiales ecológicos.
2. La universidad paga muchísimo dinero a los entrenadores *(coaches)* de los equipos atléticos.
3. No hay suficiente aparcamiento *(parking)* para los coches de los estudiantes.
4. La universidad da muchas becas *(scholarships)* para estudiar en el extranjero.
5. No se permite fumar en los salones de clase.
6. Los estudiantes necesitan estudiar una lengua para graduarse.
7. La biblioteca está abierta 24 horas al día.
8. La librería universitaria tiene un nuevo café de Starbucks.

Teaching Tip: Provide additional statements involving current or future events and policies on your campus. Use this as an opportunity to reinforce the idea that the present subjunctive is used to refer to the present and the future, not to the past.

9-22 El próximo año escolar. Con un(a) compañero(a), describan sus deseos o esperanzas sobre distintos aspectos de la vida universitaria para el próximo año escolar. Usen las siguientes expresiones:

- **Ojalá que...**
- **Espero que...**

> **MODELO** ¿la comida de la cafetería?
> TÚ: Ojalá que sirvan platos con menos grasa.
> TU COMPAÑERO(A): Yo espero que haya más opciones para vegetarianos.

1. ¿las residencias?
2. ¿el gobierno estudiantil?
3. ¿el costo de los libros?
4. ¿los equipos deportivos?
5. ¿el trabajo académico?
6. ¿las actividades extracurriculares?
7. ¿los profesores nuevos?
8. ¿tu vida social?

CD2
Track 28

Answers: piensen (pensar); puedan (poder); entiendan (entender).

Gramática

El presente del subjuntivo: los verbos con cambios en la raíz

Read along as you listen to Tito's concerns about his brother's impending divorce. How does Tito feel about the situation? Which three verbs are in the present subjunctive? What infinitives correspond to each verb in the subjunctive?

¿Qué pienso yo sobre el divorcio de mi hermano? En primer lugar, me molesta que él y su esposa piensen divorciarse antes de consultar a un consejero *(counselor)*. ¡Es increíble que ellos no puedan resolver sus problemas! Además, tengo miedo de que mis sobrinos no entiendan la situación. Realmente, es muy triste.

A. Los infinitivos -*ar, -er.* Verbs that end in **-ar** and **-er** and have stem changes in the present tense also have these very same changes in the present subjunctive. The stem changes occur in all forms, except for **nosotros** and **vosotros.**

Verbs that end in *-ar:*	e → ie	o → ue
	pensar *(to think)*	**acostarse** *(to go to bed)*
que yo	pi**e**nse	me ac**ue**ste
que tú	pi**e**nses	te ac**ue**stes
que Ud./él/ella	pi**e**nse	se ac**ue**ste
que nosotros(as)	pensemos	nos acostemos
que vosotros(as)	penséis	os acostéis
que Uds./ellos/ellas	pi**e**nsen	se ac**ue**sten

Other common stem-changing -*ar* verbs:

e → ie	o → ue
despertarse *to wake up*	acostarse *to go to bed*
empezar *to begin*	almorzar *to have lunch*
pensar *to think, to plan (to)*	contar *to count, to tell*
merendar *to snack*	encontrar *to find*
recomendar *to recommend*	jugar (u → ue) *to play (a sport, game)*
	probar *to taste, to try*

Verbs that end in *-er:*	e → ie	o → ue
	entender *(to understand)*	**volver** *(to return)*
que yo	ent**ie**nda	v**ue**lva
que tú	ent**ie**ndas	**v**ue**lvas**
que Ud./él/ella	ent**ie**nda	v**ue**lva
que nosotros(as)	entendamos	volvamos
que vosotros(as)	entendáis	volváis
que Uds./ellos/ellas	ent**ie**ndan	v**ue**lvan

Other common stem-changing -*er* verbs:

e → ie	o → ue
atender *to tend to, to assist*	poder *to be able to, can*
perder *to lose*	volver *to return, to go back*
querer *to want, to love (a person)*	

B. Los infinitivos terminados en -ir. Verbos that end in **-ir** and have stem changes in the present tense also have stem changes in the present subjunctive. However, there is one important difference: In the subjunctive, the stem changes take place in *all* persons, including **nosotros** and **vosotros.** Note carefully the three patterns in the chart.

Verbs that end in *-ir*:	e → ie/i **sentir** *(to be sorry)*	o → ue/u **dormir** *(to sleep)*	e → i/i **servir** *(to serve)*
que yo	sienta	duerma	sirva
que tú	sientas	duermas	sirvas
que Uds./él/ella	sienta	duerma	sirva
que nosotros(as)	sintamos	durmamos	sirvamos
que vosotros(as)	sintáis	durmáis	sirváis
que Uds./ellos/ellas	sientan	duerman	sirvan

Other common stem-changing *-ir* **verbs:**

e → ie/i	o → ue/u	e → i/i
divertirse *to have a good time*	morir *to die*	pedir *to ask, request*
preferir *to prefer*		repetir *to repeat*
sentir *to be sorry, to regret*		seguir *to follow*
sentirse *to feel*		vestirse *to get dressed*

Teaching Tip: Be sure to have students take note that the first two kinds of **-ir** verbs have different changes in the **nosotros/vosotros** forms than in the other persons.

Ponerlo a prueba

9-23 El compromiso de Lourdes. Lourdes está escribiendo en su diario sobre su compromiso con William. Escribe los verbos en el presente del subjuntivo.

Teaching Tip: Assign the first two activities for homework. In class, you may wish to review in each sentence the triggering phrase that prompts the use of the subjunctive.

Querido diario:

¡Este ha sido un día increíble! ¡Cuántas emociones! ¡Incredulidad *(Disbelief)*! ¡Miedo! ¡Alegría! De veras, me sorprende que William (1. pedir) __pida__ mi mano en matrimonio en este momento. Ya que nos queremos tanto, es bueno que él y yo (2. poder) __podamos__ casarnos. Sin embargo, me preocupa que mis padres (3. pensar) __piensen__ que no voy a ir nunca más a Chile. Es una lástima que Chile (4. estar) __esté__ tan lejos. Ojalá que ellos (5. entender) __entiendan__ la situación. Es bueno que mi familia (6. venir) __venga__ a visitarme este verano. Me alegra que mis padres y mi hermana (7. volver) __vuelvan__ a visitarme en los EE.UU. Es posible que la visita de mi familia (8. servir) __sirva__ para unirnos a todos. Estoy contenta de que mi familia y William (9. sentirse) __se sientan__ a gusto cuando estamos todos juntos. ¡Ojalá que todo (10. salir) __salga__ bien!

9-24 El matrimonio de Lupe y Leopoldo. Lupe y Leopoldo se casan y todo el mundo tiene una reacción diferente. Completa las oraciones con una expresión de la lista; cambia los verbos al presente del subjuntivo. **¡Ojo!** Todos estos verbos tienen un cambio en la raíz.

> **MODELO** Los abuelos de Lupe están contentos de que... su nieta **piense** vivir cerca de casa.

su mejor amigo / **no poder** ir a la boda
su hija / **preferir** una boda sencilla, no muy costosa
los jóvenes / **no repetir** sus errores
su nuera / **no servirle** los platos favoritos a su hijo
su hermano mayor / ya no **dormir** en el mismo dormitorio con él
su futuro esposo / **querer** viajar a Europa en su luna de miel

1. Al padre de Lupe le alegra que...

2. A la madre de Leopoldo le preocupa un poco que...

3. Al hermanito de Leopoldo le gusta mucho que...

4. Lupe está encantada de que...

5. Leopoldo está triste de que...

6. Los padres de Lupe están contentísimos de que...

9-25 La vida universitaria. Con un(a) compañero(a), completa los diálogos de una manera lógica. Es necesario añadir *(to add)* **que** y cambiar el verbo al presente del subjuntivo. No te olvides de añadir alguna información para completar la conversación.

> **MODELO** Tu amiga: El sábado voy con Julián al baile formal de mi sororidad. Va a ser una noche inolvidable.
>
> Tú: Ojalá / Uds. divertirse...
>
> ¡Ojalá que Uds. se diviertan mucho en la fiesta! El domingo tienes que contarme todo.

1. Aparicio: No entiendo el subjuntivo. Voy a sacar F en el examen.

   Tú: Aparicio, me preocupa / no entender...

2. Adolfo: Hace dos días que no duermo. Tengo mucho trabajo.

   Tú: Adolfo, no es bueno / no dormir...

3. Elena: Mi prometido, Agustín, está de viajes por varios días.

   Tú: Ojalá / volver...

4. Alfonso: Nunca voy a mi clase a las 8:00 porque no puedo levantarme en la mañana.

   Tú: Alfonso, es mejor / acostarse...

5. Tus vecinos: Tus perros ladran *(bark)* toda la noche y no podemos pegar ojo *(sleep a wink)*.

   Tú: Siento / (Uds.) no poder dormir...

9-26 ¿El amor? ¿En qué situación se encuentran estas personas? ¿Cómo se sienten? Con un(a) compañero(a), describe la situación y los sentimientos de cada persona. Incluye oraciones con el presente del subjuntivo en sus descripciones.

1.

2.

 9-27 ¿Y tú? ¿Qué hay de nuevo en tu vida? Conversa con dos o tres compañeros(as) sobre algunos acontecimientos importantes. Tus compañeros(as) tienen que hacerte preguntas y tú tienes que contestarlas para continuar la conversación.

> **MODELO**   Tú: Mi cumpleaños es el próximo sábado. Estoy muy contento(a) de que mis padres vengan a la universidad para celebrar conmigo.

COMPAÑERO(A) 1: ¿Cuántos años vas a cumplir?

COMPAÑERO(A) 2: ¿Van ustedes a comer en algún restaurante?

In this *Paso* you will practice:

- Indicating doubt, denial, uncertainty, and certainty
- Expressing optimism and pessimism

Grammar:

- Using the present indicative to affirm certainty and belief
- Using the present subjunctive to express doubt, denial, and uncertainty

More Information: The suggested pace for this **Paso** is 1½ to 2 class hours.

Teaching Tip: Introduce the vocabulary by asking who has recently had a job interview or taken an important test. After identifying someone who has, ask a yes/ no follow-up question: **¿Te fue bien?, ¿Te lo van a dar?,** or **¿Saliste bien?** Then refer to the expressions that express degrees of certainty and doubt. Have the students select an appropriate response. Continue this way with additional daily concerns regarding personal finances, relationship problems, etc.

Paso 3

Vocabulario temático

Cuéntame de tu vida

MATÍAS: ¿Qué hay de nuevo?

NATALIA: Acabo de tener una entrevista para una beca.

MATÍAS: ¿Sí? ¿Piensas que te la van a dar?

NATALIA: Creo que sí. Me fue muy bien en la entrevista.

Para expresar grados de certeza o duda

¡Sin ninguna duda!	Es posible.	Es dudoso.
Creo que sí.	Quizás.	Es poco probable.
Es casi seguro.	Depende.	Creo que no.
Es muy probable.		¡Imposible!

Para expresar optimismo

Me siento muy optimista.

Pienso que todo se va a arreglar.

¡No te preocupes!

Para expresar pesimismo

Me siento pesimista.

No estoy seguro(a); es muy difícil.

Creo que va a salir mal.

Ponerlo a prueba

CD2
Track 29

9-28 ¿Cómo se siente Raquel? Escucha la conversación entre Raquel y su amiga Sofía. Completa las oraciones de una manera lógica.

Teaching Tip: Assign the first two activities for homework.

_c_ 1. Raquel está...
   a. contenta.
   b. enojada.
   c. preocupada.

_c_ 2. Raquel estudió... para su examen.
   a. muy poco
   b. tres horas
   c. toda la noche

_c_ 3. Raquel piensa que va a sacar...
   a. una buena nota.
   b. una nota regular.
   c. una mala nota.

_a_ 4. La amiga de Raquel, Sofía, se siente...
   a. optimista.
   b. frustrada.
   c. pesimista.

_b_ 5. Al final de la conversación, Raquel...
   a. cambia totalmente de opinión.
   b. sigue pesimista.
   c. decide hablar con su profesor.

9-29 ¿Seguro? Completa las conversaciones de una manera lógica. Escoge la frase más apropiada en cada caso.

1. Tú: ¿Piensas que te van a dar una beca académica?
   Camila: (Es casi seguro. / Es dudoso.) Mis notas no son muy altas.

2. Tú: ¿Crees que tú y tu novio van a comprometerse pronto?
   Mía: (Sin ninguna duda. / Imposible.) Él tiene que terminar sus estudios primero.

3. Tú: ¿Vas a hacer un crucero con tu familia este verano?
   José: (Es muy probable. / Creo que no.) Sé que papá habló con el agente de viajes la semana pasada.

4. Tú: Estoy preocupado(a) por mi nota en genética.
   Rogelio: (Debes sentirte optimista. / Debes sentirte pesimista.) Siempre sacas notas muy buenas en esa clase.

5. Tú: No tengo dinero para pagar mis cuentas y he perdido mi trabajo.
   Lina: ¡No te preocupes! Yo te ayudo. (Pienso que todo se va a arreglar. / Creo que va a salir mal.)

9-30 Probabilidades. Entrevista a un(a) compañero(a) con estas preguntas. Cuando sea tu turno de contestar, usa expresiones de certeza o duda y justifica tus respuestas:

MODELO
   Tú: ¿Va a casarse tu hermano el año próximo?
   Tu compañero(a): Imposible. ¡Tiene solamente diez años!

El romance:
1. ¿Va a casarse pronto tu mejor amigo(a)?
2. ¿Piensas comprometerte antes de graduarte de la universidad?

La familia:
3. ¿Tus padres te van a comprar un coche para tu graduación?
4. ¿Te van a mandar tus abuelos un regalo especial para tu cumpleaños?

La vida estudiantil:
5. ¿Vas a sacar una "A" en la clase de español este semestre?
6. ¿Vas a poder pagar todas las cuentas este semestre?

Los viajes:
7. ¿Vas a hacer un crucero este año?
8. ¿Piensas hacer un viaje a Europa el próximo verano?

Answers: To express certainty: **es evidente, estoy segura de, creo.** To show doubt: **es posible, lo dudo.**

Gramática

Usos del presente de indicativo para expresar certeza

Read along as you listen to Emilia speculating about the future of her friend Jazmín. What words does Emilia use to express certainty about some aspects of her situation? What words does she choose to show doubt?

¿El futuro de Jazmín y Vicente? Es evidente que los jóvenes se adoran. Pero, estoy segura de que las familias de ellos no van a aceptar el matrimonio. Es posible que resuelvan sus diferencias, pero lo dudo. Creo que va a terminar en tragedia.

A. Una breve introducción. When giving opinions, we often express different degrees of doubt or uncertainty about the situations before us. For example, the following sentences convey a variety of opinions about the outcome of a job interview.

> **Estoy seguro(a) de** que me van a ofrecer el puesto.
> *I'm sure that they are going to offer me the job.*
>
> **Creo** que me van a ofrecer el puesto.
> *I believe that they are going to offer me the job.*
>
> **Dudo** que me ofrezcan el puesto.
> *I doubt that they will offer me the job.*
>
> **Es imposible** que me ofrezcan el puesto.
> *There's no way (It's impossible) that they're going to offer me the job.*

In this section you will study how Spanish expresses certainty and belief (as in the first two sentences above). Later in this **Paso** you will explore further how Spanish expresses doubt and denial (as modeled in the last two sentences).

B. Para expresar certeza. The following verbs and expressions are used in Spanish to affirm your certainty or strong belief about events and circumstances in your life.

Expresiones de certeza

saber	**Sé** que...	*I know that . . .*
creer	**Creo** que...	*I believe that . . .*
pensar (ie)	**Pienso** que...	*I think that . . .*
estar seguro(a) de	**Estoy seguro(a) de** que...	*I'm sure that . . .*
	Es seguro que...	*It's a sure thing that . . .*
	Es verdad que...	*It's true that . . .*
	Es cierto que...	*It's true that . . .*
	Es evidente que...	*It is evident that . . .*

These expressions are used as the first part in the familiar three-part sentence pattern; however, they do **not** trigger the use of the subjunctive. Instead, you must use the following verb forms in the dependent clause (that is, in the third part of the sentence).

- To refer to present and future events: the **present** (present indicative) tense
- To refer to past events: the **preterite** or the **imperfect**

	1	2		3	
Subject	Expression of Certainty/Belief	*que*	Subject	Verb in the Indicative (Present, Preterite, Imperfect)	
(Yo) *I*	Estoy seguro de *am sure*	que *that*	(yo) *I*	**voy** a vivir en Nueva York. *am going to live in New York.*	
(Yo) *I*	Creo *believe*	que *that*	(ellos) *they*	le **dieron** el puesto. *gave him the job.*	

Ponerlo a prueba

9-31 Es la pura verdad. ¡Pobre Sra. Tierno! Los vecinos le han contado muchos chismes *(gossip)* sobre su hijo Bernardo, y resulta *(it turns out)* que todos son la pura verdad. Completa el diálogo con las afirmaciones de Bernardo. Relaciona las dos columnas de una manera lógica.

Teaching Tip: Assign the first two activities for homework.

Sra. Tierno

_b_ 1. La vecina me dijo que tú y Sofía están divorciados. Yo le dije que no podía ser.

_c_ 2. Un pajarito *(A little bird)* me dijo que te casaste con tu secretaria.

_f_ 3. Pero, hijo, tú ya tienes treinta y ocho años y me parece que tu secretaria es mucho más joven.

_d_ 4. ¿Cómo pueden Uds. llevarse bien con una diferencia tan grande de edades?

_g_ 5. Mi amiga Matilde me dijo que dejaste tu puesto en la compañía.

_a_ 6. ¿Cómo vas a poder pagar todas tus cuentas?

_e_ 7. Matilde me dijo que piensas mudarte a una isla tropical en Polinesia. Hijo, dime que eso no es verdad.

_h_ 8. ¿Cómo voy a visitarte si vives en Polinesia?

Bernardo

a. Me parece que el abuelo de Lulú se murió recientemente y le dejó todo su dinero.

b. Sí, mamá, es verdad que estamos divorciados.

c. Es cierto que me casé con ella. Creo que tú ya la conoces. Se llama Lulú.

d. Lulú y yo sabemos que el amor puede vencer *(conquer)* todo.

e. Creo que las posibilidades de trabajo van a ser magníficas allí.

f. Sé que ella tiene veinticinco años. Es evidente que es una mujer madura *(mature)*.

g. Estoy seguro de que voy a encontrar otro puesto sin problemas.

h. Los boletos de avión no cuestan mucho. Estoy seguro de que puedes visitarnos con frecuencia.

9-32 Un poco de análisis. Vuelve a mirar las afirmaciones de Bernardo en la Actividad 9-31. ¿Qué expresiones usa él para expresar certeza *(certainty)*? Escribe cinco de estas expresiones.

MODELO Es verdad...

Answers 9-32: *Any five of the following answers are acceptable:* me parece, es verdad, es cierto, creo, sabemos, sé, es evidente, estoy seguro de.

9-33 Insegura. Tu amiga, Rosa, no tiene mucha confianza *(confidence)* en sí misma y además es un poco melodramática. ¿Qué le dices para calmarla? Usa expresiones de certeza y afirmación. Completa los diálogos con un(a) compañero(a) y léelos en voz alta.

> **MODELO**   ROSA: Tengo otro examen de química hoy y estoy muy nerviosa. Tengo miedo de sacar una mala nota.
>
> TÚ: Sé que vas a salir bien. Estoy seguro(a) de que vas a sacar una "A". Eres una estudiante muy buena y aplicada.

1. Tuve una entrevista ayer para un puesto para el verano. No me fue muy bien.
2. Todavía no tengo compañero para el baile y es en dos semanas. ¡Yo soy la única en mi sororidad sin compañero!
3. Si no apruebo *(pass)* la clase de matemáticas, no voy a poder graduarme en junio. Entonces mis padres me van a matar *(will kill me)*.
4. Mi compañera de cuarto y yo no nos llevamos bien. Quiero mudarme a otra residencia en la primavera.
5. Fui a la peluquería y me teñí *(dyed)* el pelo. ¡Mira qué color más horrible!
6. (Inventa una situación original.)

9-34 Este semestre. Piensa en tu vida este semestre y completa las oraciones siguientes de una manera original. Comparte tus respuestas con un(a) compañero(a).

1. Respecto al dinero, pienso que _____.
2. En cuanto a mis clases, creo que _____.
3. Cuando pienso en mis amigos, sé que _____.
4. Sobre mi compañero(a) de cuarto, es seguro que _____.
5. En cuanto a mi familia, es verdad que _____.
6. Respecto a las notas que recibo en mis clases, es cierto que _____.

Answers to Estrategia: 1. c; 2. d; 3. a; 4. b.

Estrategia *Gestures and body language*

Intercultural communication involves much more than knowing the right words to say. The way we stand and the gestures we make can greatly influence how persons in another culture perceive our intentions.

Because body language varies from country to country, what is courteous in one place or situation may sometimes be considered inappropriate in another. For example, people often stand several inches further apart for business conversations than they do for encounters among family and friends. Interestingly, in Spanish-speaking countries, both distances—the "formal" and the "friendly"—tend to be shorter than they are in the United States. When people are not aware of these varying cultural norms, misunderstandings can easily arise. For example, in a conversation between an American and a Chilean, the American may end up feeling that the Chilean is too forward or pushy, because he or she has "invaded" his/her personal space. At the same time, the Chilean may find the American cold or standoffish, because he or she has stood too far away.

The use of gestures varies greatly from country to country, as do the forms gestures take. In Spanish-speaking countries, gestures are used frequently to punctuate conversations in both informal and formal settings. Depicted below are four gestures common to most of the Hispanic world. Can you match each one to its meaning?

a. Dinero
b. ¡Ojo! ¡Ten ciudado!
c. ¡Excelente!
d. ¡Tacaño! *(Stingy!)*

 1.    2.    3.    4.

Gramática

Usos del presente del subjuntivo: la duda y la negación

CD2
Track 31

Read along as you listen to Santino and Benjamín discussing their financial difficulties. What expressions does Benjamín use to express his uncertainty about upcoming events? Which verbs are in the present subjunctive?

SANTINO: Benjamín, tenemos que pagar el alquiler *(rent)* mañana. ¿Te van a dar el dinero tus padres?

BENJAMÍN: No sé, es posible que me lo den, pero.... Mira, para decirte la verdad, todavía no he hablado con ellos.

SANTINO: No comprendo por qué no has hablado con ellos. ¿Y qué va a pasar si no te lo dan?

BENJAMÍN: Entonces, es dudoso que pueda pagar el alquiler. Lo siento.

A. Una breve introducción. In the previous **Gramática** section of this **Paso,** you learned how to express certainty and strong belief. In this section you will learn to express uncertainty, doubt, and denial.

Uncertainty:	**Dudo** que ella esté embarazada. *I **doubt** that she is pregnant.*
Denial:	**No es verdad** que ella esté embarazada. *It's **not true** that she is pregnant.*

B. Expresiones de duda y negación. Here are some common expressions of uncertainty, doubt, and denial.

▶ To say that you do **not** believe something, or that you are not completely certain about it, use these expressions:

no creer	**No creo** que...	*I don't believe that . . .*
no pensar	**No pienso** que...	*I don't think that . . .*
dudar	**Dudo** que...	*I doubt that . . .*
	Es posible que...	*It's possible that . . .*
	(No) Es probable que...	*It's (un)likely that . . .*
	Es dudoso que...	*It's doubtful that . . .*
	Quizás...	*Perhaps/Maybe . . .*

▶ To deny that something is so, use the following expressions:

No es verdad que...	*It's not true that . . .*
No es cierto que...	*It's not true that . . .*
Es imposible que...	*It's impossible that . . .*
No es posible que...	*It's not possible that . . .*

All of the expressions above are used as the first part of the familiar three-part sentence pattern. With these expressions of doubt and denial, be sure to use the subjunctive after **que.**

Heinle Grammar Tutorial:
The present subjunctive in impersonal expressions

Answers: Uncertainty: No sé, es posible, es dudoso. Present subjunctive: den, pueda.

	1		2		3
Subject	Expression of Uncertainty/Denial		*que*	Subject	Verb in Present Subjunctive
It	Es posible *is possible*		que *that*	(ella) *she*	**se comprometa.** *is getting engaged.*
It	No es verdad *isn't true*		que *that*	(ella) *she*	**se case.** *is getting married.*

C. Un contraste. When creating sentences with expressions of certainty, doubt and denial, keep in mind that you may change the meaning of the sentence entirely if you add **no** before the verb in the main clause. The choice between **present indicative** and **present subjunctive** depends ultimately on the meaning conveyed.

Indicative required: belief, certainty, affirmation	Subjunctive required: disbelief, doubt, uncertainty, denial
Creo que la clase **es** muy difícil. *I think that the class is very hard.*	No creo que la clase **sea** muy difícil. *I don't think that the class is very hard.*
Estoy seguro(a) de que todos **sacamos** una buena nota. *I'm sure that we're all getting a good grade.*	No estoy seguro(a) de que todos **saquemos** una buena nota. *I'm not sure that we're all getting a good grade.*
Es verdad que él **estudia** seis horas diarias. *It's true that he studies six hours every day.*	No es verdad que él **estudie** seis horas diarias. *It's not true that he studies six hours every day.*

Ponerlo a prueba

9-35 Pensando en el futuro. Eduardo está especulando *(is speculating)* sobre el futuro. Completa las oraciones con la forma más apropiada del verbo. Tienes que escoger entre el presente del indicativo y el presente del subjuntivo.

1. ¿Los estudios? Pienso que (yo / ir) ___voy___ a graduarme en dos años, aunque es posible que (yo / graduarse) ___me gradúe___ el próximo año. Es poco probable que (yo / hacer) ___haga___ estudios de postgrado.

2. ¿Mi novia y yo? Creo que (nosotros / ir) ___vamos___ a casarnos en cinco años. Dudo que (nosotros / casarse) ___nos casemos___ antes, porque queremos ahorrar dinero para comprar una casa. Es probable que (nosotros / vivir) ___vivamos___ en Santiago porque hay más oportunidades de trabajo.

3. ¿Mis padres? Es posible que ellos (ir) ___vayan___ a vivir en Valparaíso por motivos de trabajo. Es evidente que mi padre (estar) ___está___ frustrado con su empleo. Creo que el (querer) ___quiere___ encontrar algo nuevo.

Grammar: With more proficient classes, you may wish to point out to students that when using **pensar** and **creer** in a question, the subjunctive is almost always used.

Teaching Tip: Students may not recognize the term "present indicative." Remind them that this is the basic "present tense" that they've been practicing since the first chapter.

Teaching Tip: Assign the first activity for homework.

El presente del indicativo (present indicative) is the official term for the present tense that you've been practicing since the first chapter: **hablo, como, estoy, voy,** etc.

9-36 El optimista y el pesimista. Ignacio e Isabel siempre tienen puntos de vista completamente contrarios *(opposite)*. ¿Cómo responde Ignacio a los comentarios de Isabel sobre la boda de sus amigos, Marisa y Julio? Trabaja con un(a) compañero(a) para completar los diálogos. Sigan el modelo. **¡Ojo!** A veces hay que usar el presente del indicativo, y a veces hay que usar el presente del subjuntivo.

> **MODELO**   ISABEL: Creo que Marisa y Julio van a vivir con los padres de él.
>
>   IGNACIO: No creo que *Marisa y Julio* **quieran** *vivir con sus padres.*

1. ISABEL: Pienso que Marisa va a tener una boda sencilla *(simple)*.
   IGNACIO: Dudo que...

2. ISABEL: No creo que los padres de Marisa les den una casa como regalo de boda.
   IGNACIO: ¿No? Pues, yo creo que...

3. ISABEL: Es cierto que Marisa y Julio son felices.
   IGNACIO: En mi opinión, es posible que...

4. ISABEL: Creo que los padres de Marisa están tristes, pero no sé por qué.
   IGNACIO: Es probable que...

5. ISABEL: Es seguro que Marisa sabe adónde van de luna de miel.
   IGNACIO: Julio me dijo ayer que era un secreto, así que es imposible que...

6. ISABEL: Es posible que Marisa quiera tener muchos hijos.
   IGNACIO: Pienso que Julio...

 9-37 ¿Qué opinas? ¿Qué piensan tú y tus compañeros(as) sobre estos temas? Expresen y comparen sus opiniones. Sigan el modelo.

> **MODELO**   Todos los estudiantes deben estudiar un idioma extranjero por un mínimo de dos años.
>
>   TÚ: Es una buena idea. Creo que es importante aprender otras lenguas. ¿Y tú? ¿Qué piensas?
>
> TU COMPAÑERO(A):   No creo que sea buena idea. Debemos tener menos cursos obligatorios en la universidad. Quisiera tener más tiempo para tomar cursos propios de mi carrera.

1. La universidad debe conceder *(to award)* becas según la necesidad económica, sin tomar en cuenta otros factores (estatus minoritario, talento atlético o artístico, mérito académico, etc.).

2. Todos los estudiantes universitarios deben pasar parte de su carrera académica estudiando en el extranjero.

3. La universidad debe obligar a sus estudiantes a participar en actividades de servicio comunitario para poder graduarse.

4. Una pasantía *(apprenticeship/internship)* debe ser una parte integral de todas las carreras en la universidad.

Answers: *Sample Answers:* 1. Marisa vaya a tener una boda sencilla. 2. los padres de Marisa les dan una casa como regalo de boda. 3. Marisa y Julio no sean felices. 4. los padres de Marisa no quieran que Marisa se case. 5. Marisa sepa adónde van de luna de miel. 6. no quiere tener muchos hijos.

9-38 En el futuro. En una de tus clases, te piden que le escribas una carta al alcalde *(the mayor)* de tu comunidad. En la carta, le pides que implemente algunos cambios *(changes)* para mejorar la calidad *(the quality)* de vida de los ciudadanos. Piensa en los problemas que existen en tu comunidad: ¿el tráfico?, ¿la criminalidad?, ¿la falta de actividades para los jóvenes?, ¿las personas desamparadas *(needy)*?, ¿otro problema?, ¿otra cosa? Luego, completa las oraciones y escribe la carta.

> Estimado alcalde/Estimada alcaldesa:
>
> Me llamo _____ y soy ciudadano(a) de _____.
>
> Le escribo porque me preocupa mucho el problema de _____ que existe en nuestra comunidad.
>
> Ese problema existe porque _____.
>
> Es verdad que ese problema _____.
>
> No es cierto que todos los ciudadanos de nuestra comunidad _____.
>
> En mi opinión, es importante que _____.
>
> Para resolver el problema, es necesario que _____.
>
> Le agradezco mucho la oportunidad de poderle expresar a Ud. mis ideas sobre ese problema tan preocupante.
>
> Muy atentamente,
>
> _____

Expansion 9-39: After completing the activity, have your students make a list of the most serious problems on campus, including those not mentioned in the questions. Discuss them as a class.

9-39 La vida universitaria. La administración de tu universidad quiere que los estudiantes completen la siguiente encuesta sobre la vida universitaria. Primero, expresa tu opinión y justifica tu respuesta. Compara tus opiniones con las de dos o tres compañeros.

MODELO

El gobierno estudiantil, ¿representa bien a la población universitaria?

(Creo que / No creo que)

Tú: No creo que el gobierno estudiantil nos represente bien porque los representantes no interactúan mucho con los estudiantes. Además *(Additionally),* muy pocos estudiantes votan en las elecciones para el gobierno estudiantil. ¿Y tú? ¿Qué piensas?

1. El número de estacionamientos para los estudiantes, ¿es adecuado para estacionar sus carros?
   (Pienso que / No pienso que)

2. El laboratorio de computación, ¿tiene suficientes computadoras para todos los estudiantes?
   (Es cierto que / No es cierto que)

3. Las cafeterías, ¿sirven comida sana, rica y a precio moderado?
   (Es verdad que / No es verdad que)

4. Las residencias, ¿están en buenas condiciones?
   (Dudo que / No dudo que)

5. La biblioteca, ¿es moderna y tiene los recursos necesarios para los estudiantes?
   (Creo que / No creo que)

Un paso más

¡Vamos a hablar!

Estudiante A

Contexto: Tú (**Estudiante A**) tienes tres dibujos y tu compañero(a) (**Estudiante B**) tiene tres también. Uds. tienen que comparar los dibujos mediante *(through)* descripciones orales y descubrir *(discover)* las diferencias entre los dibujos. Ustedes necesitan describir:

- lo que pasa en el dibujo
- cómo se sienten las personas
- qué piensan las personas de las circunstancias

Tú vas a empezar así: " El dibujo número uno muestra una mujer y su esposo. Ella está embarazada. Está muy contenta porque quiere tener un bebé. Espera que sea niña. Su esposo... (Continúa con la descripción.)

Go to the **Un paso más** section in the *Cuaderno de actividades* for additional reading, writing, and listening activities that are correlated with this chapter.

1.

2.

3.

Un paso más

¡Vamos a hablar!

Estudiante B

Contexto: Tú **(Estudiante B)** tienes tres dibujos y tu compañero(a) **(Estudiante A)** tiene tres también. Uds. tienen que comparar los dibujos mediante *(through)* descripciones orales y descubrir *(discover)* las diferencias entre los dibujos. Ustedes necesitan describir:

• lo que pasa en el dibujo

• cómo se sienten las personas

• qué piensan del acontecimiento

Tu compañero(a) va a empezar. Escucha y después describe en qué se diferencia tu dibujo.

1.   2.

3.

¡Vamos a ver! | *Episodio 9*

En la Hacienda Vista Alegre

Anticipación

A. Hablando se entiende la gente. Habla con un(a) compañero(a). ¿Has tenido alguna vez una relación difícil con una persona (un amigo, un compañero de cuarto, un ex novio, etc.)? ¿Cómo era esta persona? ¿Qué pasó? ¿Cómo reaccionaste tú? ¿Cómo te sentías?

B. ¿Cómo se dice...? Relaciona las siguientes expresiones con la definición apropiada.

1. tener celos *(to be jealous of someone)*
2. espiar *(to keep watch on)*
3. machista *(sexist)*
4. enamorarse de alguien *(to fall in love with somebody)*
5. ¡Esto es el colmo! *(This is the last straw!)*

a. Cuando te gusta una persona mucho.

b. Pensar que las mujeres son inferiores.

c. Algo que llega a su punto máximo.

d. Observar disimuladamente *(surreptitiously)* las acciones de una persona.

e. Ser una persona posesiva.

Teaching Tip: Preview the video by showing a fragment of the episode without sound and have students use visual clues to anticipate content. Stop and rewind the video until they understand the gist of the episode.

Answers B: 1.e; 2.d; 3.b; 4.a; 5.c

Vamos a ver

C. De paseo por la Hacienda Vista Alegre. Primero, lee las preguntas. Después, mira el Episodio 9 del vídeo, observa a los personajes y contesta las preguntas.

1. ¿Con quién está hablando Valeria por teléfono?
2. ¿De quién está celoso *(jealous)* César? ¿Por qué?
3. ¿Por qué Valeria piensa que en la casa no hay privacidad?
4. ¿Cómo es César?
5. ¿Qué pasó con Antonio y su ex novia? ¿Por qué dejaron *(broke off)* la relación? ¿Cómo reaccionó Antonio?
6. ¿Qué van a hacer Antonio y Valeria?

Answers C: 1. con César, su ex novio; 2. de Antonio, porque Antonio le regaló un ramo de flores el día de su cumpleaños y la invitó a cenar. 3. Piensa que Antonio la está escuchando cuando habla por teléfono; no puede estar tranquila en el baño porque sus compañeros quieren entrar, etc. 4. César es muy celoso y machista. 5. Su novia se enamoró de su mejor amigo. Él los perdonó. 6. Van a cenar.

En acción

D. Charlemos. Comenta con tus compañeros(as). Si tu novio(a) se enamora de tu mejor amigo(a), ¿cómo vas a reaccionar? ¿Qué te parece la reacción de Antonio ante el comportamiento de su ex novia? ¿Piensas que Valeria tenía motivos para romper la relación con su ex novio? ¿Por qué? ¿Qué crees que va a pasar entre Antonio y Valeria?

E. 3, 2, 1 ¡Acción! Interpreten la siguiente situación en grupos de 3 ó 4 estudiantes.

Estás con tus amigos en la Hacienda Vista Alegre y ya tienen mucha confianza para contarse temas personales. Habla con ellos sobre tus sentimientos, opiniones, problemas que estás atravesando últimamente, etc. Tienen que expresar opiniones y recomendaciones según lo que les cuenten los (las) compañeros(as).

Teaching Tip: Have students practice summarizing, describing characters, sequencing events, making comparisons, and giving detailed narrations and descriptions based on what they see in the video.

Panorama cultural

DATOS ESENCIALES

Nombre oficial: República de Chile

Capital: Santiago

Población: 16 602 000 habitantes

Unidad monetaria: el peso

Economía: exportación de cobre y sal, frutas y vegetales, vino, productos industriales, incluyendo productos para la producción de alimentos, papel, productos químicos y de petróleo; agricultura; pesca

🌐 **www.cengage.com/spanish/ puentes**

Note: Copper accounts for one third of government revenue. In addition, as the European and Asian markets have opened to Chile, exports of fruit and vegetables have increased dramatically. Since 1990 tourism has grown greatly, especially to the more remote locations such as Patagonia, Atacama, and Easter Island.

Note: The majority of the population is **mestizo**; immigrants from England, Ireland, and Germany have also had significant impact on Chilean culture. Although indigenous peoples were largely decimated by war and smallpox, surviving Aymara continue to live in the north while the Mapuche populate the south-central valley. On Easter Island (**la Isla de Pascua**) the native inhabitants speak the Polynesian language Rapa Nui.

Note: El Festival de Viña was begun in 1960 and has grown from a local to a truly international event. In addition to the contest for best song, the most popular recording artists in the world are invited to perform. The crowds that attend the festival are so large and vociferous that they are known as **el monstruo.**

Note: After his election, Allende instituted Marxist social and economic reforms, including the nationalization of private companies. The economy went into a severe decline, with widespread shortages of food and consumer goods as well as an annual inflation rate of 1000%.

Festival Internacional de la Canción de Viña del Mar Todos los años en el mes de febrero la pintoresca ciudad de Viña del Mar se convierte en el centro del mundo musical. El Festival de Viña atrae a todos los grandes artistas internacionales y también a miles de espectadores. Por seis noches, todo el país está pegado a la pantalla (*glued to the screen*) mientras se transmiten en vivo las competencias para elegir las mejores canciones del año.

Un vistazo a la historia

1541	Comenzó la conquista española. Pedro de Valdivia fundó la ciudad de Santiago.	**1973– 1990**	Augusto Pinochet Ugarte se instaló en la presidencia después de un golpe de estado militar.
1810– 1818	Guerra de independencia contra España; Chile ganó con la ayuda de las tropas de José de San Martín y Bernardo O'Higgins.	**1990**	La elección de Patricio Aylwin a la presidencia marcó la transición a la democracia. Se creó una comisión para estudiar las violaciones a los derechos humanos.
1879– 1884	En la Guerra del Pacífico, Chile obtuvo territorios bolivianos y peruanos, incluyendo un área rica en minerales en el desierto de Atacama.	**2006**	Michelle Bachelet es la primera mujer en asumir el cargo de Presidenta de la República.
1970	Elección del presidente marxista Salvador Allende.		

Note: Allende was overthrown and killed by a military coup led by General Pinochet. Pinochet's authoritarian regime, which was assisted in part by the CIA, lasted 16 years. Severe human rights violations marked his rule, especially in the early years. During this time Chile moved quickly to a free market system and the economy grew rapidly.

Chile

Personajes de ayer y de hoy

El Libertador, General Bernardo O'Higgins (1778–1842)

Héroe de la independencia chilena, Bernardo O'Higgins nació en Chillán en 1778. Vivió y se educó en Perú, España e Inglaterra. Con José de San Martín, liberó al país de España y se autoproclamó Director Supremo de la República. Sus reformas contribuyeron a su destitución del cargo y a su exilio en Perú.

Note: O'Higgins championed the cause of democracy and the abolition of titles of nobility. For this reason he lost the support of the aristocracy and the Church and was ultimately forced into exile.

Pablo Neruda (1904–1973)

Este célebre poeta chileno es considerado uno de los grandes poetas del siglo XX. Ganó el Premio Nobel de Literatura en 1971. Uno de sus libros más populares es la colección *Veinte poemas de amor y una canción desesperada*. Un activista político, conocido por su apoyo al partido comunista, Neruda sirvió como senador de la República; también fue cónsul y embajador de Chile en varios países.

Note: Pablo Neruda is the pseudonym for Neftalí Reyes Pasoalto. He began publishing his works at a very young age. Moved by the death of fellow poet García Lorca, Neruda threw his support to the Republicans during the Spanish Civil War. After that time, his work became increasingly political and social in nature.

Michelle Bachelet (1951–)

Esta política y médica pediatra es la primera mujer en ser presidente de Chile. Antes de asumir la presidencia en 2006, sirvió por varios años en el Ministerio de Salud, donde implementó varias reformas en el sistema público de salud. También fue la primera mujer en ocupar el puesto de Ministra de Defensa Nacional.

Note: Bachelet's father was in charge of food distribution during the government of Salvador Allende. After Pinochet came to power, General Bachelet was arrested and he and his family were detained and tortured. After living for a time in exile with her family in Australia and East Germany, Michelle Bachelet returned to Chile in 1979.

Note: Santiago is located in the central valley and enjoys a Mediterranean type climate. With over five million residents, the area is home to about thirty-six percent of the country's population. Recent economic growth has made Santiago one of the continent's most modern capital cities.

Imágenes de Chile

Mira el vídeo y contesta las preguntas.

1. ¿Dónde está situada la capital de Chile?
2. Describe "la Alameda", la avenida principal de Santiago.
3. ¿Qué personajes históricos son conmemorados con monumentos en la capital?
4. ¿Qué diferentes estilos de arquitectura observas en Santiago?
5. ¿Cuáles de los lugares del vídeo te gustaría visitar? Explica por qué.

Additional activities on Chile and the **Panorama cultural** may be found in the **Un paso más** section of the *Cuaderno de actividades*.

Answers: *Suggested answers follow:* 1. Está al sur del río Mapocho, frente a la cordillera de los Andes. 2. Tiene diez kilómetros de largo. Hay muchos monumentos por la Alameda. La línea principal del metro corre debajo de la calle. 3. Hay monumentos a Bernardo O'Higgins, José de San Martín y Simón Bolívar. 4. Hay varios estilos. Algunos son más viejos y tradicionales, y otros son modernos. 5. *Answers will vary.*

Sustantivos

el acontecimiento *event*
la ayuda *help*
la beca *scholarship*
la boda *wedding*
el compromiso *engagement (to be married)*
el consejo *advice*
la entrevista *interview*
la noticia *news*
el trabajo escrito *a written academic report, "paper"*
la verdad *truth*

Verbos

acabar de + infinitivo *to have just (done something)*
aconsejar *to advise*
alegrar *to make happy*
casarse *to get married*
comprometerse *to get engaged*
cuidarse *to take care of oneself*
dejar *to leave, to let*
dejar de + infinitivo *to stop (doing something)*
desconectarse *to disconnect, to have some down time*
discutir *to discuss, to argue*
divorciarse *to get divorced*
dudar *to doubt*
enfadar *to anger*
entregar *to turn in*
esperar *to hope*
fumar *to smoke*
llevarse bien/mal *to get along well/ poorly*
molestar *to bother, to irritate*
morirse (ue, u) *to die*
ponerse en forma *to get in shape*
posponer *to postpone, to put off*
preocuparse *to worry*
procrastinar *to procrastinate*
prohibir (i) *to forbid, to prohibit*
romper *to break (up)*
salir bien (mal) *to do well (poorly)*
sentir (ie, i) *to regret, to be sorry*
separarse *to separate, to get a (marital) separation*
sorprender *to surprise*

Otras palabras

agotado(a) *exhausted, worn out*
balanceado(a) *balanced*
cierto(a) *true, certain*
desconsolado(a) *grief-stricken*
deprimido(a) *depressed*
diario(a) *daily*
difícil *unlikely, difficult*
dudoso(a) *doubtful*
embarazada *pregnant*
emocionado(a) *excited*
enamorado(a) *in love*
estresado(a) *stressed out*
furioso(a) *furious, very angry*
ojalá *I hope that . . . ; May . . .*
orgulloso(a) *proud*
probable *likely, probable*
quizás *maybe, perhaps*
seguro(a) *sure*
sorprendido(a) *surprised*

To react to good or bad news, pp. 307–308
To indicate degrees of certainty and doubt, p. 318
To express optimism and pessimism, p. 318

For further review, please turn to **Vocabulario temático: español e inglés** at the back of the book.

Go to the ***Puentes*** website for extra Vocabulary practice using the Flashcard program.

Gramática suplementaria

El presente progresivo

Heinle Grammar Tutorial: Present progressive tenses 29

Fifteen-year-old Felipe has just called the López home. Read his conversation with Mrs. López and answer these questions: With which two persons would Felipe like to speak? Why can't they talk on the phone just then?

Hablando por teléfono:

FELIPE: Buenos días, señora López, soy yo, Felipe. ¿Puedo hablar con Marcos?

SRA. LÓPEZ: Lo siento, Felipe, pero Marcos está haciendo la tarea ahora.

FELIPE: ¿Y Silvia? ¿Puedo hablar con ella?

SRA. LÓPEZ: Ella está estudiando también.

FELIPE: Ah, está bien. Vuelvo a llamar *(I'll call again)* más tarde.

A. La función del presente progresivo. The present progressive tense (**el presente progresivo**) is used to describe what somebody is doing or what is taking place at the moment that someone is speaking. In other words, it is used to give a vivid description of what is happening at the moment of speech. For example, in the conversation above, Marcos cannot speak on the phone because he *is doing* his homework; similarly, Silvia cannot speak because she *is studying*.

Marcos y Silvia **están estudiando.**   *Marcos and Silvia **are studying.***

B. La formación del presente progresivo. To form the present progressive, use the present tense of the verb **estar** together with the present participle of the main verb. Study the examples of this structure below:

Presente progresivo: estar + *present participle*

yo	**estoy estudiando**	*I am studying*
tú	**estás comiendo**	*you are eating*
Ud./él/ella	**está escribiendo**	*he/she is writing*
nosotros(as)	**estamos mirando**	*we are watching*
vosotros(as)	**estáis leyendo**	*you (pl.) are reading*
Uds./ellos/ellas	**están trabajando**	*they are working*

The present participle is formed by adding **-ando** to the stem of **-ar** verbs and by adding **-iendo** to the stem of most **-er** and **-ir** verbs.

▸ **-ar** verbs: hablar + ando → hablando   *talking, speaking*
▸ **-er** verbs: comer + iendo → comiendo   *eating*
▸ **-ir** verbs: escribir + iendo → escribiendo   *writing*

-Er and **-ir** verbs that have a vowel before the infinitive ending form the present participle by adding **-yendo.**

Infinitive		Present Participle	Meaning
leer + yendo →		leyendo	*reading*
construir + yendo →		construyendo	*building, constructing*

Grammar: Unlike the English present progressive, in Spanish this verb tense is never used to talk about future events. The simple present tense is used in these cases. For example: **Salimos** para Tucson mañana. *We are leaving for Tucson tomorrow.*

Ponerlo a prueba

GS1-1 El blog de Marta. Completa el blog de Marta con los verbos más lógicos de la lista. Escribe los verbos en el presente progresivo.

correr	**escribir**	**escuchar**	**trabajar**
leer	**mirar**	**montar**	**usar**

¡Qué día más tranquilo! Mi hija Daniela (**1**) _____ música en su ipod. Mis hijos, Rafael y David, (**2**) _____ su programa favorito en la tele. Mi esposo (**3**) _____ en el parque con sus amigos. Abuela (**4**) _____ el periódico en el patio. Los vecinos (**5**) _____ en el jardín y yo (**6**) _____ este blog.

GS1-2 En una escuela. Son las diez de la mañana. ¿Qué están haciendo los niños en la escuela hoy? Mira el dibujo y describe las actividades de los niños. Escribe oraciones completas en el presente progresivo.

GS1-3 Las excusas. Tu amiga Patricia te llama por teléfono constantemente, pero tú no quieres hablar con ella. Con un(a) compañero(a), crea pequeños diálogos. Sigan el modelo y usen el presente progresivo.

> **MODELO**   8:00 A.M. (a las ocho de la mañana)
>
> PATRICIA: Hola, ¿qué estás haciendo?
>
> TÚ: Hola, Patricia. Lo siento, pero no puedo hablar ahora. Estoy comiendo el desayuno (*breakfast*).

1. 9:00 A.M. (a las nueve de la mañana)
2. 11:30 A.M. (a las once y media de la mañana)
3. 2:00 P.M. (a las dos de la tarde)
4. 5:30 P.M. (a las cinco y media de la tarde)
5. 7:00 P.M. (a las siete de la tarde)
6. 9:30 P.M. (a las nueve y media de la noche)

🌐 **Heinle Grammar Tutorial:** The future tense 25

El futuro

The tour guide is explaining to your group what you will be doing on your excursion to Mexico City tomorrow. What are three of the planned activities? Identify three verbs that refer to the future.

Su tour empezará con un corto viaje en autobús. Después, nosotros visitaremos la hermosa catedral. Yo les recomendaré varios restaurantes donde ustedes podrán probar los platos típicos de la región. Por la tarde, iremos al Museo de Antropología.

A. La función del futuro. The future tense (**el futuro**) is used in two ways:

▸ to describe what will happen or what somebody will do in the future.
Notice that the English word *will* is not translated, but expressed through the *verb ending* in Spanish.

Su tour **empezará** con un corto viaje en autobús.	*Your tour **will begin** with a short trip by bus.*
Después, nosotros **visitaremos** la hermosa catedral.	*Afterward, we **will visit** the beautiful cathedral.*

▸ to speculate about what is *probably going on* or what *will probably take place* in the near future.
In English, probability is expressed by using separate words such as *probably* or *must,* while in Spanish the notion of probability is conveyed by the use of the future tense.

—¿Qué hora es, mamá?	*What time is it, Mom?*
—No sé, hija. **Serán** las cinco.	*I don't know, daughter. **It must be** five o'clock.*
—¿Cuándo va a llegar papá?	*When is Dad coming home?*
—No te preocupes. **Llegará** pronto.	*Don't worry. **He will probably arrive** soon.*

B. La formación del futuro. To form the future tense of most verbs, add the appropiate verb endings to the entire infinitive. Notice in the following examples that the same set of endings is used for -**ar,** -**er,** and -**ir** verbs.

El futuro: verbos regulares

		viajar *(to travel)*	volver *(to return)*	ir *(to go)*
yo	-é	viajar**é**	volver**é**	ir**é**
tú	-ás	viajar**ás**	volver**ás**	ir**ás**
Ud./él/ella	-á	viajar**á**	volver**á**	ir**á**
nosotros(as)	-emos	viajar**emos**	volver**emos**	ir**emos**
vosotros(as)	-éis	viajar**éis**	volver**éis**	ir**éis**
Uds./ellos/ellas	-án	viajar**án**	volver**án**	ir**án**

There are a number of irregular verbs in the future tense. These verbs use the same endings as the regular ones, but the endings are attached to an irregular stem.

El futuro: verbos irregulares

Meaning	Verb	Stem	Endings	Example
to say, to tell	decir	**dir-**	-é	yo saldré
to do, to make	hacer	**har-**	-ás	tú saldrás
to have	tener	**tendr-**	-á	Ud./él/ella saldrá
to put, to place	poner	**pondr-**	-emos	nosotros saldremos
to come	venir	**vendr-**	-éis	vosotros saldréis
to leave, to go out	salir	**saldr-**	-án	Uds./ellos/ellas saldrán
to know	saber	**sabr-**		
to want	querer	**querr-**		
to be able to	poder	**podr-**		

The future of the verb **hay (haber)** is **habrá.**

—¿**Habrá** una excursión por la tarde?

Will there be an excursion in the afternoon?

—No, pero **habrá** una por la mañana.

No, but there will be one in the morning.

Ponerlo a prueba

GS2-1 Un tour de México. El señor Pacheco quiere hacer un viaje a México. Ahora está hablando con una agente de viajes. Lee la conversación y completa los espacios en blanco con la forma correcta del futuro.

EL SEÑOR PACHECO: ¿Qué ciudades **(1)** _____ (nosotros / visitar)?

LA AGENTE: Bueno, primero, **(2)** _____ (ustedes / pasar) dos días en la capital, y después **(3)** _____ (ustedes / empezar) las excursiones a otras ciudades: Taxco, Oaxaca, Guadalajara y otros lugares.

EL SEÑOR PACHECO: ¿**(4)** _____ (Ser) posible explorar un poco las ruinas aztecas?

LA AGENTE: ¡Cómo no! También **(5)** _____ (haber) una excursión opcional a Acapulco.

EL SEÑOR PACHECO: ¿**(6)** _____ (nosotros / tener) la oportunidad de visitar Cancún?

LA AGENTE: Claro que sí. Ese tour **(7)** _____ (salir) el miércoles, dieciséis de mayo, y **(8)** _____ (volver) el martes, día veintidós.

EL SEÑOR PACHECO: ¡Fenomenal! Parece un viaje fantástico. **(9)** _____ (yo / hablar) con mi esposa y la **(10)** _____ (yo / llamar) la próxima semana con nuestra decisión.

LA AGENTE: Muy bien. Hasta pronto.

GS2-2 Los turistas. Examina el dibujo y contesta las preguntas con oraciones completas. ¿Qué pasará *(is probably happening)*? **¡Ojo!** Tienes que usar el futuro en las respuestas.

1. ¿En qué país estarán estos turistas? ¿De dónde serán?

2. ¿Quién será el señor?, ¿la señora a la izquierda *(on the left)*?

3. ¿Quién será la niña? ¿Cuántos años tendrá?

4. ¿Qué le dirá el señor a la vendedora *(vendor)*? ¿Qué le dirá la vendedora?

5. ¿Cuánto costará la piñata? ¿Comprará la piñata el señor?

6. ¿Qué querrá comprar la señora? ¿Cuánto costará?

 GS2-3 La visita de tu amigo(a). Tu nuevo(a) amigo(a) mexicano(a) viene a la universidad para visitarte por unos días. ¿Qué harán ustedes durante su visita? Describe los planes; incluye un mínimo de cinco verbos en el futuro. Comparte tus ideas con un(a) compañero(a).

> **MODELO** El primer día, **visitaremos** el campus por la mañana. Por la tarde, **iremos** al nuevo Centro de Wellness y **nadaremos** en la piscina. Por la noche, **iremos** a una fiesta en el apartamento de mis amigos. El segundo día…

Gramática suplementaria

El participio pasado

Read the conversation between Rosaura and Linda. Is everything ready for the visit of their house guests? Identify three adjectives they use to describe their preparations.

> LINDA: ¿Está todo listo para la visita de nuestros amigos?
>
> ROSAURA: Sí. Toda la casa está en orden. Las camas están hechas, los platos están lavados y la mesa está puesta.
>
> LINDA: ¿Y la comida está preparada?
>
> ROSAURA: Todavía no. Pero la voy a preparar ahora mismo.

A. La función del participio pasado. Past participles (**los participios pasados**) are often used as adjectives to describe the condition of people or things. When used in this way, they must agree in number and gender with the noun they describe.

▸ Past participles used as adjectives may be placed after the verb **estar.**

Las camas **están hechas,** los platos **están lavados** y la mesa **está puesta.**
*The beds **are made,** the dishes **are washed** and the table **is set.***

▸ Past participles used as adjectives may also be placed directly after nouns.

Mi hermano tiene un coche **hecho** en los Estados Unidos.
*My brother has a car **made** in the United States.*

B. La formación del participio pasado. To form the past participle, replace the **-ar** ending of the infinitive with **-ado,** and the **-er** or **-ir** ending with **-ido.**

Infinitive		Ending		Past Participle	Meaning
-ar verbs: preocupar	+	ado	→	**preocupado**	*worried, preoccupied*
-er verbs: vender	+	ido	→	**vendido**	*sold*
-ir verbs: aburrir	+	ido	→	**aburrido**	*bored*

A number of common verbs have irregular past participles.

Infinitive	Irregular Past Participle	Meaning
abrir	**abierto**	*open; opened*
decir	**dicho**	*said; told*
escribir	**escrito**	*written*
hacer	**hecho**	*done; made*
morir	**muerto**	*dead; died*
poner	**puesto**	*put; set; placed*
resolver	**resuelto**	*resolved; solved*
romper	**roto**	*broken*
ver	**visto**	*seen*
volver	**vuelto**	*returned*

In general, compound words based upon these irregular verbs will share the same kind of irregular past participle.

Infinitive	Past Participle	Meaning
poner	**puesto**	*put*
descom**poner**	descom**puesto**	*broken, out of order*

Ponerlo a prueba

GS3-1 Un mal día. La familia Malapata está pasando un día muy malo. Describe su día; completa los espacios en blanco con el participio pasado del infinitivo.

1. Papá está _____ (frustrar). La computadora en su oficina está _____ (descomponer) y todos los documentos importantes están _____ (borrar [to erase]).

2. Mamá está _____ (preocupar). El autobús llega en diez minutos y los niños todavía no están _____ (vestir [to dress]).

3. ¡Pobre Miguel! La ventana en su cuarto está _____ (romper) y papá se va a poner furioso con él.

4. Las gemelas, Selenia y Sabrina, están _____ (aburrir). Están _____ (resfriar [to be down with a cold]) y no pueden salir de casa.

5. Abuelita está muy _____ (agitar). La puerta de su coche está _____ (cerrar [to lock]) y la llave está _____ (perder [to lose]).

Teaching Tip: Assign the first activity for homework. Complete the remaining two in class.

Answers GS3-1: 1. frustrado; descompuesta; borrados; 2. preocupada; vestidos; 3. rota; 4. aburridas; resfriadas; 5. agitada; cerrada; perdida.

 GS3-2 ¡Cálmate! Tu amiga Sofía le va a dar una fiesta a su novio. Ella está un poco preocupada con los preparativos y tú tienes que calmarla. Con un(a) compañero(a) de clase, sigue el modelo y completa los diálogos. **¡Ojo!** Hay que usar participios pasados en las respuestas.

> **MODELO** SOFÍA: ¿Quién va a decorar el pastel?
>
> Tú: ¡No te preocupes! ¡Cálmate! El pastel ya (already) **está decorado.**

1. —¿Por qué no preparamos los sándwiches ahora?

2. —¿Quién va a poner la mesa?

3. —Ahora tenemos que hacer las camas.

4. —¿Cuándo vamos a envolver (wrap) los regalos?

5. —Debemos abrir las ventanas; hace calor hoy.

6. —¿Hay más platos sucios? Tenemos que lavarlos antes de que lleguen los invitados (before the guests arrive).

Answers GS3-2: 1. ...están preparados. 2. ...está puesta. 3. ...están hechas. 4. ...están envueltos. 5. ...están abiertas. 6. ...están lavados.

GS3-3 Los estudios. Conversa con un(a) compañero(a) acerca de los estudios. Fíjense bien en el uso de los participios pasados.

1. Normalmente, ¿estás bien **preparado(a)** para tus clases? ¿Cuántas horas estudias en un día típico?

2. ¿Estás bien **preparado(a)** para las clases de hoy? ¿Tienes **hecha** toda la tarea para hoy?

3. ¿Estás **aburrido(a)** en alguna de tus clases este semestre? ¿Qué haces cuando estás **aburrido(a)** en clase?

4. ¿En cuál de tus clases estás un poco **frustrado(a)**? Explica por qué.

CAPÍTULO
4

Gramática suplementaria

Heinle Grammar Tutorial: The present perfect tense 30

El presente perfecto

Ada and Diego are discussing their preparations for a dinner party. What have they already done to get ready? Identify the verbs for three different things they've done to prepare.

DIEGO: ¿Has comprado el vino para la fiesta?

ADA: Sí, y también he preparado las tapas.

DIEGO: Y el postre, ¿has hecho algún postre especial?

ADA: Sí, he preparado una torta de chocolate.

DIEGO: Gracias, mi amor. Me encanta la torta de chocolate.

A. La función del presente perfecto. The present perfect verb tense (**el presente perfecto**) is used to indicate what somebody *has done* or what events *have taken place.*

—¿**Has comprado** el vino para la fiesta?	*Have you bought the wine for the party?*
—Sí, y también **he preparado** las tapas.	*Yes, and I have also prepared the appetizers.*
—¿Qué **han hecho** Uds. hoy?	*What have you done today?*
—**Hemos trabajado** mucho.	*We've worked very hard.*

B. La formación del presente perfecto. To form the present perfect tense, use the helping verb **haber** *(to have)* and a past participle. The forms of **haber** are **he, has, ha, hemos, habéis, han.**

Presente perfecto: haber + *past participle*

yo	**he trabajado**	*I have worked*
tú	**has comido**	*you have eaten*
Ud./él/ella	**ha salido**	*he/she has left*
nosotros(as)	**hemos visto**	*we have seen*
vosotros(as)	**habéis escrito**	*you (pl.) have written*
Uds./ellos/ellas	**han hecho**	*they have made*

To form the *past participle* of regular verbs, drop the -**ar, -er,** or -**ir** ending of the infinitive and add -**ado** to -**ar** verbs and -**ido** to -**er** and -**ir** verbs.

Infinitive	Past Participle of Regular Verbs	Meaning
comprar	**comprado**	*bought*
comer	**comido**	*eaten*
salir	**salido**	*left, gone out*

Infinitive	Past Participle of Irregular Verbs	Meaning
abrir	**abierto**	*open; opened*
decir	**dicho**	*said; told*
escribir	**escrito**	*written*
hacer	**hecho**	*done; made*
morir	**muerto**	*dead; died*
poner	**puesto**	*put; set; placed*
resolver	**resuelto**	*resolved; solved*
romper	**roto**	*broken*
ver	**visto**	*seen*
volver	**vuelto**	*returned*

Ponerlo a prueba

GS4-1 Los preparativos. Tú y tus amigos van a dar una gran fiesta para celebrar el noviazgo *(engagement)* de su amiga Rosaura. Cada persona tiene ciertas responsabilidades. ¿Qué ha hecho cada persona? Escribe los verbos en el presente perfecto.

1. Yo (mandar) _____ las invitaciones y también (comprar) _____ el vino.

2. Pilar (hacer) _____ una tortilla. Además, (preparar) _____ la sangría.

3. Paco y Sara (poner) _____ la mesa. También (limpiar) _____ el baño.

4. Dina y yo (arreglar) _____ el jardín. Ya (pedir) _____ las flores, también.

5. ¿Y tú? ¿(Alquilar) _____ más sillas? ¿(Ir) _____ al mercado?

Teaching Tip: Assign the first activity for homework.

GS4-2 El trabajo doméstico. La familia Soto va a tener una fiesta en casa esta noche. ¿Qué han hecho todos en anticipación de esta celebración?

MODELO Elvira ha lavado los platos.

Elvira

Enriqueta

Answers GS4-2 *(continued)*: 2. Filomena ha limpiado el garaje. Ha trabajado en el jardín. 3. Gonzalo ha preparado la comida.

2.

Filomena

3.

Gonzalo

GS4-3 ¿Qué has hecho? Usa las siguientes expresiones para conversar con un(a) compañero(a) de clase sobre sus experiencias gastronómicas y culinarias. Sigan el modelo.

MODELO　　comer en un restaurante mexicano

　　　　　　Tú:　¿Has comido en un restaurante mexicano alguna vez *(ever)*?

Tu compañero(a):　Sí, he comido en un restaurante mexicano muchas veces. Me encanta la comida mexicana, especialmente los tamales. ¿Y tú?

　　　　　　O:　No, nunca he comido en un restaurante mexicano, pero me gustaría probar unos platos típicos. ¿Y tú?

1. comer en un restaurante tailandés *(Thai)*

2. probar calamares *(squid)*

3. servir comida mexicana a tus amigos alguna vez *(ever)*

4. beber champaña

5. tomar café italiano

6. cocinar para tu familia

7. trabajar de camarero(a)

8. asistir a una cena de gala *(formal dinner)*

Gramática suplementaria

CAPÍTULO 5

El condicional

🌐 **Heinle Grammar Tutorial:**
The conditional tense 22

What would Hernando do if he had more money? Read the conversation to find out. Then, identify four verbs in the conditional tense.

EUGENIA: Hernando, ¿qué harías si tuvieras más dinero?

HERNANDO: Estaría muy contento. No tendría que trabajar para pagar la matrícula *(tuition)*. Luego, me mudaría de la residencia. Me iría a vivir en un apartamento más amplio y nuevo, y para las vacaciones de primavera, mis amigos y yo haríamos un crucero a las Bahamas.

A. La función del condicional. The conditional verb tense (**el condicional**) is used in three main ways:

▸ to describe what somebody *would* or *could do* or *what would happen* under certain conditions.

English expresses this idea by adding the word *would;* Spanish uses verb endings to convey this meaning.

Si tuviera mucho dinero, **compraría** un coche nuevo.	*If I had more money **I would buy** a new car.*
También, **iría** a las Bahamas de vacaciones.	*Also, **I'd go** to the Bahamas on vacation.*

▸ to indicate politeness, especially with the verbs **gustar, poder,** and **deber.**

Me gustaría informarme sobre programas de estudios en Argentina.	*I would like to get some information about studying abroad in Argentina.*
¿Podría usted ayudarme?	*Could you help me?*
Deberías buscar la información por Internet.	*You should look for the information on the internet.*

▸ to indicate probability in the past.

—¿Por qué no fue Paco a clase hoy?	*—Why didn't Paco go to class today?*
—No sé. **Estaría** enfermo.	*—I don't know. **He must have been** sick.*

B. La formación del condicional. The conditional of most verbs is formed by adding a set of endings to the whole infinitive; the same set of endings is used for -**ar,** -**er,** and -**ir** verbs.

El condicional: verbos regulares

		llegar *(to arrive)*	volver *(to return)*	vivir *(to live)*
yo	-ía	llegaría	volvería	viviría
tú	-ías	llegarías	volverías	vivirías
Ud./él/ella	-ía	llegaría	volvería	viviría
nosotros(as)	-íamos	llegaríamos	volveríamos	viviríamos
vosotros(as)	-íais	llegaríais	volveríais	viviríais
Uds./ellos/ellas	-ían	llegarían	volverían	vivirían

For a number of common verbs, this same set of endings must be added to an *irregular stem;* these are the same irregular stems that are used to form the future tense. (See *Gramática suplementaria, Capítulo 2.*)

El condicional: verbos irregulares

Meaning	Verb	Irregular Stem	Endings	Example
to say, to tell	decir	dir-	-ía	yo haría
to do, to make	hacer	har-	-ías	tú harías
to have	tener	tendr-	-ía	Ud./él/ella haría
to put, to place	poner	pondr-	-íamos	nosotros(as) haríamos
to come	venir	vendr-	-íais	vosotros(as) haríais
to leave, to go	salir	saldr-	-ían	Uds./ellos/ellas harían
to know	saber	sabr-		
to want	querer	querr-		
to be able to	poder	podr-		

The conditional of the verb **hay (haber)** is **habría:**

Habría más gente en el tour, pero está lloviendo.	***There would be** more people on the tour, but it's raining.*

Ponerlo a prueba

GS5-1 Un viaje de estudios a Argentina. ¿Qué harían todos los estudiantes si pudieran estudiar *(if they could study)* en la Argentina? Escoge un verbo lógico de la lista y escríbelo en el condicional.

aprender	comer	hacer	ir
bailar	comprar	gustar	poder

1. Si pudiera estudiar en la Argentina, yo _____ a bailar el tango.
2. Paco _____ una excursión a las montañas de Patagonia.
3. Mis amigas Laura y Raquel _____ de compras en las boutiques de la capital.
4. A Ángel y a Carlos les _____ salir todas las noches para bailar en las discotecas.
5. Todos nosotros _____ bistec, el plato nacional.
6. También nosotros _____ practicar el español todos los días.

GS5-2 En el extranjero. Varios estudiantes en tu clase han recibido una beca *(scholarship)* para estudiar en el extranjero *(abroad)*. Con dos o tres compañeros de clase, contesten las preguntas y conversen sobre el tema. **¡Ojo!** Tienen que usar el condicional.

1. ¿En qué país te gustaría estudiar? ¿Por qué?
2. ¿Cuánto tiempo pasarías allí?
3. ¿Preferirías vivir con una familia o en una residencia con otros estudiantes?
4. ¿Qué ciudades u otros lugares visitarías durante tu estadía *(during your stay)*?
5. ¿Qué esperarías aprender de esta experiencia?

GS5-3 Situaciones hipotéticas. A veces la vida académica nos presenta con situaciones difíciles y dilemas. ¿Qué harías tú en las siguientes situaciones hipotéticas? Incluye un verbo en el condicional en tu respuesta. Compara tus respuestas con las de un(a) compañero(a).

1. Tienes que hacer una presentación oral en una clase y estás muy nervioso(a).
2. Tu carrera es Biología, pero descubres *(you discover)* que no te gustan los laboratorios.
3. Te llevas muy mal *(you don't get along at all)* con tu compañero(a) de cuarto.
4. Estás tomando un examen y observas que un(a) compañero(a) está haciendo trampa *(cheating)*.
5. Tu despertador *(alarm clock)* no sonó y te perdiste *(missed)* tu examen de Filosofía.

Gramática suplementaria

Las expresiones indefinidas y negativas

Isidro is tired of working at the store. Read his blog entry to discover why. Identify three negative expressions (that is, the Spanish equivalents of words like *nothing, nobody, never*).

Estoy harto *(fed up)* de trabajar en esta tienda. Los turistas siempre tocan todo y luego nunca compran nada. Además, no veo ningún futuro en las ventas *(sales)*. Yo quiero hacer algo más creativo.

A. Palabras indefinidas y negativas. Here are the most common negative words (words like *never, nobody, nothing*) and their indefinite or affirmative counterparts (words like *always, somebody, something*). To help you remember these words, notice that nearly all the negative words in Spanish begin with the letter **n.**

Palabras indefinidas/afirmativas y negativas

en inglés	en español
somebody, someone *anybody, anyone*	alguien
nobody, no one *not . . . anybody; not . . . anyone*	nadie no... nadie
something, anything	algo
nothing *not . . . anything*	nada no... nada
always	siempre
never *not . . . ever*	nunca no... nunca
some, any	algún (alguno), alguna, algunos, algunas
no, not one *not . . . any; not . . . a single (one)*	ningún (ninguno), ninguna no.... ningún (ninguno), ninguna
also	también
neither *not . . . either*	tampoco no... tampoco
either . . . or	o... o
neither . . . nor *not . . . or*	ni... ni no... ni... ni

B. Los usos. Spanish uses negative words in some ways that are different from English.

▸ Negative words may be placed before the verb.

Before the verb:	**nadie**	**Nadie** lleva ese estilo.	*Nobody* wears that style.
	nunca	**Nunca** llevo ese color.	I *never* wear that color.

▸ Negative words may also be placed after the verb. In this case, it is necessary to add **no** in front of the verb.

After the verb:	**no... nadie**	**No** hay **nadie** en el probador.	There isn't *anybody* in the fitting room.
	no... nunca	**No** llevo bikini **nunca.**	I *don't ever* wear a bikini.

▸ Several negative words may be used properly in the same sentence in Spanish. English avoids double negatives and generally uses a combination of just one negative word and multiple indefinite words.

Nunca haces **nada** para **nadie**.	You *never* do *anything* for *anyone*.
Nadie nunca me ayuda con **nada**.	*Nobody ever* helps me with *anything*.

C. *Alguno* y *ninguno*. The negative word **ninguno** and the indefinite word **alguno** can be used as pronouns or adjectives. Like all pronouns and adjectives, they have different forms to reflect gender (masculine / feminine) and number (singular / plural).

▸ When used as a pronoun, **alguno** has these forms: **alguno, alguna, algunos, algunas.** When used as an adjective, the forms are **algún, alguna, algunos,** and **algunas.**

Alg**unas** tiend**as** dan descuentos a los turistas.	*Some* stores give discounts to tourists.
¿Quiere comprar **alguno** de estos recuerdos?	Do you want to buy *any* of these souvenirs?

▸ When used as a pronoun, **ninguno** has these forms: **ninguno, ninguna.** When used as an adjective, the forms are **ningún, ninguna.** Notice that the plural forms are not generally used: n̶i̶n̶g̶u̶n̶o̶s̶, n̶i̶n̶g̶u̶n̶a̶s̶.

¿**No** tienes **ningún** amigo español?	*Don't* you have *any* Spanish friends?
No, **no** tengo **ningún** amigo español.	No, I *don't* have *any* Spanish friends. / No, I *don't* have *a single* Spanish friend.
No, **no** tengo **ninguno**.	No, I *don't* have *a single one*.

Ponerlo a prueba

GS6-1 La Sra. Guerra. Cuando la Sra. Guerra piensa en el comportamiento *(behavior)* de su familia, tiene reacciones positivas y negativas. Lee sus reacciones y decide en cada caso si ella está contenta o no. También, subraya *(underline)* todas las expresiones indefinidas y negativas.

> **MODELO**   Nuestros hijos <u>nunca</u> llevan ropa sucia a la escuela.   ☺ ☹

1. Nuestra hija Alicia siempre se viste bien para ir a la iglesia.   ☺ ☹
2. Nuestro hijo nunca se pone corbata cuando lleva traje.   ☺ ☹
3. Nadie quiere lavar la ropa; siempre tengo que lavarla yo.   ☺ ☹
4. Ninguno de nuestros hijos abusa de las tarjetas de crédito.   ☺ ☹
5. Mis hijos siempre me compran aretes bonitos para el Día de las Madres.   ☺ ☹
6. Nuestro hijo Adán nunca pone la ropa sucia en la cesta *(hamper)*. Tampoco quiere limpiar el polvo de los muebles en su cuarto.   ☺ ☹

GS6-2 De mal humor. Reinaldo —un chico de diez años— está de muy mal humor. Lee las conversaciones y complétalas con las palabras negativas o indefinidas más lógicas.

1. **algo**   **alguien**   **nada**   **nadie**

    ABUELITA: Mañana es el cumpleaños de tu hermanita. ¿Vas a comprarle _____ bonito?

    REINALDO: No, abuelita. No voy a comprarle _____, porque ella nunca quiere compartir *(to share)* sus juguetes conmigo.

2. **algún**   **también**   **ningún**   **tampoco**

    MAMÁ: ¿Te gusta tu chaqueta nueva? El color es muy bonito. Te queda perfectamente, _____.

    REINALDO: Yo creo que es muy fea. Y no me gustan mis nuevos pantalones _____.

3. **algunos**   **siempre**   **ninguno**   **nunca**

    PAPÁ: Vamos al centro comercial esta tarde. ¿Quieres invitar a _____ de tus amigos?

    REINALDO: No, papá, no quiero invitar a _____ de mis amigos. ¡Son todos idiotas!

4. **alguien**   **siempre**   **nadie**   **nunca**

    EL HERMANO MAYOR: Mamá, Reinaldo es un chico muy malo. _____ entra en mi dormitorio y usa mis cosas sin *(without)* permiso.

    REINALDO: ¡No es verdad, mamá! _____ entro en su cuarto. Él es un mentiroso *(liar)*.

GS6-3 Las quejas. ¿Cuáles son algunas de las quejas *(complaints)* típicas en las siguientes situaciones? Comparte tus ideas con las de un(a) compañero(a). Incluye palabras negativas o indefinidas en las quejas.

> **MODELO**   Los profesores, sobre los estudiantes.
>   —Los estudiantes **nunca** hacen la tarea.

1. Los turistas, sobre los productos en la tienda de recuerdos.
2. Los estudiantes, sobre sus clases o sus profesores.
3. Los padres, sobre sus hijos.
4. Los turistas, sobre los precios o la calidad de los artículos en el mercado.
5. Los novios o las novias, sobre su pareja *(their partner)*.

Gramática suplementaria

El pluscuamperfecto

⊕ **Heinle Grammar Tutorial:**
The pluperfect tense 33

Isabel is recounting what happened at her friend Susana's birthday party. Why was Susana's mother upset with her son Jaime? What had the family already done to celebrate Susana's birthday before Jaime arrived? Find examples of three verbs in the past perfect.

Cuando Jaime llegó por fin a casa, ya eran las seis de la tarde. Ya habíamos comido el exquisito almuerzo. Susana ya había abierto sus regalos. Y los niños ya habían roto la piñata.

Mamá estaba furiosa: —¿Por qué has llegado tan tarde para el cumpleaños de tu hermana?

A. La función del pluscuamperfecto. The past perfect tense, or pluperfect **(el pluscuamperfecto),** is used to tell what somebody *had done* or what *had happened* before another past event took place.

Susana ya **había abierto** sus regalos cuando Jaime llegó.	Susana **had** already **opened** her presents when Jaime arrived.
Cuando llamaste a Marisol, ya **había salido.**	When you called Marisol, **she had gone out** already.

B. La formación del pluscuamperfecto. To form the past perfect tense, you must use the imperfect form of the verb **haber** and a past participle. The imperfect forms of **haber** are **había, habías, había, habíamos, habíais, habían.**

Pluscuamperfecto: haber + *past participle*

yo	**había estudiado**	*I had studied*
tú	**habías conocido**	*you had met*
Ud./él/ella	**había terminado**	*he/she had finished*
nosotros(as)	**habíamos visto**	*we had seen*
vosotros(as)	**habíais tomado**	*you (pl.) had taken*
Uds./ellos/ellas	**habían hecho**	*they had done*

To form the past participle of most verbs, drop the **-ar, -er,** and **-ir** and add **-ado** to **-ar** verbs and **-ido** to **-er** and **-ir** verbs.

Infinitive	Past Participle of Regular Verbs	Meaning
estudiar	**estudiado**	*studied*
venir	**venido**	*come*
vivir	**vivido**	*lived*

Infinitive	Past Participle of Irregular Verbs	Meaning
abrir	**abierto**	*open; opened*
decir	**dicho**	*said; told*
escribir	**escrito**	*written*
hacer	**hecho**	*done; made*
morir	**muerto**	*dead; died*
poner	**puesto**	*put; set; placed*
resolver	**resuelto**	*resolved; solved*
romper	**roto**	*broken*
ver	**visto**	*seen*
volver	**vuelto**	*returned*

Ponerlo a prueba

Teaching Tip: Assign the first activity for homework.

Answers GS7-1: 1. había visitado; 2. habíamos comido; 3. había visto; 4. habíamos estudiado; 5. habían entrado.

GS7-1 Una excursión. Lee las descripciones del viaje que hicieron Yvonne y Laura. Completa las oraciones con el pluscuamperfecto de los verbos entre paréntesis.

1. El fin de semana pasado, mi amiga Laura y yo fuimos a playa Flamingo. Yo no (visitar) _____ esa playa antes de este viaje.
2. El viernes por la noche, cenamos en un restaurante conocido por sus mariscos. ¡Nosotras nunca (comer) _____ camarones tan frescos y deliciosos!
3. El sábado llovió mucho y no pudimos nadar en el mar. Nunca en mi vida yo (ver) _____ una lluvia tan fuerte.
4. El domingo exploramos el bosque tropical. Nosotras (estudiar) _____ la biodiversidad en una clase, así que reconocimos muchas de las plantas.
5. Cuando llegamos al hotel esa noche, vimos que unos monos *(monkeys)* (entrar) _____ en nuestro cuarto. ¡Qué desorden!

 GS7-2 Antes y después. Entrevista a un(a) compañero(a) sobre las experiencias antes de venir a la universidad. Sigan el modelo.

> **MODELO** estudiar química
>
> Tú: *Antes de venir a la universidad, ¿habías estudiado química?*
>
> Tu compañero(a): *Sí, ya había estudiado química por varios años. / No, no había estudiado química.*

Antes de venir a la universidad...

1. estudiar español
2. vivir lejos de tu familia
3. compartir *(share)* un dormitorio con alguien
4. lavar tu ropa
5. leer tantos libros
6. escribir un trabajo de investigación

 GS7-3 ¿Es verdad? ¿Qué cosas interesantes habías hecho antes de venir a la universidad? Escribe oraciones con cuatro o cinco de tus experiencias extraordinarias. Comparte la información con un(a) compañero(a).

> **MODELO** Cuando tenía cinco años, ya **había participado** en un concurso de belleza *(a beauty contest).*
>
> Cuando tenía diez años, ya **había ganado** una competición de golf.
>
> Cuando tenía doce años, mi familia y yo ya **habíamos visitado** treinta estados diferentes.
>
> Cuando tenía dieciséis años...

Gramática suplementaria

Los mandatos familiares

Heinle Grammar Tutorial:
Informal commands 43

Lucas asks his Ecuadorian friend Micaela for tips on his uncoming trip. What three suggestions does she give him?

LUCAS: Voy a hacer un viaje a Quito el próximo mes. ¿Qué me recomiendas?

MICAELA: Tengo tres sugerencias para ti. Primero, descansa en tu hotel los primeros días porque la altura te va a afectar mucho. Segundo, haz una excursión a las islas Galápagos; son únicas en el mundo. Y finalmente, ¡llévame contigo, porque yo quiero ir también!

A. Los mandatos familiares. Informal commands (**mandatos familiares**) are used to give directions and instructions to people you would normally address with **tú** or **vosotros.** The familiar commands use different verb forms for affirmative and negative commands.

AFFIRMATIVE:	**Habla** espanol durante tu viaje.	***Speak*** *Spanish during your trip.*
NEGATIVE:	**No hables** inglés todo el tiempo.	***Don't speak*** *English all the time.*

B. El mandato familiar afirmativo. The affirmative **tú** command uses the same verb form as the **él/ella** form of the present tense.

Infinitive	*él/ella* **Present Form**	**Affirmative *tú* Command**
respetar	respeta	**Respeta** las costumbres del país. *Respect the customs of the country.*
aprender	aprende	**Aprende** el idioma del país. *Learn the language of the country.*
pedir	pide	**Pide** información sobre las vacunas. *Ask for information about vaccines.*

Many common verbs have irregular affirmative **tú** commands:

Infinitive	Affirmative *tú* Command
decir	**di**
hacer	**haz**
ir	**ve**
poner	**pon**
salir	**sal**
ser	**sé**
tener	**ten**
venir	**ven**

C. El mandato familiar negativo. In order to tell somebody what *not* to do, you need to use a negative command. To form the negative **tú** command of most verbs, follow this two-step procedure.

- First, conjugate the verb in the **yo** form of the present tense.
- Then, drop the -**o** and add -**es** to -**ar** verbs, and -**as** to -**er** and -**ir** verbs.

Infinitive	*yo* Present Form	Negative *tú* Command
tomar	tomø + es	**no tomes**
poner	pongø + as	**no pongas**
salir	salgø + as	**no salgas**

Here are the irregular negative **tú** commands.

Infinitive	Negative *tú* Command
dar	**no des**
estar	**no estés**
ir	**no vayas**
saber	**no sepas**
ser	**no seas**

D. El mandato familiar plural. Plural commands are used to give instructions or directions to two or more people. In Latin America the **formal** plural commands (**ustedes**) may be used for friends and strangers alike. In Spain, however, the **ustedes** commands are used only for formal situations; to give commands and instructions to several friends or family members, the **vosotros** command is used.

- The affirmative **vosotros** command is formed by dropping the -**r** of the infinitive and adding -**d.**
- The negative **vosotros** command is formed by first conjugating the verb in the **yo** form of the present tense and then dropping the -**o** and adding -**éis** to -**ar** verbs and -**áis** to -**er** and -**ir** verbs.

Infinitive	Affirmative *vosotros* Command	Negative *vosotros* Command
trabajar	**¡Trabajad!**	**¡No trabajéis** tanto!
comer	**¡Comed!**	**¡No comáis** ahora!
venir	**¡Venid!**	**¡No vengáis** tan temprano!

E. Los mandatos con complementos y pronombres reflexivos. Commands are often used together with reflexive pronouns and/or with direct and indirect object pronouns.

- With affirmative commands, the pronouns are attached to the end of the command, and an accent mark is added on the third to last syllable.
- With negative commands, the pronouns are placed in front of the verb.

| AFFIRMATIVE: | ¡Levántate! | *Get up!* |
| NEGATIVE: | ¡No **te** levantes! | *Don't get up!* |

Ponerlo a prueba

GS8-1 Los consejos. Aquí tienes unos consejos para tu viaje a Ecuador. Escribe los verbos en la forma apropiada de los mandatos familiares **(tú).**

> **MODELO**   (Beber) <u>Bebe</u> el agua embotellada.
>   (No beber) <u>No bebas</u> el agua del grifo.

1. (Llevar) _____ tu medicina en una bolsa de mano.
   (No llevar) _____ más de dos maletas.

2. (Comer) _____ los platos típicos del país.
   (No comer) _____ la comida por la calle porque puedes enfermarte.

3. (Viajar) _____ en avión cuando puedas.
   (No viajar) _____ en autobús porque vas a perder mucho tiempo.

4. (Hacer) _____ un itinerario.
   (No hacer) _____ muchos planes para el primer día, porque necesitas recuperarte del *jetlag*.

5. (Poner) _____ tu pasaporte en un lugar seguro *(secure)*.
   (No ponerlo) _____ en tu maleta.

6. (Ir) _____ a la selva amazónica para ver la increíble variedad de flora y fauna.
   Pero (no ir) _____ solo(a). Es muy fácil perderse.

7. (Acostarse) _____ temprano porque necesitas conservar la energía.
   Pero (no acostarse) _____ sin mosquitero *(mosquito netting)*.

 GS8-2 Haciendo ejercicio. Tú y tu compañero(a) tienen que ponerse en forma para unas vacaciones de aventura. Aquí tienen las instrucciones para hacer ejercicios típicos de entrenamiento. Cambia los infinitivos a mandatos familiares y lee las instrucciones en voz alta. Tu compañero(a) tiene que hacer el ejercicio.

1. **Separar** los pies y **subir** los brazos. **Bajar** la mano derecha hasta tocar el pie izquierdo, y vice versa. **Repetir** el ejercicio treinta veces. Después, **inhalar** profundamente y **expulsar** el aire con lentitud.

2. **Marchar** en el mismo lugar por treinta segundos. **Comenzar** con el pie izquierdo y **flexionar** la rodilla derecha hasta llevarla a la altura del pecho. Luego, **cambiar** de pierna rápidamente, y **ejercitarse** otros treinta segundos.

3. **Correr** en el mismo lugar. **Tratar** de mantener el ritmo desde el principio hasta el final. **Contraer** los muslos *(thighs)* al subir las piernas, para relajar la espalda.

GS8-3 Por favor. Te vas de viaje por unos días y un(a) amigo(a) va a cuidar a tu perro y tu apartamento. Dale instrucciones sobre qué debe hacer durante tu ausencia. Usa mandatos familiares. Comparte tus ideas con un(a) compañero(a).

> **MODELO**   **Saca** a mi perrito a pasear todos los días.

Teaching Tip: Assign the first activity for homework.

Answers GS8-1: 1. Lleva, No lleves; 2. Come, No comas; 3. Viaja, No viajes; 4. Haz, No hagas; 5. Pon, No lo pongas; 6. Ve, no vayas; 7. Acuéstate, no te acuestes

Expansion: Have students continue giving instructions for other kinds of exercises.

Answers GS8-2: 1. Separa, sube, Baja, Repite, inhala, explusa; 2. Marcha, Comienza, flexiona, cambia, ejercítate; 3. Corre, Trata, Contrae.

Gramática suplementaria

El subjuntivo en cláusulas adjetivales

Read the conversation between Claudia and her mother, Eliana. According to Claudia, what kind of man is her fiancé Rolando? What objections does her mother have to this marriage? As you read the conversation, identify any verbs that are in the present subjunctive.

ELIANA: ¿Es cierto que vas a casarte con Rolando?

CLAUDIA: Sí, mamá. Creo que somos muy compatibles. Rolando es un hombre que vive intensamente. Es mi media naranja *(the perfect mate)*.

ELIANA: Sí, sí, ya lo creo, mi hija. Pero, por favor, piénsalo bien. Rolando ya se ha divorciado dos veces y tiene tres hijos. Debes casarte con un hombre que tenga menos obligaciones.

A. Las cláusulas adjetivales. As you know, the subjunctive is used after verbs that express wishes, feelings, uncertainty, and denial. In all these cases, the sentences follow the special three-part pattern and the subjunctive is used after the word **que.**

Main Clause			Dependent Noun Clause	
	subject + verb	+ *que*	+ subject	+ verb
(wishes/wants)	Eliana no quiere	que	su hija	**se case** con Rolando.
(feelings/ emotions)	Ella tiene miedo de	que	él	**sea** un don Juan.
(doubt/denial)	Ella duda	que	él	**ame** de verdad a su hija.

Another kind of dependent clause is known as an *adjectival* clause. Adjectival clauses describe a noun in the main part of the sentence.

	noun	+ *que*	+verb
Claudia debe casarse con	**un hombre**	que	**tenga** menos obligaciones.
Claudia should marry	***a man***	*who*	***has*** *fewer obligations.*
Claudia necesita	**un esposo**	que	**sea** más responsable.
Claudia needs	***a husband***	*who*	***is*** *more responsible.*

B. El subjuntivo en las cláusulas adjetivales. In adjectival clauses, the verb may be used in the present indicative or in the present subjunctive, depending on circumstances.

▶ Use the **present subjunctive** when the adjective clause describes a person, place, or thing that is *nonspecific, hypothetical,* or *nonexistent.*

Necesitamos una secretaria que **hable** japonés.
(We need a secretary with that talent; we have no one specific in mind.)

> Quiero encontrar un puesto que **ofrezca** oportunidades para viajar.
> *(I would like a job that offers such a possibility, but I don't know of any for certain; it is hypothetical.)*
>
> No hay nadie que **trabaje** tanto como Elisondo.
> *(There is no one who works harder; that kind of person does not exist.)*

▸ Use the **present indicative** when the adjective clause describes persons, places, or things that are *specific* or *known* to the person speaking.

> Tenemos una secretaria que **habla** francés y alemán.
> *(We already have such a person; the adjective clause describes a specific person.)*
>
> Aquí hay dos anuncios para puestos que **ofrecen** buenos beneficios.
> *(The ads refer to known, specific jobs that offer good benefits.)*

Ponerlo a prueba

GS9-1 Los profesores. ¿Qué piensa Héctor de sus profesores? Lee las descripciones y escoge entre el presente del indicativo y el presente del subjuntivo en cada caso.

1. Tengo un profesor que me (vuelve / vuelva) loco.

2. En clase, él da conferencias que no (tienen / tengan) sentido *(don't make sense)*.

3. Además, es muy quisquilloso. Siempre nos da exámenes que (son / sean) muy largos y difíciles.

4. El próximo semestre espero tener algún profesor que me (inspira / inspire) a aprender.

5. Sé que es necesario tener exámenes. Pero, los profesores deben asignarnos también algún proyecto que (estimula / estimule) la creatividad.

6. Para mí, las conferencias son un método anticuado de impartir la información. Los profesores deben emplear algún método que (incluye / incluya) los últimos avances tecnológicos.

GS9-2 Frustraciones y esperanzas. Lee los siguientes diálogos y completa los espacios en blanco con el presente del indicativo o el presente del subjuntivo, según el caso.

1. **Problemas del corazón**

    GLORIA: ¿Qué te pasa, Graciela? Parece que estás muy triste.

    GRACIELA: Sí, creo que voy a romper con Luis.

    GLORIA: Pero, ¿por qué? Luis es un hombre que te _____ (amar) mucho y que te _____ (poder) ofrecer todo lo mejor de la vida.

    GRACIELA: Sí, sé que él es muy serio y responsable. Pero yo quiero casarme con un hombre que _____ (ser) más romántico, uno que me _____ (traer) flores y que me _____ (llevar) a lugares exóticos.

    GLORIA: ¡Ay, Graciela! Te estás portando *(You are behaving)* como una adolescente de dieciséis años.

2. **Problemas de trabajo**

ALICIA: Acabo de enterarme de que dejas *(you are leaving)* la compañía, Eduardo. ¿Ya tienes otro puesto?

EDUARDO: Sí, Alicia, y es maravilloso. Es con una compañía que _____ (tener) muy buena reputación en sistemas electrónicos. Además, me han dado *(they have given)* un puesto que _____ (ofrecer) buenas posibilidades de ascenso *(promotion)*.

ALICIA: ¡Qué buena suerte! Algún día, yo también espero irme de aquí. Quiero trabajar para una compañía que _____ (estar) más cerca de la casa de mi mamá. También, sueño con *(I dream about)* tener mi propia oficina, una que yo no _____ (tener) que compartir con nadie.

EDUARDO: Mira, Alicia, en mi nueva compañía, sé que buscan un contador que _____ (saber) usar computadoras. ¿Por qué no solicitas el puesto?

GS9-3 Pensando en el futuro. ¿Cuáles son tus sueños *(dreams)* y esperanzas para el futuro? Primero, completa las siguientes frases; usa el presente del indicativo o el presente del subjuntivo, según el caso. Después, compara tus respuestas con las de tu compañero(a) de clase.

1. Ahora, vivo en (un lugar / una ciudad) que...
   Algún día, quiero vivir en (un lugar / una ciudad) que...

2. Ahora, vivo en (una residencia / una casa / un apartamento) que...
   En el futuro, espero tener (una casa / un apartamento) que...

3. Con respecto al trabajo, prefiero un puesto que...
   No quiero un puesto que...

4. Quiero vivir con (un hombre / una mujer) que...
   No quiero casarme con (un hombre / una mujer) que...

Appendices

Appendix A *Regular Verbs*

Simple Tenses

Infinitive	Present Indicative	Imperfect	Preterite	Future	Conditional	Present Subjunctive	Past Subjunctive	Commands
hablar *to speak*	hablo	hablaba	hablé	hablaré	hablaría	hable	hablara	
	hablas	hablabas	hablaste	hablarás	hablarías	hables	hablaras	habla (no hables)
	habla	hablaba	habló	hablará	hablaría	hable	hablara	(no) hable
	hablamos	hablábamos	hablamos	hablaremos	hablaríamos	hablemos	habláramos	hablemos
	habláis	hablabais	hablasteis	hablaréis	hablaríais	habléis	hablarais	hablad (no habléis)
	hablan	hablaban	hablaron	hablarán	hablarían	hablen	hablaran	(no) hablen
aprender *to learn*	aprendo	aprendía	aprendí	aprenderé	aprendería	aprenda	aprendiera	
	aprendes	aprendías	aprendiste	aprenderás	aprenderías	aprendas	aprendieras	aprende (no aprendas)
	aprende	aprendía	aprendió	aprenderá	aprendería	aprenda	aprendiera	(no) aprenda
	aprendemos	aprendíamos	aprendimos	aprenderemos	aprenderíamos	aprendamos	aprendiéramos	aprendamos
	aprendéis	aprendíais	aprendisteis	aprenderéis	aprenderíais	aprendáis	aprendierais	aprended (no aprendáis)
	aprenden	aprendían	aprendieron	aprenderán	aprenderían	aprendan	aprendieran	(no) aprendan
vivir *to live*	vivo	vivía	viví	viviré	viviría	viva	viviera	
	vives	vivías	viviste	vivirás	vivirías	vivas	vivieras	vive (no vivas)
	vive	vivía	vivió	vivirá	viviría	viva	viviera	(no) viva
	vivimos	vivíamos	vivimos	viviremos	viviríamos	vivamos	viviéramos	vivamos
	vivís	vivíais	vivisteis	viviréis	viviríais	viváis	vivierais	vivid (no viváis)
	viven	vivían	vivieron	vivirán	vivirían	vivan	vivieran	(no) vivan

Compound Tenses

Present progressive	estoy estás está estamos estáis están	hablando	aprendiendo	viviendo
Present perfect indicative	he has ha hemos habéis han	hablado	aprendido	vivido
Present perfect subjunctive	haya hayas haya hayamos hayáis hayan	hablado	aprendido	vivido
Past perfect indicative	había habías había habíamos habíais habían	hablado	aprendido	vivido

Appendix B Stem-changing Verbs

Infinitive / Present Participle / Past Participle	Present Indicative	Imperfect	Preterite	Future	Conditional	Present Subjunctive	Past Subjunctive	Commands
pensar *to think* e → ie pensando pensado	**pienso** **piensas** **piensa** pensamos pensáis **piensan**	pensaba pensabas pensaba pensábamos pensabais pensaban	pensé pensaste pensó pensamos pensasteis pensaron	pensaré pensarás pensará pensaremos pensaréis pensarán	pensaría pensarías pensaría pensaríamos pensaríais pensarían	**piense** **pienses** **piense** pensemos penséis **piensen**	pensara pensaras pensara pensáramos pensarais pensaran	**piensa** (no **pienses**) (no) **piense** pensemos pensad (no **penséis**) (no) **piensen**
acostarse *to go to bed* o → ue acostándose acostado	me **acuesto** te **acuestas** se **acuesta** nos acostamos os acostáis se **acuestan**	me acostaba te acostabas se acostaba nos acostábamos os acostabais se acostaban	me acosté te acostaste se acostó nos acostamos os acostasteis se acostaron	me acostaré te acostarás se acostará nos acostaremos os acostaréis se acostarán	me acostaría te acostarías se acostaría nos acostaríamos os acostaríais se acostarían	me **acueste** te **acuestes** se **acueste** nos acostemos os acostéis se **acuesten**	me acostara te acostaras se acostara nos acostáramos os acostarais se acostaran	acuéstate (no te acuestes) (no) acuéstese acostémonos acostaos (no os acostéis) (no) acuéstense
sentir *to be sorry* e → ie, i sintiendo sentido	**siento** **sientes** **siente** sentimos sentís **sienten**	sentía sentías sentía sentíamos sentíais sentían	sentí sentiste **sintió** sentimos sentisteis **sintieron**	sentiré sentirás sentirá sentiremos sentiréis sentirán	sentiría sentirías sentiría sentiríamos sentiríais sentirían	**sienta** **sientas** **sienta** **sintamos** **sintáis** **sientan**	**sintiera** **sintieras** **sintiera** **sintiéramos** **sintierais** **sintieran**	**siente** (no **sientas**) (no) **sienta** **sintamos** sentid (no **sintáis**) (no) **sientan**
pedir *to ask for* e → i, i pidiendo pedido	**pido** **pides** **pide** pedimos pedís **piden**	pedía pedías pedía pedíamos pedíais pedían	pedí pediste **pidió** pedimos pedisteis **pidieron**	pediré pedirás pedirá pediremos pediréis pedirán	pediría pedirías pediría pediríamos pediríais pedirían	**pida** **pidas** **pida** **pidamos** **pidáis** **pidan**	**pidiera** **pidieras** **pidiera** **pidiéramos** **pidierais** **pidieran**	**pide** (no **pidas**) (no) **pida** **pidamos** pedid (no **pidáis**) (no) **pidan**
dormir *to sleep* o → ue, u durmiendo dormido	**duermo** **duermes** **duerme** dormimos dormís **duermen**	dormía dormías dormía dormíamos dormíais dormían	dormí dormiste **durmió** dormimos dormisteis **durmieron**	dormiré dormirás dormirá dormiremos dormiréis dormirán	dormiría dormirías dormiría dormiríamos dormiríais dormirían	**duerma** **duermas** **duerma** **durmamos** **durmáis** **duerman**	**durmiera** **durmieras** **durmiera** **durmiéramos** **durmierais** **durmieran**	**duerme** (no **duermas**) (no) **duerma** **durmamos** dormid (no **durmáis**) (no) **duerman**

Appendix C Change of Spelling Verbs

Infinitive / Present Participle / Past Participle	Present Indicative	Imperfect	Preterite	Future	Conditional	Present Subjunctive	Past Subjunctive	Commands
comenzar (e → ie) to begin z → c before e comenzando comenzado	comienzo comienzas comienza comenzamos comenzáis comienzan	comenzaba comenzabas comenzaba comenzábamos comenzabais comenzaban	**comencé** comenzaste comenzó comenzamos comenzasteis comenzaron	comenzaré comenzarás comenzará comenzaremos comenzaréis comenzarán	comenzaría comenzarías comenzaría comenzaríamos comenzaríais comenzarían	**comience** **comiences** **comience** **comencemos** **comencéis** **comiencen**	comenzara comenzaras comenzara comenzáramos comenzarais comenzaran	comienza (**no comiences**) (**no**) **comience** comencemos comenzad (**no comencéis**) (**no**) **comiencen**
conocer to know c → zc before a, o conociendo conocido	**conozco** conoces conoce conocemos conocéis conocen	conocía conocías conocía conocíamos conocíais conocían	conocí conociste conoció conocimos conocisteis conocieron	conoceré conocerás conocerá conoceremos conoceréis conocerán	conocería conocerías conocería conoceríamos conoceríais conocerían	**conozca** **conozcas** **conozca** **conozcamos** **conozcáis** **conozcan**	conociera conocieras conociera conociéramos conocierais conocieran	conoce (**no conozcas**) (**no**) **conozca** conozcamos conoced (**no conozcáis**) (**no**) **conozcan**
construir to build i → y; y inserted before a, e, o construyendo construido	**construyo** **construyes** **construye** construimos construís **construyen**	construía construías construía construíamos construíais construían	construí construiste **construyó** construimos construisteis **construyeron**	construiré construirás construirá construiremos construiréis construirán	construiría construirías construiría construiríamos construiríais construirían	**construya** **construyas** **construya** **construyamos** **construyáis** **construyan**	**construyera** **construyeras** **construyera** **construyéramos** **construyerais** **construyeran**	**construye** (**no construyas**) (**no**) **construya** construyamos construid (**no construyáis**) (**no**) **construyan**
leer to read i → y; stressed i → í leyendo leído	leo lees lee leemos leéis leen	leía leías leía leíamos leíais leían	leí leíste **leyó** leímos leísteis **leyeron**	leeré leerás leerá leeremos leeréis leerán	leería leerías leería leeríamos leeríais leerían	lea leas lea leamos leáis lean	**leyera** **leyeras** **leyera** **leyéramos** **leyerais** **leyeran**	lee (no leas) (no) lea leamos leed (no leáis) (no) lean

Appendix C   Change of Spelling Verbs (continued)

Infinitive Present Participle Past Participle	Present Indicative	Imperfect	Preterite	Future	Conditional	Present Subjunctive	Past Subjunctive	Commands
pagar *to pay* **g → gu before e** pagando pagado	pago pagas paga pagamos pagáis pagan	pagaba pagabas pagaba pagábamos pagabais pagaban	**pagué** pagaste pagó pagamos pagasteis pagaron	pagaré pagarás pagará pagaremos pagaréis pagarán	pagaría pagarías pagaría pagaríamos pagaríais pagarían	**pague** **pagues** **pague** **paguemos** **paguéis** **paguen**	pagara pagaras pagara pagáramos pagarais pagaran	paga (no pagues) (no) pague paguemos pagad (no paguéis) (no) paguen
seguir (e → i, i) *to follow* **gu → g before a, o** siguiendo seguido	**sigo** sigues sigue seguimos seguís siguen	seguía seguías seguía seguíamos seguíais seguían	seguí seguiste siguió seguimos seguisteis siguieron	seguiré seguirás seguirá seguiremos seguiréis seguirán	seguiría seguirías seguiría seguiríamos seguiríais seguirían	**siga** **sigas** **siga** **sigamos** **sigáis** **sigan**	siguiera siguieras siguiera siguiéramos siguierais siguieran	sigue (no sigas) (no) siga sigamos seguid (no sigáis) (no) sigan
tocar *to play, touch* **c → qu before e** tocando tocado	toco tocas toca tocamos tocáis tocan	tocaba tocabas tocaba tocábamos tocabais tocaban	**toqué** tocaste tocó tocamos tocasteis tocaron	tocaré tocarás tocará tocaremos tocaréis tocarán	tocaría tocarías tocaría tocaríamos tocaríais tocarían	**toque** **toques** **toque** **toquemos** **toquéis** **toquen**	tocara tocaras tocara tocáramos tocarais tocaran	toca (no toques) (no) toque toquemos tocad (no toquéis) (no) toquen

Appendix D *Irregular Verbs*

Infinitive Present Participle Past Participle	Present Indicative	Imperfect	Preterite	Future	Conditional	Present Subjunctive	Past Subjunctive	Commands
andar *to walk* andando andado	ando andas anda andamos andáis andan	andaba andabas andaba andábamos andabais andaban	anduve anduviste anduvo anduvimos anduvisteis anduvieron	andaré andarás andará andaremos andaréis andarán	andaría andarías andaría andaríamos andaríais andarían	ande andes ande andemos andéis anden	anduviera anduvieras anduviera anduviéramos anduvierais anduvieran	anda (no andes) (no) ande andemos andad (no andéis) (no) anden
*caer *to fall* cayendo caído	caigo caes cae caemos caéis caen	caía caías caía caíamos caíais caían	caí caíste cayó caímos caísteis cayeron	caeré caerás caerá caeremos caeréis caerán	caería caerías caería caeríamos caeríais caerían	caiga caigas caiga caigamos caigáis caigan	cayera cayeras cayera cayéramos cayerais cayeran	cae (no caigas) (no) caiga caigamos caed (no caigáis) (no) caigan
*dar *to give* dando dado	doy das da damos dais dan	daba dabas daba dábamos dabais daban	di diste dio dimos disteis dieron	daré darás dará daremos daréis darán	daría darías daría daríamos daríais darían	dé des dé demos deis den	diera dieras diera diéramos dierais dieran	da (no des) (no) dé demos dad (no deis) (no) den
*decir to say, tell diciendo dicho	digo dices dice decimos decís dicen	decía decías decía decíamos decíais decían	dije dijiste dijo dijimos dijisteis dijeron	diré dirás dirá diremos diréis dirán	diría dirías diría diríamos diríais dirían	diga digas diga digamos digáis digan	dijera dijeras dijera dijéramos dijerais dijeran	di (no digas) (no) diga digamos decid (no digáis) (no) digan
*estar *to be* estando estado	estoy estás está estamos estáis están	estaba estabas estaba estábamos estabais estaban	estuve estuviste estuvo estuvimos estuvisteis estuvieron	estaré estarás estará estaremos estaréis estarán	estaría estarías estaría estaríamos estaríais estarían	esté estés esté estemos estéis estén	estuviera estuvieras estuviera estuviéramos estuvierais estuvieran	está (no estés) (no) esté estemos estad (no estéis) (no) estén

*Verbs with irregular *yo* forms in the present indicative

Infinitive Present Participle Past Participle	Present Indicative	Imperfect	Preterite	Future	Conditional	Present Subjunctive	Past Subjunctive	Commands
haber *to have* habiendo habido	he has ha [hay] hemos habéis han	había habías había habíamos habíais habían	hube hubiste hubo hubimos hubisteis hubieron	habré habrás habrá habremos habréis habrán	habría habrías habría habríamos habríais habrían	haya hayas haya hayamos hayáis hayan	hubiera hubieras hubiera hubiéramos hubierais hubieran	
*hacer *to make, do* haciendo hecho	hago haces hace hacemos hacéis hacen	hacía hacías hacía hacíamos hacíais hacían	hice hiciste hizo hicimos hicisteis hicieron	haré harás hará haremos haréis harán	haría harías haría haríamos haríais harían	haga hagas haga hagamos hagáis hagan	hiciera hicieras hiciera hiciéramos hicierais hicieran	haz (no hagas) (no) haga hagamos haced (no hagáis) (no) hagan
ir *to go* yendo ido	voy vas va vamos vais van	iba ibas iba íbamos ibais iban	fui fuiste fue fuimos fuisteis fueron	iré irás irá iremos iréis irán	iría irías iría iríamos iríais irían	vaya vayas vaya vayamos vayáis vayan	fuera fueras fuera fuéramos fuerais fueran	ve (no vayas) (no) vaya vayamos id (no vayáis) (no) vayan
*oír *to hear* oyendo oído	oigo oyes oye oímos oís oyen	oía oías oía oíamos oíais oían	oí oíste oyó oímos oísteis oyeron	oiré oirás oirá oiremos oiréis oirán	oiría oirías oiría oiríamos oiríais oirían	oiga oigas oiga oigamos oigáis oigan	oyera oyeras oyera oyéramos oyerais oyeran	oye (no oigas) (no) oiga oigamos oíd (no oigáis) (no) oigan
poder (o → ue) *can, to be able* pudiendo podido	puedo puedes puede podemos podéis pueden	podía podías podía podíamos podíais podían	pude pudiste pudo pudimos pudisteis pudieron	podré podrás podrá podremos podréis podrán	podría podrías podría podríamos podríais podrían	pueda puedas pueda podamos podáis puedan	pudiera pudieras pudiera pudiéramos pudierais pudieran	

*Verbs with irregular *yo* forms in the present indicative

Infinitive Present Participle Past Participle	Present Indicative	Imperfect	Preterite	Future	Conditional	Present Subjunctive	Past Subjunctive	Commands
*poner to place, put poniendo **puesto***	**pongo** pones pone ponemos ponéis ponen	ponía ponías ponía poníamos poníais ponían	**puse pusiste puso pusimos pusisteis pusieron**	**pondré pondrás pondrá pondremos pondréis pondrán**	**pondría pondrías pondría pondríamos pondríais pondrían**	**ponga pongas ponga pongamos pongáis pongan**	**pusiera pusieras pusiera pusiéramos pusierais pusieran**	**pon (no pongas)** (no) **ponga** pongamos poned (**no pongáis**) (no) **pongan**
querer (e → ie) to want, wish queriendo querido	**quiero quieres quiere** queremos queréis **quieren**	quería querías quería queríamos queríais querían	**quise quisiste quiso quisimos quisisteis quisieron**	**querré querrás querrá querremos querréis querrán**	**querría querrías querría querríamos querríais querrían**	**quiera quieras quiera** queramos queráis **quieran**	**quisiera quisieras quisiera quisiéramos quisierais quisieran**	**quiere (no quieras)** (no) **quiera** queramos quered (no queráis) (no) **quieran**
reír to laugh **riendo** **reído**	**río ríes ríe reímos** reís **ríen**	reía reías reía reíamos reíais reían	reí **reíste rio reímos reísteis rieron**	reiré reirás reirá reiremos reiréis reirán	reiría reirías reiría reiríamos reiríais reirían	**ría rías ría riamos riáis rían**	**riera rieras riera riéramos rierais rieran**	**ríe (no rías)** (no) **ría** riamos **reíd (no riáis)** (no) **rían**
saber to know sabiendo sabido	**sé** sabes sabe sabemos sabéis saben	sabía sabías sabía sabíamos sabíais sabían	**supe supiste supo supimos supisteis supieron**	**sabré sabrás sabrá sabremos sabréis sabrán**	**sabría sabrías sabría sabríamos sabríais sabrían**	**sepa sepas sepa sepamos sepáis sepan**	**supiera supieras supiera supiéramos supierais supieran**	sabe (**no sepas**) (no) **sepa** sepamos sabed (**no sepáis**) (no) **sepan**
salir to go out saliendo salido	**salgo** sales sale salimos salís salen	salía salías salía salíamos salíais salían	salí saliste salió salimos salisteis salieron	**saldré saldrás saldrá saldremos saldréis saldrán**	**saldría saldrías saldría saldríamos saldríais saldrían**	**salga salgas salga salgamos salgáis salgan**	saliera salieras saliera saliéramos salierais salieran	**sal (no salgas)** (no) **salga** salgamos salid (**no salgáis**) (no) **salgan**

*Verbs with irregular *yo* forms in the present indicative

Appendix D *Irregular Verbs (continued)*

Infinitive Present Participle Past Participle	Present Indicative	Imperfect	Preterite	Future	Conditional	Present Subjunctive	Past Subjunctive	Commands
ser *to be* siendo sido	soy eres es somos sois son	era eras era éramos erais eran	fui fuiste fue fuimos fuisteis fueron	seré serás será seremos seréis serán	sería serías sería seríamos seríais serían	sea seas sea seamos seáis sean	fuera fueras fuera fuéramos fuerais fueran	sé (no seas) (no) sea seamos sed (no seáis) (no) sean
*tener *to have* teniendo tenido	tengo tienes tiene tenemos tenéis tienen	tenía tenías tenía teníamos teníais tenían	tuve tuviste tuvo tuvimos tuvisteis tuvieron	tendré tendrás tendrá tendremos tendréis tendrán	tendría tendrías tendría tendríamos tendríais tendrían	tenga tengas tenga tengamos tengáis tengan	tuviera tuvieras tuviera tuviéramos tuvierais tuvieran	ten (no tengas) (no) tenga tengamos tened (no tengáis) (no) tengan
traer *to bring* trayendo traído	traigo traes trae traemos traéis traen	traía traías traía traíamos traíais traían	traje trajiste trajo trajimos trajisteis trajeron	traeré traerás traerá traeremos traeréis traerán	traería traerías traería traeríamos traeríais traerían	traiga traigas traiga traigamos traigáis traigan	trajera trajeras trajera trajéramos trajerais trajeran	trae (no traigas) (no) traiga traigamos traed (no traigáis) (no) traigan
*venir *to come* viniendo venido	vengo vienes viene venimos venís vienen	venía venías venía veníamos veníais venían	vine viniste vino vinimos vinisteis vinieron	vendré vendrás vendrá vendremos vendréis vendrán	vendría vendrías vendría vendríamos vendríais vendrían	venga vengas venga vengamos vengáis vengan	viniera vinieras viniera viniéramos vinierais vinieran	ven (no vengas) (no) venga vengamos venid (no vengáis) (no) vengan
ver *to see* viendo visto	veo ves ve vemos veis ven	veía veías veía veíamos veíais veían	vi viste vio vimos visteis vieron	veré verás verá veremos veréis verán	vería verías vería veríamos veríais verían	vea veas vea veamos veáis vean	viera vieras viera viéramos vierais vieran	ve (no veas) (no) vea veamos ved (no veáis) (no) vean

*Verbs with irregular *yo* forms in the present indicative

Appendix E *Pronoun Chart*

Subject pronouns

► Subject pronouns identify the topic of the sentence, and often indicate who or what is performing an action.

► Subject pronouns are generally used in Spanish only for clarification or for emphasis.

► The subject pronouns **Ud.** and **Uds.** are often used as a sign of courtesy.

► There is no Spanish equivalent for *it* as the subject of a sentence.

I	**yo**	*we*	**nosotros / nosotras**
you	{ **tú** **usted (Ud.)**	*you (plural)*	{ **vosotros / vosotras** **ustedes (Uds.)**
he	**él**	*they*	**ellos / ellas**
she	**ella**		
it	**Ø**		

Reflexive pronouns

► Reflexive pronouns are used with reflexive verbs such as **despertarse, bañarse,** and **divertirse.**

► Reflexive pronouns are often translated into English as *myself, yourself, himself,* etc.

► Sometimes the reflexive meaning is simply understood, or is expressed in other ways.

► The plural reflexive pronouns **nos, os,** and **se** may also be used reciprocally, to mean *each other* or *one another.* (Elena y Marta **se** escriben. *Elena and Marta write to each other.*)

(yo)	**me** lavo	*I wash myself*	(nosotros)	**nos** lavamos	*we wash ourselves*
(tú)	**te** lavas	*you wash yourself*	(vosotros)	**os** laváis	*you wash yourselves*
(Ud.)	**se** lava	*you wash yourself*	(Uds.)	**se** lavan	*you wash yourselves*
(él/ella)	**se** lava	*he/she washes him/herself*	(ellos/ellas)	**se** lavan	*they wash themselves*

Indirect object pronouns

► Indirect object pronouns indicate *to whom* or *for whom* something is done. Occasionally, they express the notions *from whom* or *of whom.*

► Indirect object pronouns are placed before a conjugated verb, or attached to an infinitive.

► Indirect object pronouns are used with the verb **gustar** and with similar verbs such as **encantar, importar, interesar, parecer.**

► **Le** and **les** are often used together with proper nouns or equivalent noun phrases. (**Le** escribí una carta **a mi padre.**)

► When used with direct object pronouns, **le** and **les** are replaced by **se.** (**Le** escribí una carta **a mi padre.** → **Se** la escribí ayer.)

to me	**me**	to us	**nos**
to you	{ **te** **le**	to you (plural)	{ **os** **les**
to him/her/it	**le**	to/for them	**les**

Direct object pronouns

▶ Direct object pronouns answer the questions *whom* or *what* with respect to the verb. They receive the action of the verb.

▶ Direct object pronouns are placed before a conjugated verb, or attached to an infinitive.

▶ Direct object pronouns are placed **after** any other indirect object pronoun or reflexive pronoun. (¿La falda? Mamá me **la** regaló para mi cumpleaños.)

me	**me**	*us*	**nos**
you	{ **te** **lo** (masc.) **la** (fem.)	*you* (plural)	{ **os** **los** (masc.) **las** (fem.)
him, it	**lo**	*them*	{ **los** (masc.)
her, it	**la**		**las** (fem.)

Prepositional pronouns

▶ Prepositional pronouns are used after prepositions such as **de, para, por, con, sin, cerca de,** etc.

▶ After the preposition **con,** you must use certain special forms to express *with me* (**conmigo**) and *with you* (familiar) (**contigo**).

▶ Subject pronouns, rather than prepositional pronouns, are used after the propositions **entre** *(between),* and **según** *(according to).*

mí	**nosotros / nosotras**
ti	**vosotros / vosotras**
usted (Ud.)	**ustedes (Uds.)**
él / ella	**ellos / ellas**

Possessive adjectives

▶ The forms of possessive adjectives look very much like the forms of various kinds of pronouns. These words, however, are always used together with a noun in order to indicate ownership.

▶ Since these words are adjectives, you must make them agree in number (singular / plural) and gender (masculine / feminine) with the nouns that follow them (For example, **nuestras casas**).

my	**mi(s)**	*our*	**nuestro(a) / nuestros(as)**
your	{ **tu(s)** **su(s)**	*your*	{ **vuestro(a) / vuestros(as)** **su(s)**
his / her	**su(s)**	*their*	**su(s)**

Appendix F *Rules of Accentuation*

Written accent marks

In both English and Spanish, a *stressed syllable* is the part of the word that is spoken most loudly and with the greatest force, such as <u>stu</u> - *dent* or *u* - *ni* - <u>ver</u> - *si* - *ty*.

In Spanish, stress generally falls on an easily predictable syllable of the word. Words that *do not* follow these patterns must carry a *written accent mark,* known as **un acento ortográfico** or **una tilde.**

1. Words that end in a consonant other than **-n** or **-s** are stressed on the last syllable. Words that follow this rule do not need a written accent mark:

   co - **mer**
   re - **loj**
   ge - ne - **ral**
   Ba - da - **joz**
   ciu - **dad**

   Words that *do not* follow this rule need a written accent mark on the stressed syllable:

   ár - bol
   Rod - **rí** - guez

2. Words that end in a vowel or in the consonants **-n** or **-s** are stressed on the second-to-last syllable. Most words follow this rule, and therefore do not need a written accent mark:

   ca - sa
   tra - **ba** - jo
   e - le - **fan** - tes
   vi - ven

   Words that *do not* follow this pattern carry a written accent mark on the stressed syllable:

   me - **nú**
   Á - fri - ca
   Ni - co - **lás**
   al - **bón** - di - gas *(meatballs)*
   na - **ción**

3. In order to apply the previous rule correctly, keep in mind these special vowel combinations:

   - In general, one syllable is formed when the "weak" vowels **i** or **u** are next to the "strong" vowels **a, e,** or **o.** In the following cases, for example, the stress falls on the second-to-last syllable and no written accent mark is needed.

     gra - cias
     bue - no

     A written accent mark is used, however, when the stress falls on the **i** or **u** and the vowels are divided into two syllables:

     dí - a
     ra - **íz** *(root)*
     grú - a *(crane)*

- The combination of two "strong" vowels—**a, e, o**—is generally divided into two syllables. In the following cases, for example, the stress falls naturally on the second-to-last syllable, and no written accent mark is needed:

mu - **se** - o
ma - **es** - tro

4. Written accent marks are occasionally used to distinguish two words that are spelled exactly alike but have different meanings:

Without the written accent		With the written accent	
te	*to you*	**té**	*tea*
mi	*my*	**mí**	*me* (prepositional pronoun)
el	*the*	**él**	*he*
tu	*your*	**tú**	*you*

Vocabulario

ESPAÑOL - INGLÉS

The meanings provided in this glossary are limited to those used in the contexts of this textbook. Genders of nouns are given only if they are an exception to the -**o** and -**a** endings. The number of the chapter where the vocabulary word or expression first appears is indicated in parentheses after the definition. Spelling changes in stem-changing verbs are indicated in parentheses after the verb given, where appropriate.

The following abbreviations are used in this glossary:

adj.	adjective	**m.**	masculine
conj.	conjunction	**n.**	noun
f.	feminine	**PP**	paso preliminar
form.	formal	**pl.**	plural
inf.	infinitive	**sing.**	singular
inform.	informal	**v.**	verb

A

a *prep. at, to*
  a finales de *at the end of (5)*
  a la derecha *to the right (3)*
  a la izquierda *to the left (3)*
  a la parrilla *grilled (4)*
  ¿a qué hora? *at what time? (1)*
  a veces *sometimes (3)*
abanico *fan (6)*
abierto(a) *open (2)*
abogado(a) *lawyer (5)*
abrigo *coat (6)*
abril *April (2)*
abrir *to open (PP)*
abuela *grandmother (1)*
abuelo *grandfather (1)*
abuelos *grandparents (1)*
acabar de (+ inf.) *to have just (done something) (9)*
acampar *to go camping (7)*
aceptar *to accept (6)*
aconsejar *to advise (9)*
acontecimiento *event (9)*
acostarse (ue) *to go to bed (3)*
acostumbrar (a) *to be accustomed (to) (7)*
actividad *(f.) activity (1)*
aderezo *salad dressing (4)*
¿adónde? *to where? (1)*
aeropuerto *airport (8)*
afeitarse *to shave (3)*
agencia de viajes *travel agency (2)*
agente de bienes raíces *(m., f.) real estate agent (5)*
agosto *August (2)*
agotado(a) *exhausted (9)*
agricultor(a) *farmer (5)*

agua *(f.)* **de la llave** *tap water (8)*
ají picante *(m.) chili pepper (4)*
ajustado(a) *tight-fitting (6)*
alegrar *to make happy (9)*
alegrarse *to be happy (9)*
alfombra *rug (3)*
álgebra *algebra (5)*
algo *anything, something (1)*
algodón *(m.) cotton (6)*
alimentarse *to eat, nourish oneself (9)*
allí mismo *right there (8)*
almacén *(m.) department store (6)*
  gran almacén *department store (6)*
almorzar (ue) *to eat lunch (4)*
almuerzo *(n.) lunch (3)*
alquilar *to rent (3)*
alto(a) *tall (3)*
ama de casa *homemaker (5)*
amable *friendly (3)*
amarillo(a) *yellow (6)*
amigo(a) *friend (3)*
amueblado(a) *furnished (3)*
análisis *(m.) analysis (8)*
anaranjado(a) *orange (color) (6)*
anfitrión (anfitriona) *host (hostess) (4)*
anillo *ring (9)*
animal doméstico *pet (3)*
anteojos *eyeglasses (3)*
antes (de) *before (1)*
antibiótico *antibiotic (8)*
antipático(a) *unpleasant (3)*
antropología *anthropology (5)*
año *year (2)*
  año pasado *last year (5)*
  el próximo año *next year (5)*

apagar *to put out (7)*
apartamento *apartment (1)*
aparte de *aside from (4)*
apellido *surname, last name (1)*
aplicarse *to apply, put on oneself (8)*
aprender *to learn (1)*
aprobar (ue) *to pass the basic courses (5)*
aprobarse (ue) *to be approved (1)*
apuntes *(m.) notes (5)*
aquellos(as) *those (5)*
árbol *(m.) tree (7)*
arena *sand (2)*
arete *(m.) earring (6)*
arma *weapon (2)*
arreglarse *to fix oneself up, get ready (3)*
arroz *(m.) rice (4)*
arte *(m.) art (5)*
artesanía *arts and crafts, handicraft (6)*
asado(a) *roasted (4)*
asignatura *subject (5)*
asistir a *to attend (1)*
aspirina *aspirin (8)*
atropellar *run over (6)*
aunque *even, even though (3); although (6)*
autobús *(m.) bus (2)*
  parada de autobuses *bus stop (8)*
avenida *avenue (8)*
avión *(m.) airplane (2)*
ayer *yesterday (5)*
ayuda *(n.) help (9)*
ayudar *to help (3)*
azúcar *(m.) sugar (4)*
azul *blue (6)*
azul marino *navy blue (6)*

B

bailar *to dance (1)*
bajo(a) *short (3)*
balanceado(a) *balanced (9)*
banana *banana (4)*
banco *bank (2)*
bañarse *to take a bath (3)*
bañera *bathtub (3)*
baño *bath(room) (2)*
barato(a) *cheap, inexpensive (6)*
barba *beard (3)*
barco *boat (2)*
   barco de vela *sailboat (7)*
barra (de pan) *loaf (of bread) (4)*
bastante *quite (8)*
bebé *(m., f.) baby (9)*
beber *to drink (4)*
beca *scholarship (9)*

beige *beige (6)*
bellas artes *fine arts (5)*
bendecir *to bless (1)*
bendición *(f.) blessing (1)*
biblioteca *library (1)*
bien *(adv.) well, fine (1)*
biftec *(m.) beef (4)*
bigote *(m.) moustache (3)*
boleto *(m.) ticket (2)*
billetera *wallet (6)*
biología *biology (5)*
blanco(a) *white (6)*
blusa *blouse (6)*
boca *mouth (8)*
boda *wedding (9)*
boina *beret (6)*
boleto *ticket (2)*

bolígrafo *pen (PP)*
bolsa *(n.) bag (4)*
bolso de cuero *leather purse (6)*
bordado(a) *embroidered (6)*
borrador *(m.) eraser (PP)*
bosque *(m.) forest (2)*
bota *boot (6)*
botella *bottle (4)*
brazalete de plata *(m.) silver bracelet (6)*
brazo *arm (8)*
brevemente *briefly (3)*
brindar *to toast, make a toast (7)*
brócoli *(m.) broccoli (4)*
bucear *to dive, snorkel (7)*
bueno(a) *good (3)*
buscar *to look for (6)*

C

caballo *horse*
   montar a caballo *to go horseback riding (7)*
cabeza *head (8)*
cacique *(m.) leader (1)*
cadena de oro *gold necklace (6)*
caerse *to fall down (5)*
calcetín *(m.) sock (6)*
cálculo *calculus (5)*
calendario *calendar (PP)*
caliente *hot (2)*
calle *(f.) street (1)*
calor *heat*
   hace calor *it's warm (7)*
   tener calor *to be hot (1)*
calvo(a) *bald (3)*
calzar *to wear, take (shoe size) (6)*
cama *bed (2)*
   hacer la cama *to make the bed (3)*
camarero(a) *waiter (waitress) (4)*
camarón *(m.) shrimp (4)*
cambiar *to change; to exchange (8)*
caminar *to walk (8)*
caminata: hacer caminatas *to go hiking (7)*
camisa *shirt (6)*
camiseta *T-shirt (6)*
campo *country(side) (7)*
candelabro *Menorah, candelabra (7)*
canela *cinnamon (4)*
canoso(a) *gray-haired (3)*
cansado(a) *tired (1)*
cantante *(m., f.) singer (4)*
cantar *to sing (7)*
cara *face (3)*
   lavarse la cara *to wash one's face (3)*
carácter *(m.) character, personality (3)*
caraqueño(a) *resident of Caracas (3)*
cariñoso(a) *affectionate (3)*
caro(a) *expensive (6)*
carrera *major (field of study) (5); race (3)*
   carrera de auto *auto racing (3)*
carta *letter (8); menu (4)*
cartas *(playing) cards (7)*
cartel *(m.) poster (PP)*
casa *house (1)*

casado(a) *married (1)*
casamiento *marriage (3)*
casarse *to get married (9)*
castaño(a) *chestnut (color), brown (3)*
castañuelas *castanets (6)*
catarro *(n.) cold (8)*
catedral *(f.) cathedral (8)*
catorce *fourteen (PP)*
cazar *to hunt (7)*
celebración *(f.) celebration (7)*
celebrar *to celebrate (7)*
cena *supper, dinner (3)*
cenar *to eat supper (3)*
cerca *near (by) (8)*
   cerca (de) *close to (1)*
cereal *(m.) cereal (4)*
cero *zero (PP)*
cerrado(a) *closed (2)*
cerrar (ie) *to close (2)*
cerveza *beer (4)*
césped *(m.) lawn (3)*
champaña *champagne (7)*
chaqueta *jacket (6)*
cheque de viajero *(m.) traveler's check (2)*
chico(a) *boy (girl) (3)*
chocar contra *to run into (7)*
chocolate *(m.) chocolate (4)*
chuleta de cerdo *pork chop (4)*
churro *fritter (4)*
cien *one hundred (2)*
cien mil *one-hundred thousand (2)*
ciencias naturales *natural sciences (5)*
ciencias políticas *political sciences (5)*
ciencias sociales *social sciences (5)*
ciento uno *one hundred one (2)*
cierto(a) *true, certain (9)*
cinco *five (PP)*
cinco mil *five thousand (2)*
cincuenta *fifty (1)*
cine *(m.) cinema, movie theater (7)*
cinematografía *film-making (5)*
cinturón *(m.) belt (4)*
cita *(n.) date (9)*
cliente *(m., f.) customer, client (3)*

clínica *clinic (8)*
clóset *(m.) closet (3)*
cocina *kitchen (3)*
cocinar *to cook (3)*
codo *elbow (8)*
collar *(m.) necklace (6)*
color *(m.) color (6)*
   color crema *cream color (6)*
   color miel *honey color, hazel (colored) (3)*
comedor *(m.) dining room (3)*
comer *to eat (1)*
   dar de comer *to feed (3)*
comida *food, meal (4)*
   comida rápida *fast food (1)*
comisaría *police station (8)*
¿cómo? *how? (1)*
cómoda *bureau (3)*
compañero(a) *partner (PP); date, escort (9)*
   compañero(a) de clase *classmate (1)*
   compañero(a) de cuarto *roommate (3)*
compañía *company (1)*
   compañía multinacional *multinational company (5)*
compartir *to share (4)*
completo(a) *complete; full (2)*
comprar *to buy (3)*
comprender *to understand (1)*
comprensivo(a) *comprehensive (3)*
comprometerse *to get engaged (9)*
compromiso *engagement (to be married) (9)*
computadora *computer (PP)*
con *with (1)*
   con frecuencia *frequently, often (3)*
   con lunares *polka-dotted (6)*
concierto *concert (7)*
conferencia *(n.) lecture (5)*
conjunto *(musical) group (7)*
conmigo *with me (PP)*
conocer *to know (a person) (2), to be introduced to, meet (7)*
conocido(a) *known (2)*
conseguir (i) *to get, obtain (5)*
consejero(a) *counselor (5)*
consejo *(n.) advice (9)*

consultor(a)   *consultant (5)*
contador(a)   *accountant (5)*
contar (ue)   *to tell (a story) (7)*
contento: estar contento(a)   *to be happy (1)*
contestar   *to answer (1)*
convenir (ie)   *to be helpful (2)*
convertirse (ie)   *to become (5)*
copa   *glass (4)*
  copa de vino   *glass of wine (4)*
corazón (m.)   *heart (8)*
corbata   *necktie (6)*
cordillera   *mountain range (2)*
correo   *post office (8)*
correo electrónico   *e-mail (1)*
correr   *to run (1)*
cortar   *to cut (3)*
  cortarse   *to cut oneself, get cut (8)*

cosa   *thing (1)*
costar (ue)   *to cost (2)*
creer   *to believe, think (opinion) (5)*
crema   *cream (8)*
criar   *to raise (children) (3)*
cruel   *cruel (3)*
cruzar   *to cross (8)*
cuaderno   *notebook (PP)*
cuadra   *block (of a street) (8)*
cuadro   *square (3)*
  de cuadros   *plaid (6)*
¿cuál(es)?   *which one(s)? (1)*
¿cuándo?   *when? (1)*
¿cuánto(a)?   *how much? (1)*
¿cuántos(as)?   *how many? (1)*
cuarenta   *forty (1)*
cuarto   *room (1); fourth (2)*

cuatro   *four (PP)*
cuatrocientos   *four hundred (2)*
cubierto   *place setting (4)*
cubito de hielo   *ice cube (4)*
cuchara   *spoon (4)*
cucharita   *teaspoon (4)*
cuchillo   *knife (4)*
cuello   *neck (8)*
cuenta (n.)   *bill, check (2)*
cuento   *short story (7)*
cuidado: tener cuidado   *to be careful (1)*
cuidarse   *to take care of oneself (9)*
cumbre (f.)   *peak (5)*
cumpleaños   *birthday (7)*
  pastel de cumpleaños (m.)   *birthday cake (7)*

D

daño   *damage (1)*
dar   *to give (3)*
  dar de comer   *to feed (3)*
  dar un beso   *to give a kiss (1)*
  dar un paseo   *to take a walk (7)*
  darse la mano   *to shake hands (1)*
dato   *fact, information (1)*
de   *of; from*
  de estilo moderno   *modern (in style) (3)*
  de estilo tradicional   *traditionally styled (3)*
  de ida   *one-way (2)*
  de ida y vuelta   *round-trip (2)*
  de la madrugada   A.M. *(early morning) (2)*
  de la mañana   A.M., *6 A.M. to noon (2)*
  de la noche   P.M., *sundown to midnight (2)*
  de la tarde   P.M., *noon to sundown (2)*
  de nada   *you're welcome (PP)*
  de rayas   *striped (6)*
  de tamaño mediano   *medium-sized (3)*
debajo de   *under (3)*
deber   *to owe (4)*
  deber + inf.   *must (4)*
  deberse a   *to be due to (3)*
décimo(a)   *tenth (2)*
decorar   *to decorate (7)*
dedo   *finger (8)*
dedo del pie   *toe (8)*
dejar   *to leave; to let (9)*
  dejar de (+ inf.)   *to stop (doing something) (9)*
delante de   *in front of (3)*
delgado(a)   *thin (3)*
demasiado(a)   *(too) much (5)*
dentista (m., f.)   *dentist (5)*
dentro de   *inside (3)*
depender   *to depend (9)*
deprimido(a)   *depressed (9)*
derecho (adv.)   *straight ahead (8) (n.) law (5); right (7)*
desayunar   *to eat breakfast (4)*

desayuno (n.)   *breakfast (4)*
descansar   *to rest, relax (1)*
descompuesto(a)   *out of order (3)*
desconectarse   *to disconnect; to have some down time (9)*
desconsolado(a)   *grief-stricken (9)*
descuento (n.)   *discount (2)*
desear   *to want, wish for (4)*
desfile (m.)   *parade (7)*
desocupar   *to check out (of hotel) (2)*
desordenado(a)   *messy (3)*
desorganizado(a)   *disorganized (5)*
despedirse (i, i)   *to say good-bye (3)*
despejado   *clear (7)*
despertarse (ie)   *to wake up (3)*
después   *after (1); afterwards (5)*
  después de   *after (5)*
detrás de   *behind (3)*
día (m.)   *day (2)*
  Día de Acción de Gracias (m.)   *Thanksgiving (7)*
  Día de Año Nuevo (m.)   *New Year's Day (7)*
  Día de la Independencia (m.)   *Fourth of July (7)*
  Día de las Brujas (m.)   *Halloween (7)*
  Día de los Enamorados (m.)   *St. Valentine's Day (7)*
  día festivo   *holiday (7)*
diagnóstico   *diagnosis (8)*
diario(a)   *daily (9)*
diarrea   *diarrhea (8)*
diccionario   *dictionary (PP)*
diciembre   *December (2)*
diecinueve   *nineteen (PP)*
dieciocho   *eighteen (PP)*
dieciséis   *sixteen (PP)*
diecisiete   *seventeen (PP)*
diente (m.)   *tooth (8)*

diez mil   *ten thousand (2)*
diez   *ten (PP)*
difícil   *difficult (9)*
diligencia   *errand (8)*
dimitir   *to resign (4)*
Dios   *God (1)*
dirección (f.)   *address (1)*
director(a) de personal   *personnel director (5)*
disco compacto   *compact disc (1)*
discutir   *to discuss (9)*
disfraz (m.)   *costume (7)*
disfrutar (de)   *to enjoy (7)*
divertido(a)   *funny (7)*
divertirse (ie)   *to have a good time (3)*
divorciado(a)   *divorced (1)*
divorciarse   *to get divorced (9)*
doblar   *to turn (8)*
doble   *double (2)*
  habitación doble (f.)   *double room (2)*
doce   *twelve (PP)*
docena   *dozen (4)*
doler (ue)   *to hurt, ache (8)*
dolor (m.)   *pain (8)*
domingo   *Sunday (2)*
¿dónde?   *where? (1)*
  ¿de dónde?   *from where? (1)*
dormir (ue)   *to sleep*
dormirse (ue, u)   *to fall asleep (3)*
dormitorio   *dormitory (3)*
dos millones   *two million (2)*
dos   *two (PP)*
doscientos   *two hundred (2)*
ducha (n.)   *shower (2)*
ducharse   *to take a shower (3)*
dudar   *to doubt (6)*
dudoso(a)   *doubtful (9)*
dulces (m.)   *candy (7)*
durante   *during (3)*
durazno   *peach (4)*

E

ecología   *ecology (5)*
educación (f.)   *education (5)*
educado(a)   *well-mannered (3)*
efectivo: en efectivo   *cash (2)*
ejercicio (n.)   *exercise (1)*

el   *the (sing.) (PP)*
embarazada   *pregnant (9)*
emocionado(a)   *excited (9)*
empezar   *to begin (PP)*
empleado(a)   *employee; maid (3)*

en   *on (PP)*
  en efectivo   *cash (2)*
  en el medio   *in the middle (3)*
enamorado(a)   *in love (9)*
encantar   *to love (a thing or activity) (5)*

encarcelado(a) *incarcerated (6)*
encender (ie) *to light (7)*
encima de *on top of (3)*
encontrar (ue) *to find (6); to meet (7)*
enero *January (2)*
enfadar *to anger (9)*
enfermarse *to get sick (7)*
enfermedad *(f.) illness (8)*
enfermo(a) *sick, ill (1)*
  estar enfermo(a) *to be sick (1)*
enfrente de *opposite, across from (8)*
enojado(a) *angry (1)*
  estar enojado(a) *to be angry (1)*
ensalada *salad (4)*
ensayo *essay (7)*
enseguida *right away (4)*
enterarse *to find out (9)*
entonces *then (5)*
entre *between (3)*
entregar *to hand in (9)*
entrevista *(n.) interview (9)*
envolver (ue) *to wrap (6)*
época *era (1); time (7)*
equipo *team (7)*
escalar en roca *to rock climb, go rock climbing (7)*

escalera *stairs, staircase (3)*
escaparate *(m.) window (of a shop) (6)*
escribir *to write (1)*
escuchar *to listen to (1)*
ese/esa *that, that one (6)*
esos/esas *those (3)*
espalda *back (8)*
esperar *to wait; to hope (7)*
esposo(a) *husband (wife) (3)*
esquiar *to ski (7)*
esquina *(street) corner (8)*
estación *(f.) season (of the year) (7)*
estación de tren *(f.) train station (8)*
estadidad *(f.) statehood (1)*
estadística *statistics (5)*
estado libre asociado *commonwealth (1)*
estampado(a) *printed (6)*
estante *shelf (3)*
estar *to be (1)*
  estar contento(a) *to be happy (1)*
  estar de buen/mal humor *to be in a good/bad mood (1)*
  estar enfermo(a) *to be sick (1)*
  estar enojado(a) *to be angry (1)*
  estar nervioso(a) *to be nervous (1)*
  estar ocupado(a) *to be busy (1)*

estar pendiente de *to keep track of (3)*
estar preocupado(a) *to be worried (1)*
estar triste *to be sad (1)*
este/esta *this, this one (6)*
estilo *(n.) style (3)*
  de estilo moderno *modern (in style) (3)*
  de estilo tradicional *traditionally styled (3)*
estómago *stomach (8)*
estos/estas *these, these ones(6)*
estrella *star (7)*
estresado(a) *stressed out (9)*
estudiante *(m., f.) student (PP)*
  estudiante de derecho *(m., f.) law student (6)*
estudios de postgrado *graduate school (5)*
estudios profesionales *professional studies (5)*
estufa *stove (3)*
excursión *(f.) trip, tour (2); field trip (5)*
exhibir *to be on exhibit (7)*
exigente *demanding (5)*
exigir *to require (5)*
éxito *(n.) success (1)*
explicación *(f.) explanation (PP)*
exposición *(f.) exhibition (7)*

F

fabuloso(a) *great (7)*
falda *skirt (6)*
faltar *to be short, missing, lacking (6)*
familia *family (1)*
familiar *(m.) family member (3)*
farmacia *pharmacy (8)*
fascinante *fascinating (5)*
fatal *terrible (7)*
febrero *February (2)*
fecha *(n.) date (2)*
feo(a) *ugly (3)*
festival *(m.) festival (7)*
festivo(a): día festivo *holiday (7)*
fideo *noodle (4)*
fiebre *(f.) fever (8)*
fiesta *(n.) party (1)*

fin *(m.) end*
  a finales de *at the end of (5)*
  fin de semana *weekend (1)*
  fin de semana pasado *last weekend (5)*
  por fin *finally (1)*
firmar *to sign (7)*
física *physics (5)*
flan *(m.) custard (4)*
florecer *to flourish (3)*
formal *dressy, fancy (6)*
foto *(f.) picture (1)*
fractura *(n.) fracture (8)*
frasco *jar (4)*
fregadero *kitchen sink (3)*
fresa *strawberry (4)*
fresco: hace fresco *it's cool (7)*

frijol *(m.) bean (4)*
frío(a) *cold (3)*
  hace frío *it's cold (7)*
  tener frío *to be cold (1)*
frito(a) *fried (4)*
fuego *fire*
  fuegos artificiales *fireworks (7)*
fuente *(f.) source (9)*
fumar *to smoke (9)*
función *(f.) show (7)*
fundador(a) *founder (1)*
furioso(a) *furious (9)*
fútbol *(m.): fútbol (europeo) soccer (1)*
  fútbol americano *football (1)*

G

gafas *eyeglasses (3)*
  gafas de sol *sunglasses (6)*
galleta *cookie (4)*
ganado *livestock (5)*
ganas: tener ganas de (+ inf.) *to feel like (doing something) (1)*
garganta *throat (8)*
gaseosa *soda (4)*
gato *cat (3)*
gemelos *twins (1)*

geografía *geography (5)*
gerente *(m., f.) manager (5)*
gimnasio *gym (1)*
gobernador(a) *governor (1)*
gordo(a) *fat (3)*
gorra *cap (6)*
gracias *thank you, thanks (PP)*
graduarse *to graduate (5)*
gramática *grammar (1)*
gran almacén *(m.) department store (6)*

grave *severe (8); serious, grave (9)*
gripe *(f.) flu (8)*
gris *gray (6)*
guante *(m.) glove (6)*
guapo(a) *handsome (3)*
guardar cama *to stay in bed (8)*
guayabera *loose-fitting men's shirt (6)*
guerra *war (2)*
gustar *to like, be pleasing (1)*

H

habitación *(f.) room*
  habitación doble *double room (2)*
  habitación sencilla *single room (2)*
hablar *to talk, speak (1)*

hacer *to make, do*
  hace buen(mal) tiempo *it's good (bad) weather (7)*
  hacer caminatas *to go hiking (7)*
  hacer ejercicio *to exercise, do exercise (1)*

hacer estudios de postgrado *to go to graduate school (5)*
hacer la cama *to make the bed (3)*
hacer un picnic *to have a picnic (7)*
hacerse *to become (5)*

hambre (f.): **tener hambre**   to be hungry (1)
hamburguesa   hamburger (4)
hámster (m.)   hamster (3)
hasta   until (3)
   hasta tarde   until later (3)
hay (haber)   there is/there are (PP)
helado   ice cream (4)
herido: ser herido   to be injured (6)
hermanastro(a)   stepbrother
   (stepsister) (3)

hermano(a)   brother (sister) (1)
hijastro(a)   stepson (stepdaughter) (3)
hijo(a)   son (daughter) (1)
historia   history (5)
hogar (m.)   home (3)
hoja de papel   sheet of paper (PP)
hombre (m.)   man (6)
hombro   shoulder (8)
honesto(a)   honest (3)
horario (n.)   schedule (5)

horno   oven (4)
   al horno   baked (4)
hospital (m.)   hospital (1)
hotel (m.)   hotel (2)
hoy   today (2)
   por hoy   nowadays (3)
huelga (n.)   strike (3)
huevos revueltos   scrambled eggs (4)
humanidades (f.)   humanities (5)
humilde (adj.)   humble (5)

I

ida: de ida   one-way (2)
   de ida y vuelta   round-trip (2)
iglesia   church (7)
igualmente   likewise (PP)
impermeable (m.)   raincoat (6)
importar   to matter (6)
impresora   printer (PP)
indiferente   indifferent (3)
infección (f.)   infection (8)

informática   computer science (5)
ingeniería   engineering (5)
ingeniero(a)   engineer (5)
inglés (m.)   English (language) (1)
inodoro   toilet (3)
intercambiar   to exchange (7)
interesar   to be interested in, interest (5)
internado   internship (9)
intoxicación alimenticia (f.)   food poisoning (8)

investigación (f.)   research (5)
invierno   winter (7)
inyección (f.)   shot (8)
ir   to go (1)
   ir a pie   to go on foot (8)
   ir de caza   to hunt (7)
   ir de picnic   to go on a picnic (7)
irresponsable   irresponsible (3)
isla   island (3)

J

jamón (m.)   ham (4)
Janucá   Hannukah (7)
jarabe (m.)   (cough) syrup (8)
jardín (m.)   yard (3)
joven   young (3)

joya   jewel (6)
jueves   Thursday (2)
jugador(a)   player (7)
jugar (ue)   to play (1)
jugo de naranja   orange juice (4)

julio   July (2)
junio   June (2)
juntos(as)   together (1)

K

kilo   kilo (metric pound) (4)

L

la   the (sing.) (PP)
lado: al lado de   to the side of (3)
lago   lake (2)
lámpara   lamp (3)
lana   wool (6)
langosta   lobster (4)
lápiz (m.)   pencil (PP)
lastimar   to hurt, injure (8)
lastimarse   to injure oneself, get hurt (8)
lavabo   bathroom sink (3)
lavaplatos (m.)   dishwasher (3)
lavar   to wash (3)
   lavarse el pelo/las manos/la cara   to wash
   one's hair/hands/face (3)
lechuga   lettuce (4)
leer   to read (1)

legado   legacy (6)
lejos   far (8)
   lejos (de)   far from (1)
lentamente   slowly (7)
levantamiento   uprising (2)
levantar pesas   to lift weights (7)
levantarse   to get up (3)
libertad (f.)   freedom (3)
libre   free, unoccupied (9)
   tiempo libre   free time (1)
libro   book (PP)
limpiar   to clean (1)
limpio(a)   (adj.) clean (3)
lindo(a)   wonderful (1)
literatura   literature (5)
litro   liter (4)

llave (f.)   key (2)
llegada   arrival (2)
llegar (ue)   to arrive (2)
llevar   to wear (clothing) (6); to take, carry (7)
   llevarse bien (mal)   to get along well
   (poorly) with someone (9)
llover (ue)   to rain (7)
lluvia (n.)   rain (7)
los/las   the (pl.) (PP)
luchar   to fight (3)
lucir   to stand out; to wear, show off (6)
luego   then, next, later (5)
lugar (m.)   place (2)
lunes   Monday (2)

M

madera   wood (4)
madrastra   stepmother (3)
madre (f.)   mother (1)
madrina   godmother (3)
madrugada   dawn, early morning (5)
maestría   master's degree (3)
maestro(a)   teacher (5)
maíz (m.)   corn (4)

mal de altura (m.)   altitude sickness (8)
mal(o)(a)   bad (1)
maleducado(a)   rude, ill-mannered (3)
manifestación (f.)   demonstration (5)
mano (f.)   hand
   lavarse las manos   to wash one's hands (3)
mantequilla   butter (4)
mantilla   lace scarf (6)

mañana   tomorrow (2)
   de la mañana   A.M., 6 A.M. to noon (2)
   por la mañana   in the morning (1)
mapa (m.)   map (PP)
maquillarse   to put on make-up (3)
maquinaria   machinery (5)
maracas   maracas (6)
marcar   to score (7)

mareo   *dizziness, light-headedness, motion sickness (8)*
mariscos   *shellfish (4)*
marrón   *brown (6)*
martes   *Tuesday (2)*
marzo   *March (2)*
más   *more*
   más tarde   *later on (5)*
   más... que   *more . . . than (3)*
matemáticas   *mathematics (5)*
mayo   *May (2)*
mayonesa   *mayonnaise (4)*
mayor   *older; elderly (3)*
mechado(a)   *shredded (4)*
media hermana   *half sister (3)*
mediano(a)   *medium (3)*
   de tamaño mediano   *medium-sized (3)*
medianoche *(f.)*   *midnight (2)*
medicina   *medicine (5)*
médico(a)   *doctor (5)*
medio   *half*
   de en medio   *middle (child) (3)*
   en el medio   *in the middle (3)*
medio hermano   *half brother (3)*

mediodía *(m.)*   *noon, midday (2)*
mejilla   *cheek (1)*
mejor   *better; best (3)*
melecotón *(m.)*   *peach (4)*
menor   *younger; youngest (3)*
menos... que   *less . . . than (3)*
mentiroso(a)   *lying, deceitful (3)*
menú *(m.)*   *menu (4)*
mercado   *market (6)*
merendar (ie)   *to snack (4)*
merienda   *snack; snack time (4)*
mermelada   *marmalade (4)*
mes *(m.)*   *month (2)*
   mes pasado   *last month (5)*
   mes próximo   *next month (5)*
mesa   *table (PP)*
mesita   *end table (3)*
mesita de noche   *night stand (3)*
mí mismo(a)   *myself (5)*
microondas   *microwave (3)*
miedo: tener miedo   *to be afraid (1)*
miércoles   *Wednesday (2)*
mil   *one thousand (2)*
millón *(m.)*   *million (2)*

mirar   *to watch, to look at (1)*
mochila   *backpack (PP)*
moda   *fashion (6)*
   última moda   *latest fashion (6)*
moderno(a)   *modern (3)*
molestar   *to bother; to irritate (9)*
montaña   *mountain (7)*
montar en bicicleta (a caballo)   *to ride a bike (a horse) (1)*
morado(a)   *purple (6)*
morirse (ue, u)   *to die (9)*
mostrar (ue)   *to show (6)*
moverse (ue)   *to move (a part of the body) (3)*
muchísimo(a)   *very much (7)*
mucho(a)   *much, a lot (1)*
mudarse   *to move (one's residence), move out (3)*
muebles *(m.)*   *furniture (3)*
muerte *(f.)*   *death (1)*
mujer *(f.)*   *woman (6)*
multinacional *(adj.)*   *multinational (5)*
muñeca   *wrist (8)*
museo   *museum (2)*
música   *music (1)*

N

nacer   *to be born (1)*
nadar   *to swim (7)*
nariz *(f.)*   *nose (8)*
náuseas   *nausea (8)*
navegar   *to navigate, surf (the Internet) (1)*
Navidad *(f.)*   *Christmas (7)*
necesitar   *to need (1)*
negocios   *business (5)*
negro(a)   *black (3)*
nervioso: estar nervioso(a)   *to be nervous (1)*
nevar (ie)   *to snow (7)*
nevera   *refrigerator (3)*
nieto(a)   *grandson (granddaughter) (3)*

nieve *(f.)*   *snow (7)*
niñez *(f.)*   *childhood (5)*
niño(a)   *child (4)*
noche *(f.)*   *night*
   de la noche   P.M., *sudown to midnight (2)*
   por la noche   *in the evening (1), at night (5)*
Noche Vieja *(f.)*   *New Year's Eve (7)*
Nochebuena   *Christmas Eve (7)*
nombre *(m.)*   *name (1)*
normalmente   *normally, usually (3)*
nota *(n.)*   *(academic) grade (5)*
noticias   *news (3)*
novecientos   *nine hundred (2)*

novela   *novel (1)*
noveno(a)   *ninth (2)*
noventa   *ninety (1)*
noviembre   *November (2)*
novio(a)   *boyfriend/girlfriend (1); fiancé/ fiancée (9)*
nublado   *cloudy (7)*
nueve   *nine (PP)*
nuevo(a)   *new (1)*
número   *number (1)*
nunca   *never (3)*

O

obra (de teatro)   *play, drama (7)*
obrero(a)   *laborer (5)*
observatorio   *observatory (5)*
ochenta   *eighty (PP)*
ocho   *eight (PP)*
ochocientos   *eight hundred (2)*
octavo(a)   *eighth (2)*
octubre   *October (2)*
ocupado(a)   *busy (1)*

   estar ocupado(a)   *to be busy (1)*
ocupar   *to check in (a hotel) (2)*
ocurrir   *to happen, occur (7)*
oficina   *office (1)*
   oficina de turismo   *tourism office (8)*
oficio   *occupation, trade (5)*
oído   *inner ear (8)*
ojalá   *I hope that . . . ; May . . . (9)*
ojo   *eye (3)*

once   *eleven (PP)*
optimista   *optimistic (9)*
ordenado(a)   *neat, tidy (3)*
oreja   *outer ear (8)*
organizar   *to organize (9)*
orgulloso(a)   *proud (9)*
otoño   *autumn, fall (7)*
otro(a)   *other; another (7)*

P

paciente *(m., f.)*   *patient (8)*
padecer   *to suffer (from illness) (9)*
padrastro   *stepfather (3)*
padre *(m.)*   *father (1)*
padres   *parents (1)*
padrino   *godfather (3)*
paella   *rice dish with saffron, seafood, chicken (4)*
pagar   *to pay (for) (6)*
página *(n.)*   *page (PP)*

pájaro   *bird (3)*
palta rellena   *avocado stuffed with chicken or tuna salad (4)*
pan *(m.)*   *bread (4)*
   barra (de pan)   *loaf (of bread) (4)*
   pan tostado *(m.)*   *toast (4)*
panecillo   *roll (bread) (4)*
pantalones cortos *(m.)*   *shorts (6)*
pantalones de vestir *(m.)*   *dress pants (6)*

papa   *potato (4)*
papas fritas   *French fries (4)*
papelería   *stationery store (8)*
paquete *(m.)*   *package (4)*
¿para qué?   *what for? (1)*
parada de autobuses   *bus stop (8)*
paraguas *(m.)*   *umbrella (6)*
parecer   *to seem, appear (6)*
pariente(a) *(n.)*   *relative (3)*

parilla: a la parrilla *grilled (4)*
parque *(m.)* *park (1)*
parque zoológico *(m.)* *zoo (8)*
partido *game (1); (political) party (1)*
pasado(a) *last (5)*
pasar *to spend (time) (1)*
  pasarlo bien *to have a good time (7)*
Pascua *Easter (7)*
pasear *to stroll (7)*
paseo: dar un paseo *to take a walk (7)*
pasillo *aisle (3)*
pastel *(m.)* *cake (7)*
  pastel de calabaza *(m.)* *pumpkin pie (7)*
  pastel de cumpleaños *(m.)* *birthday cake (7)*
pastilla *pill, tablet (8)*
patata *potato (4)*
paterno(a) *paternal (3)*
pavo *turkey (7)*
pecas *freckles (3)*
pecho *chest (8)*
pedir (i, i) *to ask for; to order (4)*
  pedir la bendición *to ask someone for a blessing (1)*
peinarse *to comb one's hair (3)*
película *movie (1)*
pelo *hair (3)*
  lavarse el pelo *to wash one's hair (3)*
pendiente: estar pendiente de *to keep track of (3)*
peor *worse; worst (3)*
pera *pear (4)*
perder (ie) *to lose (2)*
perdón *pardon me, excuse me (PP)*
perezoso(a) *lazy (3)*
periódico *newspaper (1)*
periodismo *journalism (5)*
periodista *(m., f.)* *journalist (4)*
perro *dog (3)*
perseguir *to pursue (8)*
personalidad *(f.)* *personality (3)*
pesa: levantar pesas *to lift weights (7)*
pesado(a) *heavy (5)*

Pésaj *(m.)* *Passover (7)*
pescado *fish (cooked) (4)*
pescar *to fish (7)*
pesimista *pessimistic (9)*
pésimo *miserable (7)*
pez tropical *tropical fish (3)*
picnic *(m.):* **ir de picnic** *to go on a picnic (7)*
pie *(m.)* *foot (8)*
  ir a pie *to go on foot (8)*
pierna *leg (8)*
pimienta *black pepper (4)*
piña *pineapple (4)*
piscina *swimming pool (2)*
piso *floor (6)*
pizarra *chalkboard (PP)*
planchar *to iron (3)*
  planta baja *ground/first floor (6)*
planta *floor (6)*
plátano *banana (4)*
plato *dish (3)*
  plato de cerámica *ceramic plate (6)*
  primer plato *first course (4)*
  segundo plato *second course (4)*
playa *beach (7)*
poco(a) *(a) little, not much (1)*
poesía *poetry (1)*
pollo asado *roast chicken (4)*
poner *to put; to turn on (TV, radio); to set (the table) (3)*
ponerse *to put on (3)*
  ponerse en forma *to get in shape (9)*
por *by*
  por casualidad *by chance (7)*
  por fin *finally (5)*
  por la mañana *in the morning (1)*
  por la noche *at night (1)*
  por la tarde *in the afternoon (1)/in the evening (5)*
¿por qué? *why? how come? (1)*
porque *because (1)*
posponer *to postpone, put off (9)*
postre *(m.)* *dessert (3)*

practicar *to play (a sport), practice (1)*
pregunta *(n.)* *question (PP)*
preguntar *to ask (PP)*
prenda (de vestir) *article of clothing (6)*
preocupado(a) *worried (1)*
  estar preocupado(a) *to be worried (1)*
preocuparse *to worry (9)*
preparar *to prepare (3)*
presentación *(f.)* *presentation (5)*
presentar *to present, to introduce (7)*
préstamo *(n.)* *loan (9)*
primavera *spring (5)*
primer plato *first course (4)*
primero(a) *first (5)*
primo(a) *cousin (3)*
principios: a principios de *at the beginning of (5)*
prisa: tener prisa *to be in a hurry (1)*
privado(a) *private (2)*
probable *likely, probable (9)*
probador *(m.)* *dressing room (6)*
probar (ue) *to taste, to try (4)*
  probarse (ue) *to try on (6)*
procrastinar *to procrastinate (9)*
profesor(a) *professor (PP), teacher (1)*
programa *(m.)* *program, show (1)*
programador(a) *programmer (5)*
prohibir *to forbid; to prohibit (9)*
pronóstico *forecast (7)*
propina *tip (4)*
proteger *to protect (5)*
próximo(a) *next (5)*
proyecto *project (5)*
psicología *psychology (5)*
psicólogo(a) *psychologist (5)*
pueblo *group of people (2)*
puesto *job (9)*
pulmones *(m.)* *lungs (8)*
punto *stitch (8)*
pupitre *(m.)* *desk (PP)*

Q

¿quién(es)? *who? (PP)*
¿qué? *what? (1)*
quedar *to fit (6)*
  quedarse *to stay, to remain (7)*
quehaceres *(m.)* *household chores (3)*
queja *complaint (9)*

quemarse *to get burned (8)*
querer (ie) *to want (PP)*
queso *cheese (4)*
química *chemistry (5)*
quince *fifteen (PP)*
quinientos *five hundred (2)*

quinto *fifth (2)*
quisquilloso(a) *picky (5)*
quitar el polvo *to dust (3)*
quitarse *to take off (clothing) (3)*
quizás *perhaps (9)*

R

radiografía *x-ray (8)*
rama *branch (3)*
rato *while (5)*
razón *(f.):* **tener razón** *to be right (1)*
rebaja: de rebaja *on sale (6)*
receta *prescription (8)*
recetar *to prescribe (8)*
rechazar *to reject (8)*
recibir *to receive (7)*
recoger *to put in order, pick up a room (3)*
recolectar *to collect (5)*
recomendar (ie) *to recommend (4)*

recuerdo *souvenir (6)*
redacción *(f.)* *writing (1)*
refresco *soda (4)*
refrigerador *(m.)* *refrigerator (3)*
regalar *to give (as a present) (7)*
regalo *present, gift (7)*
  papel de regalo *wrapping paper (6)*
regatear *to bargain, haggle over a price (6)*
regresar *to return, go back (1)*
regular *(adj.)* *average, so-so (5)*
relajarse *to relax (7)*
reloj *(m.)* *clock (PP)*

remedio *remedy (8)*
renombre *(m.)* *renown (4)*
reproductor de MP3/MP4 *(m.)* *MP3/MP4 player (PP)*
resbaloso(a) *slippery (7)*
reservación *(f.)* *reservation (2)*
resfriado *(n.)* *cold (8)*
residencia estudiantil *residence, dormitory (1)*
respuesta *(n.)* *response, answer (1)*
restaurante *(m.)* *restaurant (1)*
retrato *(n.)* *portrait (3)*
reunirse *to get together (7)*

revista *magazine (1)*
revuelto(a) *scrambled (4)*
rodilla *knee (8)*
rojo(a) *red (3)*

romper *to break (up) (9)*
romperse *to break (7)*
ropa *clothing (6)*
rosado(a) *pink (6)*

roto(a) *broken (3)*
rubio(a) *blond(e) (3)*

S

sábado *Saturday (2)*
saber *to know* (information) *(8)*
sabroso(a) *delicious (7)*
sacar *to get a grade (5)*
  sacarle *to take (out)(8)*
sal *(f.) salt (4)*
sala *living room (3)*
  sala de clase *classroom (PP)*
salida *departure (2)*
salir *to leave, go out (3); to go out* (on a social occasion) *(7)*
  salir bien (mal) *to do well (poorly) (9)*
saludar *to greet (4)*
sandalia *sandal (6)*
sandía *watermelon (4)*
sándwich *(m.) sandwich (4)*
sarape *(m.) Mexican sarape (6)*
seco(a) *dry (7)*
sed *(f.):* **tener sed** *to be thirsty (1)*
seda *silk (6)*
seguir (i, i) *to follow (3)*
segundo(a) *second (2)*
  segundo plato *second course (4)*
seguro(a) *sure (9)*
seis *six (PP)*
seiscientos *six hundred (2)*

sello (postage) *stamp (8)*
semana *week (2)*
  fin de semana *(m.) weekend (1)*
  semana pasada *last week (5)*
  Semana Santa *Holy Week (2)*
semestre *(m.) semester (1)*
sencillo(a) *simple (6)*
  habitación sencilla *(f.) single room (2)*
sentarse (ie) *to sit down (3)*
sentir (ie, i) *to regret, be sorry (9)*
  sentirse (ie, i) *to feel (3)*
señalar *to point out (9)*
septiembre *September (2)*
séptimo(a) *seventh (2)*
ser *to be (1)*
  ser herido *to be injured (6)*
serio(a) *serious (3)*
servilleta *napkin (4)*
servir (i, i) *to serve (4)*
sesenta *sixty (1)*
setecientos *seven hundred (2)*
setenta *seventy (1)*
sexto(a) *sixth (2)*
sí mismo(a) *himself, herself (1)*
siempre *always (3)*
siete *seven (PP)*

siglo *century (3)*
silla *chair (PP)*
simpático(a) *likable (3)*
sinagoga *synagogue (7)*
síntoma *(m.) symptom (8)*
sobre *above; on (3)*
sobrevivir *to survive (2)*
sobrino(a) *nephew (niece) (3)*
sociología *sociology (5)*
sofá *(m.) sofa (3)*
sol: hace sol *it's sunny (7)*
soltero(a) *single (1)*
sombrero *hat (6)*
sopa *soup (4)*
sorprender *to surprise (9)*
sorprendido(a) *surprised (9)*
sótano *basement (6)*
su *your (formal) (PP)*
sucio(a) *dirty (3)*
sudadera *sweatshirt (6)*
sueño: tener sueño *to be sleepy (1)*
suéter *(m.) sweater (6)*
suficiente *enough (9)*
supermercado *supermarket (1)*

T

talla *size (6)*
tamaño *size (5)*
tan... como *as . . . as (3)*
tanto(a) (s)... como *as much (many) . . . as (3)*
tarde *(f.) afternoon (2); (adv.) late (3)*
  de la tarde P.M., *noon to sundown (2)*
  más tarde *later on (5)*
  por la tarde *in the afternoon (1)*
tarjeta *card (2)*
  tarjeta de crédito *credit card (2)*
  tarjeta postal *postcard (8)*
taza *cup (4)*
  taza de café *cup of coffee (4)*
té *(m.) tea (4)*
teatro *theater (7)*
teléfono celular *cell phone (PP)*
televisión *(f.) television (1)*
televisor *(m.) television set (3)*
temperatura *temperature (7)*
temporal *temporary (9)*
temprano *early (3)*
tenedor *(m.) fork (4)*
tener *to have (1)*
  tener calor *to be hot (1)*
  tener cuidado *to be careful (1)*
  tener frío *to be cold (1)*
  tener ganas de (+ inf.) *to feel like* (doing something) *(1)*
  tener hambre *to be hungry (1)*

  tener miedo *to be afraid (1)*
  tener prisa *to be in a hurry (1)*
  tener razón *to be right (1)*
  tener sed *to be thirsty (1)*
  tener sueño *to be sleepy (1)*
  tener vómitos *to be vomiting (8)*
tenis *(m.) tennis (1)*
teoría *theory (5)*
tercer(o)(a) *third (2)*
terminar *to finish (7)*
tía *aunt (1)*
tiempo *weather (7)*
tiempo libre *free time (7)*
tienda *(n.) store (1)*
tímido(a) *shy (3)*
tina *bathtub (3)*
tío *uncle (1)*
tiza *chalk (PP)*
tobillo *ankle (8)*
tocar *to play* (a musical instrument); *to touch (5)*
toda la noche *all night (7)*
todos los días *every day (1)*
tomar *to take, drink (1); to take (4)*
  tomar apuntes *to take notes (5)*
  tomar el sol *to sunbathe (7)*
tomate *(m.) tomato (4)*
torcer (ue) *to twist, sprain (8)*
tormenta *storm (7)*

torta *cake (4)*
tortilla *omelette (4); flour tortilla* (Mexico) *(4)*
tos *(f.) cough (8)*
trabajador(a) *hard-working (3)*
  trabajador(a) *social social worker (5)*
trabajar *to work (1)*
trabajo *(n.) work, job (1)*
  trabajo escrito *written paper (9)*
tradicional *traditional (3)*
traje *(m.) suit (6)*
  traje de baño *(m.) bathing suit (6)*
tras *after (5)*
tratado *treaty (1)*
tratar de + inf. *to try to (do something)(9)*
  tratarse *to treat oneself (9)*
trece *thirteen (PP)*
treinta *thirty (PP)*
treinta y nueve *thirty-nine (PP)*
treinta y uno *thirty-one (PP)*
tren *(m.) train (2)*
trepar *to climb (7)*
tres *three (PP)*
trescientos *three hudred (2)*
triste *sad (1)*
  estar triste *to be sad (1)*

U

último(a)   *last (6)*
  última moda   *latest fashion (6)*

un poco (de)...   *a little (of) . . . (1)*
universidad *(f.)*   *university (1)*

uno   *one (PP)*

V

vacaciones *(f.)*   *vacation (7)*
vacunarse   *to get innoculated (8)*
valer   *to cost (6)*
vaqueros   *jeans (6)*
vaso   *glass (4)*
  vaso de leche   *glass of milk (4)*
vecino(a)   *neighbor (1)*
veinte   *twenty (PP)*
veintidós (veintitrés, veinticuatro...)   *twenty-two (twenty-three, twenty-four . . .) (PP)*
veintiuno   *twenty-one (PP)*
vela   *candle (7)*
velorio *(n.)*   *wake, vigil (9)*
vendedor(a)   *salesperson (5)*

ventaja   *advantage (8)*
ventana   *window (PP)*
ver   *to look (7)*
verano   *summer (7)*
verde   *green (3)*
vestido   *dress (6)*
vestirse (i, i)   *to get dressed (3); to wear(6)*
veterinario(a)   *veterinarian (5)*
viaje *(m.)*   *trip (2)*
vida   *life*
  vida diaria   *daily life (1)*
  vida marina   *aquatic life (5)*
vídeo   *video (1)*
viejo(a)   *old (3)*

viento: hace viento   *it's windy (7)*
viernes   *Friday (2)*
villancico   *(Christmas) carol (7)*
visitar   *to visit (1)*
vivir   *to live (1)*
vómito   *vomiting (8)*
vuelo   *airplane flight (2)*
vuelta: de ida y vuelta   *round-trip (2)*
vuestro(a)   *your (inform., pl.)(1)*

Y

y   *and (1)*

yo   *I (1)*

Vocabulario

The following abbreviations are used in this glossary:

adj.	adjective	**m.**	masculine
conj.	conjunction	**n.**	noun
f.	feminine	**PP**	paso preliminar
form.	formal	**pl.**	plural
inf.	infinitive	**sing.**	singular
inform.	informal	**v.**	verb

A

A.M. *de la mañana;* **A.M., early morning** *de la madrugada (2)*
a *un(a) (PP)*
  (a) little *poco(a) (1)*
  a lot *mucho(a) (1)*
above *sobre (3)*
accept *aceptar (6)*
accountant *contador(a) (5)*
accustomed: to be accustomed
  (to) *acostumbrar a (7)*
ache *(v.) doler (ue) (8)*
across from *enfrente de (8)*
activity *actividad (f.) (1)*
address *(n.) dirección (f.) (1)*
advice *(n.) consejo (9)*
advise *aconsejar (9)*
affectionate *cariñoso(a) (3)*
afraid: to be afraid *tener miedo (1)*
after *después (1); después de (5)*
afternoon *tarde (f.) (1)*
  in the afternoon *por la tarde (1)*
afterwards *después (5)*
ahead: straight ahead *derecho (adv.) (8)*
airplane *avión (m.) (2)*
  airplane flight *vuelo (2)*

airport *aeropuerto (8)*
aisle *pasillo (3)*
algebra *álgebra (5)*
all night *toda la noche (7)*
although *aunque (6)*
altitude sickness *mal de altura (8)*
always *siempre (3)*
analysis *análisis (m.) (8)*
and *y (1)*
anger *(v.) enfadar (9)*
angry *enojado(a) (1)*
  to be angry *estar enojado(a) (1)*
ankle *tobillo (8)*
another *otro(a) (7)*
answer *(n.) respuesta (1); (v.) contestar (1)*
anthropology *antropología (5)*
antibiotic *antibiótico (8)*
anything *algo (1)*
apartment *apartamento (1)*
appear *parecer (6)*
apply *aplicarse (8)*
approved: to be approved *aprobarse (ue) (1)*
April *abril (2)*
aquatic life *vida marina (5)*
arm *brazo (8)*

arrival *llegada (2)*
arrive *llegar (ue) (2)*
art *arte (m.) (5)*
  fine arts *bellas artes (5)*
  arts and crafts *artesanía (6)*
as . . . as *tan... como (3)*
as much (many) . . . as *tanto(a)(s)... como (3)*
aside from *aparte de (4)*
ask *preguntar (PP)*
  ask for *pedir (i, i) (4)*
asleep: to fall asleep *dormirse (ue, u) (3)*
aspirin *aspirina (8)*
at night *por la noche (1)*
at what time? *¿a qué hora? (1)*
attend *asistir a (1)*
August *agosto (2)*
aunt *tía (1)*
auto racing *(n.) carrera de autos (3)*
autumn *otoño (7)*
avenue *avenida (8)*
average *(adj.) regular (5)*
avocado stuffed with chicken or tuna salad *palta rellena (4)*

B

baby *(n.) bebé (m., f.) (9)*
back *espalda (8)*
backpack *mochila (PP)*
bad *mal(o)(a) (1)*
badly behaved *maleducado(a) (3)*
bag *(n.) bolsa (4)*
baked *al horno (4)*
balanced *balanceado(a) (9)*
bald *calvo(a) (3)*
banana *plátano, banana (4)*
bank *banco (2)*
bargain *(v.) regatear (6)*
basement *sótano (6)*

bath(room) *baño (2)*
bath: to take a bath *bañarse (3)*
bathing suit *traje de baño (m.) (6)*
bathroom sink *lavabo (3)*
bathtub *bañera, tina (3)*
be *estar, ser (1)*
  to be accustomed (to) *acostumbrar a (7)*
  to be afraid *tener miedo (1)*
  to be approved *aprobarse (ue) (1)*
  to be careful *tener cuidado (1)*
  to be cold *tener frío (1)*
  be due to *deberse a (3)*
  be happy *alegrarse (9)*

be helpful *convenir (ie) (2)*
be hot *tener calor (1)*
be hungry *tener hambre (1)*
be in a good/bad mood *estar de buen/ mal humor (1)*
be in a hurry *tener prisa (1)*
be injured *ser herido (6)*
be interested in *interesar (5)*
be introduced to *conocer (7)*
be on exhibit *exhibir (7)*
be pleasing *gustar (1)*
be right *tener razón (1)*
be short, missing, lacking *faltar (6)*

be sleepy *tener sueño (1)*
be sorry *sentir (ie, i) (9)*
be thirsty *tener sed (1)*
be vomiting *tener vómitos (8)*
beach *(n.)* *playa (7)*
bean *frijol (m.) (4)*
beard *barba (3)*
because *porque (1)*
become *convertirse (ie) (5)*
bed *cama (2)*
   go to bed *acostarse (ue) (3)*
   make the bed *hacer la cama (3)*
beef *biftec (m.) (4)*
beer *cerveza (4)*
before *antes (de) (1)*
begin *empezar (ie) (PP)*
beginning: at the beginning of *a principios de (5)*
behind *detrás de (3)*
beige *beige (6)*
believe *creer (5)*
belt *cinturón (m.) (4)*
beret *boina (6)*
better, best *mejor (3)*
between *entre (3)*

bill *(n.)* *cuenta (2)*
biology *biología (5)*
bird *pájaro (3)*
birthday *cumpleaños (m.) (7)*
   birthday cake *pastel de cumpleaños (m.) (7)*
black *negro(a) (3)*
black pepper *pimienta (4)*
bless *bendecir (1)*
blessing *bendición (f.) (1)*
   ask someone for a blessing *pedir la bendición (1)*
block *(of a street) cuadra (8)*
blond(e) *rubio(a) (3)*
blouse *blusa (6)*
blue *azul (6)*
boat *barco (2)*
book *libro (PP)*
boot *bota (6)*
born: to be born *nacer (1)*
bother *molestar (9)*
bottle *(n.)* *botella (4)*
boy *chico (3)*
boyfriend *novio (1)*
bracelet: silver bracelet *brazalete de plata (m.) (6)*

branch *rama (3)*
bread *pan (m.) (4)*
   loaf of bread *barra (de pan) (4)*
break *(v.) romperse (7)*
break up *romper (9)*
breakfast *(n.) desayuno (4)*
   eat breakfast *desayunar (4)*
briefly *brevemente (3)*
broccoli *brócoli (m.) (4)*
broken *roto(a) (3)*
brother *hermano (1)*
   half brother *medio hermano (3)*
brown *castaño (3), marrón (6)*
bureau *cómoda (3)*
burned: to get burned *quemarse (8)*
bus *(n.) autobús (m.) (2)*
bus stop *parada de autobuses (8)*
business *negocios (5)*
busy *ocupado(a) (1)*
   be busy *estar ocupado(a) (1)*
butter *mantequilla (4)*
buy *comprar (3)*
by *por (1)*
   by chance *por casualidad (7)*

C

cake *torta (4); pastel (m.) (7)*
calculus *cálculo (5)*
calendar *calendario (PP)*
candelabra *candelabro (7)*
candle *vela (7)*
candy *dulces (m.) (7)*
cap *gorra (6)*
card *tarjeta (2)*
   playing cards *cartas (7)*
   postcard *tarjeta postal (8)*
care: to take care of oneself *cuidarse (9)*
careful: to be careful *tener cuidado (1)*
carry *llevar (7)*
cash *en efectivo (2)*
castanets *castañuelas (6)*
cat *gato (3)*
cathedral *catedral (f.) (8)*
celebrate *celebrar (7)*
celebration *celebración (f.) (3)*
cell phone *teléfono celular (PP)*
century *siglo (3)*
cereal *cereal (m.) (4)*
certain *cierto(a) (9)*
chair *silla (PP)*
chalk *tiza (PP)*
chalkboard *pizarra (PP)*
champagne *champaña (7)*
change *(v.) cambiar (8)*
character *carácter (m.) (3)*
cheap *barato(a) (6)*
check *(n.) cuenta (2)*
   traveler's check *cheque de viajero (2)*
check in (a hotel) *ocupar (2)*
check out (of hotel) *desocupar (2)*
cheek *mejilla (1)*
cheese *queso (4)*
chemistry *química (5)*
chest *pecho (8)*

chestnut (color) *castaño(a) (3)*
chicken: roast chicken *pollo asado (4)*
child *niño(a) (4)*
childhood *niñez (f.) (5)*
chili pepper *ají picante (m.) (4)*
chocolate *chocolate (m.) (4)*
chores: household chores *quehaceres (m.) (3)*
Christmas *Navidad (f.) (7)*
   (Christmas) carol *villancico (7)*
Christmas Eve *Nochebuena (7)*
church *iglesia (7)*
cinema *cine (m.) (7)*
cinnamon *canela (4)*
classroom *sala de clase (PP)*
classmate *compañero(a) de clase (1)*
clean *(adj.) limpio (a) (3); (v.) limpiar (1)*
clear *despejado (7)*
client *cliente (m., f.) (3)*
climb *trepar (7)*
clinic *clínica (8)*
clock *reloj (m.) (PP)*
close *(v.) cerrar (ie) (2)*
close to *cerca (de) (1)*
closed *cerrado(a) (2)*
closet *clóset (m.) (3)*
clothing *ropa (6)*
   article of clothing *prenda (de vestir) (6)*
cloudy *nublado (7)*
coat *(n.) abrigo (8)*
cold *(n.) resfriado, catarro (8); (adj.) frío(a) (3)*
   it's cold *hace frío (7)*
   to be cold *tener frío (1)*
collect *recolectar (5)*
color *(n.) color (m.) (6)*
comb: to comb one's hair *peinarse (3)*
commonwealth *estado libre asociado (1)*
compact disc (CD) *disco compacto (1)*

company *compañía (1)*
   multinational company *compañía multinacional (5)*
complaint *queja (9)*
complete *completo(a) (2)*
comprehensive *comprensivo(a) (3)*
computer *computadora (PP)*
computer science *informática (5)*
concert *concierto (7)*
consultant *consultor(a) (5)*
cook *(v.) cocinar (3)*
cookie *galleta (4)*
cool: it's cool *hace fresco (7)*
corn *maíz (m.) (4)*
corner *esquina (8)*
cost *(v.) valer (6); costar (ue) (2)*
costume *disfraz (m.) (7)*
cotton *algodón (m.) (6)*
cough *tos (f.) (8)*
   (cough) syrup *jarabe (para la tos) (m.) (8)*
counselor *consejero(a) (5)*
country(side) *campo (7)*
course: first course *primer plato (4)*
   second course *segundo plato (4)*
cousin *primo(a) (3)*
crafts: arts and crafts *artesanía (6)*
cream color *color crema (6)*
cream *crema (8)*
credit card *tarjeta de crédito (2)*
cross *cruzar (8)*
cruel *cruel (3)*
cup *taza (4)*
   cup of coffee *taza de café (4)*
custard *flan (4)*
customer *cliente (m., f.) (3)*
cut *(v.) cortar (3)*
   cut oneself, to get cut *cortarse (8)*

D

daily *diario(a) (9)*
  daily life *vida diaria (1)*
damage *(n.) daño (1)*
dance *(v.) bailar (1)*
date *(n.) fecha (2); cita (9); compañero(a) (9)*
daughter *hija (1)*
dawn *madrugada (5)*
day *día (m.) (2)*
  every day *todos los días (1)*
death *muerte (f.) (1)*
deceitful *mentiroso(a) (3)*
December *diciembre (2)*
decorate *decorar (7)*
delicious *sabroso(a) (7)*
demanding *exigente (5)*
demonstration *manifestación (f.) (5)*
dentist *dentista (m., f.) (5)*
department: department store *gran almacén (m.) (6)*
departure *(n.) salida (2)*
depend *depender (9)*
depressed *deprimido(a) (9)*

desk *pupitre (m.) (PP)*
dessert *postre (m.) (3)*
diagnosis *diagnóstico (8)*
diarrhea *diarrea (8)*
dictionary *diccionario (PP)*
die *morirse (ue, u) (9)*
difficult *difícil (9)*
dining room *comedor (m.) (3)*
dinner *cena (3)*
dirty *sucio(a) (3)*
disconnect *desconectarse (9)*
discount *(n.) descuento (2)*
discuss *discutir (9)*
dish *(n.) plato (3)*
dishwasher *lavaplatos (m.) (3)*
disorganized *desorganizado(a) (5)*
dive *(v.) bucear (7)*
divorced *(adj.) divorciado(a) (1)*
  to get divorced *divorciarse (9)*
dizziness *mareo (8)*
do *hacer (3)*
  to do business *comerciar (6)*

to do exercise *hacer ejercicio (1)*
to do well (poorly) *salir bien (mal) (9)*
doctor *médico(a) (5)*
dog *perro (3)*
dormitory *residencia estudiantil (1); dormitorio (3)*
double *doble (2)*
  double room *habitación doble (f.) (2)*
doubt *(v.) dudar (6)*
doubtful *dudoso(a) (9)*
dozen *docena (4)*
drama *obra (de teatro) (7)*
dress pants *pantalones de vestir (6)*
dress *vestido (6)*
dressed: to get dressed *vestirse (i, i) (3)*
dressy *formal (6)*
drink *(v.) tomar (1); beber (4)*
dry *seco(a) (7)*
due: to be due to *deberse a (3)*
during *durante (3)*
dust *(v.) quitar el polvo (3)*

E

ear (inner) *oído (8); (outer) oreja (8)*
early *temprano (3)*
  early morning *madrugada (5)*
earring *arete (m.) (6)*
Easter *Pascua (7)*
eat *comer (1), alimentarse (9)*
  eat breakfast *desayunar (4)*
  eat lunch *almorzar (ue) (4)*
  eat supper *cenar (3)*
ecology *ecología (5)*
education *educación (f.) (5)*
eggs: scrambled eggs *huevos revueltos (4)*
eight hundred *ochocientos (2)*
eight *ocho (PP)*
eighteen *dieciocho (PP)*
eighth *octavo(a) (2)*
eighty *ochenta (PP)*
elbow *codo (8)*
elderly *mayor (3)*

eleven *once (PP)*
e-mail *correo electrónico (1)*
embroidered *bordado(a) (6)*
employee *empleado(a)(3)*
end *(n.) fin (m.)*
  at the end of *a finales de (5)*
engaged: to get engaged: *comprometerse (9)*
engagement (to be married): *compromiso (9)*
engineer *ingeniero(a) (5)*
engineering *ingeniería (5)*
English *(language) inglés (m.) (1)*
enjoy *disfrutar (de) (7)*
enough *suficiente (9)*
era *época (1)*
eraser *borrador (m.) (PP)*
errand *diligencia (8)*
escort *(n.) compañero(a) (9)*
essay *ensayo (7)*
even *aunque (3)*

evening *noche (1)*
  in the evening *por la noche (1)*
event *acontecimiento (9)*
every day *todos los días (1)*
exchange *(v.) cambiar (8)*
exchange *intercambiar (7)*
excited *emocionado(a) (9)*
excuse me *perdón (PP)*
exercise *(n.) ejercicio (1)*
  to exercise, to do exercise *hacer ejercicio (1)*
exhausted *agotado(a) (9)*
exhibit: to be on exhibit *exhibir (7)*
exhibition *exposición (f.) (7)*
expensive *caro(a) (6)*
explanation *explicación (f.) (PP)*
eye *ojo (3)*
eyeglasses *anteojos, gafas (3)*

F

face *(n.) cara (3); (v.) enfrentar (9)*
  wash one's face *lavarse la cara (3)*
fact *dato (1)*
fall *(n.) otoño (7); (v.) caerse (5)*
fall asleep *dormirse (ue, u) (5)*
family *familia (1)*
  family member *familiar (m.) (3)*
fan *abanico (6)*
fancy *formal (6)*
far *lejos (8)*
  far from *lejos (de) (1)*
farmer *agricultor(a) (5)*
fascinating *fascinante (5)*
fashion *moda (6)*
  latest fashion *última moda (6)*
fat *gordo(a) (3)*

father *padre (m.) (1)*
February *febrero (2)*
feed *dar de comer (3)*
feel *(v.) sentirse (ie, i) (9)*
  feel like *(doing something) tener ganas de (+ inf.) (1)*
festival *festival (m.) (7)*
fever *fiebre (f.) (8)*
fiancé (fiancée) *novio(a) (9)*
field trip *excursión (f.) (5)*
fifteen *quince (PP)*
fifth *quinto (2)*
fifty *cincuenta (1)*
fight *(v.) luchar (3)*
film-making *cinematografía (5)*
finally *por fin (5)*

find *(v.) encontrar (ue) (6)*
  find out *enterarse (9)*
fine *(adv.) bien (1)*
finger *dedo (8)*
finish *(v.) terminar (7)*
fire *fuego (7)*
fireworks *fuegos artificiales (7)*
first *primer(o)(a) (9)*
  first course *primer plato (m.) (4)*
  first floor *planta baja (3)*
  first name *nombre (m.) (1)*
fish (cooked) *pescado (4)*
fish *(v.) pescar (7)*
  tropical fish *pez tropical (m.) (3)*
fit *(v.) quedar (8)*
five *cinco (PP)*

five hundred *quinientos* (2)
five thousand *cinco mil* (2)
fix oneself up *arreglarse* (3)
flight: airplane flight *vuelo* (2)
floor *piso* (6); *planta* (3)
  ground/first floor *planta baja* (6)
flourish *florecer* (3)
flu *gripe* (f.) (8)
follow *seguir* (i, i) (3)
food *comida* (4)
  fast food *comida rápida* (1)
  food poisoning *intoxicación alimenticia* (f.) (8)
foot *pie* (m.) (8)
  go on foot *ir a pie* (8)

football *fútbol americano* (m.) (1)
forbid *prohibir* (9)
forecast (n.) *pronóstico* (7)
forest *bosque* (m.) (2)
fork *tenedor* (m.) (4)
forty *cuarenta* (2)
founder *fundador(a)* (1)
four *cuatro* (PP)
four hundred *cuatrocientos* (2)
fourth *cuarto* (2)
Fourth of July *Día de la Independencia* (m.) (7)
fracture (n.) *fractura* (8)
freckles *pecas* (3)
free (adj.) *libre* (9)
  free time *tiempo libre* (7)

freedom *libertad* (f.) (3)
French fries *papas fritas* (4)
frequently *con frecuencia* (3)
Friday *viernes* (2)
fried *frito(a)* (4)
friend *amigo(a)* (3)
friendly *amable* (3)
fritter *churro* (4)
full *completo(a)* (2)
funny *divertido(a)* (7)
furious *furioso(a)* (9)
furnished *amueblado(a)* (3)
furniture *muebles* (m.) (3)

G

game *partido* (1)
geography *geografía* (5)
get *conseguir* (i) (5)
  to get a grade (in school) *sacar* (5)
  to get along well (poorly) with someone *llevarse bien (mal)* (9)
  to get burned *quemarse* (8)
  to get cut *cortarse* (80)
  to get divorced *divorciarse* (9)
  to get dressed *vestirse* (i, i) (3)
  to get engaged *comprometerse* (9)
  to get hurt *lastimarse* (8)
  to get in shape *ponerse en forma* (9)
  to get married *casarse* (9)
  to get ready *arreglarse* (3)
  to get sick *enfermarse* (7)
  to get together *reunirse* (7)
  to get up *levantarse* (3)
gift (v.) *regalar* (7); (n.) *regalo* (7)
girl *chica* (3)
girlfriend *novia* (1)

give *dar* (3)
  give (as a present) *regalar* (7)
  give a kiss *dar un beso* (1)
glass *copa, vaso* (4)
  glass of milk *vaso de leche* (4)
  glass of wine *copa de vino* (4)
glove *guante* (m.) (6)
go *ir* (1)
  to go back *regresar* (1)
  to go camping *acampar* (7)
  to go hiking *hacer caminatas* (7)
  to go horseback riding *montar a caballo* (7)
  to go on a picnic *ir de picnic* (7)
  to go on foot *ir a pie* (8)
  to go out *salir* (3); to go out (on a social occasion) *salir* (7)
  to go to bed *acostarse* (ue) (3)
  to go to graduate school *hacer estudios de postgrado* (5)
God *Dios* (1)
godfather (godmother) *padrino (madrina)* (3)
good *bueno(a)* (3)

good bye: to say good-bye *despedirse* (i, i) (3)
governor *gobernador(a)* (1)
grade *nota* (5)
graduate (v.) *graduarse* (5)
  to go to graduate school *hacer estudios de postgrado* (5)
grammar *gramática* (1)
grandfather (grandmother) *abuelo (abuela)* (1)
grandparents *abuelos* (1)
grandson (granddaughter) *nieto(a)* (3)
grave (adj.) *grave* (9)
gray *gris* (6)
gray haired *canoso(a)* (3)
great *fabuloso(a)* (7)
green *verde* (3)
greet *saludar* (4)
grief-stricken *desconsolado(a)* (9)
grilled *a la parrilla* (4)
ground floor *planta baja* (3)
group: musical group *conjunto* (7)
gym *gimnasio* (1)

H

hacerse *to become* (5)
haggle over a price *regatear* (6)
hair *pelo* (3)
  to comb one's hair *peinarse* (3)
  to wash one's hair *lavarse el pelo* (3)
Halloween *Día de las Brujas* (m.) (7)
ham *jamón* (m.) (4)
hamburger *hamburguesa* (4)
hamster *hámster* (m.) (3)
hand (n.) *mano* (f.)
  to wash one's hands *lavarse las manos* (3)
hand in *entregar* (9)
handicraft *artesanía* (6)
handsome *guapo(a)* (3)
Hannukah *Janucá* (7)
happen *ocurrir* (7)
happy: to be happy *estar contento(a)* (1)
  to make happy *alegrar* (9)
hard-working *trabajador(a)* (3)
hat *sombrero* (6)
have *tener* (1)
  to have a good time *divertirse* (ie, i) (3), *pasarlo bien* (7)

  to have a snack *merendar* (ie) (4)
  to have just (done something) *acabar de (+ inf.)* (9)
  to have some down time *desconectarse* (9)
hazel (colored) *miel* (3)
head *cabeza* (8)
heart *corazón* (m.) (8)
heavy *pesado(a)* (5)
help (n.) *ayuda* (9); (v.) *ayudar* (3)
helpful: to be helpful *convenir* (ie) (2)
hiking: to go hiking *hacer caminatas* (7)
himself (herself) *sí mismo(a)* (1)
history *historia* (5)
holiday *día festivo* (7)
Holy Week *Semana Santa* (2)
home *hogar* (m.) (3)
homemaker *ama de casa* (5)
honest *honesto(a)* (3)
honey color *color miel* (3)
hope (v.) *esperar* (7)
  I hope that . . . *ojalá...* (9)
horse *caballo*
  to go horseback riding *montar a caballo* (7)

hospital *hospital* (m.) (1)
host (hostess) *anfitrión (anfitriona)* (4)
hot *caliente* (2)
  to be hot *tener calor* (1)
hotel *hotel* (m.) (2)
house *casa* (1)
household chores *quehaceres* (m.) (3)
how? *¿cómo?* (1)
how come? *¿por qué?*
how many? *¿cuántos(as)?* (1)
how much? *¿cuánto(a)?* (1)
humanities *humanidades* (f.) (5)
humble (adj.) *humilde* (5)
hungry: to be hungry *tener hambre* (1)
hunt *cazar, ir de caza* (7)
hurry: to be in a hurry *tener prisa* (1)
hurt (v.) *doler* (ue); *lastimar* (8)
  to get hurt *lastimarse* (8)
husband *esposo* (3)

I

ice cream   *helado (4)*
ice cube   *cubito de hielo (4)*
ill-mannered   *antipático(a) (3)*
illness   *enfermedad (f.) (8)*
in front of   *delante de (3)*
in the afternoon   *por la tarde (1)*
in the evening   *por la noche (1)*
in the morning   *por la mañana (1)*
incarcerated   *encarcelado(a) (6)*

indifferent   *indiferente (3)*
inexpensive   *barato(a) (6)*
infection   *infección (f.) (8)*
information   *dato (1)*
injure oneself   *lastimarse (8)*
injured: to be injured   *ser herido (6)*
inside   *dentro de (3)*
interest, to be interested in   *interesar (5)*
internship   *internado (9)*

interview   *(n.)   entrevista (9)*
introduce   *presentar (7)*
introduced: to be introduced to   *conocer (7)*
iron   *planchar (3)*
irresponsible   *irresponsable (3)*
irritate   *molestar (9)*
island   *isla (3)*

J

jacket   *chaqueta (6)*
January   *enero (2)*
jar   *frasco (4)*
jeans   *vaqueros (6)*

jewel   *joya (6)*
job   *puesto (9)*
journalism   *periodismo (5)*
journalist   *periodista (m., f.) (4)*

July   *julio (2)*
June   *junio (2)*

K

keep track of   *estar pendiente de (3)*
key   *(n.)   llave (f.) (2)*
kitchen   *cocina (3)*
kitchen sink   *fregadero (3)*

knee   *rodilla (8)*
knife   *cuchillo (4)*
kilo (metric pound)   *kilo (4)*

know (people)   *conocer (2),* (information)   *saber (8)*
known   *conocido(a) (2)*

L

laborer   *obrero(a) (5)*
lace scarf   *mantilla (6)*
lake   *lago (2)*
lamp   *lámpara (3)*
last   *(adj.)   pasado(a) (5)*
   last month   *mes pasado (5)*
   last week   *semana pasada (5)*
   last weekend   *fin de semana pasado (5)*
last   *(v.)   durar (9)*
late   *tarde (3)*
later   *luego (5)*
   later on   *más tarde (5)*
latest   *último(a) (6)*
   latest fashion   *última moda (6)*
law   *derecho (n.) (5)*
lawn   *césped (m.) (3)*
lawyer   *abogado(a) (5)*
lazy   *perezoso(a) (3)*
leader   *(n.)   cacique (m.) (1)*
learn   *aprender (1)*

leave (go out)   *salir (3); dejar (9)*
lecture   *(n.)   conferencia (5)*
left: to the left   *a la izquierda (3)*
leg   *pierna (8)*
legacy   *legado (6)*
less . . . than   *menos... que (3)*
let   *dejar (9)*
letter   *carta (8)*
lettuce   *lechuga (4)*
library   *biblioteca (1)*
life: daily life   *vida diaria (1)*
   aquatic life   *vida marina (5)*
lift weights   *levantar pesas (7)*
light   *(v.)   encender (ie) (7)*
light-headedness   *mareo (8)*
likable   *simpático(a) (3)*
like   *(v.)   gustar (1)*
likely   *probable (9)*
likewise   *igualmente (PP)*
listen to   *escuchar (1)*

liter   *litro (4)*
literature   *literatura (5)*
little: a little (of) . . .   *un poco (de)... (1)*
live   *(v.)   vivir (1)*
livestock   *(n.)   ganado (5)*
living room   *sala (3)*
loaf (of bread)   *barra (de pan) (4)*
loan   *(n.)   préstamo (9)*
lobster   *langosta (4)*
look   *ver (7)*
   to look at   *mirar (1)*
   to look for   *buscar (6)*
lose   *perder (ie) (2)*
love (a thing or activity)   *encantar (5)*
   in love   *enamorado(a) (9)*
lunch   *(n.)   almuerzo (3)*
   to eat lunch   *almorzar (ue) (4)*
lungs   *pulmones (m.) (8)*
lying   *mentiroso(a) (3)*

M

machinery   *maquinaria (5)*
magazine   *revista (1)*
maid   *empleado(a) (3)*
major (field of study)   *(n.)   carrera (5)*
make   *hacer (3)*
   to make happy   *alegrar (9)*
   to make the bed   *hacer la cama (3)*
man   *hombre (m.) (6)*
manager   *gerente (m., f.) (5)*
map   *(n.)   mapa (m.) (PP)*
maracas   *maracas (6)*
March   *marzo (2)*
market   *mercado (6)*
marmalade   *mermelada (4)*

marriage   *casamiento (3)*
married   *casado(a) (1)*
   to get married   *casarse (9)*
master's degree   *maestría (3)*
mathematics   *matemáticas (5)*
matter   *importar (6)*
May   *mayo (2)*
mayonnaise   *mayonesa (4)*
meal   *comida (4)*
medicine   *medicina (5)*
medium   *mediano(a) (3)*
   medium-sized   *de tamaño mediano (3)*
meet   *conocer, encontrar (ue), reunirse (7)*
Menorah   *candelabro (7)*

menu   *menú (m.), carta (4)*
messy   *desordenado(a) (3)*
microwave   *microondas (3)*
midday   *mediodía (m.) (2)*
middle (child)   *de en medio (3)*
   in the middle   *en el medio (3)*
midnight   *medianoche (f.) (2)*
million   *millón (m.) (2)*
miserable   *pésimo(a) (7)*
modern (in style)   *de estilo moderno(a) (3)*
Monday   *lunes (2)*
month   *mes (m.) (2)*
   last month   *mes pasado (5)*
   next month   *mes próximo (5)*

more . . . than *más... que (3)*
morning: in the morning *por la mañana (1)*
mother *madre (f.) (1)*
motion sickness *mareo (8)*
mountain *montaña (7)*
mountain range *cordillera (2)*
moustache *bigote (m.) (3)*
mouth *boca (8)*

move (a part of the body) *moverse (3)*
　to move (one's residence), to move
　　out *mudarse (3)*
movie *película (1)*
movie theater *cine (m.) (7)*
MP3/MP4 player *reproductor de MP3/*
　MP4 (m.) (PP)
much *mucho(a) (1)*

multinational *(adj.) multinacional (5)*
　multinational company *compañía*
　　internacional (5)
museum *museo (2)*
music *música (1)*
musical group *conjunto (7)*
must *deber + inf. (4)*
myself *mí mismo(a) (5)*

N

name *nombre (m.) (1)*
　last name *apellido (1)*
napkin *servilleta (4)*
nausea *náuseas (8)*
navigate *navegar (1)*
navy blue *azul marino (6)*
near(by) *cerca de (8)*
neat *ordenado(a) (3)*
neck *cuello (8)*
necklace *collar (m.) (6)*
　gold necklace *cadena de oro (6)*
necktie *corbata (6)*
need *(v.) necesitar (1)*
neighbor *vecino(a) (1)*
nephew *sobrino (3)*
nervous: to be nervous *estar nervioso(a) (1)*

never *nunca (3)*
new *nuevo(a) (1)*
New Year's Day *Día de Año Nuevo (m.) (7)*
New Year's Eve *Noche Vieja (f.) (7)*
news *noticias (3)*
newspaper *periódico (1)*
next *luego (5); próximo(a) (5)*
　next month *mes próximo (5)*
niece *sobrina (3)*
night *noche (f.)*
　all night *toda la noche (7)*
　at night *por la noche (5)*
night stand *mesita de noche (3)*
nine *nueve (PP)*
nine hundred *novecientos (2)*
nineteen *diecinueve (PP)*

ninety *noventa (1)*
ninth *noveno(a) (2)*
noodle *fideo (4)*
noon *mediodía (m.) (2)*
normally *normalmente (3)*
nose *nariz (f.) (8)*
not much *poco(a) (1)*
notebook *cuaderno (PP)*
notes *apuntes (m.) (5)*
nourish oneself *alimentarse (9)*
novel *novela (1)*
November *noviembre (2)*
nowadays *hoy por hoy (3)*
number *número (1)*

O

observatory *observatorio (5)*
obtain *conseguir (i) (5)*
occupation *oficio (5)*
October *octubre (2)*
office *oficina (1)*
often *con frecuencia (3)*
old *viejo(a) (3)*
older, oldest *mayor (3)*
omelette *tortilla (4)*
on *en (PP); sobre (3)*

　on top of *encima de (3)*
one hundred *cien (2)*
one hundred one *ciento uno (2)*
one thousand *mil (2)*
one-hundred thousand *cien mil (2)*
one-way *de ida (2)*
open *(v.) abrir (2)*
open *abierto(a) (2)*
opposite *(adj.) enfrente de (8)*
optimistic *optimista (9)*

orange (color) *anaranjado(a) (6)*
orange juice *jugo de naranja (4)*
order *(v.) pedir (i, i) (4)*
order: out of order *descompuesto(a) (3)*
organize *organizar (9)*
other *otro(a) (7)*
oven *horno (4)*
owe *deber (4)*

P

P.M. (afternoon) *de la tarde (2); (night) de la*
　noche (2)
package *paquete (m.) (4)*
page *(n.) página (PP)*
pain *dolor (m.) (8)*
pants: dress pants *pantalones de vestir (m.) (6)*
paper: sheet of paper *hoja de papel (PP)*
　wrapping paper *papel de regalo (6)*
parade *desfile (m.) (7)*
pardon me *perdón (PP)*
parents *padres (1)*
park *parque (m.) (1)*
partner *compañero(a) (PP)*
party *(n.) fiesta (1); (political) partido (1)*
pass the basic courses *aprobar (ue) (5)*
Passover *Pésaj (m.) (7)*
paternal *paterno(a) (3)*
patient *paciente (m., f.) (8)*
pay (for) *pagar (6)*
peach *durazno, melocotón (m.) (4)*
peak *(n.) cumbre (f.) (5)*
pear *pera (4)*

pen *bolígrafo (PP)*
pencil *lápiz (m.) (PP)*
people: group of people *pueblo (2)*
perhaps *quizás (9)*
personality *personalidad (f.) (3); carácter*
　(m.) (3)
personnel director *director(a) de personal (5)*
pessimistic *pesimista (9)*
pet *animal doméstico (3)*
pharmacy *farmacia (8)*
physics *física (5)*
picky *quisquilloso(a) (5)*
picnic: to go on a picnic *ir de picnic (7)*
　to have a picnic *hacer un picnic (7)*
picture *foto (f.) (1)*
pie: pumpkin pie *pastel de calabaza (m.) (7)*
pill *pastilla (8)*
pineapple *piña (4)*
pink *rosado(a) (6)*
place *(n.) lugar (m.) (2)*
place setting *cubierto (4)*
plaid *de cuadros (6)*

plate: ceramic plate *plato de cerámica (6)*
play *(n.) obra (de teatro) (7)*
play *(v.) jugar (ue) (1)*
　to play (a musical instrument) *tocar (5)*
　to play (a sport) *practicar (1); jugar (ue) (1)*
player *jugador(a) (7)*
pleasing: to be pleasing *gustar (1)*
poetry *poesía (1)*
point out *señalar (9)*
police station *comisaría (8)*
polka-dotted *con lunares (6)*
pool (swimming) *piscina (2)*
poorly: to do poorly *salir mal (9)*
population *población (f.) (2)*
pork chop *chuleta de cerdo (4)*
portrait *(n.) retrato (3)*
post office *correo (8)*
postage stamp *sello (8)*
postcard *tarjeta postal (8)*
poster *cartel (m.) (PP)*
postpone *posponer (9)*
potato *papa, patata (4)*

practice (v.) *practicar* (1)
pregnant *embarazada* (9)
prepare *preparar* (3)
prescribe *recetar* (8)
prescription *receta* (8)
present (n.) *regalo* (7); (v.) *presentar* (7)
presentation *presentación* (f.) (5)
printed *estampado(a)* (6)
printer *impresora* (PP)
private *privado(a)* (2)
probable *probable* (9)

procrastinate *procrastinar* (9)
professional studies *estudios profesionales* (5)
professor *profesor(a)* (PP)
program (n.) *programa* (m.) (1)
programmer *programador(a)* (5)
prohibit *prohibir* (9)
project (n.) *proyecto* (5)
protect *proteger* (5)
proud *orgulloso(a)* (9)
psychologist *psicólogo(a)* (5)
psychology *psicología* (5)

pumpkin pie *pastel de calabaza* (m.) (7)
purple *morado(a)* (6)
purse: leather purse *bolso de cuero* (6)
pursue *perseguir* (8)
put *poner* (3)
   to put in order, pick up the room *recoger* (3)
   to put off *posponer* (9)
   to put on make-up *maquillarse* (3)
   to put on oneself *ponerse* (3); *aplicarse* (8)
   to put out *apagar* (7)

Q

question (n.) *pregunta* (PP)

quite *bastante* (8)

R

race (n.) *carrera* (3)
rain (n.) *lluvia* (7); (v.) *llover* (ue) (7)
raincoat *impermeable* (m.) (6)
raise (v.) *criar* (3)
read *leer* (1)
ready: to get ready *arreglarse* (3)
real estate agent *agente* (m., f.) *de bienes raíces* (5)
receive *recibir* (7)
recommend *recomendar* (ie) (4)
red *rojo(a)* (3)
refrigerator *nevera; refrigerador* (m.) (3)
regret (v.) *sentir* (ie, i) (9)
reject *rechazar* (8)
relative (n.) *pariente* (m.) (3)
relax *descansar* (1); *relajarse* (7)
remain (v.) *quedarse* (7)
remedy *remedio* (8)
renown *renombre* (m.) (4)

rent (v.) *alquilar* (3)
require (v.) *exigir* (5)
research *investigación* (f.) (5)
reservation *reservación* (f.) (2)
residence *residencia estudiantil* (1)
resign *dimitir* (4)
response (n.) *respuesta* (1)
rest *descansar* (1)
restaurant *restaurante* (m.) (1)
return (v.) *regresar, volver* (ue) (2)
rice *arroz* (m.) (4)
   rice dish with saffron, seafood, chicken *paella* (4)
ride a bike (a horse) *montar en bicicleta (a caballo)* (1)
right (n.) *derecho* (7)
   to be right *tener razón* (9)
   to the right *a la derecha* (3)
right away *enseguida* (4)

right there *allí mismo* (8)
ring (n.) *anillo* (9)
roasted *asado(a)* (4)
rock climb, go rock climbing *escalar en roca* (7)
roll (bread) *panecillo* (4)
room *habitación* (f.) (2), *cuarto* (1)
   classroom *sala de clase* (PP)
   double room *habitación doble* (2)
   dressing room *probador* (m.) (6)
   single room *habitación sencilla* (2)
roommate *compañero(a) de cuarto* (3)
round-trip *de ida y vuelta* (2)
rude *antipático(a)* (3)
rug *alfombra* (3)
run *correr* (1)
   run into *chocar contra* (7)
   run over *atropellar* (6)

S

sad *triste* (1)
   to be sad *estar triste* (1)
sailboat *barco de vela* (7)
salad *ensalada* (4)
salad dressing *aderezo* (4)
sale: on sale *de rebaja* (6)
salesperson *vendedor(a)* (5)
salt *sal* (f.) (4)
sand *arena* (2)
sandal *sandalia* (6)
sandwich *sándwich* (m.) (4)
sarape (Mex.) *sarape* (m.) (6)
Saturday *sábado* (2)
say good-bye *despedirse* (i, i) (3)
schedule (n.) *horario* (5)
scholarship *beca* (9)
school: go to graduate school *hacer estudios de post-grado* (5)
science: natural science *ciencias naturales* (5)
   political science *ciencias políticas* (5)
   social science *ciencias sociales* (5)
score (v.) *marcar* (7)
scrambled *revuelto(a)* (4)
season (of the year) *estación* (f.) (7)
second *segundo(a)* (2)
   second course *segundo plato* (4)

seem *parecer* (6)
semester *semestre* (m.) (1)
September *septiembre* (2)
serious *serio(a)* (3); *grave* (9)
serve *servir* (i, i) (4)
set (the table) *poner* (3)
seven hundred *setecientos* (2)
seventeen *diecisiete* (PP)
seventh *séptimo(a)* (2)
seventy *setenta* (1)
severe *grave* (8)
shake hands *darse la mano* (1)
share (v.) *compartir* (4)
shave (v.) *afeitarse* (3)
sheet of paper *hoja de papel* (PP)
shelf *estante* (3)
shellfish *mariscos* (4)
shirt *camisa* (6)
   loose-fitting men's shirt *guayabera* (6)
short *bajo(a)* (3)
short story *cuento* (7)
shorts *pantalones cortos* (m.) (6)
shot *inyección* (f.) (8)
shoulder *hombro* (8)
show (n.) *función* (f.) (7); *programa* (m.) (1); (v.) *mostrar* (ue) (8)

show off *lucir* (6)
shower (n.) *ducha* (2)
   to take a shower *ducharse* (5)
shredded *mechado(a)* (4)
shrimp *camarón* (m.) (4)
shy *tímido(a)* (3)
sick, ill *enfermo(a)* (1)
sick: to get sick *enfermarse* (7)
   to be sick *estar enfermo(a)* (1)
side: to the side of *al lado de* (3)
sign (v.) *firmar* (7)
silk *seda* (6)
simple *sencillo(a)* (6)
sing *cantar* (7)
singer *cantante* (m., f.) (4)
single room *habitación sencilla* (f.) (2)
single *soltero(a)* (1)
sister *hermana* (1)
   half sister *media hermana* (3)
sit down *sentarse* (ie)(3)
six hundred *seiscientos* (2)
six *seis* (PP)
sixteen *dieciséis* (PP)
sixth *sexto(a)* (2)
sixty *sesenta* (1)
size (n.) *talla* (6)

ski (v.) esquiar (7)
skirt falda (6)
sleep (v.) dormir (ue) (2)
sleepy: to be sleepy tener sueño (1)
slippery resbaloso(a) (7)
slowly lentamente (7), despacio (PP)
smoke (v.) fumar (9)
snack, snack time merienda (4)
   to have a snack merendar (ie) (4)
snorkel (v.) bucear (7)
snow (n.) nieve (f.) (7); (v.) nevar (ie) (7)
soccer fútbol (europeo) (1)
sociology sociología (5)
sock calcetín (m.) (6)
soda gaseosa, refresco (4)
sofa sofá (m.) (3)
something algo (1)
sometimes a veces (3)
son hijo (1)
sorry: be sorry sentir (ie, i) (9)
so-so regular (5)
soup sopa (4)
source fuente (f.) (9)
souvenir recuerdo (6)
speak hablar (1)
spend (time) pasar (1)
spoon cuchara (4)
spring primavera (7)
square cuadro (3)
St. Valentine's Day Día de los Enamorados
   (m.) (7)

stairs, staircase escalera (3)
stamp (postage) sello (8)
stand out (v.) lucir (6)
star estrella (7)
statehood estadidad (f.) (1)
stationery store papelería (8)
statistics estadística (5)
stay (v.) quedarse (7)
stay in bed guardar cama (8)
stepbrother (stepsister) hermanastro(a) (3)
stepfather padrastro (3)
stepmother madrastra (3)
stepson (stepdaughter) hijastro(a) (3)
stitch punto (8)
stomach estómago (8)
stop (doing something) dejar de (+ inf.) (9)
store (n.) tienda (1)
   department store gran almacén (m.) (6)
storm tormenta (7)
story cuento (7)
stove estufa (3)
straight ahead (adv.) derecho (8)
strawberry fresa (4)
street calle (f.) (1)
street corner esquina (8)
stressed out estresado(a) (9)
strike (n.) huelga (3)
striped de rayas (6)
stroll (v.) pasear (7)
student estudiante (m., f.) (PP)
   law student estudiante de derecho (6)

style (n.) estilo (3)
   modern (in style) de estilo moderno (3)
   traditionally styled de estilo tradicional (3)
subject asignatura (5)
success (n.) éxito (1)
suffer (from illness) padecer (9)
sugar azúcar (m.) (4)
suit traje (m.) (6)
summer verano (7)
sunbathe tomar el sol (7)
Sunday domingo (2)
sunglasses gafas de sol (6)
sunny: it's sunny hace sol (7)
supermarket supermercado (1)
supper cena (3)
sure seguro(a) (9)
surf (the Internet) navegar (1)
surname apellido (1)
surprise (v.) sorprender (9)
surprised sorprendido(a) (9)
survive sobrevivir (2)
sweater suéter (m.) (6)
sweatshirt sudadera (6)
swim (v.) nadar (7)
swimming pool piscina (2)
symptom síntoma (m.) (8)
synagogue sinagoga (7)
syrup (cough) jarabe (para la tos) (m.) (6)

T

table mesa (PP)
   end table mesita (3)
tablet pastilla (8)
take (shoe size) calzar (6)
take tomar (1); llevar (7)
   to take a shower ducharse (5)
   to take a walk dar un paseo (7)
   to take care of oneself cuidarse (9)
   to take notes tomar apuntes (5)
   to take off (clothing) quitarse (3)
   to take out sacarle (8)
talk (v.) hablar (1)
tall alto(a) (3)
tap water agua de la llave (8)
taste (v.) probar (ue) (4)
tea té (m.) (4)
teacher profesor(a) (1); maestro(a) (5)
team (n.) equipo (7)
teaspoon cucharita (4)
television televisión (f.) (1)
television set televisor (m.) (3)
tell (a story) contar (ue) (7)
temperature temperatura (7)
temporary temporal (9)
ten diez (PP)
ten thousand diez mil (2)
tennis tenis (m.) (1)
tenth décimo (2)
terrible fatal (7)
thank you, thanks gracias (PP)
Thanksgiving Día de Acción de Gracias (m.) (7)
that, that one ese/esa (6)
the el (la), los (las) (PP)
theater teatro (7)

movie theater cine (m.) (7)
then luego, entonces (5)
theory teoría (5)
there is/are hay (haber) (PP)
these estos/estas (3); these ones estos/estas (6)
thin delgado(a) (3)
thing cosa (1)
think (v.) (opinion) creer (5)
third tercer(o)(a) (2)
thirsty: to be thirsty tener sed (1)
thirteen trece (PP)
thirty treinta (PP)
thirty-nine treinta y nueve (PP)
thirty-one treinta y uno (PP)
this, this one este/esta (6)
those, those ones esos/esas (6); aquellos (5)
throat garganta (8)
Thursday jueves (2)
ticket boleto (2)
tidy ordenado(a) (3)
tight-fitting ajustado(a) (6)
time tiempo (7); época (7)
   free time tiempo libre (1)
   to have a good time divertirse (ie, i) (3);
      pasarlo bien (7)
tip (n.) propina (4)
tired cansado(a) (1)
toast (v.) brindar (7); (n.) pan tostado (m.) (4)
today hoy (2)
toe dedo del pie (8)
together juntos (1)
   to get together reunirse (7)
toilet inodoro (3)
tomato tomate (m.) (4)

tomorrow mañana (2)
too much demasiado(a) (5)
tooth diente (m.) (8)
tortilla (flour) tortilla (Mex.) (4)
touch (v.) tocar (5)
tour (n.) excursión (f.) (2)
tourism office oficina de turismo (8)
trade oficio (5)
traditionally styled de estilo tradicional (3)
train (n.) tren (m.) (2)
train station estación de tren (f.) (8)
travel agency agencia de viajes (2)
travel viajar (2)
traveler's check cheque de viajero (m.) (2)
treat oneself tratarse (9)
treaty tratado (1)
tree árbol (m.) (7)
trip (n.) viaje (m.) (2); excursión (f.) (2)
true cierto(a) (9)
try (v.) tratar (9); probar (ue) (4)
   to try on probarse (ue) (6)
   to try to (do something) tratar de (+ inf.) (9)
T-shirt camiseta (6)
Tuesday martes (2)
turkey pavo (7)
turn (v.) doblar (8)
turn on (the TV, radio) poner (3)
twins gemelos (1)
twist (v.) torcer (ue) (8)
two dos (PP)
two hundred doscientos (2)
two million dos millones (2)

U

ugly *feo(a) (3)*
umbrella *paraguas (m.) (6)*
uncle *tío (1)*
under *debajo de (3)*

understand *comprender (1)*
university *universidad (f.) (1)*
unoccupied *libre (9)*
unpleasant *antipático(a) (3)*

until *hasta (3)*
  until late *hasta tarde (3)*
uprising *levantamiento (2)*
usually *normalmente (3)*

V

vacation *vacaciones (f.) (7)*
very much *muchísimo(a) (7)*
veterinarian *veterinario(a) (5)*

video *vídeo (1)*
vigil *(n.)* *velorio (9)*
visit *(v.)* *visitar (1)*

vomiting *vómito (8)*

W

wait *(v.)* *esperar (7)*
waiter (waitress) *camarero(a) (4)*
wake *(n.)* *velorio (9)*
wake up *despertarse (ie) (3)*
walk *caminar (8)*
  to take a walk *dar un paseo (7)*
wallet *billetera (6)*
want *(v.)* *desear (4); querer (ie) (PP)*
war *guerra (2)*
warm: it's warm *hace calor (7)*
wash *(v.)* *lavar (3)*
  wash one's hair/hands/face *lavarse el pelo/las manos/la cara (3)*
watch *(v.)* *mirar (1)*
watermelon *sandía (4)*
weapon *arma (2)*
wear *llevar; lucir (6); (shoe size) calzar (6)*
weather *(n.)* *tiempo (3)*
  it's good (bad) weather *hace buen (mal) tiempo (7)*
wedding *boda (9)*
Wednesday *miércoles (2)*

week *semana (2)*
  last week *semana pasada (5)*
  last weekend *fin de semana pasado (5)*
  weekend *fin de semana (m.) (1)*
weight: to lift weights *levantar pesas (7)*
welcome: you're welcome *de nada (PP)*
well *(adv.)* *bien (1)*
  to do well *salir bien (9)*
  to get along well *llevarse bien (9)*
well-mannered *educado(a) (3)*
what for? *¿para qué? (1)*
what? *¿qué? (1)*
when? *¿cuándo? (1)*
where from? *¿de dónde? (1)*
where to? *¿adónde? (1)*
where? *¿dónde? (1)*
which one(s)? *¿cuál(es)? (1)*
while *rato (5)*
white *blanco(a) (6)*
who? *¿quién(es)? (PP)*
why? *¿por qué? (1)*
wife *esposa (3)*

window *ventana (PP); escaparate (m.) (6)*
windy: it's windy *hace viento (7)*
winter *invierno (7)*
wish for *desear (4)*
with *con (1)*
  with me *conmigo (PP)*
woman *mujer (f.) (6)*
wonderful *lindo(a) (1)*
wood *madera (4)*
wool *lana (6)*
work *(n.)* *trabajo (1); (v.) trabajar (1)*
worker *trabajador(a) (3)*
  social worker *trabajador(a) social (5)*
worried *preocupado(a) (1)*
worry *(v.)* *preocuparse (9)*
  to be worried *estar preocupado(a) (1)*
worst, worse *peor (3)*
wrap *envolver (ue) (6)*
wrist *muñeca (8)*
write *escribir (1)*
writing *redacción (f.) (1)*
  written paper *trabajo escrito (9)*

X

x-ray *radiografía (8)*

Y

yard *jardín (m.) (3)*
year *año (2)*
  last year *año pasado (5)*
  next year *el próximo año (5)*

yellow *amarillo(a) (6)*
yesterday *ayer (5)*
young *joven (3)*

younger, youngest *menor (3)*
your *(form. sing.) su; (inform., pl.) vuestro(a) (1)*

Z

zoo *parque zoológico (m.) (8)*

Vocabulario temático

PASO PRELIMINAR

¿Qué hay en la sala de clase?	What is there in the classroom?
un bolígrafo	a pen
un borrador	an eraser
un calendario	a calendar
un cartel	a poster
una computadora	a computer
un cuaderno	a notebook
un diccionario	a dictionary
un estudiante	a (male) student
una estudiante	a (female) student
Hay...	There is/are . . .
una hoja de papel	a sheet of paper
una impresora	a printer
un lápiz	a pencil
un libro	a book
un mapa	a map
una mesa	a table, desk
una mochila	a bookbag/backpack
la pizarra	the chalkboard
la profesora	the (female) teacher
una puerta	a door
un pupitre	a student desk
un reloj	a clock
un reproductor de MP3/MP4	MP3/MP4 player
la sala	the room
una silla	a chair
también	also
un teléfono celular	cell phone
una tiza	a piece of chalk
una ventana	a window

El abecedario / The alphabet

—¿Qué es esto? / —What is this?
—Es *un pupitre*. / —It is *a desk*.
—¿Cómo se escribe "pupitre"? / —How do you spell it/write it?
—Se escribe *pe-u-pe-i-te-ere-e*. / —You spell it *p-u-p-i-t-r-e*.

a	a	Argentina	a	Argentina
b	be / be grande	Bolivia	b	Bolivia
c	ce	Colombia	c	Colombia
ch	che	Chile	ch	Chile
d	de	Dinamarca	d	Denmark
e	e	Ecuador	e	Ecuador
f	efe	Francia	f	France
g	ge	Guatemala	g	Guatemala
h	hache	Honduras	h	Honduras
i	i	Inglaterra	i	England
j	jota	Japón	j	Japan
k	ka	Kenia	k	Kenya
l	ele	Luxemburgo	l	Luxemburg
ll	elle	Llano	ll	Llano
m	eme	Mónaco	m	Monaco
n	ene	Nicaragua	n	Nicaragua
ñ	eñe	España	ñ	Spain
o	o	Omán	o	Oman
p	pe	Perú	p	Peru
q	cu	Quito	q	Quito
r	ere	Rusia	r	Russia
s	ese	Suiza	s	Switzerland
t	te	Tailandia	t	Thailand
u	u	Uruguay	u	Uruguay
v	ve/uve ve chica	Venezuela	v	Venezuela
w	uve doble doble ve	Washington	w	Washington
x	equis	México	x	Mexico
y	i griega	Yemen	y	Yemen
z	zeta	Nueva Zelanda	z	New Zealand

Los números de 0 a 39 / Numbers from 0–39

¿Cuántos pupitres hay? / How many desks are there?
Hay *veinte*. / There are *twenty*.

0	cero	0	zero
1	uno	1	one
2	dos	2	two
3	tres	3	three
4	cuatro	4	four
5	cinco	5	five
6	seis	6	six
7	siete	7	seven
8	ocho	8	eight
9	nueve	9	nine
10	diez	10	ten
11	once	11	eleven
12	doce	12	twelve
13	trece	13	thirteen
14	catorce	14	fourteen
15	quince	15	fifteen
16	dieciséis	16	sixteen
17	diecisiete	17	seventeen
18	dieciocho	18	eighteen
19	diecinueve	19	nineteen
20	veinte	20	twenty
21	veintiuno	21	twenty-one
22	veintidós (veintitrés, veinticuatro...)	22	twenty-two
30	treinta	30	thirty
31	treinta y uno (treinta y dos, treinta y tres...)	31	thirty-one
39	treinta y nueve	39	thirty-nine

Expresiones para la clase de español

—Hola. Me llamo *Amanda*.

—Hola, *Amanda*. Soy *Chris*.
—Mucho gusto.
—Igualmente.

Las instrucciones del profesor

Abran los libros.
Repitan.
Contesten en español.
Lean la información.
Escriban el ejercicio.
Cierren los libros.
Escuchen.
Trabajen con un(a)
   compañero(a).

Cómo hablar con tu profesor(a)

Más despacio, por favor.

Tengo una pregunta.
¿Cómo se dice...?
¿Qué quiere decir...?
¿Puede repetir, por favor?

¿En qué página?
Sí./No.
No sé.
Gracias.
De nada.
Perdón.
Con permiso.

CAPÍTULO 1

Paso 1

Las presentaciones familiares

—Hola. Soy *Francisco Martín*. ¿Cómo te llamas?
—Me llamo *Elena Suárez Lagos*.
—Mucho gusto, *Elena*.
—Mucho gusto, *Francisco*.

Las presentaciones formales

—Buenos días. Me llamo *Rafael Díaz*. ¿Cómo se llama usted?
—Soy *Carmen Acosta*.
—Encantado.
—Igualmente.

Expressions for Spanish class

—Hi. I'm (My name is) *Amanda*.
—Hi, *Amanda*. I'm *Chris*.
—Nice to meet you.
—Likewise.

Classroom instructions

Open your books.
Repeat.
Answer in Spanish.
Read the information.
Write the exercise.
Close your books.
Listen.
Work with a partner.

How to speak with your professor

(Speak) More slowly, please.
I have a question.
How do you say . . . ?
What does . . . mean?
Could you repeat that, please?
On what page?
Yes./No.
I don't know.
Thank you./Thanks.
You're welcome.
Pardon me.
Excuse me.

Introducing yourself to classmates

—Hi. I'm *Francisco Martín*. What's your name?
—I'm *Elena Suárez Lagos*.
—Nice to meet you, *Elena*.
—It's a pleasure to meet you, *Francisco*.

Introducing yourself to professors

—Good morning. My name is *Rafael Díaz*. What is your name?
—I'm *Carmen Acosta*.
—Pleased to meet you.
—Likewise./Same here.

Los saludos informales

—Hola, *Patricia*.
—Hola, *Margarita*.
—¿Cómo estás?
—*Bien*, gracias. ¿Y tú?

   Regular.
   Más o menos.
—Muy bien. *Hablamos más tarde.*
—Está bien. *Hasta luego.*
   Nos vemos.

Los saludos formales

—Buenas tardes, *profesor(a)*.

—Buenas tardes, *Roberto*.

—¿Cómo está usted?
—*Estoy bastante bien. ¿Y usted? Ocupado(a), pero bien.*
—*Bien*, gracias. Bueno, nos vemos en clase.
—Adiós. *Hasta mañana.*

Más saludos y despedidas

Buenos días.
Buenas tardes.
Buenas noches.
¿Qué tal? *(informal)*

Estoy... estupendo(a) / bastante bien / bien / regular / mal.
Chao. *(informal)*
Hasta pronto.
¡Que pases buen un fin de semana! *(informal)*
¡Que pase buen un fin de semana! *(formal)*

Algunos estados

—¿Cómo estás? *(informal)*
—Estoy muy *enfermo(a)*. ¿Y tú?
—¿Cómo está Ud.? *(formal)*
—Estoy un poco *cansado(a)*. ¿Y Ud.?

Otras expresiones

contento/contenta
de buen humor
de mal humor
enojado/enojada
nervioso/nerviosa

Greeting classmates and friends

—Hi, *Patricia*.
—Hi, *Margarita*.
—How are you?
—*Fine (Good)*, thanks. And you?
   So-so.
   So-so.
—Great. *We'll talk* later.

—O.K. *See you later.*
   See you around.

Greeting your professors

—Good afternoon, *professor*.
—Good afternoon, *Roberto*.
—How are you?
—*I'm quite well.* And you? *Busy, but well.*
—Fine, thanks. Well, see you in class.
—Good-bye. *See you tomorrow.*

More ways to greet and say good-bye

Good morning.
Good afternoon/evening.
Good evening/night.
How are you doing? *(informal)*
I'm . . . great / quite well / fine / so-so / not so good.
Bye. *(informal)*
See you soon.
Have a good weekend! *(informal)*
Have a good weekend! *(formal)*

Expressing how you feel

—How are you? *(informal)*
—I'm very *sick/ill*. And you?
—How are you? *(formal)*
—I'm a bit *tired*. And you?

Related expressions

happy
in a good mood
in a bad mood
angry
nervous

ocupado/ocupada	busy
preocupado/preocupada	worried
triste	sad

Información básica

Exchanging basic information with classmates

—¿Cuál es tu nombre completo?
—Me llamo *Victoria Lourdes Rosati Álvarez.*
—¿Cuál es tu primer nombre?

—Me llamo *Victoria Lourdes*, pero me dicen *Viki.*

—¿Cuál es tu apellido?
—Mi apellido paterno es *Rosati*, y el materno es *Álvarez.*
—¿De dónde eres?
—Soy de *Nueva York.* Nací en *San Juan, Puerto Rico.*

—¿Cuál es tu dirección local?

—Vivo en
la calle *Azalea*, número *358.*
los apartamentos *Greenbriar*, número *6-B.*
la residencia *Capstone*, número *162*
—¿En qué año de estudios estás?

—Estoy en *primer* año.

   segundo
   tercer
   cuarto
—¿Cuántas clases tienes este semestre?

—Tengo *cuatro clases y un laboratorio.*
—¿Cuál es tu número de teléfono?
—En casa, es *el 7-54-26-08 (siete, cincuenta y cuatro, veintiséis, cero, ocho).*
Mi celular es el *7-98-46-16 (siete, noventa y ocho, cuarenta y seis, dieciséis).*
—¿Cuál es tu dirección de correo electrónico?
—Es *Viki278@yahoo.com (Viki dos, siete, ocho, arroba yahoo punto com).*

—What is your full name?
—My name is *Victoria Lourdes Rosati Álvarez.*
—What is your first name?

—My name is *Victoria Lourdes*, but they call me *Viki.*
—What's your last name?
—My paternal surname is *Rosati* and my maternal surname is *Álvarez.*
—Where are you from?
—I'm from *New York.* I was born in *San Juan, Puerto Rico.*
—What's your local address?
—I live at *358 Azalea Street.*
at *Greenbriar Apartments*, in *6-B.*
Capstone Residence Hall, room *162*
—What year (of studies) are you in?
I'm in *my first year (a freshman).*
second year (a sophomore)
third year (a junior)
fourth year (a senior)
—How many classes do you have this semester?
—I have *four classes and a lab.*
—What's your phone number?
—At home, it's *754-2608.*

My cell phone is *798-4616.*

—What's your e-mail address?
—It's *Viki278@yahoo. com.*

—¿Vamos a un café más tarde?
 ¿Tomamos algo?
 ¿Estudiamos juntos?

—Sí, de acuerdo.

—*Shall we go to a café later? Shall we get something? Shall we study together?*
—*O.K.*

Los números de 40 a 100

Numbers from 40 to 100

40	cuarenta (cuarenta y uno, cuarenta y dos...)	40	forty
50	cincuenta (cincuenta y uno, cincuenta y dos...)	50	fifty
60	sesenta (sesenta y uno...)	60	sixty
70	setenta (setenta y uno...)	70	seventy
80	ochenta (ochenta y uno...)	80	eighty
90	noventa (noventa y uno...)	90	ninety
100	cien (ciento uno, ciento dos, ciento tres...)	100	one hundred

Paso 2

La familia y los amigos

Family and friends

—¿Cómo es tu familia, *Dulce*?

—Aquí tengo una foto. Mira.

Este es mi hermano mayor, *Carlos*. Tiene *veinte* años.

Esta soy yo. Tengo *diecisiete* años.
Esta es mi tía *Felicia*. Es *soltera* y vive *con nosotros.*

—Este es mi papá. Se llama *Arturo.*
—Esta es mi mamá. Se llama *Beatriz.*
—Estos son mis buenos amigos, *Marcos y Sara.*
—Esta es mi hermana menor, *Elisa.* Tiene *diez* años.

—What's your family like, *Dulce*?
—Here's a picture of us. Look.
This is my older brother, *Carlos*. He's *twenty (years old).*
This is me. I'm *seventeen.*
This is my aunt, *Felicia.* She's *single* and lives *with us.*
This is my dad. His name is *Arturo.*
This is my mom. Her name is *Beatriz.*
These are my good friends *Marcos and Sara.*
This is my younger sister, *Elisa.* She's *ten.*

Otros familiares

Other family members

los abuelos	grandparents
el abuelo	grandfather
la abuela	grandmother
los padres	parents
el padre	father
la madre	mother
los esposos	spouses/married couple
el esposo	husband
la esposa	wife
los hijos	children/sons and daughters
el hijo	son
la hija	daughter
los gemelos	twins
los tíos	uncle and aunt
el tío	uncle
la tía	aunt

Otros amigos	**Other friends**
los novios	engaged couple
el novio	boyfriend/fiancé
la novia	girlfriend/fiancée
unos (buenos) amigos	some (good) friends
un (buen) amigo	a (good) friend (male)
una (buena) amiga	a (good) friend (female)
los vecinos	neighbors
el vecino	neighbor (male)
la vecina	neighbor (female)
mis compañeros de clase	classmates
mi compañero de clase	my classmate (male)
mi compañera de clase	my classmate (female)

Dime más sobre tu familia — **Tell me more about your family life**

—¿Dónde vive tu familia? — —Where does your family live?

—Mi familia vive en *Dorado, Puerto Rico.* *un pueblo cerca de San Juan* — —My family lives in *Dorado, Puerto Rico.* *a little town near San Juan*

—¿Dónde trabajan *tus padres?* — —Where do *your parents* work?

—Mi *padre* trabaja *en su propio negocio.* *madre* *para la compañía Bacardi* — —My *dad* works *for himself.* *mom* *for the Bacardi company*

—¿Pasas mucho tiempo con *tus hermanos?* *tu familia* — —Do you spend a lot of time with *your siblings?* *your family*

—No, porque *viven lejos.* — —No, because *they live far away.*

—Sí, pasamos mucho tiempo juntos. — —Yes, we spend a lot of time together.

Dime más sobre la vida estudiantil — **More about student life**

—¿A qué universidad asistes? — —What university do you attend/go to?

—Asisto a *la Universidad de Puerto Rico.* — —I go to *the University of Puerto Rico.*

—Vives en una residencia, ¿verdad? ¿no? — —You live in a dorm, right? don't you?

—Sí, vivo en una residencia *con mi buena amiga Carola.* No, vivo *con mi familia.* *en un apartamento* — —Yes, I live in a dorm *with my close friend, Carola.* No, I live *with my family.* *in an apartment*

—¿Cuántas clases tomas este semestre? — —How many classes are you taking this semester?

—Tomo *cinco* clases *(y un laboratorio).* — —I'm taking *five* classes *(and a lab).*

—¿Tienes que *leer* mucho para tus clases? *estudiar* — —Do you have to *read* a lot for your classes? *study*

—Sí, normalmente tengo que *leer* mucho. — —Yes, I have to *read* a lot.

No, no tengo que *leer* mucho por lo general. — *No,* I don't have to *read* much.

—¿Cuándo trabajas? — —When do you work?

—No trabajo. — —I don't work/don't have a job.

Trabajo *por la mañana.* *por la tarde* *por la noche* *los fines de semana* — I work *in the mornings.* *in the afternoons* *in the evenings/at night* *on weekends*

—Después de tus clases, ¿regresas a *la residencia?* *tu trabajo casa?* — —After classes, do you go back to *the dorm?* *working home*

—Sí, regreso a *la residencia* para *descansar.* *No,* voy a *la biblioteca* para *estudiar.* *al gimnasio hacer ejercicio* — —Yes, I go *to the dorm* to *rest/relax.* *No,* I go to *the library* to *study.* *to the gym to exercise/work out*

—¿Dónde comen tú y tus amigos? — —Where do you and your friends eat?

—Por lo general, comemos *en la cafetería.* *en restaurantes de comida rápida* — —Generally, we eat *in the cafeteria.* *in fast-food restaurants*

Paso 3

El tiempo libre — **Free-time activities**

¿Qué te gusta hacer en tu tiempo libre? — What do you like to do with your free time?

Me gusta mirar *la televisión (vídeos / películas / partidos de fútbol).* — I like to watch *T.V. (videos / movies / soccer matches).*

Me gusta practicar *deportes (el fútbol americano / el básquetbol / el tenis).* — I like to play *sports (football / basketball / tennis).*

Me gusta escuchar *la radio (la música clásica / la música rock / el jazz / mi ipod).* — I like to listen to *the radio (classical music / rock music / jazz / my ipod).*

Me gusta navegar por Internet y leer *revistas (poesía / novelas / periódicos).* — I like to surf the internet and read *magazines (poetry / novels / newspapers).*

Otros pasatiempos — **Other pastimes**

—¿Qué les gusta hacer en su tiempo libre a ti y a tus amigos? — —What do you and your friends like to do in your spare time?

—Nos gusta *correr en el parque (por el campus).* *ir al cine (a fiestas / de compras)* — —We like to run *in the park (around campus).* *go to the movies (to parties / shopping)*

pasar tiempo con los amigos (con los novios[as]) — *spend time / hang out with friends (with boyfriends / girlfriends)*

bailar en clubs *montar en bicicleta (a caballo)* — *dance in clubs* *go cycling (horse-back riding)*

jugar videojuegos — *play videogames*

CAPÍTULO 2

Paso 1

Cómo hablar de horarios

—¿A qué hora sale *el vuelo 245?*

—Sale a *la una.*
—¿A qué hora llega?
—Llega a *las tres.*
—¿A qué hora abre *el museo?*

—Abre a *las nueve y media.*
—¿A qué hora cierra?
—Cierra a *la una y media.*

Cómo decir la hora

¿Qué hora es?
Perdón, ¿podría decirme la hora?

Es mediodía.
Es la una.
Es la una y media.
Son las dos.
Son las dos y cuarto.

Son las cinco.
Son las ocho menos veinte.
Es medianoche.

Para expresar "A.M." y "P.M."

—¿A qué hora llegamos?
—A las tres de la tarde.
de la mañana
de la tarde
de la noche
de la madrugada

Las fechas

—¿Cuándo salimos para
  Mérida?
—Salimos el *lunes, 28 de junio.*

—¿Cuándo regresamos?

—Regresamos el *viernes,
  2 de julio.*
—¿Cuándo está abierto
  el museo?
—Está abierto *todos los días,
  de lunes a sábado.*
—¿Cuándo está cerrado?
—Está cerrado *los domingos.*

Los días de la semana

—¿Qué día es hoy?
—Hoy es *lunes.*

Talking about schedules

—At what time does *flight
  245* leave?

—It leaves at *one o'clock.*
—What time does it arrive?
—It arrives at *three o'clock.*
—What time does *the
  museum* open?
—It opens at *nine-thirty.*
—What time does it close?
—It closes at *one-thirty.*

Telling time

What time is it?
Excuse me, could you tell
me the time?

It's noon.
It's one o'clock.
It's one-thirty.
It's two o'clock.
It's two-fifteen / a quarter
past two.
It's five.
It's a quarter to eight.
It's midnight.

Expressing A.M. and P.M.

—*What time do we arrive?*
—*At three o'clock.*
6 A.M. to noon
noon to sundown
sundown to midnight
early morning hours

Expressing days
and dates

—When do we leave
  for *Merida?*
—We leave *Monday,
  June 28th.*
—When do we come
  back?
—We come back *Friday,
  July 2nd.*
—When is *the museum*
  open?
—It's open *every day,
  Monday through Saturday*
—When is it closed?
—It's closed on *Sundays.*

Days of the week

—What day is today?
—Today is *Monday.*

lunes — Monday
martes — Tuesday
miércoles — Wednesday
jueves — Thursday
viernes — Friday
sábado — Saturday
domingo — Sunday

Los meses del año

—¿Cuál es la fecha de hoy?
—Es el 25 (veinticinco)
  de *noviembre.*
enero
febrero
marzo
abril
mayo
junio
julio
agosto
septiembre
octubre
noviembre
diciembre

Months of the year

—What is today's date?
—It's the *25th of
  November.*
January
February
March
April
May
June
July
August
September
October
November
December

En la agencia de viajes

—¿En qué puedo servirle?
—Quisiera
  hacer una excursión a Cancún.
  hacer un viaje a Guadalajara
—¿Cómo prefiere viajar?

—Me gustaría viajar
  por avión.
  en tren
  en autobús
—¿Qué día piensa salir?

—Pienso salir *el próximo jueves.*

—¿Cuándo quiere volver?

—Quiero volver *el dos de abril.*

—¿Cuánto es el boleto?
—Un *boleto de ida y vuelta*
  cuesta *tres mil pesos.*
  boleto de ida
—¿Necesita un hotel?
—Sí. ¿Qué hotel me recomienda?

—Le recomiendo el
  Hotel Miramar.
—¿Cómo quiere pagar?

—Voy a pagar
  en efectivo.
  con tarjeta de crédito
  con cheques de viajero

Making travel
arrangements

—May I help you?
—I'd like *to
  go on a day trip to Cancun.
  take a trip to Guadalajara*
—How would you prefer
  to travel?
—I would like to travel
  *by plane.
  by train
  by bus*
—What day do you plan
  to leave?
—I plan to leave
  next Thursday.
—When do you want to
  return/come back?
—I want to return on
  April 2.
—How much is the ticket?
—A *round trip ticket*
  costs *$3,000.
  a one-way ticket*
—Do you need a hotel?
—Yes. Which one do you
  recommend?
—I recommend the
  Hotel Miramar.
—How do you want
  to pay?
—I'm going to pay
  *with cash.
  by credit card
  with traveler's checks*

Paso 2

Para conseguir una habitación

—¿En qué puedo servirle?
—Quisiera
   una habitación.
   hacer una reservación.
—¿Para cuántas personas?
—Para *dos*.
—¿Para cuándo?
—Para *el ocho de abril*.
—¿Por cuántas noches?
—Por *tres noches*.
—¿Qué clase de habitación
   quiere?
—Quiero una habitación
   con dos camas.
   sencilla
   doble
—Su nombre y apellidos,
   por favor.
—*Roberto Martín Moreno*.
—Aquí tiene la llave. Su
   habitación está en el
   tercer piso.
—Gracias.

Getting a hotel room

—May I help you?
—I would like
   a room.
   to make a reservation
—For how many people?
—For *two*.
—For when?
—For *April 8*.
—For how many nights?
—For *three nights*.
—What type of room
   do you want?
—I want a room
   with two beds.
   a single
   a double
—Your first and last
   name, please.
—*Roberto Martín Moreno*.
—Here's the key. Your
   room is on the *third*
   floor.
—Thanks.

Preguntas típicas en un hotel

—¿Sabe Ud. donde está *el banco*?

—Sí, hay uno en la esquina.

—¿Conoce Ud. un buen
   restaurante típico?
—Sí, hay varios cerca del hotel.
   Casa Lolita es uno de
   los mejores.
—¿Dan descuentos
   para *estudiantes*?
—*Sí, con la tarjeta de identidad.*

   *No, lo siento, no damos
   descuentos.*
—¿A qué hora
   podemos ocupar el cuarto?
   tenemos que desocupar

—A las *dos de la tarde*.
—¿En qué piso está *la piscina*?
                el gimnasio
—Está en *la planta baja*.

Common questions in a hotel

—Do you know where
   there is *a bank*?
—Yes, there is one on the
   corner.
—Do you know of a good
   typical restaurant?
—Yes, there are several
   close to the hotel. *Casa
   Lolita* is one of the best.
—Do you give a discount
   for *students*?
—*Yes, with an
   identification card / I.D.
   No, I'm sorry, we don't
   offer discounts.*
—What time
   can we occupy the room /
   check in?
   do we have to check out
—At *two o'clock*.
—Which floor is *the pool* on?
                the gym
—It's on *the ground floor*.

Los pisos

la planta baja
el primer piso
el segundo piso
el tercer piso
el cuarto piso
el quinto piso

Floors of a building

ground floor
first floor
second floor
third floor
fourth floor
fifth floor

Los números de 100 a 10 000 000

—¿Cuánto cuesta
   una habitación doble?
   una excursión
—Mil cien (1100) pesos.

100	cien
101	ciento uno
200	doscientos
300	trescientos
400	cuatrocientos
500	quinientos
600	seiscientos
700	setecientos
800	ochocientos
900	novecientos
1000	mil
5000	cinco mil
10 000	diez mil
100 000	cien mil

750 000 setecientos
   cincuenta mil
1 000 0000 un millón
2 000 000 dos millones
10 500 000 diez millones
   quinientos mil

Numbers from 100 to 10,000,000

—How much does a
   double room cost?
   a day trip
—*One thousand one
   hundred pesos.*

100	one hundred
101	one hundred one
200	two hundred
300	three hundred
400	four hundred
500	five hundred
600	six hundred
700	seven hundred
800	eight hundred
900	nine hundred
1,000	one thousand
5,000	five thousand
10,000	ten thousand
100,000	one-hundred thousand

750,000 seven-hundred
   fifty thousand
1,000,000 one million
2,000,000 two million
10,500,000 ten million,
   five hundred thousand

CAPÍTULO 3

Paso 1

Mi familia

—¿Cómo es tu familia, *Carlos*?

—Tengo una familia
   de tamaño mediano.
   grande
   pequeña
Somos *seis*: mis padres, mis
   hermanas, mi tía Felicia y yo.

—¿Cómo son *tus hermanas*?
—*Elisa*, la menor, es una
   chica *cariñosa*.
   Dulce, la de en medio, es
   extrovertida e inteligente.
—Háblame más de *tu familia*.

—*Tía Felicia* es la hermana
   mayor de mi padre. Es *soltera* y
   vive con nosotros. Mis abuelos
   paternos viven en *Maracaibo*.
   Nos reunimos con ellos con
   frecuencia. Pero mis abuelos
   maternos se murieron
   hace años.

Talking about your family

—What's your family like,
   Carlos?
—I have a
   medium-sized family.
   large
   small
—There are *six* of us: *my
   parents, my sisters, my
   Aunt Felicia, and myself.*
—What are *your sisters* like?
—*Elisa*, the youngest, is
   an *affectionate* girl.
   Dulce, the middle child, is
   outgoing and intelligent.
—Tell me more about
   your family.
— *Aunt Felicia* is the *older*
   sister of my father. She
   is *single* and lives with us.
   My *paternal* grandparents
   live in *Maracaibo*. We get
   together frequently. But
   my *maternal* grandparents
   died years ago.

Otros parientes

el abuelo/la abuela
el nieto/la nieta
el tío/la tía
el primo/la prima

el sobrino/la sobrina
el padrino/la madrina
el padrastro/la madrastra
el medio hermano/la media hermana
el hermanastro/la hermanastra
el hijastro/la hijastra

Other relatives

grandfather/grandmother
grandson/granddaughter
uncle/aunt
cousin (male)/cousin (female)
nephew/niece
godfather/godmother
stepfather/stepmother
half brother/half sister

stepbrother/stepsister
stepson/stepdaughter

Los animales domésticos

—¿Tienen Uds. animales domésticos?
—No, no tenemos ninguno.
Sí, tenemos *varios animales domésticos.*
un perro
un gato
unos pájaros
unos peces tropicales
un hámster

Pets

—Do you have any pets?

—No, we don't have any.
Yes, we have *several pets.*
a dog
a cat
some birds
some tropical fish
a hamster

Las descripciones personales

¿Cómo es *Dulce?*
Dulce se parece mucho a *su mamá.*
No es ni *alta* ni *baja;* es *de estatura mediana.*

Tiene el pelo *castaño* y los ojos *verdes.*
¿Y *Carlos?* ¿Cómo es?
Carlos es bastante *atlético.*
Es menos *trabajador* que *su hermana Dulce.*
Es muy *sociable* y *simpático.*

Describing people

What is *Dulce* like?
Dulce looks a lot like *her mother.*
She is neither *tall* nor *short;* she is *medium-height.*
She has *brown* hair and *green* eyes.
And *Carlos?* What is he like?
Carlos is quite *athletic.*
He's not as *hard-working* as *his sister Dulce.*
He is very *friendly* and *nice.*

Rasgos físicos

Es *alto/bajo.*
de estatura mediana
delgado/gordo

joven/viejo; mayor
guapo/feo
calvo
Tiene el pelo
negro y los ojos *azules.*
rubio   *verdes*
castaño   *color miel*
rojo   *castaños*
canoso
Tiene *barba.*
bigote
pecas
Lleva *gafas/anteojos.*

Describing physical characteristics

He is *tall/short.*
of medium height
slender (thin)/fat (heavy-set)
young/old; elderly
good-looking/ugly
bald
He/She has
black hair and *blue* eyes.
blond   *green*
brown   *hazel*
red   *brown*
gray
He has *a beard.*
a mustache
freckles
He wears *glasses.*

La personalidad y el carácter

Es *simpático/antipático.*
tímido/extrovertido
amable/cruel
educado/maleducado

cariñoso/frío
honesto/mentiroso
También, es muy
comprensivo/indiferente.
serio/divertido
bueno/malo
perezoso/trabajador
optimista/pesimista
responsable/irresponsable

Describing personality and character traits

He is *nice/unpleasant.*
shy/outgoing
kind/cruel
well-mannered/rude, ill-mannered
warm, affectionate/cold
honest/a liar
He is also very
understanding/uncaring.
serious/fun (to be with)
good/bad
lazy/hard-working
optimistic/pessimistic
responsible/irresponsible

Paso 2

Los cuartos y los muebles

—¿Dónde viven tú y tu familia?

—Acabamos de
comprar una nueva casa.
mudarnos a
alquilar
—¿Cómo es tu (nueva) casa?

—Tiene *dos pisos* y hay *seis cuartos.*
En la planta baja, hay *una cocina, un comedor y una sala.*
En el primer piso, hay *dos dormitorios grandes y un baño.*
una alfombra
una bañera/una tina
una cama
una cocina
un comedor
una cómoda
un cuadro
un dormitorio
una ducha
un estante
una estufa/una cocina
un fregadero
un inodoro
una lámpara
un lavabo
un lavaplatos
una mesa
una mesita
una mesita de noche
un microondas
una nevera/un refrigerador
una sala
unas sillas

Describing rooms and furnishings

—Where do you and your family live?
—We've just
bought a new house.
moved to
rented
—What is your (new) house like?
—It has *two floors* and *six rooms.*
On the first (ground) floor, there's *a kitchen, a dining room, and a living room.*
On the second floor, there are *two large bedrooms and a bathroom.*
a rug
a bathtub
a bed
a kitchen
a dining room
a chest of drawers
a painting/a picture
a bedroom
a shower
a book shelf
a stove
a (kitchen) sink
a toilet
a lamp
a sink/lavatory
a dishwasher
a table
a small table/end table
a night stand
a microwave oven
a refrigerator
a living room
some chairs

un sillón	an easy chair
un sofá	a sofa/couch
un televisor	a TV set

Cómo describir algunas características de una casa

Mi casa es *nueva (vieja, de estilo moderno, de estilo tradicional).*

La cocina es *grande (de tamaño mediano, pequeña).*

Los muebles son *elegantes (baratos, caros, informales).*

How to describe some characteristics of a house

My house is *new (old, modern, traditionally styled).*

The kitchen is *big (medium-sized, small).*

The furniture is *elegant (inexpensive/cheap, expensive, casual).*

Cómo describir algunas condiciones de una casa

Mi apartamento está *amueblado (en buenas condiciones, en malas condiciones).*

Normalmente, mi dormitorio está *ordenado (desordenado).*

Por lo general, la cocina está *limpia (sucia).*

Por desgracia, el refrigerador está *descompuesto* y la ventana está *rota.*

How to describe some conditions of a house

My apartment is *furnished (in good condition, in bad shape/poor condition).*

Normally, my bedroom is *tidy/neat (messy).*

Generally, the kitchen is *clean (dirty).*

Unfortunately, the refrigerator is *not working* and the window is *broken.*

Para indicar relaciones espaciales

—¿Dónde está el gato?
—Está...
en las cortinas, a la izquierda del estante
en la lámpara, a la derecha del estante
sobre la cama
encima de la mesita
detrás del teléfono
entre los libros
al lado de la computadora
delante del clóset
dentro de la gaveta de la cómoda
debajo de la cama
en la mochila, en el medio del cuarto

Describing where something is located

—Where's the cat?
—It's . . .
on the curtains, to the left of the bookshelf
on the lamp, to the right of the bookshelf
on (top of) the bed
on top of the end table
behind the telephone
among/between the books
next to/beside the computer
in front of the closet
inside the drawer of the chest
under(neath) the bed
in the bookbag, in the middle of the room

Paso 3

Mi rutina

Por la mañana
Normalmente, me despierto *a las ocho (bastante temprano).*
Me levanto *a las ocho y cuarto.*

Me ducho y me visto *rápidamente.*

My daily routine

In the morning
I wake up *at eight o'clock (quite early).*
I get up *at a quarter past eight.*

I take a shower and dress *quickly.*

Salgo de casa *a las nueve menos cuarto.*
Paso el día *en clase.*
Por la tarde y por la noche

Para divertirnos, mis amigos y yo vamos con frecuencia *a un café (al centro estudiantil, al gimnasio).*
Por lo general, ceno en casa con mi familia *a las ocho y media.*
Por lo general, necesito estudiar por *dos o tres horas.*
Me acuesto *a la medianoche (a la una, bastante tarde).*

I leave the house *at quarter to nine.*
I spend the day *in class.*
In the afternoon and in the evening/at night

To have fun, my friends and I often go *to a cafe (to the student center, to the gym).*
Generally, I have supper at home with my family *at eight thirty.*
Generally, I need to study for *two or three* hours.
I go to bed *at midnight (at one o'clock, quite late).*

Los quehaceres domésticos

¿Cómo dividen Uds. las responsabilidades para los quehaceres?
Todos los días la empleada *limpia la casa y lava la ropa.*

Yo siempre *quito el polvo de los muebles y le doy de comer al perro.*
Normalmente mi hermana menor *lava los platos.*
De vez en cuando, mi hermana mayor *limpia el garaje.*
Trabaja en el jardín con frecuencia.
Normalmente, mi padre *cocina el almuerzo o la cena.*
Por lo general, *ayuda con los quehaceres.*
Mi hermanito nunca *pone la mesa.*
Nunca quiere *hacer su cama.*

Household chores

How do you divide up the chores?

Everyday, the maid *cleans the house and washes clothes.*

I always *dust the furniture and feed the dog.*

Usually my younger sister *washes the dishes.*
Now and then, my older sister *cleans the garage.*

She often *works in the garden/yard.*
Normally, my father *prepares lunch or supper.*
Generally, *he helps around the house.*
My little brother never *sets the table.*
He never wants *to make his bed.*

Expresiones de frecuencia

siempre
todos los días
una vez por semana
con frecuencia
de vez en cuando
nunca

Expressions of frequency

always
every day
once a week
frequently/often
now and then; sometimes
never

CAPÍTULO 4

Paso 1

El desayuno

—¿Qué te gusta desayunar?

—Casi siempre como...
y bebo...

Breakfast

—What do you like to have for breakfast?

—I almost always eat . . .
and drink . . .

un vaso de leche	a glass of milk
la mermelada	jam/marmalade
los huevos (revueltos)	(scrambled) eggs
la mantequilla	butter
el pan tostado	toast
el cereal	cereal
el jugo de naranja	orange juice
una taza de café con leche y azúcar	a cup of coffee with milk and sugar

El almuerzo / Lunch / Midday meal

—¿Qué almuerzas?	—What do you have for lunch?
—Por lo general, como... y bebo...	—Generally I eat . . . and drink . . .
una cerveza	a beer
el maíz	corn
los mariscos	seafood
la langosta	lobster
el brócoli	broccoli
una copa de vino	a glass of wine
los camarones	shrimp
las chuletas de cerdo	pork chops
una papa/una patata (al horno)	a (baked) potato
la torta	cake
el pollo asado	roasted chicken

La merienda / Snack

—¿Qué meriendas?	—What do have for a snack?
—Depende de la hora. Por la mañana, prefiero... Por la tarde, prefiero...	—It depends on the time of day. In the morning I prefer . . . In the afternoon, I prefer . . .
un sándwich de jamón y queso	a ham and cheese sandwich
un helado	ice cream
un refresco	a soft drink
una taza de té	a cup of tea
una tortilla (de huevos)	an omelette
unos churros	some churros (fritters)
unas galletas	some cookies
una hamburguesa	a hamburger
un vaso de té frío	a glass of iced tea
una taza de chocolate	a cup of hot chocolate

La cena / Supper

—¿Qué prefieres cenar?	—What do you prefer to have for supper?
—En los restaurantes pido... En casa como...	—In restaurants, I order . . . At home, I eat . . .
el biftec a la parrilla	grilled steak
el arroz con frijoles	rice and beans
las papas fritas	French fries
la ensalada de lechuga y tomate con aderezo	a lettuce and tomato salad with dressing
el pescado frito	fried fish
el panecillo	a roll
la sopa	soup
el flan	flan (custard)

En el restaurante / In a restaurant

Antes de pedir / Before ordering

—¡Camarero(a)!	—Waiter/Waitress!
—Necesito *un menú*, por favor.	—I need *a menu*, please.
—Aquí *lo* tiene.	—Here *it* is.
—¿Cuál es el plato del día?	—What is today's special?
—Hoy tenemos *lomo saltado*.	—Today we have *lomo saltado*.
—¿Qué ingredientes tiene el *lomo saltado*?	—What ingredients are in *lomo saltado*?
—Tiene *lomo, cebollas, papas, tomates y arroz*.	—It has *beef, onions, potatoes, tomatoes, and rice*.
—Quiero probar algo típico. ¿Qué me recomienda?	—I want to try something typical. What do you recommend?
—Le recomiendo *el lomo saltado o la palta rellena*.	—I recommend *lomo saltado* or *palta rellena (stuffed avocado)*.
—¿Tienen *corvina* hoy?	—Do you have *sea bass* today?
—No, *la* servimos solo los sábados. Sí, por supuesto.	—No, we serve *it* only on Saturdays. Yes, of course.

Para pedir / To place an order

—¿Qué desea pedir?	—What do you want to order?
—De primer plato, quiero *sopa a la criolla*. De plato principal, deseo *lomo saltado*.	—For the first course, I want *soup, creole style*. For the second course, I want *lomo saltado*.
—¿Y para beber?	—And to drink?
—Para beber, quisiera *una copa de vino*.	—To drink, I'd like *a glass of wine*.
—¿Quiere algo de postre?	—Do you want dessert?
—De postre, voy a probar *el flan*.	—For dessert, I'm going to try *the flan*.
—¿Necesita algo más?	—Do you need anything else?
—¿Me puede traer *unos cubitos de hielo*? *la sal* *la pimienta*	—Could you bring me *some ice cubes*? *salt* *pepper*

Después de comer / After eating

—La cuenta, por favor.	—The check/bill please.
—*Se la traigo enseguida*.	—*I'll bring it right to you*.
—¿Está incluida la propina en la cuenta?	—Is the tip included in the check?
—*No, no está incluida*. *Sí, está incluida*.	—No, it's not included. Yes, it's included.

El cubierto / Place setting

un tenedor	fork
un cuchillo	knife
una cuchara	spoon
una cucharita	teaspoon
una servilleta	napkin
la sal	salt

la pimienta	pepper
una copa	(wine) glass
un vaso	glass
unos cubitos de hielo	some ice cubes

Paso 2

En el mercado / In a market

—¿Qué desea Ud.?	—What would you like?
—¿Me puede dar *un kilo de manzanas*?	—Could you give me *a kilo of apples*?
—¿Necesita Ud. algo más?	—Do you need anything else?
—Sí, quiero *un melón*.	—Yes, I want *a melon/ cantaloupe.*
—*Se lo* pongo enseguida. ¿Algo más?	—I'll get *it* for you right away. Something else?
—No, gracias. Eso es todo. ¿Cuánto le debo?	—No, thanks. That's everything. How much do I owe you?

Otras frutas / Other fruits

unas bananas/unos plátanos	bananas/plantains
unos melocotones/unos duraznos	peaches
unas peras	pears
unas fresas	strawberries
una piña	pineapple
una sandía	watermelon

Otros comestibles / Other foods

un paquete de azúcar	a package of sugar
una bolsa de arroz	a bag of rice
un litro de leche	a liter of milk
un frasco de mayonesa	a jar of mayonnaise
una barra de pan	a loaf of bread
una botella de agua mineral	a bottle of mineral water
una docena de huevos	a dozen eggs

CAPÍTULO 5

Paso 1

Cómo hablar de los horarios y las especializaciones / Talking about your schedule and academic major

—¿Qué clases tomas este semestre?	—What classes are you taking this semester?
—Este semestre tomo *inglés y literatura*.	—This semester I'm taking *English and literature.*
—¿Te gusta tu horario?	—Do you like your schedule?
—Sí, me encanta. No, no me gusta porque...	—Yes, I love it. No, I don't like it because . . .
—¿A qué hora empieza tu primera clase?	—What time does your first class start?
—Mi primera clase empieza *a las ocho*.	—My first class starts at *eight o'clock.*

—¿A qué hora termina tu última clase?	—What time is your last class over?
—Mi última clase termina *a las dos y media*.	—My last class is over *at two-thirty.*
—¿Cuál es tu carrera?	—What's your major?
—Todavía no (lo) sé. Estudio *economía*.	—I don't know yet. I study *economics.*
—¿Cuándo piensas graduarte?	—When do you plan on graduating?
—Pienso graduarme *a finales de mayo. a principios de diciembre*	—I plan to graduate *at the end of May. at the beginning of December*

Las asignaturas / Courses (of study)

Humanidades y bellas artes	**Humanities and Fine Arts**
arte	art
literatura	literature
música	music
teatro	theater
Ciencias sociales	**Social sciences**
antropología	anthropology
ciencias políticas	political science
geografía	geography
historia	history
psicología	psychology
sociología	sociology
Ciencias naturales	**Natural sciences**
biología	biology
física	physics
ecología	ecology
química	chemistry
Matemáticas	**Mathematics**
álgebra	algebra
cálculo	calculus
estadística	statistics
Estudios profesionales	**Professsional studies**
derecho	law
informática	computer science
ingeniería	engineering
medicina	medicine
negocios	business
educación	education
periodismo	journalism
cinematografía	film-making

Opiniones sobre las clases / Expressing opinions about classes

—¿Qué piensas de tus clases este semestre?	—What do you think of your classes this semester?
—Pienso que mi clase de *microbiología* es *difícil / fácil*.	—I think that my *microbiology* class is *hard / easy.*
interesante / aburrida Me encanta mi clase de *historia del arte*.	*interesting / boring* I love my *art history* class.

No me gusta nada mi clase de *ciencias marinas*.

Las conferencias de *historia medieval* son *fascinantes / pesadas*.

Me interesa mucho la clase de *genética*. ¿Y tú? ¿Qué piensas?

I don't like my *marine science* class at all.

The lectures in *medieval history* are *fascinating / tedious*.

I'm very interested in *genetics* class. And you? What do you think?

Opiniones sobre los profesores

—¿Qué tal tus profesores?

—Son *bastante dinámicos(as)*.
   muy exigentes
   un poco quisquillosos(as)

Mi profesor de *química* es muy *organizado / desorganizado*.

Expressing opinions about professors

—What about your professors?

—They're *quite dynamic*.
   very demanding
   a bit/little picky

My *chemistry* professor is very *organized / unorganized*.

Las notas

—¿Cómo te va en *psicología*?

—(No) Me va bien.

Saqué una nota muy buena en *mi presentación*.

(No) Salí muy bien en el examen. Y a ti, ¿cómo te va en tus clases?

Discussing grades

—How's it going for you in *psychology*?

—It's (not) going well.

I got a good/high grade on *my presentation*.

I did (not do) well in the test. And you, how's it going for you in your classes?

Para hablar de las profesiones

—¿A qué te quieres dedicar?

—Quiero ser *enfermero(a)*.
—¿A qué se dedican tus padres?

—Mi padre es *dueño de un pequeño negocio*. Mi madre trabaja para *una agencia del estado*.

Discussing professions

—What do you want to do (for a living)?

—I want to be *a nurse*.
—What do your parents do (for a living)?

—My *dad* is the *owner of a small business*. My mother works for *a state agency*.

Los planes para el futuro

—¿Qué planes tienes para el futuro?
—No estoy seguro(a) todavía.

Me gustaría
   hacer estudios de postgrado.

   estudiar medicina
Espero trabajar
   para el gobierno.
   con una empresa multinacional

Discussing plans for the future

—What plans do you have for the future?
—I'm not sure yet.

I'd like to
   do graduate work / go to grad school.
   study medicine
I hope to work
   for the government.
   with a multinational company

Profesiones y ocupaciones

abogado(a)
agente de bienes raíces
agricultor(a)

Professions and occupations

lawyer
real estate agent
farmer

ama de casa — homemaker
consejero(a) — advisor/counselor
consultor(a) — consultant
contador(a) — accountant
dentista — dentist
director(a) de personal — director of personnel
gerente — manager
ingeniero(a) — engineer
maestro(a) — teacher
médico(a) — doctor
obrero(a) — laborer
periodista — journalist
programador(a) — programmer
psicólogo(a) — psychologist
trabajador(a) social — social worker
vendedor(a) — salesperson
veterinario(a) — veterinarian

Paso 2

Cómo hablar del pasado

¿Qué hiciste ayer?

Primero, me levanté y me vestí.

Después de comer desayuno, asistí a clases.

Luego, volví a casa y almorcé con mi familia.

Entonces, estudié para mi examen de 3 a 5.

Más tarde salí con mis amigos a un club y nos divertimos muchísimo.

Antes de acostarme, miré la tele por un rato.

Talking about the past

What did you do yesterday?

First, I got up and got dressed.

After eating breakfast, I went to class.

Next, I returned home and ate lunch with my family.

Then, I studied for my exam from 3 to 5.

Later (on), I went out to a club with my friends and we had a lot of fun.

Before I went to bed, I watched TV for a while.

Paso 3

Cómo hablar de las excursiones académicas

¿Hiciste algo interesante la semana pasada?

Sí, el viernes mi clase de *ciencia marina* hizo una excursión *al centro acuático de la universidad*.

Primero, el director del centro dio una presentación sobre *los delfines* y todos tomamos apuntes.

Luego, tuvimos que *recolectar datos* para nuestros proyectos.

Más tarde, fuimos *al observatorio del centro*.

Pudimos observar *varios animales acuáticos*.

Talking about field trips

Did you do anything interesting last week?

Yes, on Friday my *marine science* class took a field trip *to the university aquarium*.

First, the director of the center gave a presentation on *dolphins* and we all took notes.

Then, we had to *collect information* for our projects.

Later, we went to the *center's observatory*.

We were able to observe *different aquatic animals*.

CAPÍTULO 6

Paso 1

De compras en un gran almacén | Shopping in a department store

—Por favor, ¿dónde se encuentran *los zapatos para hombres*?
    mujeres
    niños (niñas)
    jóvenes
—Están en *la planta baja*.

—Excuse me, where could I find *men's shoes*?
    women's
    boy's (girl's)
    teen's
—They are on the *main (ground) floor*.

Los pisos | Floors

el sótano	basement
la planta baja	the main (ground) floor
el primer (1er) piso	first floor
el segundo (2°) piso	second floor
el tercer (3er) piso	third floor
el cuarto (4°) piso	fourth floor
el quinto (5°) piso	fifth floor
el sexto (6°) piso	sixth floor
el séptimo (7°) piso	seventh floor
el octavo (8°) piso	eighth floor
el noveno (9°) piso	ninth floor
el décimo (10°) piso	tenth floor

La ropa | Clothing

una blusa	a blouse
unas botas	boots
unos calcetines	socks
una camisa	a shirt
una camiseta	a T-shirt
una chaqueta	a jacket
un cinturón	a belt
una corbata	a necktie
una falda	a skirt
unos guantes	gloves
un impermeable	a raincoat
unos pantalones	pants/trousers
unos pantalones cortos	shorts
unas sandalias	sandals
una sudadera	a sweatshirt
un suéter	a sweater
un traje	a suit
un traje de baño	a bathing suit
unos vaqueros	jeans
un vestido	a dress

Los colores y otros detalles | Colors and other details

anaranjado	orange
amarillo	yellow
azul	blue
azul marino	navy blue
beige	beige
blanco	white
(color) crema	cream (color)
de cuadros	plaid
estampado	printed
gris	gray
con lunares	with polka dots
marrón	brown
morado	purple
negro	black
de rayas	striped
rojo	red
rosado	pink
verde	green

Para comprar la ropa | Buying clothes

—¿Qué desea?
—Estoy buscando un suéter *de lana*.
    de algodón
    de seda
—¿De qué color?
—Quiero un suéter *verde*.
No me importa el color.
—¿Qué talla lleva Ud.?
—Llevo la talla *mediana*.
    pequeña
    (extra) grande
—¿Qué le parece este suéter?

—No sé. Me parece *un poco caro*.
    demasiado formal
—¿Tiene otro *más barato*?

    más sencillo
—¿Quiere probarse este suéter?

—Sí, quiero probármelo. ¿Dónde está el probador?

—¿Cómo le queda *el suéter*?
—Me queda *bien (mal)*.
¿Tiene una talla más *grande (pequeña)*?
—¿Cuánto cuesta?
—Está de rebaja. Cuesta *40,00 euros*.
—Voy a llevárme*lo*.
—Muy bien. ¿Desea algo más?

—Eso es todo, gracias.

—What do you want?
—I'm looking for a *wool* sweater.
    cotton
    silk
—In what color?
—I want a *green* sweater.
It doesn't matter what color.
—What size do you wear?
—I wear a size *medium*.
    small
    (extra) large
—How do you like/What do you think of this sweater?
—I don't know. It seems *a little expensive*.
    too formal (dressy)
—Do you have another one *that's less expensive*?
    that's more simple / plainer
—Do you want to try this sweater on?
—Yes, I'd like to try it on. Where is the dressing room?
—How does *the sweater* fit?
—It fits *well (poorly)*.
Do you have a *bigger (smaller)* size?
—How much does it cost?
—It's on sale. It costs *40.00 euros*.
—I'll take *it*.
—Very well. Would you like anything else?
—That'll be all, thank you.

Paso 2

Los recuerdos | Souvenirs

¿Qué se puede comprar en un mercado típico?	What can you buy at a typical market?
un abanico	a fan
un anillo	a ring
unos aretes	earrings
una billetera	a wallet

una boina	a beret
un bolso de cuero	a leather purse
un brazalete de plata	a silver bracelet
una cadena de oro	a gold chain
unas castañuelas	castanets
un collar	a necklace
unas gafas de sol	sunglasses
una gorra	a cap
una guayabera	a guayabera (a shirt worn by men in warm climates)
una mantilla	a lace shawl
unas maracas	maracas
un paraguas	an umbrella
una piñata	a piñata
un plato de cerámica	a ceramic plate (dish)
un sarape	a sarape
un sombrero	a hat

Cómo regatear / Bargaining

—¿Me puede mostrar *esa camiseta*?
—Could you show me *that T-shirt*?

—Aquí *la* tiene.
—Here *it* is.

—¿Tiene Ud. *esta camiseta en azul*?
—Do you have *this T-shirt in blue*?

—Lo siento, no nos queda ninguna.
—I'm sorry, we're out.

—¿Cuánto cuesta *ese anillo*?
—How much does *that ring* cost?

—*Cuarenta euros.*
—*Forty euros.*

—¡Uy! ¡Qué caro! ¿Me puede hacer un descuento?
—Wow! That's expensive! Can you give me a discount?

—Bueno... para Ud., se lo dejo en *treinta y cinco euros*.
—Well . . . for you, I'll sell it for *35 euros*.

—Le doy *treinta euros*.
—I'll give you *30 euros*.

—No, lo siento. No puedo aceptar menos de *treinta y tres*.
—No, I'm sorry. I can't take less than *33 euros*.

—Está bien. Me *lo* llevo.
—That's fine. I'll take *it*.

CAPÍTULO 7

Paso 1

El tiempo libre: las invitaciones / Free time: Invitations

—¿Quieres ir *al cine* el sábado?
—Do you want to go *to the movies* on Saturday?

  al teatro
  al museo de arte
  a un concierto
  to the theater
  to the art museum
  to a concert

—¿Por qué no *vamos de picnic* esta tarde?
—Why don't we *go on a picnic* this afternoon?

  jugamos a las cartas
  damos un paseo
  vamos al partido de fútbol
  play cards
  take a walk
  go to the soccer match

Para aceptar la invitación / To accept an invitation

¡Qué buena idea!
What a great idea!

¡Cómo no!
Sure, why not!

¡Me encantaría!
I'd love to!

Para declinar la invitación / To decline an invitation

Lo siento, pero *tengo que estudiar*.
I'm sorry but *I have to study*.

Gracias, pero no puedo.
  Estoy cansado(a).
  Tengo otro compromiso.
Thanks, but I can't.
  I'm tired.
  I have another engagement.

No sé jugar.
I don't know how to play.

Quizás la próxima vez.
Maybe next time.

Para pedir información y hacer los planes / To ask for information and to make plans

—¿A qué hora empieza?
—What time does it start?

—Empieza *a las ocho*.
—It starts *at eight o'clock*.

—¿Dónde nos encontramos?
—Where shall we meet?

—Paso por tu casa *a las siete y media*.
—I'll come by your house / I'll pick you up *at seven-thirty*.

—¿Cuánto cuestan los boletos?
—How much do the tickets cost?

—La entrada es gratuita.
—It's free to get in.

Otras preguntas útiles / More useful questions

¿Qué película dan?
What movie are they showing?

¿Qué obra presentan?
What play are they presenting?

¿Quiénes tocan?
Who/What band is playing?

¿Quiénes juegan?
Who/What teams are playing?

Un fin de semana divertido / A fun weekend

—¿Qué tal tu fin de semana?
—How was your weekend?

—Me divertí muchísimo.
—I had a lot of fun.

—¿Adónde fuiste?
—Where did you go?

—Fui *a las montañas*.
  al lago
  a la playa
—I went *to the mountains*.
  to the lake
  to the beach

—¿Qué hiciste?
—What did you do?

—Mi amigo(a) y yo *acampamos*.
  paseamos en barco de vela
  tomamos el sol
—My friend and I *went camping*.
  went out in a sail boat
  sunbathed/lay out in the sun

—¡Qué bien!
—How nice!

—Sí, lo pasamos muy bien. ¿Y tú qué hiciste?
—Yes, we had a good time. And what did you do?

Un fin de semana regular/malo / An average/bad weekend

—¿Cómo pasaste el fin de semana?
—How did you spend the weekend?

—Lo pasé *fatal*.
  más o menos
—It was *terrible*.
  so-so

—¿Qué pasó?
—What happened?

—Me enfermé y tuve que quedarme en casa.
—I got sick and had to stay at home.

—¡Qué lástima!
—That's too bad!

—Sí, pero hoy me siento mejor. ¿Y tú cómo pasaste el fin de semana?

—Yes, but I feel better today. And you, how did you spend the weekend?

Actividades populares

En las montañas:
escalar en roca

hacer caminatas
acampar
dormir bajo las estrellas

En la playa:
bucear
esquiar
nadar
pasear en barco de vela
tomar el sol

En el campo:
montar a caballo
ir de caza
pescar

En el gimnasio:
correr
levantar pesas
hacer yoga
hacer ejercicio aeróbico

En un festival:
escuchar música
ver artesanías
probar la comida
bailar

En casa:
descansar
mirar televisión
relajarse
leer

Popular activities

In the mountains:
to rock climb/go rock climbing
to go hiking
to go camping
to sleep under the stars

At the beach:
to snorkel/go diving
to ski
to swim
to go sailing
to sunbathe

In the countryside:
to go horseback riding
to go hunting
to fish/go fishing

At the gym:
to run
to lift weights
to do yoga
to do aerobics

At a festival:
to listen to music
to look at the arts and crafts
to try/taste the food
to dance

At home:
to rest
to watch television
to relax
to read

Paso 2

Las estaciones

En las zonas templadas:
el otoño
el invierno
el verano
la primavera

En las zonas tropicales:
la estación de lluvia
la estación seca

El tiempo

¿Qué tiempo hace hoy?

Hace buen tiempo.
Hace sol y mucho calor.
El día está pésimo.
Está lloviendo mucho.
¡Destesto la lluvia!
Hace mucho frío.

Seasons

In temperate regions:
fall/autum
winter
summer
spring

In tropical regions:
rainy season
dry season

Weather

What's the weather like today?
The weather's nice/good.
It's sunny and very hot.
It's a miserable day.
It's raining hard.
I hate the rain!
It's very cold out.

Está nevando.
¡Me gusta la nieve!
Hace fresco hoy.
Hace mucho viento.

It's snowing.
I like the snow!
It's cool out today.
It's very windy.

Otras expresiones de tiempo

Hace *fresco.*
 (*mucho*) *calor.*
 (*mucho*) *frío.*
 (*mucho*) *viento.*
 (*muy*) *buen tiempo.*
 (*muy*) *mal tiempo.*
Está *lloviendo.*
 nevando
Está *despejado.*
 nublado
El día está *pésimo.*

 fatal
Creo que va a llover.
¿A cuántos grados estamos?
Estamos a 20 grados.
¿Cuál es el pronóstico para mañana?
Va a *llover.*
 nevar
 haber una tormenta

Other weather expressions

It's *cool out.*
 (*very*) *hot*
 (*very*) *cold*
 (*very*) *windy*
 (*very*) *nice weather*
 (*very*) *bad weather*
It's *raining.*
 snowing
It's *clear out.*
 cloudy
The weather's *really bad* today.
 terrible
I think it's going to rain.
What is the temperature?
It's 20 degrees.
What's the forecast for tomorrow?
It's going *to rain.*
 to snow
(There's going to be a storm.

Los días festivos y las celebraciones

—**¿Cómo celebras**
 el *Día de la Independencia*?
 el *Día de Acción de Gracias*
 tu cumpleaños
Para el Día de la Independencia, siempre vamos a ver un desfile en mi pueblo. Cuando era niño(a), *me gustaba ver los fuegos artificiales.*
Para el Día de Acción de Gracias, normalmente toda la familia se reúne en mi casa. Siempre comemos pavo y pastel de calabaza. Cuando era niño(a), *jugaba al fútbol americano con mis primos.*

Para mi cumpleaños, con frecuencia salgo a comer con mi familia. Cuando era niño(a), *tenía una fiesta todos los años.*

Holidays and celebrations

—How do you celebrate *Independence Day?*
 Thanksgiving Day
 your birthday
For Independence Day, we always go see a parade in my town. When I was little, *I used to like watching fireworks.*

For Thanksgiving, usually my whole family gets together at my house. We always eat turkey and pumpkin pie. When I was a child, *I would play football with my cousins.*

For my birthday, I often go out to eat with my family. When I was little, *I had a party every year.*

Las celebraciones y las costumbres

la Navidad
decorar un árbol y cantar villancicos

Celebrations and traditions

Christmas
decorate a tree and sing carols

la Nochebuena	Christmas Eve		
intercambiar regalos	exchange presents		
la Janucá	Hannukah		
encender las velas del candelabro	light the candles on the candelabra/Menorah		
la Noche Vieja	New Year's Eve		
brindar con champaña	make a toast with champagne		
el Día de Año Nuevo	New Year's Day		
reunirse con amigos	get together with friends		
la Pascua Florida	Easter		
ir a la iglesia	go to church		
el Pésaj	Passover		
ir a la sinagoga	go to synagogue/shul		
el Día de las Brujas	Halloween		
llevar disfraz y pedir dulces	wear a costume and go trick-or-treating		
el Día de los Enamorados	St. Valentine's Day		
regalar flores o chocolates	give flowers or chocolates (as a gift)		
el cumpleaños	birthday		
apagar las velas del pastel de cumpleaños	blow out the candles of the birthday cake		

Paso 3

Cómo contar un cuento

—¿Qué me cuentas?
—¿Sabes qué pasó?

—Dime, dime, ¿qué pasó?

—Gregorio se rompió la pierna.
—¡No me digas! ¿Cuándo ocurrió?
—Anteayer.

—¿Dónde estaba?

—Estaba en las montañas, de vacaciones.
—¿Cómo pasó?
—Gregorio hacía una caminata con sus amigos. Como llovía un poco, todo estaba resbaloso. Gregorio se cayó y se rompió la pierna.
—Ay, pobrecito.
—Sí, es una lástima.

How to tell a story

—What's new/What's up?
—Do you know what happened?

—Tell me, tell me; what happened?

—Greg broke his leg.
—You're kidding! When did that happen?
—The day before yesterday.

—Where was he (when it happened)?

—He was in the mountains, on vacation.
—How did it happen?
—Greg was hiking with his friends. Since it was raining a bit, everything was slippery. Greg fell and broke his leg.
—Oh, the poor thing!
—Yes, it's a shame/too bad.

Expresiones de interés

¡No me digas!
¿De veras?
¡Ay, pobrecito!
¡Qué horror!
¡Qué alivio!
Eso es increíble.
¡Menos mal!

¡Qué buena (mala) suerte!

Showing interest

You're kidding!
Really?
Oh, poor thing!
How awful!
What a relief!
That's incredible.
Thank goodness! / That's a relief!
What good (bad) luck!

Algunas preguntas típicas

¿Dónde estaba?
¿Cuándo ocurrió?
¿Qué hora era?
¿Qué tiempo hacía?

¿Cómo fue/pasó?
Y luego, ¿qué?

Some typical questions

Where was he/she?
When did it happen?
What time was it?
What was the weather like?
How did it happen?
And then what (happened)?

CAPÍTULO 8

Paso 1

Unas diligencias por la ciudad

—Perdón, ¿dónde se puede comprar sellos?
cambiar dinero
comprar aspirina
comprar tarjetas postales
—En el correo.
el banco
la farmacia

la papelería

Running errands around a city

—Excuse me, where can you buy stamps?
change money
buy aspirin
buy postcards
—At the post office.
the bank
the pharmacy/ drugstore
the stationery store

Unos lugares importantes

el aeropuerto	airport
el correo	post office
la clínica	clinic/hospital
la catedral	cathedral
la comisaría	police station
la estación del tren	train station
la farmacia	pharmacy
la iglesia	church
la papelería	stationery store
la parada de autobús	bus stop
la oficina de turismo	tourism office
el parque zoológico	zoo

Para indicar la ubicación

—Por favor, ¿dónde está el correo?
—Está al final de la calle.
en la esquina
a tres cuadras de aquí
—¿Se puede ir a pie?

—Sí, está bastante cerca.
—No, está lejos de aquí. Es mejor tomar el autobús.

Locating tourist destinations

—Excuse me, where's the post office?
—It's at the end of the street.
on the corner
three blocks from here
—Can you get there on foot?
—Yes, it's fairly close.
—No, it's far from here. It's better to take the bus.

Expresiones de ubicación

detrás de
delante de
a la izquierda de
a la derecha de

Expressions of location

behind
in front of
to the left of
to the right of

al lado de	next to
enfrente de	in front of/facing opposite
entre	between
al otro lado de la calle	on the other side of the street

Para pedir y dar instrucciones / Asking for and giving directions

—Por favor, ¿cómo se va a la oficina de turismo?	—Please, how do you get to the tourism office?
—Siga todo derecho. Está al final de la calle, a la izquierda.	—Keep going straight. It's at the end of the street, on the left.
—Perdone, ¿hay un banco por aquí?	—Excuse me, is there a bank around here?
—Sí, el Banco Nacional está bastante cerca. Camine 100 metros por esta calle. Está a la derecha, al lado de la farmacia.	—Yes, National Bank is fairly close. Walk 100 meters along this street. It's on the right, next to the pharmacy.

Otras instrucciones / Giving other directions

Vaya a la esquina.	Go to the corner.
Tome la Avenida de la Independencia.	Take Indepedence Avenue.
Tome la segunda calle a la izquierda.	Take the second street on the left.
Siga derecho por cuatro cuadras.	Keep going straight for four blocks.
Doble a la derecha en la calle República.	Turn to the right at Republic Street.
Camine cien metros.	Walk a hundred meters (one block).
Cruce la calle.	Cross the street.

Paso 2

Las partes del cuerpo / Parts of the body

la boca	mouth
el brazo	arm
la cabeza	head
el codo	elbow
el corazón	heart
el cuello	neck
los dedos	fingers
los dedos del pie	toes
los dientes	teeth
la espalda	back
el estómago	stomach
la garganta	throat
el hombro	shoulder
la mano	hand
la muñeca	wrist
la nariz	nose
el oído	inner ear
los ojos	eyes
la oreja	ear
el pecho	chest
el pie	foot
la pierna	leg
los pulmones	lungs
la rodilla	knee
el tobillo	ankle

Para indicar lo que te duele / To indicate what is hurting you

—¿Qué le duele?	—What's hurting you?
—Me duele el pecho.	—My chest hurts.
Me duelen los oídos.	My ears hurt.
Tengo dolor de cabeza.	I have a headache.

Las enfermedades / Illnesses

—¿Qué tiene?	—What's wrong?
—Me siento mal. Tengo tos y fiebre.	—I feel poorly/sick. I'm coughing and have a fever.

Otros síntomas / Other symptoms

Tengo *tos.*	I have *a cough.*
fiebre	have a *fever*
diarrea	have *diarrhea*
náuseas	feel *nauseous*
mareos	feel *dizzy*
vómitos	am *vomiting*
Me lastimé *la espalda.*	I hurt *my back.*
el pie	*my foot*

El diagnóstico / The diagnosis

—¿Qué tengo, doctor(a)?	—What's wrong with me, doctor?
—Ud. tiene *la gripe.*	—You have *the flu.*
un virus	*a virus*
un resfriado	*a cold*
una infección	*an infection*
una intoxicación alimenticia	*food poisoning*

Los remedios / The remedies

—¿Qué debo hacer?	—What should I do?
—Tome estas pastillas y guarde cama por unos días.	—Take these pills and stay in bed for a few days.

Otros remedios / Other remedies

Le voy a dar unas pastillas para el dolor.	I'm going to give you some pills for the pain / painkillers.
Tome *estos antibióticos dos veces al día.*	Take *these antibiotics twice a day.*
este jarabe para la tos cada cuatro horas	*this cough syrup every four hours*
Quiero que Ud.	I want you
guarde cama.	*to stay in bed.*
descanse mucho en casa	*rest a lot at home*
Le recomiendo que	I recommend that
tome aspirinas cada cuatro horas.	*you take aspirins every four hours.*
se aplique esta crema tres veces al día	*apply this cream/lotion three times a day*

CAPÍTULO 9

Paso 1

Las vicisitudes del estudiante
—¿Qué te pasa?
—Estoy totalmente estresado(a) por todas mis obligaciones.

—Sí, entiendo perfectamente. Debes encontrar la manera de desconectar un poco.

—Tienes razón, pero es difícil.

Algunas quejas comunes

Estoy agotado(a) de tanto trabajar.
Necesito volver a ponerme en forma.
Estoy furioso(a) con mi novio(a).
Mi compañero(a) de cuarto y yo no nos llevamos bien.
No tengo dinero para pagar todas mis cuentas.
Tengo que entregar un trabajo escrito mañana y todavía no lo he empezado.

Para dar consejos
Debes...
Tienes que...
    dormir ocho horas diarias

    buscar una solución
    tomarte unos días libres
    discutir el problema
    comer comidas balanceadas
    pedir ayuda
    hacer más ejercicio
    organizarte mejor
    dejar de fumar
    dejar de procrastinar

Para reaccionar a los consejos
Tienes razón.
Sí, es verdad, pero...
Es buena idea.
Bueno, no sé. No estoy seguro(a).

Paso 2

Los grandes momentos de la vida

Buenas noticias
—¿Qué me cuentas?

Student difficulties
—What's the matter?
—I'm completely stressed out with all my obligations.
—Yes, I understand completely. You need to find a way to disconnect a bit.
—You're right, but it's hard.

Some common complaints
I'm exhausted from so much work.
I need to get back into shape.
I'm furious with my boyfriend/girlfriend.
My roommate and I don't get along well.
I have no money to pay all my bills.
I have to hand in a (written) paper tomorrow and I haven't even started it.

Giving advice
You should . . .
You have to . . .
    get eight hours of sleep daily
    find a solution
    take some days off
    discuss the problem
    eat balanced meals
    ask for help
    exercise more
    organize yourself better
    stop smoking
    stop procrastinating

Reacting to the advice
You're right.
Yes, it's true, but . . .
It's a good idea.
Well, I don't know. I'm not sure.

Major events in your life

Good news
—What's new?

—Estoy *contentísimo*. ¡Tengo buenas noticias!
—¿Sí? Cuéntame qué pasa.

—*Mi hermana mayor está embarazada y voy a ser tío(a).*

—*¡Cuánto me alegro!*

Otros sentimientos
Estoy *orgulloso(a)*.
    emocionado(a)
    enamorado(a)
    muy alegre

Otras noticias buenas
Acabo de conocer al hombre (a la mujer) de mis sueños.
Mi hermana mayor va a graduarse con honores de la universidad.
Mi primo y su novia van a comprometerse.

Mis mejores amigos van a casarse.

Para reaccionar a las buenas noticias
¡Cuánto me alegro!
¡Qué buena noticia!
¡Estupendo!
¡Qué maravilloso!
¡Qué bueno!

Malas noticias
—¿Todo bien?
—En realidad, no. Estoy *muy triste.*
—¿Sí? ¿Qué te pasa?
—Acabo de recibir malas noticias. *Mis padres van a separarse.*
—¡Cuánto lo siento!

Otros sentimientos
Estoy *preocupado(a)*.
    deprimido(a)
    desconsolado(a)
    sorprendido(a)

Otras noticias malas
Mi hermano y su novia rompieron su compromiso.

Mis tíos van a divorciarse.

Se murió mi tía abuela.

—I'm *extremely happy.* I have good news!
—Really? Tell me what is going on.

—*My older sister is pregnant and I'm going to be uncle/aunt.*
—*I'm so happy (for you)!*

Other feelings
I am proud.
    excited
    in love
    very happy

Other good news
I've just met the man (woman) of my dreams.
My older sister is graduating from the university with honors.
My cousin and his girlfriend are getting engaged.
My best friends are getting married.

Reacting to good news
I'm so happy!
What great news!
Great! / Fantastic!
That's wonderful!
That's great!

Bad news
—Is everything okay?
—Actually, no. I'm *very sad.*
—Really? What's wrong?
—I just got bad news. *My parents are separating.*
—I'm so sorry!

Other feelings
I am worried.
    depressed
    grief-stricken
    surprised

Other bad news
My brother and his fiancée broke off their engagement.
My aunt and uncle are getting a divorce.
My grandaunt died.

Para reaccionar a las malas noticias

¡Cuánto lo siento!
¡Qué pena!
¡Lo siento mucho!
¡Ojalá que todo salga bien!

Reacting to bad news

I'm so sorry!
How sad!
I'm very sorry!
I hope (Hopefully) everything will be fine.

Paso 3

Cuéntame de tu vida

—¿Qué hay de nuevo?

—Acabo de tener una entrevista para una beca.
—¿Sí? ¿Piensas que te la van a dar?
—Creo que sí. La entrevista me fue muy bien.

Tell me about your life

—What's up? / What's going on?
—I just had an interview for a scholarship.
— Yeah? Do you think they will give it to you?
—I think so. The interview went really well.

Para expresar grados de certeza o duda

¡Sin ninguna duda!
Creo que sí.

Expressing certainty and doubt

Certainly! / Without a doubt!
I think so.

Es casi seguro.
Es muy probable.
Es posible.
Quizás.
Depende.
Es dudoso.
Es poco probable.
Creo que no.
¡Imposible!

It's almost a sure thing.
It's very likely.
It's possible.
Perhaps.
It depends.
It's doubtful.
It's very unlikely.
I don't think so.
Impossible!/No way!

Para expresar optimismo

Me siento muy optimista.
Pienso que todo se va a arreglar.
¡No te preocupes!

Expressing optimism

I feel very optimistic.
I think that everything will turn out fine.
Don't worry!

Para expresar pesimismo

Me siento pesimista.
No estoy seguro(a); es muy difícil.
Creo que va a salir mal.

Expressing pessimism

I feel pessimistic.
I'm not sure; it's unlikely.

I think it will turn out badly.

Index

Credits

Text Credits

Chapter 2: BUSCÁNDOLA, Words and Music by JOSE FERNANDO and EMILIO OLVERA SIERRA ©1992 TULUM MUSIC. All rights administered by WB MUSIC CORP. All Rights Reserved Used by Permission of ALFRED PUBLISHING CO.,INC.; **Chapter 3:** Source: Adapted from Revista Mia, 22 Mayo, 2000.; **Chapter 4:** Karen Publishing Company, 1995. Reprinted by permission.; **Chapter 6:** EL VESTIDO Words and Music by JUANA MOLINA ©Domino 2008 as advised by Domino. Reprinted by permission.; **Chapter 8:** "Ella y Él". © 1996 Sony/ATV Music Publishing, LLC, Insignia Music, Insignia Music Publishing Companies, MCA Music Publishing. All rights on behalf of Sony/ATV Music Publishing LLC and Insignia Music administered by Sony/ATV Music Publishing LLC, 8 Music Square West. Nashville, TN 37203. All rights reserved. Used by permission of SONY and the artist.

Photo Credits

Chapter P

1: DDB stock; **4 (b):** Index Stock Imagery/Photolibrary; **4 (t):** Heinle Image Resource Bank/Cengage Learning; **8:** ©Basque Country-Mark Baynes/Alamy.

Chapter 1

11: ©Hola Images/Photolibrary; **13:** "The Street", 1995 Oil on canvas, 56" × 42" by Fernando Botero. © Fernando Botero, courtesy, Marlborough Gallery, New York; **18:** eStock Photo/Alamy; **21:** ©Robert Fried/Alamy; **24:** ©S. Murphy-Larronde/age fotostock/Photolibrary; **25 (t):** Heinle Image Resource Bank/Cengage Learning; **25 (c):** Heinle Image Resource Bank/Cengage Learning; **25 (b):** Heinle Image Resource Bank/Cengage Learning; **30:** ©Don Hammond/Design Pics/Jupiter Images; **31:** eStock Photo/Alamy; **32:** Andersen Ross/Jupiter images; **37:** Image copyright Galina Barskaya 2009/Used under license from Shutterstock.com; **46 (b):** Heinle Image Resource Bank/Cengage Learning; **46 (t):** Heinle Image Resource Bank/Cengage Learning; **47 (t):** AP Photo/Jim Cooper; **47 (b):** ©AP Photo/Rob Carr; **48 (t):** ©AP Photo/Jim Cooper; **48 (b):** ©AP Photo/Rob Carr; **49 (t):** Heinle Image Resource Bank/Cengage Learning; **49 (b):** Heinle ~~ge Resource Bank/Cengage Learning; **50:** ©Hemera ~~ologies/Photos.com/Jupiter Images; **51 (t):** Hulton ~~e/Getty Images; **51 (c):** ©AP Photo; **51 (b):** AP Photo/ ~~Sladky; **51 (bl):** Heinle Image Resource Bank/Cengage ~~ing.

Chapter 2

53: ©Index Stock Imagery/Photolibrary; **54 (tr):** Andre Nantel, 2009/Used under license from Shutterstock.com; **54 (l):** ©Stephan Hoerold/iStockphoto; **54 (br):** Keith Wheatley, 2009/Used under license from Shutterstock.com; **55:** Image copyright Qing Ding, 2009/Used under license from Shutterstock.com; **61:** Heinle Image Resource Bank/Cengage Learning; **62 :** Chris Hermann/F1 Online/Photolibrary; **69 (t):** Heinle Image Resource Bank/Cengage Learning; **69 (c):** Heinle Image Resource Bank/Cengage Learning; **69 (b):** Heinle Image Resource Bank/Cengage Learning; **70:** ©Glowimages/Getty Images; **71:** ©Caitlin Cahill/iStockphoto; **73:** ©James Benet/iStockphoto; **80 (tl):** Dale Walsh/istockphoto.com; **81:** Heinle Image Resource Bank/Cengage Learning; **82:** Image copyright Ian D Walker, 2009/Used under license from Shutterstock.com; **83 (t):** ©Hulton Archive/Getty Images; **83 (c):** Bettmann/CORBIS; **83 (b):** ©AP Photo/Marcelo Salinas; **83 (bl):** Heinle Image Resource Bank/Cengage Learning.

Chapter 3

85: ©Ronnie Kaufman/Flirt Collection/Photolibrary; **87:** Scala/Art Resource, NY; **91:** Image copyright Andresr, 2009/Used under license from Shutterstock.com; **99:** Nikoner 2009/Used under license from Shutterstock.com; **100 (t):** Heinle Image Resource Bank/Cengage Learning; **100 (c):** Heinle Image Resource Bank/Cengage Learning; **100 (b):** Heinle Image Resource Bank/Cengage Learning; **104:** © Nicholas Pitt/Alamy; **113:** Heinle Image Resource Bank/Cengage Learning; **123:** Heinle Image Resource Bank/Cengage Learning; **124:** rm, 2009/Used under license from Shutterstock.com; **125 (t):** Bettmann/CORBIS; **125 (c):** ©AP Photo/Keystone/Urs Flueeler; **125 (b):** Rich Sugg/MCT/Landov; **125 (bl):** Heinle Image Resource Bank/Cengage Learning.

Chapter 4

127: DDB stock; **129:** ©Pilar Olivares/Reuters/Landov; **133:** Shirley Vanderbilt/Index Stock Imagery/PhotoLibrary; **134 (t):** ©Jose Luis Pelaez, Inc./CORBIS; **134 (b):** Image copyright RJ Lerich, 2009. Used under license from Shutterstock.com.; **135:** Courtesy of the Author; **140 (t):** Heinle Image Resource Bank/Cengage Learning; **140 (c):** Heinle Image Resource Bank/Cengage Learning; **140 (b):** Heinle Image Resource Bank/Cengage Learning; **143:** ©RALPH LEE HOPKINS/National Geographic Stock; **151:** Heinle Image Resource Bank/Cengage Learning; **152:** Image copyright Mike VON BERGEN, 2009. Used under license from Shutterstock.com.; **153 (t):** Bettmann/CORBIS; **153 (c):** ©Enrique Castro-Mendivil/Reuters/Landov; **153 (b):** ©AP Photo/Martin Mejia; **153 (bl):** Heinle Image Resource Bank/Cengage Learning.

Chapter 5

155: ©GoGo Images/Jupiter Images; 157: ; 158: ©Somos-Veer/Jupiter Images; 161 (t): ©iStockphoto.com/Juanmonino; 161 (b): Dale Mitchell, 2009/ Used under license from Shutterstock.com.; 162: Bananastock/Jupiter images; 165: ©iStockphoto.com/ Sean Locke; 167: ©AP Photo/Pilar Capurro; 168 (t): Heinle Image Resource Bank/Cengage Learning; 168 (c): Heinle Image Resource Bank/Cengage Learning; 168 (b): Heinle Image Resource Bank/Cengage Learning; 187: Heinle Image Resource Bank/Cengage Learning; 188: ©Michael Coyne/Lonely Planet Images; 189 (t): Bettmann/CORBIS; 189 (c): ©Max Rossi/Reuters/ Landov; 189 (b): ©Ron Sachs/pool via Bloomberg News/ Landov; 189 (bl): Heinle Image Resource Bank/Cengage Learning.

Chapter 6

191: ©Krzysztof Dydynski/Lonely Planet Images; 193: ©Angus Oborn/Lonely Planet Images; 199: Image copyright Losevsky Pavel 2009/Used under license from Shutterstock.com; 201: ©Gimmi Gimmi/Photo-library; 204: David Sanger photography/Alamy; 205 (t): Heinle Image Resource Bank/Cengage Learning; 205 (c): Heinle Image Resource Bank/Cengage Learning; 205 (b): Heinle Image Resource Bank/Cengage Learning; 209 (t): ©John Birdsall/Alamy; 209 (b): Hemis.fr/SuperStock; 217: Heinle Image Resource Bank/Cengage Learning; 218: ©Radius Images/Jupiter Images; 219 (t): Hulton Archive/ Getty Images; 219 (c): ©INTERFOTO/Alamy; 219 (b): Image copyright Terry Straehley, 2009. Used under license from Shutterstock.com; 219 (bl): Heinle Image Resource Bank/ Cengage Learning.

Chapter 7

221: ©Jon Feingersh/Blend Images/Jupiter Images; 223: Carmen Lomas Garza; 224 (t): Image copyright Elena Ray, 2009. Used under license from Shutterstock.com.; 224 (b): ©Image Source Black/Jupiter Images; 227: ©Danita Delimont/Alamy; 233 (t): Heinle Image Resource Bank/ Cengage Learning; 233 (c): Heinle Image Resource Bank/ Cengage Learning; 233 (b): Heinle Image Resource Bank/Cengage Learning; 238: ©AP Photo/Ed Andrieski; 240: ©travelib prime/Alamy; 246: ©mediacolor's/Alamy; 254: Image copyright Phil Date 2009/Used under license from Shutterstock.com; 257: Sony Pictures Classics/Everett Collection; 258: Sony Pictures Classics/Everett Collection; 259: Heinle Image Resource Bank/Cengage Learning; 260: Wolfgang Kaehler/CORBIS; 261 (t): ©ESTEBAN/ Xinhua/Landov; 261 (c): Courtesy of NASA Kennedy Space Center (NASA-KSC); 261 (bl): Heinle Image Resource Bank/ Cengage Learning.

Chapter 8

263: ©RODRIGO BUENDIA/AFP/Getty Images; 265: ©Creatas Images/Jupiter Images; 266: Robert Fried Photography; 270: ©David Frazier/PhotoEdit; 276 (t): Heinle Image Resource Bank/Cengage Learning; 276 (c): Heinle Image Resource Bank/Cengage Learning; 276 (b): Heinle Image Resource Bank/Cengage Learning; 280: ©PHOTOTAKE Inc./Alamy; 286: Image copyright rebvt 2009/Used under license from Shutterstock.com; 289 : Heinle Image Resource Bank/Cengage Learning; 290: Image copyright George Lamson, 2009. Used under license from Shutterstock. com.; 291 (t): © Lino Wchima/Photographers Direct; 291 (c): ©AP Photo/Dario Lopez-Mills; 291 (b): ©PHILIPPE DESMAZES/AFP/Getty Images; 291 (bl): Heinle Image Resource Bank/Cengage Learning.

Chapter 9

293: ©Steve Dunwell/Index Stock Imagery/Photolibrary; 295: SuperStock/SuperStock; 303: Zigy Kaluzny-Charles Thatcher/Getty Images; 304: masterfile; 306 (t): Heinle Image Resource Bank/Cengage Learning; 306 (c): Heinle Image Resource Bank/Cengage Learning; 306 (b): Heinle Image Resource Bank/Cengage Learning; 318: matzaball/istockphoto.com; 329: Heinle Image Resource Bank/Cengage Learning; 330: ©Marcelo Hernandez/LatinContent/Getty Images; 331 (c): ©AP Photo/Michel Lipchitz; 331 (b): ©CHRIS WATTIE/Reuters/ Landov; 331 (bl): Heinle Image Resource Bank/Cengage Learning.